Juanita Brooks

JUANITA BROOKS

THE LIFE STORY OF A COURAGEOUS HISTORIAN
OF THE MOUNTAIN MEADOWS MASSACRE

Levi S. Peterson

Illustrated by Royden Card

With a New Preface

THE UNIVERSITY OF UTAH PRESS
Salt Lake City

The Defiance House Man colophon is a registered trademark
of the University of Utah Press. It is based upon a four-foot-tall,
Ancient Puebloan pictograph (late PIII) near Glen Canyon, Utah.

15 14 13 12 11   2 3 4 5

Library of Congress Cataloging-in-Publication Data
Peterson, Levi S., 1933–
Juanita Brooks:
(Utah centennial series ; v. 5)
Bibliography: p.
Includes index.

ISBN 978-1-60781-151-0

1. Brooks, Juanita, 1898– 2. Historians–Utah–Biography.
3. Mormons–Utah–Historiography. 4. Utah–Biography.
5. Utah–Historiography. I. Title.
F826.B877P48   1988
979.2'0072024
[B]   88–17421

to my father and mother
Joseph Peterson and Lydia Jane Savage

CONTENTS

PREFACE

It is entirely fitting that the University of Utah Press should reprint this biography of one of Utah's most notable and influential historians. Few historical works have altered attitudes and changed minds more forcefully than Juanita Brooks's *Mountain Meadows Massacre* (1950), and *John Doyle Lee: Zealot, Pioneer Builder, Scapegoat* (1961). Although she was a loyal Mormon, Juanita resolutely set forth facts in these books that many of her faith would have preferred she had left untold. And though she feared excommunication, she felt obliged to narrate the terrible events accurately.

As early as 1962 I was aware that Juanita was one of the most respected historians Utah had ever produced. But it wasn't until she spoke to a small group at Weber State College (now University), where I was a member of the English Department, that I understood the personal qualities that were the basis of her fame. Her appearance at Weber State was in 1973. She was seventy-five years old, of small stature, and plainly dressed, but her voice was resonant and mesmerizing. She told us that day about her part in the posthumous rehabilitation of John D. Lee, the only person executed among the more than fifty participants in the massacre at Mountain Meadows.

When in the spring of 1961 the First Presidency of the LDS Church informed Lee's descendants of their ancestor's reinstatement, Juanita's biography of the scapegoated pioneer was in the process of publication. Juanita eagerly sought permission to announce the reinstatement in her book. Apostle Delbert Stapley emphatically refused, informing her that church president David O. McKay had threatened to rescind the reinstatement if it were made public. It was typical of Juanita that, though she dreaded excommunication, she included the reinstatement in her book. Fortunately, she was not excommunicated, and her conviction that President McKay would not rescind the rein-statement proved true.

Impressed by Juanita's presentation at Weber State, I read her history of the massacre and her biography of Lee. Two qualities of these works stood out for me. One was that she demonstrated a pro-found sympathy not only for the victims of the massacre but also for its perpetrators. From her perspective, the Mormon participants in the massacre were honest, decent men led by circumstances into a gory deed against which their own consciences must have quickly revolted. If there was anyone for whom she showed disdain it was LDS Church president Brigham Young, for unjustly narrowing the blame for the massacre to a single participant, John D. Lee.

The other quality of *Mountain Meadows Massacre* and *John Doyle Lee* that impressed me was their tragic dimension. It is true that they are both works of history, yet it seemed to me that at least for Mormon readers they roused the same kind of emotion that literary tragedies such as *King Lear* and *Othello* evoke—a sense of inconsolable loss softened by a renewed appreciation for what is lost. Feeling that this was an insight worth sharing, I developed it in the essay "Juanita Brooks: The Mormon Historian as Tragedian," which I read at the 1976 conference of the Mormon History Association and which was later published in the association's journal. In light of this essay, two editors from the University of Utah Press, Norma Mikkelsen and Trudy McMurrin, at different moments suggested that I write a biography of Juanita. Engaged in writing fiction, I did not immediately respond to their suggestion. However, in 1985—having come to a lull in that writing—I turned to the task of writing the biography.

I first proceeded to collect materials, which happily proved to be abundant. With the instincts of a historian, Juanita had carefully preserved her letters and manuscripts, and her children had donated these documents to the Utah Historical Society. During the summer of 1985, I spent every weekday—with few exceptions—in the archives there, taking notes and making photocopies. Throughout the following year, I interviewed numerous people who had known Juanita, and I researched other archives at colleges, universities, and public libraries in Utah and California. This research was stimulating and I approached each new document with anticipation and a degree of suspense, adding bit by bit to a growing picture of Juanita's life. It seemed a privilege to look in upon a person's life from its beginning to its end, particularly the life of a person for whom I felt a deep affinity. Although Juanita was old enough to be my mother, I tended to regard her as a sister. We both grew up in a Mormon village, we were both affectionately attached to a large number of Mormon relatives, and we were both what may be termed loyal dissenters from Mormon conformity.

By the summer of 1986 I settled into organizing and writing a first draft of the biography. This proved a tedious chore, as I had known it would. For me, writing a first draft on almost any topic is an exercise in tension and frustration. Tension and frustration notwithstanding, I forged dutifully ahead throughout the academic year of 1986–1987, typically teaching classes on weekday mornings and devoting afternoons and evenings to writing. I usually devoted Saturday and Sunday mornings to the same task. The result was that, despite many distractions, I completed a draft totaling nine-hundred double-spaced pages by mid-summer of 1987. By November of that year I completed a considerably shorter revision of the draft and delivered it to the University of Utah Press. On the day I delivered the draft to the press offices, the editor who had been assigned to work with me, a young woman whose name I unfortunately do not remember, embraced me with surprised delight. I had, I took it, exceeded her expectations by finishing the work on schedule. Almost a year later, in October of 1988, the book appeared. Its publication was honored with the David W. and Beatrice C. Evans Annual Biography Award and with the Best Book of the Year Award of the Mormon History Association.

I was pleased that the foreword to the volume was written by my brother, Charles S. Peterson, then a professor of history at Utah State University and general editor of the University of Utah Press's Utah Centennial Series, which commemorated the approaching centennial of Utah's statehood (1996). Mine was the fifth volume of the series—other volumes having focused on Native Americans, a Jewish back-to-the-land experiment, and the biography of a Greek couple who immigrated to Utah. Although Charles's foreword does not appear in the present reprint—Utah's centennial being now some fifteen years in the past—his perspective on Juanita deserves to be shared. "A product of Utah's Dixie," he wrote, "Juanita Brooks matured in one of the West's most isolated localities during its most insular era.... Left to its own resources, the Dixie of Juanita Brooks's youth was an enclave of pioneer Mormonism removed for three or four decades from many of the changes that shifted the eyes of other Utahns outward." Nonetheless, Charles judged Juanita to be "one of the truly exciting individuals Utah produced," one whose "background and habits enriched the heritage of a region."

I scarcely need say that this is a judgment with which I concur heartily.

ACKNOWLEDGMENTS

I gratefully acknowledge the assistance of numerous individuals and organizations in the preparation of this biography. I owe thanks to my own institution, Weber State College, for research funds extended through its research and professional growth committee. I am indebted to the Huntington Library, the Bancroft Library, the University of Utah Library, and the Utah State Historical Society for access to their holdings. The staff at the Utah State Historical Society, where I spent many months in research, were extraordinarily helpful. I thank Stanford University Press, University of Utah Press, Utah State University Press, and Howe Brothers Publishers for opening their files to my study. I express gratitude to the many relatives and friends of Juanita Brooks who gave encouragement and information. I am grateful to my wife Althea, my daughter Karrin, and my mother-in-law Stella Sand who listened patiently to my unending recital of biographical minutiae.

CHAPTER ONE

HEN LEAVITT'S BOY

D uring most of her life Juanita Brooks lived in St. George, Utah, the principal town of a wind-sculpted desert domain called Dixie. Settled by Mormon pioneers who had no inkling of future political boundaries, Dixie comprises the southwestern corner of Utah and contiguous areas in Arizona and Nevada. In many respects Juanita was simply one of those bright, devoted women who make a provincial town function in a civilized fashion. She was an affectionate mother, a loyal wife, a respected schoolteacher, an energetic organizer of church and civic affairs. She had, however, the unusual habit of traveling by night bus to Salt Lake City or Los Angeles. If she was lucky, a bus might be lightly loaded and she could dispose of two seats and sleep. But if the bus were crowded, it didn't matter so much. It was fortunate that she didn't need much sleep, because she lived by a harried schedule. She wanted to be a good mother and wife and community worker. But she also wanted to be a historian.

Birth placed her among one of the richest supplies of pioneer diaries ever produced by the American frontier, and temperament gave her the impetus to excel in preserving them. The pathos and drama of the old diaries drove her on to become a renowned editor, whose careful deciphering of cryptic handwriting and patient annotation of names and incidents gave new life to Utah's pioneer era. She was too ambitious to be only a collector and editor. It didn't matter that her work station was often a kitchen table and her writing instrument a portable typewriter. She produced dozens of articles and an impressive number of books in her chosen genres of biography and narrative history. With few exceptions her works were published by western presses and marketed to a western readership. Most of them were about the history of her own desert domain. Nonetheless, her reputation transcended the boundaries of Utah and the West.

Although it took her some years to appreciate the fact, her native Dixie was a miniature replica of Nathaniel Hawthorne's New

England, burdened with a deep and covert guilt. Ironically the pioneers of Dixie, sound theological Mormons who rejected the doctrine of original sin and innate depravity, acquired a guilt as devastating and ineradicable as that which afflicted the participants in the Salem witch trials of the late seventeenth century. Roused to hysteria by the approach of Johnston's army in 1857, local Mormon leaders in southwestern Utah induced a confederation of Indians to attack a wagon train of Arkansas emigrants camped in a grassy valley called Mountain Meadows. When the Indians proved incapable of subduing the emigrants, the Mormons ordered their own militiamen to assist. Close to a hundred emigrants were treacherously slaughtered.

It was a tragedy not only for the emigrants but for their murderers as well, who were not characteristically bloody-minded and predatory men. Furthermore, it was a tragedy by association for all Mormons everywhere. As members of the Church of Jesus Christ of Latter-day Saints, the Mormons have always prided themselves upon the superlative character of their Christianity, which they understand to be a restoration of the pristine Gospel. Brigham Young and other general authorities of the Church recognized that the massacre had been carried out by their best and most loyal lieutenants. Perhaps understandably, Young and his associates concealed the participants and obstructed federal attempts to bring them to justice for many years. Under extreme pressure Young finally assented to the conviction and execution of one of the local leaders, John D. Lee. By this sacrifice of one loyal follower, he purchased an amnesty from federal officials for all other participants. For many reasons Young's successors—and indeed the Mormons in general—ardently desired to bury the incident in the oblivion of the past. No other circumstance in the history of the Latter-day Saints in Utah has undermined their Christian self-esteem with such force as the Mountain Meadows massacre.

As Juanita Brooks awakened to the vocation of historian, she settled with courageous ambition upon the massacre as her principal subject. Her investigation showed that it was by no means a forgotten topic in Dixie and in other places where the descendants of the participants had migrated. Bitter battles of blame and self-exoneration still raged among those descendants. The dispassionate and objective treatment which Juanita gave the massacre and its aftermath established her reputation for integrity. But inevitably she became more than an objective historian: she became a minstrel of a gripping saga;

she became a tragedian whose compassion pointed toward catharsis and forgiveness.[1]

Her insistence upon telling the full truth led her into conflict with the general authorities of the Church. She engaged in this conflict with some relish, for she had inherited the antagonism of her pioneer ancestors toward the leaders in Salt Lake who had ordered them to the impoverished fringes of the Mormon empire. But she also engaged in this conflict with trepidation, because it placed her in danger of excommunication. Comfortably isolated from the dark folklore of the massacre which still circulated in Dixie, the general authorities were dismayed that Juanita should wish to revive a matter so injurious to the image of the Church. Her persistence in face of their disapproval gave dramatic interest to her life and raised it above the commonplace.

Protesters have traditionally fared poorly among the Mormons. Perhaps the Mormons suffered too greatly from external persecution and internal divisiveness in frontier times. Whatever the reason, the Church of the twentieth century has shown little tolerance for ideas not sanctioned by the central leadership, emphasizing conformity to an extraordinary degree. Growing ever more centralized, the modern Church notably lacks a mechanism for eliciting and capitalizing upon change from the rank-and-file membership. In such a system, inside dissenters—those loyal members who of their own initiative call for change and improvement—become of crucial importance. By means of their indirect influence the Church maintains some semblance of progressive harmony with the larger civilization surrounding it.[2] Needless to say, such a mode of change is slow, uncertain, and fraught with hazard for the reformers.

It is difficult to find a term which accurately delimits the nonconformity of Juanita Brooks. Her attachment to Mormonism was organic and profound. She did not think of Mormonism as an ecclesiastical corporation belonging to the men who governed it but as an informal federation of believers in which she had a full interest and voice. She was therefore loyal in her protest, and she propounded a simple agenda for change. Specifically, she wanted the Church to ratify her controversial interpretation of the massacre; more generally, she wanted Mormons everywhere to confront their past openly and fearlessly. Eventually she saw the partial realization of her objectives. Her influence, however, went far beyond the realm of history. Such were the combined effects of her outspoken candor and her unassailable integrity that for a quarter of a century she stood as the foremost symbol of dissent in all of Mormondom. Without conscious intent, she became the nexus of an extensive Mormon underground. Fundamentalists and liberals alike sent her letters and manuscripts and approached her in person. She responded to all of them with recognition and encouragement, having an instinctive sympathy for those who believed in a truth they feared to declare.

She became a sought-after public speaker. At home in Dixie she had been a frequent speaker on occasions of public ceremony. With the publication of her history of the massacre, her audiences quickly expanded across Utah and neighboring states. She spoke before groups of all sizes and of all sorts— academic, social, literary, and religious. She was immeasurably obliging, accepting travel reimbursement if it were offered, journeying at her own expense if it were not. She told and retold the story of the massacre and the scapegoating of John D. Lee. Often she recounted other incidents from the history of Dixie or the adventures of her own childhood. She frequently recounted her confrontations with church officials.

Her own life was so fraught with tragedy and triumph that friends urged her to record it in writing. She wrote one segment of her autobiography at midlife and another segment in old age. Salt Lake philanthropist Obert C. Tanner proposed that she finish her reminiscences with funding from a foundation he had established. He urged her, in telling her life's story, to emphasize her adventures in clarifying hitherto repressed and distorted historical facts. "So," Tanner wrote, "I sit back and think of you as one of the Lord's lie detectors, carefully separating the bogus from the genuine, and may I add, courageously writing what you find—that's so very, very, very important."[3] Unfortunately she never prepared for publication the story of her dissent. She did, however, provide the means for others to tell the story. When she began to collect pioneer diaries in earnest, she also began to preserve a record of her own doings. She wrote sporadic diaries and more consistently saved the letters others wrote her and kept carbon copies of her own letters and manuscripts.

The following pages reconstruct Juanita's complicated domestic life in considerable detail. She remained affectionately allied to an enormous host of relatives descended from pioneer stock—the Leavitts, Hafens, Pulsiphers, and Brookses. Her story gives valuable insight into that institution for which modern Mormondom is famous, the extended family. Even more important, the mundane details of her domestic life provide an indispensable context for her achievements as a historian, tragedian, and dissenter. She was a rare and anomalous human being. The night bus by which she so often traveled between the disparate worlds of the rural and the urban is an apt symbol for her remarkable ability to reconcile opposites. She belonged to both the folk and the intelligentsia, associating with equal sincerity with villagers and university professors. She insisted upon her private nonconformity and encouraged dissenters, yet she loved, affirmed, and lived with conformers. She was defiant yet loyal, indignant yet compassionate. She dressed with a deceptive simplicity and spoke in the rural idiom of Dixie. As Sterling McMurrin, distinguished professor at the University of Utah, declared, "she was a most uncommon woman draped in a very common exterior."[4]

She was born on January 15, 1898, and was named Juanita Leone. Her father was Dudley Henry Leavitt, called Henry. Her mother was Mary Hafen. An older sister, Orpha Ora, had been born in November 1896. The little family lived in a one-room adobe house in Bunkerville, Nevada. Next to the house was a hut with walls of wire screen for summer sleeping. Encircling the lot were cottonwood and fig trees; in the back were a privy, a corral, and a garden. Orpha, "a beautiful child, with a mass of golden curls and dark blue eyes," died of a fever in August 1898. On the night she died, Mary suffered a miscarriage. The funeral was held in the yard under the trees so that the bereaved Mary, lying in the screened hut, could participate. "I never got out of bed for 6 weeks," Mary would later write. "It was hard for me to gain strength, as I cried so much. I can see now that I should have been more brave about it."[5]

Mary soon bore other daughters: Charity in December 1899; Aura Ola in November 1901. Juanita and Charity attached themselves to each other. Because Juanita was small for her age and Charity large for hers, they seemed like twins. Aura toddled along behind, not always included in their play. On hot summer nights Juanita and Charity lay on top of the sheets in the hut, thankful when Mary doused the dirt floor with cooling water. In the winter they huddled in the same bed. "I would warm her back," Charity wrote, "and then we would turn and she would warm mine. We did that until the weight of the heavy quilts got us warm enough to go to sleep."[6]

In 1900 Henry erected a new house on the same site, a two-room brick structure over a half cellar. He finished one room, and the family moved into that while he worked on the other. Among the furnishings was an astonishing extravagance, a new organ for Mary. Then came a drastic dislocation. In 1902 Henry was called on a mission for the Church. He spent the fall in Provo, Utah, attending a training school, and returned to Bunkerville to say good-bye at Christmas. For over two years he proselyted without purse or scrip in the central states mission. With great satisfaction he would later record his spiritual experiences. He and his companion met a farmer who "told us to go into the house, that he would be in soon. When he came he said to his wife: 'These are the two men I saw in my dream last night.' In many instances the spirit of the Lord was upon me so strong that while speaking in the pulpit I felt so light and free that I hardly felt my feet touching the floor and was able to explain the gospel to my own astonishment."[7]

Henry's daughters mourned his absence, and every evening Mary consoled them with her guitar and an inexhaustible repertoire of songs. In March 1903 she bore her first son, Melvin Henry. "The little girls were so thrilled about him, too, especially Juanita," Mary wrote. "She came to the bed one day and said, Oh ma, Isn't he sweet! Lets surprise pa with another one! I laughed till I cried."[8] As a missionary's wife Mary qualified for a certain support from the community. Men and boys from the village plowed her lot, fulfilled her assessment of ditch cleaning, and chopped wood. Neighbors brought flour, potatoes, and fresh liver and spareribs from slaughtered animals. Uncle Wier brought by an occasional silver dollar. Mostly Mary coped by dint of her own labor and foresight. She pruned and irrigated her vineyard, hoed and harvested a large garden, picked cotton on shares, cleaned house for neighbors, and, in the fall of 1903, rented her unfinished second room to the school district for five dollars a month. She was, then and later, unrelentingly busy. Every day she planned a project: stitching a quilt, cleaning house, bottling fruit, or drying figs.[9]

As permitted by the custom of the village, Mary attended Saturday night dances, occasionally dancing but mostly looking on and gossiping with friends. She loved to sing with other women, and sometimes in Fast Meeting she bore her testimony with a song. She adorned her small house as best she could: she calcimined the walls and hung prints acquired as premiums for selling Cloverine salve; she rehabilitated window curtains someone else had abandoned; she squeezed out cash for a new linoleum. Later she would acquire a set of dishes by taking catalog orders among her neighbors. "You always wanted nice things," Juanita would write to her long after, "not just cobbled-up ones, and you wanted our home to be nice. . . . You wanted music and art and beautiful things."[10]

When a class convened in Mary's other room in the fall of 1903, the teacher left the door open for ventilation. Juanita, too young for school, sat in the doorway watching and listening. She couldn't do otherwise, being, like her mother, a gregarious person. When cold weather came and the door was closed, Juanita slipped inside. She said nothing and the teacher ignored her, yet when in the fall of 1904 it was time for her formal entrance into the first grade, the teacher placed her in the second. She was curious by instinct. Neither then nor later could she resist learning.

Henry arrived home from his mission in early March 1905, bringing with him coconuts and maple sugar. He sported a mustache, which may be seen in a photograph taken soon afterward when he and Mary traveled to St. George. At thirty-five Henry is tall, broad, and lean. His dark hair, shingled above his protruding ears, is parted near the middle. He stares with the intense eyes of a man in whom the missionary has not entirely subsided. Mary, twenty-eight, is of medium height and perhaps a little plump, and her puff-sleeved, high- collared black dress swells to the floor. She has a pretty nose, abundant dark hair, and docile eyes.

Mary cried for a long time on the day of Henry's return. She didn't like the mustache, which he shaved not long after the photograph was taken. Perhaps, too, she had come to relish her independence. She would later say in a letter to her brother: "I never felt better in my life than when Henry was on his mission. It seemed like my work was more of a pleasure to me than it is now. I often tell him I wish he could go again."[11] Yet the couple were not long in resuming old patterns of affection, as attested by the birth of their son Laurel Evan in December 1905, a scant nine months later.

The family now occupied both rooms of the brick house, and Juanita, Charity, and Aura shared a little iron trundle bed. Finan-

cially diminished by his mission, Henry undertook anew the pursuit
of prosperity. With time he acquired wagons and horses, corrals and
stackyard, cropland and pasture, and hogs, milk cows, and range cattle, the latter eventually numbering close to a hundred. He raised wheat,
barley, sorghum cane, and melons, and Mary continued to raise a
large garden and to cultivate her grapes and figs. By this bounty they
sustained their increasing family. Breakfast might consist of bacon and
eggs and ground wheat mush immersed in molasses and cream. Dinner might consist of beans, fried potatoes, summer squash, and green
beans from a garden whose season began in March and ended in
November. Supper, a simpler meal, might consist of bread and milk
or lumpydick, a thick flour gravy. There were melons banked in a
haystack to last until Christmas, figs soaked in a sugar solution and
dried, and grapes with waxed stems hanging in the rafters. There were
other grapes pickled in a fermentation of molasses and water, unquestionably alcoholic. Like many other devout Mormons of their era, the
Leavitts were comfortably imprecise in heeding the Word of Wisdom,
a revelation prohibiting the use of tobacco, coffee, tea, and alcohol.
With innocent gusto they consumed not only their fermented grapes
but also coffee, tea, and homemade wine.

The family lived by subsistence agriculture, which implied
for Juanita an intimacy with the out-of-doors: the river, the cropland,
and the desert. Ordinarily, the river followed a docile and murmuring
course thourgh willows, sloughs, and sandbars. Its water, rank with
minerals and suspended soil, was wryly called "Virgin Bloat." By the
river sat fields and settlements: Bunkerville to the south, Mesquite to
the north. The fields were bordered thickly by cottonwood trees, selectively pruned for firewood. Beyond the cropland was the desert. To
the north were red, intricately eroded hillocks hemmed in by Mormon Mesa, whose far-reaching bluffs loomed against the sky. To the
south the desert, sparsely stubbled by mesquite, yucca, prickly pear,
and Joshua trees, tilted toward the distant Virgin Mountains.

In the summer the desert radiated a lethal heat. Normal
temperature was one hundred five or ten Fahrenheit; in hot spells, it
rose to one hundred twenty. As much as possible people lived out-of-
doors in the shade of trees. Adults who had received their temple
endowments—vows assuring them of higher glories in the Hereafter—
were unfortunately obliged to wear year round sacredly marked union
suits reaching to wrist and ankle. Children went shoeless and lightly

clad. Until she was well into her teens, Juanita wore in the summertime only a loose shift and panties sewn from flour sacks. Sometimes
the seat of her panties whimsically bore the imprint of a milling company.

Ironically the village was susceptible to floods. Each spring,
a torrent fed by snowmelt from distant mountains effortlessly scoured
the diversion dam from the riverbed. Each summer and fall, thunder-
storms ruptured ditchbanks. Sometimes floods changed the geography of the village. On one occasion (it might have been the flood
afterward called "the Noah") Henry removed barbed wire and posts
from the bottom of a field and carefully stacked them against a tree
on the higher end. The next day the posts, the wire, and tree were
gone. The flood had changed the course of the river, literally washing
his field away. When the floods had abated, the men of the village
instantly began the laborious repair of dam and ditches. They hauled
loads of rock and brush which, splashing and stumbling, they anchored
in the muddy stream. In the meantime the village transported its culi-
nary water from the river by wagon. "To what economies were we
forced!" Juanita would write. "Water was literally measured by the drop.
You must never dip a full cup from the barrel; you should take only a
little bit, just what you could drink. If you were handed a full cup you
drank what you wanted and gave the rest back for the host to dispose
of. Usually he handed it to the next person, or poured it carefully into
a bucket kept for waste water, to be given later to the chickens. To
throw it out carelessly was a serious breach which always called forth
a protest."[12]

Nevertheless, Juanita flourished in the out-of-doors. Her
father liked to take Mary and their children along when he went out
to look after his cattle. They rode in a fancy white-topped buggy, his
saddle horse trailing behind. While he hunted for his cattle, the children played in the river or among the sand dunes. Afterward there
was a picnic Mary had packed. On one outing, Henry, Mary, and the
little children took a nap after lunch, while Juanita, Charity, and Aura
played in the front seat of the buggy. "We got to playing that the
horses were running away," Charity wrote. "Our cries and screams
brought Dad to his feet red-eyed. We felt so foolish when we came to
our senses. Our play was always so real and we had forgotten the folks
entirely."[13]

For village dwellers wilderness is never far away. On summer nights Juanita slept on top of a haystack where the air was cooler. Overhead the sky was a glowing arch pricked with bright points of light. Sunrise cast a transitory alpenglow on the bluffs of Mormon Mesa. She played in the sloughs with Charity and Aura and neighbor children. They inhaled the heated scent of willows and stroked the furry cylinders of the cattails. They found bird nests and returned day after day to mark the progress of the eggs and fledglings. One day she loafed in the sloughs with her cousin Charles, who liked to rob nests. For weeks she had defended the nest of a yellow peach bird. Now Charles climbed the tree and took the eggs, placing them in his mouth because his pockets bulged with eggs he had stolen from other nests. "When he came on a level with me, I was ready," she narrated. "I slapped him good and hard on both hind pockets, an act which started yellow goo running down the back of his legs. He jumped to the ground and began to yell and swear, breaking the eggs in his mouth."[14] These were happy days. She would later call them her Tom Sawyer childhood.

Very early Juanita knew the source of the necessities of life and participated in their production. She and Charity tended pigs and chickens and milked cows and drove them back and forth between home and pasture. In early spring, when the desert was green, they rode double on a bareback horse looking for their cows in the hills above the town. In the summer they took the cows to the pasture in the river bottom. They looked on when it came time to slaughter pigs or steers, and they observed the milling of wheat and the rolling of cane. They found threshing time exciting. Amid dust and chaff they watched the circling draft horses and men throwing sheaves of wheat or barley into the thresher and sifting straw with pitchforks. The girls helped by carrying dishes to the long tables under the trees where the threshing crew ate dinner.

In the summer of 1906 Henry secured, as a cash supplement, the contract for carrying the mail between Bunkerville and the railroad town of Moapa, a labor he would perform for twelve years. Three times a week he made the round trip in a buckboard, departing Bunkerville in the morning, staying overnight in Moapa, and returning to Bunkerville late the next afternoon. He maintained a string of eight or ten ponies, for the pair which pulled the buckboard at a grueling rate—thirty-five miles in seven hours—could make no more than one trip a week. The care of these ponies fell to the eight-year-old Juanita. When her father rolled in from Moapa, she baited the pair of tired ponies with grain and returned them to the pasture, then caught a fresh pair and brought them to the corral for her father's convenience. Henry had always hobbled the ponies when he put them into the field so that he could catch them easily. Juanita quickly learned to catch them unhobbled: "I learned to rattle the nose-sack with a little grain in front of me and to hold the tell-tale rope behind me. I learned to approach from the left side, just opposite the front legs, and to try never to go head-on to a new horse. So it was not long after we got any new horse until I could catch it in the pasture without a bit of trouble, though Father couldn't get near it."[15] In later years she would recall proudly that neighbors called her "Hen Leavitt's boy."

At two o'clock one morning Henry wakened Juanita and asked her to go the field and catch a replacement for a pony that had gone lame. The night was black and the pasture two miles away. She feared the dark but more than that she feared Henry's scorn. "It was one of the hardest assignments of my life, but I conquered my fear, walked to the field, caught the horse, and met father out on the road on the bare hills. After he had changed horses and put me on the lame animal, he slipped into my hand this shining piece of silver."[16] It was her first quarter.

Henry forbade Juanita to mount his riding horse, a large, spirited animal named Flax. So of course, when she was no more than eight or nine, she tried him out. At the edge of town the horse bolted, heedless of her pull upon the reins. At first she panicked. Then came the calming thought that, though she couldn't stop him, she could turn him. She steered him onto an uphill road and stuck to his back until he had run himself to exhaustion. Perhaps Henry was secretly proud; at least he didn't punish his daughter. Long afterward, he and Juanita reminded one another "of how that little bare-headed, bare-footed girl was riding that race horse that thought he was in a national contest of some kind, and just had to win."[17] From these and dozens of other incidents, Juanita gathered Henry's voice into her identity, a voice scorning fear, encouraging initiative, approving achievement. In the out-of-doors she was conditioned for future confrontations of a far different sort.

By Mormon custom Juanita was baptized during her eighth year, her father performing the ceremony on September 2, 1906.[18] Within a week or two of that date she made a memorable trip to St. George. It was Henry's duty, as counselor in the bishopric of Bunkerville ward, to attend the quarterly conference of the St. George stake. (A Mormon ward is equivalent to a parish; a stake is an administrative unit containing a dozen or less wards.[19]) Conveniently, there was also an annual county fair in St. George. The little family traveled in a wagon loaded with rock salt, which would help pay for the trip. They made their headquarters in Santa Clara at the home of Mary's sister, Rosina Gubler. On a Saturday morning the family drove into St. George. First they toured the temple grounds, where the temple stood tall, stately, and brilliantly white. The grounds were a display of beauty such as Juanita had never before seen – shade trees, clipped lawns, and flower beds in geometric designs. "I felt that if I looked close, I might see angels hovering near the spire," Juanita wrote. "But I did touch the wall at last, and I did climb up the steps to the eastern door where Aunt Rosina said the Savior would enter when He came."[20] In the afternoon they attended the fair in the basement of the tabernacle, where quilts, doilies, and loaves of bread competed for attention with squash, sheaves of wheat, and farm machinery. On Sunday they returned to the tabernacle for conference, arriving early and taking seats in the gallery. Mary called the attention of her daughters to "the beautiful frieze around where the ceiling met the walls, and the classic leaf and flower designs from which the light fixtures hung." She also pointed out the All Seeing Eye fixed to the wall high over the choir. This, Mary told Juanita and Charity, "would be looking directly at us no matter where we sat. We experimented, running along the front aisle of the balcony, she one way and I the other, and both returned certain that the eye had followed every move."[21] Juanita respectfully tried to maintain an interest in the visiting general authority, Joseph F. Smith, who, for all that he was president of the Church and thought to be God's true prophet, delivered a listless sermon. Irresistibly her attention dwelled on the All Seeing Eye.

It was during this trip that Juanita caught the first devasting glimpse of herself in a full-length mirror. She crossed the street from the tabernacle to the Dixie Drug, where ice cream was advertised. As she entered the drugstore, she saw a strange child approaching her.

"It was a second or two before I realized that the dowdy child in the calico dress with its red pipings was really myself," she would write later. "Two of the Watson or Woodbury girls, perfectly dressed, were there. They saw my confusion and laughed. One of them made a remark about my shoes. Mother always purchased with an eye to service rather than beauty, hence the square-toed stogie. The other mentioned my purse—I had my money tied in the corner of my handkerchief, which had been used for so many things that it had long since ceased to be white."[22] She retreated instantly, shocked and humiliated beyond telling.

Throughout her childhood, she believed herself irredeemably unfavored. She would describe herself as "a puny, homely child" with "shoulder-blades like sprouting wings." She was so frail that her mother sometimes wept while bathing her, provoking her father to say, "The child is all right. Don't snivel over her." For a period her mother required her to wear a harness in order to straighten her posture. Her piano teacher told her she had a "swill-pail complexion." Her mouth often hung open because she had "chronic catarrah" and couldn't breathe through her nose. She had such crooked, protuberant teeth that a neighbor said "she could eat corn off the cob through a picket fence."[23]

She was nonetheless an affectionate, sociable child who absorbed more thoroughly than children of lesser sensitivity the customs, beliefs, and attitudes of Bunkerville. She inhaled Mormonism with every breath. Each Sunday there were long meetings in Bunkerville: Sunday School at ten and Sacrament Meeting at two, with an intervening dinner at home, the most elegant meal of the week, unless it was Fast Sunday, when the meal came late in the afternoon. The watermaster zealously emptied the ditches on Saturday night so that no one would be tempted to violate the Sabbath. Assemblies of every sort began and ended with prayer. When dismissing a meeting, older men often raised their right arm to the square and delivered long and oratorical benedictions.[24]

Every night and morning the Leavitts knelt in family prayer. When it was a child's turn to pray, the utterance was brief. Mary's prayers were longer and aimed toward the exigencies of the family. Henry's prayers were replete with sonorous phrases like "Hasten the day when righteousness shall cover the earth as the waters the mighty deep." Juanita remembered: "We got so we could tell just where father was, and by the time he got to 'Help us do Thy will and keep Thy

was, and by the time he got to 'Help us do Thy will and keep Thy commandments' we could gather in our wandering thoughts and be ready to join in the Amen and jump up promptly as soon as it was said."[25]

The people among whom Juanita grew up believed fervently in the healing of the sick by prayer and anointing, a power particularly attributed to men, who were universally ordained to the priesthood. Mary found great comfort in Henry's prayers during her confinements. At none of them was a physician present. "Often I felt nervous and feverish, but so long as he was near me I felt that I'd be O.K. With his hand on my head, many sleepless hours were calmed to rest. I had much faith in his administrations, which always brot relief."[26] Henry's prayers similarly relieved his children. "I can shut my eyes now," Charity would write, "and feel that blessed sense of peace and well-being that would come over me when he laid his hands upon my head to administer to me."[27]

Juanita also acquired a belief in spirits and other immortal beings. Her aunt Lena Leavitt reported seeing, late one night, the spirit of a deceased friend leaving the house where her husband and children lived. "Aunt Lena said that the mother was watching over her children!"[28] On another occasion Lena believed herself to be wrestling with the devil. Later she would learn that at the same moment a workplace accident had injured her son and killed his fellow worker. Juanita's uncle Lister Leavitt believed himself occasionally harassed by evil spirits. Exorcism by the power of the priesthood was not uncommon. More benignly, the citizens of Bunkerville could cite numerous appearances of the Three Nephites, immortal disciples of the Lord who, according to Mormon belief, wander the earth rendering miraculous assistance to his saints. Juanita was likewise exposed to a detailed protocol of charms, incantations, and prescriptions. The mother of an infant was cautioned to pare its fingernails with her teeth rather than with scissors; otherwise the child would grow up "sticky-fingered," an instinctive thief. A nursing mother was advised not to eat rabbit meat, which would infect her infant with wanderlust.[29] Uncle Lister wouldn't "let the kids comb his hair after dark. He said it combs sorrow to your heart."[30]

As a girl of eight or ten Juanita would not have doubted this rich lore of the supernatural. Yet even then she demonstrated a certain dubiousness. On a Halloween night Juanita and Charity cos-

tumed themselves in sheets and started along the dark street toward a
party at a neighbor's house. Passing a shed, they were confronted by
an apparition, a long white figure hovering in midair. They retreated
in fright, then paused for a conference. Juanita recommended an eva-
sion. They armed themselves with staves from Henry's woodpile and
circled widely into the street. As they came abreast of the hovering
whiteness, Juanita grew bolder. She insisted that they approach, speaking to the figure to test whether it were a spirit. She led them closer
and closer and finally gave it a poke with her stave. It was a slaughtered pig, scraped clean of its bristles, dangling from a beam.[31]

It would not have occurred to Juanita to distinguish between
church and state. The bishop of Bunkerville appointed the watermaster
and organized community projects, socials, and celebrations. Saturday night dances took place in the same old rock church where Sunday services held forth. Juanita attended long before she could join in
the dancing. Men pushed benches against the walls to clear the floor;
a musician pumped his accordian; a floormaster called a numerous
variety of waltzes, quadrilles, schottisches, and polkas. The dancers,
married and unmarried alike, mingled freely and changed partners
often, and "so wholeheartedly did everyone enter into the activity,"
according to Juanita's description, "that soon there would be a general steaming, fanning, and wiping of faces, while some of the more
energetic young men sweat frankly, dark lines spreading from the arm-
pits of their shirts to the shoulders and down the center back."[32]

The Fourth and Twenty-fourth of July were gala celebrations, the birthday of the nation seeming, if anything, less important
than the arrival of the Mormon pioneers in the Salt Lake valley. On
either holiday, the day began, in Juanita's words, "with serenading by
the home-made band on a bunting-covered wagon, their instruments
a motley collection ranging from flute and drum through guitar and
banjo to triangle and clapsticks and paper-covered comb. A meeting
occupied the forenoon with songs and speeches and recitations, while
the afternoon was given over to sports where boys stumbled in sack
races, and fat men ran with ladies, and children in each age group
swarmed along to receive a stick of candy at the goal."[33] On the Twenty-
fourth there was also a parade of covered wagons and handcarts commemorating the western migration of the Mormons. Young men dis-
guised as Indians raced their ponies alongside, shooting blanks wildly
into the air. In front of the church the wagons and carts drew into a

protective circle, and a citizen dressed as Brigham Young made a treaty with the Indians. Inside the church the assembled villagers "sang the song of the plains 'Come, come ye Saints, no toil nor labor fear,' and its companion, 'Hard Times Come Again No More'. . . . The orator of the day told the story of the drivings and mobbings that led to the evacuation of Nauvoo, of the hand-cart tragedies, of the epoch-making words, 'This is the place!' We were all made to feel that we were a part of that Kingdom of God which they had sacrificed so much to establish, and which was never to be torn down or given to another people."[34] All this jubilation, it is to be noted, took place in the baking heat of a Bunkerville July.

Christmas was another major celebration. Often a Christmas tree was erected in the meeting hall, where the village assembled for an evening program of carols, skits, and scripture readings and a climactic visit from a Santa Claus. On Christmas Eve a wagon traveled from door to door, conveying a group of carolers, who always included Mary with her guitar. Juanita would remember waking before daylight on a Christmas morning in the trundle bed she shared with Charity and Aura. At the foot of the bed was a small evergreen tree. "It was lighted only by the fire from the fireplace and decorated with strands of popcorn and colored chains, with one apple, one orange, and some cookies for each of us. My doll had a porcelain head and a home-made body. I think no tree has ever looked so beautiful since, nor any Christmas given me such a thrill."[35]

Juanita was fortunate to have grandparents close at hand in Bunkerville. From infancy she had known Mary's mother, Mary Ann Stucki Hafen, who had lived in an adobe house on the block where Mary and Henry lived. Acerbly Juanita would write that her grandfather Hafen, a polygamist residing in Santa Clara, had moved Mary Ann and her children to Bunkerville "because one of his grown sons by his first wife was getting married and he wanted the house they lived in. Thus like Hagar, to whom she was often compared even in public, Grandma was sent into the wilderness with her family, and left to shift for herself."[36] As a child fresh from Switzerland, Mary Ann had crossed the plains by handcart. Ever after she phrased English like her native German. For example, she instructed a grandchild to "throw some hay the fence over" and wrote in her diary when rural electrification reached Bunkerville, "I agreed to pay the Government Electrichens dollers 7.75 to wier my House. . . . "[37] There is a photograph of her at the door of her small weathered home. She wears a black skirt and shawl; her hair is piled in a bun on her head; her face is kindly and resigned.

Mary Ann devoutly conveyed to the bishop an exact tithe of butter, eggs, and fruit from her lot and field. She also made excellent wine, convinced that because it was of her own manufacture drinking it was not against the Word of Wisdom. One day when Juanita, helping with her wash, complained of a stomachache, Mary Ann relieved her with a little sugared wine. "I was so strengthened," Juanita wrote, "I was drunk. And I said, 'Oh, when I get to be old and a drunkard, I'll tell everybody that I had my first taste of wine from my little Swiss grandmother.' And she cried and went to my father and he set me up and he said, 'Now look. There's some that can take it and there's some that can't. And you're one that can't. When you get in places where they have it don't make a scene or preach a sermon. But don't drink any of the wine.' "[38]

In 1906 Juanita's aged paternal grandparents, Dudley and Thirza Riding Leavitt, moved from their ranch at Leavittville into a small rock house next door to Henry's and Mary's home. Dudley had been the quintessential pioneer. As a youth he knew the Prophet Joseph Smith and observed the transfiguration of Brigham Young in the image of Joseph. He was among the first missionaries called to proselyte the Indians of southwestern Utah in 1854 and was a frequent companion to Jacob Hamblin, the most famous of Mormon missionaries to the Indians. Dudley helped found Santa Clara, Gunlock, Hebron, and Bunkerville. Between his return to Bunkerville in 1906 and his death in 1908, Juanita saw him nearly every day. He had, as she would remember, a white ruffle of beard under his chin and "a great shock of snow-white hair, a large trunk, powerful arms and shoulders, but crippled, bowed legs." In the winter Henry hauled loads of green cottonwood from the borders of the fields, and Dudley sat on a chair with a rawhide bottom and chopped wood while Juanita and her sisters stacked it in ricks. Juanita and Charity took milk to his home every day and often stayed to hear his tales of narrow escapes from the Indians. His stories, Juanita remembered, were "so convincing that I always got prickly sensations along my spine to the roots of my hair."[39] One evening he sang eerie Indian songs full of staccato wailing and guttural ejaculations. He paused and stared for a long time at the fireplace. Then he stretched his hands to the fire and said, "I thank God that these old hands have never been stained by human blood."[40] Juanita thought he meant Indian blood. Long afterward she would learn that he had been present at the Mountain Meadows massacre.

Juanita's grandmother Thirza Riding Leavitt was a more lasting, if less imposing, influence, for she survived her husband by almost twenty years. An English immigrant, she was punctiliously superstitious: "To break a mirror or the point of your scissors, or to open an umbrella in the house were all sure signs of disaster," Juanita wrote. "I remember how excited she became when father once took a new shovel into her house. How she fumed until he took it out, and it must be by the same door through which he had entered, for to have it go through the house would have brought on disaster twice as bad." Unlike Grandmother Mary Ann, Thirza refused to labor in the garden and yard. She kept bergamot and rose leaves in her linen drawers and had a passion for dressing well. "She was fussy about her own appearance, toggy we used to call her, because she did so enjoy a pretty pin or a fancy neckerchief or any other bit of decoration. She wore her brooches and beads and fancy back-comb with the air of a true aristocrat. She always carried two handkerchiefs, a large, coarse one for necessity and a dainty, laced-edged one for display, a 'show and a blow,' she called them."[41]

Dudley Leavitt had four other wives: Mary and Mariah Huntsman, who were sisters; Janet Smith, an Indian raised in a white home, whom Dudley married upon the request of an ecclesiastical authority; and Martha Pulsipher, a widow of one of Dudley's close friends. Dudley was not reluctant to multiply and replenish the earth; altogether his wives bore him forty-eight children. Grandmother Mariah was a notable midwife in Mesquite, having been called and anointed to her position by church authorities. When she got old, two men were assigned to transport her in a chair from her house to a waiting wagon and from the wagon into the room where a woman was in labor. The Indian wife was a subtle embarrassment to the Leavitt name. In her autobiography Juanita described her first visit to this dark-skinned relative: "Grandma Janet is an Indian lady," Henry explains to his children with vehemence. "Don't gawp and stare at her with your mouths open! She looks like an Indian because she IS an Indian. But she is a fine lady; she is one of your Grandpa's wives and her children are all your cousins. They're all very fine people, some of them smarter than some of the all-white cousins. Just remember this!"[42] Elsewhere Juanita recorded that throughout her married life Janet "maintained a separate establishment, poor enough it is true, but always by herself, while the others often lived two in a house."[43]

The death of Dudley Leavitt in October 1908 was probably the first Juanita observed closely. She would remember her grandfather's passing as dignified and quiet. "His family accepted the inevitable as he would have wished. Some walked in the yard, or wept quietly in the other room, but where he lay, all was peace. A son who sat beside him touched his lips with water or shifted him slightly, holding his pulse and watching his breath grow shorter. Death crept up so softly that it was hard to tell when the end came."[44] At his funeral, the Bunkerville church bell tolled once for each year of his long life. Following the service the large audience filed slowly by the opened coffin for a final view. Accepting at face value Dudley's faith in a glorious Hereafter, Juanita wondered why a daughter fainted and many others wept. At ten she could not appreciate, as she later would, the living connection the old man had given her with the heroic pioneer past. His vivid personality and remarkable adventures would remain in her imagination, fueling her ambition to study and write about the settlement of Dixie.

In the fall of 1908 Juanita encountered an educational reversal. As she entered the sixth grade, the teacher objected to her presence. A year ahead of her age group, she struck him as excessively frail and sickly. It is possible that he believed she had tuberculosis. In any event, he recommended a winter in the out-of-doors. Years later, he would greet Juanita: "Oh my land, are you still alive? I had no idea that you'd live till Christmas. I couldn't stand the sight of you!"[45] Her mother wept and her father bought her "a beautiful dapple-blue pony with a flaxen mane and tail" as a consolation.[46] Juanita would come to love Selah, as the pony was named, with a passion. Thus for a period, while her siblings and friends were in class, Juanita rode her new mount, with the family dog Griz at her heels, in the river bottom and across the desert hills. Ultimately she became bored and lonely. Before the year was over, she returned, not to the sixth grade, but to the fifth, where a tolerant aunt was the teacher. Left to listen and read as she wished, she considered her second sojourn in the fifth grade one of her best experiences in learning. In 1909 she belatedly entered the sixth grade, and in 1910 the seventh, where she continued to do exceptional work. Her seventh-grade teacher would recall, "Even then the superior quality of your mind was clearly apparent. I recall having frequently told . . . what a joy teaching would be if one could have more students of your type."[47]

On an autumn evening in 1910 Juanita rode with Henry in a jolting, loaded wagon to a roundup camp at the foot of the Virgin Mountains. Men from Bunkerville and Mesquite prepared to gather and sort their cattle which had grazed the public range all summer. This was sheer pleasure for Henry, who relished working with cattle far more than farming. It would be Juanita's duty to return to Bunkerville the next morning with the extra team which helped pull the loaded wagon up the ascending road. She slept in the back of the wagon, awakening at dawn to the cook's cry of breakfast. "I was keenly aware of everything," she wrote later, "the men shivering in the half-light against the misty backdrop of mountain, the red glints of fire-light on leather jackets and tin plates, the smell of the hay under me mixed with pungent mountain odors and the incense of coffee and bacon. The sense that the men, most of them, did not know that I was there made me shiver with excitement."[48] At twelve, Juanita retained a passionate attachment to the out-of-doors. In retrospect she would recognize that the fields and desert had come close to making her "a nature mystic."[49] In 1959 she told the graduating class of Virgin Valley High School: "I'm glad for children raised in a town like Mesquite—in towns like all of our small country villages, where they have space and freedom, where they know morning and evening and night, the changes of the moon, the seasons of the year."[50] Perhaps the most important lesson she learned from the outdoor circumstances of her childhood was that a girl had as much capacity for a vigorous, adventurous, and enterprising life as a boy. Later she would extend that lesson, ambitiously entering upon a professional endeavor largely dominated by men.

Juanita would continue to ride and work in the open throughout her adolescence. Nonetheless, the drift of her life was toward an indoor, more conventionally feminine pattern. If one must choose a single symbolic year when that pattern began to assert itself, 1911 serves best. During that year Juanita finished the seventh grade and entered the eighth. She was still small for her age and unchanged by puberty. Yet her status was changing.

Her parents had compounded their family on a regular basis. Mary gave birth to Daisy Ina in September 1907, to Eva in February

1909, and to Francis Hale in June 1911. The birth of Francis was a
genuine initiation for Juanita, who for the first time in her life was
asked to assist. Grandmother Mariah Leavitt, very old and decrepit,
was in charge. Aunt Theresa stood at Mary's bedside holding her hands
and giving comfort and encouragement. Juanita was at the kitchen
stove, keeping water at a boil, sterilizing cloth patches, and browning
flour which would be used as a talcum on the newborn infant. Her
mother's terrible cries were a revelation, filling Juanita with anger and
humiliation: "Soon it got so bad that I thought I couldn't stand it. I
must not run away! I crouched down, my hands over my ears, and
prayed. One final, long agonizing shriek I thought would pull me apart.
An instant's silence, and the lusty cry of an infant brought me to my
feet."[51] One must not underestimate the compelling model her mother
posed for Juanita. Mary had been a constant, affectionate, even quer-
ulous and demanding presence. She oversaw garden, larder, and table
with a vigorous efficiency. She had no end of wifely projects: a wash
to do, soap to manufacture, fruit to dry, a quilt to stitch, walls to
whitewash, curtains to starch, straw to replace beneath the rag carpet.
Above all, her frequent pregnancies inculcated that ultimate duty of
the Mormon housewife Juanita knew she must someday become.

An initiation of another sort occurred during the summer
of 1911. Aunt Theresa had asked Juanita to help her clean house. As
she straightened books in a secretary, the girl discovered a handwritten narrative bound in calico-covered pasteboard. Its author was her
great-grandmother, Sarah Studevant Leavitt. Instantly, Juanita lost
herself in the account of her ancestor's conversion to Mormonism,
her migrations to Ohio, Illinois, and Utah, and her many spiritual
experiences. "The writing was labored, generously sprinkled with capital letters and phonetic spelling. It looked as though it had been done
with a quill pen, the down strokes were so heavy; every word seemed
to have been fashioned deliberately and with an effort. The pages
were brittle, so that though I turned them carefully as I could, some of
the corners broke off and crumbled in my fingers."[52] Juanita was
ashamed when her aunt returned near dark and found the houseclean-
ing unfinished. Yet Juanita was gratified by that truant reading. The
incident was an early sign of her fascination with original, handwritten accounts of the pioneer past.

Another incident in Juanita's passage from childhood was
the loss of her pony, Selah. She had domesticated Selah to a perfect

docility, bringing her grain and scratching her ears. She still took cows to the pasture, searched the sloughs, and roamed the desert on her dappled pony. The animal remained the most visible symbol of her attachment to an outdoor life.

During November 1911, Juanita noticed the tracks of a strange man and horse entering and leaving the pasture where she relayed the milk cows. Obviously a fugitive, hiding nearby, was pasturing his horse by night. She mentioned this fact to Henry, who asked her if she was afraid of the stranger. As far as Henry was concerned, he had pasture to spare. Then one morning the stranger's jaded horse was in the pasture and Selah was gone. Juanita was devastated. "Why hadn't I told Pa I *was* afraid of this stranger? Why didn't I go myself to Uncle Jess, the Sheriff, and tell him about this man hiding in the fields? Most of all, *why* hadn't I ridden Selah home last night as I had planned? She had come at my whistle, and I had ridden a couple of turns around the field, and then I had actually gotten out of the lane gate to ride her home by the hill road, but had come back and left her. At the sight of that raw-boned big horse in the pasture, I burst into tears, sobbing myself out on the ground."[53] Henry advised her to heed her hunches thereafter. This was, in fact, her first documented experience with her intuition—a faculty she would later come to depend on a great deal. Two weeks later word came that the stranger had exchanged Selah for another horse at a ranch on the Mogotsu. Juanita's joy was short lived. The owner of the ranch, whose two small grandchildren had been recently orphaned, considered the gentle animal a godsend. When Juanita demanded that Henry retrieve her, he refused, saying: "That's how life is with everybody. We have something today and tomorrow it is gone, like the river taking the grain field, and Aunt Dora's baby dying so sudden. We have to face up to these things and take them the best we can." Then he consoled her by a promise of good things to come: "You are getting a big girl now. It's time you put away childish things. In a few months you'll be fourteen, and start in high school next fall. We'll have to start Melvin to look after the horses. When you want to ride, you can ride Flax, and maybe with some of the money we get from Selah, Ma can buy you a real riding skirt."[54]

Juanita took his words to heart and accepted the loss of Selah. Perhaps indeed the future held many good things. In any event, it seemed clear that her Tom Sawyer childhood was over.

CHAPTER TWO

WED AND WIDOWED

Mary Leavitt rounded out her family by giving birth to Dudley Maurice in July 1913 and to Mary in September 1915. Henry happily welcomed these additions to his numerous brood, as Juanita later recorded with some chagrin: " 'Seems like every one gets cuter and smarter,' he would say, and I who was oldest used to wonder ruefully what I must have been like."[1] With some astonishment one realizes that at the moment of Dudley's birth, the family still lived in the two-room house Henry had built before going on his mission. The largest room served as bedroom, kitchen, dining area, and, on Saturday afternoon, bathroom. Year around some of the children slept in the screened hut. Monday wash was always an outdoor affair; in summertime cooking went on over an outdoor fire in the shade of the fig trees. Nonetheless, bodies were layered in indoor bunks and beds like eggs in a crate. By a studied indirection of eyes, the family observed Victorian decencies when bathing, dressing, and grooming. When all had gathered for dinner, simple progress through the room required an ability to dodge and halt.

But too much was too much, even for the Hen Leavitts, and in September of 1913 they traded their little house with $175 to boot for a larger house on the west side of town—an unfinished two-story brick structure of eight rooms. The new lot had conventional accouterments: a privy, coops and sheds, a garden plot, fig trees, grapevines, and pomegranate bushes. One supposes that for a week or two after moving in, the family wandered upstairs and down exulting in the sheer spaciousness of their new quarters. Henry was not noted as a tidy farmer. His fences sagged and his gates were patched with wire and poles. Yet he took extraordinary pride in his new house. Among his earliest improvements was a bathtub, a genuine claw-footed porcelain tub transported by wagon from the railhead and ensconced in a downstairs room. The faucets, if there were any, were dry, for the house had no running water. For Saturday baths in the winter, the boys cut wood and built a huge fire beneath the cauldrons under the fig trees, from which boiling water was scooped and carried into the house. A hose drained soapy water from the tub and carried it via a hole in the floor outside to the grapevines and pomegranates. Henry also had progressive ideas about lights, bringing into the new house the latest pump-style gas lamps.[2]

In the fall of 1913 Juanita entered her second year of high school. In 1911 the state of Nevada had for the first time commissioned secondary schooling in Bunkerville—a single teacher meeting classes in a spare room of the grade school and in nearby homes. Hitherto the few children of Bunkerville who attended high school had done so by boarding in Cedar City or St. George. In 1914 the high school dissociated itself entirely from the grade school by moving into the old rock church. There were scarcely a dozen students in each class year, a fact which induced certain citizens of Las Vegas, the county seat, to protest the diversion of school monies to Bunkerville. The county commissioners persisted, however, and in late 1915 let a contract for a high school building. When in 1916 a disastrous wind flattened the framework of the new building, Bunkerville's citizenry rallied, raised more funds, and erected a concrete structure. Bearing banners in a triumphant march, the student body took possession of the completed building in 1917.[3]

Bunkerville benefited from a national trend to educate rural children. Two young couples who augmented the high school faculty in 1913, Mr. and Mrs. A. L. Kelly and Erastus and Roxey Romney, exemplified this trend. Mormons from rural Utah, they shared a widespread American faith that teaching subject matter and building character were equally the duty of the educator. They taught a healthy mixture of subjects—English, history, mathematics, athletics, agriculture, home science, and sewing, the latter class meeting during at least one year in an upstairs room of the new home of Henry and Mary Leavitt. Coached by Erastus Romney, the Bunkerville basketball team performed the unthinkable during 1915-16 by taking the state-wide high school championship. Romney gave a model of connubial duty to the men of the town by insisting, in violation of village custom, upon doing the wash for his wife. "Erastus not only filled the settling barrel from the big ditch, dipped the clear water from the lye barrel to the black tub over the brush fire, and from this to the scrubbing tub, but he rolled up his sleeves and scrubbed the clothes and unashamedly pinned the diapers on the line." Roxey Romney, Juanita's teacher in a church auxiliary, provided an innovative example by continuing to appear in public as her pregnancy advanced, again in violation of village custom. Juanita was impressed by "how lovely she looked in her maternity dress of soft dark material, with a vivid red velvet bow and a bit of a flower at the throat."[4]

In the spring of 1914 the Kellys and Romneys initiated a campaign to beautify Bunkerville. For decades the village had endured stinking corrals and swarms of flies and mosquitoes. Of flies Juanita wrote: "The kitchen was never entirely free of them; they gathered in black swarms on the screen especially in the fall and during the fruit season, and at every opening of the door they darted back in. . . . We made few attempts to kill them, probably because the task looked hopeless, though we continued to brush and shoo them out before every meal."[5] During the summer when no one could sleep indoors, mosquitoes buzzed and stung until, late in the night, they seemed to abate. "We had not connected the mosquitoes with the malaria that plagued our town; we counted them one of the normal discomforts of life. We built smudges against them and prayed for our sick, besides dosing them with quinine."[6] Inspired by the Kellys and Romneys, the townspeople now cleaned up corrals and pigpens, drained swampy places or treated them with kerosene, sprinkled privy pits with lime and ashes, bridged ditches, graveled sidewalks, and planted flowers, shrubs, and trees.

For several years the young couples produced a drama during the holiday week between Christmas and New Year. The importance of these amateur productions to the villagers may be gauged by Juanita's later description: "Though the deception was never quite complete (we knew all the actors in spite of the make-up and borrowed costumes), though the acting was stiff and the voice of the prompter often audible beyond the coal-oil foot-lights, the audience lent its imagination freely to make up for all defects. We followed the heroine with sympathy and rejoiced greatly at the final curtain kiss. Often the older people entered into it more completely than did the young. I remember one time when in a tense moment an old man leaped to his feet and shouted, 'Look behind you, you dam' fool!' to the surprised hero. At another time, in *East Lynne*, I think it was, when a wife was pleading with her husband for forgiveness, a hardened old freighter stood up and with tears streaming down his face, pleaded, 'For God's sake man, forgive her!' "[7]

The progressive spirit of Bunkerville during Juanita's high school days may be further judged by its enthusiastic support of institutes and lectures. In January 1915, a five-day Farmer's Institute sponsored by the state of Nevada featured separate morning and afternoon sessions for men and women and conjoint evening sessions. A Miss Davis lectured to the women on the principles of home economics, providing special demonstrations of cooking and of the removal of stains from fabrics. A Professor Scott lectured to the men on animal husbandry, including the care and breeding of dairy cattle and poultry raising. He demonstrated the testing of milk and obligingly judged local horses and dairy cattle.[8]

Through teachers, books, and lectures, the Outside impinged upon the adolescent Juanita. In the chapter of her autobiography entitled "The Outsider," she wrote of the liberating influence an educated visitor to Bunkerville had upon her in a slightly earlier period of her life. From the back of her pony, the girl Juanita pondered the departed visitor and made up her mind "that I would see some of the world beyond the desert, that I would go to a college or a university or whatever it was that one went to in order to learn of books, and how to talk like books. I would not wait for life to come to me, I would go out to meet it."[9] Her fascination with the Outside would accelerate during her high school years. Bright and energetic, she dreamed of challenge and scope somewhere in the world beyond Bunkerville.

In wry terms Juanita described the old rock church which the town fathers had donated to the use of the high school. "With one class in session on the stage and another around the stove in the center of the hall, the students at the few study desks in the back of the building had to exercise all their powers of interest and concentration to make their preparations." The informality increased as students went to other class areas. Mathematics classes met in an upstairs room in a nearby home equipped with blackboards and tables. Most startling, a woodshed served for the English classes of A. L. Kelly. The woodshed roof was of corrugated metal which deflected sun and occasional rain; its walls were no more than meshed chicken wire. "Being outside, there were often diversions: Inquiring sparrows hopped about; blackbirds settled in undulating swarms in the tithing office yard across the street; when the warm days came, there were lizards, little gray ones with beady eyes and wide mouths, and turned-in toes, and black-collared bull lizards whose green bellies, covered with a thin wash of gold, glistened in the sunshine." Such vivid detail testifies to the frequency with which the scholar Juanita allowed herself to be distracted. Nonetheless, she would claim that "many of the most profitable classes I ever attended were held there. We were introduced to Hamlet and MacBeth, to Adam Bede and Silas Marner and David Copperfield, to Portia and Jane Eyre and Christabel." She created a private nook for study in the hay shed of the nearby tithing office. "I hollowed out a place on the south side near one of the large uprights, where by curling up a little I could keep my back to the afternoon sun and my book in the shadow. Here I read my history and economics and German assignments. Here I lost myself completely in the books that were suggested as outside reading in English." Thus sequestered, she was sometimes late for classes or missed them entirely. "One day I became so absorbed in *Ivanhoe* that I did not hear the bell that marked the change of class, and came to myself only when the shadows were long and I was cold and the book finished."[10]

Juanita was embarrassed that puberty came so late. When at last she blossomed into a young woman, she still found little about herself to be proud of. Gazing into mirrors, she saw a slight, ungainly body; protruding, crooked teeth; a disproportionate nose; unruly hair. However, other people didn't think unfavorably of her. If she wasn't beautiful, neither was she ugly. Her naturally curly hair was an evident asset, as was her gregarious, good-humored personality. In retrospect, she judged her advantages more tolerantly: "I learned to substitute a pair of nimble heels and a cheerful 'line' for a pretty face, and found that I had my share of dances and some dates."[11]

Bunkerville youth often formed spontaneous parties at the Leavitt home. The large kitchen accommodated candy pulls. In the living room was a piano, which had come at the insistence of Mary, who loved music passionately. "Nobody knows the many hours I enjoyed hearing the girls play it," Mary wrote in her life story. "Often after I had gone to bed I listened for hours at a time, to the beautiful music and singing that was going on in the other room. Some of our neighbors thot we were foolish to buy a piano when times were so hard, and perhaps our children were barefooted, but music in the home was one all important thing for me. I knew it would keep our children at home, they wouldn't need to go away for amusement."[12]

Seated on her front porch on a summer evening, Mary strummed her guitar while her children, lolling roundabout on the Bermuda grass lawn, followed in song. "One after another the neighbor youngsters drifted in—some would even walk down town to see if the Leavitts were out on the lawn tonight. Though our repertoire was not large, we enjoyed singing the same ones over. 'Wake, Lady, Awake,' 'My Darling Nellie Gray,' 'Sweet Belle Mahone,' and dozens of others we sang, different ones trying the alto or tenor. Though not really finished music, we enjoyed it, it gave us something to do, and it made our home a gathering place for the young folks of town."[13]

When parties formed at the Leavitt home, Henry seized the opportunity to josh his daughters boisterously. Charity would remember "how embarrassed we used to be when the gang would gather at our house to have Dad offer one of his 'yeller' buckskin horses to any young man who would take one of us girls . . . off his hands. He used to tease the life out of us."[14] More soberly, Henry cautioned his adolescent daughters regarding modesty and an unprovocative demeanor toward men. It may seem to the modern reader that he expected more of women than of men in the preservation of chastity. "Another thing that impressed me," Juanita wrote of her father, "was his statement, often made, that no girl ever got into trouble without inviting it herself. 'No man wants to hurt you, or insult you if you will tend to your own business. If you have any place to go alone after night, get out and go like you knew where you were headed for, and no one will try to stop you. It is only when a girl loiters along and giggles on street corners that men approach her.' Often after coming home from the ditch at night, or where groups of men were working together he would say, 'Well, I hope that I never hear you spoken of like —— was today.' His common statement, 'Familiarity breeds contempt,' and 'make a boy respect you first and love you later' always had an effect."[15] Her father's exhortation helps explain the Victorian reserve with which the adult Juanita would regard sexual matters.

Juanita graduated from high school in June 1916 among a graduating class of five. In fine fettle at eighteen, she spent an adventurous summer at the Pine Valley ranch of Aunt Rosina and Uncle Ben Blake. Long afterward, she would recollect that summer in a speech made at the funeral of a cousin who was among her companions. All hands were busy milking cows, making cheese and butter, tending orchards and gardens, and snaking fence poles out of the mountains.

"I was useful chiefly because I could ride horses and milk cows. Ella had no experience in this line, and Marie was too young, but Archie, Clem, and I took over the milking department. I could round up the cows in the evening and the calves in the morning, and so release a boy for heavier work of hoeing or making fences or irrigating." She ranged widely on horseback. Once she and some of her cousins rode in search of snow to make ice cream for the Pioneer Day celebration. "We took such delight in visiting 'Further Water,' in riding along 'The Saddle' where we could see out over the valley, and in getting the sacks of snow from the Hidden Cave."[16] Eastward lay Zion Canyon, southward St. George, westward Nevada. The land she could claim as home expanded as she gazed upon shimmering deserts, tilted plains, and high mountain masses marked by ridges, buttes, and pinnacles.

Returning home in the fall of 1916, Juanita entered her first year of college study, for Nevada, as a part of a state-wide attempt to increase the supply of grade school teachers, was providing a year's normal course in Bunkerville. Her mentor was a regal young woman, Miss Mina Connell, fresh from studies in pedagogy at Columbia University. Miss Connell "was slender and trim, carrying her long braid of auburn hair around her head like a coronet."[17] Of cultivated values and firm convictions, she declared that this year of normal schooling would equal that available anywhere in the nation. Juanita deemed herself fortunate to be employed as janitor of the Relief Society house where the normal school met. During many after-hours conversations, she found that Miss Connell, though resistant to both the Mormon faith and Bunkerville society, was interested in transcribing the idioms and folkways of the village. Unquestionably Miss Connell was the most impressive representative of the Outside that Juanita had so far encountered.

It was probably during this year that Juanita showed an interest in creative writing, enrolling in a correspondence course from a film writing academy. "I remember going upstairs to her bedroom where she kept all her books and papers," wrote Daisy. "I think she was taking a correspondence course from Hollywood and she was practicing writing scenerios for a play. I read the manuscript of a love story she had written. I thought it was wonderful, even though I probably wasn't supposed to be reading it."[18]

In other ways the Outside courted her. LeRoy Hafen, her mother's brother, taught at Bunkerville during this year. He would remember that "a touring car with several 'good road' enthusiasts from Los Angeles came to town to boost the 'Arrowhead Trail' from Southern California to Salt Lake City. The townsfolk all gathered at the Meeting House, gave the visitors a big dinner, and listened to the prophecies of the promoters."[19] The Arrowhead Trail quickly took on symbolic significance for Juanita, who informed the graduates of Virgin Valley High School that "at the corner of our corral there stood a sign which said SLC 385 miles and LA 385 m. How important it made me feel when I went out to milk to think that I stood exactly half way between those two great cities!"[20] She was also touched indirectly by World War I in the spring of 1917. She sang "Tipperary," "Over There," and "K-K-K-Katy" and joined other young women in writing group letters to school chums whose departure for military service had left empty seats on the stage at graduation.

For some time Juanita had been in a brash and contentious mood. She had become a Sunday School dissenter "regarded as verging on apostasy by some of the older people of the town, who used me as an argument against going to school—it would surely destroy the faith."[21] The Sunday School teacher with whom she quarreled was aging, lethargic Uncle Lon, a half brother to Henry. "It took him so long to get to the end of a sentence," she wrote, "that my nimble mind would go on long excursions between every period. He wore funny side whiskers, and little glasses far down on his nose, and his trousers bagged and he didn't shine his shoes." Worse than his appearance were stories from the Old Testament which the old man narrated with an absolute credulity: of Lot's wife turned into a pillar of salt; of Jacob's purchase of Esau's birthright with a mess of pottage; of the bears which ate up the children who scoffed at the bald-headed Elisha. While Juanita vociferously challenged these tales, one after another, as being improbable or unjust, her classmates responded with glee. One of them told her, "You are so contrary that if you ever got drowned, they'd have to go up-stream to find you."[22]

At last an exasperated and injured Uncle Lon complained to her father. Henry pleaded with his headstrong daughter to consider the age and good intentions of her uncle. He also drew an analogy which Juanita would long after make famous among liberal Mormons. A cowboy who wants to turn a stampeding herd can ride neither in it nor counter to it; he must ride at the edge. "Happy sounds are generally better than cursing," she would quote him as saying, "but there are times when he must maybe swear a little and swing a whip or lariat to round in a stray or turn the leaders. So don't lose yourself, and don't ride away and desert the outfit. Ride the edge of the herd and be alert, but know your directions, and call out loud and clear. Chances are, you won't make any difference, but on the other hand, you just might."[23] A chastened Juanita returned to class the next Sunday determined to make amends, but Uncle Lon had resigned from his position as teacher. When the old man died not long afterward, she regretted that she had lacked the fortitude to apologize. Unknown to her at the moment, the episode had helped define the boundaries of her later nonconformity.

One could conjecture that, given the outside influences upon Juanita and given her critical and impatient temperament, she would migrate far from her origins, both physically and intellectually. In the spring of 1917, however, centripetal forces—ingrained beliefs and affectionate attachments—held her firmly in Bunkerville. One such force was her love for her cousin Albert Leavitt, son of another of her father's half brothers.

For months Juanita and Bert, as she called him, had associated closely as organist and chorister, respectively, of the Sunday School. At first, as a matter of duty, they had rehearsed hymns together in an otherwise empty church. Soon they began to accompany one another to choir practice and socials. Their budding romance encountered a serious obstacle when, during the spring of 1917, Albert departed on a proselyting mission. Juanita wrote of it in this manner in her autobiography: "Before we realized it, we were going steady, and becoming altogether too fond of each other. . . . Our two fathers evidently decided that we should be separated before it should become more difficult. Some of the local boys had volunteered to go to the army; one or two were drafted, but Bert was called on a mission, which would mean a full two-year absence. Few romances could survive that."[24] At the moment of Albert's departure, Juanita did not consider the relationship at an end. Temporary partings of this sort were common among engaged and married couples. Exchanging letters with the absent Albert, Juanita patiently awaited his return. At nineteen she demonstrated an ambition no larger than to marry a cousin and settle down as a rural wife, following precisely the pattern set by her mother and grandmothers.

Miss Connell had promised that each of her normal students would be placed in teaching positions for 1917-18. Juanita's
appointment was at the Bunkerville grade school. A. L. Kelly, now
district superintendent, recommended that Juanita borrow money and
go away for the summer. When her Uncle LeRoy Hafen suggested
that she accompany him and his wife to Berkeley, she accepted. Destined to become a widely recognized historian of the West, LeRoy would
return from summer school at the University of California to serve as
principal of the Bunkerville high school.

En route to the Bay Area, Juanita marveled at the red-
woods—"one so large that the train ran right through it, leaving enough
timber on both sides and in the top to insure its life." In Berkeley, the
group—composed of LeRoy, his wife, Ann, their toddler, Norma,
Juanita, and a cousin, Leah Leavitt—shared expenses and work, labor-
ing each Saturday to finish chores so that on Sunday they could cross
the bay by ferry to San Francisco. On bright days the sun sparkled on
the blue waters of the bay, and the cities roundabout, unruined by
the automobile, clustered picturesquely upon green rolling hills. At
Market Square they bought peanut butter by the half-gallon: "The
nuts were ground and ran directly into the jar while we watched and
waited."[25] Once they spent a happy Sunday afternoon in a park with
their cousin Laman Leavitt, a soldier on leave from a nearby boot
camp. There is a photograph of this occasion, in which one sees Juanita
in a white dress. Her face is pretty and girlish; her hair, copious and
somewhat wispy, is pulled back and adorned by a white flower.

Following her return from Berkeley, Juanita worked in Las
Vegas for a month to recoup her finances. Aura, Charity, and a host
of male and female cousins from Bunkerville were also there seeking
temporary employment. Their numbers allayed to some degree Henry's
fears that his daughters would come to harm. Juanita found a job in a
bakery run by a German couple, making dough, wrapping loaves, and
icing cupcakes. The German wife gave Juanita fastidious instructions
regarding eggs. "I came at seven in the morning," Juanita wrote, "and
began my day by breaking a dozen eggs in each of six large bowls,
being careful to rub the inside of the shell with my forefinger. Otherwise one- seventh of the egg white would be left in the shell."[26] Much
later an interviewer would ask whether she had adopted the same manner of scraping out eggshells in her own kitchen. "Are you kidding?"

Juanita replied scornfully. "I never cleaned an egg out that way again in my entire life."[27]

In the fall of 1917 Juanita began teaching the combined third and fourth grades in Bunkerville. During the Christmas holidays, the schoolhouse burned. Thereafter, Juanita's class met in a private home. She would remember two notable disciplinary problems. She seized a boy by the arm who had tripped another and ordered him not to return to school until he could behave himself. "I was trembling and weak as he left," she wrote, "and sank into a desk about to cry; embarrassed, ashamed that I had become so angry; humiliated both for myself and the boy." When the boy returned in a repentant mood, Juanita secured his loyalty by having him assist her in gathering student papers. Another fractious boy put a bee down a girl's back. As she furiously erased the blackboard, Juanita tried to think of a proper discipline. Unexpectedly she asked him in a kind voice whether he would like to be promoted to the fourth grade. His defiance melted and "from that day on, he worked at his books, graduating near the head of his class."[28] In both instances it seemed that an uncanny intuition had guided her. Increasingly she believed that she possessed an extra-rational instinct for solving personal problems and making difficult choices.

On the evening of January 2, 1918, Juanita participated in the exorcism of an evil spirit from the body of her elderly cousin, Orange D. Leavitt. Uncle Cull, as he was called, was a son of Dudley Leavitt's brother Lemuel; he had married two of his cousins (Henry's sisters and Juanita's aunts). On this January evening, Henry had been asked to give a blessing to Uncle Cull, who was very ill and reportedly possessed. Henry invited Juanita to accompany him. She and her father entered the sickroom with Cull's son Elmer, a cousin some six years older than Juanita. Elmer knelt and spoke to his father. "For a minute the room was quiet," Juanita recorded. "Then as Elmer stood and moved back so that the brethren could administer, [Uncle Cull] started to curse and rave. Pa had the oil and stepped up close to begin, but Uncle Cull started to laugh. I don't know how the Devil would laugh, but this curdled my blood. Then he started to repeat a part of the prayer about the Power of the Priesthood and would swear and threaten them. 'Bull Shit! I can handle you all, one at a time or all together! Wanna take me on?' "

Elmer signaled Juanita and quietly led her from the room. They crossed the street and made their way to a willow tree growing on the bank of the Big Ditch. There they knelt and in turn offered prayers that Cull might be liberated from the spirit which afflicted him. Returning to the sickroom, they found him resting quietly. Hours later he died in peace. Soon the lore of Bunkerville had it that the prayers of Elmer and Juanita had been the efficacious agent. "Later as people gathered at the home before the funeral, I heard Thodosia tell several times how her father was possessed of the Devil until he didn't even look like himself, how he laughed and cursed and raved, and then suddenly said, 'All right! All right! I'll go now! But it's not you guys here with that oil; it's them two kids up by the willow tree!' "[29]

Although, as she turned twenty, Juanita had challenged certain beliefs of Bunkerville, she continued to accept others. Nothing in her later education and career would dislodge her belief that an evil spirit had indeed been exorcised from Uncle Cull's body.[30] She was a complex mixture of the critical and the credulous. One sees in her, now and later, undulating patterns of opposites: love for home and attraction to the Outside; defiance and acquiescence; critical reason and blind faith. Fortunately she possessed an extraordinary potential for reconciling those opposites. That ability would have much to do with determining the precise nature of her later achievements.

During the winter of 1918, Albert Leavitt sundered the intimate relationship which he and Juanita had maintained by correspondence since his departure on a mission during the previous spring. It was Charity who witnessed the following. On a winter night Juanita read a letter from Albert by the light of the fire in the kitchen range. The door to the firebox was lowered, because, as Charity explained, the young Leavitt women, who had to cut wood as well as do other outside chores, frequently cut the cottonwood limbs into lengths which protruded from the range. Tears streamed down Juanita's cheeks as she read each page by the firelight and, having finished it, put it into the fire. Stricken with pity, Charity kept her silence, the occasion seeming too private for words. Later Juanita revealed that Albert had met a new love and wished to be free. Though Albert did not finally marry this young woman, the intimacy between him and Juanita was finished.[31] Of her ruined romance Juanita would write in her autobiography only this stoic and cryptic sentence: "Though for a while I was very lonely, I soon adjusted."[32]

As school ended in the spring of 1918, A. L. Kelly asked Juanita to teach during the following year in Mesquite. Enticed by the promise of a raise, she attended summer school at the University of Utah. She tersely summarized this experience in her autobiography, taking note of several companions in Carlson Hall—an Oriental girl who was phenomenal in her ability both to do mathematics and to eat without gaining weight and a woman who had married a Navajo and now lived and taught among the Navajo tribe.[33] One supposes that Juanita enjoyed the verdant campus and the moderate Salt Lake climate. Yet in her account she preserved an absolute silence about her own feelings and about the course of study she pursued, as if she had been in a period of lassitude and disillusionment.

Mesquite lay only four or five miles across the river from Bunkerville. Nonetheless, because a teacher was expected to join fully in the life of her community, Juanita moved to Mesquite in the fall of 1918. Instantly her spirits revived. From the first day her class, composed of grades three, four, and five, seemed exceptional. Greeting her with great warmth, the students joined readily in group singing and avidly pursued the reading assignments she gave each grade in turn.[34] Among the students were her sisters Daisy, eleven, and Eva, nine, whom Mary and Henry had relinquished to her care. Thus began for Juanita the role of substitute mother which she would play often and well. Over the years few of her traits would prove stronger than her compulsion to mother, besides her own children, an unending procession of sisters, brothers, nieces, nephews, and grandchildren. Of the winter in Mesquite Eva would write: "At Mesquite Juanita gave us such special attention, like rolling our long hair up in rags at night so that we would have pretty ringlets in the morning for school or church. She also got us cute new dresses and we were in 7th heaven. She was so wonderful to us that we simply adored her. Never had we had such attention in our large family at home. No wonder we did not once get homesick. . . . "[35]

Juanita and the girls returned to Bunkerville for the Christmas holidays. On certain evenings Juanita rode horseback to Mesquite to practice a part in a play. Henry, who had required Juanita at eight to ride alone in the dark to fetch his mail ponies, now insisted that she have Daisy's company: "She was an excellent rider, but Pa wouldn't let her go over there and back alone so I was chosen to go with her, as a chaperone I suppose. I rode behind the saddle as we sometimes galloped and most of the time walked along. It was a wonderful time to visit and talk. . . . I watched her pratise [*sic*] and thought she was the most glamorous and beautiful heroine there was. She had her hair in curls around her shoulders. It was naturally curly. I thought she outshone everyone."[36]

Early in the fall of 1918 a memorable relationship began between Juanita and Nephi Johnson, the aged patriarch of Mesquite. (Among the Mormons a patriarch is ordained to pronounce prophetical blessings upon individuals.) From their first meeting at church, Juanita treated the old man with extraordinary respect, as if she intuited how vital to her later interests was the dark secret that lay in his memory. He was, as a photograph shows, a man of remarkable appearance: his head bald; his cheeks sunburned; his mouth and chin lost in an effulgent white beard; his countenance wistful and sad, as if he pondered endlessly the probability of his own damnation.

One Sunday afternoon in September, Nephi Johnson proposed to give Juanita a patriarchal blessing. Although she had plans for an outing with newly found friends, Johnson refused to take no for an answer. He laid his hands upon her head and, while she herself wrote the blessing into his official ledger, he pronounced prophecies and admonitions.[37] Among his words were these: "Thou art of the lineage of Abraham, through the loins of Joseph and the blood of Ephraim. Thou hast come upon the earth in the dispensation of the fulness [*sic*] of times to help establish the principles of eternal truth upon the earth."[38] It was not an extraordinary blessing by the standards of the time, yet in all probability, like other believers, Juanita took it with great seriousness, having faith that by pondering and praying about it she could extract guidance for her life.

At a Saturday night dance in the early fall of 1918 Juanita began an even more momentous relationship. As he danced with her, Ernest Pulsipher addressed her with these not-so-original words: "The thing I can't understand is where you have been all my life. How come I didn't see you long ago?"[39] On subsequent Saturday nights Juanita danced with Ernest and on Sundays saw him in church. During the Christmas holidays, he entered the Bunkerville store where she helped out as a clerk. He seemed flustered by her presence. One afternoon early in the spring of 1919, when the apricots and plums had precociously bloomed, Juanita found herself as Ernest's partner for an excursion with another couple into a nearby canyon. The young women had brought baked beans, sandwiches, potato salad, and a custard pie. Ernest, who had never before tasted potato salad, declared it inedible. Juanita clapped a lid on the salad and sulked. After the meal Ernest suggested she and he take a walk. They ascended the canyon, observing the stream, the giant rocks, the groves of quaking aspen. Juanita's words complete the story: "Ernest pulled me toward him, 'I've waited six long months for this,' he said and gave me a kiss that I thought would smother me. Then into my hands he slipped a little velvet case. A diamond! An honest-to-goodness diamond! Not very large, but genuine!"[40] When they returned from their stroll, they had tentatively set a wedding date for early September when the fair was on in St. George.

Leonard Ernest Pulsipher was born in Hebron, Utah, on February 29, 1892, to John David Pulsipher and Ann Elizabeth Bowler. His grandfather, John Pulsipher, had been a prominent pioneer of Dixie. In 1900, following a sojourn in Gunlock, Utah, John and Elizabeth moved their family of four sons and a daughter to the vicinity of Mesquite, clearing a farm on undeveloped land. In 1901 John was stricken with typhoid and pneumonia; thereafter he remained an invalid. His sons assumed support of the family. Lewis, fifteen, provided cash by herding sheep away from home. Stanley, eleven, Ernest, nine, and Howard, seven, raised abundant crops of grain, melons, corn, cane, and pumpkins. Howard would reminisce: "We were so small that it took two of us to put the harness on the horses. One would get on the horse and the other working from under. I being the youngest would have to be on the wagon when we hauled hay. Stanley and Ernie would pitch the hay on. They were so small they had to get some alfalfa on the fork then put the end of the handle in the ground then raise it on the wagon."[41] Ernest was, as Juanita remembered him, "the only one of the family with dark hair; all the others were blonde. He was not so tall as Howard, nor so heavy-set as Stan, but he was wiry and strong, and had a wonderful sense of humor, even in the worst of his sickness."[42] Despite his small stature, he excelled in athletics. He was also, according to Howard, "very religious and clean in every respect—never any tea, coffee, liquor or tobacco, and never any foul language."[43]

In October 1913 Ernest departed for the northwestern states mission. Presiding over the mission from headquarters in Spokane was Melvin J. Ballard, whom Ernest learned "to love and idealize."[44] Ernest returned from his mission in June 1915, having been released early because his family's finances had failed. A private reclamation company building a dam at the mouth of the Virgin Narrows had contracted for Pulsipher hay. When its check for over $1200 bounced, the family was in a crisis. Ernest and Howard briefly worked the farm together, but since there was no market for their crops, Howard went away to work in a mine. He soon married and entered the army to serve in World War I. Ernest remained on the farm with his father and mother. He was living there when he became engaged to Juanita in the spring of 1919.

The Pulsipher farm lay downriver about two miles from Mesquite on a bench opposite Bunkerville. (Today a freeway skirts the property and a casino occupies a portion of its acreage.) It pleased Juanita and Ernest to wander this property arm in arm. They would cultivate a part of the farm in behalf of Ernest's aging parents; another part they would develop as their own. "Ernest loved this large farm," Juanita wrote. "Here we were on the high ground near the red sandhills, and we could take in the full expanse of green, so large and beautiful. We would build our place on the higher ground where we had a magnificent view, not only of the farm, but of the distant mountains."[45] With apparent good cheer, Juanita informed A. L. Kelly that she would not teach when school opened next September. Her conservative self had emerged; the call of the Outside was distant, perhaps inaudible.

As school neared its close in the spring of 1919, Nephi Johnson made what seemed a whimsical request of Juanita. His cane tapping, the old man made his way into her classroom and sat patiently until Juanita had dismissed her students. "He told me that he wanted me to do some writing for him," she recorded. " 'My eyes have witnessed things that my tongue has never uttered, and before I die I want it written down. And I want you to do it.'"[46] She listened politely; then, having other things to do, she promised to accommodate him some other day. It was one of those events which at their occurrence seem commonplace and only with time are seen in their true urgency. Juanita had no inkling of how often nor with what vehemence she would in her later life denounce her procrastination.

Juanita moved home to Bunkerville and put Nephi Johnson from her mind. Shortly word arrived that the old man was dying and calling for "the little school teacher." Juanita rode into Mesquite before sunrise the next morning. She pressed her cheek against the forehead of the dying man and he seemed comforted. She waited patiently, pen in hand, for nearly two days at the bedside, but he was too far gone to do more than babble. Toward the end his babblings became terrifying: "He seemed troubled; he rambled in delirium—he prayed, he yelled, he preached, and once his eyes opened wide to the ceiling and he yelled, 'Blood! BLOOD! BLOOD!' "[47] It was then that Lister Leavitt, Juanita's uncle and the dying man's son-in-law, revealed that Nephi Johnson had been at the Mountain Meadows massacre.

It is possible that Uncle List made his revelation without elaboration and that for days Juanita mulled it in silence. But sooner or later she asked for more detail—from Henry, surely, and probably from other relatives as well. The lore of the massacre with which she was familiar from childhood discounted it as an Indian attack upon California-bound emigrants, a frontier slaughter so unrelated to the affairs of Bunkerville as to be insignificant. Now came a shocking enlightenment. Numerous Mormons had participated in the massacre. Among them had been not only Nephi Johnson but also Dudley Leavitt. One supposes that Juanita's informants spoke reluctantly. Perhaps they emphasized mitigating circumstances or tried to exonerate the private Mormon soldiers and to lay double blame upon their officers. In particular, they conveyed to Juanita her grandfather's self-exoneration, which she would record at a much later date: "My own grandfather, Dudley Leavitt, was there, from all I have been able to learn, a picket riding guard on the hill. He might have been with the group in the valley, though all his life he denied that—as all the others did. He cautioned his children not to marry Higbees or Haights or Dames or Klingensmiths, because he believed that the sins of the fathers would be visited upon the heads of the children until the third and fourth generation."[48] Yet from the very apologetics of her relatives Juanita inferred their unwitting, vicarious assumption of responsibility. At the deathbed of Nephi Johnson she had stumbled upon an astounding truth: within the collective heart of her homeland nestled a dark and damning guilt.

As the sweltering summer of 1919 grew on, Juanita removed to the cooler clime of Cabin Spring, her family's summer homestead at the mouth of a canyon in the Virgin Mountains some twelve miles south of Bunkerville. For over a decade the family had maintained an orchard of peach, pear, and apple trees, kept dairy cattle, and cultivated large gardens in this pleasant place. The family slept in a screened cabin having a wood floor and canvas roof and cooked on an outdoor stove. A small concrete dam backed up the creek during the night. According to Juanita's brother Dudley, "We kids would jump in there and take out the plug and out would come the water and we'd irrigate during the day time."[49] It was a favorite place, and the Leavitt siblings vied for turns to stay there. Over the years Juanita had indulged her appetite for the out-of-doors at Cabin Spring. She milked, irrigated, and labored in the garden and orchard. She often used Henry's .22 rifle to provide squirrels and cottontail rabbits for the family frying pan. Once when she and Charity, in their teens, were alone at the homestead, Juanita had perhaps too much of violence. She shot a fox through the eyes, immobilizing but not killing it. Hoping the wounded animal would recover, she placed it under their bed in the cabin, where it thrashed all night. The next day men from Bunkerville happened by and earned Juanita's gratitude by finishing off the suffering creature.[50]

Ernest visited Juanita at Cabin Spring twice during the summer of 1919. The first occasion was in July, when he arrived astride a beautiful horse. To Juanita's sisters, who would remember his arrival, he seemed very handsome, even romantic. Around his neck he wore a silk scarf, an unusual accouterment for a Nevada summer. The scarf covered an ominous lump. Shortly before his engagement to Juanita, he had begun to complain of a painful neck. Since Juanita had last seen him, the pain had increased alarmingly. "Although he was taking four or five aspirins at a time, he still was suffering pain in his neck," Juanita wrote. "It seemed to be localized on the right side, down from his ear and inside his collarbone."[51] The engaged couple sought privacy. Perhaps they climbed afoot to a remarkable granite outcropping that protrudes like a giant tooth on the ridge above Cabin Spring; or perhaps they rode among the nearby foothills where high desert vegetation—Joshua trees, yucca, and cacti of many kinds—grows in abundance. Ernest was pessimistic; he doubted whether they should get married until he had found a remedy for his mysterious affliction. He came again in August. He informed Juanita that Dr. McGregor of St. George had a hunch that the swelling in his neck derived from infected tonsils; he would therefore have his tonsils out in early September—the time when he and Juanita had planned to marry. Gloomily he pondered whether they should not postpone the wedding indefinitely. "He wondered," Juanita would write, "if we should not cancel the engagement, let me teach school in Bunkerville, and wait to see how things went with him, for he felt that it would not be fair to me."[52]

One infers that Juanita, for her part, was very undecided. It is a telling fact that during the entire summer of 1919 she did not once ride down to Bunkerville—an easy jog of no more than three hours—where she could have been with Ernest at greater length. One can only assume that even before his malady became an issue she was not entirely sure she wanted to marry him.

In September Juanita learned from friends who were harvesting pine nuts near Cabin Spring that Ernest had indeed been to St. George and had his tonsils out. At her father's request, she finally returned to Bunkerville on September 27, 1919, to play the piano at the funeral of Leila Hardy. Juanita could scarcely control her emotions during the funeral. Leila, near Juanita's age, had left behind a bereaved young husband and two small children. Informed that Ernest had returned to the Pulsipher ranch following his tonsillectomy and was in much pain, Juanita mounted her horse and crossed the river at dusk. She tapped at the door and entered the darkened house, finding Ernest on a cot in the living room. She sat in a large rocking chair facing him. "After a few minutes, he said to me, 'I had a strange experience just before you came in. You must have been within a few rods, but I didn't know you were coming. I thought I saw you sitting right where you are now, holding a white-headed baby boy in your arms, and the impression was that in one year from now this will be yours.' "[53] It was a stunning announcement. Ernest had had a spiritual manifestation too immediate and uncanny to be doubted. Gratefully she acquiesced. Their marriage now seemed right and necessary, entirely ordained of God. Perhaps she also wept. Inevitably, she associated this propitious moment with the burial of Leila Hardy, from the shock of which she had not yet recovered.

On an October day the young couple traveled to St. George in a white-topped buggy pulled by a team of matched horses. Ernest's affliction had intruded upon the divine confirmation of their union, for their first stop was at the office of Dr. McGregor. " 'I'm not a well man,' Ernest said, 'and I don't want to tie this girl up to me if I am not going to be able to take care of her.' "[54] The physician suggested that they proceed with their wedding. After they had enjoyed themselves for a few days, he would cut into the growth on Ernest's neck. Probably McGregor had by now begun to suspect the truth. If so, in giving his fateful advice he was taking Ernest's part rather than Juanita's. According to Mormon belief, a temple marriage would give Ernest a mate for eternity; it would also drastically reduce his widow's oppor-tunities for remarriage during the remainder of her mortal existence.

On October 10, 1919, Juanita and Ernest were married for time and eternity in the St. George temple. While in the temple, Juanita was deeply disturbed by the ceremony of the endowment which pre-ceded the solemnization of her marriage. The washings and anoint-ings seemed indecent; the robe, cap, and apron—borrowed and too large—seemed undignified. She would write later of "a desire to giggle, a wish that I could nudge somebody and talk about it, a nervousness, a consciousness of my clothes. . . . "[55] Worse, she was shocked and made indignant by references to blood and violence. She would remem-ber that her arm, as it was anointed, was blessed to "be strong in the defense of Zion and in avenging the blood of the prophet"; at one point, an officiator brandished, as a sign of the flaming sword at the gates of Eden, "an actual long, shining, sharp sword."[56] In after years, the Church would soften the references to vengeance in the rite of the endowment. The ceremony as she first participated in it would serve Juanita as a window upon the past. She would come to think of it as a vestige of the pioneer era and could therefore understand more readily the vengeful anger which actuated the men who committed the Moun-tain Meadows massacre.

That night there was a family wedding party at Aunt Rosina's house in Santa Clara, but it seemed listless and empty to Juanita. She offended her mother with irreverent remarks about the temple ceremony, and Ernest paced the floor constantly because of the pain in his neck and shoulders. The next day he returned to Dr. McGregor, who proceeded to cut a white, fibrous, tentacled growth from the muscles of his neck.[57] The newlyweds returned to St. George in early November, when McGregor performed a second operation of an hour and a half, which Ernest underwent without anesthetic. At this point McGregor advised Ernest to consult physicians at the LDS hospital in Salt Lake. On a card of referral he wrote his diagnosis: "Sarcoma, evidently malignant."[58]

In the meantime, Juanita busied herself with preparations for the first reunion of the extended Dudley Leavitt family. Gathering in Mesquite on November 5, 1919, the multitudinous Leavitts played, conversed, feasted, and sermonized. In accordance with the Mormon belief that families had the obligation to provide genealogical information so that saving rituals could be performed vicariously for the unbaptized dead in the several temples, the family appointed as its official genealogist Aunt Selena H. Leavitt, to whom Juanita would defer in matters of Leavitt genealogy even after she had become a famous historian.[59] At Juanita's behest, the family sang "Come, Let Us Anew," the hymn which Grandfather Dudley and, before him, Great-grandfather Jeremiah had sung on their deathbeds; henceforth, it would be known as the official Leavitt hymn. During the summer at Cabin Spring Juanita had persuaded her sisters to memorize the hymn. She had also whiled away her time at Cabin Spring by copying the life story of her great-grandmother, Sarah Studevant Leavitt. This she recorded in her mother's family record book, where it covered some forty pages.

At the reunion, Juanita distributed a typed mimeographed copy of the memoir. In a preface she declared: "I have made no effort to revise it in any way, except to put in an occasional punctuation mark or correct an error in spelling. I hope that it may find a place in the hearts and homes of her descendants; that they may profit by her experiences."[60] Instinctively Juanita possessed an exceptional reverence for and sensitivity to pioneer documents. With her it would be pioneer diaries and sketches, rather than novels, movies, or even history books, that would convey most directly and movingly the saga of the heroic frontier. Interestingly, she admitted in her preface to an aesthetic correction of spelling and punctuation. Later, when she had become famous as a preserver of old diaries, she would abjure such editorial interventions.

The narrative of Sarah Studevant Leavitt recounted its small portion of the frontier saga in fascinating terms. The everyday details of Sarah's pious childhood and of her migrations to Nauvoo and Utah were sparse. More abundant were her reflections and her spiritual experiences. The death of her first daughter was accompanied by events so arcane that she refused to describe them. Months after the birth of her second daughter, a vision of hell filled her with the anguish of the damned, from which she at length found relief in a marvelous vision featuring bright, palpable lights. When she heard rumors that the Mormon leaders in Nauvoo were taking plural wives, she sought and received a vision of the celestial world and saw that polygamy was a part of it: "I saw that was the order there and oh how beautiful. I was filled with love and joy that was unspeakable. I waked my husband and told him of the views I had and that the ordinance was from the Lord; but it would damn thousands. . . . I have seen so much wrong connected with this ordinance that had I not had it revealed to me from Him that cannot lie I should sometimes have doubted the truth of it, but there has never a doubt crossed my mind concerning the truth of it since the Lord made it known to me by a heavenly vision."[61]

Ernest left for Salt Lake on November 19, 1919. It was understood that Juanita would take a suddenly vacated teaching position in Bunkerville and earn desperately needed cash. However, she quickly joined her afflicted husband in Utah's capital, recording in her diary: "I could not content myself,—it seemed as if I should be with him. So after two days I followed."[62] Shortly before her departure, Juanita received a patriarchal blessing at the hands of Joseph I. Earl of Mesquite. Undoubtedly she hoped this patriarch would promise her husband's recovery. However, like the blessing she had had from Nephi Johnson, this was not an exceptional pronouncement, making only vague predictions about her future usefulness: "You will become a kind and loving wife and mother and all with whom you are surrounded will call you blessed for your kind and charitable deeds."[63]

Five physicians connected with the LDS hospital examined Ernest and pronounced his disease incurable. Ernest apparently did not understand that cancer had spread throughout his body, for he turned to a practitioner who promised to heal the prominent tumors on his neck. For three terrible months the young man, only partially numbed by large doses of morphine, underwent the application of a flesh-killing salve to both sides of his neck. "He had three pieces drawn from the right side of his neck and one from the left, each one from a half inch to an inch and a quarter thick and nearly as large around as a saucer."[64]

During these three months Ernest and Juanita, essentially paupers, lived with Ernest's distant cousin Zillie Laub Earl and her husband, Perry, whose house stood not far from the capitol building in the northeast section of Salt Lake. Though the Earls were kind, they were near strangers to both Juanita and Ernest and their small house allowed little privacy. Ernest bore the intense pain with courage and even optimism, being, from all evidence, a man of remarkable tenacity. So far as Juanita could see, he remained undaunted by the gloomy prognosis of the physicians at the LDS hospital: "He seemed to have no fear and would only laugh at mine when they said he could not live. He had been promised by the servants of God that he would live and overcome the disease and he knew he would."[65] Accordingly, he asked that local elders give him a blessing nearly every night. Under their ministering hands he often found temporary relief.

On the night of December 17, 1919, when all was quiet in the house, Ernest woke Juanita and told her of a marvelous vision which had come to him while the hands of the elders had been upon his head. He had seen a street in a heavenly city and at the end of the street "a building so wonderful that he could find no words to express it—its pure snowy whiteness, the carvings and the flowers and gardens that surrounded it."[66] Elevated and happy, Ernest went on with his description at great length while Juanita listened solemnly, so impressed that as she recorded it a year later she could remember not only its details but also the date of its occurrence. Long after, writing to a grandson descended from her union with Ernest, she granted the possibility that morphine had something to do with the vision. Under the desperate circumstances of the moment, however, she would admit no such thought: "We both felt that he had caught just a breath, a brief vision of what the after-life might be, and fleeting as it was, were much impressed and somewhat comforted by it. Hence, my desire to preserve it."[67]

Not long afterward occurred another miraculous event which could not be attributed to Ernest's medication. It was holiday time, an evening in late December. Juanita and Ernest had been alone in the house for several days, the Earls having left town for a two-week visit. Ernest seemed more ill than usual, and Juanita could only sit by in helpless despair. A knock came at the door. A bizarre little one-eyed man stood there asking whether there was trouble in the house. Overcome by emotion, Juanita could only point toward Ernest's bed. The little man anointed him with oil and blessed him, and Ernest quickly fell into a deep, restful sleep. As he slept, the man told Juanita his story: "He said he came from below Twenty-seventh South, and that he had felt impressed to catch a bus, and he came up Main Street to wherever the bus changed and got on another bus. And then he had to walk a block and a half to where we were. He'd never seen me, but he was directed to this place. He wasn't a large man; he was kind of a spare man, more slender. And he had a heavy, heavy kind of iron grey hair that he had parted in the middle, but he wasn't an old man. He'd lost the sight of one eye. He was a convert; very very wonderful. He was full of the spirit. . . . Could he be one of the three Nephites? I wondered. But the three Nephites would surely have had both eyes. And he seemed so earthy. He looked more like a farmer, like just a common everyday type of man."[68]

When Ernest woke the next morning, he seemed regenerated, perhaps healed and destined for recovery. Juanita wrote in her autobiography: "For months he had not been so near his old self as he was the next few days; I myself came to feel more like a wife and less like only a nurse."[69] Wherein might Juanita have felt more like a wife? The Earls were absent and Ernest was invigorated. Precisely nine months later their son Ernie would be born.

In early February 1920, the practitioner declared Ernest cured, and the couple decided to return to Mesquite. Before leaving Salt Lake, both Ernest and Juanita received blessings from the presiding patriarch of the Church, Hyrum G. Smith. Juanita recorded that the patriarch gave Ernest "another blessing and promise of life. I had a blessing at the same time which I hope to be able to live up to."[70] The text of Ernest's blessing is not available. Juanita's blessing, her third and last patriarchal blessing, does not imply Ernest's survival. Elder Smith exhorted her to use her talents well, promised her future positions of responsibility, and extended consolation to her: "Therefore be comforted and acknowledge the hand of the Lord in His blessings unto thee, and He will not forget thee but will comfort and sustain thee. . . . "[71]

The couple stayed at the Pulsipher ranch for almost two months, during which Ernest's condition worsened. At the end of March, encouraged by stories of healings among temple workers, they moved to St. George intending to participate in the temple ceremonies on a daily basis. Vastly humbled by her husband's grim prospects, Juanita now banished all vestiges of impiety and indignation from her consciousness. "We went to the temple three weeks and Ernest seemed to be getting better. I rubbed his neck with oil several times each day and it began to get smaller. But he still was to be tried further—he has always considered this sickness a test to try his faith or to prepare him for some work God has in store for him."[72] He was shortly afflicted with erysipelas, a painful streptococcus inflammation of the skin. Then came nosebleeds and a throat so swollen that he could not swallow water. Disillusioned, the couple returned to the ranch around the first of June. Summer heat now added to Ernest's misery, for despite the shade of overhanging cottonwood trees, the frame ranch house was little better than an oven.

Juanita wasn't idle. She cranked the milk separator and washed its innumerable parts. She often operated the telephone central for Mesquite, which had been installed in the Pulsipher house. At night she took long walks with Ernest, who found relief in restless motion. "For twenty-four hours a day he rested at short intervals as he could, but mostly he walked himself to exhaustion. Hardly a night passed that we didn't walk the road out toward Lew's place, and pass by the turn and go on to the end of the fence and back again. By that time Ern would be weary, and so would I, for the child I was carrying was becoming active."[73]

Sometimes Juanita had visitors from home. "I rode over horseback quite often," Charity would write, "and always came back feeling so depressed. Her husband was in so much pain. She was big with child, and it seemed like she was always struggling with and washing those large milk separator tanks and utensils. She was so frail, but had an indomitable spirit."[74] One day while Henry and Mary were working in a field, little Mary disappeared. Fearful of her drowning in the ditches or river, Henry followed her tracks along the dusty road. They led him to the river crossing, where his brother Lister reported having transported her across on his horse. Henry knew then she was going to visit Juanita and returned to his labor. There was, Mary would remember, a splendid swing dangling from the cottonwoods at the Pulsipher ranch.[75]

As the birth of her child approached, Juanita demonstrated that she was as capable of an adamant faith as Ernest. Relying on his vision of a white-haired son in her arms, she was sure the child would be born exactly one year from the day of Leila Hardy's funeral. On September 10, 1920, she packed her clothes in a wagon and traveled to her parents' house for her lying-in. "I saw Warren Hardy [Leila's widower] pass just as we drove up, and asked him when his wife died, and when he told me, I said, 'We are too early. We must go back to the ranch for another couple of weeks.'"[76] With supreme confidence Juanita waited until the morning of September 27 before returning to her parents' house.

That afternoon a difficult delivery began. The autonomic function of her abdominal and back muscles astonished her: "Strange how one forgets the pains of childbirth. But though the memory of the pain grew dim, that of my complete helplessness before the great creative force did not. I was not I. I had no control over me. I was only an atom in the hands of some mighty power." The bed being too soft, the midwife put her on a pallet on the floor. Toward midnight the midwife grew alarmed, for her patient seemed to be weakening. Juanita heard frightened, whispered calculations of the time it would take to send to St. George for a doctor. Then her father entered the room, laid his hands on her head, and commanded the birth to achieve itself. "As though by the force of his will, by the very weight of his hands on my head, I felt a blessed relaxation, and then a lusty cry. My son was born, white hair and all."[77] The family clock showed five past midnight, and the birth of Leonard Ernest Pulsipher, Jr., was recorded on September 28, 1920. The clock was fast, Juanita would later assert.[78] As far as she was concerned, this miracle child had arrived as prophesied.

After eight days Juanita returned with Ernie to the Pulsipher ranch. Her husband's affliction now accelerated. "His pain was so severe," Juanita recorded in her diary, "he could not sit or lie down, and his mouth and face so badly swollen he could not eat. For ten days he did not lie down 15 minutes at a time, but would walk, walk, walk, and nearly scream with pain. When it would ease a little he would sit across a chair and put his arms on the back of it and lean his head down. That is the nearest thing to rest that he got. He had often said that the Lord would have to provide some way if he was to be permitted to live—and it truly seemed so."[79]

Hopeful word came that Salt Lake physicians had mastered the new technology of radium as a treatment for cancer. Ernest was elated, being sure this was God's way of fulfilling his promises. It was decided that Elizabeth would accompany her son to Salt Lake and that Juanita and Ernie would remain at the ranch with John. During the three months which followed, Juanita was perhaps happier than she had been for a long time. Although Ernest did not write, Elizabeth's occasional letters were encouraging. Juanita was busy keeping house, helping her father-in-law with chores, and serving as telephone operator. She was charmed by her baby's good nature and took delight in seeing how John loved his grandson, "trotting him on his knee, chanting rhyme songs and fitting folk games with his fingers and toes."[80]

While Ernest and Elizabeth were in Salt Lake, Juanita made good use of her spare time by copying the diary of John Pulsipher, Ernest's pioneer grandfather, who had participated in the Utah War. "I got an old Remington typewriter and a ream of paper, and worked at them at odd times, when there was nothing else to do and the baby was asleep. I still think that this record is the most eloquent and detailed of any I have seen, made in 1857 during that time of suspense, when the Mormons were faced with an army, approaching in spite of all their efforts to stop it." She also learned that the daughter of another pioneer, Myron Abbott, thought his old diary so worthless that she intended to use it for starting fires. Juanita telephoned her and exchanged a new Sears Roebuck catalog for the diary. This diary would later prove invaluable in water conservation studies on the Virgin, for Myron Abbott, as watermaster of early Bunkerville, had "recorded every flood, and the number of loads of rock and brush and days of labor it took to get the water back into the ditch." Thus during the fall of 1920 Juanita came to understand many things about history: the nature of the Utah War, the struggle of early Virgin settlers against Old Lady River, and even the esoteric fact that in pioneer times "the town of Bunkerville had a moving population. Every year several families would leave, their empty homes sometimes taken over by newly-married couples."[81]

Shortly before Christmas Ernest and Elizabeth returned to the ranch. They came by train as far as Moapa, where they spent a night with Howard and Myrtle Pulsipher. It was a night Howard would never forget. The brothers talked all night, Ernest being in too much pain to sleep. He had not conceded to his illness. While in Salt Lake he had received a blessing from his former mission president, Apostle Melvin J. Ballard, a man in whom, so he told Howard, he had as much faith as in Christ himself. Elder Ballard, he said, had promised him that he would be saved by the power of the priesthood and would live to assist in the return of the lost ten tribes of Israel. Lately Ernest had been lapsing into periods of unconsciousness; he feared that the family might fail in its faith and abandon him to death. He exhorted Howard to revive him should he fall into a coma. "I'll be helpless," he said; "I'll depend upon the Priesthood; that's all that will save me."[82]

The next day, December 22, 1920, Ernest and Elizabeth rode on to Mesquite. Elizabeth's letters had led Juanita to expect a significant improvement in Ernest. His actual condition staggered her. That night she recorded in her diary: "Instead of being nearly well he is almost helpless, sent home again to die by the best doctors in the west. They have been using the radium on his neck and have used it more than it has ever been used on a human before. It was put on 15 times. Well, his neck is down to normal, the lump gone but a raw sore on each side. He also had it put under his cheek bone, up through his nose—a very painful operation. Now he has such severe pains across his back and legs and they are so badly swollen he is not able to walk. He looks as though he has dropsy, but there are such hard pains with it."[83]

Men from Ernest's priesthood quorum now came by shifts every night to sit by his bedside. By the custom of the village such a vigil signified his imminent death. On the morning of January 8, 1921, Ernest asked Juanita to sit beside him. "I did, and that half hour with him will always be remembered as one of the most beautiful of my life. He wanted to know if I had ever regretted marrying him and said how much he thought of me and how glad and proud he was that he had a wife and son. He then spoke of how good everyone had been, his own folks especially and how much he appreciated it all. He asked for the baby and talked to him a little and then asked for something to eat."[84] It was a valediction, for while Juanita was in the kitchen preparing his breakfast he fell into a coma. Though his pulse and breathing seemed normal, he did not regain consciousness. That evening he died. It was exactly one week before Juanita's twenty-third birthday.

The next day, when Howard arrived at the ranch house and viewed Ernest's body, which had been prepared for burial, he became alarmed. Although Ernest was not breathing, he seemed life-like and his limbs were flexible.[85] Howard declared that he was not satisfied; the members of the family had not attempted to revive Ernest by the power of the priesthood as he had instructed. Then ensued an astonishing episode which is best recounted by William E. Abbott, the bishop of Mesquite, who conducted the funeral service:

> I had announced the time of the funeral and full arrangements were made. The people began assembling from our town as well as from neighboring towns. I was at the church waiting for the family to come with the corpse. Presently the father and brother of the dead man came

up to see me and they said they were not willing to have Ernest buried and wanted me to come down to the house and bring a number of the elders. They said they believed he was to live, Apostle Ballard had promised him life, and they felt that he was to be called back to life. I went to the ranch two miles away where the body was lying. There I met about forty or fifty men and boys. I conversed with the family and the wife of the young man. They felt that he could and should be called back to life. A grave reponsibility was upon me. It was so sudden. I stood upon the porch in front of the house and spoke to the crowd. I said, "Brothers and sisters, I know that such things have been done and can be done again, but I am not certain what the will of the Lord is in this case. However, all who have faith that such can be, may enter the room." They did so. We formed a circle around the casket and I asked each to take his turn in prayer. "But," I said, "I don't want any one of you to attempt to call him back unless you be moved upon to do so by the power of the Holy Spirit to do so." We each took our turn in prayer and at or near the close of the session, Ernest's dear wife and his youngest brother, Howard, walked up arm in arm, knelt beside the casket. Each of them took a turn in prayer and they pled earnestly with the Lord to permit him to return. But all of no avail. I then advised that we all return to the church and hold the funeral services and lay the body away. I did not know to what extent, if any, would I be censured for such a vain attempt.[86]

At the funeral the coffin rested upon sheet-draped chairs in the space between the congregation and the stage where speakers and members of a choir sat. Artificial flowers stood in vases. A coverlet lay over Ernest's body in the open coffin. Sitting in the first pew immediately before the coffin, both Howard and Juanita expected Ernest to awaken. At one moment Howard was so sure that he had seen the coverlet move that he stood half up, eager to greet his reviving brother. When nothing further transpired, he concluded it had been only a breeze.[87] According to the bishop's daughter, who observed from the choir, Juanita frequently craned her neck in order to scrutinize the covered body; the young observor was impressed by Juanita's demonstration of faith.[88] Suspending all sense of the probable and real, Juanita had adopted Ernest's blind, extravagant hope. By her desperate fervor she sought to coerce God to perform a stunning miracle. She looked for no less than Ernest's utter and instantaneous restoration to life and health.

After the service, the coverlet was removed and the congregation filed past the coffin for a final view. Then all repaired to the Mesquite cemetery where Ernest was buried in a plot devoid of other graves. His father and mother would later be buried next to him. Juanita's brother Melvin stood with her at the burial; the rest of her family were unfortunately out of town paying a visit to Charity. By now Juanita was benumbed and detached. After the last shovelful of earth had been placed, she said good-bye to Melvin and, her son in her arms, took a seat in the buggy which would convey her to the Pulsipher ranch.

CHAPTER • THREE

MOVING UP

On the day after the funeral, Ernest's mother departed for a visit with relatives in Idaho. Again his father proved an amiable companion to Juanita, and again Juanita added substantially to the economy of the household, operating the switchboard, milking cows, and separating cream. At least once during the winter or spring of 1921, she took the mail buckboard to Moapa to visit Howard and Myrtle. There is a photograph of Juanita and Myrtle out-of-doors with their infants, Ernie and Berniece. They squat at the edge of a pool. In the background are rails and a handcar; beyond those are desert hills. Juanita, in a white dress, has dipped a bare foot into the water. Her thick, fine hair is brushed back and bunched. She clasps Ernie, a husky, white-haired baby, about the chest. Both babies stare at the ripple Juanita's toe makes in the water.

"After Ernest left me, I stayed at the ranch and tried to help his parents," Juanita recorded in her diary.[1] In reality her purpose was larger. Although she planned to teach school to earn her living, she also planned to take possession of the portion of the Pulsipher farm that had been promised to Ernest. She planned to develop it, farm it, and hand it on to his son. From her perspective, it was not an extraordinary aspiration. In her grandmother Mary Ann Hafen she had a model of a woman who had successfully wrested a living from a small acreage without the help of a husband. She owed this much to Ernest, who was not dead but merely abroad—who "has left me for a while," as she told her diary.[2] Her loyalty was intense and adamant. She would raise Ernie well and through him give Ernest the posterity which Mormons considered the greatest of earthly attainments. It was her way of assuaging that anomalous guilt which afflicts those whose loved ones die a hard and unseasonable death.

She found little consolation in her resolve. Her despair centered upon the failure of the promises men of God had made to Ernest. While he lived, she had made every effort to cajole, plead, and bargain with God. She had prayed a dozen times a day, had had patriarchal blessings, and had gone to the temple. At the end, she had swallowed every doubt and, before a crowd of people, had called aloud upon God for the ultimate miracle of raising Ernest from his coffin. Now, as she went about the house where he had died, she was consumed by God's perfidy. The view of the world she had inherited from Bunkerville gave no explanations. According to it, God blessed the righteous with long life and prosperity and his servants didn't err. Long afterward, she described her disillusionment in the present tense: "I batter my soul against the WHY of innocent suffering until I am sick. I think God has not kept faith with us."[3]

For months, perhaps for years, Juanita remained in a spiritual crisis. In retrospect, she would measure the lesson she learned during this trying period: "I am sure that the sick have been restored through administration and the Spirit of the Lord. I have seen it many times. But I also learned, as I watched my young husband die of cancer at the age of 27, that no number of blessings—Patriarchal or otherwise—gave more than temporary relief, although they did promise without qualification that he should be restored, should live to be a father in Israel and to perform a great work. It really shook me at the time. . . . Now I realize what a terrible responsibility one assumes when he presumes to speak FOR God. I can petition Him, but cannot order Him."[4] Juanita's Christian faith would remain permanently sobered. If she had not abandoned her belief in God, she at least had lost her confidence in his servants.

In the early spring of 1921, Elizabeth returned from Idaho, further altering the tenor of Juanita's life. From the beginning the two women had disliked each other. During his illness, Ernest had asked his mother to enter Juanita as the beneficiary of his insurance policy. Elizabeth had agreed but quietly procrastinated. A larger matter loomed in the silent war of wills between the two women, for Elizabeth intended to forestall Juanita's possession of Ernest's portion of the farm. Upon her return, the cold cordiality that had existed between them while Ernest was alive became a painful estrangement. "She would make breakfast for herself and Grandpa while I bathed and dressed the baby," Juanita wrote. "Then I'd go in and get something for myself, for I knew that I must eat and have plenty of good food if *he* were to thrive. I felt no guilt about eating anything there was, especially eggs and milk and vegetables from the garden. . . . Always I waited until they had finished their meal before I went into the kitchen to get my own."[5]

Late in the spring Juanita accepted a suddenly vacated position in the Bunkerville junior high school. For seven weeks she lived at home with Henry and Mary, saving her prorated stipend of $120 per month to further her own schooling. When school ended she returned to the Pulsipher ranch. Her strategy was simple. She would stubbornly remain on the ranch, knowing that in time she would have to be accommodated. Elizabeth soon struck upon a sufficient gesture. She prevailed on John to come away for a visit with their relatives in Idaho and for a tour of Yellowstone National Park. Juanita bitterly assumed that Ernest's insurance paid for this vacation. In any event, she found the vacant premises intolerable. "As I couldn't live on the ranch alone, I went back to my parents for the summer,"[6] she recorded in her diary. She didn't think of her removal as permanent. "When I pulled out," she wrote long afterward, "I had no idea that I would NEVER go back to even stay over night."[7] Likely she did not comprehend at first that she had been outmaneuvered. But with time she would know it, and her sense of outrage and injury would grow. To the end of her days, she would hold a deep and inveterate grudge against Elizabeth Pulsipher.

Juanita maintained a friendship with others among Ernest's relatives. At midsummer Elizabeth's sister, Florie Truman, invited Juanita to her ranch on Mogotsu Creek near the village of Gunlock, Utah. The Truman family took Juanita and Ernie along on a wagon trip to Enterprise to celebrate the Twenty-fourth of July. The primitive road led through Mountain Meadows. For the first time in her life Juanita gazed upon the site of the massacre. Between round, low hills lay a valley a half mile wide and perhaps five miles long, no longer grassy and well watered as it had been in pioneer times, but dry, gullied, and thick with sagebrush and scrub oak. The remoteness of the spot impressed Juanita, preparing her to believe that the massacre had its origin in prayerful councils far removed from the site: "Men did not gather here by chance or mere hearsay. If they were here, they had come because they were ordered to come. And whatever went on was done because it had been ordered, not because individuals had acted upon impulse."[8]

Further assistance from Ernest's relatives came in the offer of a rent-free house in St. George during the coming school year.

Elizabeth's brother proposed that Juanita be a chaperone for his daughters who wished to attend high school. The proposal quickly expanded to include Juanita's sister Aura and other young women from out of town. For Juanita the opportunity to attend college seemed a gift from heaven, the first of many unexpected openings by which her life would resume a hopeful progress. "My folks were even more delighted than I," she wrote. "They lost no time loading—in addition to Aura and her things—bottled fruit, dried figs, apricots, molasses, honey, flour, cracked wheat cereal, ham and bacon, homemade soap, and bedding, towels, dish towels, and dishes."[9]

It was a lean year, even for country girls accustomed to a subsistence economy. Juanita and Aura signed notes for their tuition and found part-time jobs. For much of the year Juanita graded English papers at twenty-five cents an hour. Undoubtedly the one year old Ernie basked in a plethora of feminine attention. It would not be the last time he found himself the mascot of his mother's house companions. Next to his mother, his most solicitous caretaker was Aura. Aura attended classes in the morning, Juanita in the afternoon. Midday, Juanita trundled Ernie in a little wagon toward the college and handed him over to Aura. Aura was a fine cook, an accomplished seamstress, and a skilled pianist. Of an intense personality, she determined to take first place in a college piano competition. Obsessively practicing four or five hours a day, she achieved her ambition.

Dixie Normal College occupied a three-story building of hewn rock. Over the arch of its main entrance was a sculpture in relief of a hand holding the lamp of education. The church-owned institution offered four years of high school and two years of college studies in pedagogy.[10] Juanita appeared in a photograph of the College Class in the yearbook, *The Dixie 1922*. Accompanying the photograph was an explanation: "Whenever you saw a student dig diligently at one task for over ten minutes, or sit so lost in thought that he could not hear his underclassmate's giggles, you might conclude at once that he was one of the College Class."[11] In the photograph, Juanita has brushed back and bunched her long hair. She hangs her head and looks dour and miserable. Of this year at Dixie she would write: "I never really felt like I belonged all that winter. Miss Phillips and other of the teachers were cordial, but I had little companionship with my classmates."[12] As a young widow she belonged with neither the married nor the unmarried. Furthermore, she suffered still from the acute sense of social ineptitude which had afflicted her before the mirror of Dixie Drug during her first visit to St. George long ago. Although it may have seemed small and insignificant to others, for Juanita St. George represented a grace and dignity to which she had not attained.

Viewed objectively, Juanita's year as a student at Dixie College was successful. In time her English teacher, Lucy Phillips, asked her to join the college debate team. Juanita declined, having no time to spare from grading papers each afternoon at four-thirty. The next day the college president, Joseph K. Nicholes, called her into his office and forgave her tuition loan, in essence giving her a debate scholarship. A man of immense goodwill, Nicholes would remain a lifetime friend. Juanita was superlatively fitted for debate, having a ready command of ideas, a fluent English, and a competitive temperament. Her partner was Paul Thurston, "an enthusiastic nineteen-year-old, tall, lanky, all arms and legs and hands and feet," who sometimes tossed pebbles against Juanita's bedroom window at night and for hours talked through the open window about strategies of debate.[13] Juanita was embarrassed by her impoverished wardrobe. Her old dresses might do for mingling in an audience, but when she stood at the front, she had to have something better. Aura came to the rescue. Fifty years later she could recall her handiwork in minute detail: "I selected a dress with five panels, one across the front and two on each side. I embroidered the five panels with various colored embroidery thread. After sewing the panels together, I gathered them to a bask waist. The waist was embroidered around the neck and sleeves. On each side of the waist was a small design. After it was steamed and pressed, it looked just "wonderful and professional."[14]

Juanita and Paul, as disparately yoked as a horse and an ox, won their share of victories. In particular, Juanita relished their triumph over the debate team from Cedar City. Her heart quailed when her opponent "came onstage in an expensive tailored suit, the style and quality eloquent of price."[15] Perhaps her very trepidation provoked her to a redoubled effort, for the decision of the judges was unanimously in favor of the Dixie team.

During this year Juanita also wrote a story, her first original piece, "The Usual Dilemma," published in *The Dixie – The Girl's Edition 1922*. The story's protagonist is in an agony of embarrassment because a young man from town is calling on her at her farm home. "She couldn't, she simply could not have him come here. Why the furniture was all old, the carpets faded and worn, and mother had never served a meal in courses in her life!" The young man is interested in the farm work, responds warmly to her numerous brothers and sisters, and delights in the homey affection of her mother. To her great surprise, he wishes to return. Raised by an elegant, cold stepmother, he has found comfort among these plain but loving people: "This afternoon has made me see what I have been missing. This is the first glimpse of a real mother and real home life I have ever had."[16] Like much fiction appearing in pious American magazines of the time, this story demonstrated a functional style and a didactic plot. In writing it, Juanita had undoubtedly been influenced by the so-called home literature of the Latter-day Saints, which she would have read in *Juvenile Instructor*, *Relief Society Magazine*, and *The Improvement Era*. Her story could have appeared with full propriety in any of these official magazines of the Church.

As school closed in the spring of 1922, Juanita joined in celebrating D Day. During this annual activity faculty and students renovated and whitewashed a large block letter D which had been outlined in rock on the face of Black Ridge in view of the town below. It is possible that Juanita took Ernie along, for other children were present. Afterward forceful students took vigilante action against malingerers. Among those shorn of their hair as a punishment was the young man scheduled to deliver the farewell speech of the graduating class. Too embarrassed to appear, he ceded his place to the next in line, Juanita Pulsipher, who capped her graduation from Dixie Normal College by delivering the official student oration. For this occasion she wore the handsome dress Aura had made her. She wrote, "I don't know what I did for shoes, but I think I stood in the pulpit where they couldn't be seen."[17]

She was lucky enough, as she moved home to Bunkerville, to secure a contract to teach there during the coming year. Most of the summer she spent at Cabin Spring, tending Ernie, reading, and helping with the chores. In July her sister Charity departed on a mission. Supporting Charity posed a problem for Henry, whose only cash derived from the infrequent sale of range cattle. Juanita volunteered to support her during the school year. Her monthly stipend was $120, which she divided thus: $40 to Charity, $30 to Mary and Henry for board and room, $42 for herself, and $8 as a tithe. The tithe, calculated after she had subtracted her donation to Charity, brought her into conflict with the bishop of Bunkerville when, as is expected of Latter-day Saints, she reviewed her tithe with him at New Year. "I should have paid my $12.00 tithing first, he said, and then do whatever I wished to with the remainder. I insisted that the $40 went first to the Church, leaving me only $80.00 to use for myself. But he would not be convinced."[18] Juanita angrily refused to concede and went down on the records as a partial tithe payer.

Expressly trained for rural schools, Juanita was comfortable teaching two grades in a single room in the Relief Society building. She was especially interested in a daily hour of world history. She furnished her room with an unabridged dictionary, a globe, a five-volume encyclopedia, and "cardboard-mounted pictures of the Colosseum, the Colossus of Rhodes, a mosque, the three Great Pyramids, the Great Sphinx, and many other examples of the Ancients' engineering skills which our modern civilization could not match."[19] It was a happy year for Ernie, who quickly learned to call Henry and Mary Pa and Ma. Juanita's brothers and sisters made much of him, and Henry frequently took him along to the fields. Ordinarily, Juanita could concentrate on her teaching without worrying about him. At least twice, however, she experienced astonishing premonitions of danger. One of them occurred on a day when Henry had taken Ernie to the grist mill. As she taught a history lesson, Juanita was suddenly "so overcome with something that I caught my breath, turned ghastly pale, and almost fell to the floor. In just an instant it had passed, and I went on with my work. . . . That night after supper, Pa said, 'I don't know whether I should tell you this or not. But this afternoon Little Ernest had a close call. Someone had left the trap off the hole in the floor, just over the two big rollers. I caught him by the back of his pants just as he was stepping into it. He would have been instantly ground into pulp.' "[20]

In the summer of 1923 Howard Pulsipher secured Juanita a job at $100 a month as a cook at a gypsum mill. The mill, surrounded by dormitory tents for a hundred laborers, stood in the high Nevada desert where days were hot and nights mercifully cool. Juanita and Ernie slept in a tent, she on an upper bunk, Ernie below. Almost three, Ernie was toilet trained, and she kept a little chamber pot to serve his midnight needs. She found satisfaction in learning to cook in quantities. The company fed its mill hands well, since in this hot, isolated place they had little other than good food to distract and please them. The laborers were divided between white American and Spanish-speaking Mexican nationals. The latter group impressed Juanita as the more clean and polite. She was able to earn an additional $20 a week teaching them English in the evenings.

Occasionally she suffered sexual harassment from a brutal Anglo laborer, whom she privately called Old Judas. Once when he cornered her in a storeroom, she flourished a butcher knife: " 'Damn your dirty heart!' I said slowly. 'You dare to touch me, and I'll split you from stern to gudgeon!' "[21] For the moment the warning sufficed. At the end of the summer, however, she came more ominously into his power. Her employment ended, she was riding toward Moapa in the mail truck, which Old Judas was driving. In a remote, forested spot he stopped:

> This time he didn't mean to be cheated as he had been once before. Had I forgotten what an exciting experience it was to "have connection"? I had been married; I ought to know that some sex experience was necessary for good health. It was the finest, most genuine thrill that life could offer.
>
> This time I had no defense; I did not dare argue or discuss this matter; I could only pray silently: "Dear Lord, God help me!"
>
> Little Ernie had gone to sleep; he was lying between us, his head in my lap; it would be easy to slip out and slip a cushion under it, but I had no intention of doing it. I would remain where I was; he would have to drag me out.[22]

Then came another of the minor miracles of her life. Into this remote clearing walked a man leading a lame horse. With cheerful aplomb the stranger unsaddled his animal, tied it to a tree, and climbed into the mail truck. Old Judas fumed but could do nothing but drive on.

It was September 1923. At Moapa Juanita boarded the train for Provo to enroll at Brigham Young University. She had worked at the mill as long as possible and therefore had no time to return to Bunkerville. In any event, Henry and Mary were worried about her going so far away. They had pleaded with her at least to leave Ernie with them. She had said no. Unfortunately, she became nauseated on the train. Sometimes in childhood she had been so afflicted with motion sickness that she had left a swaying wagon and climbed onto one of the horses pulling it. Probably her condition was aggravated by the uncertainties before her. Despite her fixed determination, she was profoundly worried. Never before had she felt so intimidated and untested.

As the train rocked and swayed northward, a kind woman took Ernie on her lap and conversed with the queasy Juanita. Soon this self-assured person was giving Juanita advice on how to dress well on a limited budget: "Get *one* good dress. Don't go to Penney's or the little shops; go to Dixon-Taylor-Russell and get yourself one *good* dress, an all-wool, hard weave, navy blue, that fits well, and then get several sets of accesssories: different collar and cuff sets, at least four. Then you can wear just a pin or some beads for a change. But you will always be well-dressed. If you give the dress good care, it will last the whole winter long, and you'll look better than if you had three cheap dresses."[23] The advice seemed eminently sensible to Juanita and fixed in her mind a permanent prejudice against inexpensive dresses. Once settled in Provo, she would waste little time before making her visit to an expensive dress shop.

Getting settled was miraculously easy. An inquiry of a housewife in a front yard, a phone call to her friend, another phone call to the friend's friend – before noon of her first full day in Provo, Juanita had arranged to live with Geneva Larson on Fifth West and Seventh North. Geneva's husband, B. F. Larson, a professor of art, was leaving for a sabbatical in France. Geneva was happy to let a back bedroom to Juanita and to care for Ernie while she was in class. In return Juanita would cook supper, wash dishes, iron on Saturday, and pay $20 a month for expenses. There was, it is to be noted, an indoor bathroom, a luxury she had rarely enjoyed before.

Juanita had a busy schedule of classes on the old campus in downtown Provo. One class, "Quantity Cooking," involved working in the school cafeteria, where she also ate a free lunch. Following her noon work, she rested on a couch in the ladies' room before going to afternoon classes. Later she would explain why she so religiously took her daily rest: "Dr. Carroll at the BYU observed that while I wrote a test paper with my right hand, I had my left finger-tips on this spot [the ganglion of her right shoulder]. He called me in and explained to me that I was evidently working under too much tension, and that I must give myself at least 20-minutes of complete relaxation between lunch and my first afternoon class. Under his guidance I worked out a schedule which brought me through that year and the next in good health – especially since I grew in confidence."[24]

Near Easter Ernie broke out with measles. While on the toilet on a Saturday morning, he cried out and fainted. Juanita, pressing her good dress, abandoned the iron and ran to his rescue. Remembering that her mother's brother had died from measles, she swept up her limp son and rushed to Geneva, who ran to the door and called in a man from the street. The man, a Mormon elder, blessed the child, who finally caught a deep breath and revived. For Juanita it was a miracle. But now the odor of scorched wool filled the house, the iron having burned through the dress and the ironing board cover. At noon of the same day, the postman brought another miracle, a package from Mary in Bunkerville containing a beautiful gingham dress checkered in lavender and yellow.

On Monday morning as Juanita entered her psychology classroom, Professor M. Wilford Poulson exclaimed, "Why, Mrs. Pulsipher, how delightful to see you in a different dress!"[25] Smothered by embarrassment, Juanita could not muster the laughter which the situation required. As a friend of the Larsons, the blunt and crusty Poulson knew Juanita's circumstances and meant her no harm. A collector of books about Mormonism, he possessed an inquiring, skeptical mind which had brought him into a covert disagreement with the Church. Poulson was the first of many Mormon dissenters whose friendship Juanita would cultivate and cherish.

When Juanita and Ernie returned to Bunkerville for the summer, Aura was home from her first year of teaching at a remote Nevada ranch. Melvin had just graduated from high school and conjointly owned with Henry a little red Maxwell racing car. Laurel, larger than Melvin though a year behind him in school, was restless. Las Vegas, a squalid railroad town simmering in the desert, beckoned. Juanita would write: " 'If you want to keep out of the Devil's hands, keep off the Devil's ground,' Pa used to say, and for him, Las Vegas was literally The Devil's Ground. 'On the other hand,' he argued, 'there's safety in numbers.' "[26] Leaving Ernie with her parents, Juanita spent the summer of 1924 in Las Vegas, sharing with Aura, Melvin, and Laurel a small house with a cool rock-walled basement and a shady outside bower. She found a job in the same bakery where she had received instructions on carefully wiping egg white from the shell some seven years earlier. Now she wrapped bread and sold at the counter.

At the end of the summer the brothers and sisters went home to Bunkerville in a larger car for which Melvin had traded the racer. On September 12, 1924, all but Laurel departed for Provo. Packed into the flivver were Juanita, Ernie, Aura, Melvin, and a welter of "bedding, clothing, cases of fruit; preserves, jams, and jelly; cured ham and bacon; flour and whole-wheat cereal. On one running board was a five-gallon can of water; on the other a three-gallon can of gas."[27] They made the trip in two days, camping along the way. They put-putted sedately along the graveled Highway 91, crossing unbridged streams and stirring dust. At Nephi, forty-five miles from Provo, they at last encountered pavement.

In Provo they found convenient quarters with a Mr. and Mrs. Johnson across the street from the B. F. Larsons. Things dovetailed incredibly. Juanita, Aura, and Ernie domiciled in the Johnsons' remodeled granary, using an outdoor toilet. Aura took showers at the women's gymnasium. Juanita arranged with Geneva for use of her tub for her and Ernie. Melvin shared a room in the Johnsons' house with one of their nephews. Juanita did ironing and other housework for Geneva on Saturdays. By now B. F. had returned from his sabbatical and Juanita came to know and admire him. Throughout her life the Larsons would remain warm, concerned friends.

Within two weeks the transplanted Leavitt siblings were joined by Charity, who had returned from her mission. "How could we manage?" Juanita wrote. "Simply by moving over. Aura and I already slept in an extra-size double bed with good springs; we just moved over, which placed me in the middle."[28] Life in the Leavitt commune was not opulent. There was food aplenty, little else. Melvin did barnyard chores for the Johnsons and worked for local farmers, bringing home potatoes, squash, and apples. Charity, who had arrived dead broke, earned $1.50 a week cleaning for a local housewife. Juanita paid her tuition. "She even bought me a winter coat for $35.00," Charity reminisced, "and then, let it be said to my shame, she wore my old one. I was so proud of my new coat!"[29] There were abundant exchanges of clothing as the three sisters sorted and matched, managing to keep each other in some semblance of social respectability. Their common wardrobe extended even to the regalia they donned for going to the privy: "Our toilet facility was the two-holer outhouse at the back of the lot. Aura had made herself an elegant bathrobe from a bright-colored Navajo blanket, and finished it with a twisted silk rope with an extra tie around the waist. We named it 'Old Donder & Blitzen.' It was the only really warm item we had, so we all used it. Interested neighbors might see 'Old Donder & Blitzen' hurry down to the outhouse and back three times every morning."[30] "Donder & Blitzen," translating as "thunder & lightning," was an appropriate if not altogether delicate name for an article of clothing associated with a toilet. It was not an isolated instance of barnyard humor with the Leavitt sisters, who typically maintained a frivolous banter among themselves.

As at Dixie College, Aura was the relief for Juanita in the care of Ernie. She was the first to leave for the campus each morning. Juanita studied at home with Ernie until the hour of the college devotional. Aura recalled: "You would dress Ern and bring him in the cart, cutting through the city Park at 5th West and 5th North, over the canal of water and on toward BYU. I would meet you and haul Ernest back home."[31] At home Aura would study through the afternoon while Ernie took his nap or played with the Johnson and Larson boys. Neither Juanita nor Aura could attend the devotional. Juanita heard only one of the inspirational ten-minute sermons for which college president George H. Brimhall was famous.

During the winter and spring of 1925 Juanita enrolled in debate and engaged in interclass competition with a bellicose fervor. Sherman Christensen, later a federal judge, was one of her opponents. "Even then he was a good Republican and I an ardent Democrat," she wrote, "so we instinctively took the opposite sides on debate questions."[32] The high point of her year occurred when she and her partner—she in a rented dress—triumphed by a unanimous decision over a team from UCLA. Among her rewards was initiation into Tau Kappa Alpha, a national debating society whose key she wore with pride.

This was a more sociable year for Juanita. Among her friends were Donald and Augusta Flake, a brother and sister from Snowflake, Arizona. "We were good friends because she was a pioneer spirit like the rest of us," Augusta explained, alluding to the affinity that a shared privation gave those raised on the edges of the Mormon domain.[33] There is a photograph of Juanita with a group of students and professors—probably the BYU debate squad. Sitting are three professors in ankle-high shoes and vested suits; one is as sombre as a Puritan divine, another as lanky as Ichabod Crane. Standing behind are three young women and nine young men. Juanita's dress has elbow-length sleeves, broad white cuffs, and a white collar. Her hair is short, pulled back on the right and combed across her forehead and over her ear on the left. One realizes that her mood has changed since her Dixie year. She is self-confident and serene. Perhaps she goes for days at a time without thinking about the husband she buried in Mesquite.

As spring quarter of 1925 closed, Juanita prepared for graduation. The official record declared that her degree was bachelor of science and that her major was foods and nutrition. Certainly she had not undergone a radical change of intellect because of her college education. She had often selected courses simply because they coincided with the hours when Aura could tend Ernie. Furthermore, BYU was distinctly parochial, its faculty sheltered from national trends by their Mormon piety. Yet it was Juanita's nature to learn eagerly. By accident if not by design, the mix of her courses at BYU had not been bad. She had taken rudimentary courses in economics, chemistry, psychology, botany, and sociology and advanced courses in education, home economics, English, speech, and debate.[34] Through them she had taken a further step toward the Outside. If she revealed no impulse to emulate cultural patterns beyond Utah, at least she was prepared to understand them.

Always one to relish ceremonies, Juanita looked forward to the baccalaureate and commencement exercises. Her pleasure was doubled by the fact that a letter from E. M. Jenson, president of Dixie College, had offered her a position in the high school division. Unfortunately, an incident marred her anticipation. While she looked on, an Arizona friend, George A. Smith, applied at the university financial office for a loan of $100. He did so with great insouciance, as if it were the most casual matter. A day later, observing with astonishment that the loan had been granted, Juanita decided to try for $50. She would rent a graduation robe and buy new shoes and a yearbook. The financial office instantly refused her on the grounds of depleted funds. She believed otherwise; she had been refused because she was "not a fit candidate for a loan."[35] It made no difference that she was the head of a household and breadwinner of a family; because she was a woman, she was considered a poor credit risk. Flustered and humiliated, she retreated without insisting upon the prospects of her position at Dixie College. She borrowed money from Geneva Larson to rent a robe and went without new shoes and a yearbook. She smoldered wretchedly throughout the graduation ceremonies, shaping a lasting grudge against BYU.

Unknown to Juanita, Henry and Mary sat in the audience at commencement, having traveled most of the previous night. Afterward there were hugs, kisses, and perhaps tears as the couple from Bunkerville congratulated the first of their offspring to graduate from college. In time most of Juanita's siblings would duplicate the achievement. The desire of Henry and Mary for the schooling of their children was intense; education was a bridge to a new world of money, machines, and progress which they themselves were too old to cross.

Shortly after graduation Juanita found a bank that would lend her $100 against her earnings at Dixie College. Her grudge notwithstanding, she enrolled in the BYU summer school at Aspen Grove. An alpine camp high in a tributary of Provo Canyon, Aspen Grove was an idyllic setting. Flowery meadows bordered a gurgling creek, and the forested slopes and stratified cliffs of Mt. Timpanogos loomed in the background. Juanita and Ernie shared a tent with Julia Alleman, one of Juanita's debate partners. They cooked over a primitive outdoor stove and washed their clothes by hand. Geneva and B. F. Larson and their children occupied a nearby tent. Ernie, almost five, sorted through the trash pile near the commissary looking for caps from pop bottles with which to make badges. One day he found a silver dollar, which Juanita let him keep. An unseasonal rain fell for fourteen consecutive days, during which she and he huddled long hours in bed. She read to him from Lewis Carroll:

> "Beware the Jabberwock, my son!
> The jaws that bite, the claws that catch!
> Beware the Jubjub bird, and shun
> The frumious Bandersnatch!"

The fascinated Ernie wanted more: "I'd get her to read that to me and it scared my pants off, yet I couldn't stay away from it."[36]

Juanita had come to Aspen Grove to take creative writing from a Dr. Brown. There were writing assignments, critiques of style and structure, admonitions to "keep a pocket notebook in which we could write ideas as they came to us or the names of stories we might wish to return to, and sketch plots briefly. A writer was like a bee, he suggested—he gathers his pollen from many sources, but in the end it is his own handling that makes it honey."[37] She had recently written a short story in a class on the BYU campus. Entitled "But Thinking Makes It So," this story climaxes in the decision of a pioneer woman to accept an impoverished desert village as her true home. It was based, as a note Juanita penciled in a margin clarifies, "on an experience of

Grandma Hafen's mother's." Though competent in style, the story is static in plot and wooden in characterization. Neither now nor later did Juanita show the imagination necessary for writing good fiction. With accurate self-assessment, she concluded her marginal note: "No good except for background."[38] At Aspen Grove, she more candidly chose to write family biography without disguising it as fiction. She recounted the story of Grandfather Dudley Leavitt's escape from Indians when an opportune clap of thunder convinced his captors that he was in communication with the Great Spirit. Her instructor liked the narrative and suggested that it would appear at its best in a cycle of similar accounts.

At the end of summer school Juanita and Ernie made their way south to Dixie. They found board and room with Leland and Elsie Hafen, whose home was obliquely across the intersection from the main college building. Elsie's meals were splendid, and Ernie mixed well with the Hafen children. Leland, a college coach, was such an outgoing man that Ernie once remarked: "Mother, I think I'd like to have Uncle Lee for my Daddy!"[39]

The St. George to which Juanita had moved was by no means a city. Sheltering scarcely two thousand inhabitants, its modest residences clustered around four imposing buildings—the courthouse, the tabernacle, the temple, and the college. To the west loomed Black Ridge with its whitewashed D. To the north rose a bluff of red rock capped by the Sugar Loaf, a small knoll on which an earlier generation had whitewashed the word DIXIE. To the east was Middleton Ridge; the graveled track of Highway 91 pierced this ridge by means of a tunnel. To the south a vista opened upon the Virgin bottom. A serpentine hedge of trees marked the course of the river; on either side spread green, handsome fields. Farther to the south a succession of desert ridges moved to a distant horizon in the Arizona Strip.

There had been changes at the college since Juanita's tenure as a student there. In 1923 the Church had changed the name to Dixie Junior College and had dropped the first two years of high school. Thus blossomed a unique campus nomenclature: students who would have been called high school juniors elsewhere were here known as freshmen; high school seniors as sophomores; college freshmen as juniors; college sophomores as seniors. Juanita was listed in the 1926 yearbook as instructor of English and debate. Her English classes were probably high school, her debate classes college. Her photograph in the yearbook shows an attractive woman. Her short hair is elegantly marcelled and combed forward on the left until it almost covers her eye. So coifed, she entered her assigned third-story room on the first day of instruction. Taking roll, she found a student missing. Suddenly she saw hands gripping the sill of a rear window. According to Ernest's account: "In a moment a face, definitely not a pretty face, with a big jack-o-lantern grin and badly crossed eyes, appeared between the hands. . . . Then this person adroitly jumped into the room. With great dignity he brushed the dust from his clothes and took a seat in the front row. It was Milt Walker who had so startled her. He had climbed up the rainspout to make his unusual and dramatic entrance."[40] Juanita responded positively to young Walker's innovative ways and became his close friend. Some years later she would encourage him to undergo corrective eye surgery. At his insistence, she would be present during the operation.

As her year began, Juanita worried about failing. She spent long hours at night and on weekends preparing for her daily stint of six or seven hours in the classroom. Her expectations of students were so high that she got, as she wrote, "the name of being hard." By her own perception she softened with time; students would continue throughout her career to perceive her as one of the most demanding of instructors. She liked her students and quickly saw that they liked her. In particular she relished coaching debate, becoming "so engrossed in it that it takes all my extra time."[41] She would later judge the year to be successful. "My classes had been crowded, my debating classes enthusiastic, so I faced the second year with confidence."[42]

Juanita went home to Bunkerville for Christmas 1925. Returning early to St. George at New Year, she heard for the first time in her life the midnight tolling of the tabernacle bell.[43] Of such trifles a future is made. One detects a sprouting of new roots for Juanita, a broadening of her sense of home. As 1926 dawned, she recognized herself to be a native, not simply of Bunkerville, but of Dixie.

That is not to say that she found herself acceptable to the elite of St. George. She sensed particularly her exclusion from the self-satisfied ranks of the Athena Club, a ladies' literary society which had evolved from a Red Cross auxiliary organized during World War I. She was not, however, excluded from a friendship with Roxey Romney, a charter member of the Athena Club. Roxey and her husband, Erastus, it will be remembered, had added much to Bunkerville during Juanita's high school years. Now a widow and county librarian, Roxey pursued an enlightened policy of sending quantities of books to out-of-the-way places—"to ranches and villages, and to lonely sheep-herders, wherever people wanted them and she could find transportation for them."[44] Juanita was lucky enough to form an even closer friendship with Mabel Jarvis, an unmarried telephone operator who devoted herself to the care of her aging parents. A homespun author of talent, Mabel composed pageants for holidays and wrote poems for weddings, missionary farewells, and funerals. There is a photograph of her in one of Juanita's published essays.[45] Her freckled face, utterly innocent of cosmetics, shows an elemental integrity and kindness.

In the summer of 1926 Juanita and Ernie escaped the desert heat by returning to Aspen Grove. Again they lived in a tent village scattered among aspens and maples and cooked their meals over wood fires in a camp stove, and again Juanita attended outdoor classes. As the term neared its end, Henry and Mary and some of their children still living at home arrived for a brief visit. Juanita and Ernie joined them for a notable hike to the top of Mt. Timpanogos. It was, Ernest later mused, "the longest hike Uncle Hen [one of various names he called his grandfather] ever made. He always rode horses."[46] At the top the hikers rested and signed their names in a registry in a small observation building. A startling vista greeted these desert folk: in the valley below, Provo and an amethyst Utah Lake; eastward, the craggy summits of the Uintas; westward, an endless succession of desert ranges. The view inspired Juanita to write a poem, "Sunrise from the Top of Mount Timp." Published in *The Improvement Era* of September 1926, the four-stanza poem describes the heavenliness of the dawning world:

> The endless stretching away of the earth,
> The wide dome over me bent,
> An inexpressible soul-stirring within,
> And I return to my home content.

Simple in prosody, romantic in sentiment, it is the work of a novice. Poetry would not prove to be a genre for which Juanita had a gift nor, indeed, even a sustained interest.

Returning to St. George, Juanita rented a large house a half block east of the college. With an affectionate enthusiasm, she proselyted Laurel and Daisy and a cousin, Sarah Leavitt, to live with her and attend Dixie College. Daisy described the arrangement later:

"We were to help with the house work, cook, and tend Ernest for our board and room. I'm sure she put out a lot more than we did as she even bought us clothes, besides the groceries, and rent. It was a wonderful year to be with her."[47] Juanita's generosity reached further. During the Christmas holidays 1926, Melvin married Myrtle Wittwer. Knowing that he led an impoverished scholar's life at BYU, Juanita sent him money for a wedding ring. For Christmas she gave Henry and Mary a magnificent leather davenport and chair. On the day of Eva's graduation in the spring of 1927, Juanita arrived in Bunkerville with a new dress. Eva could remember it years later: "It was of real silk crepe-de-chine, white, and lavishly beaded with tiny seed pearls around the scalloped waist. . . . I was speechless, almost in a state of shock. It was truly a 'dream dress' beyond my wildest imaginings, and it fit me perfectly. I felt like a queen indeed. It cost the unheard of sum of $18." Mabel Jarvis accompanied Juanita. The two brought a tub of sweet pea blossoms, with which they decorated the stage and devised bouquets for the graduates. "This was typical of Juanita," wrote Eva, "always sensing your needs and wants without a word being said."[48]

During the 1926–27 year Juanita fixed her ambition upon a large silver bowl promised to the junior college debate team winning the most contests. She coached, exhorted, and scolded and, of course, watched every debate in an agony of anticipation. By sheer determination she propelled her squad to a clean sweep: "It seems incredible, but the records show that Dixie Junior College won every debate without a dissenting vote."[49] A photograph shows Juanita, flanked by three young men and a young woman, proudly holding a silver bowl and pedestal some twenty-four inches high. Behind them is a flivver with mud-caked wheels, reminding one that there was no pavement in St. George. The young woman smiles wanly; the young men stand clench-fisted, their heads swallowed by enormous fedoras. Juanita wears a splendid dress: a V-neck rimmed by two-inch ruffles, a skirt with a foundation and four ruffled tiers. Her hair is bobbed and marcelled. Obviously she is spending a part of her paycheck on herself.

Sometime during the spring of 1927 Juanita attended a lecture in which a visiting professor asserted that "the villages on the Virgin River were certainly the most inbred in the state, and perhaps in all the world." He was referring to Juanita's relatives, for the numerous descendants of Dudley Leavitt had intermarried extensively in the communities of the lower Virgin. Juanita was sufficiently provoked to engage in a minor study of intermarriage in Bunkerville. Her source was James G. Bleak's manuscript journal, "Annals of the Southern Mission," a four-volume record of the settlement of St. George and nearby villages. Juanita had first caught sight of the "Annals" while waiting in the telephone office for Mabel Jarvis to finish her shift so that they could attend a wedding reception. Perched on a roll-top desk, the volumes were, Juanita would write, "so large they looked like the crack of doom with St. Peter to open them. The black letters on the back were fully two inches tall on a white band."[50] On later occasions as she waited for Mabel to finish her shift, Juanita studied the old volumes and sometimes copied matters relating to Bunkerville. When school was out, she wrote a brief essay about the founding of Bunkerville, drawing principally from Books B and C.[51] Some years afterward she would send this essay to her brother Francis to assist him in graduate research, and it would become lost. In 1927 she had no visible motive for writing it—no prospective audience, no interested colleague to encourage and stimulate her. Written for no other reason than to please herself, it was an impulsive stirring of the historian's vocation.

Juanita accepted an unusual business proposition in the summer of 1927. A strawberry grower in Orem, near Provo, needed pickers. Juanita agreed to be his labor broker. She recruited a crew of some fifteen teenaged girls from Dixie, including Daisy and Eva, hired a truck, and hauled them and their bedding and clothing to Orem. The girls slept in tents and ate in a frame-and-screen dining hall. They rose at five each morning and by six were in the fields, filling small baskets with strawberries for immediate transport to market. Juanita did not pick. She shopped, cooked, supervised, and counseled; at night she "would go to each tent and rub the aching backs and give words of encouragement."[52] Ernest was there too, free to investigate the mysteries of hedgerow and ditch. Juanita enjoyed the girls' banter: "At the time, I thought that I should take notes and write up some of the stories that were told as the girls lolled around on the grass in the shade of the tall trees on the banks of the canal."[53]

When the strawberry season ended, Juanita delivered her young charges safely home to Dixie. Immediately, she and Ernest departed with Aura and a friend for Yellowstone Park, where Charity was working for the summer. They rented a tent cottage, visited Charity, saw Old Faithful, and fed bears. Shortly after the travelers had returned, Grandmother Thirza Riding Leavitt died. Thirza had been promised that she would not die before the coming of the Savior unless she herself should wish to depart. On August 26, 1927, she called in her son Thomas and told him she was ready. He gave her a blessing and on the following day she died.[54] Not long before her death someone took a photograph of Thirza and Ernest. The aged woman and the white-haired boy stand on a weedy Bunkerville sidewalk. On one side is a ragged picket fence, on the other a water-filled ditch. Thirza wears a black skirt, a light blouse, and a full white apron. She wears wire-rimmed glasses, and her lips cave in upon her toothless gums. Ernest is barefooted and he wears bib overalls and a shortsleeved shirt. He smiles at the photographer. Thirza's arm rests on his shoulder. She seems abstracted and solemn, as if she knows her time is at hand.

During 1927–28, Daisy and Eva lived with Juanita and Ernest while attending Dixie College. Juanita had rented a more imposing house. Her successes of the previous year had given her a status requiring a dignified style of living, "especially with regard to the home I was to live in. My responsibility was larger than just schoolwork. I must maintain a home setting in which I could invite family and friends without embarrassment. . . . "[55] It is possible that she had by now joined the St. George Business and Professional Women's Association. She was on the rise.

Juanita taught English B and C and courses in debate and public speaking. She took roll every day and recorded assignment grades in ink in tiny, carefully formed letters. In the debate classes, assignments included oral reports, orations, criticism of high school debates, and conferences. There was one Saturday morning assignment for a religious speech entitled "Home Mission." In her English classes, assignments included a short story, a book report, and a report on a three-act play. Her final grades included a few A minuses and B's, many C's, some D's, and a few F's. Her reputation for severe grading continued to grow.[56]

In the spring of 1928 came a great stroke of fortune. In a faculty meeting the president of the college announced the availability of a single sabbatical leave for the following year. In order of seniority he offered it to one faculty member after another. All refused until he came to Juanita, who said, "Don't look at me. I'll take it so quick it'll make your head swim."[57] Her stipend would be $85 a month. It was settled that she would pursue a master's degree. The only question was the university. Juanita's heart must have pounded as she remembered that prim young woman with a coronet of braided hair, Miss Mina Connell, who had been, it will be remembered, an alumna of Columbia. Juanita retained an unsatisfied curiosity about distant, fabulous places of which her mentor had spoken. Juanita knew something of Utah and the West. The East she didn't know at all. She would go to Columbia.

Juanita returned to Orem with an even larger group of Dixie girls to pick strawberries during the summer of 1928. Daisy and Eva were among the pickers. Charity had also come along to help cook and supervise. When the berry season ended, Juanita returned to St. George and made preparations for her departure for New York City. Ernest would stay in Bunkerville. He was welcome with Mary and Henry, and there was not money enough to arrange for his care in New York.

In mid-September she boarded the Union Pacific Flyer. By day she sat in a coach car watching America rush by; at night she slept in a Pullman berth. She described the Pennsylvania hills and the New Jersey coast as a "lovely wooded land, the trees, other than pine, being entirely new to me. There was a thick undergrowth of ferns & other vines. We crossed the Mississippi, the Wabash, and the Susquehanna Rivers. I can understand why someone should write 'On the Banks of the Wabash.' It's such a beautiful stream."[58]

She had hoped to be met by a friend, Clarissa, a native of Mesquite who was now a social worker in New York. However, she saw no familiar face when she detrained at Penn Station on Sunday afternoon, September 16. At an information desk she received the address of the Morningside, a women's residence club near the university. Having rented a room at $7.50 a week, she climbed seven stories to her apartment. She liked it even before turning on the light. She pulled up a window and looked over the city. A carillon in a nearby church played "Lead, Kindly Light." The haunting melody comforted her, and she resolved to listen to vespers each evening.[59] She unpacked her bags, had a hot bath, washed her hair, and laundered her bloomers and stockings. Then she wrote a letter home: "When I came across that picture of Ernest and I, I just had to weep a little, though I have promised myself faithfully that I wouldn't get homesick. He looks so darn cute—and I can't help but worry just a little about how he'll get along. I want you to write me the truth about him."[60]

On Monday she made her way to Clarissa's office by means of three changes on the subway, a ride on the elevated, and a hike along six blocks of much greater magnitude than St. George blocks. Clarissa and her husband took her to supper and gave her a tour of the city in their car. The Bowery horrified her. "Such filth I never imagined, and such swarms of children—and such smells! It was sickening. Then we rode down the sections where the wealthy live and past some of the great tall buildings. It was a wonderful trip. Saw more than I would have done in weeks alone."[61]

At Columbia, Juanita enrolled in a program leading to a degree in English. Her studies would be largely tutorial and self-guided. She could attend classes and lectures if she wished. She would have to write a major seminar paper and at the end of the year take a comprehensive examination in English and American literature. The topic of her seminar paper seemed enormous: "American Poetry Before Anne Bradstreet." She settled into an assigned study space in the library and oriented herself to the comprehensive examination by scanning a ten-year accumulation of previous examinations. Panic seized her: "Never before or since have I felt so ignorant, so totally lost. Who was I to come to an institution like this for a Master's degree, with a background like mine? A high school of forty students! Credits in a Normal school geared to teaching in the sage flats of Nevada! College classes taken because the time scheduled fitted the exchange in hours for caring for the baby and preparing meals! Surely I had made a major mistake to come here!"[62] Juanita decided not to retreat. She started research on her seminar topic and began a methodical survey of English and American literature. For five days a week, from twelve to fifteen hours a day, she labored in the library, reading, memorizing, and ruminating.

Back home in Bunkerville, the arrival of her letters was a major event. "I would rush to the mail every day," wrote her sister Mary, "looking anxiously for her letters to bring home to Dad & Mother. Dad would just glow when I would come home running packing a letter from New York and Juanita. Immediately Dad would sit in his big Chair and ORDER Mother to stop what ever she was doing and come and read to him Nitas letters, Over & Over—so that he would get every word straight in his mind—so that he could retell & retell the news to all his friends and relatives of her Activitys. He was so proud of her."[63] Sometimes Juanita's absence weighed heavily on the family. On Christmas day Francis played records on the family's windup phonograph. One of the songs was called "Mammy Is Gone." Ernest would remember that "at the end of the first chorus a couple of tears found their way down my cheeks, Grandma saw and dropped a couple to match. Before the record was finished the whole family was having a good cry, even the men-folks—including Pa. He, of course, just sat up straight as a rod and let his tears fall into his lap. No sniffling for him!"[64]

On Sundays Juanita made the long trip across town by subway to attend the Mormon branch in Manhattan. She also fraternized with Harold and Verna Bentley from Utah. Harold worked in the university bookstore while he pursued a doctorate. The couple had Juanita to dinner and often asked her to baby-sit their infant daughter. Otherwise Juanita's life was an utter exposure to the Outside. She frequently attended the sermons of Harry Emerson Fosdick in a nearby church, a fact which she very well may have failed to mention in her letters home. Other representatives of the Outside were Clarissa and her husband, who exhorted Juanita to adopt a greater worldliness. Clarissa, Juanita would write, "had taken up tobacco with an emphasis—smoked constantly, even drizzled ashes in her cooking. She insisted that I should learn, that I should try, at least. Sometimes I wonder now why I didn't. . . . I had an idea that it would make me sick, and I don't like to be sick. I could have taken a calomel course with as much logic."[65]

Another outside influence was Polly, a petite girl of eighteen who at first lived down the hall in the Morningside. A friendship blossomed as Juanita nursed Polly through an illness, and the two agreed to share an apartment. The roommates went out together on weekends, taking turns in choosing their destination—Coney Island, the Statue of Liberty, Greenwich Village, and various theatres and musical stages.[66] Sometimes they were joined by Ethel, a waitress in the cafe where Polly worked. Juanita found the irregularity of Ethel's life fascinating. An English immigrant, Ethel had lived for ten years as the mistress of a married man, who contributed to her support, visiting her often in her Bronx apartment and "taking a father's interest in their now eight-year-old daughter." Impressed by the sincerity of the affection between Ethel and her lover, Juanita suggested "that she was really living in polygamy. After a pause she answered, 'I guess it does amount to about the same thing.' "[67]

Juanita formed a study group with four or five other female students. Two of them, Carrie and Metta, were picturesque girls of some wealth from South Carolina. Metta can be identified as "the one who bought a car to match her gloves. Her boyfriend had given her a pair of kind of dark, plum-colored gloves. She had a car, but the gloves didn't match, so she traded until she got a car to match her gloves."[68] Carrie and Metta arranged blind dates for Juanita and another friend for the annual Alumni Banquet of the Naval Academy. It was an elegant affair requiring a rented gown and a ride in a taxicab. While the orchestra played "The Bells of St. Mary's," the revelers, drunk on illegal liquor, struck their goblets with spoons. The uproar continued during the introduction of the speaker; this unfortunate person soon sat down without finishing his speech. Juanita's date opened a flask and began filling her glass. "Now the proper thing, of course, would have been for me to smile and say quietly, 'Enough, thank you.' I should have known that, yet instinctively and on the impulse I said, 'Whoa!' If a bomb had exploded in the middle of the table, the effect could not have been more startling. The young man's mouth dropped open, his arm froze in mid-air."[69] The ensuing conversation showed her to be too rustic or perhaps too hardy for the young man's sensibilities. In any event, his evening was ruined and he became morose. Afterward he passed out on a couch and Juanita took unceremonious leave of him.

As the academic year closed, Juanita completed her paper on American poetry before Anne Bradstreet. Her grade was A minus. Long afterward she would judge this work to be "valueless at the time and still worth nothing— except that it proved me capable of doing research." She assembled with the other master's candidates for the comprehensive examination. She labored through the objective part three times, answering no more than half the questions. She left in despair, later writing: "I, who have always thought I was so honest, would even have cheated if I could have done so."[70] Although she believed the three essays she wrote on the following day were adequate, she did not at first have the courage to ask whether she had passed. Finally she steeled herself to call from the privacy of a telephone booth. She had passed in the next to top category. She could only believe that Providence had helped her. "So I just hung up the receiver, said 'Thank you, Lord,' again, and collected myself enough to hurry out onto the street."[71]

She returned to Bunkerville indirectly. She and Polly took a night boat to Boston and visited Polly's home in Lynn, Massachusetts. Saying good-bye to Polly, Juanita joined a teachers' tour of historical and literary sites along the eastern coast. Then she boarded a train and traveled west. Perhaps, as she gazed out the window at the speeding American scene, she had a clearer definition of herself than ever before. In June 1929, Juanita Pulsipher was an educated person, a career teacher, a citizen of the world. She had experienced the Outside at first hand and had discovered she had a tolerance and even a sympathy for it. Finally, however, she had no compulsion to hew her identity to its dimensions. She was happy to be going home. "The big city is all right," she would write, "but I do not belong there."[72]

When Dixie College convened in the fall of 1929, Juanita rented a small house. Characteristically, she persuaded Francis and Dudley to live with her and Ernest, Francis for his first year of college, Dudley for his third year of high school. As school began, Laurel arrived home from his mission, and he too moved in with Juanita. However, as soon as he had recovered from an attack of ulcers, he migrated on for a late registration at BYU. For Francis Juanita purchased a trumpet, "a most gorgeous instrument," at the staggering price of $110.[73] For Dudley she bought a suit, his first, so that he could attend dances and church meetings with pride. Because Dudley's eyes were chronically afflicted, she twice took him by bus to Provo for treatment. On one trip she bought a pillow en route to make his ride more comfortable.[74]

Her brothers helped out by milking the cow Henry had furnished Juanita. They also did her laundry on Saturdays. Undaunted by the derision of other young men, they built a fire under the cauldrons in the backyard, boiled the clothes, scrubbed them on the board, and hung them to dry on the line. Local rumor had it that the extraordinary whiteness of Juanita's drying sheets had come up in conversations among the Athena Club. Juanita attributed this social triumph to her mother's homemade soap.[75] It is possible that vigorous masculine arms at the scrub board had something to do with it.

Joseph K. Nicholes, president of the college, gave Juanita a $200 raise and appointed her dean of women. She was disappointed that she would no longer serve as debate coach; she would, however, continue as an instructor of English, assuming the English literature survey in recognition of her advanced status. As dean of women, she was quickly disabused of any illusion she might have had that her charges were immune to the griefs and vices of humanity at large. When a girl from California, "small, and so pale as to be ashen," infected a number of Dixie boys with gonorrhea, a local physician called Juanita greatly concerned about the boys, "for one or two were from prominent families."[76] Juanita did not ask the physician to name the boys. She pressured the girl to accept treatment and sent her home to California. In describing the affair, she was scornful not of the boys but of the girl. Unwittingly she held to a double standard.

In the spring of 1930, at Ernest's request, Juanita bought a house. It was a small white frame structure in the northwestern precinct of St. George called Mount Hope. It boasted a vineyard, pomegranate bushes, and a front lawn bordered by marigolds. Ernest's love for the place was not diminished by the fact that skunks lived underneath the porch. As Juanita, Ernest, Francis, and Dudley moved in, family weddings were afoot. Charity married Vernon Rowley on May 19. Aura married Carl Allen on June 27. Both had met their fiancés in towns where they had gone to teach. It was only the beginning of a notable nuptial year for Henry and Mary. Daisy married Leonard Reber on October 1. Ten days later Laurel married Marva Durrant. Because Laurel was living far away in Provo, none of his family attended his wedding. Juanita would make amends later. Eva married Walter Miles on May 19, 1931. Times being hard, Eva expected no reception. "Juanita, however, surpised us with a nice 'shower' in St. George. It was a wonderful party filled with fun and laughter, and we were so happy to get so many nice and useful gifts to start housekeeping with. Juanita, bless her heart, had always known how much I admired her pair of blue all wool blankets, and much to our delight, presented us with an exact pair, my greatest treasure for many years."[77]

Francis and Dudley continued to live with Juanita during the 1930-31 school year. Employed as a college chauffeur, Francis once drove Juanita to Kanab, where she had an official speaking engagement. While she spoke, he and Dudley, who had also come along, gave a couple of girls a ride around town. Juanita interpreted this as a dereliction of duty. "She reminded me in no uncertain terms," Francis reported, "of my responsibility both to her and to the college but more particularly to our relationship as brother and sister. I have never forgotten it—the one time in my life I felt truly repentant."[78] On another occasion, when Dudley had got drunk on liquor he and some friends had manufactured, Juanita turned him in to President Nicholes for disciplinary action.[79] If anything, she expected a greater rectitude from her brothers than from other students.

One evening in the winter of 1931, Juanita trudged up the steep hill to her home, fatigued by a grueling day at the college. Although she expected Francis soon, the house was empty when she arrived. She lay on her bed and dozed. Shortly she felt as if her spirit had separated from her body. In fact, she could see herself, mouth open, upon the bed. She concluded that she had died: "Then suddenly, without the lapse of any time, I was at my father's home in Bunkerville. I thought how sad that two who had had so many children should be there alone now. They were in the living room; there was a fire in the fire-place, and mother was stirring some mush in a saucepan over the coals. The house was so large and cold that they had not gone into the kitchen to make a fire, and Daddy liked mush for his supper. He was shaking some cream in a two quart jar, because their one cow did not give enough to use the big churn. And he was telling her how one of the horses had got another into the manger and was kicking it."[80]

In an instant she awakened on the bed in St. George. Francis came in then and she told him the experience. Two days later on Sunday they visited Henry and Mary in Bunkerville, where with much marveling her parents confirmed every detail she had seen and heard. Thereafter, in solemn moods she would assure friends and family of the reality of the resurrection, which hitherto she had sometimes doubted. She narrated the story in a letter to the grieving parents of a young man killed in an accident, concluding: "The experience took the horror out of death for me. It gave me the positive knowledge that we are alive and conscious and intelligent after. I think that the Lord probably had things for me to do here, or I never would have come back."[81]

In the spring of 1931 Juanita was appointed a member of the St. George Stake Board of the Mutual Improvement Association (a church auxiliary, often called Mutual or MIA). In fulfillment of her new duties, Juanita attended the general conference of the Church in Salt Lake. Returned, she caught a ride to Blanding in southeastern Utah where Charity and Vernon resided. Her ride was with William Brooks, county sheriff, who was on his way to Colorado to extradite a prisoner. Juanita and Will chatted amiably on innumerable topics.

They stopped for the night in a hotel in Moab, where Will carefully arranged for rooms on separate floors. As they passed through Monticello, where Will had lived as a young man, Juanita saw that he was remembered with great love and respect. In Blanding they said a cordial good-bye, for Juanita would find other means for getting home to St. George.[82] A married man with a family, Will had been the essence of propriety; so had Juanita, a widow sealed by a temple marriage. Nonetheless, one is tempted to give further meaning to this ride. Too proper to admit it to themselves, they had unconsciously learned that they could love each other.

In the summer of 1931, Daisy left her home in Mesquite and moved in with Juanita to await the birth of her first child. "Early one morning, Aug 30, 1931 I knew the time had come. I was real frightened, but she was so calm and masterful. She called Dr. Reichmann and his nurse Mrs Seegmiller, and they came to her home to deliver the baby."[83] In honor of Juanita, affectionately called Nita, Daisy and Leonard named their girl Anita Rae. In the fall of 1931 Francis went to BYU. Penniless, he faced his first Christmas away from home. "I'll never know how [Juanita] knew, but a few days before Christmas I received a small check with a note that I should come home and be with the family. I was the happiest young man on the entire BYU campus."[84]

Early in 1932 an enormous change in Juanita's life began to take shape. On February 19, Nellie Brooks, the sheriff's wife, died unexpectedly of a cerebral hemorrhage. If Mabel Jarvis or another suitable companion had invited her, Juanita would have gone to the viewing. She didn't dare go of her own initiative for fear of seeming interested in the new widower. In such matters Juanita adhered to a punctilious protocol. "I knew the whole Athena Club would be there in groups of three or four, or perhaps as a whole group to sit together. I hadn't the heart to face them."[85]

An unabashed matchmaker in the person of Joseph K. Nicholes now stepped forward. For months following Nellie's death, the college president lost no opportunity to speak well of Will Brooks in Juanita's presence. When legislators visited St. George and when Dixie fans loyally traveled to a ball game in Cedar City, Nicholes arranged to have Juanita ride in Will's car. For months, the widow and the widower maintained a studious silence upon the question of marriage. Will broke that silence following their attendance at the dedication of a monument to the victims of the Mountain Meadows massacre.

The date was September 10, 1932. Will invited Mabel Jarvis and others who worked at the courthouse to ride with him and suggested they bring along Juanita and Ernest, the latter to serve as company for Will's son Clair. Riding in the backseat on the outward journey, Juanita became carsick and had to call a stop while she vomited at the side of the road. Will's practice of maintaining "car speed by alternately floorboarding and releasing the accelerator,"[86] as Ernest later described it, had aggravated her susceptibility to nausea. A crowd of some 400 persons had assembled at Mountain Meadows—state and county officials, representatives of various churches and lodges, schoolteachers, interested citizens. The monument consisted of a stone wall four feet high and thirty feet square enclosing the burial place of the murdered emigrants. Fixed to the wall was a bronze plaque which read:

> In this vicinity September 7th, 1857, occurred one of the most lamentable tragedies in the history annals of the West. A company of about 140 emigrants from Arkansas and Missouri led by Captain Charles Fancher, enroute to California, was attacked by white men and Indians. All but 17 small children were killed. John D. Lee, who confessed participation as leader, was legally executed here March 23rd, 1877.

The memorial had been erected by the Utah Pioneer Trails and Landmarks Association. The most responsible individual was William R. Palmer, storekeeper and stake president from Cedar City. An accomplished amateur historian with a special interest in the Paiute Indians, Palmer had the most complete and objective grasp of the massacre of anyone alive in 1932. It was he who had raised money for the monument by public subscription and had persuaded dubious general authorities of the Church not to oppose the venture.

It was a bright, hot day. The once grassy meadows were now a sagebrush plain, and the many springs had become a deep gully bearing a trickle of water. The proceedings were as hushed as a funeral. There were solemn hymns, speeches that neither justified nor condemned, and moments of silence. Juanita could not have helped grasping the scandalous fact that this mass grave had been neglected for nearly eight decades; nor could she have helped recognizing that the massacre had been a tragedy for the aggressors as well as for the victims. She was especially moved by the prayer of dedication offered by her colleague, theology teacher John T. Woodbury. "How many times since have I wished that that prayer might have been preserved, with all its richness of tone and inflection, upon a tape recorder! When it was finished, we were all welded into one great unity. We were humbled before the enormity of what had been done here; we were lifted by a hope and a desire that we should help to right the wrong. At least, we felt that we would each resolve that our lives would be cast upon a higher plane. Gone were all thoughts of bitterness, or revenge, or scorn."[87]

When they had returned to St. George, Will let off his other passengers before taking Juanita and Ernest to the little house on the hill. Ernest led Clair into the vineyard and soon brought Will clusters of ripe grapes:

> Will picked at them and seemed pleased to take them, and stood awhile until he had sampled them all. Then as he turned to go he said seriously, "I'm not looking anywhere yet, but when I do start, *you'd* better watch out."
>
> "Oh, I don't know," I parried. "I'll have something to say about that, remember."
>
> "I'm just warning you," and he walked away, to stop and call back, "Thanks for the grapes, and for the company."[88]

In this maladroit fashion, they broached the question whether or not they should marry. In effect, Will had announced his interest, and Juanita at least had not said no.

One surmises that Juanita went about her campus duties during the fall of 1932 in a state of painful indecision. She considered her frequent bouts of loneliness, her recurring sense of incompletion. She weighed the intensity of her need to be loved by a man, to have babies, to devote herself singlemindedly to the housekeeping by which her community defined womanhood. But she also measured her life as a professional woman. She took into account the genuine pleasure and fulfillment she had found in teaching and counseling. She thought about her freedom of movement and her interest in traveling in America and Europe. She considered the very plausible prospect of a Ph.D. and a university appointment. Finally she weighed Will's shortcomings. He was after all something less than a romantic hero. At fifty-two, he was seventeen years her senior. He had three sons at home and another on a mission. He was short, bald, and stout and had false teeth.

Near Thanksgiving Henry and Mary arrived in town with their daughter Mary, seventeen, who had suddenly decided to marry her long-time boyfriend, Fenton Frehner. All were despondent, the father and mother because of Mary's age, Mary because she had no prospects for a beautiful wedding. Juanita cheered them up. She proposed that Mary and Fenton take possession of her little house for their honeymoon while she attended a conference in Salt Lake. Then, as she had taken her other sisters, she took Mary to a dress shop and spent astounding sums on two splendid garments, which Mary would affectionately remember: "a beautiful black street dress, with round collar with a soft furry white material interwoven with black velvet so neat" and "a long bright red red dress cut on the bias, with a large round lace collar that came way down, that was just gorgeous, for my reception at Bunkerville."[89]

At Christmas Juanita went home to Bunkerville. As she left St. George, she mailed a Christmas card to Will Brooks. On New Year's Day she went across the river to Mesquite for dinner at the home of Mary and Fenton. As dinnertime approached, a knock came at the door. It was Will Brooks boldly announcing that he had come to give Juanita a ride back to St. George. He had, it seems, taken the Christmas card as her acceptance of the indirect proposal he had made following the trip to Mountain Meadows. Perhaps unwittingly that was how she had intended the card be taken.

Mary invited Will to stay for dinner. Afterward, while Will and Fenton conversed in the living room, Juanita helped in the kitchen. "Out of their hearing, Mary took me by my two arms and shook me. 'You crazy kid!' she said. 'He's not either *old*, and *fat*, and *funny*! He's *nice*! You'll do well to get a man like that. Don't you make fun of him ever again!' "[90] In this case, the younger sister had the sounder advice. On the return to St. George, Juanita sat in the front seat with Will while Ernest and Dudley sat in the rear. Ernest and Dudley got out at the little house. Will drove on past the Sugar Loaf and parked behind some willows. There the county sheriff and the dean of women embraced, kissed, and murmured endearments, perhaps awkwardly and with a certain inevitable shame.

For three months it was a private engagement. Juanita and Will did not dance with each other nor attend church together. Will arrived at her house by a back road, and they drove away to have dinner in out-of-town cafes. It was Juanita, one supposes, who insisted that they not publicly slight Nellie's memory by marrying in indecent haste. On April 19, 1933, they drove to Bunkerville to celebrate Henry's birthday, taking a freezer of ice cream, a cake, and some oranges. At a fitting moment during the celebration, they asked for the attention of their assembled relatives and made public their intent to marry.

CHAPTER FOUR

AN UNDEFINED
AMBITION

During the winter of 1933 Juanita wrote two brief poems, which were published in the April 1933 issue of *The Improvement Era*. The poems express her ambivalence toward her approaching marriage, which would be both confining and fulfilling. In "Resignation" she is a caged bird; she longs to "be free, to aspire, to soar," but is imprisoned by timidity in the cage of conformity, "so sheltered, so safe, so secure." Yet in "Awakening," she is a discordant harp suddenly set in tune by the touch of her beloved.

On May 23, 1933, Washington County issued a marriage license to Miss Juanita L. Pulsipher and Mr. William Brooks.[1] On May 25 the couple were married in the St. George temple for the duration of their mortal lives. A host of relatives and friends clad in solemn white attended. Juanita responded to the temple ceremony far differently than she had on the occasion of her first wedding. She found in it, she later wrote, "a beauty and a symbolism that will make for better life." She was particularly impressed by the appearance of her grandmother, Mary Ann Hafen. "A shaft of light from the high arched window falls across her face. The softness of the white veil, her naturally wavy hair, her hands brown and gnarled from hard work, but her expression of peace, of more than that—of spiritual illumination—make me think that I have never seen old age so beautiful."[2] Following the ceremony there was a wedding dinner at Will's home. Some twenty-five adults crowded onto the front porch for a group photograph. In the photo Will holds a little girl, a niece perhaps, and Juanita grasps the child's arm and smilingly speaks into her ear. It is as if the newlyweds desire a buffer between them.

Juanita now moved, both literally and figuratively, into the center of St. George. Will's house was at 65 North 100 East, a scant remove from the courthouse, the post office, the county library, the college, and the tabernacle. From her little house on the hill Juanita brought a new bedroom set and other furniture. A particular novelty was a new refrigerator, her wedding gift to Will and herself. Nonetheless, she felt the suffocating presence of the dead Nellie in every room—in the curtains, the wallpaper, the knickknacks. Her only recourse was respectful silence. Later she would offer advice to others who might be marrying a family: "First, never try to compete with the first mother. Any comparison is to your disadvantage. . . . Never say or allow anyone else to say a single disparaging word of the woman who preceded you. If you feel that you will smother to death among her things, give them to the children to be kept as treasures against the time when they will have homes of their own, or scatter them among doting relatives, or remove them quietly, without comment, one at a time."[3]

A more serious problem for Juanita centered upon Will's three younger sons, Bob, sixteen, Grant, fourteen, and Clair, eight. His eldest son, Walter, twenty-one, was serving a Spanish-speaking mission in Texas. Difficulties were compounded by the fact that Ernest, twelve, fought with Grant and Bob. Large for his age but unaggressive, Ernest was regularly reduced to tears. Juanita wrote: "Perhaps I didn't realize how hard it was for him to see the little home on the hill broken up, the new furniture brought down to this big house, the dog taken to Bunkerville."[4] Ernest quickly followed the dog to Bunkerville, and Juanita resigned herself to his absence, relieved to know that at least he would be a help and a comfort to Henry and Mary. For several years Ernest would return to St. George only for brief visits.

Almost instantly Juanita won over Clair, a small, frail boy whom she described as "mother-hungry." On the day she and Will returned from their brief honeymoon, Clair came home sunburned from swimming in the river. Will medicated him with Mentholatum, causing the boy to scream. Juanita pushed Will aside and gently patted cream, skimmed from cool milk in the cellar, onto Clair's burned back and shoulders. "It was so soothing and he was so worn out that he fell asleep almost instantly. He never forgot it; from that time on he saw me differently. One day he came home from school with his shirt torn and his hair disheveled. He had been in a fight with a kid who said that I was his step-mother. I was nothing of the kind! I was his real mother."[5]

Grant at first seemed unreliable and rebellious. Juanita candidly noted in her diary that he "will take things that do not belong to him and will not always tell the truth."[6] Once when Grant returned muddy and bedraggled from a truant day of hunting birds' nests in the river bottom, Will angrily decided upon a whipping. Again Juanita intervened. As she gave Grant supper, she suggested that he make a formal hobby of collecting nests. She would buy him a glass display case, show him how to make identification cards, and pack him a lunch for his ventures, which, of course, had to be restricted to Saturdays. Scarcely a month after her wedding, she recorded that Grant had already collected nests from twenty-two varieties of birds. Thereafter he was more amenable to discipline.

Bob appeared unapproachable. "Always a gentleman, he was cold toward me, just seemed to have nothing to say. I found it hard to make conversation with him at all."[7] Nonetheless, at Christmas Juanita pleased him by fitting his room with "new curtains, bedspread and matching rug and table lamp. He still says it was the best Christmas gift of his life."[8] One assumes that with Will's children Juanita followed scrupulously the advice she offered others: "Never order a child to do anything in a tone or words that will give a chance for an open refusal. Ask him if he would like to, or if he will—and then if he does not, do not make an issue of it. . . . You can afford to be patient. After all, you hold the trump cards, if you only know how to play them. Just as you must not seem to compete with the first wife, so you must not be in competition with the children."[9]

On July 5, 1933, Juanita recorded in her diary the fact of her pregnancy. Odors, particularly the odor of Will's breath, offended her. Admitting that Will had been generous in helping with the housework, she lamented that "somehow the edge is gone from things. It's not so much fun after all." Then came a frank evaluation of wedded love, perhaps unfairly colored by her nausea: "I think that of all things in the world sex gratification is the *least* satisfying. It leaves not even a memory that is pleasant; in fact it can't be enjoyed in anticipation or retrospect at all. For a few seconds there is a type of excitement and that is all. It's not even especially pleasant."[10]

Scarcely six weeks married, Juanita was understandably disillusioned. The abrupt abortion of her academic career depressed her. She had onerous new housekeeping duties—and she had never relished housework. She was unsure of the love of Will and his sons, and her commitment to them had diminished her relationship with her own son. However, she was not one to languish long. By July 13 she had recovered her spirits, having just read a stimulating book called

Life Begins at Forty. "In spite of my marriage I refuse to be 'shelved' and to do nothing. I need to dig up my old ambition to write, if it's only for my own entertainment & amusement." She described Will's attentiveness, adding a doubtful note: "Sometimes I wonder if he really likes me as much as he pretends. I don't see how he can."[11] On July 15 she wrote that her nausea had disappeared entirely and that she had been riding horses several times a week. She would be free from morning sickness during the remainder of this pregnancy and during the three that would follow. She gradually came to believe in her husband's devotion, so much so that in November she recorded: "Will is such a dear. I don't believe a man ever lived who was as good to his wife. I'm getting big and awkward and ugly, but he doesn't seem to mind. Is better than ever, in fact."[12]

It was propitious that Juanita should "dig up her old ambition to write," for the role of free-lance author gave an outlet to an otherwise frustrated energy. Throughout the rest of her life she would remain willing to write in any genre that promised publication. It would require almost a decade, moreover, for her ambition to confine itself chiefly to historiography. For whatever it is worth to Mormondom and the world at large, her achievements as historian, tragedian, and dissenter derived entirely from her deflection from a conventional academic career. If she had not married Will Brooks, she would in all probability have achieved a Ph.D. and an appointment in a university English department. She would have written books, but they would have been works of literary criticism and would not have been controversial.

Juanita's ambition to be a writer was given immediate direction by Nels Anderson, who on July 18, 1933, telephoned from New York asking her to prepare an article on the polygamous family of her grandfather Dudley Leavitt. During the spring and early summer Nels Anderson had lived with his wife and son in a house just around the corner from the Brooks home. He had frequently dropped in via a backyard trail, entering their kitchen without knocking. Anderson had come to St. George armed with research grants from Columbia, where he was pursuing a doctorate. His purpose was to write a history of the Mormon frontier in Utah. He had been attracted to St. George by the most unlikely of circumstances. As a teenage hobo in 1908 he had been put off a freight train in Clover Valley, Nevada, where Mormon ranchers took him in. In 1909 he was baptized a Mormon to please his benefactors, and he later attended Dixie College and BYU. He did not claim to be a believer.

It appears that Anderson wanted Juanita to prepare an account of her grandfather's family for inclusion, more or less complete, in his book. On the day following his request, Juanita recorded that the project "completely fascinates me." She then fell to musing upon the multitudes of her grandfather's children: "I wonder how he got acquainted with them all. I doubt that he did."[13] In the days that followed she tallied Dudley's wives and children and soon expanded the project to include the polygamous families of her maternal grandfather, John Hafen. By summer's end the paper was complete. In the meantime, Will had forgotten to remove Anderson's address from his shirt pocket and the address had been obliterated by a journey through Juanita's Maytag wringer. Deciding to venture on her own, Juanita mailed the manuscript to *Harper's* and with great trepidation awaited a result.[14]

Juanita's desire to write was compromised by circumstances. Her status as the wife of Sheriff Brooks required that she join the redoubtable Athena Club. She now attended monthly parties where charades and Rook ruled, she herself serving as hostess when her turn came. Far more demanding was her call in September 1933 to the highest local church position to which a woman could be appointed, stake Relief Society president. Her duties were endless. She held regular consultations with her counselors, the stake president, and the eight or ten ward Relief Society presidents whom she supervised. She attended Relief Society general conference in Salt Lake and organized a Relief Society assembly at each quarterly conference of St. George Stake. She entertained visiting dignitaries in her home, once serving over 200 guests at a reception honoring one of them.[15]

In the fall of 1933 Juanita persuaded her brothers Francis and Dudley to continue their education at the University of Nevada in Reno, where as Nevada residents they would receive favorable tuition rates. Because of the Great Depression, neither young man had been able to find employment. On a beautiful autumn day Juanita and Will drove them to Reno. Francis wrote: "I remember following the Truckee River up to Reno and all the brilliant lights and the arched sign over Virginia Street 'The Biggest Little City in the World.' They helped us find 'batching quarters' next day before returning home. Juanita spent a sleepless night worrying about leaving us in the wicked city of Reno."[16]

Juanita sent occasional gifts of cash and, even more important for Francis, research materials which would help him write a master's thesis on the Mormon settlement of the Virgin Valley. These included the brief essay she had written about Bunkerville and other materials drawn from the early journals of James G. Bleak, which she had first seen at the telephone office in 1927. These records were now deposited in the temple, to which, as stake Relief Society president, she had unfettered access. In December 1933 she made one of several references in her diary to her research in the temple: "I am copying from Bro. Blakes old record on the early history of Bunkerville. Have finished that on the Muddy Valley. Francis should find it valuable. I may be able to use some of it myself."[17]

In the meantime, as deer season approached in October, Juanita and Will had the sharpest confrontation of their brief married life. By Juanita's reckoning, Will behaved like a man possessed. He pulled red hats and boots from closets, oiled guns, went target shooting, tied a bedroll, prepared a grub box, and fell into frequent reveries about early deer hunts. She remonstrated vigorously: "My sympathies were all with the deer; in my opinion, beef was better than venison and much cheaper. At last Will sat me down, pulled another chair up close and said, 'Now you get this! Some men get their recreation one way, some another. They get drunk, gamble with cards, chase the women. I hunt deer. I have gone every year since I could carry a gun. I'll take care of all the preparations, but it would be pleasanter all around if you would cooperate just a little. If you can't help, at least don't fight it.' "[18]

Will would remain an inveterate outdoorsman. He often hunted cottontail rabbits, quail, and pheasants. Sometimes he shot running jackrabbits with a revolver. He also loved fishing as long as he could cast, spin, or troll. His son Walter wrote: "He had a little stream up in Pine Valley that we would take him to, drop him off there and then we'd go on up the creek farther. . . . He'd fish up this little Spring Branch, as it was called, up toward Pine Valley Mountain, then fish back. By the time he got back he always had his limit. Then the limit was 30 fish."[19] Unquestionably Will's favorite sport was deer hunting. He initiated each of his sons, including Ernest, at fifteen, at which age, a year short of legally carrying a rifle, the boy was considered fit for camp chores and brushing out deer. A typical Brooks deer camp of the 1930s could number twenty-five men and boys.[20] Brothers, cousins, and friends gathered on the day before the opening among the aspens or junipers in the mountains north of St. George. They erected tents, cooked Dutch oven suppers, and retold adventures from previous hunts. Before dawn they scattered through the hills. Will rarely failed to bag his deer.

All of this Juanita learned to tolerate if not respect. Despite Will's customary deference to Juanita, he had an unassailable masculinity that she admired and depended on. As sheriff, Will was an anomalous mixture of the congenial and the heroic, the docile and the belligerent. He had a warm, contagious smile and wore a white shirt and tie, round wire-rimmed spectacles, an unformed, low-crowned Stetson, and a long-barreled .38 Colt. His adventures in law enforcement ranged from the trivial to the tragic: he wiped up urine around a toilet for a wife who had called him in to force her careless husband to do the task; he adjudicated a supposed theft of eggs; he delivered a convicted rapist to the state penitentiary in Salt Lake; he investigated the suicide by strychnine of a girl made pregnant by a CCC boy.

Juanita was fascinated by his activities and was herself drawn into them, relaying phone calls, taking meals to prisoners in the little adobe jail behind the courthouse, and receiving into her home women or children for whom jailing seemed inappropriate. One night Will brought her two prisoners arrested for stealing a car in Las Vegas and driving it to St. George. "I was surprised when I saw them," Juanita wrote; "eleven and twelve years old they were, barefoot, (such black, dirty feet!), bare headed, dusty, tired little kids. They had decided that they wanted to see the world, so had taken this car. . . . After they were bathed and combed they looked quite different. Their table manners were above reproach and their general attitude gave evidence of good training. Before they went to bed they both knelt down and said their prayers."[21]

Inevitably Juanita viewed these experiences as material for her writing. As her pregnancy progressed during the fall of 1933, she granted herself a furlough from other duties and devoted some time to writing. In November a letter from the *Relief Society Magazine* announced the acceptance of a revision she had made of "But Thinking Makes It So," a story she had written at BYU. The reworked story, named "With New Vision," would be published in 1935.[22] She was also cheered by word of an incredible success: *Harper's* had accepted her article on polygamy. On November 27 a check for $150 arrived, more than a month's salary for Will, provoking Juanita to record ecstatically: "It's just like finding the money for our baby expenses and I had so worried about how we would squeeze out enough to pay doctor bills, hospital fees, etc. I acted just like a tickled little kid, but I couldn't help it. Had to tell all the family. Our boys here at home were so appreciative that it was worth a lot. . . . I must write more."[23]

Appearing in February 1934, "A Close-up of Polygamy" was a foretaste of Juanita Brooks at her best. Her style was simple, her tone sympathetic, her details realistic. She introduced her polygamous ancestors on both sides, totaled their numerous progeny, assessed their physical stature and intelligence, and found them normal or better. For illustration, she portrayed her Uncle Tom, who lived across the street from her childhood home, assigning morning work to his countless sons: "He always drawled the first name or two and became more staccato as he proceeded until the last few sounded with a pop, 'Tommie, John-nie, Myron, Eldon, Will, Lem, Vincen, Lorin,' etc. Somehow he kept order among them all, and co-operation to the extent that his haystacks were larger, his granaries better filled, and his children better dressed than any of his neighbors."[24]

This article was a major Mormon event. Suddenly the name of Juanita Brooks was known among educated Mormons. A letter arrived from Harold and Verna Bentley at Columbia: "We congratulate you on your ability to tell in such a clear and unbiased, yet sympathetic, way the inside story of a social organization, unique to the Mormon people, among western nations."[25] The superintendent of the Sevier school district in central Utah wrote: "It is so unusual to see anything from a Utah writer in the quality magazines that one cannot restrain a feeling of pride and a thrill of exhilaration when a person from one's own state gets such recognition."[26] From Provo Joseph K. Nicholes, now a professor of chemistry at BYU, wrote: "All the teachers here are praising you, and claiming you—and I join them and add 'I taught with her at Dixie College.' You can't buy another Harper's in Utah Co—nor in Salt Lake." In the same letter Olive Nicholes quoted a lyceum lecturer as saying, "Salt Lake City is agog over it."[27]

A special case among her correspondents was Newel K. Young, the aging principal of the Mormon seminary at Richfield. Young himself had plural wives whom he had married before the Church had outlawed polygamy. "How did you ever do it?" Young wrote Juanita. "The theme is such a delicate one for some of us, and such an abhorrent one for others of us, that to discuss it frankly and freely and do it with a grace and supreme good-taste that no can can fail to be pleased is a real achievement."[28] She replied warmly, suggesting, perhaps idly, that he and she collaborate on a book about polygamy. Young responded with a pathetic eagerness. In earlier years he had served as a specially ordained counselor in a polygamous village. The sorrows and tribulations he had witnessed from that vantage had left him permanently saddened. "And many men and women came to me in their trials and weaknesses and discouragements and heart-breaks," he wrote Juanita. "Old and young, men and women came. . . . As memory recalls many of these good Friends and the incidents connected with them my eyes are swimming in mists till I can hardly see to type."[29] Although their story begged to be told, nothing would come of the proposed book. Juanita was too busy with other matters. Young, for his part, was fearful that the Church would resent a book seeming to encourage that small, zealous minority of fundamentalists who continued to contract clandestine plural marriages. Nonetheless, the correspondence between Juanita and Young gives the first clear evidence of Juanita as a public confessor, a published writer so frank and yet so friendly that polygamists, noncomformists, and eccentrics of many kinds would seek out her safe and sympathetic ear.

On February 9, 1934, Juanita gave birth to a girl of delicate, pale complexion and fine blond hair. Joseph K. and Olive Nicholes had already suggested a name. "I think of you often, and hope 'Will-am-*ita*' makes *her* safe arrival," Olive had written in the letter congratulating Juanita on the *Harper's* article. Juanita toyed with other names, scribbling "Ila Marie" and "Nita Marie" on the back of an envelope which arrived while she was in the hospital.[30] Finally the name became Willa Nita. Juanita was happy to have a girl; the males of the family, large and small, were ecstatic. Hitherto, Bob and Grant had refused to call Juanita by any name, but now they began to call her Mom. Juanita's affection for her stepsons enlarged as she saw their love for Willa. "I could never scold big, teen-age boys who were so tender and kind to my babies. I wondered then and I wonder still how the young-ones survived some of the fondling they received. I remember the time when I left our 8-months-old girl with the three boys to tend, and their game of cops and robbers became so realistic that they kidnapped her and lowered her from an upstairs window by a rope and swished her away to hide in the cellar. And she loved it!"[31]

During the spring and summer of 1934 Juanita tried her hand at a variety of stories and articles. She wrote another article about polygamy, based on pioneer diaries she had discovered in the temple archives. She mailed it first to *Harper's*. After ten weeks, this magazine politely rejected it with the suggestion that she consider writing a novel about polygamy. She shortened the piece and mailed it to *Atlantic Monthly*, eliciting "a letter saying that had they received it before the piece came out in Harper's they might have used it but as it was they did not care to follow up a discussion which had been started by a rival magazine."[32] She resubmitted the shortened version to *Harper's*. When this magazine again rejected the article, Juanita was despairful: "To say I was disappointed is putting it mildly. I felt all afternoon that I'd never touch my pen to paper again."[33]

In the meantime changes were afoot in the family. On July 1, 1934, Will resigned as sheriff and accepted the position of acting postmaster of St. George. Later, having passed an examination, he received a permanent appointment. If the position was less glamorous than that of sheriff, it was also more regular in its hours and better in its pay. It was also less dangerous, a quality which Will, starting a new family at fifty-three, could not ignore. The St. George post office, located in a store building, was a third-class establishment. Though it was furnished with postal boxes, most mail was distributed through the general delivery window. Will was methodical and well organized, receiving, sorting, and sending mail carefully and promptly. He worked comfortably with his small staff. He and his men and their wives quickly evolved the custom of hosting one another at a monthly dinner.

In early September Walter Brooks returned from his mission. Shortly before his arrival, Juanita confided to her diary that she was very depressed. She complained briefly about the irresponsibility of Bob, Grant, and Clair, then admitted that the real reason for her despondency was Nellie. Grant had commented on his mother's beautiful hands, which she had protected by wearing rubber gloves while doing housework. Juanita lamented: "I seem never to get time to even file my nails properly, tho' I know I should *take* it. I only answered that I had ruined my hands milking cows and doing heavy work when I was a girl. Then later there was a discussion of perfume & Will told

how Nellie always kept some of the best & had a bit on her handkerchiefs—some he paid $5.50 a bottle for and here I'm worrying about
getting enough together to pay the light bills."[34]

A town girl, Nellie had refused to remain in the remote village of Monticello where Will had hoped to develop a dry farm. From
the birth of Walter, her first child, she suffered poor health. She grieved,
as did Will, over the death of two sons, William Dee, who died of
pneumonia in 1914 at the age of eight months, and Paul, who died of
rheumatic fever in 1927 at twelve years. Nellie was a meticulous house-
keeper, and at any hour of the day her hair was coifed and her dress
handsome. She sang well and was called on almost weekly to sing at
funerals, church services, and civic functions. Her penmanship was
beautiful. "She was Recorder in the County Court House," Walt wrote,
"and had the job of writing, by hand, all the descriptions of the properties in Washington County so that they could be read well. She was
always very exact. I spent many hours proof-reading with her, her
descriptions, so they would be exact."[35]

If Walt's imminent arrival had something to do with Juanita's
feelings of inferiority, his presence quickly dispelled those feelings. Tall,
thin, and handsome, he proved to have an affable personality. Following the example of his brothers he readily fell into the habit of calling
Juanita Mom. "Mom at first thought I resented her for taking the
place of my own mother," Walt remembered, "but in a few months
she accepted the fact that she didn't take the place of my mother, but
was my father's wife and would make her own place in our lives."[36] He
soon left for BYU where he found a berth on the basketball team.
When he returned in the summer, Juanita depended on him to settle
quarrels between the younger boys; as a method of discipline it had
the virtue of directing the boys' wrath toward their elder brother rather
than toward their stepmother.

By early December Juanita's brother Dudley was in Salt
Lake, preparing for a mission in England. Henry and Mary had had
their doubts, but Juanita had persuaded them that Dudley should go.
As the year ended, she lamented to her diary that for months she had
written only letters. She had not, however, been entirely inactive. She
had sent a few news items to the *Salt Lake Tribune*, which would soon
appoint her a permanent correspondent. She had also written an outline for a Relief Society study of the Scriptures, which she distributed
in her stake and later submitted to the *Relief Society Magazine*. That

outline, entitled "The Old Testament," appeared in the December 1934 issue of the magazine.

In November 1934 a momentous letter arrived from Nels Anderson, who was now an advisor on labor relations to the Emergency Relief Administration in Washington, D.C. "It occurs to me that you should initiate a white collar work project for the unemployed in your area," Anderson wrote Juanita. The project would be the preservation of historical sources: "Documents, pictures and original materials concerning Dixie places including Silver Reef. All kinds of stories that people can remember about the Reef. Good and bad stories. Even the fictions and myths should be gathered. Each should be written and filed away."[37]

Anderson sent a copy of his letter to Dorothy Nyswander of the University of Utah, in charge of women's projects for the Utah ERA. Within a few days Nyswander wrote Juanita suggesting that she consult the administrator of federal relief funds in Dixie, stake president William O. Bentley. Bentley, with whom Juanita already worked closely, appointed her supervisor, and a preservation project went quickly forward. Juanita knew that old diaries lay in storage in many homes. As stake Relief Society president she was eager for additional assistance for widowed mothers and single women who could find no employment in Dixie's depressed economy. Her only reservation was that the project might stifle her writing. "I don't know whether to view it as a sort of preparation for and an aid to the novel I wish to write, or as a diversion which will lead me away from it. For I am determined to write one. When, I don't know."[38]

Juanita and Will donated the use of a back bedroom which had an outside door. They set up a long table, typewriters, and a filing cabinet. About a dozen women were employed at a stipend of $30 a month. Those who could type copied diaries and narratives in quadruplicate. Others ranged abroad, holding interviews and collecting oral history from elderly citizens. "They were to encourage reminiscences, impressions of visiting church leaders, of local leaders, of the polygamy raids, of anything in which the informant was interested," Juanita wrote. "They would take notes, write them up as best they could, return to visit the person and read what they had written, supplement or change the story as needed, and finally bring it to us to be typed in a preliminary form before we made the final copy with carbons." For her part, Juanita supervised, proofread, and, most important, hunted for diaries. "We announced in a general stake conference that this project was beginning, that if people who had diaries or other originial records in their possession would bring them in, we would copy them free of charge and return the original and a copy to the owner."[39] Following numerous leads, Juanita wrote letters and made personal visits to towns and ranches throughout southwestern Utah and nearby Arizona and Nevada. By the time the project had expended its funds in the summer of 1935, some fifty-seven diaries and personal narratives had been copied.[40]

The Brooks family frequently drove to Bunkerville for birthdays and holidays. Between visits Mary wrote Juanita a weekly letter. Ernest continued to spend most of his time in Bunkerville. His grandparents' two-story brick home had been gutted by fire ten days before Juanita's wedding, and they now lived in a smaller structure rebuilt from the burned bricks. For Ernest, Bunkerville was a happy refuge where he duplicated his mother's idyllic childhood. Henry furthered Ernest's ambition to become a cattleman by giving him an occasional calf, which they branded by placing Henry's brand, a combined HL, on the ribs rather than on the customary right hip. Ernest would long remember his grandfather's vivid personality. Uncle Hen, as he sometimes called him, drank a medicinal cup of coffee for breakfast and kept a jug of wine under his bed from which he took small daily samples. "He was a man of unusual, earthy expressions. If something was of infinitesimal amount, to him it 'wasn't enough to physic a piss ant.' If something impressed him as not being very important it 'didn't amount to a pinch of manure'. . . . But I never did hear him use real profanity, nor vulgarity. 'Hell' and 'damn,' creatively employed, sufficed for him."[41]

During the spring of 1935, Juanita was exasperated to find herself pregnant again. Presumably she had depended upon Bunkerville folk beliefs regarding contraception. Summer came with its heat. At night the house cooled off a little, but by afternoon it was an oven. There was a small fan that could be set in a window to stir the hot air.

In the autumn, as her pregnancy approached its term, a colorful episode culminated. In late 1934, comparing her electric bill with that of a friend, Juanita had discovered that she was paying $2.00 more for the same kilowatt hours. A district manager of the power company informed her that her rate was higher than her friend's because she lived in a larger house with more ceiling drops. She countered by pointing out that her friend had an electric stove and water heater which she didn't have. That didn't matter. What mattered was her potential use of power, calculated on basis of ceiling drops. Undaunted, Juanita visited the power company's lawyer. He referred her to the utilities commission in Salt Lake. She wrote to that body. In its reply the commission enclosed a response from the St. George district manager, who claimed that he had, in Juanita's words, "tried to explain the regulations to me and that I had refused to understand. From what he could learn, Mrs. Brooks was something of a trouble-maker and an agitator, and nothing further could be done." Juanita called on the district manager again, asking what remodeling she would have to undertake to qualify for the lower schedule. He said that he could have his workers reduce her ceiling drops to four. She told him to send them over. "When I explained that I could get along without ceiling drops everywhere except in the kitchen, bath, dining room, and cellar, they explained that the lights on the porch and in the hall, stairways, and cellar didn't count. I decided to substitute the babies' bed room for the cellar. The others could go. They removed those from my living room, my bed room, and the two bedrooms upstairs, knowing as well as I did that I had wall plugs for floor lamps in the living room and bed lamps in the bed rooms. This was only a pretense to satisfy the letter of the law and to shut me up."[42]

On November 7, 1935, scarcely a month after this little drama concluded, Juanita gave birth to Karl Francis Brooks. A new baby meant that Juanita burned extra lights and operated her Maytag washer twice as often. Furthermore, she installed an electric heater in the infant's room. She was enormously pleased to note that her electric bills were lower than ever before. One sees in the foregoing an early instance of Juanita's impatience with arbitrary authority. One also remembers that she was a villager by birth. Accustomed to direct, cooperative action in the production of the common necessities of life, she had a native distaste for corporate organization and bureaucracy.

In the fall of 1935, Nels Anderson, by now director of labor relations in the Works Progress Administration in Washington, wrote the Utah WPA asking permission to borrow carbon copies of the documents Juanita had gathered, which had been transferred to the WPA upon the demise of the ERA. Anderson hoped that Juanita would be allowed to renew her collection project under the WPA.[43] Utah WPA officials were in fact so impressed with her work that, by early spring 1936, she was drawing a salary of $60 a month and travel reimbursement as an assistant state supervisor of the newly created Historical Records Survey. In this position, she put several women to work in the courthouse making an inventory of city and county records. Later that inventory would expand to school and church records. Simultaneously she served as an undesignated agent of the Federal Writers' Project. In this capacity she again set up tables, typewriters, and a filing cabinet in her back bedroom and put to work a group of unemployed women as typists, interviewers, and writers of biographical sketches. Again she searched for diaries, proofread typed copy, and created name indexes to some of the diaries. Her foremost assistant in both programs was Mabel Jarvis, an intelligent, tireless worker.[44]

In the meantime, Juanita kept up a pretense of writing. During the spring of 1936, she prepared and submitted two free-lance articles to *The Utah* magazine. "The Romance of Highway 91," appearing serially in the May and July issues, pointed out historical and natural features along Highway 91 between St. George and the Beaver Dam Mountains. "St. George: The City with a Heritage," appearing in the August issue, briefly narrated the founding of the town. Interestingly, in August 1936 Juanita resigned as correspondent to the *Salt Lake Tribune*. News articles were not the kind of writing she hoped to pursue.

During the summer of 1936 all members of Juanita's and Will's compound-complex family were living at home. Ernest had moved from Bunkerville. Walter had graduated from BYU and was supervising a county recreational project. In the fall he would begin coaching basketball at the high school in nearby Hurricane. Bob and Grant had summer jobs. At two and a half, Willa ruled the household. "She is an unusually brilliant child, learns songs and poems very readily and talks so grown-up that she is a constant surprise," Juanita wrote in her diary. Karl, who weighed twenty-two pounds at nine months, was "the happiest, best-natured little fellow I ever saw. When I think of how I resented his coming so soon and his being a boy too, I am genuinely ashamed of myself."[45]

One summer night, Juanita wheeled Karl from the stifling house and placed him near the hedge along the sidewalk where the air was cooler. Inside she settled down to her typewriter:

Soon everyone else was abed and asleep. It was one of those times when my writing seemed to be going so well that I was almost drunk from my own wine. It is a pleasure like nothing else, and rarely felt.

By two a.m. I had finished, dead tired. I stripped, pulled on my nightgown, and rolled in, asleep almost before I hit the pillow. At six a.m., by signs which every nursing mother would easily know, it was time to feed the baby. I reached blindly for the crib. Horrors! He wasn't there!

"Where's the baby?" I said, jumping up.

"I don't know," said Will, rousing. "Where did you put him?"

"I don't know!" But once on my feet, I did know, and ran through the house to the hedge. He was sleeping peacefuly as an angel, his little hands above his head.[46]

Juanita had not entirely conceded that Karl was a boy. She dressed him in gowns, and as his hair grew long she curled it into ring-lets. Comments of friends on the street about the pretty little girl roused other family members to resentment. Ernest wrote: "Finally, Dad could stand it no longer and gave Karl a haircut, much to the relief of the rest of the family. Mom pleaded and wept to no avail. This was some-thing that just had to be done—one of the few times I know of that Dad overruled Mom. It wasn't that he kowtowed to her, rather that in most things he gave her total support."[47]

As stake Relief Society president, Juanita helped prepare for St. George's Homecoming during the summer of 1936. For three days in early September the town, festooned with bunting, indulged its appetite for parades, programs, dances, and exhibits. Sam and Winnie Brooks, Will's brother and sister-in-law, were house guests for a week. There were dinners and long sessions of reminiscence with Will's brothers and sisters who resided in St. George: Emma, May, Rozilla, George, and Edward.

Family and church affairs gave Juanita a steady satisfaction. More extraordinary was her search for pioneer diaries, an activity which made 1936 a memorable year. Sometimes her finds were incredible. In an upper room of the St. George temple she came upon a collection of old records. "I feel sure," she wrote, "that no one else even knows of its existence; at least it appears that no one does."[48] Her success in pres-ervation fed upon itself. "More and more I am surprised at the amount there is. It seems that every person who joined the Mormons felt it his duty to keep a record. And some of them tell things which I am sure some of our good Leaders would prefer remain untold."[49] Word of an old diary roused her predatory instincts. She became eager, even cunning and calculating. Already she had learned that the official Church was a competitor to be subverted and outdone. To her WPA supervisor she confessed: "I have purposely avoided contacting any of the general church authorities because I was afraid they would try to get all the personal stuff I knew about into the Church Historian's Office before I could get at it."[50]

Juanita's letters frequently recognized Will's contribution to her effort. He gave her leads and carefully read every diary she acquired. He also drove her on innumerable searches, for she had never learned to drive. "Will is even more interested than I," she wrote Nels Anderson. "He has been influential in securing most of the material I have found."[51] She dealt chiefly with common folk, rank-and-file Mormons on farms and ranches, in villages and even cities, into whose hands had come an ancestral diary. Her speech smacked of a common Utah idiom, her allusions were familiar, her face beamed with respect and reliability. She made a quick evaluation of each diary shown to her. If it seemed worthwhile, she asked to copy it: "My arguments for this are that I will give the owner the first carbon copy, and that the original is too valuable to be handled by everybody; if their children are to really know of the doings of their grandparents their records must be typewritten. I assure the owner that I consider such material as priceless, and wish to help them preserve it and make it permanent. . . . "[52]

Not infrequently she arrived too late, finding that a family had already burned or discarded an old document. Once in awhile she rescued a diary from the brink of oblivion. Such an occasion occurred in September 1936 when she found the diary of Henry W. Bigler, a member of the Mormon Battalion who reported the discovery of gold at Sutter's Mill in California. Bigler's diary, Juanita wrote, "gives full detail of the march of the Mormon Battalion down to the time when he and some of his companions were employed by Brannan to dig the mill race where the discovery was made. Then several pages are missing, but the return trip to Utah is given day-by-day. It is interestingly written and full of detail. But there is a catch—it has been used as a scrap book and the pages pasted over completely with newspaper clippings, some with flour paste and some with glue."[53] Ernest, who had decided to attend high school in St. George, helped

his mother resuscitate the mutilated diary. Soaking the glued pages by
means of hot, wet towels, he and Juanita uncovered the original handwriting. "Many times we worked together until two or three in the
morning cleaning off those pages," Ernest remembered. "That winter
I learned to tolerate heat on my hands. There we would be, Dad asleep
in his big rocking chair, Mom at the table being ever so careful not to
damage those precious pages, and I making like a honey bee carrying
hot towels back and forth from the boiling kettle."[54]

Juanita was happy to have Ernest at home. At sixteen, her
eldest son found a niche in the family economy as the cow milker and
animal tender. He got up at five-thirty or six, built a fire in the range,
studied a while, and, before leaving to milk, put on oatmeal and water
for cocoa. The Brooks milk cow, a gift from Henry, was a range animal of doubtful qualities. "It looked like she'd be an ideal milk cow,"
Ernest reported. "What we didn't realize was she was as wild as a deer
and she wouldn't ever tame. I was the only one in the famiy that could
get in the corral with her. If Grant even walked in the lot her head
would come up and her tail would come up and she'd head for the
other side of the corral."[55]

The Brooks corral was on the lot where the old George
Brooks home stood. The small rock house in which Will had been
born and raised stood high up Main Street on Mount Hope, not far
from the house Juanita had bought in 1930. At a family reunion in
1934, Juanita casually asked Will's brother, a real estate agent, about
the worth of the old place. Currently untended, it was the common
property of the Brooks siblings. Soon after, Juanita proposed that she
and Will buy out the shares of the others. In haphazard installments,
they would complete the purchase by 1940. From the mid-1930s they
made use of the place, renting the house and maintaining coops, pens,
and garden in the large backyard. It had a private water supply, a
spring flowing from a crevice beneath the Sugar Loaf. It also gave a
splendid view of St. George, the Virgin bottom, and the receding ridges
beyond.

In early autumn 1936 Juanita realized that she was pregnant. It seems to have been an expected pregnancy, for she left no
record of remonstrance or dismay. As he had during her previous
pregnancies, Will showed an extraordinary attentiveness. According
to Ernest, "Hardly a day passed that Dad didn't squeeze a glass of
orange juice and take it to her. He often took her complete breakfast

in bed."[56] On April 23, 1937, Juanita gave birth to Joseph K. Brooks in the home of Rosina Blake, Juanita's aunt, a midwife in whom Juanita had complete trust. Remembering the near disaster of Ernest's birth, Juanita had entered the hospital to have Willa. That birth having proved uneventful, Juanita gave in to her ingrained suspicion of physicians and to the penury of the family finances and elected to go to Aunt Rosina's home for her subsequent deliveries. Walt would remember "Dad taking me down each time, with the rest of the children that were already born, to see his new son."[57] In this case, the new son, named in honor of friend and mentor Joseph K. Nicholes, would be called Kay.

Kay was born on Will's fifty-sixth birthday. Will, for his part, was a happy man. He loved children, no matter to whom they belonged. He rarely disciplined his own children, who tended to repay his cheerful affection with good behavior. He relished community involvement, serving on committees and supporting public projects with cash and labor. He was Sunday School superintendent in his ward—as he had been for years. Furthermore, he had the pleasure in 1937 of overseeing the construction and dedication of a post office building a short half block from his own residence. During the first five years of his tenure as postmaster business tripled, rising from $8,000 to $27,000 per year. Early in that period, his post office had moved from a third- to a second-class category, making St. George eligible for a federal building.[58] Will took delight in his daily work, greeting townspeople by the score and joshing congenially with his half-dozen subordinates.

Shortly after Kay's birth, Juanita resigned from the WPA. Besides having new duties at home, she perhaps foresaw a dwindling of federal support. As early as July 1936 the Utah WPA had threatened to reduce funds for typists, revoke travel reimbursement, and deny Juanita the right to deposit a copy of each diary in the Washington County library.[59] Her federal employment as a collector of diaries had been brief: about a half year in 1935 with the ERA and a little more than a year in 1936 and 1937 with the WPA. As brief as it had been, her collecting had established her reputation among her state and national superiors. In July 1936 she accepted an invitation to describe the work she directed at a regional conference of the Historical Records Survey in Salt Lake. In September the national director wired a request for several original diaries and accompanying typed copies for display at the Joint Survey Writers' Exhibition in the National Museum in Washington.[60] It was a tribute to Juanita's personality and procedure that the WPA had permitted preservation as well as surveying of historical records in Utah. She wrote to a friend: "We are the only section in the nation which is being allowed to concentrate on the collection and copying of these old records."[61]

The diaries which Juanita helped preserve made their way into various archives. The original typescript of each was eventually transferred to Washington. Today some 450 documents compose the "Library of Congress Collection of Mormon Diaries, Journals, and Life Sketches."[62] A carbon copy of each diary was returned with the original to its owner. Another carbon copy was temporarily stored in Utah WPA files; the Utah Historical Society now holds this accumulation. Juanita succeeded in placing a carbon copy of many of the diaries in the Washington County library where she would have ready access to them. Today that library houses perhaps 200 diaries and personal narratives in looseleaf binders; their pages are yellowed with age and frayed from extensive use.

The recognition Juanita achieved through her brief federal employment stimulated her interest in writing history. She lived amid an awakening esteem for Utah's past. In 1937, following a lapse of four years, the state legislature again funded a quarterly journal for the struggling Utah Historical Society. Throughout the 1930s, the Daughters of the Utah Pioneers organized chapters in many towns and villages, claiming 18,000 members by 1939.[63] In 1938 the St. George chapter of this organization dedicated a handsome colonial-style museum donated by a wealthy New York businesswoman and St. George native, Hortense McQuarrie. In 1939 the parent organization published the first annual volume of *Heart Throbs of the West*, an anthology of historical sketches and excerpts from pioneer documents. There were other impulses toward preservation. Wilford Poulson, Juanita's former instructor in psychology, had begun to collect copies of diaries for the BYU library; frequently he and Juanita exchanged copies.[64] The Church Historian's Office had become more aggressive. When the St. George temple was renovated in the late 1930s, church officials carried away to Salt Lake many of its pioneer records, a fact which would later vex Juanita when she wanted to use sources she had surveyed in the temple but had not had time to copy. Juanita could not help responding to the spirit of the times. At forty, she was sizing up the vocation of a historian. She knew by now that Mormon country was a rich ore field of pioneer diaries, and she had confidence in her ability to find them. Though she had resigned from the WPA, she would remain alert for exceptional diaries, having appointed herself a "Quorum of One"[65] in researching the past.

Juanita continued to be active as stake Relief Society president. As the occasion demanded, she briskly reorganized ward Relief Society presidencies. In 1936 she wrote a letter of encouragement to a timid new president in a remote village. With refreshing independence, Juanita instructed the sister to proceed with her duties even though she and her counselors had not been approved by priesthood officials. "I hope the Bishop will be able to have you sustained tomorrow, but if he does not, you go ahead anyway. If you let things drop it will be all the harder to start again. I shall talk to President Bentley and see if some of the Stake Presidency cannot come up and set you all apart soon, or we may have the visiting Authority do it at the December Conference."[66] Juanita vigorously promulgated the directives of the general Relief Society board in Salt Lake. She addressed a fervent letter to the sisters of the several wards who had been appointed to sell the *Relief Society Magazine*. "No home in the stake, Mormon or otherwise, can afford to be without our high class publication," she wrote. "The subscription price of the magazine is only $1.00, three pounds of butter or two more chickens marketed during the year would pay for it. When we consider the possibility of getting so much for so little it seems that every home in the land would be provided with our splendid, faith-promoting magazine."[67]

Juanita's duties sometimes led her to the remote ranches of Mt. Trumbull in the Arizona Strip, a rough, eroded country bordering the Grand Canyon. On one occasion Walt accompanied her. They arrived to find the tiny church deserted. "They had a big bell there, so Mom said, 'You go ring that bell, that's the way we do it!' So I went over and pulled the bell four or five times and within a half hour we had a great church congregation. . . . They held their own ward meetings at a set time, but on the missionary and visiting Sunday they waited till the people came, because the roads were so rough they didn't know whether they'd ever get there. . . ."[68] On another Sunday Juanita called at a ranch where a solitary woman observed a private worship. Juanita wrote: "Her guitar was lying on the bed, her hymn book beside it, opened to 'God Moves in a Mysterious Way', her Testament with a mark in it." An accidental gunshot had recently killed the woman's son. She confided to Juanita: "I could have grieved and worried until I lost my reason. Sometimes I was afraid I would. I thought at first that I would have to put Jack's things away where I could not see them. But I knew that was not the way to conquer myself. So I got his leather coat, the one he had on when he was shot, washed the blood from it, and wore it to do my chores. After I was able to do that, I felt better."[69] By such experiences Juanita understood better the lonely borderlands of Dixie.

Juanita was also active in helping to implement the new Mormon welfare plan. Announced at a general conference of the Church in April 1936, this ambitious project for providing for unemployed and needy Mormons emphasized self-help and local initiative. In the fall of 1936 Harold B. Lee of the Church Welfare Committee organized the Zion Park Welfare Region, comprised of five stakes: Parowan, St. George, Zion Park, Kanab, and Moapa. In each stake, Lee established a welfare committee headed by the stake president. By the spring of 1937 projects were afoot in every stake.

In St. George, workers constructed canning boilers in the college science building where, during the summer of 1937, volunteers processed 14,000 cans of peaches from Hurricane. Priesthood quorums conducted a sugar beet seed project, from which they realized a profit of $300. A beautification project went forward on the tabernacle grounds with local labor and matching funds from Salt Lake. Numerous persons made contributions in kind, which by the end of 1937 had amounted to 5,000 pounds of coal, 21,382 pounds of potatoes, 489 pounds of dried beans, and 3,528 pounds of fresh apples.[70] All who worked or donated received receipts with which they could draw upon the pool of goods they had helped create.

It was Juanita's duty as a member of the St. George stake welfare committee to enlist the women of the stake in canning and sewing projects. At a stake conference early in 1937, she called upon the ward Relief Society presidents to induce their members to can and sew for their own families and to contribute to stake canning and sewing projects. At a conference in June she gave even more detailed directions.[71] Of particular concern were the poor and the unskilled. For indigent families the local bishop provided cans and produce, and Relief Society sisters provided cookers. Mothers remodeled used clothing for their children, sewing in their own homes or in the local

Relief Society hall where a skilled seamstress helped the less experienced.

Juanita devoted much time to establishing a stake sewing center in St. George where used clothing could be cleaned and renovated. Workers constructed enormous storage closets in a business shop on Tabernacle Street. Ward Relief Societies donated quilts; three large wooden chests contained as many as forty-five at a time. Juanita also initiated a minor industry in burial clothing. Because her house was across the street from a mortuary, people often inquired where to buy the special attire for persons who had been endowed in the temple. Obtaining money from the stake welfare committee, she instructed the director of the sewing center to purchase material for temple robes, caps, veils, and aprons. The project quickly showed a profit.

Juanita was never persuaded, as many Mormons were, that church welfare was a sufficient substitute for the recovery programs of the federal government. In an unpublished article she declared that she had failed to find a single Mormon voluntarily "going off a government project of any kind. If they are put off for any reason, they may turn to the church, but they evidently prefer the uniformity and regularity of the government checks to the supplying of their needs by the church."[72] Nonetheless, Juanita was greatly impressed by the local solidarity which the church program evoked. Of a fruit-canning project she reported: "A wonderful spirit of love and good will prevailed. Men donated their trucks, baskets and time; taking as many young boys as were needed to pick their loads. Women and girls donated their time, and brought their own pans, paring knives, towels, buckets, tubs, etc. A leveling process was going on. Rich and poor worked side by side and liked it."[73] It was an instance of classless cooperation of which the village-born Juanita could not fail to approve.

In late 1937 she found herself pregnant again, a scant six months following Kay's birth. This was probably an intentional pregnancy, a last exasperated try for a girl. On July 7, 1938, Juanita paused in her efforts to enlarge canning and sewing projects to give birth to Antone Leavitt Brooks. He would be called Tony. Again Juanita chose to have her baby at Aunt Rosina's, and again she was deeply disappointed that he wasn't a girl. There were dubious feelings of a different sort among her older children. Upon her return to a bed in her own home, an unusual delegation called on her. Bob, Grant, Clair, and Ernest desired to protest the embarrassing frequency of births in the Brooks family. Ernest was the spokesman. "We lined up at the bedside, and after several moments of foot shuffling and 'ahem-ing' I launched into my speech as I had been instructed by Bob and Grant. It went something like this, 'Now look here, Mom, the town is starting to talk about when you and Dad are going to stop having kids. It is becoming almost a scandal. We hear whispers everywhere we go. Besides that WE think we have got all the family we need. We don't want any more brothers and sisters. Enough is enough!' "[74]

Juanita and Will had four children under five years of age. She was forty, he fifty-seven. A friend said to Juanita, "I have often wondered how you justify yourselves in having children at your age." The friend cited his chronic heart condition as a reason why he and his wife had no offspring. Juanita answered: "You are denying yourselves the finest thing in life, and you are denying a child the right to help himself. We will have little to leave our children except happy memories. They are all normal and healthy, and it should be a satisfaction for them to help make their own way."[75] One can scarcely overemphasize the satisfaction Juanita found in her domestic life. Like Will, she loved her children utterly. Now and later she would further their interests and give them advantages at every opportunity.

If Juanita and Will enjoyed the pleasures of parenthood, they also suffered the anxieties: fevers, gashed knees, morose moods, and angry altercations among their beloved offspring. Once as the family was returning from a trip to Las Vegas, Willa accidentally opened a door and tumbled from the speeding automobile. Halted, Will and Juanita sat paralyzed while Walt leaped out and raced back to Willa. The little girl was up and running: "She was a bawling and a bawling. I asked her, 'What's the matter, are you hurt?' She answered, amid her cries, 'No, but they're going to leave me and I've got to get there fast!' I picked her up and brought her back. Dad and Mom couldn't even move because they were so scared; both of them were as white as I have ever seen two people."[76]

During the late 1930s, Juanita plied her typewriter often enough to accumulate a stockpile of manuscripts and to score a few publications. Among the several articles and reports she wrote about the Mormon welfare program was "Background for Mormon Social Security," which she prepared in the fall of 1937 for a meeting of the Utah Academy of Sciences, Arts, and Letters. At the invitation of Harrison R. Merrill, BYU librarian and president of the Academy,

Juanita had become a member during the previous year. Unable to attend the meeting, she asked Merrill to read her paper. This document, which brought her a number of complimentary letters,[77] declared that the cooperation upon which the welfare program depended was nothing new to Mormonism. Quoting copiously from pioneer diaries, she described the organized migration of the Mormons across the plains, their cooperative colonization of the intermountain region, and their unusual social experiments of polygamy and the United Order.[78] In this paper one sees the scholar's mind at work, moving from the specific to the general and amalgamating particulars into trends and movements.

The few publications Juanita achieved were of a historical or documentary sort. In 1937 she submitted two articles on pioneer history in Dixie to a small newspaper in Piedmont, California, the *Pony Express Courier*. They were accepted and probably published in June or July.[79] She placed a number of articles in church magazines. In *The Improvement Era* of October 1938 appeared "Whose Business Is Recreation?," an explanation of the community dances held in St. George. The three church wards and the college had cooperated to provide—and control—weekly dances for the town's youth. A recreation committee (of which Will was a member) maintained "high standards by prohibiting smoking or drinking in the hall, and by quietly removing anyone who gives evidence of being intoxicated. . . . Strangers not of our people uniformly remark as to the order and general tone of the dances."[80] In 1939 an article on the St. George temple appeared in the same magazine. In it, Juanita reported the recent renovation of the building at a cost of over $105,000 and described a subsequent doubling of temple attendance. In 1939 the *Relief Society Magazine* published "Recreation of the Pioneers," a short piece documenting pioneer social events and holidays from the diaries Juanita had been collecting.

Juanita also tried her hand at fiction. Typical of a number of unpublished short stories from the 1930s is "Lucy," the narrative of an Indian girl raised by a white family. Lucy bears an illegitimate child whose father, a white youth, commits suicide following a bishop's court. Lucy wanders in confusion and finally dies, leaving her little girl to be raised by the white couple who have raised her. Based upon a historical incident recounted in the diary of Priddy Meeks, this story suffers from wooden dialogue and a shifting point of view.[81]

During the spring of 1939 Juanita entered an essay contest, co-sponsored by the *Salt Lake Tribune* and the Salt Lake Chamber of Commerce. She won the first prize of $25 with an essay entitled, "Why You Should Vacation in the Intermountain West this Summer."[82] In 1940 she exhumed her forensic skills and entered a speech contest sponsored by the women's division of the State Democratic Committee. Competing in Salt Lake in early September, she won third place.[83] One sees that, despite her undoubted satisfactions as a wife and mother, Juanita constantly desired challenge and creative expression. She satisfied that desire in part through the energetic prosecution of her duties as stake Relief Society president—but only in part, for her desire obviously pointed toward a larger stage than St. George. One also sees that as the 1940s dawned her professional ambition remained indiscriminate and undefined. She had only tentatively conceived of herself as a historian. Her vocation still stood aloof, like a stranger hesitating at her door.

Yet the saga of Mountain Meadows tantalized her. Repeatedly she had encountered among old families of southern Utah a living guilt and grief over the massacre. Among her papers is a copy of a letter from William R. Palmer to a descendant of Isaac C. Haight, the stake president who gave the strategic commands from which the massacre devolved. Alluding to his correspondent's desire to write a biography of Haight, Palmer agreed that the pioneer leader's heroic achievements should be emphasized. Nonetheless, Palmer insisted upon Haight's participation in the massacre, mentioning his "one great mistake" and the "skeleton in the family closet." He concluded: "You need not be ashamed of your lineage. You cannot wipe away the one stain, but you can honor a great sire by helping tactfully to put out that greater, better side of his life."[84] The drama of contrition and guilt implicit in such a letter could not have been lost upon Juanita.

In 1936 Juanita's interest was heightened by her acquisition of a primary account of the massacre. In August she visited the elderly Emma Seegmiller Higbee of Cedar City, ostensibly to converse on polygamy and the United Order.[85] During the visit, she confirmed the existence of a handwritten account by John M. Higbee, one of the leaders at the massacre site. In October 1936, the elderly woman's son, Myron F. Higbee, allowed Juanita to make a typed copy of the account.[86] Written long after the massacre, it was curiously signed "Bull Valley Snort," probably because for a period Higbee had gone into hiding in the Bull Valley Mountains west of Cedar City. It was a stunning find. Juanita was exultant, mentioning her acquisition in almost every letter she wrote for weeks. In fact, she talked so volubly that Mrs. Higbee anxiously wrote concerning a rumor that Juanita intended to sell the account. "It is strange how things can go," Juanita replied. "I think that in time—*Sometime*—that should be published in justice to the family, but I am not ready to do it yet, and would not think of it without the full consent of the family. . . . "[87]

The truth is that Juanita very much wanted to refer to the account in an article which she hoped to deliver at the meeting of the Utah Academy in the fall of 1937. In September, she tried to persuade Myron Higbee of the advantages of discussing the massacre before the scholarly members of the Academy: "I believe that this would be a good group to present this to, because it includes some of the best educated people in the state and some of the most broad minded. It has been my experience that misunderstanding and prejudice and bitterness regarding that affair are worse among our own people than anywhere else. I think that the first place to tell the truth is at home, and I am sure I have a slant on that affair that has not been presented."[88] Higbee refused to give the desired permission, citing the wishes of "older members of the family," a denial to which Juanita conceded with an assurance that in the future "I shall do nothing without your full knowledge and consent."[89] For the Academy, Juanita substituted the paper on the Mormon welfare program.

During 1940 Juanita renewed her request to the Higbee family and received permission to refer to the Bull Valley Snort document. Her eagerness had been whetted by her recent acquisition of another primary account of the massacre, a legal affidavit made by Nephi Johnson. Thus she prepared and read before the Utah Academy in 1940 a paper entitled "Sidelights on the Mountain Meadows Massacre." Naively, she declared her documents "the only two known to be in existence." With less naiveté, she attributed the massacre chiefly to "the wave of war hysteria which swept over Utah at the approach of Johnston's army." She absolved Brigham Young of complicity, but firmly asserted that "the local church leaders must be held responsible. The white men who were present were there at their orders."[90] In these conclusions her paper remarkably anticipated the famous book she would later write. It was, however, no more than a sketch, a first unwitting step into a dense and tangled thicket.

CHAPTER FIVE

AN INDISPENSABLE
APPRENTICESHIP

In December 1940 Juanita received a copy of Maurine Whipple's *Giant Joshua*, published by Houghton Mifflin. Signing herself as "Rene," Whipple inscribed the book: "To 'Nita, for whom there aren't words grateful enough. All my wishes for the dreams of your heart!" Juanita had first made Whipple's acquaintance while a student at Dixie College. A precocious senior in the high school division, Whipple had been editor of *The Dixie 1922*. During the late 1930s, she returned to St. George supported by a $1,000 Houghton Mifflin fellowship for writing a novel about the founding of her native town.

Inevitably she called upon Juanita for information. Despite the fact that Whipple was launched upon a work which she herself had fancied writing, Juanita complied. "I read every line of her book," she wrote, "before it went in the first time, and then again went over the printer's dummy with her. I knew of some historical discrepencies [sic] which I could not get her to change. I found many things which she did modify or cut, and I gave her an abundance of local items and folk-lore."[1] Juanita's feelings for Whipple swung between fascination and disgust. She admired Whipple's style of writing, marveled over her breathless loquacity, and sympathized with her vacillations between euphoria and despair. She also considered Whipple to be an exploiter who borrowed much and returned little. Of particular concern were historical incidents which Juanita herself planned to write about. "I've been so roaring mad at her a few times that I have told her off in no uncertain terms, but she always comes back with, 'But, after all, Nita, what difference will it make? The way I use it would not be like you would'. . . . I just had to learn not to say a word that I didn't want her to use."[2]

In her spare time Juanita continued to write free-lance articles. In February 1941 she placed a trifling thing with *Writer's Digest*, which published it in *Writer's 1941 Year Book*. This piece, "A Bonanza for Writers," explained how authors could live in St. George for no more than a dollar a day. Juanita also published a brief article in *The Democratic Digest* of March 1941, a journal sponsored by the women's leadership of the National Democratic Committee. Near the same time she scored another incredible success with *Harper's*. Since 1934, when that magazine had published "A Close-up of Polygamy," she had doggedly submitted a succession of manuscripts, which the magazine had steadfastly, if politely, rejected. Her latest attempt was an article about the scarcity of water in Bunkerville. Having typed a final draft and sealed it in a manila envelope, she composed a coy note to Frederick Lewis Allen of *Harper's* in something like the following words:

> You remind me of the kind old lady who warmed the water in which she drowned the cat. You say NO so beautifully.
> I know you said that you would not be interested in this, but glance through it and fire it back to me in the same envelope. Address and stamps are supplied.[3]

Allen shortly informed Juanita of *Harper's* acceptance of "The Water's In!" and promised that a check for $200 would follow.

At Easter Willa underwent an appendectomy. The blond seven year old was now in the first grade. Juanita, who responded to any illness of her children with inordinate anxiety, was particularly distressed by this episode, as she explained in a letter: "Lately I feel as if Life had picked me up and given me a good shaking, much as a puppy might do to a rag doll. My only little girl has had a serious operation, and complications following that have left me pretty limp. They tell us she has passed the crisis now, though."[4]

The spring of 1941 was also notable for Juanita's participation in a campaign to establish a municipal power plant in St. George. Hitherto a private company had provided electricity. As its franchise expired, the company mounted a vigorous campaign for a renewal. Partisans for the company dourly warned in the local newspaper that a municipal utility endangered the American institution of free enterprise. Irked by such rhetoric, Juanita joined a little group of impromptu journalists who, before dawn for ten days preceding the bonding election, delivered a polemical newsletter, *The Beacon*, to every doorstep in town. As Juanita later explained, the newsletter argued that a municipal power plant, far from being un-American, was a sign of "real, grass-roots Democracy, government for the benefit of the people administered by representatives of the people."[5] To her great satisfaction, on

May 6, 1941, her fellow citizens voted three to one in favor of the municipal plant.

The incident demonstrates a penchant for political contention which Juanita had restrained during her tenure as stake Relief Society president. Having been released from that position during 1940, she was very willing to enter into disputes with those Mormons for whom the superiority of free enterprise and the Republican Party was an essential tenet of faith. She would remain suspicious of private corporations and the profit motive. A dyed-in-the-wool Democrat, she believed that government existed to make life better for little people. By every instinct she was an agrarian and a populist.

Juanita was gratified to see her article in the May 1941 issue of *Harper's*. Numerous friends sent their congratulations. Her delight grew when a letter from *Harper's* announced that the piece would appear in condensed form in the June issue of *The Reader's Digest*, paying her $150. "The Water's In!" was another example of Juanita's writing at its best. Evoking in picturesque detail the Bunkerville of her childhood, it described the irascible river and the stony patience of the men who rebuilt an unending succession of broken canals and washed-out dams. Its style was simple and concrete, its tone wry and good-humored. "And when I say heat," Juanita wrote of the Bunkerville summer, "I mean the kind that thickens the whites of eggs left in the coop and that makes the lizards, scurrying from the shelter of one little bush to another, flip over on their backs and blow their toes."[6]

In August Juanita attended the Writers Round-Up in Salt Lake, a two-day gathering of aspiring authors. She participated on a panel discussing whether the great Mormon novel would ever be written.[7] She returned to St. George charged with energy, having determined to apply for a Knopf Fellowship in Biography for a study of Jacob Hamblin. She thought of Hamblin as a subject not only because she had accumulated much material about him but also because he had become the most legendary of Dixie's pioneers. She asked two scholarly friends to write recommendations, explaining that the Knopf fellowship gave "an advance on the work which would enable me to do the necessary research, and would give me help in my home so that I might have time to write."[8] One of those friends was Nels Anderson. The other was Dale Morgan. Juanita's correspondence with Anderson would remain cordial and sporadic. Her correspondence with Morgan would accelerate remarkably. Few eventualities of Juanita's life were more momentous than her epistolary friendship with Dale Morgan.

A Salt Lake native, Morgan had lost his hearing from meningitis at fourteen. Immured in the introspective world of the deaf, he majored in commercial art and advertising at the University of Utah. In 1938 he secured a job with the Utah WPA Historical Records Survey and unexpectedly discovered his life's vocation in western history. In 1940 he became state supervisor of the Utah Writers' Project. In that position he oversaw the completion of the multifarious reference work *Utah: A Guide to the State*, published in 1941. Such was his promise that as early as 1939 Farrar & Rinehart issued him a contract in its American river series for a history of the Humboldt River of Nevada.[9] Although he had abandoned his Mormon faith, Morgan aspired to write an exhaustive history of Mormonism. Although he would never complete that work, he was destined to become one of the most distinguished historians of the West.

Through his subordinates, Morgan enlarged the WPA collection of pioneer diaries Juanita had begun. The correspondence between the deaf administrator and the St. George housewife began in a mutually advantageous exchange of diaries. When *The Utah Guide* appeared, she wrote her praises: "Not only are you to become Utah's top historian, but you are to leave the state a collection of records that will be priceless."[10] He readily agreed to recommend her for the Knopf fellowship and offered his services in locating sources for her intended biography. As the fall of 1941 advanced, their letters became more frequent and friendly. In November he suggested that they drop the formality of "Mrs. Brooks" and "Mr. Morgan." Accordingly Juanita began her next letter: "Dear Dale: (Thanks for the suggestion. I'm for it!)"[11] Morgan boundlessly admired Juanita's unique amalgamation of agrarian practicality, homey domesticity, and critical reason. Believing her to be a living remnant of the pioneer era, he relied on her expertise in frontier conditions. For her part, Juanita accepted Morgan as her mentor in scholarly and literary matters, finding in their correspondence an intellectual stimulation otherwise absent from her life. His technical advice would profoundly influence the form and content of her first major writings. His articulate dissent would lend vitality to her growing nonconformity in matters of faith, and his confidence in her would encourage her to persist with her history of the massacre despite the threat of excommunication.

On Morgan's advice, Juanita exchanged a series of letters late in the summer of 1941 with that crusty anti-Mormon, Charles Kelly, who maintained that Jacob Hamblin had participated in the Mountain Meadows massacre. Juanita was nonplussed by Kelly's dating of the massacre, which conveniently put Hamblin into its vicinity. "The point that puzzles me," Juanita remonstrated, "is that *no one* has ever suggested that he was there. I have talked to so many, and they have talked so freely. They do not hesitate to name the others who were present. . . . "[12] For the moment she was unable to disprove Kelly's claim. Considering the massacre with a renewed curiosity, she concluded that, whether or not Hamblin was a participant, she would have to treat that violent affair in some detail in her account of his life.

Among the sources Dale Morgan sent Juanita were carbon copies of old records he had been laboriously typing in the Church Historian's Office during his lunch hour. One was a short diary of Jacob Hamblin, which Morgan had copied without permission. He candidly admitted that "I haven't always been quite ethical in drawing upon the Historian's Office for stuff." He claimed, however, that he would use such material "only within the canons of the highest historical objectivty. I have therefore felt justified, and my conscience has never bothered me."[13] As for Juanita's citation of this purloined copy in her biography, Morgan advised that she too engage in a deception: "If anybody asks awkward questions and you don't mind imperilling your immortal soul, you can always say that that sterling old gentleman, Andrew Jenson [assistant church historian], some years since dug out the journal and let you make some excerpts from it. All you would have to do is to be suitably vague as to the exact date this happened . . . and nobody could ever say a word in rebuttal, because Andrew is now among the immortals and he had a free hand around the H.O."[14]

Juanita was amenable to dissemblance where valuable historical sources were concerned. In return for his favor, she sent Morgan a forbidden copy of the proceedings of bishops' courts in pioneer Dixie. The woman who possessed the original had been advised to submit it to the Church Historian's Office. "She was reluctant to let me see it—did not want it taken from the home," Juanita informed Morgan. "Well, I wanted to be on the level with her, but I wanted a copy of that material, too, so I phoned home and had them bring my typewriter out. I was by myself in a cold room, but I worked like fury and got it all — Took from 4 to 10:30 p.m."[15]

In 1941 Juanita solidified a habit she had tentatively assumed during the late 1930s. In recognition of her inconsistency in keeping a diary, she began to document her life by preserving incoming letters and by saving carbons of her replies. To the casual reader, her numerous letters to Dale Morgan are a mixture of the lively and the dull. She filled them chiefly with technical ruminations upon the historical sources, personalities, and events with which she was currently preoccupied. But she rarely failed to make some mention of her personal feelings and domestic activities. Often she mentioned the latter by way of explaining why she was not spending more time at research and writing. In fact, her letters would for years sound a recurrent theme of frustration over domestic interruptions.

Despite its distractions, the fall of 1941 proved highly stimulating. Focused intently upon the life of Hamblin, Juanita encountered new sources with heady excitement. It was, she wrote, "like piecing together parts of a cross-word puzzle, or a jig-saw from which many parts are missing, so that the picture is never complete."[16] In addition to the Hamblin journal, she studied for the first time John D. Lee's *Confessions*, Thomas D. Brown's "Journal of the Southern Indian Mission," and John L. Ginn's *Early Perils of the Far West*. At first she doubted the authenticity of Lee's *Confessions*, published following his execution. She concluded that, since "the style is not like him," his attorney had written the account from conversations with Lee, perhaps without the latter's knowledge.[17] It was a judgment she would later revise.

The application for the Knopf fellowship, due in February, required an outline and several chapters of the proposed biography. Having written sixty- five pages by early November, Juanita was perplexed whether to paraphrase or quote and whether to invent scenes and dialogue. She likened herself to "a person testing a food until he loses the sense of taste and doesn't know whether it is salty enough or not."[18] In early December she mailed three chapters to Morgan, requesting his criticism. Such was her esteem that now and later she would accept his red-pencilings with great deference. A month later Morgan returned the chapters with a long commentary. He reminded her that she must relate Hamblin, an unknown for most Americans, to the larger American scene; she should therefore shape her submission to Knopf toward the events of 1857 and 1858, the period of the Utah War and the Mountain Meadows massacre. He found her chapters confusingly astraddle the line between fiction and biography. He warned her to make it more clearly an expository work yet inconsistently advised her to "break up some of your material into dramatic scenes, submerging yourself in it and letting the characters speak for themselves; at other times, you ought to take over the book like God, and tell us frankly what we are to think about the people, their lives, their times, and their society."[19]

In January 1942 Juanita accepted a half-time teaching position for winter quarter at Dixie College. She taught classes at eight and one o'clock and hired a college girl to help with her housework.[20] She took a break from the biography, mailing to Morgan a brief article she had written on the Indian wives and half-breed children of pioneer men in Dixie. Apologetically she wrote: "I sort of let myself get this Indian thing wished off onto me. . . . " Furthermore, she stole time to scan Wallace Stegner's newly published *Mormon Country.* Stegner, she told Morgan, "has said some of the things I have been trying to say, only infinitely better."[21]

As the Knopf deadline approached, Juanita could not repress her fervent hope: "I think it must be sort of wicked to want anything as desperately as I do this Fellowship."[22] However, as she mailed her application in mid- February, she was dubious of her prospects: "I think I should wash my hands in a disinfectant and forget it."[23] As March came on she told Morgan that she was simply marking time: "I do contrive to keep busy, all right, but somehow it seems sort of an empty business, a frittering about to kill time. I have gone to a few afternoon clubs where I have been served a bit of a wafer and salad or a glass of punch, where everyone else has gone on with their interminable knitting or crocheting, and where the talk has been, largely, idle chatter." Such trifles reinforced her chronic distaste for herself: "I think sometimes that I am like that salt grass that grew so luxuriantly on the alkali river bottoms of the Virgin – not to be put down by any amount of trampling, but valueless at best."[24]

Actually, she was not idle at all, for during the six weeks following her Knopf submission she wrote one of her finest books, *Dudley Leavitt: Pioneer to Southern Utah.* It is indicative of her diffidence toward this work that she neglected to tell Morgan that she was busy with it. In her estimation, her subject was slight and her treatment superficial.

During the previous fall someone had told her father that she was at work on a biography of Jacob Hamblin. The seventy-year-old Henry, who had rented his farm and sold his cattle and who showed his age by mounting his horse from a stump as he prepared for a daily ride through Bunkerville, reacted jealously. Everyone spoke of Hamblin's heroic achievements; no one remembered the equally heroic achievements of his associates, among whom was Dudley Leavitt. Accordingly, Henry showed up unannounced at Juanita's door in St. George. As Juanita later described it, his protest amounted to a command that she write the life story of her grandfather.

Near the end of March Juanita visited Morgan in Salt Lake. Her delighted friend took her on a tour of local libraries and archives, orienting her to further historical sources. One can see them driving along Salt Lake streets in Morgan's car or walking side by side into the Church Historian's Office. Juanita wears, one supposes, rimless glasses, a long-sleeved dress, and shoes with thick half-high heels. Morgan wears a double-breasted suit, and his hair mounts like a clump of unruly grass over his shingled temples. He lectures his deferential friend in a high, eerie voice, pausing only to read new questions or comments she pens on slips of paper.

Despite their pleasure in one another's company, they parted in a state of subtle tension, for in their next exchange of letters they clarified their difference of opinion regarding the Mormon religion. Juanita's letter, written on Easter Sunday, expressed her freedom within the faith. She was angry over recent restrictions upon local initiative imposed by the general authorites in Salt Lake, which struck her as bureaucratic regimentation. Still, if she was a dissenter, she was, as she had always been, an inside dissenter. "I retain my fellowship in the church because I like it and I need it and I want my children to have its benefits, but I refuse to surrender my intellectual independence to it. I'm amazed with the things I can get away with, with the fact that they have me teach a Sunday School class – students in their early twenties – and we do not follow the lesson outline. Neither do we always present the orthodox point of view. Do I sound on the verge of apostasy? Some would say so." Shortly her pleasant discourse was terminated by the clamor of her returning children. "The cubs

storm in. They've been to see Walt Disney's *Dumbo* this afternoon. . . .
Now I must hear their excited versions of it."[25]

Morgan responded with a remarkable three-page summary
of his life, his historiographical ambitions, and his credo. He alluded
to the meningitis that had deafened him, confessed that he hoped
someday to marry, and came finally to the subject of his irreligion. He
had lost his faith without rancor or tempest during his final year of
college. "I do not see the necessity of a God in the scheme of things,
and on the plane of ethics think that things are in a hell of a state if
we order our behavior purely in hope of reward or fear of punishment
in a hereafter; if I have a religion, it is a belief in what I call 'the decencies of human relationships.' I live life as I see it from day to day and
hour to hour, and in my way I think I am a better Mormon than
those who go to church on Sunday and pay their tithing."[26] With
that, the matter seemed at an end, for neither he nor Juanita mentioned it in subsequent letters.

In May Juanita received word that her application for a
Knopf fellowship had been denied. Morgan urged her to continue
with the biography. At first she could not muster a renewed interest
in it and busied herself with desultory reading in the history of Indian
and white relations in early Dixie. She allowed Maurine Whipple and
another friend, Donald Seegmiller, to read the chapters which she
had submitted with her application. Both advised that she abandon a
formal biography and write a historical novel based on Hamblin's life.
She considered their advice carefully but finally concluded to resume
work on the biography: "I've felt that I must stay close to fact, and
that pretty unvarnished. . . . I know I cannot write in the same style
that 'Rene does any more than a sparrow can sing like a canary, but I
have assumed that the type of thing I can do is still worth doing."[27]

Late in May, measles struck her family. Willa was afflicted
first and then, as she recovered, two of the boys fell into "the fever and
sick-at-the-stomach stage."[28] In early June Juanita apologized for typing errors in a letter to Morgan, reminding him "that my nights have
been pretty well occupied with getting up and down for a while. . . .
The last child is now a red mass with swollen eyes, but anyway it looks
as if things are due now to be better."[29]

In May Juanita also learned of the publication of Nels
Anderson's *Desert Saints*, a book which Anderson had researched in
St. George some nine years earlier. Church officials in Salt Lake had

underlined passages of an advance copy and mailed it to the president
of the St. George stake demanding to know who had given Anderson
access to records held in the temple. Juanita wrote Anderson of this
turn of events; she also asked to buy a copy of the new book as a gift
for Will. With quixotic pride, Anderson replied that he was mailing
her a gift copy which she must not give away even if it meant buying
an extra copy for Will; he also warned her against lending the gift
copy "because bookborrowers can't be trusted." He was irritated that
the general authorities considered his book anti-Mormon, though he
admitted that he had included the last four chapters because he knew
"that much of the material available to me would never again be
available." At the time of his research he had written honest letters of
intent to the incumbent temple president and stake president assuring them "I was going to treat the Saints with respect and all the facts
with scientific objectivity." He had by his light exercised great restraint,
for "had I been interested in smearing, I could have done a masterly
job with some of the stuff that I did not use."[30]

Anderson had little cause for excitement. The success of
his book did not depend on Mormon readers, and the disapproval of
church leaders could only hasten an alienation from Mormonism
already well under way. It was otherwise for Juanita. Observing the
response of the general authorities, she felt more keenly the hazard of
the kind of writing she wished to do.

By mid-June the biography of Dudley Leavitt was ready for
distribution. For $600 a local printer had produced 250 bound copies
and 250 copies which would be bound later if a demand should
develop.[31] The book boasted a medium- blue clothbound cover, large,
sharp print, and generous margins. It did not occur to Juanita to copyright the work. Unabashedly she advertised it among her relatives at
the break-even price of $1.50 per copy. Sales were such that in Sep-
tember she would order the second binding.[32]

She mailed a gift copy to Dale Morgan. Although he pro-
fessed to be pleased, he pointed out the book's errata in considerable
detail.[33] She gave another copy to LeRoy and Ann Hafen. Juanita
and Will hosted this couple, who were en route from California to
Colorado, at a Dutch-oven cookout on the Sugar Loaf. One imagines
hot biscuits and fried chicken, a moon in a balmy sky, and the twinkling lights of the town below. Hafen wrote his thanks for the evening
and for the book, which he called "the best pioneer biography I have

ever read."[34] This compliment from Juanita's maternal uncle was more than conventional urbanity. Few persons were in a better position to make a sound evaluation of her book than LeRoy Hafen. By 1942 Hafen had achieved a doctorate in history from Berkeley under Spanish borderlands historian Herbert E. Bolton and was well launched upon a distinguished career as director of the Colorado State Historical Society and as author and editor of numerous works dealing with the Rocky Mountain frontier. Hafen's achievement unquestionably contributed to Juanita's solidifying determination to write history of an objective, professional quality.

Dudley Leavitt: Pioneer to Southern Utah remains one of Juanita's finest works. Like her two *Harper's* articles, it is written in a simple, concrete style. Utterly devoid of footnotes and other scholarly apparatus, it convinces through detail. The zeal which characterized Dudley Leavitt and the pioneering adventures which tested that zeal emerge in the pages of this book as palpable, immediate, and real. He was a credible giant, a believable doer of unbelievable deeds.

At fourteen, Dudley filed by the bier where the martyred Joseph Smith and his brother Hyrum lay in state in Nauvoo. He was present at the assembly where Brigham Young was transfigured as Joseph Smith, an event which Dudley fervently recounted many times later. With his family he suffered the privations of the exodus to Utah. As a young man with two wives, he accepted a call to serve as an Indian missionary in southern Utah under the leadership of Jacob Hamblin. He participated in the Mountain Meadows massacre, a fact which Juanita attempted to ameliorate by stressing the family tradition that he had served as a scout on the periphery of the bloody event.

During the winter following the massacre Dudley was robbed of his horse and provisions while on a mission to Las Vegas. He attempted to return afoot over a hundred miles to Santa Clara. After he had lain down to die from hunger and exhaustion in the Beaver Dam Mountains, friendly Indians discovered and saved him. In the fall of 1858 he accompanied Jacob Hamblin and others on a proselyting mission to the Hopis of Arizona. Returning across barren wastes, the group saved itself from starvation by eating a horse—Dudley's mount, which without hesitation he offered for the good of the party.

He was not ashamed of his virility, siring upon his five wives 48 children, who honored his name with some 273 grandchildren. As the settlements in Dixie became more numerous, Dudley restlessly moved his families to new locations, none of them prosperous: Gunlock, Clover Valley, Hebron, Bunkerville, Mesquite, and Leavittville. Damming and redamming intractable streams, constructing shanties and adobe huts, enduring fierce summer heat, he and his loved ones practiced a subsistence agriculture so meagre that establishing themselves in a new location was scarcely less rigorous than maintaining an old one. The very precariousness of their existence made him and his wives hospitable to every traveling stranger. In summing up his life, Juanita aptly expressed the nostalgia and reverence Americans everywhere feel toward those pioneer ancestors who from wilderness created a new civilization: "Without education, without culture in the common mean ing of that word, without wealth, he still had left his imprint upon the whole of a section in which he lived. He had blazed the way for the conquering of the desert; he had helped to establish friendly relations with the Indians. Most of all he had left in the hearts of his many children a standard of conduct which would include honesty, integrity, christian fellowship toward their neighbors, and an unwavering trust in God."[35]

Juanita found the summer of 1942 a poor season for research and writing. Willa and Karl, released from school, joined Kay and Tony in cluttering the house; dozens of canning projects clamored for attention; the desert heat, alleviated only by a tiny electric fan, vitiated Juanita's strength. In September, when the weather moderated and school opened, new distractions loomed. Laurel's wife, Melva, entered the St. George hospital to recover from gangrene following an instrument delivery. Every night for more than a month, Juanita faithfully visited her sister-in-law, bringing fresh laundry because the hospital did not launder the personal clothing of its patients. She also kept freshly baked brown bread in the hospital kitchen, Melva having found the hospital food indigestible.[36] Furthermore, World War II had by now intimately affected Juanita's life. Bob had entered the Army and was in training at an eastern military base. In September Ernest enlisted in the Navy despite Juanita's desire that he wait until drafted. During his final days in Dixie, he was feted, as Bob had been, by dinners and gatherings of family and friends.[37]

Working as she could on the Hamblin biography during September 1942, Juanita concluded that a detailed treatment of the Mountain Meadows massacre would be inappropriate within its pages.

Considering again a separate article, she asked Morgan to review the piece on the massacre she had read before the Utah Academy in 1940. "I didn't want to publish it," she explained, "because I didn't want to be called in by the Authorities, and I was afraid I would be. I don't want to be branded as 'an old apostate,' . . . and I didn't want them to say to me, 'Sister Brooks, we command you in the name of the Lord to stop this'—because I know I couldn't stop even were I so commanded. So I set it up until a few of the older generation should move ahead."[38] Endorsing her ambition, Morgan suggested that she write a *monograph*—a term which he later had to define for the unknowing Juanita as "an intensive written study" implying "a degree of thoroughness and completeness that 'article', for instance, does not." Judging her present article to be little more than a reminiscence, he set forth detailed criteria for "an essential scientific approach" which would include an accurate dating of the Fancher party's progress through Utah, a clarification of the membership of the Fancher party, a determination of its behavior toward Indians and Mormons, and an identification of the Mormons responsible for each stage of the developing massacre.[39] Nothing immediate resulted from Morgan's instructions, for Juanita continued to work on the Hamblin biography. However, when she would at last boldly commit herself to a study of the massacre, his criteria would provide a systematic and scholarly procedure.

In light of wartime food rationing, Juanita looked with greater tolerance than usual on Will's hunting. She reported a dinner of fourteen quail, which Will had bagged on the Arizona Strip. He had also brought home a large Brigham tea plant, which he thought made a delicious steeped beverage. Will's fondness for Brigham tea was, Juanita explained to Morgan, "the only thing upon which he and Maurine Whipple are wholly agreed. Did you ever taste it? I can't say that I'm too enthusiastic about it, though I can make a pretense of getting a serving out of the way."[40] As deer season approached, Will performed his usual rituals of preparation. Out came rifles, boots, red sweatshirts, tents, water cans, and Dutch ovens. His success was such that venison overflowed the Brooks cold storage locker and Juanita made jerky of two hind quarters. With considerable gusto, she described the process for Morgan:

> [I] cut it in steaks, dipped it in boiling water, heavily salted, sprinkled it generously with black pepper, strung it on a heavy twine and hung it out in the sun. I found that the Indian way was the only one that

would keep the flies off. In spite of the searing and the pepper, huge blue- black ones gathered from all over the county. I had ten yards of cheesecloth which I tried to fasten around it, but they found every tiny opening. So after the first string, I built a smudge in the furnace where I heat my wash-water outside, set up one post and fastened the line from it to another that was there. It gave the meat a better flavor, and not a fly ventured near. I gave quite a bit away, I was so proud of my venture, sent some to our boys in the service—one in the army and one in the navy, both great jerky-eaters—and thought I should still have enough for a long time yet. Today when I went to get some, I found an empty sack. The whole crowd of youngsters and their friends have been filching from it, just a piece at a time, evidently. Else I should have sent you some, instructed you how to eat it, with a little parched corn, to see if you could feel like Jacob.[41]

By Thanksgiving 1942 Morgan had moved from Salt Lake to Washington, D.C. There he hoped to find employment in a defense agency that would leave him time to search for western historical documents in the National Archives and Library of Congress. He settled in a one-room apartment across the Potomac in Arlington, Virginia, where, as Nels Anderson reported to Juanita, he "lives alone with his typewriter."[42] In December, Juanita worked part-time at the post office. In addition, she kept a couple of her sister Aura's children for extended periods, Aura having suffered a nervous breakdown. Fortunately, it was a balmy Dixie winter. The days were so bright and warm that the children played outdoors without coats. At Christmas Juanita mailed Morgan a gift of cookies, a bundle of Brigham tea, and the ingredients for what she called Dixie salad—pomegranates, apples, raisins, and nuts, which were to be diced and mixed with whipped cream. She sent similar gifts to Bob and Ernest.

In the meantime, Juanita had suffered a setback in the Hamblin biography. By mail she had courted an elderly cousin, Mary Hamblin Beeler of Mesa, Arizona, a daughter of Jacob Hamblin and Priscilla Leavitt who owned a wealth of original Hamblin documents. Juanita was particularly interested in a letter in which Brigham Young instructed Hamblin that men desiring to marry Indian women were to bring them to the Endowment House in Salt Lake. Pioneer diaries and the lore of her own family had convinced Juanita that Hamblin himself had Indian wives; she hoped the letter would reveal when he had been sealed to them.

Shortly before Thanksgiving 1942, Mary Beeler visited Juanita at home in St. George, embracing her and promising her access to her Hamblin records. Upon her return to Mesa, Beeler bluntly reneged on her promise. Juanita attributed her reversal to Pearson Corbett, a teacher of Mormon theology at Dixie College who was writing a biography of Jacob Hamblin as a master's thesis at BYU. Although Juanita had known of Corbett's project for over a year, she had persuaded herself that she and he were not competing for the same group of readers.[43] Furthermore, Corbett had maintained a friendly attitude, offering to exchange materials and asking Juanita to read his manuscript.[44] According to Juanita, Corbett conversed with Mary Beeler and gained access to her Hamblin records during her visit to St. George in the fall of 1942. "Now, as you may guess," Juanita fumed to Morgan, "Mr. Corbett has convinced her that I should see nothing until his book is safely off the press. She is a good church member, and he has had Brother Sessions write her, and has the holy cloak of Church Approval cast upon his work, while I am supposed to be some upstart who would place a false light on all the doings of the man. It burns me up completely."[45] Perhaps Corbett had also informed Beeler of Juanita's contention that Hamblin had married Indian women, a contention to which Beeler would have taken angry exception.

Smarting from her elderly cousin's rebuff, Juanita determined upon an appropriate revenge. She mailed to Marguerite Sinclair, secretary and treasurer of the Utah Historical Society, the brief article on the relations of Mormons and Indians in pioneer Utah on which she had worked in a desultory way for well over a year. Much of what it revealed would strike many Mormons as unsavory; the probability that Jacob Hamblin had Indian wives would be a particular annoyance for his proud descendants. Sinclair handed the piece to her superior, Cecil J. Alter, editor of the *Utah Historical Quarterly*. Juanita conjectured that Alter would wish to eliminate certain offensive quotations from diaries. In this she anticipated Dale Morgan's assessment of Utah's state historian. "Alter is not a Mormon," Morgan later wrote her, "so that he has a certain independence of viewpoint, but also he is not altogether honest—or rather, he evades certain realities in Mormon history—so as not to stir up any hornet's nests. He tends, I think, and therefore Marguerite does also, to flee at shadows: he is more sensitive about some things of anti-Mormon potentiality than Mormons would be."[46]

However, Alter liked the draft, and in early December Juanita received "a most enthusiastic letter from Miss Sinclair. It seems that they want more of the same kind of thing. 'The sky's the limit', according to her over- enthusiastic reaction."[47] In January 1943 Juanita mailed an expanded draft to Morgan, declaring that she couldn't return it to Sinclair and Alter "until you pass on it first—It's your own fault for making yourself so important."[48] After a few days Morgan returned a detailed critique. Juanita did not work on the article again until she learned in late February that Corbett's biography would soon be approved as a finished thesis at BYU. Quickly she mailed a second revision for Morgan's scrutiny, saying, "I'd like to get it off my hands, and (Does this sound too wicked?) I'd like it published before the Corbett thesis is all wound up. Just a streak of the Devil in me, I guess."[49]

Near the end of May 1943 she mailed the finished article to Marguerite Sinclair. In all Morgan had given it three red-pencilings. After the last of these Juanita offered him rueful thanks: "I think you would have saved time to have written the thing in the first place—but I am glad for your chiseling down and trimming up my efforts."[50] Morgan praised the part of her paper dealing with southwestern Utah and urged her to provide even more detail: "Discuss the feelings of white wives toward Indian wives, and so on. Nobody has so much information on the subject as you have, and you ought to do as thorough a job as you can, so that others hereafter will be able to stand on your shoulders, instead of having to start from the ground up."[51] However, he found her treatment of Mormon and Indian relations elsewhere in Utah and the West to be severely lacking and proceeded to educate her. In her finished paper Juanita dutifully included many of his insights. In a few instances, with his blanket permission, she borrowed his very wording. With only a slight change she offered as her own the following sentence: "The importance of the Indian relationships to the Mormons, and its non-casual character, is illustrated by the fact the original settlement in Salt Lake Valley was made because Brigham had learned from Jim Bridger that Salt Lake Valley was something of a no-man's-land between the Utes of the south and the Shoshoni of the north."[52]

Early in 1943 Juanita wrote Wallace Stegner in praise of *Mormon Country*. Stegner replied expressing his pleasure that "someone who knows as much about the Mormon country as you writes to

say that my book hasn't offended his sense of history or fact too much."
He paid her the high compliment of being familiar with her *Harper's*
articles, saying that the article on polygamy "persuaded me that I must
do something in my book on the Mormon family as an
institution."[53] Stegner mentioned *Arrows into the Sun*, a novel by
Jonreed Lauritzen, which Juanita thereupon read. Lauritzen and his
wife, Verda, who had made their home at Short Creek in the Arizona
Strip, some forty miles southeast of St. George, were by now well-
established friends of Juanita's and Will's. This first novel by Lauritzen,
published by Alfred Knopf, featured a young half-breed Navajo who
saved a Mormon wagon train from a Navajo attack. Although Juanita
admired Lauritzen's style and landscape, she was skeptical of the speed
with which his young protagonist mastered the ability to speak flaw-
less English and read Shakespeare, Milton, Dante, and Homer. "The
suggestion, too, that he learned his perfect pronunciation and enun-
ciation from a combination of Emerson's essays and the sounds of
nature amazed me," she wrote Morgan. "I told Jonreed that I had
taught school just long enough to know that the average run of teen-
age boys do not do that."[54]

In early February 1943 Juanita made a trip to Salt Lake.
Finding the hotels full of wartime travelers, she checked her portable
typewriter and suitcase at Temple Square Hotel and spent the night
with Sam and Winnie Brooks. On Sunday evening she called on Dale
Morgan's mother and brother Jim. "So now I feel that I know your
back-ground a little," she subsequently wrote. On Monday she called
at the office of the Utah Historical Society in the capitol building. She
discussed her paper on Indian and white relations with Marguerite
Sinclair, who also showed her the files, stacked upside down and presently inaccessible, in which Morgan had deposited carbon copies of
the diaries and other historical sources gathered by WPA workers.
This large and for the moment ill-organized collection marked the
entry of the Utah Historical Society into the business of gathering
original sources. Juanita found herself incarcerated in the capitol building by the heaviest snowfall of the winter. Eager to catch a bus for
Provo, she ventured into the storm with two young men who delivered her safely to the bus station. "The one with the largest feet broke
trail, the other followed, stepping in his tracks, and I brought up the
rear," she wrote. She spent Tuesday in the BYU library examining
sources. Tuesday evening she caught a bus for St. George, where she

arrived "in the morning in time to get the youngsters off to school, wash, bake bread, and set things to rights generally."[55] She had two choices of buses, the Greyhound, which stopped in St. George at the Big Hand Cafe, and the Trailways, which stopped at Dick Hammer's Cafe. In either case she had less than two blocks to walk to home, leaving her luggage for Will to pick up later with the car.

On a Sunday afternoon in late February, Juanita began a letter to Morgan with a familiar complaint about interruptions: "If Fate is kind I may get this finished before someone comes to call, or the youngsters storm in from the show, or my good husband wakes up." Warming to her subject, she went on to explain an ingenious procedure she had evolved for dealing with unexpected callers:

> I long ago hit upon the expedient of keeping my ironing set-up out with everything ready, so that as soon as there was a knock I could plug in the iron on my way to answer the door. Then it would be easy to say, "Excuse me, please, my iron is burning," or "Come on in. I'm ironing." Then as soon as they left I'd pull out the plug. It isn't economical, I know, and it kept the clothes lying dampened too long sometimes. My next neighbor to the south has a habit of running in every morning about 11 o'clock and she finally said, "My, you must have big ironings. You have been at it for three mornings now."
>
> I didn't tell her, but I should have, that all the ironing I had done she had watched me do. Once that is out of the way for a week, I keep the most urgent of the mending in a neat pile on the table, with a threaded needle stuck into it, so that I can shift to that when I am interrupted. But as soon as she gets what she wants, I go immediately back to the typewriter without taking another stitch. The trouble is, I get more ironing and mending done than I do writing.[56]

This procedure would become famous in later years as Juanita spoke of it repeatedly before delighted audiences. One of her motivations was efficiency. If she couldn't write, at least she could make a dent in her never finished housework. Another motivation, which she emphasized before audiences, was her desire to disguise the fact that she was a writer. By St. George standards, writing was a trifling and pretentious pastime for a housewife, who by all means should have something better to do. A final motivation was Juanita's hope that an obvious stack of ironing or ready bundle of mending would convey a message of urgency to her callers. Her energetic prosecution of her ironing and sewing in effect said, "Please don't tarry. As you can see,

I'm terribly busy this morning." Writing was not an adequate reason for slighting a neighbor's visit; housework was.

In late February the Brookses agreed to trade their house for a fruit farm in the nearby village of Hurricane. The thirty-five-acre farm consisted of an ample house, barn, corrals, and pens; orchards of peaches, cherries, plums, and other fruit; and an alfalfa field sufficient to support a horse and cow. Walt, who was now married, a father, and a coach at Hurricane High School, would live on the farm. Juanita and Will would move into the little red rock house on the hill which they had rented out since the mid-1930s. They would have to remodel the rock house: new floors, closets, and porches; an entire bathroom; a finished basement for the boys' bedroom. Even remodeled, it would squeeze the Brooks family terribly. However, according to the college agronomy teacher and the county agent, the farm was too good a bargain to turn down. It would also make a good place for the family to move upon Will's retirement from the post office, only seven years in the future. Furthermore, Juanita had always begrudged the meager lot on which the downtown house stood. It is possible, too, that she wished to escape the memories of Nellie which still haunted that house.

The prospect of moving brought Juanita new perturbations and awakened her chronic melancholy. As February closed, she guiltily expressed a longing to be free of Aura's children, for whom she had cared much of the winter. "Did you ever hear of the old, old man who passed a pretty girl on the street, looked at her long, sighed deeply, and said, 'Oh, to be sixty again!' In the same way I find myself thinking of the time when my family will number only seven again—instead of nine."[57] In March she wrote: "I've been so low this week that the under side of a snake's belly would look like a strip of the milky way." Though it was supposedly a good week for writing—"the rain shutting me in and others out (the children aren't much of a distraction; I'm used to them)"—she couldn't force herself to consistent writing. It was she rather than Will who decided whether to place the bathtub crosswise or lengthwise, whether to put the laundry room in the basement or on the back porch, and whether to line the fireplace with firebrick or install a circulator.[58]

Her mood changed immediately. At noon on the same rainy day she had written the foregoing, Will brought home a letter from the editor of *Arizona Highways* asking Juanita to write a 3,500-word article on Jacob Hamblin. Within a few days, Juanita was on her way to Phoenix and Mesa in search of Hamblin sources, vowing expressly to "beard Mrs. Beeler in her den." Suffering motion sickness on the swaying buses that carried her via Kanab and Flagstaff, she nonetheless enjoyed a varied new landscape: the Vermillion Cliffs, the Navajo reservation, the San Francisco Peaks, and the saguaro- studded Sonoran desert. In Phoenix and Mesa, her diplomacy served her well, for she gained access to a number of Hamblin documents, including Mrs. Beeler's. She found Hamblin's children, though divided on certain other questions concerning a biography of their father, united on "the matter of the Indian wives. They won't have it mentioned." More startling, Juanita discovered the existence of "a Hamblin-Lee feud." Hamblin's name, she learned, seemed a spontaneous trigger for a discussion of John D. Lee and the Mountain Meadows massacre. "I didn't realize that there was still so much bitterness over a matter so long since passed."[59] Her cousin, Dudley J. Hamblin, accused Lee of masterminding the massacre months before it occurred and, during its course, of violating emigrant girls before cutting their throats. (The latter accusation seems to have been an elaboration of Jacob Hamblin's testimony at Lee's last trial that Lee had cut the throat of one hiding girl and had permitted an Indian to shoot another.) When Juanita defended Lee, her elderly cousin "blew up completely, so we agreed that it was a subject which we would not discuss."[60] A calmer informant, Hamblin's niece and Lee's daughter-in-law, told Juanita that Lee's descendants harbored a bitter resentment over what they considered a blackhearted perjury on Hamblin's part, which had insured Lee's execution and his family's perpetual disgrace.

Juanita also learned that a dispute of "state-wide proportions" had flamed up in the late 1920s over the naming of the Navajo Bridge in northern Arizona. Partisans from both families argued the propriety of naming it for their respective ancestor. So heated did the issue become that it threatened to disrupt more than one Mormon stake in Phoenix and Mesa. When members of the Arizona legislature proposed calling it the Lee's Ferry Bridge, no less a person than church president Heber J. Grant traveled to Phoenix and argued against that name before the legislature.[61]

Juanita returned from Arizona with a new determination to write an article upon the forbidden subject of the Mountain Meadows massacre. For the first time in her life she had understood that in allowing John D. Lee alone to bear the official blame for the massacre, his fellow Mormons had dealt him and his posterity a terrible injustice. An article on the massacre, she wrote Morgan, "is sorely needed, more for members within the church than without, for it is among the church people where it is most misunderstood and least known, and it is among them that the interest is most keen." Fearing repercussions, she plaintively added, "But what would happen to me???"[62] For his part, Morgan pondered the possibility of a covert guilt among the Hamblin descendents: "Psychologically, there may be something significant in the extreme vindictiveness displayed by the Hamblin family toward Lee." Morgan confessed a long-standing interest in writing a biography of Lee, a project he had not seen a means for doing since it would require research among Lee descendants. "But since this has come up, let me mention it to you as a possible collaboration we might pull off some day, you to do the local research, I to do the more remote research—in the Midwest and so on."[63] Herewith another promising idea took root in Juanita's mind. Fifteen years later, unassisted by Morgan, she would write the life of John D. Lee.

While in Phoenix, Juanita consulted the editor of *Arizona Highways*, who insisted that her article on Hamblin "must have something the Mormons would like."[64] The article appeared in the April issue of the magazine. The editor was pleased and asked her to write an article on the march of the Mormon Battalion, which she completed in time for the May issue. She did not test either article on Morgan, partly from lack of time, partly from her sense that she was writing superficially. Only when she was trying to do her best did she submit manuscripts for Morgan's critique.

"Jacob Hamblin: Apostle to the Indians" dealt chiefly with Hamblin's missionary journeys and explorations among the Indians of northern Arizona, emphasizing his ability to pacify angry natives through persistence and integrity. Between Indians and whites, Juanita concluded, Hamblin had done "more single-handed to bring about a mutual understanding than all the soldiers that ever marched into Arizona."[65] This image of an unfaltering and heroic Hamblin stands in sharp contrast to Juanita's comments about Hamblin in her letters to Morgan. Advised to please Mormon readers, she had complied. In fact, she succeeded so well that the article would be reprinted word for word, with the same photographs of the frontiersman and his Santa Clara home, in *The Improvement Era* of April 1944. Her article, "The Mormon Battalion," was less infused by the heroic yet was equally absorbing. It followed 500 young Mormon men, engaged by the U.S. Army during the war against Mexico, in an epic march from Iowa to California. Relying extensively on the diary of Henry W. Bigler, Juanita selected details indicative of both the routine and the adventurous. Privation was already evident, for example, on the plains between Fort Leavenworth and Santa Fe: "The ponds of water were made filthy by the buffalo, and offensive by the sun, 'as thick as gruel,' one man said, 'but we drank it.' "[66]

During the spring of 1943 Morgan's *The Humboldt: High Road of the West* appeared. Morgan had also begun a history of the Great Salt Lake, for which he had a prospective publisher. Juanita wrote rueful congratulations: "Looks as if you have a full life's work all cut out before you, a genuine contribution to American culture. It seems that you have laid the foundation for a Tabernacle while I've been trying to pitch a pup- tent." She also promised to send some oose root which Morgan had requested. Oose root, as Juanita's ancestors had called yucca root, contained a sudsing fiber which the pioneers had used for shampooing hair and scrubbing floors. She planned to dig up a yucca when the family drove to Bunkerville in mid-April to celebrate Henry's birthday. "We always stop to let the children run and so that Will can gather some of his precious Brigham tea, and we'll just combine my errands with it. The desert should be in bloom by that time, too, so who knows what other interesting things we may find at the same time. I promise not to include any horned toads or turtles though."[67]

Eventually Juanita mailed the oose root, afterward sending instructions for its use: "First pound it or cut it up—pounding was the regular procedure—and set it in a dish of water several hours to soak. Strain it through a cloth. Shake it up a little or stir it. Does it suds? Warm it and wash your hair, rinsing it in clear water. That's all there is to it. It usually leaves the hair clean and with a fine luster—only I don't like the smell. Perhaps you will."[68] One imagines the gaunt, solitary Morgan in his bathroom, stripped to the waist, vigorously massaging his thick mat of curly hair with this natural shampoo.

Late in May the Brooks family moved into the house on the hill. Juanita domesticated her new surroundings by immediately setting up her typewriter and attending to neglected correspondence. To Morgan she sent a detailed description of the long, narrow kitchen which would serve as her writing place. There were a refrigerator, a wood-burning range, and a dining table. "On the west wall—against it, rather—are my files and my battered old table with this ancient machine. I don't even have to move out of my chair to answer the telephone, which is something. Then, too, it is the main line of travel for the family. Whenever there is a cut or a sliver or a stubbed toe, they don't have to come so far to find me. I keep Mentholatum and gauze and string in the drawer. I can start a fire in the morning, dash off a letter while the water heats, and as Will says, do a line or two between stirring in the mush."[69]

Although there were already cherries from the new farm to be canned, Juanita spent a day in early June in the village of New Harmony interviewing old-timers about Jacob Hamblin. More striking than the meager material she gathered on Hamblin were the stories about John D. Lee which her aged informants were eager to relate. Several characterized Lee as a good neighbor and a man of deep and lachrymose sympathies, but others cast him as the villain of dark folktales. According to one, Lee cut the throats of children saved from the massacre who had recognized objects belonging to their dead parents. Another said that Lee murdered one of his sons-in-law who failed to meet Lee's standards. Another claimed "that John D. had a secret powder which he might put into food or drink and any young girl who got any of it would be in his power. He had just come from Washington and had on a load of early fruit, a great treat to the people of Harmony. He broke an apple in half and handed it to two young girls, but they, hungry as they were, didn't dare eat it for fear it had some of the love powder in."[70]

Despite their crowded new quarters, the Brookses had a houseguest during the summer of 1943, Clara Hamblin, adult daughter of Dudley J. Hamblin. Hamblin was in town negotiating the purchase of her grandfather's two-story rock house in Santa Clara. On July 23 Will, a notary public as well as postmaster, notarized the sale contract. As escrow agent, he would also hold the deed while Hamblin and her relatives paid off the place in installments.[71] It was their wish, eventually realized, that the old home be dedicated as a public historical site. In the meantime, having established herself as a friend to the Hamblin family, Juanita would have freer access to sources for her biography.

In early July 1943, Juanita underwent an appendectomy and for a mandatory ten days was bedfast in the St. George hospital. The experience so impressed her that afterward she wrote a free-lance article about it. Though the piece never found a publisher, it should have. It is chatty, good-humored, and affectionate. Under the duress of "persistent, maddening pain," Juanita had consented to the operation. There had been "the suffocating fumes of ether" and, the next morning, the doctor's cheerful testimony that the operation had come just in the nick of time. Because of the war the hospital was sorely understaffed. Among the volunteer aids was a mother of eight whose "rough, honest hands rubbed my back in long strokes, as though she were wiping up her kitchen floor." Juanita sent some of her flowers and a joke book into the room of a young woman suffering from a nervous breakdown. She heard the screams of a young man who the doctors and nurses believed would shortly die from a ruptured appendix. One night the patient's father came into her room because he had to share with someone the spiritual assurance he had just received that his son would live. Immediately the young man began to mend. Juanita concluded her article: "I left behind a perfectly useless appendix and the money with which I was going to fix up the house, but I took away a feeling of neighborliness that will warm my heart for years to come, and examples of high courage, and of faith that moveth mountains."[72]

Following her stay in the hospital, Juanita canned bushels of peaches and pears from the Hurricane farm. A frequent visitor was Maurine Whipple, returned from a prolonged residence in Salt Lake. Soon, having received a contract from Alfred Knopf for a pictorial review of Utah, Whipple asked Juanita's help in locating photographs. Juanita complied, explaining to Morgan, "She does write very much better than I ever can, and I've decided that there is no reason why I should be a dog in the manger and try to hold onto things that I can't use myself."[73] Jonreed Lauritzen also called at the Brooks home on his frequent trips to St. George for mail and library books. With a mixture of envy and ridicule, Juanita observed Lauritzen's determined effort to sell a second novel extant only in a first chapter and an outline. She wrote to Morgan: "Well, he submitted it to Knopf with the terms that they might have it for a $2,400 advance, $800 to be paid down and the remainder in monthly payments of $400 each. It may be that good, but it didn't seem so to me."[74]

In late August 1943 Juanita spent nearly a week in Provo and Salt Lake. In Provo she made a splendid find, an original handwritten diary of Thales Haskell. "It was so human that I spent one whole day copying at it and visiting with the daughter who owned it. She played for me on Thales' accordian; she showed me pictures of the girl [Haskell's young wife] who was shot by the Indian, and told me the family version of the affair."[75] Of equal moment, she also made the acquaintance of Fawn McKay Brodie, who was at work upon what would become the most controversial of all biographies of Joseph Smith, *No Man Knows My History.* In early September Morgan wrote that Brodie had returned to Washington, where her husband was stationed as a military officer, and had mentioned meeting Juanita in Salt Lake. "I suppose," wrote Morgan, "you heard from her the story she tells me about her run-in with her uncle [David O. McKay]. I must say, I don't envy her situation, trying to write a scrupulously honest (and naturalistic) biography of Joseph Smith when her father [Thomas McKay] is an assistant apostle and her uncle a counselor in the First Presidency."[76] Encouraged that Brodie had mentioned her name, Juanita wrote a letter which opened an infrequent yet long-lasting and respectful correspondence between the two women.[77] Immediately Juanita began to watch for sources that Brodie might find useful in her biography, in one instance, the ledger of the Prophet's tailor. "It's just a detail," Juanita explained to Morgan, "but she might like it, and if I can, I'll get it and send it to her. I admire her courage, and will be glad to furnish anything I can."[78]

In the meantime, Juanita was fretting over a redaction Marguerite Sinclair had made of the Indian relations article she had submitted to the *Utah Historical Quarterly* in May. Assuring Juanita that there was still time to reverse the changes if she objected to them, Sinclair wrote, "I did want to present it to Mr. Alter in the best possible way, for your sake, and did quite a lot of hard work on it, myself, believe it or not!"[79] Sinclair had corrected the spelling of quotations from pioneer accounts and had rewritten a number of paragraphs. "For example," Juanita fumed to Morgan, "I say that the Indians were baptized and presented with new shirts as part of the ceremony and she changes it to read that they were ceremoniously presented with new shirts. . . . This sounds childish to you, maybe. But, dammit, I worked the thing over carefully more than once, and since it is to be printed under my name, I wonder why my own work can't stand."[80]

In September Cecil Alter defended Sinclair's revision of the piece. With considerable condescension, he informed Juanita that he would welcome her inspection of her article, ready for printing, if she happened to be in Salt Lake. He did not offer to mail it. He had, he wrote her, placed some of her footnotes "at the point of first and greatest interest, as is now pretty general standard practice" and had eliminated others entirely. "Only those who are inclined to try to make up a loss of reader interest will overload their manuscripts by learned appearances of many profuse footnotes. They should be used sparingly, frugally, to keep the manuscript from looking like a gipsy overhung with tinkles tassels and trinkets."[81] Thus Alter inveighed against the close documentation which Morgan had painstakingly taught Juanita to use.

During the fall of 1943 the war became more ominous. As Ernest shipped for Hawaii, Juanita wrote, "I'm trying hard not to be disturbed by the fact—I tell myself that, after all, there isn't much I can do by worrying. My head has a hard time keeping my heart under control at times."[82] Soon Clair received orders to report for induction into the army. Not shaving at eighteen, he seemed to Juanita to be "so young and immature for his years." At the same time Bob was bound for England on a troopship, provoking her to write: "The news of added sinkings of ships by the sub-marines keeps us worried until we know he has landed somewhere. I only hope to live to see this thing over and settled and the fellows home again. Though only one is mine by the accident of birth, the others seem no less mine."[83]

In St. George life went on tranquilly. On an October afternoon Juanita interrupted a letter to Morgan to carry in juniper wood, heat her range, and bake five loaves of bread which had been rising while she typed. The loaves were ready for supper. The Brookses protected their garden from a November frost and anticipated having tomatoes until well into December. Will bagged several deer during the annual hunt. Shortly afterward, he butchered two pigs, "with the result," Juanita wrote, "that I've been rendering lard and making headcheese and sausage and curing the rest of it. There's one comfort, though—we have our meat for a year ahead, between the venison and pork and a dozen or two chickens. I'll enjoy thumbing my nose at the rationing board."[84] Her basement was packed with jars of fruit and vegetables as well as jars of meat. She would boast to Morgan "that we lived six whole weeks without using a single food stamp. We rarely use any, except for sugar and shoes."[85]

In the meantime, she battled to preserve her Indian-relations article. In early October she took a night bus to Salt Lake and spent a day reviewing the piece with Marguerite Sinclair. She wrote Morgan that, although she and Sinclair had come "to a unity on most everything, thank goodness," Sinclair still wanted her "to re-do it and turn it hind-side before, because she thinks the human interest stories in the second part are so much more interesting than the historical material in the first part."[86] The weary Juanita seemed ready to concede to Sinclair's wish. Ultimately she did not. The article that would finally appear in print would be very close to the one Juanita had originally submitted, replete with eighty-three footnotes. Furthermore, in early December she found positive proof in the records of the Salt Lake Endowment House that Jacob Hamblin had been sealed to an Indian wife. At Juanita's request, this fact was added to the article.[87]

In early 1944 Juanita suddenly decided upon a new direction in her writing. It derived from Morgan's casual observation that she was a living remnant of the frontier. Alluding to his suggestion "that the frontier is right inside me," she agreed that at least the "southern desert frontier is. . . . It is a fact of which I have never been very proud, and which has sometimes caused me some embarrassment. . . ."[88] For Morgan, her connection with the frontier was nothing to be ashamed of. She should, he insistently replied, write her autobiography.

Immediately Juanita forgot her other projects and began to write about her girlhood in Bunkerville. Surrendering to a rush of memory, she elicited from her clattering typewriter a host of images, incidents, and personalities. In early February she mailed Morgan a sheaf of half-formed chapters. Typically, she was dubious of their worth: "While I had the time of my young life writing some of these sketches, now that they are beginning to cool, they don't sound so good. . . . To tell you the truth, I doubt that any publisher would find in my experiences material for a book."[89]

Morgan's response was ecstatic. Writing Madeline McQuown, a correspondent with whom he had a romantic understanding, he proudly detailed his own part in the genesis of Juanita's nascent autobiography. "The material is absolutely wonderful! She tells some of the most marvelous stories you ever heard; but more than that, the tone of all she writes is warm, human, witty, and wise, and as I have just written her, it is full of sunlight. It'll be a really notable book; I was never more sure of anything."[90] Morgan's concurrent letter to Juanita not only praised but instructed. On the one hand, she was to write her book thematically, elaborating, for example, "upon your frontier experience with birth and death, even though this discussion ranges over thirty or forty years of your life." On the other hand, she was to interweave the chronology of her life. Above all she was not to doubt herself as a proper subject for a book. "You are a far more interesting person than you have ever realized; I say it as one equipped to pass judgment, for I have known a good many people of all sorts, and I consider you one of the most extraordinary persons it has been my good fortune to meet."[91]

Morgan recommended that Juanita apply for an award in the Houghton Mifflin Life in America Series. Obediently she wrote the publisher and learned that, in order to qualify for the award of $2,500, a book had to "contribute to the understanding of our country by presenting a true and vivid account of Life in America."[92] Juanita morosely doubted that her autobiography would meet that qualification. Morgan responded explosively. "For Chrissake, Juanita, what do you imagine your book is? It would, by elementary definition, be exactly that kind of book." Alfred Knopf had awarded Fawn Brodie a fellowship for the Joseph Smith biography on the basis of an outline and four or five good chapters; Morgan was certain Houghton Mifflin would respond favorably to a similar submission from Juanita. By way of reassurance, he inserted himself explicitly into the process: "Accordingly, I command you to let me see what you are developing, and how you plan to develop it; let me make what suggestions I can, and let's get the book thoroughly clear in your mind before you try to build up a picture of it in their mind."[93]

It was also during early 1944 that Juanita began her long and fruitful association with the Huntington Library. Then as now, this prestigious institution in San Marino, a suburb of Los Angeles, consisted of a private research library, an art gallery, and botanical gardens established by philanthropist Henry E. Huntington. In January 1944 Morgan mentioned that the Huntington held the transcripts of the John D. Lee trials. Instantly Juanita was eager to examine them. Aware that the library admitted scholars selectively, she inquired with a certain trepidation, citing her membership in the Utah Historical Society as evidence of her scholarly status.[94] With an ingratiating alacrity, Leslie E. Bliss, chief librarian, granted her permission to examine the transcripts, either in the original or, if she could not come to the library, in microfilm or photostat. He hoped that she would apply for reader privileges and come in person, since he wished to talk to her about another matter, which in this first letter he approached indirectly. The library had recently received a $50,000 grant from the Rockefeller Foundation for the acquisition of research materials in the history of the Southwest. The library had also recently acquired a copy of Juanita's biography of Dudley Leavitt, which Bliss praised, declaring that "you made very good use of the material in hand. . . . "[95] Noting that in her introduction she spoke of herself as a collector of pioneer diaries, he inquired whether she would donate them to the Huntington. He closed cordially without having quite offered to hire her as a collector.

Regardless of expense, Juanita and Will agreed that she would buy a microfilm in order to make a leisurely study of the transcripts. Because Morgan had the means to project a microfilm and she did not, she proposed that he copy the text from the microfilm. "Reminds me of the two pioneer women," she wrote; "one had a dutch oven but no lid; the other had a lid but no oven. So by pooling their resources and timing their baking they did just as well."[96]

During the spring of 1944, Juanita was in a mood to write. Predictably, her letters to Morgan provide a lengthy catalog of interruptions. Maurine Whipple remained a major distraction. Whipple phoned one day, urgently requesting that Juanita come by. Complying in haste, Juanita found she had been summoned because her friend esteemed it a more effective tactic to ask a favor in person than by phone. She wanted Juanita to furnish material about the Mountain Meadows massacre for her pictorial review of Utah. Juanita wrote Morgan in a huff. "I told her to lay off the subject. She can't quote anything and knows nothing of sources, but she will try to re-tell and will garble everything. I insisted she leave it alone, though she maintained that she only wanted me to have the benefit of some good advertising. She'll use it, I know she will. —and if she does I'll write her a letter for her scrap book that she won't want to put into it."[97]

Such time as Juanita had for writing during the spring of 1944 she devoted to the autobiography. As she wrote new sketches, she groped for a theme which would transform the swarming incidents of her life into a statement about America. She thought about the attraction of the Outside as a theme: "the right of a child to dream, and the right of a person to move from one place to another or from one way of life to another if he has ambition and desire." She wondered whether a better theme would be neighborliness, which she saw as "the one characteristic of most small towns, and the one thing we must learn—that where people live together and come to know one another they find that they are not so different after all."[98] A little later she decided to call a chapter "A Hot-cap for Democracy," alluding to the protective covers gardeners put over delicate plants in the spring. "My idea," she told Morgan, "was that in the small community Democracy is fostered and protected, and in homes where children assume their portion of the responsibility is it nourished."[99] As he returned a second sampling of her chapters in April, Morgan declared her themes to be petty. Neighborliness "can be important," he wrote, "but you need something more arresting as the basis for your book." It was imperative that she succeed in formulating a unifying theme with impressive implications. "The various stories you tell are wonderful anecdotes and would go fine as separate articles, but gathered together into a book, they must add up to something more than the sum of their parts."[100]

For weeks Juanita fretted about a title. In late March she found what she had been looking for. "Will has suggested 'Cactus Bloom,'" she wrote Morgan, "his idea being that with all its spiny hardness, life on the edge of the desert does have some beauty, no matter how brief. My father used to hum a little ditty with a line about 'With quicksand in the river bed and cactus on the bank' which seems expressive of the country so I've been turning over 'Quicksand and Cactus.'"[101] Morgan, who had made fun of her hurry to find a title, conceded. If she wanted a provisional title, "Quicksand and Cactus" would do "because it has exciting connotations and its elements are associated with romantic ideas."[102] It was more than provisional. Ever after, there was no other name for the work.

By early May summer seemed to have arrived. The children clamored to go swimming and weeds flourished in the backyard. Corn, sweet potatoes, and tomatoes were well along in the garden, and the fruit trees on the Hurricane farm promised a rich harvest. The local Democrats (chiefly Will, who had been elected county chairman in 1942) solicited Juanita's efforts for the coming campaign. The only issue about which Juanita felt passionate was peace. "I'd be glad to throw whatever little weight I might have toward anything that would assure a peace that would last." She judged war with the feel-

ings of a mother. Clair was headed overseas "for hand-to-hand fighting on some island of the Pacific." Bob was "with a combat group in
England 'on line for the invasion.'" Grant had been sent to cook and
baker school in Colorado. Ernest remained in Hawaii, where he worked
as an aviation machinist in an air transport squadron.[103]

In May Morgan asked Juanita for information about the
colony of excommunicated Mormon polygamists at Short Creek,
whom, so he had read, Utah law officers intended to prosecute. Juanita
replied that what little she knew came from Jonreed and Verda, who
lived in Short Creek. The colony had transplanted itself there from
Lee's Ferry and in a twelve-year period had grown to 150 members,
pursuing a cooperative way of life called the "United Effort." She
believed the citizens of St. George generally favored allowing the polygamists to live unmolested. "Those folks out there have the fight of
their lives for a bare existence; if they believe the thing ardently enough
to live there in order to practice it, more power to them."[104]

Near the same time Juanita saw the movie *Buffalo Bill*, which
inspired her to write Houghton Mifflin about her prospective biography of Jacob Hamblin. Hamblin, she believed, had experienced Indian
adventures equal to those of William Cody. The publishing firm proved
cordially uninterested. Juanita now applied a renewed energy to her
autobiography, demonstrating her serious intent by again keeping her
ironing and mending handy in case visitors interrupted.[105] Within a
few days of establishing this routine she received an early morning
call from Ernest. He was on furlough and would shortly arrive in St.
George with a fiancée and plans for an immediate wedding. With an
urgent friendliness the Brooks family welcomed Margie Johnson, a
thin young woman with long, curly, golden hair. For two weeks Juanita
set aside her writing and performed her duties as chief hostess in the
happy, hectic round of visits, parties, and celebrations which accompanied the wedding. As May ended, Ernest returned to Hawaii and
Margie to her parents' home in Wyoming.[106]

On a Saturday evening in June 1944, Juanita departed by
bus for her long postponed visit to the Huntington. Sunday morning
she arrived at the home of her brother Dudley in Los Angeles. Later
in the day she visited Aura; before departing Los Angeles she would
take her chronically disturbed sister to a physician whom she trusted.
That physician was Joseph Walker, a native of St. George with whom
Juanita would shortly develop a warm correspondence.

On Monday morning, Juanita visited the Huntington in San Marino, where Leslie Bliss greeted her with an outstretched hand. On a table before him lay the small blue-bound volume of her biography of Dudley Leavitt. Bliss introduced her to Robert Glass Cleland, distinguished professor of history at Occidental College, who served as overseer of the Rockefeller grant. The two men proposed that Juanita share in the grant as a field representative. For a stipend of $50 a month and expenses, she would collect pioneer diaries and other sources of Utah history. Juanita agreed on the condition that the library photostat or otherwise copy the originals and return them to the families who owned them. "I told them that I could not be enthusiastic about getting originals for them except in cases where they were not being cared for, or where people were poor and needed to sell them."[107]

Upon her return to St. George, Juanita found waiting Morgan's cheerful endorsement of her latest chapters from "Quicksand and Cactus." He advised that she immediately submit them to Houghton Mifflin. He was sure the firm would accept them, but cautioned her to insist upon an award in the Life in America Series rather than an ordinary contract. "I can tell you, Juanita," he exulted, "I feel proud to have played any part in the conception and development of this book. It is a rich and mature statement of life, and a glowing (if unconscious) revelation of a wise and gallant personality. It will be a memorable book when it is finished, and no one else could have written it so well. I am sure it will be a great success in every way, artistic and financial."[108] On the evening of July 3 Juanita wrote Morgan that the chapters had been mailed. She also reported frantic holiday activities in the neighborhood. Willa, ten, had visitors—two cousins from out of town and two friends from down the street. The girls had returned from swimming, shampooed their hair, made lunches for a slumber party on the south porch, and noted with a provisional eye the soda pop and watermelon with which the refrigerator was laden. They spoke of pajama parades and visits to the neighbors for setting off rockets and sparklers. In the meantime, Juanita's sons, bolstered by friends, threatened attacks upon the girls. "Life promises not to be dull for the next few hours, anyway," Juanita wrote, "and I have restocked my first aid kit." Some paragraphs later she ended the letter abruptly: "Things are developing outside which demand a referee."[109]

In July 1944 Juanita started her work for the Huntington. She modestly wrote that she did not expect reimbursement for travel unless she was successful in locating historical materials. A library official quickly replied: "I am afraid you are taking too literally our formal phrase. . . . Not every trip of investigation will result in the immediate procurement of materials for the Library and I hope you will not feel that you must include a parcel of manuscript every time you send in an expense account."[110] Her first shipment included a handwritten newspaper from St. George. Soon she shipped volumes of the early *Millennial Star* and *Journal of Discourses*, which she had acquired in a strenuous manner. "If you could have seen me," she wrote Leslie E. Bliss, "dressed in some old slacks, climbing up a rickety ladder on the outside of a house, up three stories to a little attic window, and then making four trips down with dusty books, you would know that I am eager to dig out some of these old volumes. An elderly lady called me, saying that there were some books stored there, and that for forty years they had been undisturbed. If I thought you would like them, I might go up and examine them. Hence my escapade."[111]

For a decade Juanita would conduct a voluminous correspondence with Bliss. In his original letters and her carbons, which she carefully preserved, one may identify the diaries, minute books, antique printed works, and other historical matter which she forwarded to the Huntington. The correspondence maintained an utterly business-like tone, Bliss remaining cordially reserved from beginning to end. It is therefore notably lacking in the touches of dialogue and color and the biographical detail which enliven the correspondence between Juanita and Dale Morgan.

At the end of July Juanita attended the Writers Roundup in Salt Lake, where she combined business with pleasure by inquiring after diaries and old printed materials. She was particularly excited to have acquired a box full of small diaries of L. John Nuttal, an early superintendent of public instruction in Utah. Upon her return to St. George, Juanita shipped the Huntington a very gratifying package including the journal of Thales Haskell and twenty-seven small Nuttal diaries. She also submitted a frugal expense account: $15 for bus fare, $15 for four nights lodging, and $6.50 for meals averaging 50 cents each.[112]

While in Salt Lake Juanita examined the research her friend Vesta Crawford, an editorial assistant for the *Relief Society Magazine*, had done regarding the plural wives of Joseph Smith. Long ago Dale Morgan had made Juanita aware that in her biography Fawn Brodie intended to attribute numerous sexual partners to the Prophet. On the basis of Crawford's research, Juanita renewed her disagreement with Morgan over this matter. She was persuaded, she wrote, by the sheer number of women sealed to the Prophet, by the absence of children known to have been sired by him, and by the fact that men as well as women had been sealed to him. Of the numerous wives Juanita wrote: "Instead of leading to the conclusion that he was a libertine and sensual, they make me think he was a—well, I can't think of a single word to express it, but a person who dwelt quite largely in the realm of the spirit."[113]

The pleasure of the Writers Roundup was marred for Juanita when she phoned home to Will and learned that Houghton Mifflin had rejected "Quicksand and Cactus." Dejectedly she informed Morgan of the fact in a letter penned on Newhouse Hotel stationery: "I must fight the instinct to shelve the thing and forget it; if you can still have faith in it perhaps I can."[114] Morgan now insisted that she put the manuscript in his hands, in effect making him her unpaid literary agent. Not waiting for the manuscript to arrive, he decided to capitalize on his friendship with literary critic and historian Bernard DeVoto. He wrote DeVoto a long eulogy of the incomplete autobiography: "Its materials are wonderful, alive and colorful; it gives you a renewed sense of the dignity of the human soul and the worth of human living; and it also gives you a great feeling of admiration for a modest woman who is a valiant woman in all the meaning of that term."[115] Unimpressed, DeVoto refused to burden himself with an unfinished manuscript by an obscure denizen of rural Utah.

Juanita's spirits remained low. In mid-August Maurine Whipple gave a reading from the text of her book of Utah photographs. "Boy, how she does write in some places!" Juanita wrote Morgan. "It is lovely. It is the best writing that she has ever done, I think, and I have always been a booster for 'Joshua'. It makes me feel that I lack the spark somehow, or the touch which distinguishes between just writing and art. I have always said that a quail has its place as well as a canary, but I feel like a quail. Perhaps I should stay with the one thing which I have been able to do—collect material for others to work into best selling novels." Irresolutely she pondered a variety of projects, including the Hamblin biography, the monograph about the massacre, and a movie script based on Hamblin's life. Dismally she came around to her chronic problem, interruptions: "The point is, I would like to be able to write, openly and unashamedly, to hire some one to come in and take over much of the routine of my home and set up where I could make a business of writing."[116]

Almost immediately her spirits were elevated by a letter from E. P. Dutton & Co. soliciting a submission of her autobiography. The firm had learned of it through Ray B. West, whose *Rocky Mountain Anthology* Dutton was in the process of publishing.[117] West, Juanita believed, had learned of it through Dale Morgan, to whom she cheerfully forwarded the Dutton letter. She had been busy at the Hurricane farm helping to sort peaches—158 bushels shipped one day, 110 the next. Now she was ready to attend a conference at the Huntington. When she returned from that, she promised, things would be different: "I'm going to be less of a hewer of wood and hauler of water and spend my time at the typewriter. On the basis of it I have already turned down two church positions and resigned from one literary (?) club."[118]

Juanita and Will set out for Los Angeles on a Saturday night in late August. They found both the Greyhound and the Trailways buses booked full by wartime travelers. By sheer luck a young woman with a baby was in one of the stations seeking a driving companion for crossing the desert by night. Juanita and Will gratefully accepted seats in her new DeSoto, Will relieving the young woman at the wheel from time to time. On Monday the unassuming couple from St. George showed up on the sumptuous grounds of the Huntington to mingle with certified scholars and academicians, who for the most part were working on projects funded by the library's Rockefeller grant. Undoubtedly Juanita suffered an enormous reticence among the assembled illuminati. She had hoped to learn more about the John D. Lee diaries which Morgan had recently told her were deposited in the Huntington. "There was a convention on and many important PhD'ers present (and some that seemed not so important)," she wrote Morgan. "Anyway, Dr. Clelland [sic] was pretty much occupied with playing host to the crowd and I didn't want to force the issue."[119] As for Will, one supposes that in his utter innocence of academic hauteur he got along famously. He was not a bashful man and had an enviable ability to make everyone like him.

When it came time to go home, Juanita and Will faced the fact that no bus seats were available for days ahead. With a considerable foreboding they accepted the offer of an ancient coupe, a 1931

Buick, which Juanita's brother Dudley wished to have driven to Bunkerville as a gift for Henry. Setting out across the desert on Wednesday afternoon, they soon resigned themselves to a top speed of thirty miles an hour. They fixed a flat tire and after dark, because the vehicle had no dash lights, Juanita repeatedly struck matches to give a reading of the gauges. "We had planned to rest a while at Las Vegas, figuring that we would get there about 2:30 a.m., but when we beat our own time and arrived at 2:10, we shook hands with ourselves, patted the car, and decided to go on to Bunkerville. I never dreamed what a cup of black coffee would do to a fellow, for after I had been reinforced with one, I was not only wide awake, I was mildly hilarious. I grin now to think how I sang—everything from nonsense jingles to anthems—how I quoted Shakespeare and Henry W. Longfellow, how good the whole world seemed as that little car clicked along through a tunnel of darkness."[120]

Juanita's search for materials for the Huntington led her into a renewed contact with her former mother-in-law, Elizabeth Pulsipher. In early August Juanita attended the funeral of Ernest's grandfather in Mesquite. Following the funeral she secured from Elizabeth the splendid pioneer diary of John Pulsipher, which she had copied while her husband had taken radium treatments in Salt Lake. She also concluded a delicate negotiation with her former brother-in-law Stanley over two bound volumes of the *Deseret News* from the pioneer era, which he had reluctantly given her some years before. He now accepted her proposal that she sell the volumes to the Huntington for $100 and split the sum with him.[121] In September Elizabeth wrote Juanita, fretting that the diary had not been returned. Signing herself "Mother Pulsipher," the aged woman also complained that Juanita had not dropped in to visit her a few days earlier when the Brookses had brought LeRoy and Ann Hafen to Bunkerville and Mesquite.[122] At Juanita's urging, Leslie Bliss wrote Elizabeth assuring her that the diary would be safely returned. On a Saturday in mid-September Elizabeth called on Juanita in St. George, apologizing for having been unduly anxious.[123]

One is reminded that according to Mormon belief Juanita was still the eternal mate of Ernest Pulsipher. One Sunday Tony returned from Sunday School in tears because his teacher had told him his father and mother would not be united in the Hereafter. Juanita calmly reassured him that if she had any choice in the matter she would elect to stay with Will. In any event, it was not something to worry about; God would arrange it for the happiness of all.[124] Presumably Tony was pacified. The issue, however, would smolder and break out long afterward in discussions among the descendants of Juanita and her two husbands.[125] The intensity of Juanita's feelings, duly concealed from her children, may be measured by her frequent declaration among her liberal friends that wild horses couldn't pull her apart from Will Brooks in the Hereafter.

On September 9 and 10, 1944, Juanita made three appearances in Provo and Pleasant Grove as the featured speaker before local chapters of the Daughters of the Utah Pioneers.[126] Already she had a reputation among the amateurs, if not the professionals, of Utah history. While there, she promised Marba C. Josephson, editor of *The Improvement Era*, a long article on the first Mormon mission to the Indians of southern Utah. At home in mid-September she tied herself to her typewriter and quickly prepared the article. Drawn chiefly from the journal of Thomas D. Brown, it would appear serially as "The Southern Indian Mission" in the April, May, and June 1945 issues of this official church magazine.

She felt obliged to apologize to Morgan for wasting time on this project: "I thought it might be an opportunity to let Bro. [John A.] Widtsoe and some of the others who have been so suspicious of me know that maybe I'm not so bad, after all."[127] Undoubtedly her desire to enhance her status among the orthodox was sincere. Yet such was her ambivalence that she could not refrain from subtly teasing Marba Josephson. In her letter of submission, Juanita quoted passages from Brown's journal which she had deliberately omitted from the article. Some of the quotations had reference to the consumption of tobacco and beer by the Mormon missionaries and to Brown's resentment of local church authorities. One passage described an Indian woman so terrified of the missionaries that she seemed about to urinate: "Oh! how she feared to approach us; . . . she trembled and sweat and held her limbs together as if required to keep her reins steady that there should be no apparent leakage; such was her fear." Juanita concluded the quotations with an innocent comment: "To me they only show the humanness of the men, but I felt that they would be inappropriate for *The Era*."[128] She knew Josephson did not need a reminder of their inappropriateness. It was her oblique way of registering a protest against the

tendency of the Church to excise the indelicate and unsavory from
its past.

As September ended, Juanita wrote Marguerite Sinclair proposing that the *Utah Historical Quarterly* publish the Thales Haskell
diary Juanita had located over a year earlier. The diary, some of whose
pages were written in the arcane Deseret alphabet, gave a detailed
account of the second mission of Jacob Hamblin and his fellow missionaries to the Hopis of northern Arizona. Sinclair, agreeing that it
would make a good companion piece to Juanita's Indian relations article, urged haste in its preparation, for the quarterly had at last succeeded in purchasing paper and the typesetter was requesting copy.[129]
In mid-October Juanita reported satisfactory progress to Morgan. For
the most part the diary needed "very little editing; in fact, aside from
inserting periods, it could stand without change or comment."[130]

For a month preceding election day in 1944 Juanita enlisted
in the local Democratic campaign. As a Democratic victory loomed,
she labored with gusto and passion. She was irritated by the ostenta-
tion of local Republicans, whom she described as having "fancy 'TEAS'
in the afternoon, with formal dresses and flowers and pourers – and
speakers" financed from a rich campaign chest. In contrast, the Democrats organized small, austere evening study groups.[131] She and Will
joined a dozen other Democrats to produce a semiweekly newsletter
called "The Citizen," which the conspirators planned and wrote in
the Brooks kitchen. Girls typed stencils and boys ran off copies on a
mimeograph machine hidden in a vacant downtown building. A "host
of youngsters" distributed the newsletter. All was done with such telling bellicosity that the opposition called it a "low, contemptible, scandal sheet" and muttered about reprisals if the identity of the polemi-
cists were made known. "I wouldn't be bullied, so I put a notice in the
second-to-the-last issue, saying that I was proud of the small part that
I had been able to play in the publication, and that I was willing to
assume full responsibility for every word in every issue, and daring
them to do their worst. . . . "[132]

In the meantime Juanita awaited the result of Morgan's
efforts to secure a publisher's contract for the incomplete "Quicksand
and Cactus." In the early fall, she was dubious, writing Morgan, "I
have great faith in your judgment on most things, but I confess that
from the first I have felt that you were over-optimistic on this."[133]
Shortly, however, Morgan informed her that he was submitting her

outline and chapters to Farrar & Rinehart, who had responded positively to his inquiry; if that initiative failed, he would submit to E. P. Dutton. Juanita's spirits soared. She wrote, "I daren't hope too much; I daren't say a word except to Will, but if ever we really land anything, I'll stage a celebration for sure!" She also insisted that if the work found a publisher, Morgan was to "have the regular agent's fees. . . . Now listen, Old Dear, I'll have no back-talk on this point."[134]

In his next letter Morgan wrote that Farrar & Rinehart had rejected the manuscript; he would now submit to Dutton. He also refused an agent's fee: "I am not an agent, I am a friend of my friends— and in this case I am godfather to the book. So let that be an end to all such frivolous remarks."[135] In mid-November he reported Dutton's rejection. He advised against further preliminary submissions; she should finish the work before submitting it to other publishers. He pointed out that both publishers had recommended that she abandon the outline of her adult life and concentrate entirely upon her childhood in Bunkerville. For the fourth or fifth time, he tried to define the qualities with which he hoped she would infuse the work. It should have a cohesiveness now lacking, a unity of theme or tone among its disparate incidents. It should also seek a more harmonious and vivid style: "Don't be in such a hurry to say things that you say them in pedestrian fashion. . . . Build up what you are saying with the richness of all the sensory perceptions so that what you are writing becomes an experience in itself, not just a narration of an experience."[136]

Juanita absorbed his advice soberly, relieved that at least she could limit the work to her early life. She promised to press on despite a reawakened distaste for the project. "My natural impulse would be to put the Ms far back in a drawer, pile a lot of other things on top of it, and lock the drawer." As she wrote these lines, it was Thanksgiving. Although the Brooks family often went to Bunkerville for Thanksgiving, they had used up their gas stamps this year and would have to remain in St. George. The weather was balmy and clear. "I picked some gorgeous yellow chrysanthemums yesterday, and this morning got some fresh tomatoes from the vines. The mulberry leaves haven't started to turn at all yet, though the cotton-woods are getting yellow."[137] Across the street lived elderly Mary Conger, an ailing and eccentric woman for whom the Brooks family had assumed the role of caretaker for well over a year. "I take her breakfast over every morning and start a fire in the heater," Juanita wrote Conger's relative. "She comes here for her noon meal each day. I feed the children at about 12:30 and start them back to school, and then she and Will and Mr. Lorimer (a hired man) eat about 1:30."[138] The Mr. Lorimer to whom Juanita referred was a transient who boarded with the Brooks family for several years, doing odd jobs around the house and yard as payment for his keep. One sees that Juanita and Will had made their home into a cross between a rescue mission and a family hostel.

On December 2, 1944, Juanita received an alarming phone call from Bunkerville. Her father was critically ill and she was to bring a doctor at once. One of the St. George physicians was out of town and the other was occupied. Juanita filled a prescription which the latter gave and caught a bus for Bunkerville. By the time she arrived, Henry had been dead several hours.[139]

On the day before he died, Henry went to the post office, returning with letters from Francis and Laurel, which he read to Mary twice, as was his custom. He saddled his horse and rode about town visiting with friends. He went to bed early, leaving open the bedroom door so that he could converse with Mary, who sat up quilting. When she went to bed, according to her account, he "turned to me with open arms and said, 'Oh, you darling! You precious thing! Stay up and work all night till you're worn out!' He smothered me with kisses and it seem [sic] like he could not praise me enough; I think he was just over-flowing with love and affection."[140] Suddenly he fainted. Mary shook him and when he revived gave him a little wine. She ran for help. When she returned with neighbors he was unconscious. He died peacefully at seven in the morning. The funeral, attended by numerous friends and relatives, was held in the Bunkerville schoolhouse. His ten living children and their spouses were present. His six sons-in-law served as pallbearers. Ernest and Margie also attended, Ernest having taken emergency leave; one remembers that Henry had been a father to Ernest.

During January 1945 Juanita asserted her self-confidence by acquiring attractive personal stationery, each sheet of which bore, on its upper left hand corner, an embossed "Juanita Brooks." Throughout the winter she made a number of quick trips to Provo and Salt Lake, traveling by night and relying on the Huntington expense account. Among the materials she forwarded to the Huntington were records pertaining to Bunkerville's United Order, Book B of James G.

Bleak's "Annals of the Southern Mission" (a major source on the set-tling of St. George), and the diaries of Hosea Stout. She described the trip on which she acquired the Stout volumes as a near failure, telling Leslie Bliss, "I think I never put in more time with less results."[141] Iron-ically, she failed to appreciate the exceptional value of the Stout record, which alone would have justified ten such trips. In late February Juanita resumed work on "Quicksand and Cactus." In March she apologeti-cally mailed a revision to Morgan, admitting that she had reorganized but not radically rewritten her material. She also accepted a flattering request to deliver the Founders' Day Address at Dixie College in March, writing Morgan, "If they are fool enough to think I can do it, I'm just fool enough to try."[142]

Juanita continued to worry over the war that raged in Europe and the Pacific during the spring of 1945. Ernest, an aircraft mechanic in Hawaii, was in no danger. In March Grant was medically discharged from the Navy, blinded in an eye by the concussion of a cannon. Clair served as an ammunition carrier with a combat unit in the Pacific. For weeks Bob had been in thick fighting in Belgium and Germany; in December he had been in the Battle of the Bulge. In February a doctor ordered him to bed for a few days and he received a week's furlough to England: "Not long enough or far enough," Bob wrote, "but anywhere to get out of this for a while."[143]

During this spring Juanita was pleased to see the long-delayed winter 1944 issue of the *Utah Historical Quarterly* bearing her article, "Indian Relations on the Mormon Frontier," and her edited piece, "Journal of Thales Haskell." The journal, her first printed edi-tion of a pioneer document, bore testimony to her passion for an accu-rate reproduction of a handwritten original. The Indian relations arti-cle was an even greater scholarly achievement. Her loyal friend Joseph K. Nicholes, informing her that he ranked her with B. H. Roberts as a Mormon historian, judged her article to be "the most scholarly ever written on that subject."[144] Long afterward, western historian Charles Peterson would call it the "best article ever written on the history of Utah's Indian women."[145] Concentrating especially upon southwest-ern Utah, the article discussed Mormon attempts to civilize Indians by teaching them a settled, farming life and to assimilate them through the purchase of Indian children and intermarriage. Somberly, Juanita judged the process of assimilation to have been a failure: "Everything combined to create a feeling of inferiority, if not in childhood, at least by the time they reached maturity. No matter how excellent their training, Indian girls were usually forced to accept whom they could as white husbands; Indian boys rarely married."[146]

In April 1945 Juanita received a letter from Blanche Knopf, wife of Alfred A. Knopf, inviting her to submit a manuscript on the Mountain Meadows massacre. Robert Glass Cleland of the Huntington, Knopf reported, had informed her that Juanita was engaged in such a work. All at once, Juanita's projected monograph on the massacre became a projected book and took on an inevitable preeminence among her several endeavors. She immediately sent Knopf's letter to Morgan, who admiringly wrote back, "You're on your own, Sister Brooks! The letter from Mrs. Knopf is, incidentally, an interesting illustration of how one thing leads to another in this world."[147] A week later Juanita departed on a collecting trip to Salt Lake. While the bus paused at Cedar City, she heard the news that President Franklin D. Roosevelt had died of a cerebral hemorrhage. She was momentarily desolated. "My impulse was to wait and catch the next bus back home—I felt the need of support somehow, for it gave me such an empty, sick feeling. I went on, however." In the letter in which she described this incident, she congratulated Morgan for his appointment to a Guggenheim Fellowship and revealed that she herself had returned to a writing mood. "My ironing-board is all set up beside me with the iron ready to connect and what is left of the ironing after my session with Maurine Whipple yesterday afternoon still to do."[148]

Upon receiving Blanche Knopf's letter, Juanita also wrote to Robert Glass Cleland. Encouraged to know that he had recommended her, she made an astonishing request for an official assignment from the Huntington to write a history of the massacre. Such an appointment was essential to a scheme she had devised to gain access to documents in the Church Historian's Office. Of particular concern were a number of affidavits made by eyewitnesses to the massacre. Juanita knew the affidavits existed because they had once been in the possession of her friend St. George attorney and judge David H. Morris, before whom they had been sworn. Morris had invited her to inspect these affidavits while she had collected diaries for the WPA. Each time Juanita had called at his home, she had found him either ill or reluctant to show the documents before his adult children who happened to be present. Following his death, Juanita called on his adopted daughter, a Mrs. Hafen, who, upon Juanita's inquiry about the affidavits, "burst into tears. 'How did you know about them?' she asked. 'I thought that I was the only person in the world who knew of their existence.' Then she told how she had read some of them – there were eight, signed by local people who were there – and had been so shocked by the story, that she took them in to Salt Lake, since she didn't want to trust them to the mail, and gave them to David O. McKay."[149]

Few men in Mormondom were more powerful than David O. McKay, formerly second counselor to church president Heber J. Grant and presently first counselor to George Albert Smith. For months Juanita had brooded about ways of persuading McKay to allow her to inspect the affidavits. She now believed she saw a means. It was necessary that she appear to have a commission from a scholarly institution to write an objective account of the massacre. "If I can say," she wrote Cleland, "that I am doing a serious study, under the direction of the H. L. or under the R. F. Fund – that I have been assigned the task in an effort to get at the truth rather than just to be sensational, etc.etc. I believe that I could get the cooperation of enough of the church leaders to secure these documents."[150] In a letter to Morgan she further refined her purpose in asking for an official commission. If the Church "knew that it was a subject which was to be assigned for further study under the Rockefeller Grant, and that someone was to do it, perhaps they would prefer a person with a church background, and would cooperate with me."[151]

In May Cleland tardily responded to Juanita's request. It would be satisfactory to him, he wrote, if she were to include a study of the massacre among the duties of her appointment as field representative of the Huntington. Juanita cheerfully replied that she would devote most of her time during the coming year to the massacre. Since Cleland had made no mention of an increased stipend, she predicted: "I may not be able to make the extended trips which I had planned before in the interest of the library."[152] Cleland answered by return mail, concerned not to interrupt her "extraordinarily fine and satisfactory job in gathering material for the Library." He had assumed that she had wished only to confirm that her grant allowed her to study the massacre as well as collect diaries. Now, however, he countenanced the possibility of expanding the grant. "If you feel the grant should be increased to enable you to devote more time to both projects, we shall be glad to consider your request and I think something of the kind could be arranged."[153]

This letter, intended to mollify Juanita, had the opposite effect. It reminded her that Cleland and Bliss had not thought of her as one of the illustrious historians assembled at the Huntington during the previous August. Those scholars had included at least two persons whom Juanita considered her peers, LeRoy and Ann Hafen, who, supported by a Rockefeller grant, were writing a history of the Salt Lake to San Bernardino trail. In her next letter Juanita reviewed the economies she had practiced in behalf of the Huntington and declared that she most certainly could not research the massacre and continue to collect other sources without increased support. With a tone of deep injury, she wrote, "Perhaps I was foolish to assume that I might be given an assignment such as others had, since I am not now connected with any educational institution."[154] Again by return mail Cleland attempted to placate his offended field representative. He proposed doubling her monthly stipend to $100, an offer which Juanita instantly accepted.

In her letter of acceptance, she reiterated her desire that Cleland assist her in levering the massacre affidavits from David O. McKay. During a recent trip to Salt Lake, she had attempted to arrange an interview with the apostle, but had been thwarted by his secretary. "After I had given her a full account of my mission, she said she had been employed there for the past ten years and had never received such papers nor seen them and therefore was sure that they had never been brought in." It was Juanita's plan to arm herself with letters that might have impact upon McKay. One would be from Mrs. Hafen, the woman who had given the affidavits to McKay, which would force the apostle to admit he had them. Another would be from her stake president certifying Juanita to be a faithful Mormon. A third would be an official commission from Cleland for a study of the massacre—a commission which Juanita specified should be shown to derive from the Rockefeller Foundation rather than from the Huntington Library. "In Utah," she explained, "California is considered just another state and there is a hint of rivalry or jealousy toward her, while the Rockefeller Foundation carries a connotation of national importance. It is only a detail, as I said before, but in this particular undertaking every detail is important. And I MUST get these accounts written by men who actually participated in that thing."[155]

One supposes that Cleland choked over her latest request, for, as he wrote, "the Rockefeller Foundation does not consider those who receive fellowships or grants-in-aid as working under them but under the institution to which the money has been given."[156] To his credit, however, he produced a delicately worded document that satisfied his punctilious correspondent:

> This is to certify that Mrs. Juanita Brooks is authorized, under the Rockefeller grant to the Huntington Library for a Study of the Economic, Social, and Cultural Development of the Southwest, to make a study of the Mountain Meadows Massacre. Any assistance that may be given Mrs. Brooks in the course of her study will be greatly appreciated.[157]

At last Juanita had a fellowship for a writing project. Although it increased her meager stipend by only $600 a year, its effect upon her spirits was immense. She wrote Morgan: "Now I can frankly admit that I am writing, can send out my laundry, can hire more of my routine house work done, can refuse church and club jobs with the excuse that I have not time."[158] There is every reason to believe that without the grant she would never have written the chief book of her career.

The Fourth of July came with "its sleeping parties that tear around all night and its pop and watermelon and gangs of kids," Juanita reported to Morgan. Following the Fourth, Tony's seventh birthday loomed, "and the rumble of the approaching party already makes itself heard." She ended her letter when the noon whistle sounded. An hour later, Will would arrive from the post office, and she would have ready a lunch of green corn and summer squash from the garden and homemade ice cream from the refrigerator.[159] In mid-July Juanita mailed snapshots to Morgan. There was one of the rock house on the hill at the time she and Will had moved in. She had to explain their additions. They had torn down the front fence, built rock ditches and walks, added a white porch over the outside entrance to the basement, and established a trellis now aswarm with roses and morning glories. Invisible in the snapshot were the giant ancient trees that Will remembered from his childhood. Juanita also included photographs of the children, ordered at Clair's request. She had charged Willa with the responsibility of corralling her brothers, combing their hair, and getting them to the photographer. Willa, Juanita mused, "[is] quite a mature little eleven-year-old, and accustomed to looking after the others. . . . Karl is my student. He reads and reads, everything he can get his hands on. He'll be in the fourth grade next year, but already has nearly worn out my Book of Knowledge set. Kay is not so good in school, but is all around boy, full of mischief and pranks and acrobatics—swims like a fish, walks on his hands, etc. He ranks in the upper third of his class, but doesn't go all out for reading like Karl does. If I have a genius in the family it is Tony, only he's geared so high that I'm afraid sometime that he will snap. . . . Anyway he is so thin that he looks like a caricature of famine."[160]

During the summer of 1945 the Brooks home was in shambles. In April Juanita and Will had decided to build a bedroom for Willa over the back porch and to remodel the "cubby-hole" in which their daughter had hitherto slept. This tiny space adjoining the living room would become Juanita's study. The Brookses also planned to paint and paper other rooms and to replace Juanita's venerable cast-iron kitchen range with a new electric stove when one should become available.[161] An electric stove would mean less hewing and hauling of wood and a cooler kitchen in summer. The old range of course had had its advantages; in winter its sturdy oven door, lowered, sometimes served as a warm seat for Juanita as she typed. The remodeling dragged on through the summer, workmen being in short supply because of the war. In mid-July Will acquired a used cooler for Juanita, the first the old house had ever seen. "You have no idea the difference it makes," she wrote Morgan. "It gives me a new lease on life, and makes me feel that MAYBE I can get going again."[162] Not until autumn would Juanita assure Morgan that the carpenters, painters, and paperhangers had at last brought order from chaos: "The net result was that the place was torn limb from limb. Now it is all finally straight again, the walls clean and new, the kitchen shining, even the basement painted."[163] Happily she would take possession of the cubby-hole as her place of intellectual labor.

Mid-summer Juanita listened eagerly to rumors of peace. Bob was still in Europe, presumably safe following the end of hostilities there, though the family had not heard from him since March. In the Philippines Clair's division had recently gone forward into action.[164] Then one August day, while Juanita was at her typewriter, a neighbor shouted the news of the Japanese surrender. Juanita crossed the fence and listened on the neighbor's radio, since her own did not receive well during daylight. The tabernacle bell began to toll and the town emptied its houses and filled its streets. "We got into our little one-seated car with all our kids and our neighbors in the back, and went down town. . . . The fire engine with two big flags led the line of cars—we were in the middle of it—all honking and clattering, around and around the town. Kids on bicycles ran in groups, with bunches of tin cans tied to their fenders. War widows collected and laughed and cried and hugged each other." The next morning the town made a formal celebration. Bands played in the street and a crowd assembled in the tabernacle for prayers and speeches. Juanita fought to control her tears. "It seems that the combined joy and gratitude are almost more than I can contain, certainly more than I can express—at least by any noise making devices that I know. I think that the combined prayers of gratefulness of all the mothers of the earth must rock the throne of heaven."[165]

Following V-J Day Juanita applied herself to "Quicksand and Cactus" with a new vigor. For months she had worked on her autobiography in a desultory, dispirited fashion. In April Morgan had asked Fawn Brodie and Darel McConkey, a former colleague on the Utah Writers' Project, to read Juanita's latest revision. According to Morgan, they liked her work yet found much lacking in it. He used a summary of their criticism to reinforce his own. He agreed with Brodie that Juanita's prose was "flat" and "colloquial to the point where it sounds like careless writing." He agreed with McConkey that the work was disunified and smacked too much of fiction and folklore. "Conversations are remembered too facilely for them to have been actually remembered, and by 're-imagining' those conversations, you are working in the borderland of fiction. The difficulty is compounded by the fact that you have several chapters in which one strongly suspects the things you describe never happened, that you have merely fashioned your own vehicle for saying some things you want to say."[166] In June, Juanita rallied and mailed another revision. In July Morgan returned another negative critique, repeating his old refrain that the work lacked organic unity. "These chapters are very nearly static. One gets practically no feeling of direction or movement, and without this to sustain them, the chapters add up to little more that a collection of stories. . . ."[167] His criticism, which had always been highly abstract, simply augmented Juanita's despondency. In early August she wrote: "I don't know when I've been so nearly discouraged—I mean to the point that I've been tempted to quit and dump things overboard. There's no use listing the distractions and all the reasons; it would sound too much like whining."[168]

Within days the war ended, and Juanita found new energy. She reorganized episodes and polished sentences until she could think of no further improvements. She believed herself ready now to submit the manuscript to Alfred A. Knopf, who had agreed to look at it. If Knopf rejected it, she planned to submit to E. P. Dutton, whose editor had agreed to take a second look. Ambivalently, she dallied in mailing the draft, perhaps because, as she had told Morgan, she had "felt all along that this is not something in which Knopf will be interested." In early September Juanita, Will, and their children visited her sister Charity in Blanding. Juanita took along the manuscript, thinking she would mail it from Salt Lake, where the family first stopped. Instead, she carried it on to Blanding to let Charity read it, since she had frequently mentioned her sister in its pages. However, she couldn't bring herself to show it to Charity. "Of all the family, only Francis, who is safely in Guam, knows of the undertaking at all," she wrote Morgan. "So I carried it around for the twelve hundred miles, never taking it out of the case enroute and came back to working conditions worse than ever—fruit that must be canned, etc.etc. All of which adds up to show what a fool I am."[169] Near the first of October she at last mailed the manuscript, slightly amended, to Knopf. Anticipating rejection, she gave instructions that the firm return the document, not to her, but to Morgan, who she hoped would give the chapters another critique.

In November Knopf would indeed reject the work, and Morgan would submit it to Dutton with a fervent endorsement: "The manuscript I send you is probably the fifth version I have seen since she wrote me the first tentative sketches to stake out the boundaries of the book, and each version has been enriched with new thought and feeling."[170] In April 1946 Dutton too rejected the manuscript. Morgan advised that Juanita let the project rest awhile. It was advice which she heeded only too willingly. For several years Morgan continued to mention the work to eastern publishers. In 1948 Juanita submitted a compilation of chapters to Rinehart & Co. That firm gave the manuscript a long, close look but decided finally against publication. Describing it as "pleasant, honest and often very entertaining," Rinehart's editor-in-chief apologized: "We came to the conclusion reluctantly that there simply was not enough sales possibilities in the book to make it a profitable venture for you or for us."[171] In 1949 Bobbs-Merrill would ask to see it. For the first time since 1945 Juanita invested major time in revision, creating a fictionalized version narrated in the third person and featuring a girl named Sal. "While I can see that it may lose something in authenticity," Juanita wrote the firm, "I hope that it may gain in vitality. I had felt that, to justify a book, the subject of an autobiography should have achieved distinction in some field, while a good story may be just a good story."[172] In time Bobbs-Merrill rejected this version. For many years "Quicksand and Cactus" would remain in Juanita's inactive file, disturbed only when she rifled through it for material with which to enrich a speech.

The unpublished chapters which feature Juanita as the first-person narrator were composed between January 1944 and October 1945. With little exception, they confine themselves to the first thirteen years of her life. Bearing such titles as "More than Meat," "Let Us Be United," "Five Grandmas," "Old Lady River," and "Hen Leavitt's Boy," they offer a motley welter of events. In many, the precise chronology of Juanita's life is indistinct, and one often finds in proceeding from one chapter to another a confusing recombination of the same episodes and descriptions. From these manuscript pieces, an editor would extract twenty-one brief chapters which would appear in 1982 as the first half of the published *Quicksand and Cactus*. (Juanita wrote the chapters which would comprise the second half of her published autobiography during the early 1970s. These chapters follow her life through adolescence and early adulthood. Ending with her wedding to Will, her autobiography would remain a forever unfinished work.)

The first half of the published *Quicksand and Cactus* represents the best writing Juanita did in 1944 and 1945 about her childhood in Bunkerville. She herself of course figured importantly in these early chapters. Often she appeared in a comic light, physically stunted, naive, and unsure. Hence, when her father preposterously suggested that she prepare him a cloth belt filled with tea leaves to wrap about his waist, she did so and suffered from his merciless laughter. At other times, particularly when in an out-of-doors setting, she appeared competent, active, and happy. Sometimes she responded to the lure of the Outside, anticipating the time when she would leave the village. In addition to characterizing the girl Juanita, these chapters characterized Bunkerville. In its stark, moody surroundings of desert and river, the village had its own fascinating, picturesque personality. In these pages its collective life stood forth, lovingly if comically recreated: its public works, its crafts and trades, its church services, dances, and celebrations, its courts and disciplines, its lore and tradition.

Each autumn the men of the village cooperated in shoveling silt from its ditches. "Before work began each morning, the Watermaster stepped off the stints and drove in a peg to mark the place of each man. At eight o'clock each was in his place and did his stint, going ahead to do another at the head of the line as soon as he finished."[173] Relaxing at lunch, the laborers engaged in hearty, ribald gossip. "Men who would shrink from speaking from the pulpit would wax eloquent over the shovel handle; men who turned to stone if asked to address the meeting could entertain the crowd with ease. Here the cloak of sanctity was torn off, tainted jokes were told, testimonies of the over-zealous were repeated amid hilarity that was suppressed in church. Here, too, originated tall tales that became legend."[174] Juanita provided a liberal sampling of those tales. For example, a man named Chris heard an evil spirit in his house one night, which he commanded in the name of the priesthood to depart. Hearing further noises his wife rammed a broom handle under the bed. "The Spirit of Evil gave a squeal and came out so fast it knocked Chris down, tipped the table over, and scattered tinware from hell to breakfast!"[175] It was of course a pig.

The folktales of Bunkerville influenced *Quicksand and Cactus* in form as well as content. It is little wonder that Juanita, who had an exceptional gift for the oral tale, should have infused her chapters with a storied effect. A few of the published chapters have, like "The Outsider," the consistency and structure of a formal short story. But many others advance in a highly episodic fashion, their fabric loosely woven of a variety of lesser narratives—Juanita's own adventures, pioneer experiences handed down by generations of tellers, and universal tall tales recast in the particulars of Bunkerville, all having in common the simplicity of the oral folktale rather than the elaboration of the literary short story.

A mingling of autobiography, folklore, and fiction occurs, for example, in the chapter entitled "Simon and the Magic Sack." Simon was an Indian comrade from Henry's boyhood whom Henry invited to dinner and to whom he lent his rifle. Although Henry's white neighbors invidiously warned that he would never see his rifle again, Simon returned it in due time, bearing a gift of a large sack of pine nuts. This narrative Juanita developed chiefly through dialogue—a distinct fictionalization, since she could not have remembered the precise content of conversations she heard in childhood. She introduced another fictionalization by attributing evocative powers to the sack of pine nuts. "Certainly we had never tasted nuts quite like these before, and might never again," she continued, "for nuts that we parched on top of the stove or baked in the oven lost much of their moistness and flavor. These had been slow-cooked in the cone, in a pit and left covered to steam. We learned to think of them as coming from a Magic Sack, because the older folks who ate them at once began to remember stories from the past, and how it was when they were young."[176] Then came a variety of tales about Indians and village industry in early Santa Clara, supposedly quoted from the mouth of one of the best of the storytellers, grandmother Maria Leavitt.

These chapters composing the first half of the published *Quicksand and Cactus* lack the thematic consistency and expansive philosophic insight which Dale Morgan repeatedly recommended. They are in fact mixed in approach and treatment. Demonstrating traits of the memoir, the folktale, the short story, and the personal essay, they defy easy classification. Their very confusion adds to their appeal. If they seem unstructured and episodic, they also offer pace, variety, and unending human interest. Furthermore, they demonstrate a frequent felicity of style. Their sentences are arranged in simple, harmonious rhythms; their concrete, wry diction is richly evocative of scene and setting. These chapters are clearly of a high literary quality.

Soon after submitting her manuscript to Knopf in the fall of 1945, Juanita proceeded with her scheme to extricate the affidavits from David O. McKay. She decided first to seek the support of George Albert Smith, president of the Church. In a less than ingenuous letter to Smith, she alluded to her commission to write about the massacre as "a Fellowship from the Rockefeller Institute through the Huntington Library." She claimed that "a rabid anti-Mormon" had a book almost ready for publication—she meant Charles Kelly (who actually had not progressed beyond research on the topic). A Mormon in good standing, she reasoned, should preempt the topic with an interpretation that put the best possible light on it: "As in anything else, it is good to get there with the first blow; an 'answer' is never so effective." She claimed to have expressly refused "offers from publishers in the East" in order to avoid sensationalizing the massacre—a not altogether honest assertion, given the fact that her interest in the subject had been recently escalated by Knopf's solicitation.[177]

In a gracious reply Smith granted her request for an audience.[178] At four o'clock on a Thursday in mid-October, she called at the church administration building for her appointment. She was impressed by the contrast between Smith's receptionist and McKay's. "When I went some time ago to talk to David O. McKay the attitude of the girl was one of suspicion and her business seemed to be to keep people out. Now when the girl answered the telephone, she always said, 'The President is busy right now, but I am sure that he will be glad to see you.' "[179] During the interview Smith said he would prefer that the massacre not be "stirred up" but listened sympathetically to Juanita's reasons for wishing to write about it. He told her that he knew nothing of the affidavits and recommended that she speak directly to McKay about them. As they parted, he twice shook her hand and said, "I hope that whatever you do in this matter, you will be happy about it, permanently happy." Greatly encouraged, Juanita went to McKay's office and found Joseph Anderson, secretary to the First Presidency, who knew of the affidavits because he had received them from Mrs. Hafen. McKay was unavailable. Anderson suggested that Juanita return, which she did on Friday morning. After she had waited an hour and a half, Anderson disappeared into McKay's office and "explained what I wanted, and Bro. McKay referred me to Joseph Fielding [Smith]. I said no, that Joseph Fielding did not know of the papers and I preferred to wait until I could talk to David O."[180] Rebuffed, she vowed to return at a later date.

Thanksgiving 1945 was made extraordinary by Bob's return from Germany. Ernest had called that he was in Wyoming with Margie and would shortly bring her and their baby to St. George. Clair was on duty in the Philippines. The day was bright and clear, and the children swarmed in the yard and took a hike to the Sugar Loaf. In mid-December an unheard-of snowstorm struck St. George. "You never saw youngsters more thrilled than mine, either," Juanita wrote Morgan. "They want to be out in it all the time, rolling snow men and pelting each other with snow balls. I could be more thrilled myself if the kitchen floor didn't get such a mess."[181] Juanita helped at the post office for long hours, decorated a Christmas tree, and wrapped gifts. Shortly before Christmas, the weather became balmy again: "Today it has been really growing weather, with all the children in their shirt sleeves raking leaves and playing marbles. The kind of weather St. George should capitalize on."[182]

In November Juanita was amused to read in *Saturday Review of Literature*, to which she subscribed, Dale Morgan's review of Maurine Whipple's photographic book, *This Is the Place: Utah*. Morgan bluntly accused Whipple of having plagiarized significant portions of her commentary. After Thanksgiving, Whipple called on Juanita, angrily defending herself. "I told her I thought she could well let it stand as it was," Juanita wrote Morgan, "but she insists that she did not borrow."[183] Shortly Whipple wrote a protest to Alfred Knopf, her publisher. Knopf forwarded the letter to Morgan. Piqued by this "dishonest squawk," as he described the letter to Juanita, Morgan wrote a four-page documentation of the alleged plagiarism and mailed the ribbon copy to Whipple and the carbon to Knopf.[184] In late December Juanita reported that Whipple had set off for Salt Lake to write her next book. "She severed diplomatic relations with me when your review first came out. She came here full of accusations and complaints; she just couldn't understand *why* you should have it in for her; goodness knows, she had tried hard enough to be friendly to you. I couldn't agree with all her line, so she left in a miff and has never been back nor spoken to me since. I don't mind, really. I know that when she needs something that I can help her with she will come, soon enough."[185]

In November Morgan informed Juanita that *Saturday Review* had also asked him to review an advance copy of Fawn Brodie's *No Man Knows My History*. "I will," he wrote her, "be interested to know what you think of her book, almost more than any other single person. When my own opus [a projected history of the Mormons] is finished, one of these years, you are one of the persons I am going to ask to read the manuscript, for the sake of the perspective I'll derive from your mind, which is both rarely independent and essentially sympathetic to the Mormon point of view."[186]

Early in December 1945, Juanita read Brodie's book. On a Sunday afternoon, prompted by Morgan's review, she wrote a remarkable four-page letter giving Morgan the response he desired. It was the clearest, completest expression of her Latter-day Saint faith that she would ever make in writing.

Brodie's biography was, she judged, both scholarly and literary and established a new and necessary perspective on Joseph Smith. The book would have little impact upon rank-and-file Mormons, who would simply dismiss it as another anti-Mormon work. Upon Mormon scholars, however, it would "have its effect, and in the long run, a very profound effect." In certain crucial matters Juanita disagreed strongly with Brodie. She saw no reason to overemphasize the Prophet's youthful treasure hunting or even his trial for disorderly conduct related to treasure hunting, which seemed to Juanita "but the normal activities of a growing boy." Above all, she could not agree with Brodie that the Prophet "was a conscious fraud and imposter. . . . For a fraud, he inspired loyalties too deep in too many. Certainly he had SOMETHING. Men, catching their spark from him, were willing to sacrifice too much to further his cause." As a prime example of his devoted followers, she named her grandfather, who had spoken of the Prophet "in a tone and with an expression that made me quiver inside. To him, Joseph was second only to Christ himself, and a close second, at that." She cited her own spiritual experiences as reasons for believing in the Prophet's spiritual experiences. In particular, she narrated for Morgan the miraculous appearance of the strange little man who long ago in Salt Lake had blessed and comforted the dying Ernest. "What I am trying to say is this: I believe that it is possible for human beings to tap the great source of all good—to contact God direct, if you will. I believe that there were times, rare, perhaps, when Joseph Smith did that. I believe that it was those times that held his people to him in spite of all his human blunderings and frailities [sic] and mistakes."[187]

Morgan replied quickly with an equally remarkable, unequivocal statement of his obverse faith. He praised Juanita for her tolerance: "Juanita, if every member of the church united your feeling for the Mormon way of life with your intellectual objectivity and reasonableness, no religion on earth would rival Mormonism, and the Kingdom of God would have a fair chance of early realization." He particularly valued the fact that she could read Brodie's book candidly and "then discuss it without rancor, appreciating its merits without accepting its arguments." He found, however, that he and Juanita stood on opposite sides of "a Great Divide." He was, he declared, essentially an atheist, though he preferred to speak of himself as an agnostic because he found positive proof lacking either for or against the existence of God. His premise clarified, he proceeded to reason. "If God does not exist, how can Joseph Smith's story have any possible validity? I will look everywhere for explanations except to the ONE explanation that is the position of the church." Though he had once inclined toward believing that Joseph had suffered from delusion, the verbatim Isaiah texts in the Book of Mormon had persuaded him that Joseph was "indeed a conscious fraud and imposter." He could not agree with Juanita's point that the loyalty of his followers proved the Prophet's authenticity. "Fundamentally it was Joseph's personal magnetism that bound people to him originally; and then after the church began to grow, it acquired an almost independent existence. It acquired a dignity from the lives of its converts; it became a social force energizing the lives of innumerable people swept up in its course."[188]

The exchange was not quite complete. Mailing Juanita's letter to Fawn Brodie, Morgan expressed his great admiration for his Dixie friend: "One of these days I am going to put Juanita into a book. Maybe even the Great Salt Lake book, though not referred to specifically by name, merely an example of the hard core of integrity and common sense that can be found in the Mormon way of life and the Mormon society if you are willing to look around a little."[189]

Juanita, for her part, brooded about Morgan's skeptical position. Between Christmas and New Year 1945, she wrote an ambivalent letter. She had handed a copy of Brodie's book to her mother, who, refusing to read it, asked whether Juanita remembered how her father had always said that he would as readily expose his children to a dread disease as to anti-Mormon literature. "Yes, I do remember," Juanita wrote to Morgan in answer to her mother, "and I remember how that only made me more eager to hear the other side of the story." In another paragraph, recognizing her own budding dissent, she vacillated between guilt and defiance: "I am in fact in a state of apostacy [sic], perhaps, with many of the practices and teachings of our church. I simply cannot accept them and retain my intellectual independence, which I do try to maintain. And yet, I am loyal to it. I think it is as much my church as it is J. Reuben Clark's or anyone elses [sic]."

Nonetheless, she affirmed that she and Morgan were on opposite sides of the "Great Divide." She recounted having attended, just the evening before, a program honoring the pioneers of Santa Clara, in particular Samuel Stucki, her great-grandfather on her mother's side. Seemingly forgetful of Morgan's affliction, she drew a cruel parallel between deafness and disbelief. "I know that analogies are often dangerous, but it occurred to me that a deaf person could as well criticize a grand opera from what he could get of the actions of the characters and without hearing the music that was basic to it all as for a person to whom there is no God could evaluate the life of a man like Samuel Stucki. To you, God is not; to him, He was very real and very near; an ever-ready help in time of trouble." She concluded that she and Morgan would have to make their historical judgments according to their opposite biases. "I hope," she said with a return to her customary respect for her friend, "that mine can be as fair in my way as I know that yours will be in your way."[190]

CHAPTER SIX

THE STORY SHE WAS BORN TO TELL

In January 1946 Juanita addressed the employees of Zion National Park on the subject of Toab, a Paiute chief who in pioneer times had inhabited the Arizona Strip. As a consequence of her speech, the National Geological Survey gave the official name of Mt. Toab to a hitherto unnamed peak southwest of the park. A further consequence was that Juanita published a minor article, "Old Toab," in the April 1946 issue of the recently revived *Utah Magazine*. The article recounted absorbing anecdotes. For example, while on trial Toab listened to his white lawyer emphasize Toab's fear of an Indian whom he had killed. The incensed Toab leaped to his feet and shouted that he had not been afraid of his opponent but had readily struck him down with a hoe. Thereby Toab lost his case and went to the Utah penitentiary.

The editor liked the article so much that he solicited another. Juanita obliged, her "Beauty Beckons in the Parks of Southern Utah" appearing in the June issue. This travelogue contains some of Juanita's most vivid natural description. She wrote of her first visit to the Grand Canyon: "The far reaches of it took all the elastic out of the imagination. Here on the edge the narrow bands of rock lay in irregular scallops, each gathering tightly in its hand flutings and ruffles of sand in horizontal stripes of orange and yellow and red. . . . The immensity of it, the utter silence of it, the sun pointing up the ridges with gold and shimmering the purple shadows in the gullies, all combined into an impression which after ten years still shakes me to the grass roots."[1]

In January 1946 Juanita's grandmother Mary Ann Hafen died. Juanita arrived home from a collecting trip to Salt Lake and Ogden in time to help her mother prepare Mary Ann's body for burial. "Mother had already washed it," she wrote Morgan, "and put on the underwear and shampooed her hair—Grandma had a dread of having a man handle her body, turn the hose on it, etc.etc." After the funeral, Juanita's brothers and sisters and their spouses held an informal family reunion, making the Brooks home their headquarters. "It has meant beds all over the place and meals in installments and at all hours."[2]

As 1946 advanced Juanita settled into serious work on the massacre. During February she was able to validate a major source in the possession of the Huntington—a transcript of the trials of John D. Lee held at Beaver, Utah, in 1875 and 1876. That validation came in a letter from W. L. Cook of San Francisco, the court stenographer who had recorded the proceedings of the trials in shorthand. "The Judge said he wanted to write a book on the said trials," the aged Cook wrote Juanita, "and that if I would make the transcript he would give me a third of the profits of the book he would write."[3] The judge had never completed the book and his impecunious son had eventually sold his copy of the transcript to the Huntington. The unpaid Cook had refused to certify that he had made the document. Now his letter to Juanita put the origin of the Huntington's transcript beyond question.

In early March Juanita made a quick trip to the Huntington, riding night buses in both directions, in order to examine the transcript directly. She had found her microfilm too dim for her overworked eyes. Returned, she wrote Morgan of the perplexities which her sources aroused. The massacre was "a mixed up affair. Everyone who tells it tries to shield himself and blame the other fellow. Klingen Smith does not mention Indians at all; Nephi Johnson says there were between 150 and 300; Higbee says they number 600."[4] In light of these counterclaims, Juanita pondered attaching to her narrative a massive appendix of original accounts from which readers could form their own opinions. Furthermore, the horror of the incident made her research a depressing affair. She wrote to Leslie Bliss: "Interesting as it is, it still is such a ghastly thing that I shall be glad and relieved to feel that it is finally done."[5]

Early in 1946, Bob left home again, having decided to reenlist in the army. In February Clair arrived home from duty in the Pacific. At first his skin had a yellow pallor and his hands shook violently. At home he improved rapidly and talked freely of his experiences. Once as Will dressed an infection on Karl's arm, Clair reminisced about a buddy who had fainted when he saw the blood of a wounded friend. "And yet when we were out on patrol, crawling through the jungle, we had to stay flat on our bellies because there was still shooting at us. Well, this same kid could go right over Japs with their heads all shot to pieces or their bodies all torn, crawl right over them and never bat an eye." On another occasion Clair chided Tony for complaining of hunger: "Why, Tony, I saw hundreds of Japs starve to death, just lay down and die for want of food. I think I counted over two hundred myself."[6] The listening Juanita enlarged her understanding of war—an important education, for the more she studied the massacre the more she was disposed to interpret it as a military action carried out by men in a state of war hysteria.

In April Juanita hunted for diaries in Provo and Salt Lake and made another assault on the affidavits held by David O. McKay. By telephone she was able to make an appointment to speak to the apostle. However, when she presented herself in person, McKay's secretary denied her entrance. Instead, Juanita was again shown into the presence of Joseph Anderson, who agreed to present her request to the First Presidency. She called again the next morning at the church administration building, where she sat opposite Anderson at a table. On the table lay "a large brown envelope, so old that it was cracking and full of folded papers." J. Reuben Clark, second counselor in the First Presidency, had reviewed the materials with Anderson and had instructed him to tell Juanita that there was nothing among them that would be of any value to her study. To her insistent questions Anderson made certain half-compromising replies. The envelope contained typed documents, signed and notarized. There were only three affidavits, two by Nephi Johnson (one of which Juanita already possessed) and one by Samuel Knight. There was also a telegram from an earlier First Presidency instructing David H. Morris to gather the affidavits. "How I wanted the date of that telegram!" Juanita wrote. "I'd have given anything to have it. But he didn't remember and he didn't dare take the material from the envelope."[7] Juanita at last accepted the fact that she would have to proceed without the affidavits. She consoled herself that she would be less beholden to the official Church.

Before she left Salt Lake, Juanita called on a Mr. Tidwell in search of a record. Eager to help, Tidwell phoned numerous relatives and was told that the record was in Linden, near Provo. He offered to drive Juanita there. In Linden they were told that the record was in Mt. Pleasant in Sanpete County. Depositing Juanita's luggage at the Provo bus station, they drove on. Arriving in Mt. Pleasant, they discovered the woman thought to have the record had moved to Salt Lake. Because it was nearly dark and his car had poor lights, Tidwell decided to stay the night with relatives in Mt. Pleasant. A vexed Juanita hired a taxi to drive her some seventy miles to Provo, a conveyance she would apologetically charge to her Huntington expense account. She arrived home the next morning in time to get her children off to Sunday School.[8]

Other affairs enlivened Juanita's spring. Her ward bishopric was selling subscriptions to the *Deseret News* to finance a movie projector. When ward representatives dropped by, Juanita made clear her attitude toward the Republican orientation of the church-owned newspaper. "Anyway, when they came here," she wrote Morgan, "I told them that I wanted to be a good member of the church, but I hadn't a chance if I read the News: it made me so blankety-mad that I lost even my standing as a Christian. . . . I might add that I contributed $3.00 to the movie machine, but did not subscribe for the News. So now I'll be counted as an Apostate for sure."[9]

As school ended, the Brooks house seemed extraordinarily busy. Clair was living at home, and Ernest, Margie, and their daughter had moved next door into a house Juanita and Will had bought from Will's brother Ed. (Juanita's mother would soon move into this small house, which she would occupy for twenty-five years.) Juanita suffered from fatigued eyes and headaches that kept her awake at night. Sometimes she typed with her eyes closed. Nonetheless, early one morning she was in the mood to write Morgan a relaxed letter. The children were still asleep, and Will, after listening to the six o'clock news, had gone out to do the morning chores. She proceeded to satisfy Morgan's curiosity on personal sanitation among the pioneers. Throughout each day of travel emigrant trains made regular stops near bushes or gullies, it being understood that men went to the right and women to the left. "I have heard my grandmother tell how, when they were on the open prairie, without even a bush to squat behind, the women would walk in groups to the left and several would stand in a line or semi-circle to shelter each other. With their long, full skirts, they formed an effective screen and retained some bit of their womanly modesty."[10] For Morgan, Juanita remained a living repository of pioneer history.

In June 1946 Juanita informed Morgan of the excommunication of Fawn Brodie. Juanita had naively hoped for a less punitive response to Brodie's biography of Joseph Smith. "Now that it has done its duty on that point," she sarcastically wrote, "the Church can feel much more righteous, I imagine." For the leaders of the Church it was more than a matter of feeling righteous, for few other works in the literature of Mormonism directed such a lethal attack upon the Church's faith in its founder's heroic perfection and upon its claim to represent an exclusive restoration of the authentic Christianity. Inevitably Brodie's excommunication augmented the suspense in which Juanita lived. Although the massacre was a topic of less importance, Juanita knew that an objective treatment of it would seriously impugn the moral stature of those cherished pioneers who had established the Church in the Rocky Mountains. In the foregoing letter, Juanita also informed Morgan of the appearance in *The Improvement Era* of her article on the St. George temple, submitted long before. Dolefully she commented: "I consider it my final bow to the Mormon audience, for I feel sure that as soon as the MMM study is finished I'll be OUT."[11] Juanita had a far greater stake in remaining a Mormon than Fawn Brodie. Long before her excommunication, Brodie had moved beyond the borders of Utah and had married a non-Mormon. Juanita could expect the support and encouragement of only a handful of friends and loved ones in the event of her excommunication. In overwhelming numbers the people with whom she associated would have interpreted her ejection from the Church as a shocking disgrace.

In June Juanita accompanied Will to Salt Lake for a postmaster's convention. In mid-July the couple combined a family vacation and a working visit to the Huntingon. The final few days before departure were an agony of waiting for the four Brooks children. Setting out on a Thursday noon, the family traveled in Will's Chevrolet, well stocked with bedrolls, food, and water. They crossed the desert in the light of a full moon, pausing to sleep briefly beside the highway. In the morning they drove to the Huntington and toured the grounds and buildings so that the children would know their mother's working environment. Then Juanita remained at the library to study the transcripts of the Lee trials, and Will and the children began what Juanita described as "a four-day whirl of beach bathing, zoos, uptown shows, parks, shopping, etc.etc.—oh, yes, and a boat trip."[12] When the family returned, they paused to sleep beside the highway in the desert. "In the morning as we were building a fire, and preparing some breakfast," Kay would later write, "a sports car went by, and someone yelled out the window 'Oakies.' That really upset Willa, but I didn't know why at the time."[13]

Upon her return, Juanita wrote a letter to Leslie Bliss proposing that she show the manuscript of her study of the massacre to the president of the Church, "explaining that I have written the truth as I have found it, but if he or any of his historical consultants can point out defects in my research, in my thinking, or the pattern of my facts, I shall be glad to make proper corrections."[14] She had first suggested this drastic eventuality to Morgan, who surprisingly had endorsed it as a means of achieving a complete objectivity. Bliss responded with alarm to the possibility of an expurgated manuscript. He had understood, he told Juanita, that Robert Glass Cleland was to have the first look at the preliminary draft. Hastily Juanita assured Bliss that indeed Cleland should have the first look and therewith dropped the idea of showing it to any Mormon official.

One sees in such behavior an unmistakable pattern. Earlier Juanita had asked Cleland to assist in a subterfuge by certifying that she had been recruited to research the massacre. Next she had revealed her project to church president George Albert Smith and had rejoiced when he had not expressly forbidden her to undertake it. She had assiduously pursued the affidavits in the keeping of David O. McKay not only because they would have proved valuable as sources but because McKay's cooperation would have amounted to a tacit approval of her project. And now, during the summer of 1946, she briefly considered allowing the Church to censor her manuscript. The pattern would persist. From time to time during the next fifteen years she would attempt to elicit an official approval of her interpretation of the massacre. One surmises that conformity had an undeniable appeal to Juanita. Everywhere in Mormondom conformity was preached and practiced and reinforced by an abundant folklore as to the dire consequences of dissent. Besides fearing excommunication, Juanita suffered the guilt of disloyalty. In certain moods she regarded her dissent as perverse and reprehensible. In short, she was a complex and ambivalent person.

On August 20, 1946, Juanita penned a letter in ink to Morgan. It was Clair's wedding day, and she was under a hair dryer in a local beauty parlor "with the blower making a miniature hurricane around my head and burning my ears off—as hot as the winds that used to come off the mesa." Clair and his bride, LaVon Adams, would be married at four o'clock in the temple. At eight there would be a reception in the ward recreation hall. Juanita would wear "a gray-blue formal and a corsage of a rose-colored camillia (if that's how you spell it)." She and Will would take their place in a reception line with the bride and groom, the parents of the bride, and sundry best men and maids of honor. A crowd of well-wishers would yield gifts to little girls in frilly dresses and patiently file by to give their congratulations. Clair and LaVon struck Juanita as terribly young. "After seeing these two gum-chewing youngsters dance blithely into matrimony I feel as ancient and wise as a Sphinx. How much they do have to learn! She'd better be a good getter-uppper in the morning if she gets him to school on time. He's 21 and she 19—full of energy and pep heretofore quite undirected."[15]

In the early fall Aura suffered another nervous breakdown. Within an hour of receiving Carl's plea for help, Juanita was on a bus for Los Angeles. When she entered Aura's bedroom, her sister burst into tears and wondered whether someone had died or had been hurt in an accident. Juanita gave her a hot bath and massage and lay in bed with her answering her questions. Late in the night Aura awoke with a start and commenced to sing, whistle, and speak incoherently. Eventually Juanita calmed her with another hot bath and massage. Several days later she assisted Carl in committing Aura to the psychiatric ward of the Los Angeles general hospital. It was a difficult ordeal for Juanita, who had a horror of what she called insane asylums. Upon her return to St. George Juanita wrote Morgan that she could discern a dizzying momentum in her sister from childhood. Aura had always applied herself compulsively, practicing the piano for hours and engaging in great stints of housework. "Now she is like a machine that gathers strength and speed and runs so fast that it must fly apart and disintegrate entirely from its own inner force."[16]

In early November 1946 Juanita read *No, Ma'am, That's Not History*, a rebuttal of Brodie's biography by Hugh Nibley, a prominent professor of ancient scripture at BYU. Juanita soon wrote Nibley a not altogether polite critique of his rebuttal. She declared her own loyalty to the Church and chided those Mormons who by reacting hysterically to Brodie had given her work "an importance greater than it deserves." Brodie's book could have no compelling power over the faithful because its original premise—that there was no God—invalidated its successive conclusions. "For those of us to whom God is a reality, there is no common ground in all her study. We cannot accept her major premise, hence cannot follow her logic." Juanita twitted

Nibley for certain nonsensical assertions, among them these brash words: "The gospel as the Mormons know it sprang full grown from the words of Joseph Smith. It has never been worked over or touched up in any way, and is free of revisions and alterations." Derisively she commented: "What a delight that should be to the Fundamentalists!" Had there been no revision in the law of consecration, she asked? What about polygamy? The United Order? The old doctrines of the geographical location of the Ten Tribes of Israel and of the imminent return of the Saints to Jackson County, Missouri? "I think I see in our church evidence[s] of change—even since President Smith has come into the head of it—that are wholesome and healthy and a good reason for alert and progressive people to have faith in it," she concluded. "I can think of nothing more terrible than one that was immune to revisions or alterations, one that could not claim continuous revelation."[17]

Juanita produced two Thanksgiving dinners, one on Thursday for Brooks relatives, another on Friday for Leavitt relatives. Among a number of holiday phone calls was one from Aura and Carl. Having responded well to electroshock therapy, Aura had been leaving the hospital to shop and visit and expected to leave permanently before Christmas. "In counting our blessings," Juanita wrote, "that ranked first."[18]

On November 28, 1946, Juanita received a letter that opened a long and fateful friendship. It was a handwritten note from Miss Ettie Lee of Los Angeles, who had heard that Juanita was writing a book about her grandfather, John D. Lee. "If that be true please advise me as our family has some documentary material that should be used if the *true* John D. Lee is to be introduced to the reading public."[19] Juanita replied on the same day, needing no other bait than the prospect of fresh sources for her study of the massacre. She praised John D. Lee as "a man of superior intelligence and of unquestioning loyalty to the church" and mentioned that her own grandfather had also been involved in the massacre. "If you can trust me enough to let me see your material, I shall be glad."[20] A chain reaction had been set up. Ettie Lee quickly replied that she had asked her relatives, most of whom lived in Arizona, to send their materials to her in order to make them accessible to Juanita. Then with a hint of regal condescension, she asked to know Juanita's credentials: "Being a teacher, it is natural for me perhaps to observe that your letter was particularly well expressed and that pleased me since English teaching in the high schools and both colleges of this city has been my work since 1914. If it is not presumptious [*sic*] may I ask about your background so that I may pass it on to my family, who are jurists, teachers, and bank officials as well as one journalist; and I will, therefore, be questioned."[21] Juanita immediately mailed a brief vita. Ettie Lee, for her part, had been raised in Arizona and had taught English principally in the junior high schools of Los Angeles. Shrewd and determined, she had become wealthy during World War II by buying and renting old apartment buildings. At the moment of first writing Juanita, she also owned a large commercial apricot orchard.

Juanita mailed Christmas gifts of molasses and butter. One package went to Morgan, who returned from a prolonged visit to his sister's house in New York to find the molasses can sprung open and the butter turned rancid. "Anyhow," he wrote, "you were sweet to think of sending me this present, and it was through no fault of yours that I wasn't on hand to take proper care of it on its arrival."[22] An embarrassed Juanita replied: "You know, I told Will way before Christmas that something had happend to that crazy molasses. Damn funny that it had to be yours that got smashed. . . . And the butter! Anyway, I think my face will be red every time I think of it for the next twenty years. There is no smell in the world quite like that of stale butter, and how well I know it!"[23]

In February 1947 Juanita mailed *Arizona Highways* a brief article about the St. George temple, which the editor had solicited some time before. Appearing in the April 1947 issue, "To the Glory of God" featured the construction of the sacred building, giving particular emphasis to the communal effort of the temple builders. "After seventy years it remains impressive as ever, rising like a block of light to stir the heart of the most skeptical with a feeling akin to awe. Let us not say simply that it cost nearly a million dollars; let us say that it cost the reverent labor of a community for seven years."[24] This was Juanita's third brief publication about the St. George temple. A fourth, "Symbol of a People's Faith," would appear in the July 1947 issue of *Utah Magazine*.

In early March Juanita declared that spring had long since arrived: "My jonquils and pansies have never been nicer; the vegetable garden is up, the trees are showing green." Her sons delivered newspapers every morning now; eating breakfast at seven, they came home ravenous from school at noon. Willa had been elected "bobby-sox girl" of the seventh grade and would compete for a school title against girls from the eighth, ninth, and tenth grades. "She couldn't be more excited if she were running for 'Miss America.' "[25]

In late March 1947 Juanita took an extraordinarily fast-paced and far-ranging trip at the expense of the Huntington. She left St. George by bus late on a Monday evening. On Tuesday she flew from Salt Lake to San Francisco. Wednesday, Thursday, and Friday she spent in the Bancroft Library at the University of California at Berkeley. She found few materials relating to her study of the massacre, but could at least boast that she had inspected the Bancroft. More significantly, she listed 247 items relating to Utah history which the Huntington would consider photostating for its own collection. Friday night she took a bus for Los Angeles. Saturday she spent in the Huntington. Sunday morning found her in the Los Angeles airport, penciling a letter to Morgan. She would shortly take off in a commuter airplane for Cedar City. She didn't know whether she would catch a bus or thumb a ride to St. George. "But I'll be there in time to cook the evening meal, I'll bet." Will had played cook and comforter of children long enough. Besides having routine reports to prepare, Will would begin "installing city delivery of mail on Monday. It's the end of the quarter for him and the end of the month, so I must take over my responsibilities."[26]

During Easter vacation in early April the folklorists Austin and Alta Fife were visitors in the Brooks home. Juanita and Will had first become acquainted with the couple in 1939 when Mabel Jarvis had led them to their door in search of folktales about the Three Nephites. Several of Juanita's contributions were thereafter cited in their article "The Legend of the Three Nephites Among the Mormons," published in *The Journal of American Folklore* in 1940. At Easter 1947, Juanita and Will again assisted the Fifes by assembling friends and relatives to sing folk songs which the Fifes recorded.

Perhaps the most interesting aspect of the Fifes' visit was Austin's account of censorship at the University of Utah. In the summer of 1946, Hector Lee, director of the Utah Humanities Research Foundation, had solicited an article for the first issue of the *Utah Humanities Review* (later the *Western Humanities Review*). Fife's article, "Folk Belief and Mormon Cultural Autonomy," described a host of cherished Mormon beliefs and practices in the dispassionate and perhaps too naturalistic language of the professional folklorist. A member of Hector Lee's staff alerted church officials, who protested the publication of the article. Although Fife revised the piece, Lee's staff continued to disagree about it. Lee placed it in the hands of university president A. Ray Olpin, who decided against publication.[27] Juanita responded to Austin's tale of censorship with understandable dismay. She was particularly disillusioned with the university president. "I could hardly believe it of him, for I had hoped that in him the University would have a liberal, courageous leader."[28]

Near the same time an incident occurred in St. George which, by demonstrating the dynamics of a mob, clarified the massacre for Juanita. Young telephone operators—Juanita called them girls—had been picketing the telephone building. Men of anti-union sentiment—two physicians, a lawyer, several merchants and service station operators—were indignant. Someone produced a key to the garage where the volunteer fire department kept the city fire truck. The girls refused to leave and the men turned a high-pressure hose on them. "When they stood and took their drenching, some of the men in the crowd reacted against the whole thing, and when they learned that one was a GI's wife nearly five months pregnant, they all left the scene hurriedly." When the union threatened to sue, no one knew anything about the incident. "Now, though they did not approve of the doing, witnesses will not testify in court. On a small and unimportant scale, it's a dead-ringer for the thing that went on at the Meadows."[29]

In mid-April Washington County held its official celebration of the centennial of the arrival of the Mormon pioneers in Utah. For months Juanita had taken very seriously her membership on the county centennial committee. As she had traveled, she had been dismayed elsewhere by confusion and inappropriate preparations. In February she returned from Provo and Salt Lake in great indignation over plans for a "modernistic art show entirely divorced from Utah or her people or her accomplishments"[30] and for a "fool show RAMROD, a fourth rate western, filmed in the vicinity of Zion Canyon and so labeled a Utah Centennial product."[31] Juanita's contempt extended to Kate B. Carter, the powerful president of the Daughters of the Utah Pioneers. Juanita approved of Carter's desire to orient the centennial celebration toward pioneer history and of her organization's ongoing publication of pioneer diaries and records. However, she listened with mounting disgust as on a Sunday evening Carter told a

BYU faculty group that she insisted upon purging documents of offensive passages before permitting their publication. For Juanita, such bowdlerizing of historical sources was as alien to the authentic Utah as a modernistic art show or a fourth-rate Western: "When [Carter] talked of 'editing' journals, one of the audience . . . asked specifically what it was that she called 'editing.' She explained that she omitted material that seemed not important or that was repetitious and then said, 'I never allow anything into print that I think will be injurious to my church, or that will in any way reflect discredit upon our pioneers. I hope that if I ever do, I shall lose my position and my power to do.' "[32]

Juanita was pleased to assist the other members of the county committee in preparing an appropriately historical celebration. She collaborated with Mabel Jarvis and Grace Woodbury in writing the script of an elaborate pageant. She hurriedly wrote a summary history of the settlement of Washington County for publication as a souvenir pamphlet. She promised a copy to Leslie Bliss since she was eager that he not think she had been shirking her duties for the Huntington: "While it is not documented, it is accurate, I believe, and may be of use. I feel sure that it will help to unearth other records in different parts of the state, since there will be 7,000 copies printed and circulated."[33] From the ninth to the fifteenth of April 1947 the celebration unfolded in a satisfying manner. One evening there was a formal centennial ball in Hurricane. On the last two evenings the pageant, "The Spirit of Dixie," held forth on the temple grounds. "The pageant was so much better than I had hoped for," Juanita wrote, "the music score simply super, the 300-odd characters all local people. Anyway, it was honest, an outgrowth of the culture of this section and our tribute to the founders of the Cotton Mission."[34]

During the celebration, eight-year-old Tony contracted an ear infection. He reacted to sulfa with a scarlet rash, and when his fever abated, a side of his face was paralyzed. "In all my experience, nothing has simply got me worse. His funny little face, so peaked and pale anyway, now dead on one side. When he would laugh or cry it was positively sickening. I insisted all the time that it must be temporary. It HAD to be. But I was beset by such a heavy fear." Juanita wrote these words to Morgan two weeks following the first sign of Tony's infection. At last he could smile a little and blink his eye. "Tony is singing, so I've decided that if Tony can sing, I can finally write to you." She had received Morgan's gift copy of *The Great Salt Lake* and had found it a merciful distraction from Tony's affliction. "It's superb how you have managed to give the impression of all your great research and your rich background without making the book heavy with it." As for her own writing, she had at last, after many false starts, mailed the manuscript of her history of the Mountain Meadows massacre to Robert Glass Cleland at the Huntington.[35]

In early May Juanita read a brief paper before the Arts and Letters section of the Utah Academy at the University of Utah. Faced with a last-minute cancellation, the chairman of the section had asked Juanita to substitute. Her paper, "The First One Hundred Years of Southern Utah History," would be published in the Academy's *Proceedings* of 1946–47, appearing belatedly in 1949.

It was one of the best expressions of a historian's credo Juanita would ever make. It was, furthermore, an open denunciation of Kate Carter's editorial practices. Juanita repeated her conviction that many of the centennial observances throughout the state were failing to celebrate the authentic Utah past, either by ignoring it through art and entertainment having nothing to do with Utah or by prettifying it in a dishonest manner. Citing the Daughters of the Utah Pioneers, she declared: "They do not wish to see their pioneers realistically as tough frontiersmen, sometimes disagreeing among themselves, quarreling upon occasion, swearing under provocation, drinking a little once-in-a-while, loyal to each other, but cheating Gentiles with impunity. Like the pink-and-white portraits of the leaders, all smoothed of character wrinkles, they lack only a halo. Yet to guild the lily is not more ridiculous than to put powder and rouge on their leathered, weatherbeaten faces."[36] The saga of the pioneers, Juanita asserted, was replete with failures: failed enterprises like the manufacture of iron at Cedar City and the mining of lead at Las Vegas and failed social experiments like polygamy, the Law of Consecration, and the United Order. Nonetheless, the pioneers had survived, leaving "a residue of achievement worthy of respect." While the first settlers of St. George were still living in their wagons, they had organized a lyceum and at its first meeting listened to a lecture on English grammar. "Imagine men who had gee'd and haw'd at oxen all day and women who had managed a camping-out household in December sitting on the ground in a candle lit tent to listen to a lecture on the better use of the English language."[37] For these reasons, Juanita concluded, Mormons should strive to understand their *real* past. "We should study our history in a dispassionate and objective manner, not as proselyters of the faith, but as historians. We should reproduce the diaries and journals of our pioneers without deletion or modification."[38]

In late June Juanita conferred with Cleland at the Huntington about her history of the massacre—some three months after mailing her manuscript. He recommended further revision and urged her to submit the work to a commercial publisher or a university press. Juanita understood him to promise that the Huntington would publish it if no other publisher were found.[39] She brought the draft away and worked intermittently at revising it during the summer and fall.

Mid-summer the Brookses bought a new car and went on a combined collecting trip and family vacation, which Will narrated in a letter to Bob. The family stayed three days in Provo, where Juanita hunted diaries while Will and the children fished, went to movies, took drives up Provo Canyon, and visited relatives. On the Twenty-fourth of July they stationed themselves on Eighth South and Main in Salt Lake and watched the Pioneer Day parade—the biggest ever in commemoration of the centennial. In Yellowstone Park, they gazed at Old Faithful, did a little fishing, and ate at a cafeteria. "Tony got quite a kick out of collecting his own dish of food, I think he picked up about $1.15 for his feed, he found that he could not quite consume it." Having visited Ernest and Margie in Graybull, Wyoming, the family drove homeward via Jackson Hole, the Teton Pass, and Idaho Falls, where, faithful Mormons that they were, they toured the Idaho Falls temple grounds.[40]

In October 1947 Juanita made another trip to the Huntington, taking her revision of the history of the massacre. Because Cleland was out of town for an extended period, Bliss suggested that she keep the draft. Disappointed, she continued in her letters to remind Bliss of potential buyers for her projected book. While in Los Angeles she had called on Ettie Lee, whom she described as "a woman of considerable means, I would judge, and a very intelligent person all around." The wealthy spinster claimed that the descendants of her grandfather, John D. Lee, 4,000 strong by her count, would all want to buy a copy of the book. "I think she is over estimating the number, but at any rate she is very militant about seeing that he has justice done him. I insisted that I was not writing to clear him of blame, but she feels that anything that is done will be better for them than the present interpretation."[41] Similarly she did not fail to report to Bliss her discussion of the massacre before a group in Cedar City at the invitation of William R. Palmer, who next to Juanita was the foremost authority on the massacre. She and Will drove to Cedar City with friends, where they found an audience of some sixty prominent citizens. She was very pleased with the response. "In spite of any official stand by the church, they in that area know the facts quite well and are anxious to have them presented and very liberal in their own interpretation. So many are eager to see the work in print and say that they want copies. . . . "[42]

At Thanksgiving Ettie Lee penned Juanita a note on flowered stationery and enclosed an early Christmas gift, a check to be spent on "whatever will give you the most joy and satisfaction." It was clear that Juanita had already emerged in Ettie's mind as a champion and defender. She declared Juanita's recent visit in her home "one of the genuinely happy experiences of my life. Ever since I learned of the tragic experiences of my worthy grandfather when I was a mere child I have prayed almost daily for his vindication and for a greater understanding of all of the whole unfortunate affair."[43] Juanita responded with effusive thanks.

Despite the usual interruptions of the Christmas season, Juanita pushed hard to finish her revision of the massacre manuscript. Since Cleland had last seen it, she had added a preliminary chapter and had entirely rewritten the other chapters. In mid-December she mailed it to him, expressing her optimistic belief "that the L.D.S. people as a whole will accept my conclusions and will welcome this frank study."[44] On January 2, 1948, Cleland wrote a disturbing letter. He would not read the manuscript until he returned from the East, and he wanted Juanita to understand "that the Library has no claim of any kind upon the manuscript; nor any authority to tell you by whom it is to be published." Juanita took that to mean that the Huntington was not interested in publishing the work. "Will says it is O.K.," she wrote Morgan, "but I feel a little like I'd been slapped, and can't tell why." Her pessimism, accumulated from numerous rejections, had asserted itself: "I have felt that someone will publish it, but I dread to start the merry-go-round of finding who."[45]

In early February she asked Cleland to return the manuscript. He soon complied, apparently without having given it more than a cursory reading. He recommended that she submit it to Alfred Knopf. He had recently spoken of it to Mrs. Knopf, whose interest in a book-length study of the massacre had triggered Juanita's ambition two years earlier. If Knopf turned it down, Cleland recommended that she submit it to Stanford University Press. "You have made what seems to me to be the most authoritative study of the Mountain Meadows Massacre yet undertaken," he complimented her. "So far as I can tell it conforms to all of the canons of scholarship and I believe it will be of great value to the students of various phases of American history. . . . "[46] She did not submit to Knopf, appreciating too keenly that Knopf was in poor repute in Utah for having published *No Man Knows My History.* Instead, she responded to an inquiry from Rinehart & Co. and in mid-February mailed that firm the manuscripts of both "Quicksand and Cactus" and "The Mountain Meadows Massacre."

During the winter and spring of 1948 Juanita worked on an article for *The Pacific Spectator,* a humanities journal published at Stanford University. In November 1947, the editor had solicited a piece on an undefined topic.[47] An agreeable Juanita had proposed Jacob Hamblin. In February 1948 she submitted a first draft, which the editor returned for minor revision. Near the end of April she submitted the finished piece, "Jacob Hamblin: Apostle to the Lamanites," which would appear in the summer 1948 issue.

It was Juanita's best statement about this frontiersman, far surpassing in quality if not in length the biography of Hamblin she would write in 1952 (unpublished until 1980). The article had no footnotes yet achieved a satisfactory documentation through textual references to pioneer records. Briefly surveying Hamblin's life, it focused upon his attempts to convert and civilize the Paiutes, Navajos, and Hopis. It cast him as a hero yet delineated his failures. It cited his despair over the irredeemable Paiutes of the desert: "They are in a very low, degraded condition indeed, loathsome and filthy beyond description. I have wished many times for the moment that my lot was cast among a more cleanly people; where there could be found something desirable, something cheering to a person accustomed to civilized life."[48] The article absolved Hamblin of participation in the Mountain Meadows massacre; however, it admitted that "there might be reason to hold that he was accessory after the fact, in that he learned all about the tragedy and yet did nothing to bring any of the guilty to justice. . . . "[49] It conveyed the futility of his later years and the igno-

minious obscurity of his death in New Mexico: "Few men have seemed
less heroic at their passing. His wife Louisa prepared his body for burial
on her 'off chill day' [she being afflicted with malaria]; passing strangers dug his grave; there were not enough well people in the village to
hold a funeral ceremony. Not a flower, not a song relieved the "stark-
ness of it all."[50]

In April Rinehart rejected both "Quicksand and Cactus"
and "The Mountain Meadows Massacre." In May Juanita carried the
manuscript of the latter work on a collecting trip to Salt Lake. It was
her great pleasure to visit Dale Morgan and deliver the manuscript for
his scrutiny.[51] For months her correspondence with Morgan had been
infrequent. As he returned to Utah from Washington, determined to
begin a three-volume history of the Mormons, Morgan had slowly followed their westward trail across the nation, gathering documents and
scouting local landscapes. During Juanita's May visit, he escorted her
and Vesta Crawford, by now an associate editor of the *Relief Society
Magazine*, on a Sunday tour of Parleys and Emigration canyons to orient them to the route by which the pioneers had entered the Salt
Lake Valley.[52] One imagines the outing. Morgan is at the wheel of his
1942 Hudson. While he drives he carries on a monologue, for Juanita
cannot pass notes to him. The two women listen respectfully because
he is an encyclopedia of historical lore. On top of Little Mountain the
friends, dressed in their Sunday best, stroll through the sagebrush
and oak, examining the still visible track of pioneer wagons and gazing westward where the canyon opens into the valley. Juanita freely
writes notes to Morgan, asking questions and noting the observations
she and Vesta have made to one another. She is utterly solicitous of
the deaf man. Therefore it is still he who does most of the talking.

Before returning to St. George, Juanita attempted to effect
an exchange of copied documents between the Huntington and the
Daughters of the Utah Pioneers. Kate Carter had recently issued an
edict against members conveying documents "to anyone working for
libraries or interests outside the state,"[53] a proscription aimed chiefly
at Juanita. Under Carter's imperious guidance, the organization opened
its well-stocked archives only to members, limited to women descended
from persons having arrived in Utah before the advent of the railroad
in 1869. Failing to gain an audience with Carter, Juanita wrote a letter
from home. She explained that the Huntington retained copies of pioneer documents and returned the originals to their Utah owners; she

also specified the advantages of an exchange: "For every original which you will allow Huntington to photograph, you may have a photostatic copy of another original which you do not have. In this way you can also build up your own collection at the same time that you keep all you have."[54] Piqued by Juanita's recent utterances against her editorial practices, Carter for the moment ignored her proposal.

It is not apparent why Juanita was not a member of the Daughters of the Utah Pioneers, a chapter of which had long existed in St. George. Perhaps the group's policy of exclusiveness had violated her ideal of equality. In any event, as she took measure of the central organization's proscriptive ruling in late 1947, she persuaded her mother to join. Mary Leavitt obligingly went through the elaborate process of attesting to her pioneer ancestry. On March 15, 1948, Kate Carter affixed her bold signature to the application.[55] It is unlikely that she took the time to peruse the document. If she had, she might have realized that Juanita had thereby gained an indirect access to her society's restricted archives.

In the meantime, Juanita tactlessly prepared another article which could only offend Carter. For some time Juanita had exchanged documents with Hector Lee, under whose direction the Utah Humanities Research Foundation at the University of Utah had begun to collect pioneer records. In the spring of 1948 she complied with Lee's request for an article for the *Utah Humanities Review*. Appearing in the July 1948 issue, "Let's Preserve Our Records" offered a hearty draught of Juanita's adventures in collecting diaries and urged her readers to preserve conscientiously their ancestral records. Earnestly she admonished that "the first requirement in the preservation of documents is that they should stand *absolutely unchanged*." With the archives of the Daughters of the Utah Pioneers in mind, she further admonished that "once preserved, these records should be made available not only to members of the family, but to responsible students in any field."[56]

During the summer of 1948 Juanita busied herself with other writing and editing tasks. At Hector Lee's request, she edited excerpts from the journal of John Pulsipher. The first installment appeared in the October 1948 issue of the *Utah Humanities Review*; the second installment appeared in the January 1949 issue of the renamed *Western Humanities Review*. Juanita also prepared for *The Improvement Era* an article featuring the adventures of Jacob Hamblin and his associ-

ates. Titled "Ye Who Are Called to Labor," it appeared serially in the
August and September 1948 issues. Although it was generally an undis-
tinguished piece, it achieved moving emotion in recounting the death
of Maria Haskell. Accidentally shot by an Indian boy, the pregnant
Maria lingered in agony, being delivered of a stillborn child before she
died. No one in the tiny settlement was immune to horror, least of all
her stunned husband as he stood at the side of her coffin: "Thales
looked at her long, his face working and tears streaming down his
cheeks. She lay so still and white, with the wee baby nestled in her
arm—all his hopes and his dreams gone. The chalky, drawn face with
the purple streak along the neck did not seem like the Maria of a few
days ago. Only the crown of her braids and the little curling tendrils
about her face seemed natural. He picked up one end of the coffin lid
and motioned for Jacob to help him replace it."[57]

One knows that Juanita shed tears as she wrote this passage. Her friends and children observed that she often wept as she
read them passages from pioneer diaries; she had internalized the grief
of her ancestors and to it added her own misfortunes. Yet her moods
shifted readily. She also wrote in the summer of 1948 a light piece
called "Trippingly Off the Tongue," which took second place in a contest sponsored by the League of Utah Writers and the *Deseret News*.
Appearing in that paper in September, the article presented colorful
coinages of language from Bunkerville. Among her sources was her
father: " 'Don't stand there like the fifth calf,' he often said, when urging a person to sit up and join us at a meal. Anyone who knows the
anatomy of a cow knows that there are but four places at the table,
and the fifth calf must fare poorly indeed."[58]

She also worked to improve the manuscript of "The Mountain Meadows Massacre," which Morgan had returned with his comments late in May. In July she mailed it back, having "typed it all over
again—the third complete re-writing—from the first page to the
last."[59] Morgan was impressed but in August sent further suggestions
and in September followed with detailed instructions for her bibliography, to which he added titles hitherto missing.[60] In the meantime,
he wrote Wallace Stegner at Stanford asking whether the university
press would be interested in the manuscript. Stegner quickly wrote
letters to Morgan and Juanita, making a generous offer. "Since I have
connections both with Houghton Mifflin and with the Stanford University Press, I'd be delighted to do whatever I can in either quarter."[61]

As September closed Juanita mailed the much revised manuscript to Stegner, who carried it east to Houghton Mifflin, for whom he served as West Coast editor. A month later that firm declined the manuscript, whereupon Stegner put it into the hands of Donald Bean, director of Stanford University Press.

In September Juanita joined Morgan in a memorable tour of historical sites in southern Utah. Short of funds, Morgan had postponed work on his history of the Mormons to undertake a historical trails map for the publicity department of the Utah state government. The two friends met in Cedar City and drove in Morgan's car to Mountain Meadows. Wandering afoot "through something less than a thousand miles of sage,"[62] they failed to locate the massacre site. The next morning they returned with Will, who led them to the spot. The next day they explored the Virgin Narrows, the Beaver Dam Mountains, and the Virgin Valley. The following day, they traversed the Hurricane Cliffs and traveled into the Arizona Strip, dropping in for good measure on Jonreed and Verda Lauritzen at Short Creek. In these peregrinations, Will continued as their indispensable guide.

In October 1948 Juanita, Will, and their children attended the annual Leavitt reunion in Bunkerville. There were hundreds in attendance. Registration was at nine, a business meeting at ten, a barbecue at noon, a variety show at three, a dance at eight. The next day there were excursions to the St. George temple for the pious and to Hoover Dam for the curious. Because all nine of Juanita's siblings and their spouses had gathered, dinners and visits went on for days after the official end of the reunion.[63]

The clutter in the Brooks home was exacerbated by Will's preparations for the deer hunt, which opened on the Saturday following the reunion. It was a memorable hunt. On Friday afternoon Will, his sons Walt, Grant, and Clair, his brother Ed, and various cousins and friends assembled in a camp among the junipers north of the Pine Valley Mountains—an area to which Will would return each fall during the next thirty years. There is a photograph of Will in camp. He stands in a state of unhygienic joy amidst a litter of tarps, mattresses, and cookware. His ample belly, half concealed by a baggy red sweatshirt, hangs over a tightly cinched belt. On his head is a battered Stetson around which he has wound a red bandanna.

As dawn broke Will fired the first shot of the hunt, missing a large buck. Before nine he had knocked down a four point with a spread of twenty-four inches. As he gutted the animal, a seven-point buck rushed by. Will's bloody fingers slipped repeatedly from the cocking mechanism of his .30-.40 Krag. When he finally shouldered the rifle and pulled the trigger, he discovered he had forgotten to eject the spent shell. By noon on Sunday the party had filled every permit with a large buck—and had given away three. "It does seem exaggerated," Will wrote Bob, "but the story is correct; I will send you a picture if they turn out good."[64] The hunters had generated, as Juanita had predicted they would, "a new edition of stories to add to the ones we have listened to for the past year. With the mountains as lovely as they are now, I can well understand the urge to get out in them."[65]

In late October Juanita met with Kate Carter in Salt Lake. Carter declared herself too distracted by her efforts to negotiate state funding for a Daughters of the Utah Pioneers museum to consider Juanita's proposal for an exchange of documents. "As I left," Juanita wrote Leslie Bliss, "she followed me out into the hall to ask if I could help her locate a suitable diary for her next publication of *Heart Throbs*. I promised that I would see what I could do."[66] Juanita could scent victory.

Juanita had begun to think seriously of writing a biography of John D. Lee, as Ettie Lee constantly urged her to do. In order to explore this possibility, she attempted in November to examine the Lee diaries held by the Church. She and Manetta Henrie, a granddaughter of Lee who lived in Provo, called at the Church Historian's Office where Juanita signed Henrie's name to a request for a Lee diary. A young man naively brought out three small handwritten volumes, which Juanita eagerly perused near a window. Only narrowly did the two confederates avoid a sudden eviction. "While we were examining the last two volumes, we heard Brother [A. William] Lund begin to scold him loudly and angrily, asking if he did not know that NO ONE should see these except after permission from Bro. Joseph Fielding [Smith]. I sat quietly and read as fast as I could, determined to get all that I could before I was literally kicked out, while Mrs. Henrie went in to explain that she had meant to break no rules, she thought she had a right to see the records of her grandfather. 'How do I know that you are his grand-daughter?' Brother Lund demanded, and she quietly unrolled her long sheet of genealogical research. He finally quieted down, and we stayed until quitting time."[67]

In late November Juanita spent several afternoons in the library of Dixie College making arrangements for a John D. Lee memorial bookshelf. Some months earlier, Ettie Lee had offered a gift of $1,000 for a collection of books—a part of the businesswoman's determined strategy to renovate the reputation of her grandfather. Heartily endorsing the proposal, the college president, Glenn E. Snow, provided a locked, glass-enclosed case and appointed a committee to select the books. As winter approached, Juanita submitted an announcement of the gift to the local newspaper. Citizens reacted positively with the exception of a woman who delivered Juanita a whispered protest at a club meeting.[68]

On a snowy Sunday in January 1949, Juanita attended stake conference in the St. George tabernacle, where she saw the young wife of Stanton Schmutz, a missionary whom Juanita had taught in Sunday School. A week later she wrote the absent missionary a comforting description of his wife: "She looked so like a pale Madonna to me that I could hardly keep my eyes off her—her skin so clear that it was almost transparent and her hair so lovely in the light of the sun from the south window." Then Juanita responded to a request Stanton had made in a Christmas card for information about John D. Lee. Eloquently she reviewed both Lee's astonishing achievements and his disgraceful part in the massacre. She emphasized that Lee "was not the most responsible for it, nor was he the leader." As for his having been singled out for trial and execution, "it seemed the best thing to do, the easiest way to quiet all the stir, to just let him take all the blame and close the incident once and for all."[69]

Upon completing the three-page letter, she was alarmed by the thought that it would pass into hands other than Stanton's. Thereupon she retyped a precise duplicate with a carbon. She mailed the original ribbon sheet to Stanton, placed the carbon in her own files, and mailed the second ribbon sheet to Apostle Harold B. Lee with a cover letter requesting the opportunity for a face-to-face discussion of John D. Lee. "I am in touch with many of the Lee descendants and find them people of extra-ordinary ability of firm faith in the gospel—but with the feeling that they have suffered a grave injustice and have carried a heavy load through three generations."[70] She also expressed a hope that the apostle would file the letter where it would be available in case someone called it into question. Anxiously expecting that sooner or later she would be summoned before a church court, Juanita wished to ensure that the indictment be based upon her actual writings and statements rather than upon the distortions of rumor and malice.

If she had hoped for a friend in Elder Lee, she was quickly undeceived. The apostle's polite answer made it clear that there was no connection between his ancestors and those of John D. Lee. Ignoring her request for an audience, he expressed a fear that her defense of the executed pioneer would lend credence to the accusation that "the leaders of the Church directed this killing." He passed on to Juanita the recommendation of Anthony W. Ivins, a deceased apostle from Dixie. "On one occasion he discussed with me some of these matters pertaining to the Mountain Meadows Massacre and at a certain point he stopped and said, 'Well, Brother Lee, I think I shouldn't make any further statement—too much has already been said—I think the wisest thing is to avoid unnecessary discussion of this subject."[71]

During the severe winter of 1949, which brought deep snow and frozen plumbing to Dixie, Juanita's sister Mary came from Mesquite to await the birth of her eighth child. Three times Mary had awakened in the night with labor pains and Fenton had driven her during heavy snowstorms over the Beaver Dam Mountains. "Cars would be stalled and slipped off into gutters all the way up the mountain. But we kept [going] each time—plowing our way thro. Never stopping—or we would never get started again. And on the north side going down was even worse. (Some one had to be watching over us.)"[72] Twice her labor pains halted and Mary returned to Mesquite. The third time she decided to stay with Juanita and Will. On February 5, she bore a ten-pound son. Leaving the hospital after a few days, she stayed a week with the Brookses.

As a belated Dixie spring bloomed in March, Juanita had startling news for her friends: "I had the surprise of my young life last week when His Excellency, Governor J. Bracken Lee, appointed me to the Utah State Historical Society Board of Control. I'm sure he does not know what an ardent Democrat I have always been. He couldn't and ever put me where I could say a word."[73] Thus began Juanita's long and influential tenure on the Board of State History. Dale Morgan, who had known of the appointment in advance, expressed his pleasure. "The Society is badly in need of people like you, who have its interests at heart and will stand up and fight for it when need be. The Board has had too many people who were on it just for the ride—

or with the intent to sabotage it if it crowds any pressure group like the Daughters of the Utah Pioneers."[74]

By March Juanita had begun to worry about the silence of the Stanford University Press. She had in fact begun to think of publishing the history of the massacre privately. Following Morgan's advice, she wrote Donald Bean, asking for a prompt decision about the manuscript and expressing her confidence that she could sell 1,000 copies to the Lee family. Shortly Bean wrote that the manuscript had received the approval of his editorial committee in February but could not be scheduled for publication because of limited funds. A guarantee of the purchase of 1,000 copies by the Lee family, he suggested, would vastly improve its prospects.[75] It was a momentous break for Juanita, her first success in placing a long manuscript. Having written the good news to Ettie Lee, she inquired of Bean whether the press would expect payment in advance and whether it could effect an early publication to accommodate the Lee family, who had postponed a reunion pending the appearance of her book.[76] A month later she informed Bean that haste was not mandatory, for Ettie Lee had written her these calming words: "I think the publication of Stanford Press well worth waiting for. Let us cooperate with them in every way."[77] Bean replied that the press was ready to offer a formal contract if Juanita could give "a firm agreement" for 1,000 copies at $3 each; the press would also print another 1,000, which it would sell at a regular rate of $5 each.[78]

Juanita forwarded Bean's proposal to Ettie, who interpreted it to mean that most of the money would have to be paid in advance. "That is a blow between the eyes right now with all my other expenses—heavy taxes in April," Ettie wrote, "but the more I think about it the more I know we must have the prestige of Stanford back of the research. . . . "[79] Ettie's accountant had come up with a solution to her problem. Ettie would place Juanita on her payroll and send her a monthly stipend, which Juanita would bank against the day when the press called for its money. For tax purposes the shrewd businesswoman could then claim the sum as a business expense. Juanita agreed to the ruse and gave Ettie permission to secure a social security number for her, which she had not hitherto had reason to obtain. She offered to match $1,000 of Ettie's with $500 of her own and outlined a plan for aggressively vending the published work. "It certainly does not seem right for you to feel that you must subsidize me for doing what should be my natural job to do," Juanita wrote Ettie,[80] sturdily ignoring that her friend was several times over a millionaire.

In May 1949 Juanita revised an article, "The Arizona Strip," which she had earlier submitted to *The Pacific Spectator*. In returning her piece, the editor had included a check to sweeten the task of revision. As she resubmitted, Juanita wrote: "If you feel that it is still 'woody,' please do not hesitate to use the clippers further."[81] Appearing in the summer 1949 issue, the article gave a poetic characterization of that fractured, sparsely peopled land lying between the southern border of Utah and the Grand Canyon in northern Arizona. Among its polygamists, ranchers, and occasional outlaws, she wrote, the observer might discern the mysterious alchemy by which the American character had been formed upon the frontier: "For most of us, away from it, living for this day and for these few years, still guided by the gleam of Democracy in action, the Arizona Strip could well be an experimental plot upon which to test some theories. Here, perhaps, isolated as it is, we could segregate the elements which combine to form 'The American Way of Life,' and see if they could be fitted together so that they would tick."[82]

On June 6, 1949, Juanita and Will left St. George by automobile on a circuitous, two-week search for diaries. By a fantastic coincidence, in Salt Lake Juanita acquired a diary written by John D. Lee. Somewhat earlier, Mozelle Bickley of Salt Lake, a granddaughter of Lee, had provided Juanita a typed copy of a brief early diary in which her grandfather had written acrostics. Bickley's sister in Panguitch possessed a second Lee diary but had refused to allow Bickley to copy it. Shortly before Memorial Day the sister had arrived from Panguitch, bringing all her family records. Mercurially she changed her mind at once and refused to let Bickley examine a single sheet. After the sister had departed, Bickley found the second diary inexplicably lying upon her bed. Precisely at that juncture Juanita and Will called on her. Bickley surrendered the diary upon Juanita's promise to return it with a free photostat. "She justifies herself," Juanita wrote Bliss as she mailed the volume to the Huntington, "because she contends that it did not belong to the elder sister more than to other members of the family, and because others are so eager to have access to it also, she will make typed copies for them from the photostat."[83]

Having driven to Vernal in eastern Utah, Juanita and Will attended the annual convention of the Utah Association of Postmasters. The couple banqueted and socialized amidst a welter of statistical reports and motivational speeches. Will was happy to be elected vice-president of the organization and to secure St. George as the location of the convention for the following year.[84] For several days thereafter, the couple wandered in their car in eastern and central Utah in search of diaries. On June 16 they returned to Salt Lake where Juanita appeared as a featured speaker in a writing seminar conducted by *The Improvement Era*. "I am glad for this opportunity to demonstrate that I am a member of the church in good standing," Juanita wrote Ettie before the event. "It has been so easy for some to point the finger and scream APOSTATE! at any one whose views are not the accepted and traditional ones on any subject. I shall try to make my discussion such that the ones who are there will feel that I am sincere, at least."[85] On a Saturday evening Juanita and Will arrived home to a happy greeting from their children. The next day—Father's Day—Will had the pleasure of ordaining Kay to the office of deacon in the Aaronic Priesthood.

In July 1949 Juanita read in the *Tribune* about the death of Roderic Korns, an amateur Utah historian and a close friend of Dale Morgan. The deeply affected Morgan immediately wrote Juanita that he intended to complete Korns' project of editing and annotating diaries related to emigrant trails in Utah. "I feel a special responsibility to Rod now, being the only one who can get his ideas down in print so they will survive him, and I mean to finish the editorial work on these 1846 journals as soon as possible." In the same letter Morgan reported Fawn Brodie's recent adversity. Brodie had flown into Salt Lake to be with her father after he had suffered a heart attack. While in Salt Lake, the pregnant Brodie underwent a miscarriage, hemorrhaging severely and coming close to death. "She had gone through a pretty black period after returning from the hospital," Morgan told Juanita, "but hopes that she will yet be able to have another child."[86]

In mid-July Donald Bean sent Juanita an unintentionally volatile letter. It would be necessary, he said, for Stanford University Press to demand $3,000 from the Lee family in advance, and in light of a warning from a reader of Juanita's manuscript, he wanted to have in writing her attitude toward the possibility of a disciplinary action on the part of the Church after her book had appeared.[87] Juanita replied immediately, her urbanity obviously strained. She pointed out the injustice of demanding in advance the full price of a book none of

the Lee family had ever examined. She suggested a compromise of half
the sum, but warned that the family "may not be willing to accept
your terms, in which case, I assume, our negotiations will automati-
cally be at an end." As for her attitude toward possible discipline, she
reviewed her interest in the massacre from the day she had first learned
of it at the deathbed of Nephi Johnson to the latest moment, concluding with one of the most splendid statements of her life: "I do not
want to be excommunicated from my church for many reasons, but if
that is the price that I must pay for intellectual honesty, I shall pay
it – I hope without bitterness."[88] This statement was apparently satisfactory, for no more was said about possible retribution by either Juanita
or Bean.

Juanita remained distraught over the question of an advance
payment. Writing Ettie Lee, she wisely suggested in one paragraph
that the two allies make a counter-offer of half the sum and rashly
suggested in another that they withdraw the manuscript from Stanford
and seek another publisher.[89] A few days later, she fired off an angry,
injured letter to Bean. Whereas she had thought her manuscript had
been accepted "because you considered it worthy of publication, and
on the same basis that you would accept any other manuscript," it
now appeared that its acceptance had been contingent upon an autho-
rial subsidy. "I have not heard from Miss Lee," the tight-lipped Juanita
continued. "I doubt that she will accept your terms; I know that I
would not."[90]

The next day's mail brought a pacifying letter from Ettie,
who enclosed a check for $1,000 and promised $1,000 more by
September, most of which would probably come from the supposed payroll funds Juanita had been banking each month. Instantly
Juanita wrote Bean a polite letter, arguing that the press should accept
$2,000 as a sufficient gesture of good faith on the part of the Lee
family. "Their faith in both of us surprises – and humbles me. Many
of them, I know, will be disappointed in my treatment, for their
chief wish is to have their grandfather vindicated, as he cannot be."[91]
A conciliatory Bean replied that "Miss Lee's very helpful attitude
straightens everything out."[92] He enclosed a formal contract calling
for $1,000 immediately, $1,000 by September 1, and $1,000 when the
books were ready for shipment. This Juanita forwarded to Ettie, whose
signature removed the last serious obstacle to publication. The printing would ultimately exceed Bean's early estimate; it would consist of

1,000 copies for the Lee family and 1,945 copies for the general trade.[93]

On July 27, 1949, Juanita attended a meeting of the Board of State History in Salt Lake, probably her first. She went carefully instructed by Dale Morgan to support a proposal that the entire 1950 volume of the *Utah Historical Quarterly* be devoted to Roderic Korns' compilation of early Utah trails journals. Morgan knew that Joel E. Ricks, chairman of the board, wished to devote that volume to a work on Father Escalante by California historian Herbert E. Bolton. When Juanita arrived, she discovered that seven members of the ten-member board had been constituted as an executive committee. Since she was not on it, she was required to wait in a hall for several hours while the committee met. Vouchsafed entrance at last, she found that the committee had in effect decided to publish the Bolton manuscript.[94] Indignantly she planned to voice her protest at subsequent meetings. Coached by Morgan, she eventually did her part in effecting a more equable organization of the board. Between them, she and Morgan ensured that the 1951 volume of the quarterly would consist of Korns' *West from Fort Bridger: The Pioneering of the Immigrant Trails across Utah, 1846–1850*, as redacted and polished by Morgan.

In late July Juanita traveled to Blanding to attend the funeral of Marilyn Rowley, Charity's thirteen-year-old daughter who had been crushed by a backing truck. During August Juanita made a number of minor revisions of her pending book in light of her recent findings. She worked with a firm discipline, getting up earlier than usual and sending her children to the farm in Hurricane, where the fruit harvest was in full swing. In September she accepted a suddenly vacated part-time teaching position at Dixie College. Will warned that it would divert her from more important work, but she believed it good policy to accommodate the college president against the day when Will would retire and she would want a permanent teaching position. She had an assigned room in which she taught three high school classes daily and two college classes which met at the same hour on alternate days.

Near the time she began teaching, she spoke about the massacre before the convention of the Utah Municipal League in St. George. She wrote: "More than 100 people stayed to hear the discussion, and I was pleased with the reception I got."[95] On a weekend in late September, she and Will and their children joined others from Cedar City and St. George in a camp-out at Lee's Ferry on the

Colorado River. The men cooked a Dutch-oven supper over a camp-fire, and all bedded down under the bright desert sky. In the morning they hiked to Lee's Lookout east of the ferry and with binoculars scrutinized the barren cliffs, gorges, and buttes. As they returned to their homes, the campers paused at Pipe Springs National Monument. Her friends asked Juanita to talk about John D. Lee at the campfire, on the lookout, and at the monument. She complied, emphasizing, as she told Ettie, "that I am just finding out more and more about him, and that the further I go, the more convinced I am that he was in every way a superior man."[96] Juanita was entering upon an endless circuit of speeches about the massacre and the scapegoating of John D. Lee. Over the next quarter of a century she would recount that saga before hundreds of audiences. Her oral elaboration gave the grim details an immediacy that no written work could achieve. She appeared before audiences with a deceptive simplicity. Her attire was plain and her demeanor unassuming. Invariably she began her account with quiet hesitation. Yet she quickly intuited the heartbeat of her listeners, and her husky voice assumed a confident, mesmerizing cadence. She belonged to the race of wandering bards whose eloquent voices have from time immemorial vivified the triumphs and tragedies of humanity.

In early November Pamela Faust, a text editor at Stanford University Press, informed Juanita that she had made a two-page deletion in her manuscript. No one at the press, she said, could accept the analogy Juanita had drawn "between the Mormon emotions and actions of September 1857 and the behavior of American soldiers in the recent war." The implication that modern American soldiers had committed atrocities, Faust declared, was "sure to draw a storm of criticism" upon Juanita's head.[97] As the operational files of the press show, there was indeed widespread indignation among its staff over this matter. As early as January 1949, the primary reader of the manuscript had doubted "as to the inclusion of any references to cruelty or to conduct in the World War."[98] In a response to the question whether the manuscript contained anything libelous, Bean informed his editor-in-chief that there was "only that one question of good taste in throwing the same situation up to the American Army in Europe."[99] In another memo Faust told Bean that she had "deleted or toned down all the objectionable comparisons of the Mormons and our fine spirited soldiers."[100]

Juanita delayed her reply for over a week, then wrote sarcastically, "Because I am so new at this, I am not sure whose book this is to be." She defended the pages in question by referring to her sons' experiences in combat. "What I was trying to say is that in any age war is hell, that it releases the beast in man, and that in spite of our so-called civilization, we have not changed essentially. It is easy to point out the atrocities of our enemies, but we should realize that our own men react in a similar manner to the emotions engendered by war."[101] Her point was crucial, for it implied that the Mormon militiamen who committed the massacre deserved as much understanding and forgiveness as the soldiers of any war.

Faust proposed a compromise: rather than entire pages, they would delete several paragraphs.[102] It was not truly a compromise because it substituted a pallid statement about mob psychology in general for the reference to American soldiers in World War II. Weary of the matter, Juanita conceded without further protest.[103] In the meantime Morgan had sent Juanita his acid comment on Faust and the press: "The kind of sensitivity she exhibits toward the suggestion that American soldiers were not always angels in the war just past, is precisely the kind of sensitivity which has prevented until now the chronicling of the Mountain Meadows Massacre in any rational manner. . . . You could say that you felt that the Stanford University Press of all people would have understood this. . . . "[104]

During the winter of 1950 Juanita taught her classes and cared for her family. In February came a request from the press for the names of the publishers of the books cited in her bibliography, which she had neglected to provide. Some of the books she had at hand. For others she had to make a quick trip to Salt Lake. A few which Morgan had provided were harder to reach, his books being in storage because he had recently returned to Washington, D.C., in order to be near the Library of Congress. "You have no doubt heard of the man who scattered a bag of feathers and then tried to gather them up," Juanita wrote the press, likening herself to that man.[105] Later she acquired and mailed an old map of Mountain Meadows which the press would use as endsheet plates. The galleys came in early summer with a request for a quick return. In the fall a frantic call came for an index. Juanita was startled because someone had told her that publishers always prepared the index to a book. "I locked myself up over the week-end," she wrote the press, "and hardly came out for air."[106]

When she had completed a patched and messy first draft, her fatigued eyes persuaded her to mail it without further ado.

During the spring of 1950 Juanita devoted much time to helping Will prepare for the postmaster's convention. During its three-day course in late May, she kept detailed minutes of its assemblies, banquets, and entertainments. A typical speech was delivered by the postmaster from Tremonton, who claimed that "the post offices of the nation were being run a good deal more efficiently than many businesses that are operating today."[107] Letters of thanks followed, one of which complimented the couple for providing "the ultimate in fine entertainment, food, and fellowship."[108] Creating happy occasions for ordinary people was something both Will and Juanita were skilled at.

When her part-time teaching ended in May 1950, Juanita signed a contract for full-time instruction during the following year. Accordingly, she gave Leslie Bliss notice that she would resign as the Huntington's field representative in September. Bliss acquiesced but attempted to entice her to collect during subsequent summers by promising to increase her stipend, currently $75, to $100 per month.[109] During the summer of 1950 Juanita conscientiously gathered documents. Of particular value were the records of Anthony W. Ivins, deceased apostle, made available by his son Stanley. Juanita spent two rainy days in June inspecting these materials in Salt Lake, from which she shipped selections to the Huntington.[110] Of independent means and a skeptical turn of mind, Stanley Ivins had collected numerous documents relating to polygamy. Ivins was representative of the liberal, dissenting Mormons to whom Juanita was increasingly drawn. Until his death many years later, she and he would remain good friends, each attracted by the irreverent ebullience of the other.

During the summer of 1950 Juanita participated as a board member in the selection of a permanent executive secretary-editor for the Utah Historical Society, a position later designated as director. Among the applicants was A. Russell Mortensen, a high-voltage great-grandson of John D. Lee and a widower with six children. Juanita already knew Mortensen. One day while he had been doing research at the Huntington for his doctoral dissertation, Leslie Bliss had asked him to give Juanita a lift into Los Angeles. Instantly they had liked each other. During the selection process in 1950 Juanita threw her support behind Mortensen and was gratified when on September 1 he was appointed.[111] For over a decade they would stand as close allies in many a fracas on the Board of State History.

In September 1950, Juanita became a full-time teacher at Dixie College for the first time in seventeen years. Among the students thronging the halls was Willa, sixteen, her short golden hair beautifully coifed, her skirts full and long in the fashion of the moment. By the peculiar union of senior high school and junior college at Dixie, Willa was a freshman—the equivalent of a junior in high school elsewhere. For her part, Juanita wore rimless glasses and combed her dark hair back into a bun at the nape of her neck. She held an unillusioned view of her students, whom she accused of "trying to inflate a 60-word vocabulary to make something that will sound like an oration, or their idea of one."[112] She was enthusiastic and amiable, yet maintained an utter rigor in assignments and grading, as her roll book for English Composition, a year-long sequence of courses, shows. Reading assignments included Arthurian romances, "Lady MacBeth," "She Stoops to Conquer," and *The Pickwick Papers.* Exercises included speeches, book reports, business letters, themes, and sentence diagramming. As final grades she assigned a few A minuses and B's, many C's, and a few D's and E's. She gave no unqualified A's.[113]

In November 1950 *The Mountain Meadows Massacre* at last appeared. Before Juanita saw a copy, a letter arrived from Joseph Walker, her loquacious physician friend in Los Angeles. "Dear Juanita, dearest Juanita, Blessed Juanita, Wonderful Juanita, Courageous Juanita, Artistic Juanita, The Only Juanita. . . . Oh, goddammit, what-in-hell is a dictionary for when it never has the words one wants and needs?" The previous day he had bought her book and had stayed up most of the night "in an exciting romp from cover to cover." Generously he offered: "If it becomes necessary for you to wear a bullet-proof brassiere, or to buy wings with which to flee, please count on me for a liberal contribution."[114]

The style in which she had written her book was simple and muted, unemphatic almost to a fault, as if she had been loath to express her terrifying message, and sometimes her narrative was digressive and indirect. Yet her book was extraordinary, for with an utter integrity it gave shape to an electrifying drama. It was more than a history; it was a tragedy.

In its preface she declared her dual loyalty to her church and to historical fact. "This study is not designed either to smear or to clear any individual; its purpose is to present the truth. I feel sure that nothing but the truth can be good enough for the church to which I belong."[115] In the first chapter she explained the motivation of the participants: the persecutions they had suffered in Missouri and Illinois, the incendiary rhetoric of general authorites preaching moral reformation, the war hysteria induced by the approach of Johnston's army, and the abrasive behavior of the members of the Fancher train. Next came an account of the massacre. The stake high council in Cedar City made simultaneous decisions to set the Indians upon the Fancher train camped at Mountain Meadows and to send a messenger asking Brigham Young whether it was proper to do so. The messenger carrying Young's order to leave the emigrants unmolested arrived too late. John D. Lee—who had not been present at the original meeting of the high council—was sent to direct the Indians, but failed to forestall an injudicious attack which the emigrants repulsed. For several days the excited Indians besieged the train while Mormon militia gathered nearby. On Friday, September 11, 1857, John D. Lee lured the emigrants from their fortification with a promise of safe conduct to Cedar City. After the emigrants had surrendered their arms and marched clear of their wagons, Mormon militiamen shot the men and the Indians slaughtered the women and older children. Close to a hundred died. The only survivors were seventeen small children considered too young to tell tales.

Beyond these undisputed details lay the perplexity of determining who had ordered the Mormon participation in the killing. Juanita allowed the witnesses whose scattered accounts she had gathered to make their contradictory accusations. She wrote a detailed paraphrase of John D. Lee's version in his *Confessions* and shorter paraphrases of accounts by Nephi Johnson, Philip Klingonsmith, John M. Higbee, and Daniel S. Macfarlane. These latter accounts she reproduced in their entirety as appendices. Lee, Klingonsmith, and Johnson agreed that the orders for the massacre had come from the militia colonel, William H. Dame, and the stake president, Isaac C. Haight, neither of whom were on the field. Higbee and Macfarlane, leaving Haight out of their account, asserted that John D. Lee had exceeded Dame's orders to conciliate the Indians if possible; they implied that Lee had coerced the militiamen through his overbearing personality. For her part, Juanita did not take sides but assigned responsibility hierarchically, insisting that, despite the participation of Indians, "the final responsibility must rest squarely upon the Mormons, William H. Dame as commander, and those under him who helped to form the policy and to carry out the orders."[116]

Juanita moved on to consider the ineffectual efforts of federal authorities to bring the leaders of the massacre to justice. Although she cleared Brigham Young of ordering the slaughter, she accused him of complicity in sheltering the participants for many years after the fact. She also blamed him for the eventual scapegoating of John D. Lee. By Young's orders or consent, Lee was exiled to the barren wastes of Lee's Ferry, excommunicated from the Church without a hearing, and finally convicted in a rigged second trial. At that trial, hitherto unavailable Mormon witnesses appeared, among them Jacob Hamblin. Whereas the jury in the first trial had split along Mormon and non-Mormon lines, in the second trial an all-Mormon jury unanimously declared Lee guilty. "Why, then, were his own people so willing to sacrifice him, to let him take the punishment for both himself and his immediate superiors?" For years the federal authorities had doggedly attempted to implicate Brigham Young in the massacre. If the sacrifice of one man—who after all had admitted taking part—would close the case, it was a small price. And in the process it was not pleasant to remember his extraordinary devotion to the Mormon cause. "To brand him as an 'apostate' was much simpler and easier."[117]

In her closing pages, Juanita gave Lee his due, detailing his generosity to his neighbors and service to his church and noting that some five hundred persons signed a petition asking for his pardon. She described his helpful and trustworthy behavior as he awaited trial in the penitentiary and his struggle to resign himself to the betrayal of those he had thought his friends and comrades. Through carefully selected details, she evoked a profound sympathy for Lee and, by extension, for his fellow participants. Not only had the massacre been a tragedy for the slaughtered emigrants; it had been a tragedy for the otherwise upright and admirable men who perpetrated it.

As for her own anger, Juanita reserved it, not for any participant, nor even for those who first scapegoated Lee, but for the modern church authorities whose devious behavior perpetuated the injustice. As she ended her book, she indignantly censured David O. McKay and J. Reuben Clark for their humiliating manner of denying her access to the affidavits in their care. She also rebuked Joseph Fielding Smith for conscious distortion of the truth about the massacre in his *Essentials in Church History*, published in 1945. Pointing out that Smith had quoted Hubert H. Bancroft's assertion that the massacre "was the crime of an individual, the crime of a fanatic of the worst stamp," Juanita observed that as church historian Smith commanded abundant evidence to the contrary. "Even the most superficial research," she scathingly concluded, "would show the utter ridiculousness of such a statement."[118]

The book made a respectable showing in the reading world. The *San Francisco Examiner* called it "an absorbing and dramatic story."[119] According to *The Oregonian* of Portland, this "carefully done study, with extensive appendices and immense bibliography, should be welcomed by all, Mormon or not, as an important contribution to an understanding of a West that now seems as remote as the Dark Ages."[120] Scholarly and literary reviews accumulated. Most laudatory was a review by Henry Nash Smith, distinguished interpreter of the significance of the American frontier. Writing in the New York *Herald Tribune Book Review*, Smith asserted: "In gathering evidence, in evaluating the numerous and conflicting accounts of the massacre, in comprehending the motive and biases of the various people involved, and in placing an isolated event against a richly documented social background, Miss Brooks proves herself a skilled historian. Her courage and devotion to truth are even more remarkable. Whatever stigma may be cast upon the Mormons by the revelation that some of them were responsible for the crime is more than offset by Miss Brooks's demonstration that the society shaped by the Church can foster scholarly probity of a high order."[121]

Of more immediate impact upon Juanita were oral reviews conducted by local clubs and reading groups. By April 1951 she could report over sixteen oral reviews in St. George, Cedar City, Enterprise, Hurricane, Veyo, and Zion Park, "with a very good reception at each."[122] She was encouraged by abundant letters—over fifty within two months. In one, Ettie Lee described the response of Lee relatives gathered on Thanksgiving in Mesa, Arizona, where the Stanford University Press had directed fifty copies of the book. "We wept over some of your statements and your understanding. . . . We had a happy get-to-gether; everyone's nose was in a book and each would come up with—'Now what do you think about this?' or Wouldn't some of this family or that wish they had not been so uncharitable in their remarks. Claude Lee couldn't be budged from what he was reading. . . . Finally he said, 'This cheers my very soul. You see I bear the name and have been snubbed often but never again will I be annoyed. I'll answer back knowing I am bolstered with facts.' "[123]

Fawn Brodie wrote in a tone close to veneration. "I can't tell you how much I admire the delicacy, dispassionateness, and understatement with which you have handled a potentially lurid and sensational problem."[124] Dale Morgan, stating that he was placing the book "among the most cherished books in my library," predicted that its objectivity and thoroughness would influence the course of future Mormon historiography. "Your book will serve to shape, even as it now expresses, the social force that will bring it about."[125] Charles Kelly complimented her highly and offered "a nice cave in the cliffs" in case Juanita should need to flee from the wrath of the Church.[126] The book also brought new friends from the ranks of Mormon liberals, among them J. Golden Taylor, at the time an assistant professor of English at BYU. The book, he wrote, "fits my definition of loyalty and is the essence of integrity. . . . I admire your courage even though I am too expedient to emulate it."[127]

There was also some negative correspondence. Frank H. Jonas, associate professor of political science at the University of Utah, emitted a provocative questionnaire aimed at gathering information for a review which he apparently never completed. Jonas' correspondents included general authorities and Mormon scholars Joseph Fielding Smith, Milton R. Hunter, Preston Nibley, and Levi Edgar Young, who to a man replied that they had not read the book. Hunter wrote Jonas that he had surveyed all the members of the First Council of the Seventy and found that none of them had read it. Some of them had, like Hunter, talked with a William H. Reeder, who claimed to have read it and was highly incensed.[128] Jonas also asked Juanita to elaborate upon her attitude toward the general authorities who had denied her access to the affidavits. Juanita replied matter-of-factly, explaining that she had been assigned to write on the massacre and refusing to conjecture how the missing affidavits might have altered her book.[129]

Of greater personal interest to Juanita was correspondence set in motion when Charity asked Albert R. Lyman, the most prominent Mormon of San Juan County, for his opinion of her sister's book. In January 1951, Lyman responded with a stern denunciation. He declared himself profoundly shocked that Juanita would accuse Brigham Young of being an accessory after the fact to the massacre.

Challenging her evidence, he called the book "the most vicious thing published against the Church since the days of John C. Benned [sic], William Laws and the men who contrived at and finally accomplished the death of Joseph Smith."[130] Charity soon wrote Lyman a protest. She enumerated his praises in one list and his criticisms in another, much longer list. Chiding him for failing to look for value in the work, she expressed her faith that good would come from it: "I know my sister well. She is honest and fearless, and I am sure willing to let her work *stand on* or *fall from* the foundation of truth."[131]

Charity mailed Juanita Lyman's letter and a carbon of her reply. On the back of her carbon she penned an anguished note. She was not at all sure that the restitution which the book made in behalf of John D. Lee justified the unedifying display it gave to terrible events. "The book doesn't leave a good feeling," she admonished Juanita. "It doesn't give the impression of being written by a good Latter-day Saint. . . . I sympathized with you in your feelings of resentment for not getting the full cooperation of the church authorities in collecting your data, but again, since they are men of God and doing the best they can, I hated to see your resentment flare against them. Your book gives me the impression of *you* sitting in judgment upon men & events."[132]

Juanita wrote Lyman, asking him not to judge her book harshly. "You think I have done an evil thing; I believe sincerely that I have done a wholesome thing and done the church I love a service."[133] On the same day she wrote Charity: "You are a dear to defend me so warmly. And I appreciate it all the more when I sense the great love and respect you have for Brother Lyman." Most of her letter to Charity consisted of homey detail. Their widowed brother Dudley, now an insurance agent in Cedar City, was in the process of choosing a new wife. Mother Mary Leavitt was making quilts "by the score, almost." Charity's son Conrad, who was attending Dixie College, had come to dinner twice; Juanita was embarrassed to have served him beans each time. As Juanita wrote the letter, Tony was taking a bath and Karl and Kay were "wrestling all over the front room."[134] Behind such comforting domestic facts Juanita could momentarily hide from her new and perplexing celebrity.

CHAPTER SEVEN

GIVING VOICE TO
JOHN D. LEE

In March 1951 Charity's daughter Janice, recently married, was killed when the truck she was driving failed to negotiate a curve near Blanding. In less than a year Charity and Vernon had lost both their daughters in truck accidents. At the request of Janice's husband, her body was brought to St. George for burial. Juanita and Will arranged a graveside service – a speaker and music accompanied by a piano stationed on a rented truck – and afterward hosted the bereaved Rowleys at a family dinner.[1]

On May 1, 1951, Will retired as postmaster of St. George, having served seventeen years. The *Washington County News* observed his retirement with an appreciative article and a photograph. The photograph shows him at seventy to be still rustically appealing – his bald head gleaming, his eyes windowed by wire-rimmed spectacles, his round face transfused by cheerfulness and tolerance.

On a Saturday in May, following an all-night bus trip, Juanita called on Robert Glass Cleland at the Huntington to discuss the possibility of a conjoint publication of the John D. Lee diaries held by the Huntington and those held by the Church Historian's Office. It appeared that the Lee family was close to gaining permission to publish the latter. Cleland was mildly interested – enough so that he allowed her to carry back to St. George on the Saturday night bus typescripts of the Lee diaries in the Huntington.[2] It was also understood that for the summer she would again be on the Huntington's payroll as a field representative.

When school was out, the Brooks family moved for the summer to the fruit farm in Hurricane, where it was Will's notion to occupy himself with horticulture. Dry foxtail covered the yard and the house was dusty from disuse. Working frantically to finish before the cherry crop ripened, Will and Walt plastered and painted a basement room to serve as Juanita's study. Even after she had begun to cook for the cherry picking crew, Juanita found time for research and writing. Willa was away working full time at Zion Park, and the boys spent the day under Will's supervision in the orchards.[3]

For most of the summer Juanita submerged herself in the Lee diaries, browsing through each and then, as was her custom when mastering a diary, making an index of names and topics. Breathlessly she came upon passage after passage which confirmed her earlier surmises—and posed new problems for those who wished to interpret Brigham Young as an unerring and superhuman leader. She found the date of Lee's excommunication, October 8, 1870—otherwise unrecorded even in official registers. She found Lee's paraphrase of Brigham Young's after-the-fact endorsement of the massacre, which she excitedly copied into a letter to Dale Morgan: "I never saw Pres BY feed better. . . . After meeting I had some private conversation with him he advised me relative to my future location. . . . Pres Young said that the company that was used up at the Mountain Meadows were the fathers, mothers, bros sisters & connections of those that Muerders [sic] the Prophets, they merritd their fate, & the only thing that ever troubled him was the lives of the Women & children but that under the circumstances could not be avoided. . . ."[4] Morgan responded with an equal excitement: "The remarkable extracts you send me go to show all over again that there is hardly a Mormon diarist who can be ranked with him for getting the inside story down on paper. What a fellow! . . . if Huntington doesn't do right by the Lee journals and publish them in full, I am going to buckle on my guns and go to San Marino and shoot up the place. It will be a wonderful day when I can study all these journals at my leisure. . . ."[5]

In early September, as she prepared to return to the classroom, Juanita attended the Utah Conference on Higher Education at Cedar City. At the end of the conference, she and William R. Palmer accompanied a group of educators from northern Utah to the massacre site. The day was sunny and warm. Standing in turn upon the steps of the monument, Juanita and Palmer addressed the group, she narrating the massacre, he detailing its aftermath, including his own strenuous efforts to obtain permission from the Church for establishing the monument in 1932.[6] Among her listeners were three academicians from Salt Lake: from the University of Utah, William Mulder, professor of English, and Sterling McMurrin, professor of philosophy; and from the LDS Institute of Religion attached to the university, George Boyd, instructor of theology. That night Mulder, McMurrin, and Boyd visited the Brooks home in Hurricane, eating peaches and grapes and listening until a late hour as Juanita read fascinating excerpts from Lee's diaries.[7] They invited Juanita to appear before an informal group which met monthly on the university campus to discuss Mormon topics. Accordingly, she would journey to Salt Lake in the late autumn to address "the Mormon Seminar," as the group then called itself, or "the Swearing Elders," as later commentators have named it.[8] Among other notable liberal Mormons whom Juanita could well have met on the occasion of her address were the following: from the University of Utah, Jack Adamson, professor of English, and Obert C. Tanner, professor of philosophy (Tanner was also a wealthy jeweler and philanthropist); from the LDS Institute of Religion, Lowell Bennion, instructor of theology; from Brigham Young University, Richard Poll and Brigham Madsen, professors of history; and from Weber College in Ogden, Jennings Olson, instructor in philosophy.

The Swearing Elders had a brief and controversial existence. Some of the members of this group were in open disagreement with essential doctrines of the Church. Jennings Olson, for example, would soon cheerfully accept excommunication. Others saw their participation as harmonious with their Latter-day Saint faith. Lowell Bennion believed that his attendance at the seminar helped him reconcile the conflicts between faith and secular learning that his institute students encountered at the university. Inevitably, certain conservative apostles regarded the seminar as no more than a seedbed for heresy and disbelief. During the summer of 1952, Joseph Fielding Smith and Harold B. Lee arranged an interview with Sterling McMurrin, whom they regarded as the leader of the group. McMurrin attempted to persuade these elders that it was not a conspiracy against the faith but a forum for free inquiry into Mormon culture. Only partially reassured, the apostles asked McMurrin to clarify for his fellow participants the position of the Church on each issue which they would thereafter discuss. This the astonished professor refused to do.[9] In late 1954, at one of its last meetings, the group staged a debate between an advocate of organic evolution and an advocate of creationism, a debate made timely by the recent publication of Joseph Fielding Smith's *Man: His Origin and Destiny*, a treatise propounding that Christian faith and organic evolution are irreconcilable. Smith's views were quietly opposed by no less a person than church president David O. McKay, who repeatedly assured questioners that the Church took no official stand on the question of evolution. McKay went so far as to intervene in excommunication proceedings brought against Sterling McMurrin in the wake of the debate held before the seminar.[10] Ultimately the conflict between conservative and liberal Mormons over the question of organic evolution arrived at a stalemate, the Church today having no official position thereon.

Three hundred miles away in St. George, Juanita was indirectly affected by the controversies of the Swearing Elders. She probably believed in organic evolution yet had such little interest in the topic that she failed to discuss it in any of her published or unpublished writings. Of greater importance to her than any particular issue was the fact that the group bolstered the legitimacy of free inquiry among Mormons. Admittedly its victory was minor, for the large majority of Mormons, great and small, would remain highly suspicious of debate on matters of belief. Nonetheless, the Swearing Elders made the central leaders of the Church a little more tolerant of nonconformity, a liberalization of which Juanita would be a beneficiary. As she doggedly attempted to force those leaders to admit that her interpretation of the massacre was correct, she would find them inclined, not to excommunicate, but merely to scold her. Furthermore, most of the highly educated men who belonged to the Swearing Elders would remain Juanita's firm, fast friends. Her single appearance before that group in the fall of 1951 was therefore a planting of a future crop. There she discovered, if she had not already begun to suspect it, that liberal Mormonism claimed her for its own. Recognizing her membership in an informal community of dissent, she was encouraged and enheartened.

On a Friday evening in early September, Juanita received a phone call from a Brian Foy, production manager for Warner Brothers in Hollywood. The firm wanted to create a movie in which the Mountain Meadows massacre would be a prominent feature, portraying local participants but not depicting Brigham Young. Foy wished to retain Juanita as a consultant on location. Fearful of offending the Church, he asked her to seek approval from the general authorities. The ecstatic Juanita was enormously flattered. To Morgan she would write, "After all Maurine's frantic efforts to hit the movies and Jonreed's long stays in Hollywood trying to sell his books, I can't help being just a little inflated at even receiving a telephone call."[11]

Within three hours of Foy's call, Juanita was on a night bus for Salt Lake. On Saturday morning she phoned William H. Reeder, who she believed had been officially assigned to read *The Mountain Meadows Massacre*. According to the correspondence which Frank Jonas had conducted with church officials, each denied having read it, relying instead upon Reeder's negative interpretation. On the phone Reeder was suspicious, but finally agreed to meet Juanita. When she showed him a copy of her book, he was astonished, saying he had never seen it before. The book he had read and reported upon to the general authorities had been smaller and released by a different publisher. Assured her book demonstrated that Brigham Young had not ordered the massacre, Reeder seemed mollified and recommended that she phone Joseph Fielding Smith. That apostle answered the phone, but referred her to William Lund. Lund having no listed phone, she dialed five other apostles, all of whom proved to be out of town. Finally she found Stephen L. Richards, first counselor to David O. McKay in the First Presidency, which had been reorganized following the death of George Albert Smith during the previous spring. "I explained that Warner Brothers wanted to do a western in the setting of 1857 in Southern Utah, that they did not plan to portray on the screen either Joseph Smith or Brigham Young, but would use Jacob Hamblin, John D. Lee, Thales Haskell, Ira Hatch, James Haslam, and other local characters." Richards' response struck Juanita as fair. He said that the Church could not officially give approval for a commercial movie, but that "if I felt that the presentation was to be historical and fair, I should not hesitate to cooperate in such an activity."[12] Before attending faculty meeting on the following Monday morning, Juanita wrote Foy, arguing that Richards' attitude "is as good as you could expect or want."[13] In recommendation of her own participation in creating the movie, she confidently cited her qualifications as an offspring and historian of the Mormon frontier.

In mid-October, Finlay McDermid of Warner Brothers wrote that Juanita's services would not be required "until we have some sort of rough screenplay prepared, which should take two or three months."[14] Warning McDermid that she would have to give thirty days notice at the college, she expressed the hope that she might not be needed at the studio until after winter quarter.[15] Shortly McDermid announced a change of plans. Brian Foy wished her presence within a week—or at the end of thirty days if giving notice to the college was inevitable. McDermid also conveyed word of her prospective remuneration: round-trip train travel to Hollywood and a stipend of $250 per week for four weeks.[16]

Juanita was vastly disappointed. She phoned Donald Bean and learned that Warner Brothers had offered Stanford University Press $3,500 for the movie rights, half of which sum would be hers by terms of her contract.[17] Armed with that information, she wrote McDermid that she wished to withdraw from the venture. Compared to her years of labor, her half of $3,500 was insignificant. Furthermore, the $1,000 she stood to earn as a consultant would barely pay for living expenses and a replacement at the college. "Most important of all to me, in the eyes of my community and of my people generally, I would be held responsible for the finished product—a responsibility which I certainly do not want to assume under the present arrangements. Since this is only history, and hence anyone's province, I suggest that you go ahead without me."[18]

It had been a dubious enterprise from the beginning, as the astonished Morgan had suggested: "I am floored by your letter, and am in fact surprised that you aren't still lying unconscious on the floor in Hurricane, long distance telephone clutched in your hand. No one yields to me in admiration for your book, but if I had been asked to pick out the least likely candidate for a movie among the books published in 1950, *The Mountain Meadows Massacre* would have figured prominently in my ruminations."[19] Even during the exciting weeks when it had seemed that she might actually achieve a Hollywood success, Juanita had experienced a dismal dream which signified failure: "I saw a nest of about eight eggs, with one or two chickens hatched, and a third just pecking through the shell and cheeping loudly as if for help. I turned and walked away, saying that a chicken that could not peck its way out of its own shell would be too weak to live if I helped it out. So I told the family the next morning that the moving picture would die a-borning, as indeed it did."[20]

Warner Brothers went forward briefly with its plans to make the movie. When an announcement of its intention appeared in *Publisher's Weekly*, Mormon officials acted. J. Reuben Clark, second counselor in the First Presidency, pressured the movie firm to abandon the project.[21] Extraordinarily sensitive about the disapproval of the Church from the beginning, Warner Brothers proposed a rewording of their contract with Stanford University Press, which, in the words of Donald Bean, would have placed upon the press "any onus that might develop."[22] The press rejected the rewording and the venture died.

The national publicity forced Juanita to explain the project's demise. Though she candidly confessed to Morgan that the film company's stingy offer had provoked her withdrawal, she offered other correspondents a better sounding motive. To Leslie Bliss she wrote: "From the first I had my doubts about what kind of picture they could make of it, and when I saw what the scenario writer had outlined, I knew at once that I wanted nothing to do with it. If he had read my book at all, there was little evidence of the fact."[23] She repeated this assertion in letters to Robert Glass Cleland, William R. Palmer, and Virginia Sorensen. As late as 1973 she would recall that she had been invited to Las Vegas where, "I was met by the representative [of Warner Brothers], who took me out to a 'farm' several miles from the city, gave me the manuscript, and left me for a couple of hours to read it and make up my mind."[24] This was a face-saving fib. There was, however, a potential, if not actual, truth behind her claim to have reviewed and rejected an unsatisfactory script. She had accurately inferred from Warner Brothers' niggardly offer that a typical Hollywood romance having little resemblance to the historical event she had set forth was in the making.

In early 1952 the Stanford University Press reported sales of 1,215 copies of Juanita's work in addition to 1,000 copies delivered to the Lee family.[25] Juanita continued to receive letters of praise. Louis C. Zucker, a prominent Jew and professor of English at the University of Utah, wrote that the book was "one of the most exemplary acts ever done by a loyal member of any church. An act of this kind, so tragically rare, is an invaluable service to The Church as instrument of progress towards the achievement of the Kingdom of Heaven on earth."[26] By now, more than a year after the book's appearance, Juanita had set aside her fear of excommunication. The Church had received her work, she wrote Charles Kelly, "by silence, total and absolute. Not a word anywhere. My local people, the bishop and the president of the Stake, and all the authorities here never refer to the book—they evade it with the delicacy and solicitude they might show to a mother who has given birth to a monster child. No one among the higher ups will admit that he has read it—as near as I can tell, few have. At any rate, no official action has been taken, which must mean that I have a few friends in camp."[27] In her private feelings Juanita was less than amused by the studied silence of local church officials. It seemed to her that they practiced a subtle ostracism, calling upon her and Will less often than formerly to serve on committees and to give lessons, prayers, and sermons. There were others who ostracized them as well. Certain friends said a curt hello and hurried away or avoided them altogether. A number of relatives expressed strong disapproval. All this Juanita resented more for Will's sake than for her own. She regretted deeply that such a good and guileless man should have to feel to some degree like an outcast.

Knowing that the support of even a single apostle would dramatically alter her status, Juanita made an attempt during the fall of 1951 to persuade Stephen L. Richards that her interpretation of the massacre was correct. She selected Richards because he had responded tolerantly to her request to proceed with the movie. Calling on him in his Salt Lake office, Juanita explained her evidence and conclusions. Afterward she mailed him a copy of her book. In January, Richards wrote thanking her for the book, which he had not read, and reiterating the negative position he had taken during her visit to his office: "I confess it is a little difficult to understand how a member of the Church, with a record of devotion and service such as you enjoy, should desire to recreate such a sad chapter in the history of southern Utah."[28] Stung by the apostle's rebuke, Juanita replied angrily, chiding Richards for implying that the massacre had been comfortably buried until her book had given it fresh publicity. "I did not think it had ever been out of public attention, especially since President Grant went before the Arizona legislature and protested the naming of the Lee's Ferry Bridge [Navajo Bridge]. That really broke it wide open, this time within the Church, among the many friends and descendants of John D. Lee."[29]

Why did Juanita risk offending a powerful man who, by a phone call to her stake president, could effect her speedy excommunication? She desired no less than an official admission that Brigham Young and his colleagues in Salt Lake had helped create the bellicose atmosphere from which the massacre devolved, that they had treated John D. Lee with great injustice, and that their successors had perpetuated that injustice to the latest moment. Among her many motivations for declaring the truth about the massacre was this: that she wished the Church at large to assume a portion of the shame which hitherto her native Dixie had borne alone. She had long since grasped that the guilt of the massacre was collective. It was a deed to which many assented and to which many more contributed. The sincere and prayerful men who carried it out were representative Mormons. The vengeful heart of an entire people had been prepared to commit the crime which circumstances thrust in the way of the pioneers of southwestern Utah. Because she was a daughter of Dixie, Juanita accepted the guilt as her own. But because she was a daughter of Dixie, she also resented profoundly those who had contrived to make it the guilt of only Dixie. In her book she had spoken for more than John D. Lee. She had spoken for Dudley Leavitt and Nephi Johnson and, yes, even for William H. Dame and Isaac C. Haight, those principal leaders who had gone unpunished. She had spoken for Dixie.

As 1952 dawned, the Brooks family embarked upon a novel adventure in hostelry. During the fall of 1951, they had returned from the farm to their house on the hill in St. George. As winter began, Ettie Lee made a down payment on the Lyn-Mor Motel at 420 East St. George Boulevard and proposed that the Brookses undertake its management and move into the residential unit attached to the office. Disillusioned with fruit farming, Will was agreeable. It is perhaps an indication of Juanita's long-standing dissatisfaction with the cramped house on the hill that she consented. During the Christmas holidays, the family moved, and Juanita found herself performing domestic duties in the renamed Lee Motel. It would be some time before the family became accustomed to traffic noise—their bedrooms gave upon the street, the route by which Highway 91 passed through town. There was also the annoyance of Ettie's parsimony. The refurbishing of the deteriorated motel went forward slowly. From Los Angeles Ettie transported used office and cabin furniture which she had bought at frugal prices. "I want to set it up so that Will can lie down while he waits for customers," she wrote in March. "I have a good comfortable couch. We will look quite awake too, for our colors are a tiny bit noisy." She apologized for the fact that the Brookses had been forced to make payments in her behalf and promised to put the motel's finances on a sound business basis: "I have a plan to help with our income there that will be an asset to the place I am sure. I'll advise you, that is, we'll go into a huddle when I arrive."[30]

The idea of the Brooks family in the motel aroused Dale Morgan to a macabre humor. He proposed to Juanita that Ettie name her property the John D. Lee Motel. "Just consider how fascinating: Each room to be decorated with portraits of Lee, engravings of the massacre, and framed photostatic copies of Brigham Young's remarks of 1861 to Lee on the subject. A pamphlet setting forth the facts of Lee's life. A notice in your window that copies of a book on the subject can be purchased at the office."[31] Ironically, Morgan's fancies were partially realized. The congenial Juanita and Will frequently engaged their guests in conversations. Sometimes Juanita explained the massacre and gave away copies of her book, as she did to an administrator from Iowa State College at Ames, who afterwards thanked her in a letter for the warm hospitality she and Will had shown him and his wife. "What a joy it is to come into a clean and well-managed unit after a long drive in the heat – most especially when that unit is air-cooled, has a beautiful bath and rents for only $4.00. Lee's Motel was our shining example of what a motel should be."[32]

During the unusually rainy spring of 1952, Juanita declared herself to be overworked. Dale Morgan repeatedly advised her to buy a hammock and relax as soon as school had ended. In early June Will was bruised and shaken in an automobile accident – "not seriously, but bad enough to keep him down a couple of weeks."[33] The family car, struck broadside in an intersection, was a total loss. On the heels of that, Juanita taught a brief session of summer school at the Branch Agricultural College at Cedar City, a subsidiary of Utah State Agricultural College at Logan. While there she got leads on pioneer journals, which she pursued in behalf of the Huntington, although that institution had not formally retained her for the summer.

Mid-summer, Juanita undertook a substantial free-lance writing project. She recast her unpublished chapters on the life of Jacob Hamblin into a simple biography which she hoped to sell to a movie company as the basis of a Western. In late July, she mailed four carbon copies of her finished manuscript to the Library of Congress for copyright registration and sent a hopeful inquiry to Warner Brothers in Los Angeles. In November 1952, after Warner Brothers had declined the work, she offered it to a free-lance scenario writer residing in Big Sur, California.[34] Shortly that initiative also died, and she retired the manuscript to her inactive files, where it would sit unmolested for many years. In 1980, Westwater Press (later Howe Brothers) of Salt Lake would publish it as *Jacob Hamblin: Mormon Apostle to the Indians*, almost precisely as Juanita wrote it in 1952.

This biography emphasized episodes that Juanita hoped would appeal to film makers. Slanted toward juvenile readers, it was susceptible to the same charge she had laid against Paul Bailey's biography of Hamblin in her review of 1948: the work was "neither fiction nor biography, but an uncertain combination of both."[35] Nonetheless, it was quick paced and often moving and eloquent. Perhaps its most compelling chapter was entitled "Young George A." As Hamblin prepared for his third journey to the Hopis of northern Arizona, Apostle George A. Smith asked him to take along his son, George A., Jr. A precocious adventurer of fifteen, Young George A. decorated his superbly trained horse, Vittick, with spangled trappings. When the men of Hamblin's party quailed before the high waters of the Colorado, Young George A. fearlessly swam Vittick across. However, his indiscreet valor brought him to an ignominious end. Ranging alone, he fell prey to Navajos who riddled his body with bullets and arrows. Hamblin and his men retreated in haste, transporting the groaning youth until death mercifully ended his agony. Afraid to pause for a burial, they left his body wrapped in a blanket beside the trail. Months later, Hamblin returned to the scene and gathered his skull, pelvis, and a few other bones and soldered them into an airtight box. Meeting Navajos who had Young George A.'s revolver and clothing in their possession, he could do no more than converse peacefully with them. When he delivered the sealed box to the murdered youth's father, Hamblin declined payment for his effort.

Here then was Juanita's idea of good material for a movie. Truly this and other episodes from Hamblin's life made for real-life drama. Of themselves, however, they lacked the pointed structure of a Hollywood Western, and Juanita did not know how to adapt them to that structure.

The recent publication of Pearson Corbett's biography, submitted earlier as a thesis at BYU, had added to Juanita's impetus to write an adventurous life of Jacob Hamblin. Mid-summer 1952 she agreed to review Corbett's volume, *Jacob Hamblin, the Peacemaker*, for the *Pacific Historical Review*. Throughout the summer and fall, Dale Morgan urged her to be sharply criticial of Corbett's failure to allude to details of Hamblin's life which Juanita had established in *The Mountain Meadows Massacre*. In November Morgan wrote: "If a book isn't up to snuff, it is up to the critics to say so, or the level of mediocrity will just keep on sinking lower and lower."[36] The brief review, published in 1953, was not severe. Juanita chided Corbett for slavishly following an earlier biography and for slanting his work toward Hamblin's descendants rather than toward scholars. "Yet one closes the book," she concluded, "with the feeling that here was a man who was truly great. . . . For a better knowledge of him we are indebted greatly to his current biographer, Pearson H. Corbett."[37] Corbett was, after all, her colleague at Dixie College—no distinction being made in St. George between the state-operated college and the adjoining LDS Institute of Religion at which Corbett taught.

In September 1952 Juanita returned to teaching at the college on a half-time basis. To allow for writing, she scheduled her classes in the afternoon.[38] As school began, she and Will responded to a claim by the Internal Revenue Service for $107.68 in unpaid taxes for 1951. Having lost a W2 form, they had failed to report $1,006.60 which Juanita had received from the college. Will enclosed money orders for the required sum with an apology. Juanita was not contrite. She conceded to the demand of the IRS only because the couple's duplicate tax form had been misplaced in the several moves they had made between the house on the hill, the farm, and the motel. She reminded the IRS that it had harrassed them during the previous year over their claim of four dependent children: "Some one, in studying our report, decided that the dates must be wrong. People of our age could not possibly have children so young. So we had to dig up birth certificates and affidavits to prove that we were born and that our children were our own. Perhaps it is unusual for a man of nearly 72 and a wife of 54 to have four teen-age youngsters, but it can happen."[39]

The autumn of 1952 was a happy one for the Brooks family. Willa, a college junior and active as a cheerleader, dated a tall basketball player. Karl, a freshman, was proving to be exceptionally adept on the high school football team. Walt, who lived in St. George with his wife and children, was his coach. Clair also enrolled at Dixie. In the fall of 1950, as a member of the National Guard, he had been mobilized and had engaged in combat in Korea. On his return at New Year 1952, he had worked at a service station. Now, in the fall of 1952, he tried his luck at college football but soon suffered sprained ankles. Grant, a postman, resided in St. George with his wife and children. Only Ernest and Bob were away. Ernest and Margie had moved their growing family to Grand Junction, Colorado. Bob was stationed at Fort Dix, New Jersey, and had recently married a woman

unknown to the family. "Your room is here and ready," Will wrote
Bob on motel stationery; "we know you are getting a good girl, bring
her home as soon as convenient."[40]

On November 14, 1952, Juanita participated in a panel discussion on Mormon culture at the meetings of the Utah Academy at
Utah State Agricultural College in Logan. Having agreed many weeks
before to address a matter of Mormon history, she joined scholars
William Mulder, Leonard Arrington, and Gaylon L. Caldwell on the
panel. Her remarks, "St. George—A Community Portrait," were published with those of the other participants in a mimeographed pamphlet entitled "Symposium on Mormon Culture." Juanita's paper, duly
documented from pioneer diaries, elaborated upon the image of St.
George which she had presented in brief magazine articles. She emphasized industry and economics in the pioneer town. Discussing the production of wine, she made assertions that Mormons of her own day,
who practiced total abstinence from alcoholic beverages, might have
found distressing: "From the first, the brethren were counseled not to
drink their own product, but many of them began tasting and ended
by guzzling. . . . Wine was served for the sacrament in all the wards.
Though the brethren were counseled to take only a sip or one small
swallow, some grew over-enthusiastic until the pitcher had to follow
along to keep the goblets filled. Finally, on July 9, 1892, the High
Council issued a ruling that no more wine be served for sacrament.
The problem of drinking became so great that by 1900 people were
counseled to dig up their vineyards."[41]

In January 1953, Juanita traveled to the Huntington and
held a long-delayed interview with Robert Glass Cleland concerning
the disposition of the John D. Lee diaries. Cleland proposed that he
and she collaborate on a formal edition of the five diaries in possession of the Huntington. In return for a grant-in- aid of $150 a month
for twenty-four months, Juanita would edit four of the diaries, providing such annotation as might seem necessary, and write brief connect-
ing accounts. Cleland would edit one of the volumes, write a general
introduction, and oversee the publication of the work.[42] Without hesitation, Juanita accepted. It was an exciting, even flattering proposal,
a mark of Cleland's respect. "I have been informed," Morgan wrote
her, "that as Cleland is getting a little old and ineffectual, he is inclined
to be a little jealous of male historians who are young and vigorous.
On the other hand, I have also been informed that you carry more

weight with Cleland than you might expect, for as you spade a some-what different field and are a woman, he does not feel himself in com-petition with you."[43]

The five Huntington diaries covered, respectively, 1848–49, 1857–61, 1866–73, 1873–74, and 1875–76. The library had acquired them in May 1929 from Miss Esther Nelson, daughter of William Nelson, U.S. Marshall for Utah Territory, to whom John D. Lee had given his personal papers as he prepared for his execution. Cleland had agreed to edit the first, Juanita the final four. She had held type-scripts of all the diaries since June 1951. As need arose, the Huntington would provide photostatic copies of the orginals for comparison.

At first, Juanita wrote Cleland deferential letters inquiring about procedure and wondering whether their project should not include the Lee diaries in the Church Historian's Office. Cleland instructed her to proceed with her editing and leave such matters for later consideration. Ultimately she fell into a satisfying routine. In the middle of the night or in the early morning before her children arose, she sat at her desk in her housecoat and slippers. She hovered over the typescript, surveying a promiscuous welter of eccentric spellings and unpunctuated clauses. Then her fingers tapped upon the keyboard of her portable typewriter, creating a fresh draft, providing capitals and punctuation but for the most part leaving the bizarre spellings unchanged. Consulting the photostat, she sometimes concluded that the Huntington's typescript had misinterpreted a word and she pro-vided another in her draft. As she encountered names and allusions, she paused to create a separate annotation, calling upon her own well-stocked memory or rummaging among her large collection of diaries and books to identify persons and to explain events and policies.[44]

In the meantime, the free-lance writer in Juanita had not entirely died. During the winter of 1953 she submitted a small travel article to Ford Times, the magazine of the Ford Motor Company. Titled "Way Out West in Dixie," the article told how, as the Civil War had threatened to cut off supplies of cotton, Brigham Young had called the Cotton Mission to St. George, thereafter dubbed Utah's Dixie. During the summer, she submitted an article on Bunkerville to the same magazine, for which she was paid $300.[45]

In the summer of 1953 Juanita finished editing and annotating her first diary and mailed the manuscript to Cleland. Discovering that he had gone for the summer to a guest ranch in

Montana, she asked his secretary to return it. She proceeded with editing the second. Willa worked for the summer in the lodge at Zion Park. Karl and Kay held full-time summer jobs while Tony spent considerable time fishing. Will supervised the construction of a new unit at the motel, channeling profits from rentals into payments for construction. Each month he made an escrow payment of $418 from rental receipts. On weekends during July, his units were full. However, on week nights his vacancy sign often glowed all night. "We hope you will not be too disappointed with the results," Will concluded a report to Ettie Lee; "we will keep moving along just as fast as we can."[46]

Sometimes good friends stayed at the motel. Fawn Brodie and her family stayed overnight, as did Sterling McMurrin and his family, en route to Los Angeles where McMurrin would teach summer school. It is possible that Ansel Adams and Dorothea Lange, noted photographers, stayed in the motel, for both spent time in Dixie during the summer of 1953. Adams photographed the nearby national parks for travel promotion, and Lange documented rural people in their daily pursuits.[47] The San Francisco-based Lange had become acquainted with the Brooks family while taking photographs of the rural West for the Farm Security Administration in the 1930s. During the summer of 1953 Lange took many photographs of Mary Leavitt. One of the photographs would be published in the summer 1971 issue of *Dialogue* as part of a photo essay entitled "Mormon Country Women." That photograph shows Mary seated in a rocking chair in front of Juanita's house on the hill. She holds a guitar and sings. At her feet sit two little girls and Juanita. Juanita, simply dressed and coifed, holds an infant nephew on her lap. Clair squats on the nearby steps.[48] In this context Juanita seems no more than a picturesque country housewife.

In mid-summer Juanita reacted indignantly to the mass arrest of the polygamists of Short Creek. Before dawn on Sunday, July 26, 1953, over a hundred highway patrolmen and deputy sheriffs, mostly from Arizona, invaded the tiny settlement on the Utah-Arizona border, entering with red lights flashing and sirens screaming, hoping to take the Mormon fundamentalists by surprise. They found men and women, dressed in their Sunday best, assembled around a flagpole in the schoolyard soberly singing "America." Arizona judges set up temporary courts and arraigned thirty-one men and fifty-six women. The men were remanded to the Mohave County jail in Kingman, Arizona, and the women, accompanied by 263 children, were parceled out among Mormon families throughout Arizona to await disposition by juvenile courts and social agencies. Jonreed and Verda Lauritzen were among the five adult residents of Short Creek who were not arrested.[49]

Juanita's physician friend Joseph Walker, reacting to coverage in the Los Angeles papers, disparaged the polygamists: "Who cares about their frolicksome fornications and sexual whoopies?" he wrote. "It doesn't look as tho some future Longfellow will write such a poem about the Short Creekers as he wrote about the Acadians."[50] Juanita was not in accord with her friend, but she could at least thank him for drawing her attention to Longfellow's poem "Evangeline." She soon wrote an essay called "Short Creek: Arizona's Grand Pre," and attempted to place it with national magazines. It was not accepted and went into her inactive file. It was nonetheless a remarkable expression of her sympathy for Mormon polygamists.

In it, she described Short Creek as she saw it soon after the raid. "I counted 18 windmills, each furnishing water for a fine garden, a small vineyard, and a few fruit trees. There was corn in the tassel; corn two feet high; corn just coming up; beans were thrifty, grapevines loaded." It struck her as timelessly agrarian. It could have been "Evangeline's home town, or . . . any other village in Arizona or Russia or Peru. Seedtime and harvest, the cycles of the moon, the uncertainty of frost or rain, the daily chores, the home-made entertainment – the basic life strands are of a common color." She defended the arrested polygamists as decent, moral, hard-working people. "For entertainment they have dances, they have organized an orchestra, they enjoy group singing, they have a home dramatic organization. By most of the measures applied they cannot be classed as anything other than rural folk, isolated but not criminal." She was especially angry over the permanent separation of parents and children which Arizona proposed, an intervention of the state in the home which created an ominous precedent: "A part of the glory of America," she declared, "has always been the right to be different, the right to be wrong, even. Always we have protested regimentation of ideas. Parents may be food-faddists, nudists, atheists, Jehovah's Witnesses, Shakers, Catholics, Fundamentalist Mormons, but the state has not presumed to supervise the conversations in the home."[51]

Juanita soon prepared a protest on another subject. On Friday, August 28, 1953, she attended a special convention of the Utah Education Association in Salt Lake. More than 3,300 members had gathered in the Rainbow Randevu to debate and vote whether to open public schools as usual in September. The crux of their discussion was the adamant refusal of Governor J. Bracken Lee to call a special session of the legislature to alleviate a severe underfunding of Utah schools. Plans were already afoot in the large Salt Lake districts to cut second grade classes to a half day. There was talk of returning Dixie College and Weber College to the Church. The vociferous chatter in the Rainbow Randevu ranged from the angry and militant to the despairful and resigned. The vote, taken after five hours of debate and speeches, was 2,204 in favor of opening, 1,120 against.[52] Unquestionably Juanita voted against.

Juanita went home and wrote an angry essay which concluded: "This is government unworthy of Governor Lee and unworthy of the State of Utah."[53] The draft, never polished, reveals her intense partisanship over matters of educational funding. She believed in labor unions and regarded the Utah Education Association as a union, as an incident involving her sister Charity demonstrates. Charity had recently resumed school teaching in San Juan County. Privately Charity disagreed with those teachers who insisted on negotiating for higher salaries. Nonetheless, as she told Juanita during a visit, she accepted the raise her colleagues had won for all. Juanita hissed a scathing ejaculation: "Scab!" Then, ashamed of herself, she apologized to her sister.[54]

In September 1953 Juanita and Will acquired a house in Provo. Clair wished to attend BYU to pursue a teaching certificate in physical education. He and LaVon, who was pregnant with their second child, searched Provo for a rental and, finding decent places impossibly expensive, returned to St. George in discouragement. Alarmed by Clair's talk of surrendering his ambition for an education, Juanita took a night bus for Provo, searched for a day, and contracted to purchase a two-bedroom house near the BYU campus. She bought out the owner's equity with $4,000 she and Will had saved for the construction of a new house for themselves and arranged monthly payments of $50, which Clair would pay as rent. The new home would have to wait, for, as Will later expressed it, "Nita had chosen to invest what we had in a boy rather than a house."[55] Clair and LaVon would live in the house for three years; later other Brooks relatives attending BYU would live in it.

On October 10, 1953, Juanita spoke about the Mountain Meadows massacre to an invited assembly at the University of Utah. The event was marred by a minor incident reminding one that, if Juanita's book had given the descendants of John D. Lee cause to rejoice, it had intensified the anguish among descendants of some of the other participants. As Juanita prepared to speak, a friend warned her that Caroline Keturah Parry, a granddaughter of Isaac C. Haight, had joined the audience without invitation. Parry, who was preparing a biography of her grandfather, was known to disagree with Juanita's contention that Haight bore a major responsibility for the massacre. "I soon identified her," Juanita later wrote, "though I had never met her, by the extreme pallor of her face. She heard me through in silence, asked no questions, made no comment, but left immediately as soon as I had finished."[56] Her wordless exit in fact came after Juanita had approached her and ingratiatingly offered to share information relevant to the biography of her grandfather. After three years Parry belatedly accepted Juanita's offer; in doing so she expressed a hope that Juanita would understand why she had rushed wordlessly away on that October day in 1953: "I was deeply hurt by the publication of your *Mountain Meadow Massacre.*[57]

In October Juanita received a request from a college dean in Los Angeles for documented information regarding the influence of members of the Mormon Battalion upon the Gadsden Purchase and the California Gold Rush. The dean desired the information for the dedication of a sculpted wall and fountain commemorating the raising of the first American flag at Fort Moore in 1847. Unfortunately, he could offer Juanita no remuneration.[58] Characteristically, she complied, promising that, if the information were required at once, she would drop other matters and get it out to you immediately."[59] This minor incident is entirely typical of Juanita's compulsive response to a plea for historiographical help. Her files are replete with requests from persons great and small and with her detailed responses giving whatever she knew of names, dates, and sources.

In December Juanita wrote Russell Mortensen and offered to resign from the Board of State History for having failed to organize a local chapter of the Utah Historical Society in St. George. Mortensen quickly returned a reassuring letter. As far as he was concerned, she could forget all about forming a local chapter. Local chapters were Joel Ricks' enthusiasm, not Mortensen's. "And forget that business of resigning. There are too few people like you and Dale to uphold the banner of objective scholarship without voluntarily withdrawing yourself from a position of influence weak as you may think it is."[60]

She had neglected her duty to the society, as she conceived it, because she had been "burning the before-daylight oil consistently," in an attempt to complete the editing of the Lee diaries within the time Cleland had allotted. As usual she found numerous distractions. Although she was on furlough from the college during this year, she was anomalously enrolled as both student and moderator in a Great Books extension course from the University of Utah which met at the college one night a week. She had recently given the literary lesson at Relief Society and had served on a club committee. "Sometimes I feel that one more complication & I'll do like the old Tramp who lay sleeping under the tree who patiently permitted the gnats and flies and ants to explore his face until a bee lit on his nose and stung it. 'Now just for that, you'll all have to move,' he said, and with one angry swoop cleared out the whole outfit."[61]

On the evening of Wednesday, January 13, 1954, Juanita attended a reception in Salt Lake. On Thursday she had lunch with Dale Morgan. It was another moment of saying good-bye. Morgan had returned briefly to Salt Lake following a long residence in Washington; now he was departing for Berkeley, where he would take a position organizing the manuscript collection of the Bancroft Library. On Friday afternoon Juanita penned Morgan a letter on Hotel Temple Square stationery. That morning, after hours of waiting, she had seen Dr. Leland Cowan, who examined her for a disorder of the cervix. "When he had finished with me I was a bit dazed," she wrote. She attempted, however, to be optimistic: "I'm sure everything is O.K. It just *can't* be malignant. And it will be such a relief to be rid of the uncertainty."[62]

On Saturday she entered the LDS hospital to await a minor operation on Monday. While she waited, two interns gave her unexplained uterine examinations. One was a Nicaraguan who spoke little English; his procedure, as Juanita later described it, "was like a play-doctor business. I assumed that he needed practice and I was willing to humor him and help him get it." With the other intern, whose English was better, her anger boiled over—to no effect, for he proceeded with the examination. "When he had finished I said, 'Dr., I'm supposed to be in here for a tumor. Would you say that said tumor is as big as a pea or a grape or an orange?' A shadow crossed his face . . . and he said, 'Well—I'm not sure that I'd call it a tumor exactly. There's an excoriation about the size of a dime.' "[63] During the day, when she could read, write letters, and receive visitors, she was in control of her emotions, but at night she was wracked by frightful memories of Ernest's death.

On Monday Cowan performed the operation and biopsy and left the hospital before Juanita had recovered from the anesthetic. For several days she remained in Salt Lake. Though she repeatedly inquired of staff nurses and the two interns, she could learn nothing about the biopsy. She drew a terrifying conclusion: if the biopsy had been favorable, the hospital staff would have told her so; their silence meant that the unfavorable results had been passed on to Will or Dr. Reichmann in St. George, whose duty it would be to inform her. In a state of shock she took a bus home. Will greeted her so cheerfully that she knew he had received no bad news. Telling him all was well, she grimly waited for a call from Reichmann, which never came. Gradually it dawned on her that no news was good news.

Not until the summer would she write Cowan for a formal report. When he assured her she had no malignancy, she wrote another letter explaining that his failure to inform her earlier had caused her great distress: "If you had deliberately tried to create a fear psychology, you could not have succeeded better," she wrote.[64] In August, Cowan sent a belated bill for $125. Juanita was startled, having assumed that when she had paid her hospital bill, she had settled her entire account. "Your bill . . . gives me the opportunity to do what I have wanted to do ever since I left the LDS Hospital," she replied with undisguised anger. "I pride myself upon paying my bills promptly, but before I pay this one, I think I should have some satisfaction as to the services." She reviewed the indignity of the unnecessary uterine examinations by the two interns. She heatedly emphasized that she did not know what Cowan had done to her during the operation and that she had never received a laboratory report on the biopsy. It is a testimony as to the sting of Juanita's pen that Cowan replied with a full explanation of the biopsy procedure and an assertion of personal injury: "This is one of the very few letters in all my practice that I have received in great dissatisfaction."[65]

In February 1954 Juanita traveled to the Huntington for a conference with Cleland. She stayed at night with Joseph and Tina Walker in Los Angeles. In anticipation of her visit Walker had written with typical ebullience, promising "heaps of grapefruit and dates" and "free meals"—with the cautionary note that the meals could not equal the breakfasts of "17 little hotcakes" followed by "eggs and bacon and toast" which Will customarily cooked when the Walkers came to St. George. "Anyway, romp along," Walker had concluded, "and we'll gossip about something. There's always the weather, the Reds, and arthritis. Even if we have to fall back onto 'rhumatiz,' dammit, we can still gossip."[66]

Juanita's interview with Cleland was encouraging. She had recently mailed him edited, annotated drafts of two of the four Lee diaries assigned to her. He seemed so pleased with her work that upon her return to St. George she wrote him a letter again proposing to include in their forthcoming publication as many as possible of the half-dozen or more unpublished Lee diaries not in the possession of the Huntington.[67] Through Lee's granddaughters Mozelle Bickley and Manetta Henrie, Juanita had obtained typescripts of four: the diary of Lee's first mission, 1841; the diary of his second mission, 1844; his Camp of Israel journal, 1846; and his Mormon Battalion journal, 1846. Cleland replied dubiously. He believed the Huntington would not have funds for so large a work, and he foresaw the improbability of the Church giving the necessary approval. He ended his letter most cordially: "I greatly enjoyed your visit to the Library. I think we're getting somewhere rather fast."[68] Juanita resigned herself to the fact that only the five Huntington diaries would be published. The others, as she told Cleland, would furnish material for the annotation of those five and for the brief transitional narratives which she would write to bridge the gaps between them.[69]

In April Cleland mailed Juanita a draft of the introduction to the work, which he had written, and the edited typescript of the diary of 1848–49, which an assistant had prepared. Cleland asked for Juanita's close scrutiny of both documents. She responded with detailed comments in a cover letter and on the margins of the manuscripts. A typical criticism was that Mountain Meadows was not a "site on the Santa Clara River," as Cleland had asserted: "There is no river at or near the Meadows. At the time of the massacre there was a small spring there which eventually found its way into the small Santa Clara

Creek." She complimented the introduction emphatically, calling it "a wonderful piece of work" and noting Cleland's excellent "balance and perspective" in condensing historical facts.[70] Accepting most of her suggestions, Cleland declared that her praise had pleased him "immensely."[71] He had, after all, trod upon a ground where she, rather than he, was the recognized authority.

In the meantime another change was afoot in the Brooks domicile. In March Ettie Lee sold the Lee Motel and instructed the Brookses to turn it over to its new managers on April 1. Juanita and Will immediately began the laborious process of vacating their house on the hill of its tenants and refurbishing it with fresh paint and new linoleum and carpet. On April 12, the new owners of the motel, with whom the Brookses had shared living quarters for some days, reneged on their purchase and departed. Ettie pleaded with the Brookses to remain as managers while she searched for another buyer. Because they had moved most of their furniture to their house, Juanita and the children moved there while Will remained at the motel. Juanita was greatly annoyed that, as they waited from one week to the next for Ettie to effect a sale, she and Will resided in separate quarters.[72]

In May 1954 Willa graduated from Dixie. Her presence in her parents' home thereafter would be infrequent, because, following another summer at the lodge in Zion Park, she would migrate to BYU to pursue a teaching certificate. She left Dixie with flourish, having been elected D-Day Queen. A photograph in the 1954 yearbook shows her beneath an arch, flanked by six attendants clad in white. She wears a dark strapless formal. Beneath a glittering tiara, her face is serene and attractive.

As the school year ended, Juanita wrote a long evaluation of the evening course in Great Books which she had both taken for credit and moderated. The course had been, as she described it, "an experiment in adult education." Students could apparently elect credit from either Dixie College or the University of Utah. Three times each quarter professors from the latter institution visited the class; otherwise, Juanita gave leadership to the course. The reading list ranged from *The Odyssey* and *The Nicomachean Ethics* to *The Brothers Karamozov* and *Lord Jim*, all the more remarkable for the fact that the enrollees were ordinary citizens of St. George, "all rural folk with western-desert background." Except for three or four young men the enrollees were women, all but two married. Juanita alluded to the elementary school teacher "who hereafter will include Socrates in her work with the 7th grade" and to the Dixie Mormons "who will hereafter see in the worship of others a sacred, meaningful matter, as genuine before God as is their own pattern." As for herself, Juanita would exploit the course in her later teaching by assigning many of the books in her college literature classes.

One supposes that the discussions Juanita led each week were both heated and exhilarating. The course was for her a renewed encounter with the Outside. For example, while reading *Walden* she found a kindred spirit in Thoreau, whom she judged to be "not a mystic, but a keen observer who took a sensuous delight in the sights and sounds around him." She conjectured on what the result would have been had Thoreau's landscape been the desert she knew rather than the forests of Massachusetts: "Could he have endured the barren distances and unbroken silence? Would the nightly sunset pageant when the hills bloom lavender and rose in the reflected splendor, and the benediction of the night with the stars hanging low and clear compensate for the threat and glare of mid-day? Perhaps on the desert he would have become a second Jeremiah, for it seems not exactly an accident that the major prophets all came up out of the desert."[73]

During May Juanita also wrote a review of Leonard Arrington's *Orderville, Utah: A Pioneer Mormon Experiment in Economic Organization*, a review soon appearing in the *Western Humanities Review*. Juanita praised Arrington, a good friend and a noted Mormon historian, for a "scholarly, fair presentation."[74] However, she devoted much of her review not to Arrington's book but to her own observations on the failure of the experimental United Order in communities other than Orderville. On the first weekend in June, she attended a reunion of the John D. Lee family at Lee's Ferry on the Colorado River. There were sightseeing excursions, Dutch oven meals, and campfire assemblies with reports, prayers, and hymns. As an honorary member of the family, Juanita addressed the group on Lee's experiences at the ferry, a topic about which she now knew a great deal.[75]

Throughout the summer of 1954, Will spent his nights at the motel. At home, Juanita moved her desk, typewriter, and cooler into Willa's upstairs bedroom, where she found contentment editing the final Lee diary. Occasionally she recruited Karl, Kay, and Tony for labor in the backyard. "Only this morning I got out with the boys to encourage a campaign against the weeds," she wrote Morgan, "and was digging in a bit by way of demonstration, when a wasp attacked me—just struck with such lightning speed that I didn't know what hit the knuckle of my thumb. I'd forgotten how one of those things can hurt! This afternoon the back of my right hand looks like a boxing glove."[76]

During the fall Ettie Lee sold the motel and Juanita and Will were reunited under one roof. In the meantime, Juanita had returned to full-time teaching at the college. In October, while the college took recess for the annual convention of the Utah Education Association, Juanita traveled to the Huntington to confer with Cleland. She was gratified by his satisfaction with her work, but was distressed to find him greatly debilitated by a recent heart attack.[77] Henceforth he would affix his signature to letters with a scrawling, shaky hand. Juanita paused in Los Angeles after her interview with Cleland only long enough to phone Aura, then took a night bus for St. George. Dale Morgan would shortly inform her of the astonishment her travel habits engendered among observers. He had his information from a Bancroft cataloguer formerly employed by the Huntington: "You have no idea how you impressed them there, the women in particular, for the nonchalant way you would take the bus home, weekends, to fix for your family. It wasn't every day someone commuted to Huntington from St. George or any comparably distant place."[78]

In early 1955 Juanita's stepson Grant Brooks, thirty-six and the father of four children, died from a stroke. On the evening of January 21, Grant's daughter Dawn phoned Juanita—Will being out doing his monthly ward teaching—with the news that her father was in the hospital near death. Juanita arrived to find Grant paralyzed on one side and suffering muscular convulsions on the other. When his breathing stopped and a doctor ordered resuscitation equipment, Juanita protested. The doctor heeded her remonstrance and shortly declared Grant dead. Will approved, as he made clear in a later account: "In an instant more he was beyond recall. It was all over before I got there. Knowing Grant and his condition, I was glad my wife took a firm stand not to prolong his suffering."[79]

Will insisted that the funeral be held in the tabernacle. Maxine, Grant's widow, expected few attenders; to her astonishment, a crowd filled the building. After the funeral, the nineteen-year-old Karl put an arm around Maxine and promised to be a father to her son Bill. When Bill proved difficult to manage at home, Maxine sent him to live with Juanita and Will. For a year Bill remained at the house on the hill, where Karl, Kay, and Tony made a project of reforming his fastidious eating habits. They offered a running commentary upon the desirability of foods which the boy loathed—oranges, eggs, spinach, and so on. By Will's calculation, the effort paid dividends: "Before long Bill ate whatever was served, and prided himself upon how strong and active he was growing because of it."[80]

During the spring of 1955 the staff at the Huntington were proofreading the galleys of the Lee diaries and otherwise preparing them for printing. Juanita was now without a major writing project. She toyed with various possibilities, including a history of Nevada for use as a text in Nevada public schools.[81] She was, however, amply distracted by a renovation and enlargement of the house on the hill. That project represented a major concession on Juanita's part. She had come to dislike the cramped, inelegant house to whose two original rooms had been appended a hodgepodge of peripheral rooms. She had contemplated the purchase of a modern house in Provo or Salt Lake, where her children seemed destined to go for their university education, or the construction of a new house in St. George. In this, however, she came up against a rare resistance in Will. A disagreement ensued which he described as, not a quarrel, but "a sort of a 'cold war' between us."[82] Will did not want to move to Provo or Salt Lake, nor did he relish the idea of building a new home high on the hill just under the Sugar Loaf next to the spring which the family owned. Furthermore, he could not tolerate the thought of razing or plastering over the rock house, nor of felling the giant trees which had shaded the structure from his infancy and before.

In a gesture of compromise, Juanita called in an architect from Cedar City, L. Robert Gardner, who designed an addition to the old house. It was to be a wing running perpendicularly southward from the rock house, a single story over a half buried basement. Using Gardner's plans, Will supervised the construction. The design called for cut rock matching the old house, which had been made from imperfect pieces left over from the construction of the tabernacle, where Will's father, George Brooks, had been a master mason. Such rock was available in a ravine east of town where workers had recently dumped rubble from a house the county school board had bought and razed. Juanita called on the school board and received permission to take the abandoned rock. Her sons transported it in a borrowed pickup, and Will hired an expert rock worker to set the stone while he himself mixed mortar and carried hod. "We worked at our own pace," Will wrote, "visiting and really enjoying it."[83] In the late fall of 1955, the structure was roofed, plastered, and painted, and the family expanded into its lovely new space.

The residence at 346 North Main was now an eloquent amalgamation of pioneer and modern architecture, justly meriting the listing in the Utah Registry of Historical Homes which it would later achieve. A walk led to a new front door, the former door having been converted into a window. The new wing consisted of a kitchen and a spacious living room with exposed modernistic rafters and southerly picture windows overlooking St. George. Below, the basement was divided into commodious bedrooms. "We have already told everyone who looks at our place that we feel the best money we spent was what we paid the architect," Juanita would write to Gardner. "So many here have felt that they can cut a picture from a home magazine and make that do. I honestly believe that our place, and our great delight with it, may help establish the idea that in the problem of building we need expert help as much as we laymen need help in medicine or other specialized fields."[84]

In early September 1955 Juanita delivered a speech in Harrison, Arkansas, where the Fancher train had assembled in the spring of 1857 before striking west toward its destiny at Mountain Meadows, Utah. The occasion was the dedication of a monument erected to the victims of the massacre by the Richard Fancher Society of America. J. K. Fancher, president of the society, had requested a representation from Utah. Accordingly, Russell Mortensen arranged to pay Juanita's travel expenses through a gift from Nicholas G. Morgan, Sr., a member of the Board of State History.

Five hundred persons gathered in the Harrison court park on the morning of Sunday, September 4, and listened to hymns, prayers, and speeches. One supposes that Juanita anticipated condemnation and blame, since she had been announced in the Friday *Harrison Daily Times* as a Latter-day Saint who would "give the Mormon version of the massacre."[85] When the crowd adjourned at noon for a box lunch at a nearby American Legion hall, Juanita inadvertently communicated her disconsolation to J. K. Fancher, who ten years afterward reminded her of the following incident: "You must have been lonely, because you said, 'Don't you guess I'd better go to a cafe and

get my dinner,' and I told you not to do so as the people would feel
hurt. And I told you about Franklin D. Roosevelt once as a graduation exercise speaker what he told [a woman who] was to talk before
he did—she said, 'I am scared,' and he replied, 'I am scared too—just
think of others instead of yourself and that will help.' I remember a
very sweet inspiring smile come over your face, and your feeling of
loneliness and fear seemed to vanish and from then on you seemed as
one of us, a Christian sister and a true and loyal friend. And I could
see on your face renewed inspiration for the wonderful address you
were soon to give!"[86]

Following lunch, a local historian recounted the horrifying
details of the massacre. Then members of the local Masonic lodge,
attired in business suits and white waist aprons, unveiled the imposing granite shaft, and a pretty eight-year-old girl, said to be the great-
great-granddaughter of Captain Alexander Fancher, leader of the murdered emigrants, laid a large wreath of flowers against it. Juanita was
composed. She now stood and delivered with a kinetic eloquence the
most important speech of her life.

"My dear friends," she began. "My text for today comes
from Proverbs 4:7—'And with all thy getting, get understanding.' "
She explained why the Mormons had committed the massacre, alluding to the persecutions of Missouri and Illinois, to the approach of
Johnston's army, and to the excitement of the Indians. Admitting that
the massacre was "one of the most despicable mass murders of history,"
she emphasized that it had nonetheless been uncharacteristic of the
Mormons who had carried it out. "It was tragic for those who were
killed and for the children left orphans, but it was also tragic for the
fine men who now became murderers, and for their children who for
four generations now have lived under that shadow."[87]

"You impressed the people most favorably," Fancher wrote
shortly afterward, "and your coming has done much to establish a
spirit of love and forgiveness. The Mormon Church owes you much
because now the people in this section feel much better toward the
Mormon people."[88] Back home in Utah her address struck a similar
chord in many. Russell Mortensen published it in the winter 1956
issue of *Utah Historical Quarterly*. In 1958 Mortensen and William
Mulder would reprint it in their *Among the Mormons: Historical Accounts
by Contemporary Observers*, an anthology published by Alfred A. Knopf.
One is reminded that penitence was prominent among Juanita's pur-

poses in writing and speaking about the massacre. She had become the public voice, otherwise silent, of confession and contrition for the most shameful deed in Mormon history.

During September 1955 Juanita also carried out minor literary projects. One was the writing of a note on Fort Pierce, a guard station built in 1863 and shortly abandoned, scarcely a dozen miles from St. George on a would-be route to Arizona. This brief piece appeared in the October 1955 issue of *SUP News*, the monthly publication of the Sons of the Utah Pioneers. Another project was the reprinting of *Dudley Leavitt: Pioneer to Southern Utah*, the little volume about her grandfather which she had written and published in 1942. She contracted with a Salt Lake firm for a precise reproduction by offset press of the original work.[89] Thereafter she sold copies at a price about five times greater than her cost.

Having decided to retire from teaching in the fall of 1955, Juanita made arrangements to go on Social Security. Because Will's Social Security payments included an allowance for their dependent children, the couple hoped the family could get by while Juanita devoted her time to writing. However, when school opened with unexpectedly high enrollments, she agreed to teach a single course in college English for $72 a month, a stipend allowable under Social Security regulations. Always susceptible to a plea for help, she agreed to coach the high school debate team without pay. At the beginning of winter quarter she would agree to take on a second English class for pay, thereby disqualifying herself for Social Security payments.[90]

Perhaps it was during this year that Karl took an English class from his mother. Once, as he labored to compose a paper, he asked her how a person could write well. "Her answer was," he recorded, " 'You can't write well. Nobody writes well. With enough patience some people develop an ability to rewrite well if they are willing to do it enough times.' "[91] This was Karl's final year at Dixie. Turning twenty during the fall, he played aggressively on the football team, much to the delight of Will, who attended every home game. As student-body president, Karl was noted for his affable good humor. His photograph appears on the official letterhead of the Associated Students. His utterly blond hair glistens; his handsome face beams. He seems intelligent, sociable, and happy.

Around November 1, 1955, *A Mormon Chronicle: The Diaries of John D. Lee – 1848–1876* made its appearance. A two-volume work totaling 856 pages, it sold for what was at the time a forbidding price of $15. The text of the diaries had been coherently rendered without effacing Lee's charming linguistic license: on the one hand, phonetic spellings and eccentric capitalizations had been preserved; on the other hand, obscure words had been deciphered, inexorable ambiguities had been bracketed, and conventional commas and periods had been inserted. For scholars the diaries would prove invaluable, a rich treasure of fact and intimation. For the general reader too they would have great appeal. As gripping as a novel, they opened a marvelous corridor into the daily doings of Lee and his pioneer associates. In vivid detail emerged their labor, tools, and entertainments; their love, jealousy, and petty striving for status; their narrow escapes, miraculous healings, and inevitable tragedies. Permeating every passage was the paradoxical personality of the author, a man irascible, domineering, and shrewd, yet philanthropic, God-fearing, and compassionate. John D. Lee could at last speak for himself, establishing by his own pen his integrity, humanity, and dignity.

Often Lee's pen transfused ordinary events with a fascinating vitality, as in the following description of a Pioneer Day celebration. In attendance were various friends and relatives "besides some 45 of my wives and children, Making in all about 58 souls who sat down togeather at my Table to a Rich & well got up Dinner. . . . I was also placed to represent the Pioneers & was Selected for one of the speakers of the day. I enJoyed myself well. Dancing comenced at 1 P.m. & continud till midnight."[92]

Even more compelling were the adventures of pioneer life. On a journey with companions during a stormy November, Lee recorded efforts to recover a fugitive mule. Lee pursued the animal through a cold rainstorm for miles before fatigue drove him back to camp. The next day, ignoring Lee's objections, a companion rode into the storm on another mule in search of the first. When after two days and nights the man had not returned, Lee feared that "he had a fit of insanity & had likely Perished." Late on the third night the man returned, his mount utterly fatigued. Lee wrote: "I have no doubt but he rode the mule for 40 hours without stopping to Eat or drink. Through the Night I dreamed Where my Mule was & that I caught it without much Trouble. So on the following Morning Chas. A. & I set out, & at the distance of 4 ms., at the very spot where I saw them in the Dream, we caught the mule with the Saddle still on."[93]

As Lee returned home, finding refuge in villages along the
way, he was more than once called upon to practice his widely recognized powers of healing. An old man, learning of his approach, sent
for him in haste: "I accordingly administered to him, anointing him
with oil in connection with D. Dority & the old man arose, Praised
god & Eat his Brakefast, saying, I knew if you would reach me before
I died, that I would be healed." Lee arrived home in Harmony to find
that between negligent herders and unseasonal rains, his crops were
damaged to the extent of $2,000. "The stock & Rain togeather
destroyed nearly all my crop, including my Hay, & here I was likely to
encounter a Severe Winter without feed for my animals & more than
1/2 of the Bread to sustain my Family to Bye. It was one of the darkest
times I had witnessed for some time."[94]

Lee was by no means loath to attribute a turbulent, earthy
language to his beloved leader Brigham Young, whose words he
recorded as attentively as Boswell had those of Samuel Johnson. Once
when Lee sued a couple for payment for goods which the wife denied
receiving, Brigham Young persuaded Lee to drop the suit and forgive
the debt. Young praised Lee lavishly in court and indirectly castigated the fraudulent wife by unleashing a tirade against the meddling
of women generally in public affairs. "All their council & wisdom
(although there are many good women) don't weigh as much with me
as the weight of a Fly Tird," Lee quoted Young as saying. "Excuse me
for my vulgarity. It is not common for me to use such Language, but I
know of no Language to mean to suit the case before us."[95]

By the modest criteria of western historiography, *A Mormon Chronicle* was an instant success. Two reviews in national publications, appearing within a month of its publication, gave it a more
than local celebrity. A review in *Time* emphasized the contention and
ribaldry of Lee and his fellow pioneers. It called the two-volume work
"one of the most extraordinary documents ever written by an
American."[96] A review in the *New York Times Book Review* doubted
the objectivity of Lee's observations, yet expressed a general admiration for him as "a bold, resourceful, incredibly persistent pioneer."[97]
Among local reviews of note was one by Russell Mortensen, who hurried it into the galleys of the *Utah Historical Quarterly*. Though critical
of errors in the introduction and notes, Mortensen judged that other
Mormon frontier journals "pale into insignificance" when compared
to Lee's diaries.[98] Mortensen published his seemingly bland review with

trepidation, thereafter noting with relief: "I have been prepared to
have coals piled on my head for my review . . . ; so far there has been
no criticism, at least it hasn't been brought to my attention."[99] That
his anxiety was not entirely unfounded is evidenced in the experience of Juanita's longtime friend Olive Burt of the staff of the *Deseret
News*, who had prepared a review which her superiors refused to print.
"Last Sunday," wrote Mortensen to Juanita, "she told me that she
now goes around the office mumbling to herself and out loud to anybody who will listen—Cowards! Cowards! Cowards!"[100]

As 1956 opened, Juanita basked in the glow of an augmented
fame. Friends in great numbers wrote their congratulations. Among
them was Virginia Sorensen, prominent Mormon novelist currently
living in Pennsylvania, with whom Juanita conducted an intermittent
correspondence: "I've been tossing my hat in the air about the wonderful notices! I'm so glad and so proud. I wish to heaven I could see
you for a celebration—and that you're sure-enough having one. The
very notion of you gives me health and strength and always has. Bless
you and your work and your honesty and your good sound sense."[101]
Leonard Arrington, however, confided to Juanita that the diaries had
disillusioned him. He regretted that they revealed the unsavory aspect
of Mormonism, "the crudity and narrowness and littleness of it," and
that they depicted the non-Mormons who had dealt with Lee as "mean
and petty, and base." Ruefully Arrington wondered: "Did Lee bring
out the worst in people; or are his reports an accurate picture of people as they are?"[102] Soon replying, Juanita defended Lee, alluding to
his praise for many of his associates and pointing out that the petty
bickerings he reported were characteristic of the Bunkerville of her
childhood. "I had thought," she wrote, "that it was typical of the daily
trivialities that fill many of our lives, that if I were to write faithfully at
the end of every day, I might record some differences and misunder-
standings—more perhaps if I were weary when I set myself down to
write."[103]

From the Huntington came word of jubilation as sales of
the expensive volumes quickly surpassed expectations—by May over
1,000 sets of a printing of 1,500 would sell. Martha Padve of the library's
publication department wrote Juanita: "I only wish you and Dr. Cleland
could be here to share the whoops of joy with which these old walls
resound when we receive news of another call, another review, another
wire, another large order."[104] In October 1956 it would be Juanita's

pleasure to learn that the American Association for State and Local History had extended an Award of Merit to *A Mormon Chronicle* as an outstanding contribution in biography. The honor was not diminished by the fact that her faithful ally in Salt Lake, Russell Mortensen, was a member of the association's awards committee. His furtherance of *A Mormon Chronicle* and of Juanita's reputation generally was an unconscious strategy in the unequal battle for the liberalization of Mormonism. For Mortensen, as for an ever growing number of liberal Mormons, Juanita was a preeminent front-line soldier, a faithful Mormon who had the courage for open dissent.

CHAPTER • EIGHT

A LIFE AT ITS PEAK

During the fall of 1955 a friend of Juanita's requested the opinion of Elder LeGrand Richards regarding *The Mountain Meadows Massacre*. In his reply the apostle cast doubt upon Juanita's friendliness toward the Church. Perhaps unwisely, the friend forwarded the letter to Juanita, who immediately wrote the apostle defending herself: "Anyone who knows me will tell you that I have always been active in the Church: MIA Ward President, MIA Stake Board, Stake S.S. Board, Stake Pres. of Relief Society. I financed, practically alone, a brother and a sister on missions; we have sent two sons on missions and have three more growing up to go. I went to the Temple just last Saturday."[1]

In his prompt reply, Richards complimented Juanita's good deeds but reiterated his negative judgment. Even if her interpretation of the massacre were correct, he asserted, it was not in the interest of the Church "to bring it up at this late date." He was reminded of a mother who cautioned a tactless son who wished to inform a man that his nose was big and red: "All the truth does not always need to be told."[2] Quickly mailing a rebuttal, Juanita claimed that time would prove her book to have been in the best interest of the Church. As for the man with the red nose, it seemed "that if he had a mirror, no one would need to tell him of it. He could see plainly enough himself."[3] Richards agreed to accept the test of time but affirmed his prior position: "I love the church so much and have defended it so many times that I don't like to see statements coming from within that in any way cast a shadow upon the integrity of the leaders of the church." He declared that he intended to read the book, "hoping that by so doing I will obtain a more favorable impression than I now have."[4]

Some weeks later, his reading completed, Richards wrote that he was unwilling to believe that Brigham Young and other leaders had inflamed their zealous followers before the massacre, had concealed their misdeed afterward, and had sacrificed John D. Lee in the interest of the Church at large. "I am at a loss to understand your motive for writing the book," he asserted. "In view of your statement that you are a loyal member of the church, and interested in its reputation, surely you cannot truthfully say that your book does not injure the reputation of your church and its leaders." He exhorted her to turn her gifted pen to a work that promoted rather than destroyed faith. With that, he insisted the matter be closed.[5]

Once again Juanita had vainly sought vindication for her interpretation of the massacre. The foremost issue between Juanita and the Church at large was the reputation of Brigham Young. According to a cherished Mormon belief, the president of the Church, God's anointed mouthpiece, is the most infallible and perfect of living persons. Among the presidents of the Church, Brigham Young has ranked a close second to Joseph Smith in the esteem of the Latter-day Saints. Unquestionably, his success in planting Mormon colonies throughout the strategic center of the mountain West explains the vigor of the modern Church, which claims over six million members. Without denying his prophetical calling, Juanita repudiated the heroic perfection of Brigham Young. She in fact held a lifelong grudge against him for having sent her ancestors into an impoverished exile on the ragged edge of the Mormon empire. A recurrent minor theme in her historical writing, early and late, was Brigham Young's callous treatment of his obedient followers. "The deepest anger in her was something I've thought a lot about," wrote one of Juanita's associates at the Utah Historical Society. "She inherited the feeling that the Church was at fault for sending all those people into those incredible places. They felt that they had been abandoned, that people from [Salt Lake] had all the advantages and that they thought they were superior to their wilderness brothers and sisters. She carried in her a paranoia rooted in that situation that colored so many things that she did and said. Her favorite story was one about Brigham Young's daughter coming to St. George to tell the sisters they must retrench. After listening to the lavishly dressed woman, one of the sisters got up and said, 'What do you want us to retrench from, the bread or the molasses?' "[6]

In January 1956 Juanita protested the prosecution of Vera Black, a polygamous wife who, because her residence was in Utah, had not been arrested in the raid of July 1953. In 1954 Vera Black had provided a test case for Utah officials who proposed to separate children from parents who would not sign an affidavit promising neither to teach nor practice polygamy. Juanita was present at Short Creek on June 4, 1954, when officers came to transport seven of Black's eight children to Provo where they would be placed in a foster home. With Juanita's encouragement, Black insisted on riding to St. George with her children, then on to Cedar City, where by a judge's order she was evicted from the automobile. An appellate judge soon overturned the order of separation and the children and mother were reunited.[7]

By January 1956 Utah officials had refined their case against Black. After an abortive initial effort, law officers and welfare workers succeeded in transporting Vera Black and her children to Provo, where for more than two hours officials made a last attempt to persuade the woman to renounce polygamy and keep her children. She refused and her children were again placed in a foster home in Provo under orders to have no communication with former loved ones or friends. A photograph in the *Daily Herald* of January 13 shows the weeping Black and two of her daughters at the heartrending moment of separation.

At home, Juanita followed this development with seething emotion. She wrote a welfare officer in Provo pleading that the children at least be kept together so that the younger children could find support among the older. Of particular concern was a little boy named Wilford whose fragile temperament reminded Juanita of Tony's. Alluding to the first attempt to separate the Black children from their mother, Juanita wrote: "Only a mother who has nursed along such a frail, sensitive child, could realize what that experience did to Wilford, and how deeply and irreparably he is being injured by this one."[8]

It was, however, an editorial in the *Deseret News* of Saturday, January 28, entitled "Stamp Out Polygamy," which triggered Juanita's full anger. She composed letters to the editors of the Salt Lake and Provo newspapers, which the *Tribune* obligingly printed and the *Deseret News* and the *Daily Herald* stolidly ignored. Few statements of her entire life were as eloquent of indignation as her unacknowledged letter to the *Deseret News*. "That the official organ of the Church of Jesus Christ of Latter-day Saints should approve such a basically cruel and wicked thing as the taking of little children and babies from their mother strains the faith of many, many of us." Predicting that like action against other polygamists would sunder the Church, she likened it to the treatment of slaves in early America. Never in their most oppressive zeal had federal prosecutors of Mormon polygamists in the nineteenth century attempted to separate mothers from their children. "In trying to stamp out one evil," she pleaded, "let us not commit another so black that it will shame us for ages to come."[9]

Juanita's letters would be published in the March 1956 issue of *Truth*, a Salt Lake fundamentalist magazine. From California, Samuel W. Taylor—author and maverick grandson of church president John Taylor and son of apostle John W. Taylor—wrote his praise of these letters: "I admire your courage and wish more of us had some of it."[10] Juanita would shortly write an affirmative review, appearing in the *Utah Historical Quarterly*, of Taylor's *I Have Six Wives*, a factual treatment of a polygamous family in contemporary Utah. Taylor's book reminded Juanita that the student of nineteenth-century polygamy would find among modern polygamists "a repetition of the same words, the same fervor, and the same aura of religious exaltation which surrounnded the Saints before the Manifesto. To these people the forgotten story of the Angel with the Drawn Sword is alive and vital; the sermons of Brigham Young and his contemporaries ring with counsel and command not to be ignored."[11]

Juanita's protest in early 1956 of the treatment of Vera Black and her children had no immediate result. It would be with satisfaction but no sense of personal achievement that Juanita would learn in June that Black and her children had been reunited after the woman had unexpectedly reversed her position and agreed to renounce polygamy.[12] Nonetheless, Juanita's indignation and that of a swelling number of other liberal-minded persons would ultimately effect an undeclared amnesty for Utah's polygamists. Although legislation prohibiting polygamy remains upon the books, officials today quietly neglect its enforcement.

In January 1956, BYU religion professor Anthony I. Bentley sent Juanita a questionnaire soliciting her opinion on the place of creative thinking within the Church. Initially she was suspicious, for she constantly feared that her written statements, come into the wrong hands, might be used against her in a church court. Though guarded, her response to the questionnaire was an admirable elaboration of her liberal outlook. Human beings honor God, she asserted, when they fully exploit the intellectual gifts with which he has endowed them. "We should bring the best we have to the consideration of every problem and accept what seems truth to us regardless of dictums from any Authority. By the 'best we have' I include not only mental faculties but spiritual intuition. Nor would I exclude the possibility of . . . re-examination and modification of a conclusion or stand." For members who might be fearful of freely expressing themselves, she could only adduce her own insistence upon speaking out as a free American. She had, she avowed, repeatedly criticized annoying alterations in church rituals such as the banning of background music from the sacrament service and the military-like regimentation of the deacons who passed the bread and water to the congregation. More important, she would continue to speak out in condemnation of the Church's treatment of fundamentalists, in particular of its role in the prosecution of Vera Black, which, she went on to assert, was "the most wicked thing that has been done in our state since the Mountain Meadows Massacre."[13]

On a Sunday afternoon in February Juanita appeared for a discussion of A Mormon Chronicle on "Cavalcade of Books" on Los Angeles TV channel two. Cleland was not present, for at that moment her coeditor lay critically ill in a hospital. Juanita was pleased that Aura sat in the studio audience. Of all her siblings, Aura had seemed the most willing to ostracize her for having written the history of the massacre. At six o'clock Monday morning Juanita arrived home by bus and at eight was in her classroom.[14]

Her appearance on Los Angeles TV stimulated a flurry of literary solicitations. At the studio an agent from Colliers encouraged her to write and submit an article about Emma, the wife of John D. Lee who accompanied him into exile at Lee's Ferry.[15] With characteristic luck, Juanita would soon see the piece rejected. An agent from Harper's traveled to St. George and urged her to submit an unspecified work to his firm. Turnley Walker, Juanita's interlocutor on the TV program, expressed an interest in creating a movie script based on The Mountain Meadows Massacre. Perpetually lured by the big money and splashy fame of a successful Hollywood production, Juanita entered a correspondence with Walker. As a first condition, he insisted that she secure the copyright to her book.[16] Since her contract with Stanford University Press allowed for a reversion of the copyright to the author when sales became negligible, Juanita made a hopeful inquiry as to when the work would be sold out. The press returned the discouraging estimate of eighteen months. After a period of ineffectual brooding, Juanita reworded her inquiry. How many copies were actually on hand? Back came the encouraging news of a prior miscalculation: only eighty-two remained. Juanita immediately mailed a check for the entire stock[17] and thereafter barraged the press with pleas that it release the copyright. One of the first acts of a new director of the press in May 1956 was to rescind the copyright to Juanita,[18] who immediately proceeded to register the work in her own name. Walker declared himself greatly cheered by the news. "I am now doing final rewrite on a picture to be filmed in August and September, and, if we can get things properly set up, should have time to get started on 'Massacre' in the meantime."[19] However, no movie was ever made. There is, in fact, no evidence that Walker completed a script. Possibly he eventually recognized that the massacre did not lend itself to a conventional romantic plot.

In June, Juanita and Will attended Willa's graduation from BYU. As she departed for Provo, Juanita suffered from a painfully swollen eyelid. When Ettie Lee phoned following her departure, Karl described his mother's affliction with some alarm. Deciding it was a serious matter, Ettie wrote revealing that she was fasting and praying in Juanita's behalf and urging Juanita to visit a tumor specialist in Salt Lake. From Los Angeles, physician Joseph Walker also wrote, for, unknown to Karl and Ettie, Juanita had consulted him by phone and received a calming diagnosis. She had a sty, for which he was forwarding ointments. Its Latin name was "Hordeolum Meibomianum," which Juanita must use when persuading her bishop to excuse her from Sunday duties. "I further prescribe: Each Sunday morning a couple of cups of coffee with Will's Little Anti-sty hotcakes, a comfortable nest in the new home, keeping on your pajamas, and whether you are a Christian or not, for the one day at least of Sunday, believing the good Lord knew what he was talking about when he ordered one day of rest."[20]

Ettie was willing to fast and pray because she was convinced, as she wrote Juanita, that "God has set you apart for special services."[21] The calling she had in mind was a biography of John D. Lee. A month earlier Ettie had reported a conversation at a dinner party in Los Angeles in which it been generally agreed that Juanita was "Utah's first lady." "No matter who may speak of a biography of Grandfather," Ettie went on, "there is just one person really equipped to do one worthy of his life and sacrifice and that is you.[22] Accordingly, in mid-June Juanita attended the reunion of the Lee family in the mountain village of Alpine, Arizona. Departing from Los Angeles, Ettie, Juanita, and two of Ettie's sisters drove across the southern Arizona desert and on into the White Mountains. Returning via St. George, the travelers passed through places of importance in John D. Lee's final years—Tuba City, Moencopi, Moenavi, and Lonely Dell.

At home, Juanita was moved to write a piece which she had promised Russell Mortensen some time earlier. Her new grasp of Arizona's geography became immediately useful as she put the finishing touches to "Lee's Ferry at Lonely Dell," which would appear in *Utah Historical Quarterly* in 1957. The article ends with a pedestrian consideration of the ferry in the years after it had passed out of the hands of John D. and Emma Lee. In its early pages, however, it is a gripping narrative of the struggle of the exiled Lee and his heroic wife to raise food in an arid, denuded gorge and to maintain the ferry against the hazards of the treacherous Colorado. In June 1872, following a flash flood on the Paria, Lee battled for twenty-one days to construct a dam eight feet high and seven rods long. In July came another flood. Having barely revived his crops, he began again. He was assisted by four small sons and Emma, who nursed a newborn baby. Such drama had long attracted Juanita. Now, following the trip to Alpine and the completion of her article, she became resolute. She announced to her friends that she considered herself launched upon a full-fledged biography of John D. Lee.[23]

Juanita agreed to teach full-time in the fall of 1956. On her schedule of instruction was a high school English course for which she was required to renew her teaching certificate. She therefore enrolled in two extension graduate courses from the University of Utah. Under William Mulder she would pursue a directed readings course in Western American literature; under Henry Webb, a bibliography and research course.[24] She decided to dispose first of Mulder's course. Her reports on books Mulder assigned revealed her fundamental educability. She reacted intensely to Henry Nash Smith's *Virgin Land*, which dispelled many of her favorite myths about the West—its refuge for the unfortunate, the independence of its yeoman farmers, the success of the Homestead Act. "To have each held up, turned around, examined, and then discarded as unsound forces me to look at history and at the general philosophy of government with a more critical eye. . . . I had no idea of the contrast between the image of the West and the fact, the ideal and the actual."[25]

On a Saturday evening in October, she began to read A. B. Guthrie's *The Big Sky*—reluctantly, because she was not interested in mountain men. Quickly the novel seized her and she stayed home from stake conference on the following day and read on, "so engrossed," she reported, "that I came up out of it as though I had been on a cheap drunk." She liked the descriptions of the Rocky Mountain wilderness and was fascinated by the primitive masculinity of Guthrie's characters. "All the crudity and stamina, the savagery and brutality are here. After his detail of the sex life of the mountain men, I fully expected him to bring in a few perverts—what John D. Lee called sodomy or another diarist spoke of as 'having to do with a mare.' I was pleased that he did not get to that, though I think he might have done without exaggeration."[26]

During the following week, though her eyes ached, Juanita read Willa Cather's *My Antonia* at a forced pace. She taught five classes a day and entertained Bob's wife and children at home while Bob, on leave, accompanied his father and brothers on the deer hunt. She helped Willa, who taught in Provo but was home for a weekend, prepare a shower for a roommate who was getting married. She also tried to complete a brief paper on John D. Lee's prison experiences for the November meeting of the Utah Academy.[27] Not surprisingly she delivered a short, negative report on Cather's novel of the Nebraska sod-busting frontier. Mulder responded tactfully. At her leisure she was to read about Cather in a secondary source. She was not to be deceived by Cather's seeming simplicity. "Give her—and yourself—the break of a considered critical second look," Mulder urged.[28]

Her final report was on Andy Adams' *The Log of a Cowboy.* In mid-November, she carried the book as she journeyed north to attend the Academy meetings. Ensconced in Willa's apartment in Provo, she read on a Thursday evening and Friday morning. Friday afternoon, she traveled to Weber College in Ogden where she read her paper. She snatched a couple of hours of reading at the home of Golden and Ethyl Taylor in Logan where, after speaking to a group on a historical topic, she spent Friday night. Making her way to Provo by noon Saturday, she finished the book in Willa's apartment. She arrived in St. George on the bus at 3:45 Sunday morning. When she had seen Will, Kay, and Tony off to Priesthood Meeting, she settled down to write a report. With great relish she recited episodes from this novel about a trail drive from Texas to Montana and digressed into memories of cowboys and cattle from her own childhood: "Little things like hog-tieing the mule and pulling it across the river stirred many memories. I once helped to build a fire under the belly of a recalcitrant burro. I remember a neighbor with a team of horses pulling a live mule down the street by the neck. As he came past our place, Dad called out goodnaturedly to him and he stopped the horses. As soon as the rope slacked, the mule scrambled to its feet and from there on followed along as tractable [sic] as Mary's lamb."[29] With this Juanita finished the course. Unquestionably her papers were hurried and undisciplined, rambling rather than structured, reminiscent rather than scholarly. Impressed by the vitality of her responses, Mulder nevertheless cheerfully granted a grade.

When Christmas vacation arrived, Juanita wrote Henry Webb that she had suffered a loss of incentive regarding his course. On basis of Mulder's course she had received the desired recertification for high school teaching. Ironically, college enrollments were so high that she was not scheduled to teach high school courses for winter quarter. Exposure in Webb's course to the British Museum's *Catalogue of Printed Books* and the French Biblioteque Nationale's *Catalogue général des livres imprimés* seemed irrelevant to her biography of John D. Lee. Furthermore, she was at a great distance from the university library. The situation, she concluded, was "one of those things which curses him that gives and him that takes because it makes it difficult for you to maintain the standards which you have set for all who receive credit for this course and difficult for me to meet them."[30]

Nonetheless she submitted a preliminary assignment. In January 1957, she mailed another assignment and announced herself compelled to continue: "My pioneer sense of economy demands that I do not waste the good money I paid for registration fee; my own stubborn pride will not let me admit that I am incapable of completing it."[31] In March she mailed a biographical sketch of John Doyle, the maternal grandfather of John D. Lee. It was, Juanita emphasized in her cover letter, "a good example of research done by mail," for she had been busily engaged in correspondence with the Historical Society of Illinois and with governmental offices in Illinois and Virginia in pursuit of information about the ancestors of her pioneer subject.[32]

On April 12, Juanita traveled to Provo and addressed an assembly of English faculty and students at BYU. At home, she enlarged her speech into a documented paper, which she mailed to Webb, hoping that it would satisfy a requirement in his course. If it would not, she wrote, "it is not too important, because I wanted to do it anyway."[33] Webb accepted the paper, an advanced if not entirely polished draft called "A Tentative Examination of Some Basic Mormon Concepts." In it Juanita discussed some disparities between historical fact and present belief among the Mormons. Temperance societies had propounded the dicta of the Word of Wisdom regarding abstinence from alcohol, tobacco, coffee, and tea long before Joseph Smith had emitted that revelation, and a myriad of cooperative communities in Europe and America had preceded the United Order of the Mormons. There were disturbing similarities between the Book of Mormon and a contemporary nineteenth-century American book, *A View of the Hebrews*, as Mormon historian and general authority B. H. Roberts had demonstrated in his surreptitious manuscript "Parallel" (a copy of which Juanita had come by twenty years earlier from Newel K. Young, the polygamous principal of the Richfield seminary).

It was lamentable, Juanita argued, that the Church sought to excise its past, conveniently practicing "denial by omission." Whatever the borrowings of the early Mormons from their neighboring societies, whatever their failings and excesses, the "magnitude of their accomplishment justifies them. Whatever its surroundings, our early church was a great dynamo, generating such energy, such unshakable conviction and strong emotion that after many years and thousands of miles it could establish itself in this forbidding land." Moreover, as God's people, the Latter-day Saints had a calling to liberality. "We should be the most progressive and open-minded of all men, as well as the most tolerant and kindly. We should really incorporate into our lives the 13th article of faith and keep it as a lamp to our feet."[34]

Although Henry Webb was not a Mormon, he could appreciate the local import of this paper as in June 1957 he gave a final reading to it and other papers Juanita had submitted. He had been tempted, he wrote, "to take red pencil in hand and strike out a few things here and there, but I soon decided that what I would have taken away would have been part of your personality. There is a discursive, digressive, highly personal quality in your style that must be associated with subjectivity rather than with objectivity. . . . Now this *might* be considered 'bad.' However, since whatever else it does, it creates interest (and thus leads one to read on and to learn), I put the pencil down. . . . There are too many boring historians in the world for me to carp at an interesting one."[35] Thus ended for Juanita a profitable if unorthodox experience in graduate education with the University of Utah.

Near the same time Juanita and Will looked on as Kay graduated from Dixie College. Kay planned to work for the summer and in the fall join Karl at BYU. In July, Juanita and Will bought a year-old Plymouth from a dealer in Cedar City—a pink sedan having swept-back fins, a powerful engine, and an air conditioner. At $2,500, it was one of the most luxurious cars of their career—and destined to become the most famous, for as time passed and its splendor regressed into oxidized paint and dented fenders, the Brooks offspring would give it the affectionate name of "the Pink Bomb."

In July 1957 Juanita attempted to organize an on-site centennial commemoration of the Mountain Meadows massacre. She had heard talk favorable to the idea among the trustees of the Utah Historical Society; a board member had even promised to donate a bronze plaque and marker on the highway near the site—a promise that failed to materialize. In town for a brief visit, Maurine Whipple informed Juanita on July 20 that Newsweek would be interested in a photographic story if representatives of the Fancher family in Arkansas could be persuaded to attend the ceremony at Mountain Meadows. Juanita wrote J. K. Fancher—Kenner, as she now familiarly called him—urging him to organize a family excursion.[36] Traveling to Salt Lake, she encountered an entrenched apathy which she suspected was owing to opposition from church leaders. At home on August 1, she wrote Fancher urging him to forget the matter.[37] The aborted initiative marked the beginning of a minor obsession which Juanita would exhibit over the next fifteen years: a penitential need to dignify the site of the massacre by making it a place of public pilgrimage.

In September Juanita received word of the death of Robert Glass Cleland, whose patronage had been indispensable to her success as the historian of the massacre. As she entered another year of full-time teaching at Dixie College, Juanita continued with the Lee biography. Among a number of extraordinary distractions was Kay's sudden decision to go on a mission, a decision he made in conjunction with his close friend, R. J. Snow. Kay and R. J. enrolled in the college for fall quarter as they awaited their mission calls. In December they arranged their own farewell testimonial, a marathon affair featuring talks by the departing missionaries and eight others, including Juanita and Will, and ending with a favorite Mormon hymn, "The Spirit of God Like a Fire Is Burning."[38]

Kay was scheduled to leave on January 8, 1958, for a Spanish-speaking mission with headquarters in San Antonio, Texas. He bought luggage, received a patriarchal blessing, and took the vows of the temple endowment ceremony. On New Year's Eve his left knee became stiff and painful. Hot packs and massages followed, then a visit to the local physician, then a quick trip to Salt Lake where a specialist recommended surgery. Kay refused, his knee having improved remarkably, and declared himself ready to go on his mission. By now, however, the departure quotas of missionaries had been met, and he would have to wait for a spring departure. Without delay Juanita and Will packed him off to BYU, where he enrolled in Spanish courses. January 15, 1958—the day after Kay had left for BYU—was Juanita's sixtieth birthday. She went to faculty meeting at seven and stayed at the college until five. In the evening she and Will had "a bread-and-milk-and-onion supper, and went to bed early."[39] Before retiring, she had a phone call from Ernest and another from Willa, Karl, and Kay who had got together in Provo and now sang a long-distance Happy Birthday.

In May the Utah Academy bestowed upon Juanita a Distinguished Service Award in Letters. "We have, in the truest sense," wrote Leonard Arrington in a subsequent letter, "honored the Academy by honoring you!"[40] When school ended in May, Juanita had her teeth extracted and a set of dentures constructed. It was withal a traumatic experience. Her terror of dentists was great and the extraction seemed a major surgery to her. Furthermore, as she wrote Morgan, the following "adjustment has been difficult, psychological as well as physical."[41] Still it was not an entirely negative exchange. Since childhood she had hated her protuberant, misaligned teeth (in almost all photographs her lips are closed), and in recent years she had suffered from repeated abscesses. When she smiled hereafter, her teeth would not be an embarrassment.

During the summer of 1958 Juanita and Will made a trip to the Midwest to reconnoiter the geography of John D. Lee's early years. Fortuitous events so smoothed Juanita's way that in retrospect she was sure she could see "the Hand of the Lord clearly in it all."[42] Shortly before they left St. George, Juanita received a letter from a midwestern admirer of *The Mountain Meadows Massacre*. She replied, asking

his help in securing the services of a guide. When the couple disem-
barked at the Omaha airport, the man met them, took them to a
hotel, and acquainted them with a Beth Andrews. A recent convert
to Mormonism, Andrews cheerfully spent several days guiding Juanita
and Will over the sites of camps, villages, and cemeteries established
by the Saints upon the Iowa and Nebraska plains. Thereafter Juanita
and Will traveled by bus to Kaskaskia, Vandalia, and Nauvoo, Illinois, at each place unexpectedly finding "a person prepared and eager
to give us the information we needed."[43] After the trip was over, she
received by interlibrary loan from the Illinois State Library a "large
book which compiled the early history of the state," by means of which
she was "able to verify almost every item of Lee's early life as he gave it
in the *Confessions*."[44]

July 1958 also saw the publication in the *Utah Historical
Quarterly* of Juanita's travelogue, "The Land That God Forgot," on
which she had worked during the spring. Tracing Highways 91 and
89 through the villages and scenic wonders of Dixie and neighboring
areas, the article was a pleasant amalgam of natural description and
historical fact. The following characterization of Fredonia, Arizona, is
an example of the latter: "During the years when the Mormons were
living polygamy proudly and defiantly, this town was a refuge for plural wives. Safe over the line in Arizona, they were secure against arrest
by Utah officers, while still near enough to friends and neighbors at
Kanab. So great was the annual crop of babies that some wag called it
'the lambing ground.' "[45] Shortly the editor of the magazine of the
Automobile Club of Southern California solicited a shorter piece in
the same vein. Accordingly Juanita prepared "There's a Dixieland in
Utah," a brief travelogue appearing in the December 1958 issue of
Westways.

In the fall of 1958 Juanita became a minor actor in one of
the most comic episodes in the career of the Utah Historical Society.
Near the intersection of Third South and Sixth East in Salt Lake
stood the branchless trunk of an ancient juniper (called a cedar by
Utah custom) protected by a peristyle and adorned by a bronze plaque.
The plaque explained that the original Mormon pioneers, as they
entered the Great Salt Lake Valley, had "found growing near this site
a lone cedar and paused beneath its shade." On the night of September 21, 1958, a vandal sawed down the trunk and carried it away. The
next day, the *Deseret News* reported the destruction and quoted Rus-

sell Mortensen as saying that the tree was a "historical fraud." It was foolish, Mortensen declared, to suppose, as many did, that the cedar had been the only tree growing in the valley when the pioneers arrived: "It's only an old dead stump with little historical value."[46] Fact was on Mortensen's side, for upon their arrival in the valley, the pioneers had found that cottonwoods and box elders lined the numerous creeks, in some places spreading into considerable groves. Nonetheless, Mortensen did not go unchided. There were indignant letters to the editor and an editorial in the *Deseret News* which denounced with equal vehemence vandals who defaced beloved public monuments and historians who scoffed at those monuments because of their doubtful authenticity.[47]

Contributing to the episode, a practical joker dropped an envelope at the city desk of the rival *Tribune* and dashed away unidentified. The envelope contained the key to a locker at the Greyhound depot and a note stating, "Here is a clue to the whereabouts of the missing 'lone cedar tree.'" In the locker police found a paper sack filled with charred wood. Scientists at the University of Utah examined the charred remains and declared them to be Douglas fir. The hoax was worth a half page in the *Tribune*.[48]

For Mortensen, the incident had coalesced a dangerous opposition in the Utah Historical Society, as he realized when he read in the *Tribune* a statement by his superiors, Leland H. Creer and Nicholas G. Morgan, chairman and vice chairman of the board of trustees. These men deplored the vandalism and apologized for "the unfortunate comments made by our director which appear to have been interpreted as condoning this regretable [sic] deed."[49] Behind Creer and Morgan stood, among others, Kate B. Carter, with whom Mortensen had an uneasy relationship because the state government funded the Daughters of the Utah Pioneers through the Historical Society's budget. It was a chastened Mortensen who met with Juanita and seven of her fellow trustees at their regular quarterly meeting on October 4, 1958. They had asssembled in the splendor of the Kearns Mansion at 603 East South Temple, which in 1957 had become the official home of the Utah Historical Society. Following routine business, Mortensen was called upon to state his position on the "'cedar tree' episode, in support of which he quoted at length from the newspaper files of the library, going back as early as 1919."[50] Then the worried Mortensen sat in discrete silence while Juanita and her ally on

the board, William H. McCrea, director of public relations of Amal-
gamated Sugar in Ogden, took up his defense. According to
Mortensen's later account, "When Juanita would run out of breath,
[McCrea] would take on. When he would run out of breath, Juanita
would take it back. She said what kind of a board was it that wouldn't
support the person they hired. The upshot of it was, they decided
maybe they were a little premature. I survived."[51]

At home another adventure awaited Juanita. She had
retained Winifred "Peg" Gregory to assist her in the preparation of
the Lee biography by proofing the data and critiquing the composition. It was Peg Gregory, wife of a naval officer, who had edited the
single Lee diary for which Cleland had been responsible in the preparation of *A Mormon Chronicle*. While Juanita returned from the board
meeting, Peg arrived in St. George for a relaxed two-and-a-half-week
orientation to places of importance to John D. Lee. Mid-week while
Juanita met her classes, Peg made enthusiastic sorties in many directions. On Friday afternoon the two women drove in Peg's car by a
devious route to Kanab, where they spent the night. On Saturday
they visited the ruins of Lee's tiny settlement at Skutumpah ranch
and then made their way to Lonely Dell on the Colorado, spending
the night in a motel at nearby Marble Canyon. On Sunday they hired
a Texan with a four-wheel-drive vehicle to guide them to Jacob's Pools,
where at the base of the towering Vermillion Cliffs John D. Lee had
established a tiny hideout and ranch in 1872. Its stark aridity stunned
Juanita. "Totally barren, hot even in mid-October, the talus a blue
formation, dark blue nearer the bottom and shading to gray near the
top, a poisonous accumulation that reminded me of blue vitrol [*sic*]
and that our Texan said was an arsenic combination. Anyway, not
one blade of anything could grow on it. . . . If I have never looked
upon desolation before, I saw it there."[52]

At the end of her stay, Peg bore away to California the first
eight chapters of Juanita's biography. There would soon be twelve more,
for Juanita had been writing vigorously since returning from Omaha
and Kaskaskia. The two women had formed a friendship which they
would keep alive for many years. Peg was impressed by Juanita's rural
ability to "intimidate a whole field of young bulls" with a flourish of
her arms.[53] Juanita relished Peg's whimsical claim to be a reincarna-
tion of one of John D. Lee's wives. "I never saw anyone, not even
members of the family, so emotionally wound up in the story as she

is," Juanita wrote. "She carried a boquet [sic] of wild flowers from the grave yard at Harmony to Panguitch and put on Lee's grave there—that's just how sentimental she is."[54]

For the first time since Juanita and Will had married, their home was empty of children. Tony, having graduated from Dixie in the spring, had decided to enter the University of Utah to major in biochemistry. Kay served as a missionary in Santa Fe, New Mexico. Karl was serving a six-month hitch in the army. Willa had taught elementary school for two years in Provo and was now teaching in Las Vegas.

Among Juanita's college students during the fall of 1958 was Wayne Hinton of Hurricane, who long afterward would describe her teaching. The English course in which Hinton had enrolled, meeting three days a week, combined the study of literature and frequent writing assignments on personal and literary topics. Juanita marked each paper copiously with red ink, affixing a none-too-generous grade at the beginning and a comment at the end. While teaching, she had the nervous habit of fingering the bun into which she had pulled her hair at the nape of her neck. Willing by moments to digress into humorous anecdotes, she once told a story about a rural acquaintance who was so overcome by his newborn son "that he just couldn't express his emotions and he would stroke its head and he'd say, 'Daddy's little sonny bitch, Daddy's little sonny bitch.' "[55] One is reminded that occupationally Juanita was a teacher rather than a historian. Firm and friendly, she informed and pleased generations of students.

In February 1959 Juanita received from Boyd Mathias a copy of an unpublished article, "The Mormon Church and Its Negro Doctrine." Mathias, a professor at the University of Kansas City, had for some years circulated articles and letters protesting the Church's refusal to extend the priesthood and temple blessings to blacks. Writing Mathias earlier, Juanita had deplored a story her mother had narrated. According to Mary's story, a temple president intuited that a young woman who had come to the temple to be married carried a trace of Negro blood; he of course halted the wedding. "Now the point that Mother was trying to make was that our leaders ARE inspired to discern such things. To me, it was all ghastly. . . . I hope that it did not happen anywhere. The mere telling of it as inspired truth is terrible enough, I think."[56] In February 1959, as Juanita filed Mathias' article for future reference, she reiterated her conviction that the Church's policy regarding blacks was erroneous and encouraged Mathias to believe that his article would "set some ripples into motion and strike some sympathetic hearers. I think also that it is wholesome for some of us to be willing to take a stand openly and defend it. On this I am with you."[57]

In March 1959 the Brooks family celebrated Willa's wedding. On a January night Willa had phoned her plans from Las Vegas, interrupting Juanita at her typewriter and rendering her incapable of further concentration.[58] Willa's fiancé was Thales A. Derrick, a fighter pilot temporarily stationed at Nellis Air Base near Las Vegas. His credentials were impeccable: he was a faithful Mormon and a great-grandson of Thales Haskell of pioneer fame. In order to qualify for favorable housing near Luke Air Base in Arizona, to which Thales would shortly return, the young couple planned an immediate wedding. Juanita objected strenuously on two counts. It would require Willa to break her teaching contract, and it would require Juanita, as mother of the bride, to stage a formal reception while preoccupied by the duties of a teacher. Juanita, who could confront disapproving apostles with aplomb, could not readily face such an event, seemingly fraught with opportunities for social misdemeanor. The wedding nonetheless took place on March 7, 1959, in the St. George temple. Willa's school superintendent, a Mormon, had willingly annulled her contract. As for the reception, friends and relatives rallied to plan, decorate, and serve. While gifts accumulated in embarrassing numbers, a happy, chattering multitude filed by to congratulate the bride and groom and their parents and honored friends. Within a few days, the newlyweds, driving two cars and pulling a trailer, departed for their home near Phoenix.

During the summer of 1959 Juanita made many public appearances. In May she addressed the graduates of Virgin Valley High School, urging them to proceed to college since the nation needed scientists in order to remain competitive with the Soviet Union in the post-Sputnik era.[59] In June she participated on the staff of the Rocky Mountain Writers Conference at Utah State University in Logan, delivering a lecture, sitting on a panel, and serving as a consultant to students offering manuscripts on historical topics.[60] In August she addressed the Provo chapter of the League of Utah Writers. The caption beneath her photograph in the *Daily Herald* called her a "distinguished Utah writer."[61]

Throughout the summer Juanita worked diligently on the Lee biography. By August she hurried to complete a manuscript for mailing to a prospective publisher. "I have a typist going on a draft which I hope to send out for consideration, but I myself have five more chapters to do, plus the preface or foreword. When this is done, there'll be the real work of final proofing, footnotes, bibliography, etc. etc."[62] Chatty, encouraging letters frequently arrived from Kay in the mission. He and his companion had organized a parade among the Primary children of his branch to celebrate Pioneer Day on July 24. The event featured some forty children, nine covered wagons made of cardboard and butcher paper, and a subsequent supper. "Only one thing tho," Kay wrote. "We made some punch in a galvanized bucket, and nearly all the kids got sick from drinking it. My companion even got sick. I guess I have too strong of a stomach, because it didn't even affect me."[63]

In September 1959 Juanita and Will purchased a piece of land in Mesquite on which Karl could park a trailer home. Having graduated from BYU at the end of the summer term, Karl had signed a contract to teach at Virgin Valley High School. In this, as in earlier real estate transactions, it was Juanita who drove the bargains, insisting that the land come with water rights[64] and that the proposed price of the trailer be cut by $100.[65]

In October Juanita mailed Alfred A. Knopf the manuscript of her biography, entitled "John D. Lee, Builder in the Kingdom."[66] Knopf shortly rejected the work. In December, following a lead from Provo novelist Frank Robertson, she submitted the manuscript to Curtis Brown, Ltd.[67] That firm also shortly rejected it. During the winter of 1960 Juanita continued to enlarge and refine the work. During the spring she mailed it to Peg Gregory, now an editor at the University of New Mexico Press in Albuquerque. In June 1960, Peg returned the draft with extensive commentary. She had compared Juanita's quotations from the Lee diaries with the actual text in *A Mormon Chronicle*, for, as she explained, "I saw so much of scholarly sniping, *particularly among historians*, while at the Huntington, that I am sure I am not the only reader who will compare the biography with the *Diaries*." She also suggested some revision in content. She doubted that sufficient evidence lay behind a dialogue Juanita had attributed to William H. Dame and Isaac C. Haight following the massacre. "I believe every word of it, because it is logical and because I want to," Peg wrote. "But what of the descendants of Dame and Haight among your readers? What is backing up this chapter?"[68] The published work shows that Juanita did not entirely delete the dialogue to which Peg objected.

On June 15, 1960, Juanita traveled by Greyhound to Los Angeles to show her manuscript to Arthur H. Clark, proprietor of a small publishing firm specializing in western history. She went at the recommendation of her uncle, LeRoy Hafen, many of whose works Clark had published. She was met at the bus station and conveyed to Clark's office in nearby Glendale by J. Wesley Williamson, a great-grandson of John D. Lee. At this moment Williamson, a resident of Whittier, was simply another of the multitudinous Lees with whom Juanita had a cordial relationship. Arthur Clark was impressed by Juanita's manuscript and would soon offer to publish it. She would not make up her mind immediately. She had a feeler from the University of Indiana Press, and it worried her that Clark's firm was generally unknown. Peg Gregory would urge her to sign with Clark: "University presses don't really *extend* themselves to sell. As for the prestige factor, with Stanford and the Huntington behind you, you couldn't care less."[69] By mid-summer Juanita would accept Clark's offer.

On the day after her visit with Clark in June, Juanita flew from Los Angeles to Phoenix. When she walked off the plane at Skyharbor, Willa and Thales, with their infant son David in their arms, met her. Will was also waiting, for he had risen early that morning in St. George and had caught a commuter plane for Phoenix. Remaining with Willa and Thales for four days, Juanita and Will visited Luke Air Base and observed fighter planes flying in formation. They departed for St. George in an aging Chevrolet which Juanita had bought from Willa for $400. They had furnished Kay with a used Chevrolet for his missionary work and had helped Karl buy a used Chevrolet. Now they intended to treat Tony equally by making him a gift of Willa's vehicle.[70]

Upon their return, Juanita and Will prepared to move to Salt Lake, Juanita having accepted an offer from Russell Mortensen to join the staff of the Utah Historical Society as a research associate. The appointment would run from July 1, 1960, to December 31, 1961, and would pay $505 a month.[71] Salt Lake was also made attractive by the presence of many friends and relatives. Tony and Kay—the latter nearing the end of his mission—would live with Juanita and Will while attending the University of Utah. Clair and LaVon resided in Salt

Lake, Clair teaching in a junior high school. Also in Salt Lake were Will's brother and sister-in-law, Sam and Winnie, and Juanita's former brother- and sister-in-law, Howard and Myrtle Pulsipher. As usual, Juanita found that housing arrangements fell into place with predestined ease. A young physician rented their St. George house for $125 a month, and for $130 a month they rented the house of Frank H. Jonas at 1218 Third Avenue, not far from the university. Leaving St. George in their pink Plymouth on June 25, 1960, Juanita and Will paused for a few days in Provo to visit Karl, who was pursuing graduate studies at BYU during the summer term and living with companions in Juanita's and Will's Provo house. Unflagging in his interest in athletics, Will enjoyed watching Karl play city-league softball during the evenings.[72]

Juanita's duties at the Utah Historical Society had a pleasing informality. With some regularity she arrived at the Kearns Mansion at eight and left at five, although no one monitored her comings and goings. Her office was a convenient place of work from which she frequently emerged to consult books and research materials in the library or to chat comfortably with the other staff members. Her foremost assignment was editing the Hosea Stout diaries, which ranked with the diaries of John D. Lee in importance. She would also engage in the production of small educational pamphlets on various aspects of Utah history.

In August Juanita and Will attended the Lee family reunion in Panguitch, where they were joined by Peg Gregory and her husband, Reginald. In a letter Peg had eagerly anticipated the adventure, revealing that she had dreamed of laying a wreath of metal leaves on the grave of John D. Lee.[73] Significantly, a more substantial memorial had recently been placed upon the grave in preparation for the reunion. For decades a simple marble shaft had marked the repose of Lee's body in the Panguitch cemetery. Now at the behest of Ettie Lee and through the arrangements of Wesley Williamson, a Utah monument maker had installed upon the grave a large flat rectangle of polished granite. For the descendants of the executed pioneer who assembled for its dedication, the words carved upon the blanket stone were charged with emotion: "Ye shall know the truth and the truth shall make you free."

The group also assembled in a Panguitch meetinghouse for speeches and entertainments. Of primary interest was a book listing

Lee's descendants, compiled by Manetta Henrie of Provo. Both Juanita and Peg were asked to speak. Juanita spoke of the forthcoming biography and wondered whether the numerous delays in its publication implied that a fact as yet undiscovered was destined to appear in its pages. She asserted her conviction that similar delays in the publication of *The Mountain Meadows Massacre* had been providential, for "the most important thing in it [information from a letter from the father of two of the victims], came after it was being set up in the galleys."[74] Immediately after Juanita had ended her remarks, Merrit L. Norton, a descendant of John D. Lee and an ordained officiator in the Salt Lake temple, moved that the group pass a resolution requesting that the Church officially restore their grandfather to membership and to his temple blessings. Although many were doubtful of its realization, the congregation approved the resolution.

By September 1960, Juanita's domestic life had become pleasantly complicated. Kay had returned from his mission and joined Juanita, Will, and Tony in Salt Lake, as had R. J. Snow, who would board with the Brooks family during the school year. The young men left for classes, jobs, and church events by an uncoordinated schedule that multiplied kitchen chores for Juanita and Will—particularly for Will, who cheerfully assumed many housekeeping duties. Out-of-town relatives and friends dropped in with incredible frequency. Fortunately, the two-story house easily accommodated a crowd, its convenience enhanced by a large dining table, a piano, and a pleasant fireplace.[75]

Among the friends whom Juanita enjoyed at the Kearns Mansion was receptionist Marjorie Walker. Juanita often joined Walker for morning and afternoon breaks in the marble kitchen of the mansion, where she drank a convivial cup of weak coffee, invariably buffered by a slice of bread and butter. She also paused regularly at Walker's desk on the first floor as she trekked to the library upstairs. "Sometimes the few minutes stretched into an hour as I answered two phones and took care of patrons who came in," Walker wrote. "She was always interested in the people who came and often knew them so the talk would move out to include them. If it was someone who wanted to talk to her and she didn't know them she would be courteous but cautious and when she was asked a question that she couldn't answer at once she would take refuge in these words, 'Well, I married Will Brooks in. . . . ' Of course these were people who were interested in her life or something about the continuity of her work. But you could see that she was getting her bearings that way as if her marriage had been a water mark of some sort to divide her life and keep it all fixed in her mind."[76]

Juanita mused confidentially to Walker about apparent sexual irregularities among their acquaintances. According to Walker, Juanita "definitely had the old nineteenth century attitude toward the double standard—that is she believed that men had greater sexual needs than women and that it was more allowable for them to satisfy them in other than conventional ways." Hence, more than once Juanita rationalized the philandering of a male acquaintance "by saying that it was something that happened to men often as they approached middle age or indeed anytime." On the topic of female sexuality, Juanita became more cautious. Once she asked Walker "about a young woman we knew who kept taking her alcoholic husband into their home time and time again in spite of vowing never to take him back so many times. She asked me if it was because she needed him sexually. It seemed a little daring as if she would only risk saying it to me since it was such a delicate matter."[77]

Often Juanita pumped visiting researchers for information that would facilitate her own research. One such person was George Ellsworth, professor of history at Utah State University, whom Juanita took home to supper one evening. As she departed she told Walker that she would give Ellsworth bread and milk and in return he would give her knowledge. For a time B. F. Larson came by to seek advice on the editing of his mother's diary. In reply to a scolding Juanita gave him for correcting his mother's grammar, he insisted that because she had made him look good, he would also make her look good. Others dropped in for conviviality rather than research. Stanley Ivins came at least once a week, as did Charles Kelly and Wilford Poulson. Ivins and Poulson, disaffected Mormons, and Kelly, a notorious anti-Mormon, engaged in an irreverent banter in which Juanita took a full and delighted part.[78]

More completely than in any other period of her life, Juanita sensed her citizenship in an underground community of dissenting Mormons. A minor episode of January 1961 demonstrates how seriously she took that citizenship. For some years she had maintained a correspondence with A. C. Lambert. After many years as a professor of educational administration at BYU, Lambert had become Dean of Los Angeles State College of Applied Arts and Sciences in 1951, in which position he supervised the construction of a new campus.[79] Besides authoring an impressive array of articles and reports on educational matters, he wrote with amazing fecundity on the inconsistencies of early Mormonism, specifying in his self-annotated bibliography that they were "not for Publication but for Personal Private Use."[80]

Lambert had assumed the habit of mailing Juanita his manuscripts, some for her files, others to be read and returned. A timid man, he frequently admonished her to secrecy. In late November 1960 he mailed a 529-page manuscript entitled "The Great Dilemma of the Early Mormons," asking her to return it within sixty days. It was a detailed comparison of Joseph Smith's early and later revelations, emphasizing "the dilemmas that were created for the believers by the significant changes that were made in the revelations and by the changing explanations that were advanced for the non-fulfillment of the prophecies and promises."[81]

It was probably this manuscript over which the following furor arose in January 1961. One day Wilford Poulson, Juanita's former instructor in psychology at BYU and her collaborator in acquiring pioneer documents, saw the manuscript on Juanita's desk. A closet dissenter, Poulson expressed great interest in the document and asked to take it home. "I read your letter to him," Juanita wrote Lambert later, "explained that the work was NOT for general circulation and that this was a private copy." Poulson took the work, promising to return it within a week. Near the end of the week he phoned that LaMar Petersen, a music instructor and dissenter, wished to read the manuscript. Petersen being among her new friends, Juanita agreed. A few days later, during one of his frequent visits to the mansion, Stanley Ivins casually mentioned that his barber, a Mr. Wardle, had informed him that he was having a photostat made of a remarkable book by an unknown Dr. Lambert. "Well, I hit the ceiling," Juanita reported. "I tried to call Wardle and found that he had no telephone. I did get Poulson and asked him what-the-hell! He was incoherent, talked in circles, tried to explain that this man Wardle was really a fine fellow, that he had the most amazing collection of early-day Mormon material and was most generous with it. . . . I was so angry that I was fit to be tied: called him things I don't care to recall."[82]

Juanita next phoned the microfilm shop and ordered that the film be held until she could call for it. Alerted by Poulson, Wardle

quickly called Juanita and insisted that he would not release the microfilm until she had examined his collection of covert Mormon materials. Without mincing words, she informed him that she would meet
him only at the microfilm shop where she intended to take possession
of the film. The next morning on schedule she arrived at the shop and
received from the contrite Wardle a typed statement "clearing himself
of any intent to steal or to take material not meant for him and releasing the film to me." She mailed Lambert both his manuscript and the
microfilm. In her letter of explanation she laid responsibility directly
upon the aging Poulson, concluding that he had intended from the
beginning to have the work surreptitiously copied. "I told him that I
could never trust him again in anything, and I cannot."[83]

On January 13, 1961, Will embarked upon an adventure.
David O. McKay had commissioned the Sons of the Utah Pioneers to
raise an honorary Mormon Battalion who, clad in historical uniforms,
would parade at the inauguration of John F. Kennedy in Washington,
D.C. Though his brother Sam urged him to enlist, Will at first decided
it would be unfair to leave Juanita. After she had chastised him for his
reluctance, Will happily changed his mind and signed up. He bought
a new uniform, a suit, a belt, a cap, and white gloves, commenting, "I
did feel proud of the very fine and sharp looking outfit."[84] The convoy
of buses paused to allow the travelers, 107 strong, to inspect Mormon
historical sites along the way. Will was wide-eyed with interest and,
with a characteristic egalitarianism, quickly conceived a fondness for
his bus driver: "We soon had full confidence and great respect for
him, a wise and careful driver to whom we looked for answers to all
questions."[85] In Denver the group made an initial march in a parade
of thirty-eight blocks, apparently learning maneuvers by dint of trial
and error. "I soon learned forward march, left, left, left," Will wrote.
"The easiest command was *halt*. We done that well, some times our
step was right sometimes not."[86] On January 20, Inauguration Day,
the Battalion presumably marched with satisfactory precision through
the streets of the nation's capital.

Shortly after his return, Juanita gave Will a diary, having
sensed that time hung heavily on his hands. Immediately he began to
keep a daily record of his own putterings about the house, the comings and goings of Tony, Kay, and R. J., the arrival and departure of
relatives and friends, and the daily whereabouts of his famous wife.
He would keep diaries for 1961, 1962, and 1963, the period of the

Brookses' stay in Salt Lake, with the consequence that for few other periods of Juanita's life is so much known of her daily activities.

It was a period of great intellectual stimulation for Juanita. She appeared in public at least once a week, invited before groups of all kinds along the Wasatch Front—informal gatherings, clubs, church firesides, and academic assemblies. Her topics included the Mountain Meadows massacre, John D. Lee, the settling of Dixie, her childhood, and her experiences in gathering and writing history. Even more satisfying was the association she and Will had with many couples of professional status. They were frequently invited out, and they frequently invited others in. Hilarity often characterized their gatherings—irreverent laughter offering a convenient vent for their dissident emotions. Juanita's catalytic humor and high enjoyment— and Will's too—may be discerned in Marjorie Walker's description of a dinner party at the Brooks home to which she and her husband were invited: "It was pure magic. [Juanita] somehow brought out all the native wit in those people. The sparkling conversation was all about the local culture—that is no one who wasn't raised in Mormondom could have understood what was going on. There seemed to be no end to the 'in' stories they could think up. The ball never dropped and Juanita was having the time of her life. Of course Will loved a good joke and he laughed so hard I thought he might choke on his food."[87]

On the last Saturday evening of each month Juanita and Will met with a circle of friends for a lecture by an invited guest on a topic related to Mormonism. This group had been organized by Angus and Grace Woodbury, who liked to call it the Mormon Forum. Angus Woodbury, who had been Juanita's colleague years before at Dixie College, was a professor of zoology at the University of Utah. His announced credo in the study of Mormonism was "an intellectual analysis, not an emotional crusade." Others in this group included Brigham Madsen, professor of history, and his wife, Betty; Ray Canning, professor of sociology, and his wife, Lois; LaMar Petersen, a professional instructor in piano and organ, and his wife, Faye; Gordon Howard, a dentist, and his wife, Alta; Allen Crockett, chief justice of the Utah State Supreme Court, and his wife, Eulalia; and John Fitzgerald, an elementary school principal, and his wife, Mary.[88] (The liberal character of the group may be measured by the fact that in 1975 LaMar Petersen would publish an irreverent and whimsical book, *Hearts Made*

Glad: The Charges of Intemperance Against Joseph Smith the Mormon Prophet, whereupon he and his wife would be excommunicated.) On the evening of Saturday, March 25, 1961, it was Juanita's and Will's turn to entertain. Some twenty-seven persons attended, enjoying refreshments and a talk which Juanita delivered about the aftermath of the Mountain Meadows massacre.[89]

In March, Willa and David arrived for a stay with Juanita and Will while Thales attended survival school. In the weeks that followed Will enjoyed particularly the company of his grandson, whose behavior he described with doting affection: "Had a good day with Willa and David. David telling us what to do. He is very much advanced for a child one year and one week old. He entertains us by dancing, saying bye bye, winking at us, throwing kisses and says many words, hat, clock, Dad, apple, and trys many other words he's our Pride and Joy."[90] General conference in early April brought a crowd to the Brooks home. Juanita and Will complicated matters by deciding just at that moment, in anticipation of the return of Frank Jonas in July, to buy a house at 1295 East Crystal Avenue. On April 5 Will made a down payment of $900 and a first monthly payment of $101.[91] The family would make its move with great deliberation, puttering away at cleaning and painting its latest acquisition until the end of June.

For Will's eightieth birthday, a great crowd gathered, some sleeping at Juanita's and Will's newly acquired house, others at the homes of other relatives. On Saturday, April 22, fifty-three had lunch in the Brooks home on Third Avenue. All the living children of Juanita and Will were there with spouses and most of their children. In the afternoon friends arrived for an open house, congratulating Will, chatting noisily with his assembled kin, and partaking of the refreshments which Willa and a bevy of granddaughters served. On Monday the *Tribune* took note of the celebration, conveying "belated wishes to youngish friendly Will Brooks" and declaring that he "is a cheerful philsopher and a great story teller. His own story needs to be written."[92] In the meantime, Will and Juanita went on Sunday to the Salt Lake airport with some of their children and with Thales' parents to watch Willa, Thales, and David enplane for England, where Thales was now assigned. Will sadly wrote: "After the plane had gone out of sight we came home feeling that we were seperated from some children very dear to us."[93]

During the winter and spring of 1961 Juanita paused in her work on the Stout diaries and prepared an entire summer issue of the *Utah Historical Quarterly* celebrating the centennial of the founding of St. George. For an outline, she relied upon her unpublished article presented before the Utah Academy in 1952, "St. George, Utah—A Community Portrait." She called on her former student Lorraine Taylor Washburn to write about pioneer entertainments and education and on her colleague at Dixie College Karl Larson to write about agriculture in early Dixie. She herself wrote the rest. In keeping with recent special issues, Russell Mortensen aspired to produce this issue in commercial quantities on slick paper and with an abundance of color photographs. In late March Juanita and Will traveled with Mortensen and his wife to St. George. After a night at her mother's house, Juanita joined Mortensen for a grueling day of calling on persons known to have historical photographs. Will spent the day rambling, commenting in his diary, "I did really enjoy all the visits in St. George after several months away."[94] Despite his manifest good cheer while living in Salt Lake, Will's heart never left the town of his birth.

In mid-April Juanita's work on the Dixie issue was impeded by the arrival of galleys for the biography of John D. Lee. For days she spent every spare moment proofreading what would prove to be a book of nearly 400 pages. She was so preoccupied, in fact, that when Will's brother-in-law, J. W. Pace, died and Will traveled to St. George to speak at his funeral, she did not accompany him. On May 1, she finished and Will mailed the galleys. On June 1, Juanita and Will accompanied the Mortensens on a promotion trip to St. George, bearing with them an advance copy of the Dixie issue. The next morning at ten, Juanita and Mortensen met with mayor William A. Barlocker, the Chamber of Commerce, and the St. George Centennial Committee. Brandishing the advance copy, Mortensen delivered an enthusiastic sales pitch: "Look," he would remember saying, "you're going to have thousands of people come to this celebration, and a lot of them will be strangers, tourists, but a lot of them will be people who have had roots in St. George who are 'coming home.' "[95] An order for 5,000 copies followed.[96]

The Dixie issue of the *Utah Historical Quarterly* was attractive. The commercial version sported a special cover entitled *Utah's Dixie: The Cotton Mission.* To accompany a section of color photographs Juanita wrote an eloquent travelogue much like her previously published travelogues. Her article "The Cotton Mission" borrowed some of the wording of her 1952 Academy paper but added details about the settling of St. George which she had newly mined from pioneer records. Her article "Early Buildings" contributed little that she had not published elsewhere about the tabernacle, courthouse, and temple. Her brief article "Silver Reef" made an interesting if superficial introduction to the history of the gentile mining camp that had provided a market for Mormon produce between 1880 and 1900. Under the title "Vignettes" she published reminiscences gleaned in part from the letters of her irrepressible correspondent, Joseph Walker. Walker claimed that pioneer physician J. T. Affleck, operating on his kitchen table, had successfully removed a Dixie woman's diseased kidney: "He nursed her through without benefit of any post-operative aids such as intravenous salines, transfusions, sulfa drugs, or penicillin, and with no other nursing than the clumsy, no matter how willing, hands of her neighbors. . . . He put his skill and judgment against the outstretched, clutching fingers of Death. He won."[97]

While in St. George promoting the issue, Juanita and Will had a midday dinner with Juanita's sister Eva and her husband—a "sumptious spread," as Will called it, of chicken and trimmings and currant pie. In the afternoon, the Mortensens and Brookses toured St. George and the surrounding countryside. They visited the new campus, astir with construction, to which Dixie College would move in 1962. That evening, Juanita and Will attended the fiftieth annual commencement of the combined college and high school.[98] Of special note were awards of "Merit and Respect" made to none other than Juanita and Will Brooks, presented by president Arthur F. Bruhn. The citation for Juanita called her a "distinguished educator, author, and woman of affairs who has always exhibited during her life the indomitable spirit of her pioneer progenitors who knew not the word defeat." The citation for Will declared him to be a man "whose capacity for seeing the best in everyone has won the confidence, respect, and love of children and young people; who has been no small factor in his distinguished wife's success as an educator and author; and who, by his admirable qualities and services, has been an influence for good as lasting as the enduring masterpiece carved in stone by his pioneer artist father at the entrance of Dixie College."[99]

On Monday June 5 Juanita and Will attended commencement at the University of Utah where Tony received a bachelor's degree. R. J. would shortly leave for a summer with his parents in Washington, D.C., and Kay and Tony would begin summer jobs at service stations. Karl would visit a few days before entering summer school at BYU for continued work on a master's degree in history.

In the meantime, Juanita was in the midst of one of the most rigorous trials of her life. It had begun in May when Ettie Lee ecstatically informed Juanita that John D. Lee had been posthumously restored to membership in the Church. The resolution passed by the Lee family at the Panguitch reunion in 1960, conveyed to the general authorities by Merrit L. Norton, had borne fruit. On April 20, 1961, a meeting of the First Presidency and the Quorum of Twelve Apostles had authorized the necessary rituals. On May 8, Norton was baptized in proxy for his grandfather, and on May 9 Elder Ezra Taft Benson officiated in the endowment and sealing ceremonies. This had been made known, Ettie informed Juanita, "with the admonition that it would be wise for this information to be given only to members of the family and that there be no unnecessary publicity."[100]

It was more than a restitution for the disgraced pioneer; it was a personal vindication for Juanita, who had for years suffered a shadowy disgrace among her conservative friends and relatives for having espoused his cause. She immediately wrote Arthur H. Clark, calling the reinstatement "a thing that I have not expected to live to see." She enclosed a brief announcement to be added at the end of the biography, which she asked Clark to hold pending her attempt to negotiate appproval, for she did "not dare to use it without official consent."[101] At the same time, she sent the statement to Merrit Norton, suggesting that it be included in the biography. "Since the edition is small, and the purchasers will be chiefly members of the family, I see no harm in putting it in, though I would not do so without permission."[102]

That permission would not be forthcoming. By reinstating Lee, the Church had tacitly admitted that Juanita's accusations against Brigham Young were correct. Understandably, the Church was reluctant to grant that its recognition of the all too human conduct of the great colonizer be published before the world at large. It is possible that Juanita could have been dissuaded by polite arguments. In effect, however, the Church commanded her not to publish the reinstatement. She was not a woman to be commanded.

Pressure came first through the Lee family. On June 7, 1961, Elder Delbert E. Stapley, a native of Arizona, phoned Jesse Udall in Phoenix. Udall was a stake president, justice of the Arizona State Supreme Court, and husband to a granddaughter of John D. Lee. The apostle informed Udall that the aged prophet David O. McKay was, in Udall's words, "greatly disturbed because of Juanita's presumption to put this confidential matter in a book. He was so distressed that he was considering rescinding the action that had been taken if Juanita persisted in her attempt to publicize it."[103] Udall phoned Ettie, who in turn phoned Juanita. Juanita argued that, while McKay might well excommunicate her for publishing forbidden information, he could not prove so unjust to John D. Lee as to reverse the reinstatement. Taking McKay's threat seriously, Ettie remained adamant. Reluctantly Juanita promised to omit the reinstatement from a first edition of the biography, to be printed chiefly for members of the Lee family. She would not omit it from a later general edition. By this means the onus for its publication would not fall upon the family. Ettie acquiesced, satisfied that the second edition was comfortably in the future.

Udall and Stapley were suspicious. Stapley now requested that Juanita confer with him in the church office building in Salt Lake. According to Will's diary, the meeting took place on Tuesday, June 13, 1961, and the result was "Definately No do not print it in her biography of the Life of J. D. Lee, Order of Pres David O McKay." Juanita and Stapley were alone in the room, and she spoke to him "as one person to another, not as a humble member to an Apostle of the Lord."[104] She pointed out the futility of repressing the news, telling him that she had had word from four other persons before Ettie Lee's letter had arrived. She showed him *The Mountain Meadows Massacre* and *A Mormon Chronicle*, attempting to explain why publishing the reinstatement would be appropriate. "He seemed not to hear what I said, but repeated over and over like a broken victrola record the words, 'If this appears in print *anywhere*—in the book, on the jacket, in a review—President McKay will rescind the action.' " She attempted to express her conviction that God had purposely delayed the printing of the book so that this news could be included, whereupon the apostle "just slapped the table and said, 'IT IS FROM THE DEVIL.' "[105] Juanita ended the interview insisting "that I had made a promise to keep it out of the First Edition; more than that I would not promise."[106]

For the moment Stapley and his allies among the Lee family were satisfied. Ettie amiably sought to assuage Juanita's affronted feelings by insisting that at all costs she must attend the next Lee reunion.[107] Jesse Udall anxiously phoned Juanita for assurance that she had ordered Arthur H. Clark to halt plans for printing word of the reinstatement. Believing he had that assurance, he wrote his gratitude for her cooperation.[108] Ironically that letter struck Juanita as a culminating indignity. Her reply was eloquent with anger and a sense of violation: "I do think that as an honest historian – as I have tried to be – I owe it to myself and to my readers to tell all the truth, for truth suppressed is its own kind of a lie. So to protect *your* integrity and to help you keep *your* word, I must act the part of a prevaricator myself in that I fail to use important and pertinent information or deliberately pretend that I do not have it. This is a role which I do not enjoy playing." She also declared that President McKay's threat to rescind the reinstatement was "only a bluff," an assertion which, according to her note scribbled later on her carbon copy of the letter, "shook them all up." Ominously she hinted that the second edition of the biography would appear upon the heels of the first.[109]

As these negotiations went on, the Brooks family prepared to move. On Saturday, June 24, Will borrowed Clair's pickup and began to transport furniture to the house on Crystal Avenue. Kay and Tony assisted as their work schedules allowed, as did Bill Brooks, Grant's son, who was paying his grandparents an extended visit. During the ensuing week they conscientiously cleaned the house they were vacating. Will's diary noted with satisfaction that Tony and Bill made an excellent window washing team: "Bill on one side with Tony the other they wash the glass on each side, pointing out the misty places on the opposite sides of the glass."[110] Although their belongings were in great disarray, the family moved on July 1, the appointed day, into the Crystal Avenue house. The next day they attended services in their new ward where they were made welcome. Karl was present for the weekend. In the afternoon he and Juanita discussed his thesis topic, the life of A. Milton Musser. Will offered his observations on the topic but found himself "just poo-pood."

Jesse Udall now applied new pressure to Juanita. Through another round of frantic phone calls, he and Ettie proposed that Juanita fly at their expense to Phoenix to discuss the threatened appearance of a second edition of the biography. For obscure reasons,

Juanita agreed to go. Wesley Williamson phoned from California, offering to appear uninvited at the meeting. He was out of sorts with many of his Lee cousins and intended to bring a tape recorder.[111] Juanita gratefully accepted his offer, desiring a precise recording of her words in case a church court should later be convened against her.

On Saturday, July 8, 1961, she caught a plane to Phoenix and by mid-afternoon found herself in the home of Jesse and Lela Lee Udall among a group of about twenty-five persons. The meeting began with a long prayer for harmony. Then Jesse Udall spoke, "bearing his testimony to the fact that Pres. McKay was God's mouth-piece on earth, and that if we did not obey his demands, he would rescind the earlier action." In succession Udall called upon others to deliver a similar message. These included a few women, Ettie among them, and a host of male Lee descendants, most of whom were bishops or other leaders in their stakes and wards and some of whom had traveled great distances to be present. At last Juanita was allowed to speak. Bitterly, she renewed the arguments she had asserted in her letter to Udall. She spunkily pitted her own righteousness against that of the prior speakers. "I told them that I could bear as fervent a testimony as any there, that I had seen instances of healing, of answer to prayer; that I had worked in every organization of the Church where women work, from organist in Primary to Stake President of Relief Society; that I always carried a Temple Recommend in my purse, though I did not often use it."[112]

Udall initiated "a second round of speeches in which each in turn pled, implored, urged, – I've forgotten all the terms – me NOT to do this terrible thing. To each I had to answer: 'Sorry, the answer is NO.'" The meeting was an exceedingly difficult ordeal – a "horrible, horrible afternoon," as she later called it. Inferring that arrangements had been made to overwhelm her by sheer numbers, she felt a desperate gratitude for the few who remained conspicuously silent and for Wesley Williamson, who knelt on the floor by his tape recorder. Discomfited by Williamson's unexpected presence, Udall had ordered the recorder turned off while he spoke. At the end, Williamson claimed a right to be heard. "As to this fact appearing in print," Juanita quoted him as saying, "I have already put it out in print in the family *News-letter* of which I have mailed out more than a hundred copies. And I am so proud of it that I tell everyone. I turned off the highway to the town of Harmony where I scattered the good word to all I knew, so that we could rejoice together."[113]

Afterward, while his wife served an elegant lunch, Udall chatted pleasantly with Juanita, who "couldn't choke down a bite, I was so tied into knots." On Sunday she returned to Salt Lake in time to share a roast beef dinner Will had prepared. "Mother felt good about her trip to Phoenix," Will recorded that night in his diary, "as things were cleared up and an understanding was reached."[114] Juanita had concealed her actual feelings in order to preserve Will's amiable view of the world.

An exchange of letters between Juanita and Arthur H. Clark now firmed up a previously conceived plan. Clark would print 200 copies of the first edition of the biography of John D. Lee, dated 1961. He would immediately proceed to print a second edition, dated 1962 and ending with the announcement of the reinstatement. There would be minor differences between the two editions in the color of the binding, dust jacket design, and page trimming.[115]

On the last Saturday in July, Juanita and Will attended the Mormon Forum at the summer cabin of Angus and Grace Woodbury in Mill Creek Canyon. Grace, always waggish, suggested that the beer drinkers in the group toss their empty cans onto the tennis court of the next-door neighbor, Elder Joseph Fielding Smith.[116] Good taste prevailed and no one disposed of cans in this manner. On a Sunday in August the Brooks family provided the program at Sacrament Meeting in their new ward. Tony, Kay, Karl, Juanita, and Will spoke; a visiting nephew, Kenneth Reber, sang a solo. "The entire audience seemed to like the meeting," Will recorded.[117] The next Wednesday Juanita attended a luncheon in honor of Russell Mortensen, who had resigned as director of the Utah Historical Society in order to become the director of the University of Utah Press.

In early September, the Brooks family gathered in St. George for the Dixie centennial, sleeping in the house on the hill, unrented for the moment, and taking meals next door with Mary. On Sunday evening Juanita and Will attended a crowded opening service in the tabernacle where a martial band played pioneer tunes and an impressive roster of dignitaries spoke. On Monday evening they attended a musical pageant in the fine arts building on the new Dixie campus, an event of exceptional interest because Eva had composed the music and lyrics. At noon on Tuesday they relished a barbecue at the city park, and in the evening they attended a melodrama, "East Lynne," a play in which Juanita had acted while she was an unmarried school-teacher in Mesquite. That ended the celebration for Juanita, who took a late bus for Salt Lake in order to resume the urgent labor of compiling an index to the biography.

Will remained in St. George. One morning he mused in his diary about his birth and childhood in the rock house. "I do wonder just how we managed to make room, furnish food and the necessary clothing for our growing family until it reached the number fifteen members. Twelve children, father and mother with Uncle Frank Brooks, fathers only living brother, a single man, being a cripple all his life; he was hauled across the great plains with a handcart . . . ."[118] Unquestionably the celebration was a happy occasion for Will, as Juanita remarked in a letter: "It warms my heart to see how genuinely glad people are to see him. I don't think he has an enemy in all the world, or a person that would doubt his word."[119]

In the summer of 1961 Juanita finished an article, "Indian Sketches from the Journals of T. D. Brown and Jacob Hamblin," which would appear in the October issue of the *Utah Historical Quarterly*. Quoting abundantly from the journals of two pioneer missionaries, Juanita delineated the character and habits of the Paiutes of south-western Utah. It was an article of exceptional interest. For example, an excerpt from Brown's journal described a healing by a medicine man, who held a sick woman in his arms, chanted, and sucked the disease from her, repeatedly spitting out a small stone which he, in Brown's words, "would carry off, crawling in a stooping posture some 20 yards and hide it among the brushes or in the earth, burying the disease or evil spirit."[120] Early in the year Juanita had reviewed for the *Utah Historical Quarterly* Norman F. Furniss' *The Mormon Conflict 1850–1859*, a study of the relations between Mormons and non-Mormons in Utah during a turbulent frontier decade. In October she accepted an invitation to review the same book for the *New Mexico Quarterly*, promising to write a substantially different review.[121] In each review, she praised Furniss' interpretation but corrected his rendering of various incidents.

Between frequent interruptions, Juanita went on with the editing of the Stout diaries. During September she began working on the diaries on Saturdays as well as on weekdays. Everett L. Cooley, the new director of the Utah Historical Society, had reluctantly informed her that because of depleted funds her employment would end upon the expiration of her contract on January 1, 1962. She planned by that date to have completed about half the task—some 660 typed pages composing a first of two projected volumes. In late October she asked Wallace Stegner, temporarily serving as assistant to Secretary of the Interior Stewart Udall, whether he might use her services as a pamphlet writer.[122] Stegner promised to inquire whether Udall could find her a position.[123] It says much of Juanita's character that at sixty-three she declared herself "thrilled beyond words" at the prospect. (A nephew of Jesse Udall and a great-grandson of John D. Lee, Stewart Udall heartily approved of Juanita's publication of his ancestor's reinstatement.) Stegner also asked whether she might provide him with an annotated bibliography of Mormon journals relating to his projected book, *The Gathering of Zion: The Story of the Mormon Trail*. She promised a preliminary list within a week and apologized for her sudden disinterest in a position with the Department of the Interior. Everett Cooley had found new funds and would hire her for a half year more at $500 a month so that she could finish editing the second volume of the Stout diaries. "This record is significant enough," she explained to Stegner, "that it should be finished and I cannot stand leaving a job half done to either dangle unfinished indefinitely or to fall into the hands of someone else to do."[124]

Thus Juanita continued to edit the Stout diaries. She worked with some "thirteen hundred typewritten pages of daily entries plus another three hundred of miscellanea," as she explained in a paper she delivered before the history section of the Utah Academy on October 27, 1961, at the University of Utah.[125] Although she wished to preserve the integrity of the original document, she accepted that certain minor interventions were mandatory, for, as she wrote an acquaintance, "the editor is a go-between from the writer to his audience, and a part of the business of the editor is to be interpreter and guide." She could not, she went on, "expect every reader to take as much time to decide what this man is trying to say as I have had to do."[126] Accordingly, she divided the long entries into paragraphs and sometimes inserted punctuation to prevent misreading. She left unchanged the variant spellings of names and indicated accepted spellings in her notes. She did not correct the misspelling of other words, adding a cautionary *sic* only when she feared the reader might suspect a typographical error.

In the fall of 1961 Kay and Tony enrolled again in the university, Kay majoring in Spanish, Tony entering graduate studies in zoology. They continued to chum with R. J. Snow, who lived with a nearby aunt. During September Juanita suffered a minor accident. As she sat on a folding stool while Will trimmed her hair, the stool collapsed, sending her sprawling backward. For a few minutes she could not move. Then Will helped her up and continued to trim. He recorded: "We both got a scare and she had a painful bruise."[127] Another notable event was a cablegram from England announcing the birth of Willa's and Thales' second son, Daniel. Will wrote that he no longer knew how to properly celebrate such an event: "Thirty years ago I could have purchased five gallons of good wine and invited my friends to help wet its head."[128]

In mid-October, in an attempt to mend fences, Juanita attended the reunion of the Lee family at the Navajo Bridge in Arizona, where they would dedicate a monument to their grandfather. On the day before the reunion she shopped for sturdy walking shoes before catching a commuter plane for Page, Arizona. Wesley and Sana Williamson met her at the airport under a full moon. The next day the three drove to Jacob's Pools to inspect the remnants of John D. Lee's ranch nestling at the base of the Vermillion Cliffs. Juanita put her walking shoes to good use while Wesley took photographs. In the evening they met Peg Gregory at the airport. Wesley had by this time become intoxicated and surly. Juanita wrote: "I never had such a frightful ride in my life as the one he took us on—with the speedometer not working and the machine at the fullest speed of which it was capable, and four of us in the front seat." They arrived late for the first meeting at the monument site. The next morning Wesley apologized for his behavior. Juanita believed she could discern a softening in some of the men who had been affronted by her insistence upon publishing the reinstatement. However, the day was not to be pleasant. Ettie declared "that she was going to tear off the top of the monument and re-build it because it was out of proportion,"[129] an insult to Wesley, who had designed it. Furthermore, Juanita's contribution to the wording of the monument went unnoticed. It was, she would write long after, "my ultimate disgrace, and Peg's embarrassment, too. She had made such great efforts to be present. We were both totally ignored, as much as if we had been a couple of cock-roaches. . . . I cannot put into words my humiliation. Peg said then that she was through with the Lee family, and she has stayed with it."[130]

In late November, Juanita received her first copies of *John Doyle Lee: Zealot – Pioneer Builder – Scapegoat*. Not surprisingly, the limited first edition had instantly become a book collector's item. Intending to oblige her friends by selling at a discount, she ordered a number of copies of this edition. The publisher's office informed her that she did not qualify for the full discount allowed book dealers. With a not so subtle sarcasm, she replied: "Thank you for . . . explaining why an author must not expect to be classed with a dealer, even though she pays cash in advance and sells twice as many books. I feel that authors should be kept in their places also and have no hard feelings in this matter. Huntington Library had spoiled me; that's why I asked."[131]

Predictably, reviewers would note certain inadequacies in the biography. Paul Hubbard expressed "reservations about Mrs. Brooks' use of direct quotes of conversations for which there cannot possibly be any reliable documenation." Juanita had characteristically refused to distinguish between the techniques of fiction and those of objective historiography. Hubbard also lamented the "spotty" documentation, which he dryly excused on the grounds of "the economics of publishing and the public contempt for footnotes."[132] Norman Furniss similarly found it "regrettable that her bibliography is so sketchy."[133] Juanita's secondary sources were indeed few, and as usual her primary sources were chiefly pioneer diaries and accounts. She sometimes named her sources in her text, but often did not; even when naming them, she failed to cite page numbers. Her few footnotes were informational rather than documentary.

Nonetheless, the biography achieved extraordinary praise. Numerous western newspapers responded favorably. The *San Francisco Chronicle* called it "the most towering biography ever written about any character of the American West."[134] The *Los Angeles Times* asserted: "There is in this account some measure of Christian tragedy, at least a kind of grandeur and awe which harks back to characters of Biblical times."[135] Scholarly reviewers were equally complimentary. Dale Morgan declared: "In recent Mormon historiography there is no figure to compare with this gallant seeker after the truth who has gone on the principle that 'nothing but the truth is good enough for the Church to which I belong,' and I for one am honored to account Juanita Brooks my friend."[136] Leonard Arrington wrote: "Inherently significant and interesting, scholarly and simply and superbly written, *John Doyle Lee* is surely one of the finest biographies yet written of a Westerner."[137] Paul Bailey emphasized the work's dramatic interest: "The book is no arid plowing through academic dust—it is one of the most readable and interesting studies of this decade."[138]

The primary achievement of the work was its depiction of a remarkable personality. Born in 1812 and orphaned early, John D. Lee grew up unhappily in an uncle's home. In 1838, he and his wife converted to Mormonism and joined the embattled Saints in Missouri. By 1843 he had established his wife and children in Nauvoo, Illinois, and had completed five brief proselyting missions, during which he had preached to more than a thousand people and converted over a hundred. By May of 1845, under the laws of celestial marriage, he had taken five additional wives, including the sister and mother of his first wife. He would eventually marry a total of nineteen women by whom he would sire sixty children. Many of his wives left him, some of them soon after he had married them.

During the spring of 1846 Lee and his dependents joined in the exodus from Nauvoo. Lee enjoyed the confidence and affection of Brigham Young and rendered the Mormon leader a loyal, indefatigable service. Of particular note was a dangerous journey he made from Iowa to Santa Fe and back in the fall of 1846 to retrieve the payroll of the Mormon Battalion for Brigham Young. Lee was a member of the Council of Fifty, the secret committee through which the Saints were governed during the migration to Utah and for some time after. He obediently stifled his desire to join the vanguard of Saints forging westward to the Rocky Mountains in 1847 and remained behind to assist in Iowa. Arriving in Salt Lake in 1848, he happily laid out farms and built houses. In the fall of 1850, called to the Iron Mission, he sadly disposed of his property and joined in the winter trek to southwestern Utah. In the south Lee's peregrinations at last seemed at an end and he began to prosper. By 1855 he had completed enough of a spacious fort at Harmony to house his enlarged families. His participation in the Mountain Meadows massacre in 1857 seemed only a slight disarrangement of his flourishing affairs. Soon his ambition to found a mighty settlement and to live with baronial largess seemed likely to be realized. His fields, mills, wives, children, and hired hands were numerous, and he used his large houses as inns for California-bound emigrants and as halls of hospitality for his neighbors and for visiting church dignitaries.

Eventually his life turned bitter. In the winter of 1862 unseasonal rains crumbled his adobe fort at Harmony, crushing two children and forcing Lee to evacuate and rebuild his settlement some miles away at New Harmony. Ugly rumors about his part in the massacre circulated, and many of his immediate neighbors became cold and insulting. Early in 1870, Brigham Young advised Lee to seek anonymity by pioneering along the trail to Arizona. Sorrowfully Lee disposed of his property in Harmony and Washington and placed his few faithful wives in Panguitch, Skutumpah, Lonely Dell, and Jacob's Pools. During the fall of 1870 he was excommunicated from the Church without a trial. Nonetheless, he deemed it a privilege to assist in the Mormon migrations to Arizona by operating the ferry across the Colorado at Lonely Dell.

As she followed Lee's waning fortunes, Juanita skillfully emphasized his virtues, arousing the reader to pity and indignation over his sufferings. It is probable that Lee's aggressive personality made it easy for his neighbors to join in making a scapegoat of him, for he was feudal in his ability to gather dependents, quick to contend, and uncompromising once he had entered upon a quarrel. He was, however, deeply affectionate toward his own, competent in frontier survival, public-spirited, and inveterately loyal to Mormonism. Perhaps nothing was more becoming to Lee than his refusal while in prison to make a plea bargain which would have freed him or reduced the severity of his sentence in return for detailed testimony about the massacre. To those who tempted him he replied that he "chose to die like a man then live a villain, that the Truth they did not want & as for lies, they must call on some other person to tell them besides me."[139] Nor was any circumstance of his life more heartrending than his second trial when his former friends—some of them participants in the massacre—stepped forward to deliver a damning testimony against him: "So carefully had the questions been placed; so patient and delicate had the lawyers been with the witnesses, that the combined sins of all the fifty men who were present [at the massacre] were laid on the shoulders of John D. Lee. By the time the arguments were finished he had been made responsible for planning and executing the murder, in defiance of his superior officers and contrary to their orders."[140]

The biography culminated a restitution of John D. Lee on which Juanita had worked for nearly two decades. One is reminded that she was a tragedian as well as a biographer and historian. As she had cast him, Lee surpassed even Joseph Smith as a tragic personality, not simply because the Prophet's martyrdom had with time taken on a triumphant color but because Lee more closely fit a classical pattern of tragedy. He was more than the victim of disloyal friends and unfortunate circumstances, whereby his labors were frustrated, his life cut short, and his name handed down in ignominy. A good man who had committed an evil deed, he was, like many tragic figures of literature, the victim of his own flawed character. He had hungered after righteousness yet had assented to the massacre of the innocent.

Lee's exile, trial, and execution gave his life a dramatic climax. Juanita's life had no such dramatic structure. Her existence, like that of most people, peaked momentarily and then went on in its mundane fashion. If there was a single summit year in Juanita's life, it was 1961. If there were summit moments in that year, they occurred on June 13 and July 8 when she courageously confronted Elder Stapley and the assembled Lees and insisted that for a complete catharsis, the century-old tragedy required the publication of the posthumous restoration of John D. Lee to full and honorable status in the church he had loved so much. Time quickly proved that her instinct was right. Many of the reviewers alluded with sincere satisfaction to the reinstatement. Perhaps their affirmative response disarmed the potential criticism of the general authorities, for as Juanita had predicted, the Church did not rescind the reinstatement, nor did it bring disciplinary action against her. Although the Deseret Book Store refused to stock the book on the grounds that it falsified Brigham Young's involvement in the fate of John D. Lee,[141] the Church Historian's Office blithely requested two complimentary copies. Juanita provided one, explaining apologetically that she had had only five free copies from the publisher.[142]

CHAPTER NINE

REFUSING TO RETIRE

In January 1962 the Brookses again changed residences in Salt Lake. The house on Crystal Avenue was too distant from the university and the Kearns Mansion, and its mortgage seemed too large. Juanita and Will therefore struck a bargain with a university administrator who had accepted a temporary position in Ethiopia. For his equity in a small house at 98 U Street they traded a lot in St. George and $1,000, assuming a loan which would pay off in six years at $85 per month.[1] On New Year's Day the family, reinforced by Karl and Mary, who had come from Dixie for the holiday, launched a major attack upon the soiled interior of the little house. While the women laundered curtains and washed windows, the men scrubbed cupboards and appliances and set up scaffolding and washed the walls and ceilings, which turned, in Will's words, "a white and delightsome shade."[2] Mid-January, Will, Kay, and Tony searched J. C. Penney's for suitable gifts for Juanita's birthday but came away with only minor items for which Will felt it necessary to apologize. His tribute to her in his diary was an adequate compensation: "She is one of the great women of the day. Never quarles, never too busy to give her time for her family or anyone in need of help. Her money is free to any of us needing it. Many times she has said, 'One thing that will never make trouble between us is money.' "[3]

During the holidays, Juanita received an astonishing phone call from Savoie Lottinville, director of the University of Oklahoma Press, informing her that his organization wished to publish a second edition of *The Mountain Meadows Massacre*. A contract was in the mail, and a typescript of the first edition which his staff had prepared awaited the insertion of her revisions. Juanita now remembered that two years earlier Russell Mortensen had, with her consent, sent a copy of the book to Lottinville with a proposal that he reprint it.[4] Despite Lottinville's enthusiasm, Juanita vacillated for several weeks, for Arthur

H. Clark had also shown interest in reprinting the work. Ultimately she signed the contract the University of Oklahoma Press had offered.

Through the snowy winter of 1962, Juanita continued to edit the Stout diaries. Her labor included an exacting comparison of the microfilm copy of the originals of Stout's diaries with a typescript which had been in existence since Dale Morgan's tenure on the Utah Writers' Project. "You were right about Hosea's journals being about ready to publish," she wrote Morgan. "In fact, if we had a clearer ribbon copy, I'd protest even copying them again." Suffering greatly from eye fatigue, she limited herself to only a few hours a day with the microfilm. She soon relieved her eyes by getting a new prescription for her glasses. Seeking help wherever she could find it, she casually offered Morgan her interpretation of an unusual word. "On p 90," she wrote, "where the young Indian was 'arrested & tried & *nepoed* today' I have taken *nepo* as the root of *nepotism* and assumed that the boy was put into the custody of white parents who would be responsible for him. Any suggestions?"[5] Morgan quickly returned a startling correction: *Nepo*, he wrote, "should be read in reverse, like Ytfif, and . . . symbolically if not in actual fact, it means opening up a man's belly, filling it with rocks, and sinking it in a river."[6] The enlightened Juanita composed a long footnote documenting from other sources that *nepo* meant to execute and that, indeed, an Indian had been executed in Salt Lake at the time of the entry in Stout's diary.[7]

In her turn, Juanita helped others. She provided valuable insights on the Council of Fifty to Klaus Hansen, a young man writing a doctoral dissertation. She offered evidence that Hosea Stout was not a member of the Fifty—although he had, she believed, "carried out the decisions of the Council, especially with regard to some of the 'necessary' killings both in Nauvoo and later. . . . "[8] She also lived up to her promise to assist Wallace Stegner in collecting diaries for *The Gathering of Zion: The Story of the Mormon Trail*. When Juanita billed Stegner for a modest $20, saying she had done most of her work in his behalf during her coffee breaks, he paid a double amount with this remonstrance: "I shall begin to feel very guilty about imposing on your time if you don't charge me for it, for I know that every hour you give me you are stealing from your own research—or from your coffee breaks. And what is a coffee break doing in a Brigham street office anyway? What ever happened to the Word of Wisdom?"[9]

As the Stout diaries neared completion, Juanita restlessly cast about for a new project. She wrote a number of futile inquiries to magazines about free-lance articles. She went so far as to inquire, also futilely, about a position at the University of Nevada at Las Vegas where she might divide her time between teaching English and doing research in Nevada history.[10] As the spring advanced, she served as a prominent member of the state Democratic Committee, sitting on both the platform committee and the rules committee. On the former she advocated a Civil Rights plank. She wrote her friend, John Fitzgerald, a liberal Mormon long concerned with the Church's discrimination against blacks: "I think we should join the Legislative groups, the A.A.U.W., and others who are working for a decent, or at least a more liberal Civil Rights program for our colored citizens. It was a disgrace that the last legislature would not even pass that watered down bill."[11]

On a Sunday in May, Kay left a pot of soup boiling on the stove. When others returned, the house was full of acrid smoke which the family labored some days to eradicate from the drapes and carpets.[12] During the following week, Will began the first of many happy hours of donated labor with shovel and hammer at the construction site of a new ward chapel. On the first Sunday in June Juanita replaced the regular teacher in her Sunday School class, and in Fast Meeting she bore her testimony. Tony was out of town that morning collecting samples of milk and soil for radiation testing; he also tried his hand at fishing in a mountain stream. With him was his fiancée, Janet Paulsen, who, while hiking, dislodged a boulder which injured her foot. For a few days Janet rested at the Brooks home, Juanita and Will becoming solicitous nurses to "our little Janie,"[13] as Will affectionately called her in his diary.

As June 1962 ended, Will departed upon an adventure. At a viewing, Howard Pulsipher offered him a job at a summer resort at Bear Lake which Howard and his partners owned. "His great delight at this opportunity made me conscious that he must have been more frustrated than I realized," Juanita wrote Peg Gregory.[14] Called "New Ideal Beach," the resort consisted of a motel, restaurant, dance hall, skating rink, campground, swimming beach, and boat dock. As he assisted in the construction of a fence on the day of his arrival, a length of high webbed wire fell on Will, pinning him helplessly until others freed him. Though unscathed, he reported, "I felt like a chipmunk in a dead-fall trap."[15] For four weeks he collected entrance fees at the gate, disciplining himself to bear patiently the wrath that the unpopular charge provoked. When Juanita's infrequent letters arrived, he was greatly cheered, recording on one occasion: "Today I got a love letter from my Salt Lake sweetheart, very lovely and interesting and newsy."[16] He returned from this employment too late to accompany Juanita to the wedding of Tony and Janet in the Los Angeles temple. However, on July 27 he stood beside her at an open house for the newlyweds on Eva's and Walter's back lawn in St. George.

Juanita now put herself vigorously to a revision of *The Mountain Meadows Massacre*. Although she was no longer on the payroll of the Utah Historical Society, she continued to occupy an office in the Kearns Mansion. The revision was minor and quickly finished. She persuaded an obliging librarian at the University of Utah to update her bibliography of recent works about the massacre—a perfunctory gesture to satisfy the expectations of academic readers.[17] A hitherto unknown diary or affidavit would have interested Juanita; speculations by other scholars did not. Soon she returned to the Stout diaries and at the end of August completed the transcription and annotation. For many weeks thereafter she would collaborate with Marjorie Walker, who was typing a finished draft from Juanita's notes.

On August 31 Juanita traveled to St. George. Will, who had preceded her by ten days, had been painting and cleaning their residence in preparation for new renters; he had also been enticed into a fishing trip to Enterprise reservoir with Walt and Karl. On September 1, Juanita, Will, and Karl attended a Hafen reunion in Santa Clara. At noon, at the request of Dixie College president Arthur Bruhn, Juanita and Will joined a Chamber of Commerce tour where Juanita recounted local history for representatives of a national TV network. Of particular interest were the Brigham Young winter home in St. George, the Jacob Hamblin home in Santa Clara, and Snow Canyon, a nearby scenic area, all of which the Utah State Parks and Recreation Commission was developing as visitor sites. Juanita had contributed much to the preservation of the two homes.[18] One is reminded that she constantly advocated historical preservation. In early 1963 she would, for example, join others in an effective protest against the destruction of the old county courthouse in St. George.[19]

During their prolonged visit in September 1962, Juanita and Will attended a Rook party of the Athena Club. "It was nice to meet with the old crowd," Will wrote. "We all admit that we are not just what we used to be. Our eyes are dim we cannnot tell Red from Yellow. So we have good hands, but some times they don't win on account of not being trumps."[20] Early on a Saturday Juanita and Will arrived at the temple to attend the double wedding of Walt's twin daughters Lida and Leona. They were momentarily discomfited to discover that their bishop in Salt Lake had not signed their temple recommends. After three long distance calls and a promise to mail the signed certificates to the temple president, they entered the temple. Following the wedding, Walt hosted a chicken dinner at the Sugar Loaf Cafe for over fifty persons, provoking one of Leona's in-laws to comment, "I did not think a person could acquire so many relatives in such a short time."[21]

When classes commenced at BYU in late September, Kay enrolled as a graduate student and teaching assistant in Spanish. He and Ida Jean Taylor from Provo would soon announce their engagement. Juanita and Will were by no means solitary, however, since Kay returned on many weekends and Clair and Lavon and Tony and Janet dropped in frequently. A crowd converged upon them for general conference in early October. A notable visitor was J. K. Fancher, with whom Juanita had corresponded since her speech in Harrison, Arkansas, in September 1955. Fancher, on a return trip from California, phoned from St. George expressing his desire to visit Mountain Meadows. Juanita in turn phoned friends, who conveyed Fancher to the site where his great-grandfather and the party he had led had been slaughtered. Fancher traveled on to Salt Lake, and Juanita invited him, his wife, and nephew to breakfast on a Saturday morning. Fancher expressed satisfaction over his visit to Mountain Meadows. "Mr. Fancher," Will wrote, "is a good Christian man, has no bad feelings against our people, he has a beautiful Christian spirit with him, would like all feelings eradicated."[22] Afterward Juanita, chauffeured by Russell Mortensen, gave the Fanchers a guided tour of Salt Lake.

In October 1962 Juanita secured temporary employment in the office of the United States Attorney for Utah. Her new quarters were on the top floor of the Federal Building at Fourth South and Main, and her supervisor would be assistant U.S. attorney Parker M. Nielson.[23] Her job was to research and write a report on the history of navigation on the Green River in Utah. Her study would be useful in countering an attempt by the state of Utah to take possession of the riverbed within its borders. The question of navigability was crucial, for legal precedent favored state control of a riverbed if it could be proven that the river was navigable at the time statehood was granted. Within days of occupying her new office, Juanita was steeped in the journals of early explorers and fur trappers and in authoritative histories of the fur trade. Of particular importance was Dale Morgan's *Jedediah Smith*, which in a letter to Morgan she called "my Bible."[24]

In late October Will's brother Sam suffered a severe heart attack. Visiting Sam in the hospital, Will promised that he would not go deer hunting. "He did not approve of me going," Will wrote. "So my hunting this year is called off."[25] Wistfully, Will monitored the hunt by phone and found it had been a great success. On the Tuesday following the hunt, Sam died. Amidst the phone calls, visits, and viewings, Will filled his diary entries with a bereaved appreciation of his departed brother. In the evening after the funeral, the surviving siblings and numerous other relatives crowded into Juanita's and Will's home for supper and thoughtful reminiscence.

In October Juanita had lunch in downtown Salt Lake with Boyd Mathias, with whom she had frequently corresponded regarding the policy of the Church toward blacks. Mathias spoke about his plans to annotate and publish "Parallel," the underground manuscript in which B. H. Roberts had made a disconcerting correlation between the Book of Mormon and a nineteenth-century treatise, *A View of the Hebrews*. Juanita encouraged Mathias in this endeavor—which he would not complete—but she was disturbed that his angry disbelief seemed likely to rupture his family life. In subsequent letters she appealed for compromise: "Perhaps I have placed too high a value on harmony in our home, but I know that children, even very young ones, are sensitive to frictions between their parents—or situations in which, in spite of themselves, they have to take sides."[26] Her own accommodation to Mormonism, she told Mathias, had been greatly influenced by her desire to give her children, not a dogmatic faith, but a Christian stability. "Somehow I have always felt that a basic faith in God (without undue emphasis of body, parts, and passions) gives depth and direction to life; a God who loves all his children equally, and who expects them to treat each other as brothers. I also think that the basic teachings of Jesus Christ are worth trying to live, and the weekly pledge that I will try to keep His commandments that I may have His spirit to be with me is one that I am glad to make."[27] Whatever effect her letters may have had upon Mathias, they remain a valuable elaboration of her personal religion.

In November Juanita took a bus to Cedar City where she spoke at the farewell testimonial of her nephew Carrick, who was preparing to leave for a mission to England. Some days later her bishop asked Juanita to supervise and edit a project for publishing brief biographies of every member of the Federal Heights Ward, a task she accepted. Following Thanksgiving, she and Marjorie Walker worked diligently after hours at the Kearns Mansion to complete the typescript of the Stout diaries. The reason for their haste was a deadline for sending the manuscript to the University of Oklahoma Press, which Everett Cooley hoped would publish the work. Months earlier, Russell Mortensen had irritated Cooley by publishing a brochure announcing that the University of Utah Press would print the diaries. Although Juanita remained neutral in this matter, she had on occasion released a shower of sparks in Mortensen's presence. One day as she took lunch in the kitchen of the Kearns Mansion, Mortensen dropped by and proposed that she edit the papers of Reed Smoot, an early senator from Utah. She declined the offer bluntly: "Now, don't you ask me to edit the Smoot Papers because I will not do it. I did not admire him in life and I do not honor him in death—so I would not be qualified emotionally to edit them, besides which, they cover a period with which I am only slightly familiar."[28]

In December Juanita flew to Los Angeles at the invitation of George T. Boyd, instructor at the LDS Institute of Religion at the University of Southern California. "I can't think of anything I could say that would be worth half the cost of transportation,"[29] she had protested as she offered Boyd an opportunity to renege on his invitation. Speaking before groups of liberal Mormons on Saturday and Sunday evenings, Juanita rambled widely over the massacre, Hosea Stout, and the pioneering of Dixie. She later apologized to Boyd for possibly offending some of her listeners "with my comments on the use of wine in the sacrament or by intimating that 'the testimonies went on until sundown,' after the proper spiking of the noon meal. We in Dixie have not taken this matter so seriously as some members of the church who have not been so close to it."[30]

While in Los Angeles, she stayed at night with Aura and Carl, enjoying the immaculate order of her sister's home. Returning to Salt Lake on Monday morning, she phoned Will from her office at

eleven. She had worried about him because he suffered from a painfully swollen knee. That night, heeding Aura's advice, she applied cold
packs to the knee, inducing a speedy improvement which did much to
raise Will's spirits. She also arranged her hair with large pins Aura
had given her and pondered in a letter to her sister whether she might
not "cut my hair short in front of the ears and see if I can get away
from this tight, pull-back effect. I'm a little scared of it, though, and
I'm so old and ugly that there's nothing that can be done about it."[31]

After the holidays, Juanita resumed her work on the Green
River project in the Federal Building. In her spare time, she gave direction to the project for publishing a collection of brief biographies of
the members of the Federal Heights Ward. Throughout the winter
and spring of 1963, she met at night with a ward committee, devising
means of motivating the members to write their accounts. Juanita had
also agreed when Will's brothers and sisters gathered for Sam's funeral
to write a biography of their father, George Brooks. That book, Juanita
wrote Alfred Bush in January 1963, "is waiting to be finished, and it's
a tremendous story. It's one that I should postpone no longer."[32] (As a
graduate student in Utah, Alfred L. Bush had shown great respect for
Juanita; having become curator of western Americana at Princeton
University library by 1963, he remained one of her regular correspondents.) For the moment the biography of George Brooks chiefly involved
Will, who found it a pleasant pastime to sift family files in search of
material relating to his father's life, which, Will assured his diary, was
very interesting—"from Wales to Utah via Handcart to S.L.C. to St.
George, his work as a stone cutter, raising 12 children, [serving as]
county sheriff and city marshall."[33] Occasionally Juanita paused on a
Saturday morning to write a few tentative paragraphs, causing Will to
record, not altogether optimistically, that she was "getting warmed up
some" to the project.[34]

During the spring of 1963, Juanita also evaluated for a fee
the manuscript of a history of Nauvoo for the University of Oklahoma Press. As she contemplated the end of her employment by the
U.S. Attorney, she cast about for more significant labor: "All this
seems just busy work for children, or finger exercise," she wrote Alfred
Bush in January: "I want something that will present more of a challenge and offer more of a reward. I don't mean just a financial reward—
I mean a satisfaction of having done something that is worth doing."[35]
Perhaps the question of her future was made acute by her sixty-fifth

birthday and the beginning of monthly Utah Public Employees retirement checks. With admirable pluck, she inquired whether the Huntington would hire her to catalogue its Mormon collection or whether the U.S. National Archives would hire her to edit the territorial papers of Utah.[36] "I may be like a child reaching for the moon. Who was it said, 'A man's reach should exceed his grasp, or what's a heaven for?'" she wrote A. C. Lambert. "Like Tennyson's 'Ulysses,' I'm just not ready to admit that I'm done and finished."[37]

In January 1963, Juanita was cheered by the appearance of the second edition of *The Mountain Meadows Massacre*. "My sincere thanks to all the Oklahoma Press staff," she wrote to Savoie Lottinville, "for the excellent way in which this book of mine has been prepared."[38] The changes were minor. Endnotes had become footnotes; a map of Utah, photographs of John D. Lee, and chapter titles had been added; the bibliography had been enlarged; slight emendations of the text had occurred. The *Los Angeles Times* called it "a definitive and beautifully written history of one of the most tragic events in the history of the West."[39] Respectful reviews appeared in many other newspapers, including the Bridgeport, Connecticut, *Post*, the *Tulsa World*, and the *Dallas Times-Herald*. In their leisurely fashion, scholarly journals also gave it favorable attention. Wyoming historian T. A. Larson, writing for the *New Mexico Historical Review*, commended Juanita "for remarkable resourcefulness in running down evidence, a passion for justice, and rare objectivity."[40] An exception was the review of Merlin Stonehouse in *Southern California Quarterly*. Unimpressed by Juanita's attempt to mitigate the guilt of John D. Lee by reference to war hysteria, Stonehouse declared her assertion that Brigham Young had been an accessory after the fact to be "a dreadful calumny upon a great man."[41]

The success of the second edition can also be measured by sales. Within three months of publication, the second edition had sold nearly 1,350 copies—"little short of amazing," a proud Lottinville informed Juanita.[42] For many years Juanita would receive royalty checks of some substance. By the end of November 1985, the edition would have gone through eight printings with cumulative sales of 16,542 copies.[43] An indisputable Mormon classic, *The Mountain Meadows Massacre* remains in print as of the present writing.

In February 1963, Juanita and Will joined a trek of the Mormon Battalion unit of the Sons of the Utah Pioneers. The group had agreed to march in a Tucson parade observing the centennial of Arizona's investiture as a U.S. territory. Their participation was appropriate, for it had been the original Mormon Battalion that, in 1846 at Old Fort Tucson, had raised the first American flag over Arizona soil. Departing from Salt Lake, the tour buses stopped in Nephi and, according to Will, "picked up a jolly bunch of Nephites who soon showed themselves as good neighbors and good sports." The travelers, taking advantage of the loudspeakers on the buses, entertained themselves with "songs, storeys, jokes and speaches,"[44] the general tenor of which remained respectable, there being but "very few that needed screening."[45] In Kanab, Utah, and Mesa, Arizona, they stayed overnight and paraded. Both men and women, dressed in formal uniforms and long flowered dresses, participated. Arriving in Tucson on a Thursday morning, the Battalion marched in a massive two-hour parade, eliciting vigorous applause from a large crowd along the three-and-a-half-mile route. Juanita and Will found it exhilarating. The buses returned to Utah via Four Corners. At that spot, wrote Will, "I stood one foot in Utah, one in Colorado, Nita one foot in New Mex and one in Arizona as I gave her a four-cornered kiss."[46]

In March Juanita intensified her efforts on the Green River project. By mid-April she had finished her report and was proofreading the draft as a secretary typed it. She remained on the job until after May 1 preparing a brief. Her 145-page document was entitled "A Report on the History and Uses of the Green River from the Point Where It Enters the State of Utah to Its Confluence with the San Rafael." In it she provided a preliminary bibliography of convincing length, citing diaries, exploration reports, biographies, and histories. She devoted over two-thirds of the report to early explorations, giving emphasis to the John Wesley Powell expeditions down the Green because Powell's reports and journals described the river and its sparse inhabitants in great detail. Drawing upon modern accounts and census reports, she also treated recent development along the river course.

It was an admittedly biased document. With the bellicose fervor of a college debater, Juanita hammered out her thesis: the river was not now navigable, nor had it ever been. Its narrow canyons and brutal rapids made up-and-down traffic impossible, as she demonstrated by reference to numerous accounts of the explorers. Even in its open stretches the river had not fostered settlements of note. In 1930, Daggett County, into which the river flowed from Wyoming, had a population of 411; in 1960, 329. When formed in 1917, the county boasted two towns, Manila and Linwood; by 1960, Linwood had disappeared. In earlier years the citizens of Linwood cooperated in an effort to estab-lish river travel upstream to the railroad town of Green River, Wyo-ming. Although their motorboat was troubled by "several delays on sandbars," its initial voyage from Green River to Linwood seemed sat-isfactory. "Steaming back up the stream posed an entirely different set of problems. The boat simply would not go, and the attempts to pry it loose from sandbars, to secure extra fuel, to make any headway at all provide material for many a hilarious tale. Travel on the Green River was abandoned then and there, and with the coming of automobiles and highways, has never been attempted since."[47]

The finishing of her study did not end Juanita's connection with the suit. As late as October 1963, she examined the opposing report of the plaintiff and provided Parker Nielson with a rebuttal.[48] Although she stood ready to testify in court, she was not called upon. Following various hearings, the case would be settled amicably in early 1965 by a compromise. Long stretches of the river passing through relatively flat, open land were defined as navigable and therefore sus-ceptible to ownership by the state. Other stretches passsing through mountainous canyons and filled with rapids were defined as un-navigable and would therefore remain in the ownership of the federal government.[49] The compromise did not satisfy Juanita, who remained convinced of the river's unnavigability. She would write to Nielson: "And yet both sides were willing to try to make it so for somebody's private benefit."[50]

Through the winter and spring of 1963, Juanita and Will flourished socially. On a Friday evening they attended a reading from Shakespeare in the company of Sterling and Natalie McMurrin. On a Monday evening, they had a Mexican supper at the home of Gordon and Alta Howard in Farmington; afterward the couples attended the play *Peter Pan* in the new Pioneer Memorial Theatre on the university campus, Juanita and Will buying the tickets. The next evening, Juanita and Will attended a lecture delivered by the famous anthropaleontolo-gist, Louis Leakey, whose topic was early man in the Olduvai Gorge of Africa. "The house was crowded," Will reported; "all liked his knowl-edge and wit. His delivery was just a little English accent which made it difficult to grasp."[51] On another evening Fae Dix, a friend whom Juanita had first met long ago in Cedar City, took her to see an art exhibit at Auerbach's; some of the paintings, according to Will, were valued at over $100,000.

Two happy family events occurred as spring turned to summer in 1963. On April 25 Juanita and Will became grandparents again as Janet gave birth to Mark Leavitt Brooks. Later in the month the Brookses entertained Janet's parents, who came from southern California to see the newborn, whom Will affably described as "a remarkable child; he meets every expectation, beautiful, good natured, much black hair, already likes to show off to his folks."[52] On June 5, 1963, the Brooks clan gathered in Logan for Kay's and Ida Jean's wedding. Following a temple ceremony, Juanita and Will, as parents of the groom, hosted a wedding breakfast at a Logan restaurant. The next evening they attended a reception at a private home in Provo, hosted by Ida Jean's parents, Mr. and Mrs. John W. Taylor. Following a brief honeymoon, Kay and Ida Jean would move into Juanita's and Will's rental house in Provo, and Kay would continue graduate work in Spanish at BYU.[53]

Amidst such domestic doings Juanita maintained a busy schedule of talks and addresses. Of particular note was a regional conference of the American Folklore Society in Logan, where Juanita delivered a paper entitled "Beliefs, Practices, and Customs of the Mormon Pioneer Household."[54] Early in 1963 Juanita had accepted a position on the governing board of the Utah Folklore Society.[55] There she established a beneficial relationship with such stalwarts of Utah folklore as Austin and Alta Fife and Thomas E. Cheney.

Juanita now hoped to complete neglected free-lance writing projects. In May she vowed she would spend eight hours a day for thirty days writing in her tiny basement study at 98 U Street, which she described to Alfred Bush as "this black hole of Calcutta where there are no distractions." With a characteristic uncertainty she admitted that her projects might come to nothing even if she should succeed in completing them: "As Bill Bracken so aptly said, 'No man lives as far from the market as the one who has nothing to sell.' "[56] She did not in fact get much writing done, for she found other people's projects more compelling. For a modest honorarium, she verified the historical accuracy of Wallace Stegner's partially completed *The Gathering of Zion: The Story of the Mormon Trail*. "You are at your superlative best here," she complimented the California author when she returned his manuscript. She pointed out, by way of correction, that

Brigham Young had played only a minor role in the evacuation of the beleaguered Mormons from Missouri in 1838 and that Porter Rockwell had not committed anything close to the hundred killings that Charles Kelly had attributed to him.[57] She had her information on Rockwell from Harold Schindler, a young writer for the *Salt Lake Tribune* whose research for a biography of the famous Mormon gunman Juanita both respected and assisted. Stegner accepted her compliments and corrections with equal gratitude, replying, "You're a good angel, or at the very least a good Saint."[58] Juanita also advised Tony and R. J. Snow about their master's theses. Tony had vowed not to shave until his thesis had been accepted, "which," Juanita wrote Peg Gregory, "I hope will be before he looks like Rip Van Winkle. He did compromise and clear off all but a chin beard, though."[59]

June found Juanita hurrying to complete the Federal Heights biographies, the publication of which in multilith form coincided with the dedication of the new Federal Heights meetinghouse. She made slight redactions in the 147 accounts which the genealogical committee had solicited and wrote a brief history of the ward's official life, which had begun in 1950 with its separation from University Ward. The compilation provided a roster of the illustrious Mormons with whom Juanita and Will worshiped while living at 98 U Street. Among them were Alexander Schreiner, Salt Lake tabernacle organist; Harold B. Lee, member of the Quorum of Twelve Apostles; Henry D. Moyle, first counselor in the First Presidency; A. Ray Olpin, president of the University of Utah; and George D. Clyde, governor of the State of Utah.

As the summer of 1963 advanced, Juanita and Will prepared for a trans-Atlantic trip, receiving smallpox vaccinations and applying for passports. As a corollary to this process, Juanita changed the legal spelling of her name from "Waneta," as it had appeared on the church records in Bunkerville at the time of her birth. Moreover, Mary Leavitt prepared to accompany her daughter and son-in-law to Europe. "Bless her, she's so excited and thrilled about it all," Juanita wrote to R. J.'s parents, Laura and Glen Snow. "Her grandchildren joined in a 'send Grandma to Europe' fund drive which will supplement her savings enough so that she will not have to use all she has."[60]

As the time for departure drew near, Juanita observed a minor drama touching upon the publication of the Hosea Stout diaries. In May the University of Oklahoma Press sent Everett Cooley a signed contract by whose terms that press would underwrite the entire cost of the project. It is probable that Russell Mortensen lobbied against Cooley with the trustees of the Utah Historical Society, for at a meeting of June 28, the Board, after "literally days of discussion and debate," instructed Cooley to accept a contract from the University of Utah Press if Mortensen could produce a favorable counteroffer within two weeks. Mortensen did so,[61] paring an earlier bid and condemning his press to economies of production that his successor, Richard Thurman, would regret. Thereafter, it was Cooley's painful duty to inform Lottinville that the trustees had ordained "that the publication program of the Society should be kept within the state where it is possible to do so."[62]

On Sunday morning, July 21, 1963, Juanita, Will, and Mary were escorted to the Salt Lake airport by nearly forty of their loved ones and friends. On Monday morning Willa, Thales, and their sons met them at the London airport and drove them to their home near Lakenheath Air Base, where Thales' fighter squadron was stationed. On the following Thursday, having arranged a baby-sitter for David and Daniel, Willa took her visitors to a session of the London temple. She aroused their admiration by her skillful negotiation of metropolitan traffic. Staying overnight in London, they took in Buckingham Palace, Madame Tussaud's Waxworks, and "The Sound of Music." On Sunday, Juanita and Will addressed the Mormon congregation at Bury St. Edmunds, where Thales was branch president and Willa was Relief Society president and organist.[63]

The next day, Willa and her visitors departed on a four-day circle through Wales. Their first stop was Green Knowe, a manor in rural Hampshire belonging to Lucy M. Boston, an author of children's books, to whom Juanita carried a message from a friend in Logan, Utah. Juanita was exceptionally pleased by this experience. Woods, hedges, and lawns enhanced the grounds, and the stone manor house boasted arched windows, quilted drapes, and a great fireplace. "The carved and embellished furniture, the old kettles, pitchers, dishes, tongs, candles, all seemed from another civilization almost," Juanita would write. Boston proved to be "a lovely lady, her dark hair graying just a little, dressed in a simple denim dress of a brown-green combination, with hands that showed how she loved to work out of doors as well as at the typewriter or the needle."[64] Next the travelers visited Stratford-on-Avon and then traversed Wales, arriving at a lonely lighthouse at Point of Ayr on the Welsh coast. They plodded through the dunes at the base of the lighthouse and looked out on the heaving sea with a hushed reverence, for this was the birthplace of Will's father.

They returned to Willa's home via Cambridge, and after a four-day rest, Juanita, Will, and Mary entrained for London. Willa's eyes, her father reported, "filled with tears as she left us at the station."[65] They flew to Frankfurt, Germany, and made their way via Nuremburg to Bern, Switzerland, where circumstances forced them to take a more expensive hotel than they wished. "We did see the way some people entertain each other with champaign, whiskey and wine," Will commented.[66] Perhaps craving the familiar, they transferred the next day to a pension near the Mormon temple at Zollikofen, where they attended a German-speaking session. Soon they returned to Bern, a point of pilgrimage because it was here that Mary's mother had lived before migrating to Utah during her childhood. Mary was particularly happy to find the famous bear pit of Bern exactly as her mother had described it. They also took a bus into the Alps and rode a chairlift to a scenic overlook. Returning on the lift, Mary occupied a chair alone. Wrote Juanita: "Soon I could hear her singing, the 'Tra la la la' of the Swiss song floating clear on the air. She was just so happy she had to sing."[67] It was withal a congenial journey, though at times Mary practiced an excessive frugality. "She did fear the high prices of meals, food and Hotels," Will complained, noting that she "did willingly eat food from our orders if she thought it would be wasted."[68]

The travelers arrived in Salt Lake on August 16, 1963. Mary returned to St. George, and Juanita and Will shortly followed, intending to rent their place for another year. They went so far as to promise the new part of their house to a couple, leaving the old part for Karl, who had accepted a position as coach and social sciences teacher in the high school division of Dixie College. Within hours of agreeing to rent the place, Juanita reneged. As she explained to Peg Gregory, "Will's desire to stay here and live was so deep and so evident that I decided to do that."[69]

There were matters to attend to in Salt Lake. Foremost among them was saying good-bye to Tony and Janet. Tony had completed a master's degree at the University of Utah and accepted a handsome $6,000 fellowship at Cornell, where he would pursue doctoral studies in the effect of radiation upon living tissues. During the first weekend of September, the little house at 98 U Street bulged with visitors—Janet's parents and siblings and Margie and Sharon, Ernest's wife and daughter, who had come to Salt Lake to establish Sharon at the LDS Business College. Harold Schindler dropped by on Saturday to consult Juanita about his biography of Porter Rockwell; he considerately relieved the bedding problem by offering sleeping quarters in his home. On Monday afternoon Tony and Janet made a tardy departure. Sadly Will wrote: "After dinner and our farewells they got into their car taking little Mark with all his smiles and joy out of our life."[70]

On September 21, Clair and Kay helped their parents move to Dixie. Despairing of the clutter, Will wrote: "Oh my, oh my, what a pile of junk, some of which is well worth saving, some questionable."[71] Before Kay and Clair returned to Provo and Salt Lake, Juanita took Connie and Julie, Clair's daughters, on a hike on the Sugar Loaf. The hike was, one supposes, a gesture of homecoming on Juanita's part. For days she and Will labored to put their home on the hill in order. While Will trimmed the oleander bushes and planted a mailbox on a post at the front of the lot, Juanita was busy indoors, going "about her cleaning just as any other good scrubwoman would do."[72] Karl helped as he could. Each morning as he drove to school, he delivered Mary to the temple where she attended daylong sessions.

Will stopped keeping a regular diary, having too many other things to do. "His delight to be home is beautiful to see," Juanita told Peg Gregory. "Here he has busyness; here he has space and sunshine and friendly neighbors; here he can drive the Old Pink Bomb with comparative safety." Juanita adapted less joyfully. "I think that perhaps I can write with as much purpose as I could in Salt Lake City," she wrote Peg. "If I can only be reconciled to this 'rook game' level of society! There are other things, to be sure, and I'll have to help make some of them."[73] She accepted a call to teach a regular lesson in her ward Relief Society class and another to teach an MIA class in the college ward. In late October she spent four days in Salt Lake attending the meetings of the Western History Association. While there she phoned Grace Woodbury, uttering words for which she later felt compelled to write a letter of apology. "It was inappropriate and—well, just crude. Forgive me. I must have just had a cup of coffee. It sometimes turns the Devil loose in me."[74]

Above the piano in the Brooks home hung a photograph of John F. Kennedy. On November 23, 1963, that photograph took

on a tragic aura with the assassination of the young president. Joining
in the shock and grief of the nation, Juanita sat before the TV
"unashamedly weeping." On the first day she turned off the TV "for
long periods in the afternoon; I simply could not stand it. The last
evening program after the funeral with the symphony music and the
changing pictures, with the brief readings between, I thought was most
appropriate and lovely."[75] Juanita was soon confronted by another
loss. In early December she was asked to speak at the funeral of Roxey
Romney, with whom she had often visited during her recent sojourn
in Salt Lake. With great respect, Juanita outlined the life of this remarkable woman who had served as county librarian in St. George, as
Democratic National Committeewoman, and as member of the Board
of Regents of the University of Utah.[76]

During the fall of 1963 Juanita roughed out four chapters
of a biography of George Brooks. In late January 1964, she applied
herself to gathering materials for a fifth chapter covering George's life
from 1862 to 1872. Because he had left no records for this period, she
was forced to fit him into events revealed in the journals of others. "I
must assume," she wrote Wesley and Sana Williamson, "that he was
present when the telegraph wires were connected, and when the Washington factory was dedicated, and at the various fairs and 24th of July
celebrations."[77]

She was, however, easily diverted by more interesting
projects. One such project would result in the publication of three
chapters from "Quicksand and Cactus." Often, when audiences
had asked her to discuss her own life, Juanita had mined anecdotes
from her dormant autobiography. In December came two requests
to publish her chapter "The Outsider." One came from Golden
Taylor at Utah State University, who, according to his letter, intended
to compile an anthology of short stories "genuinely representative
of life in the West. I would like to include your story 'The Outsider' which I have heard you tell on several occasions with such
charm. I realize that you tell it with the utmost fidelity as autobiography, but just a touch of fiction would justify its inclusion."[78]
Ten days later Juanita received a similar request from John Greenway,
editor of the *Journal of American Folklore*, who had heard her
rendition of "The Outsider" at the folklore conference in Logan
in July 1963. Desiring to publish it as an example of folklore
having literary values, he declared it "to be as excellent a picture of

the old days on our frontier as anything written by Hamlin Garland."[79]

Having promised "The Outsider" to Taylor, Juanita proposed that Greenway take "Old Tubucks" or "Selah." Greenway boldly wrote Taylor, whereupon Taylor graciously agreed – not without regret – to give Greenway the right of first publication.[80] Having scented other game, Greenway offered to publish "Old Tubucks" and "Selah" as well as "The Outsider." Entirely agreeable, Juanita forwarded the three narrratives to Greenway at intervals, and in late March, having made further slight revisions of each, proposed "Memories of a Mormon Girlhood" as an inclusive title.[81] She did not disabuse Greenway and Taylor of their assumption that she was putting the accounts into writing for the first time. Perhaps she feared that they would lose interest should they know how many editors, nearly twenty years earlier, had rejected these and other chapters from her autobiography.

In any event, "Old Tubucks," "The Outsider," and "Selah" first saw print in the *Journal of American Folkore* of July–September 1964. Greenway handsomely commented in a prefatory note: "It is good now and then to remind ourselves that there is still a small place in folk scholarship for the human observer – not only the illiterate informant whose reminiscences never leave our archives except in the form of statistics, but those eminently literate persons whose memories of lives begun in folk societies can give us not only understanding of such cultures but sheer gladness in the reading."[82] For his part, Golden Taylor would go forward with his plan to publish "The Outsider" as a work of short fiction. It would appear in *Great Western Short Stories* in 1967, honorably positioned between Willa Cather's "Neighbour Rosicky" and Hamblin Garland's "Under the Lion's Paw."

On April 11, 1964, Juanita participated on a panel at a workshop for women at the College of Southern Utah in Cedar City. Assigned the topic of "Women in the Arts,"[83] Juanita emphatically declared marriage to be the primary role of women. "Do, by all means," she advised her young listeners, "get a ring on your third-finger left. And do support your husband in every way. We all know that the success of any man depends very largely upon his wife. . . . And DO share your children's interests and encourage them – see that they have their opportunity to be trained in basic skills and arts." Within this domestic context, she went on, the arts could provide a vital rejuvenation. "Every woman needs to have some creative activity – handwork, flower culture, flower arrangement, interior decoration, music – vocal or instrumental – or any one of many other hobbies. She needs some bit of 'aloneness,' some time to herself, and some place of her own."[84] Juanita illustrated her points by reference to her own reconciliation of family life and historical research and writing, a topic which audiences with increasing frequency asked her to discuss. With a polite deference, she likened her professional career to the handwork and flower arrangement she had recommended to her listeners: it was a mere hobby, a pleasant pastime. In part, Juanita slighted her professional achievement in this astonishing manner because she judged the young women of this rural college to have exclusively domestic interests. But in part she slighted it because she herself doubted its significance. Despite her publishing triumphs, she continued to identify herself chiefly as a wife and mother, and despite her happy association with bright and accomplished people in the cities of the Wasatch Front, she thought of herself as one of the folk.

Another project which diverted Juanita from the George Brooks biography was an article about the Mormons in northwestern Nevada at the time when that region was part of Utah Territory. Having agreed in December to prepare the article for a conference in Reno, she procrastinated until nearly April, when a deadline loomed, before settling down to hard work. It was a project for which she could stir up little enthusiasm, because Mormon settlement in the region had been ephemeral. "It seems to me literally Much Ado about Nothing," she wrote Peg Gregory. "They were called there in the spring of 1856, made the six weeks-long journey, pitched in, built houses, erected mills, cleared land – and then were recalled in the fall of 1857."[85] In May she traveled by automobile to Reno and delivered her paper at the first annual Nevada History Conference, cosponsored by the Nevada Historical Society and the University of Nevada.[86] In the spring of 1965 her paper, "The Mormons in Carson County, Utah Territory," would appear in the *Nevada Historical Society Quarterly*. It was one of the least polished scholarly publications of her career. In the published version, the contents of what had been an extensive footnote in the manuscript were clumsily inserted in the main text, presumably by the editor. It is probable that Juanita herself was responsible for several citations from H. H. Bancroft's *History of Nevada, Colorado and Wyoming* which mingled paraphrase and quotation in a promiscuous manner—a lapse from professional standards indicative of her indifference to her topic.

Throughout the spring of 1964 Juanita was agitated over neglect of the site of the Mountain Meadows massacre. The present monument was, she wrote, "a disgrace to the whole of southern Utah. The walls have cracked some two-feet apart on the two eastern corners, and that section is ready to fall. . . . In another season or two the bones will be washed out and scattered."[87] Grasping at straws, she hoped that the Lee family might be encouraged to purchase the site and donate it to the Forest Service, the family having, with considerable courage, agreed to hold its 1964 reunion at Mountain Meadows and nearby Pine Valley. Accordingly, she and Will drove with Wesley and Sana Williamson, who were on their way to Denver, to the ranch of Ezra Lytle, owner of the site. After a chat with the absent rancher's wife, they drove on to Cedar City and conversed with the forest ranger. Juanita and Will then accompanied Wesley and Sana as far as Provo, where the next evening Juanita would speak to the Sons of the Utah Pioneers. For the moment, Lytle was reluctant to sell to any party and the site would continue to deteriorate.

On June 6, 1964, Utah State University awarded Juanita an honorary doctorate of letters. At the same commencement it made a similar award to LeGrand Richards—an irony not lost upon Juanita, who reminisced in a letter about her heated exchange with the apostle regarding her history of the massacre. "Life is full of paradoxes, certainly," she mused.[88] Attending baccalaureate services with Will and Karl on the evening before the award, she became jammed in a crowd and missed a banquet at which she was expected. The next day officials assigned a professor the duty of escorting her promptly to a luncheon. Her citation summarized her achievements as a collector, editor, and author, noting too her "wealth of influence upon educational, civic, and religious institutions and communities."[89]

On June 19, Juanita met with a small number of Lee family members at Mountain Meadows, then accompanied them to Pine Valley, where all enjoyed a dinner and a program. The next day Juanita and Will invited friends and relatives to meet the Lees at a luncheon in their home. In the midst of their merriment, a package arrived, which Will opened. It was Juanita's honorary doctoral hood, resplendent with velvet color. "Yes, I must even model it over my kitchen apron and a nephew pointed his camera at me. I didn't mean it to be a desecration; I wasn't being flippant either. So I hope there was no film in the camera," she sheepishly wrote to an official at Utah State University.[90] In the afternoon, Evan and Ettie Lee, brother and sister, escorted the group to a scenic point in Kolob Canyon, where Evan had subdivided properties for summer homes. The properties lay near a high overlook from which the fugitive John D. Lee had once observed his settlement of Harmony, an event he had recorded with great emotion in his diary. Casually Juanita spoke of buying a single acre. Evan responded with serious intent, and within a few days she and Will had paid $500 for a site. Shortly, Ettie refunded the purchase price. "Never in my life, Juanita," she wrote, "have I wanted so much to make a gift to anyone as I desire you to have this particular spot from me. It is symbolical in a way of what you and your pen have done for me and all the John D. Lee Family. Father told me when I was a mere child about Grandfather's Look Out and how the strength of the hills, the clearness of the sky, the beauty of nature's carvings helped his father to grow strong in stature and tall in spirit and become equal to the sacrifice ahead of him."[91] For unapparent reasons, the Brooks family would never build a cabin on the spot.

In early July, Juanita and Will attended the World's Fair in New York City. They traveled by bus to Grand Junction where they joined Ernest and Margie. Then all drove on in the Pulsiphers' new automobile, Juanita and Will paying for gas and lodging. In Nauvoo, their friend T. Edgar Lyon, a prominent Mormon historian involved in the restoration of the frontier city, gave them a detailed tour. In Ithaca, they stayed three nights with Tony and Janet, who took them on a tour of Cornell University and a picnic at a nearby lake. Crowding the young family into Ernest's car, they drove on to New York City. One morning at the fair, Will watched over the sleeping Mark in the comfort of the Mormon Pavillion while the others attended a science exhibit. That evening the weary Juanita and Will stayed in the hotel with Mark while Ernest, Margie, Tony, and Janet went out on the town. Saying good-bye to Tony and Janet, the travelers went on to Washington, D.C., where they visited the Lincoln Memorial and Arlington National Cemetery. As they drove west, Will grumbled in a little diary: "Ern succeeds quite well in keeping us from know[ing] just where we are, he leaves the highway for an hour or so knowing well where he will return, we must guess where we are. . . . " They arrived in Grand Junction on July 23, after a drive of "5216 miles in Erns Ford without any trouble not even a flat tire."⁹²

Upon their return, Will acquired a hearing aid. It was an annoyance but served him well during a visit of Willa and her sons; she and Thales had returned to the United States and would soon be stationed in Clovis, New Mexico. Juanita and Will were also pleased that Kay had finished initial schooling with the FBI and was now stationed in Oklahoma City. In early August came shocking news: Angus and Grace Woodbury had been killed in an automobile accident. Juanita took a night bus to Salt Lake and attended the viewing and funeral. She sought comfort from many old friends and found the proceedings dignified and appropriate. Yet, as she wrote to Gordon and Alta Howard upon her return, "the bleak, stark fact is that they are *gone*, and with them so much that made life richer for so many."⁹³ In September, she returned to Salt Lake for the annual meeting of the Utah Historical Society. Patiently she sat through morning and afternoon sessions, listening to scholarly papers while jotting notes on her program. Among her scribblings may be reconstructed the following adage, her judgment, perhaps, of the proceedings: "A speech that is read is like making love through a hedge fence; you can hear the voice, but contact is poor."⁹⁴

During the heated political campaign of the fall of 1964, the Brooks family threw their energies wholeheartedly behind the Democratic cause. Will and Karl attended the Democratic State Convention as delegates from Washington County. Juanita helped to open and to staff headquarters for the party in St. George. A candidate for whom the Brookses worked diligently, William Bruhn, was one of the few Utah Democrats to fail of election. Otherwise Juanita rejoiced in the Lyndon Johnson landslide: "I have been a virtual outcast among the elite of the town," she wrote Dale Morgan. "Everyone who is anyone, in the Church especially, was Goldwater, so that the day after election was a day of mourning much more deep than that shown here at the death of President Kennedy. It was as if a pall had settled over the town, a pall so deep that I felt guilty of my jack-o-lantern grin."⁹⁵

During the 1964–65 school year the Brooks household was augmented by Gerry Pulsipher, Ernest's and Margie's eldest son, whom Juanita described for Dale Morgan: "nearly 18; in his last year of high school, 6 ft 3 and loosely hung together, so not athletic—so thin he doesn't cast a shadow unless he stands broadside. But a very fine boy nonetheless."⁹⁶ During the fall Juanita taught two morning classes at Dixie College and continued to collaborate with Thomas Cheney on a folklore project. As president of the Utah Folklore Society, Cheney had enlisted her help in editing a collection of articles about Utah folklore, a collection which would find a belated publication in 1971 as *Lore of Faith and Folly*. Juanita was to contribute two items of Dixie folklore as well as to evaluate the manuscripts of other authors. By the end of the summer she had in fact read twenty or thirty pieces. Among the articles which she recommended that Cheney eliminate was a discussion of Brigham Young that seemed naively eulogistic. Facetiously she suggested Cheney solicit an article of an opposite bias toward the Mormon leader: "Plenty of authentic material could be gathered to put under a title such as 'The Shearer of the Sheep' or 'The Supreme Dictator' if you know anyone who would like to undertake it."⁹⁷

The project culminated in the annual meeting of the Utah Folklore Society in St. George on December 4, 1964.⁹⁸ Serving as local arrangements chairman, Juanita provided an evening program of Dixie folk song and tales by local performers. Following the successful conference, Juanita polished the pieces she had promised to contribute. One, "Our Annual Visitors," was a description of the Paiute Indians who visited Bunkerville each winter during her childhood. It is probable that she had written this sketch in the 1940s as a part of "Quicksand and Cactus." The other piece, "Pranks and Pranksters," was a review of shivarees, practical jokes, and pranks in Bunkerville. This she probably composed freshly. She narrated the story of a bridegroom, unaccustomed to drink, who had been enticed into complete inebriation by designing comrades. "When finally his young bride came to look for him, no one knew where he was exactly, but one had seen him enter the back room of a neighboring house. Following this lead, the girl opened the door to see him asleep on a bed, a young squaw sitting beside him fanning him and brushing the flies away with a leafy branch—a situation carefully arranged for the bride's benefit."⁹⁹

Near the end of January 1965 Juanita traveled to Logan for a series of appearances. She spoke before the Cache Valley chapter of the Utah Historical Society, several history classes at Utah State University, and a ladies' literary club. As a climax, she addressed the Associated Women Students at the university on the role of women in a changing world. Instead of stressing marriage as the proper role of women as she had done at the College of Southern Utah, she here emphasized professional achievement. She alluded with a self-deprecating humor to the common prejudices against achieving women, quoting Daniel Webster as having said, "A woman speaker is like a dog walking on its hind legs; you don't expect that it will be done well. You are surprised that it is ever done at all."[100] Among a number of achieving woman whom she advanced as examples was Esther Morris, who had persuaded the legislature of Wyoming Territory to accord the franchise to women in 1869—the first territory or state in the Union to do so.

Before returning to St. George Juanita shopped happily with Florence and Mary, Bob's wife and daughter, buying on Florence's advice a pair of shoes and a purse for herself and a birthday gift for Willa. Otherwise her trip to Logan had seemed frantic. "I was so rushed there," she wrote Willa and Thales as she mailed the gift, "that I hardly had time to breathe. Felt like a monkey on a chain."[101] Writing other family members, she assessed her speeches as mediocre and pondered whether in the future she would refuse invitations to give talks in far-away places: "They're too expensive of time and energy."[102]

Not long afterward, she dreamed about the trip, as she explained to Gladys Harrison, a friend from Logan. In the dream she was in an airport waiting for a plane. On her feet were boots that were not mates; nearby stood a third unmated boot. Her plane was called and she rushed to an elevator whose door closed before she could enter. Dashing down some stairs she saw a limousine pulling away without her. "There I stood in these silly boots, with my purse and my ancient black zipper bag. I opened it to find that it was *empty*!" The empty briefcase reminded her, in her later ruminations upon the dream, that she had misplaced her speech while in Logan. The clumsy boots were like a pair she had seen on a little girl on a bus. Above all, the dream seemed to signify that she must make up her mind "whether my major work from here on is to be editing other diaries or writing things of my own."[103]

In early February all of Will's surviving brothers and sisters except Llewellyn assembled in St. George on the occasion of an honor paid to their sister May by her literary club. Juanita took the opportunity to pump her brothers- and sisters-in-law for details about their father, for she was at last ready to write the biography of this pioneer stonemason and sheriff. Not long before she had written to Dale Morgan, "But the completion of this short biography of George Brooks must be placed first on my list, and to it I will now turn my attention."[104] It was not to be a complicated project; from the first she had thought of it as a simple narrative of little interest beyond the family. Accordingly, when she finished the draft in June 1965, she arranged with a St. George printer for a private publication. It is also to be noted that in March 1965 Juanita was reappointed to the board of trustees of the Utah Historical Society and so soon began again to travel north for the meetings of that body.[105] She would remain on the board, from which she had been absent since 1960, for twelve years, making a total service of twenty-four years.

During the spring of 1965 Alfred Bush suggested that Juanita apply for a research grant from the American Philosophical Society. Supported by recommendations from Leonard Arrington and Sterling McMurrin, Juanita proposed a single-volume edition of John D. Lee's diaries written before those published in *A Mormon Chronicle*. In June 1965, the society awarded her $1,000 for travel related to research.[106] "I hardly know where to begin," a nonplussed Juanita wrote to Peg Gregory. "The early missionary diaries are such a hodge-podge of poor verse, 'acrostics,' and sermons, that I think I should only excerpt them. Then of the Nauvoo Journal I can use nothing because I am not supposed to have it."[107] Although she would expend most of her travel allowance during the coming autumn, she would not begin to edit for almost a year.

Domestic matters went on as usual. Mother Mary suffered from a tenacious shin infection, which temporarily kept her from making her accustomed daily sessions in the temple. Will worked on the lot, visited about town, and kept up with his church duties, which included supplying the local motels with copies of the Book of Mormon for sale to itinerant gentiles. For a period Juanita took a fancy to riding Karl's horse. Will fretted because on a number of occasions girls whom Karl had allowed to ride the horse had returned afoot. Juanita experienced no difficulties. "The animal needs the training and exercise and I do enjoy the ride, though it lasts only about a half hour," she wrote Bob and Florence, who had sent her riding pants and shirt. "I go up the hill past the Sugar Loaf and the water tank, then detour off toward the mountain on a different trail each time to explore a bit and get the horse used to trying different routes."[108]

In the late spring Willa gave birth to her third son. The FBI transferred Kay to Washington, D.C., where he would work among Spanish-speaking people. At Cornell, Tony passed his preliminary examinations for a doctorate in radiation biology. Perhaps the most momentous family event was Karl's wedding. Mid-spring he had become engaged to Carla Hoyt, a high school English teacher whom Juanita described as "beautiful and accomplished." On June 4, Juanita and Will witnessed the wedding in Kamas, Carla's home town, and that night stood in the greeting line at the reception. On June 12, they hosted an open house for the newlyweds in St. George.[109]

The first half of 1965 was a time of property consolidation for Juanita and Will. They paid off the mortgage on their house at 98 U Street in Salt Lake, which they continued to rent out. One day in March, as she walked to the post office, Juanita allowed a realtor to give her a tour of a house near their home on the hill. Without consulting Will, she offered $2,000 under the list price of $14,500. Although Will believed she had paid too much, she immediately rented the place unfurnished at $80 a month.[110] In June she and Will instituted foreclosure on a mortgage they held on the house next to the 98 U Street address in Salt Lake by virtue of having lent its owner $1,200 while they lived in Salt Lake. After considerable anxiety over the matter, they received a settlement of over $1,900, $325 of which they paid an attorney.[111]

The summer of 1965 was made memorable by the long awaited appearance of *On the Mormon Frontier: The Diary of Hosea Stout – 1844–1861*. The dust jacket of each of the two volumes featured a portrait of Stout painted by University of Utah art professor Alvin Gittins. Employing broad, heavily textured strokes, Gittins gave the frontier policeman an intense, even ominous countenance. An impressed board of trustees of the Utah Historical Society had thanked Gittins for the portrait: "It is not only a beautiful piece of art, but it captures the whole tragedy of the life of Hosea Stout."[112] According to Everett Cooley, Gittins believed the portrait to have "the most penetrating eyes he had ever painted."[113] Thereafter Gittins would strive to create a similar countenance for a haunting life-sized portrait of Porter Rockwell which would adorn a wall in the Kearns Mansion.

Unfortunately there was anguish at the University of Utah Press over the quality of the paper and print in the new publication. In mid-production, Russell Mortensen had resigned as director of the press. The new director, Richard Thurman, judged that the firm to which the printing had been let was incapable of a superior job. Thurman apologetically explained to an irate reader: "There was really nothing basic I could do about the printing at that stage, except to insist that certain, totally unacceptable lines be re-set in unbroken, or slightly less broken type. But this was a surface touching up, a little like giving a single aspirin tablet to a man dying of cancer." The printing firm had, Thurman insisted, outdone itself, rising "to heroic heights to turn out the product as you see it. It strains credulity, I know, to hear that this book is far, far better than anything they have ever done before."[114]

Nonetheless, journalists and scholars gave the diary one of the most copious and enthusiastic reviewings of any work with which Juanita had a connection. Perhaps the most negative review, by Leonard Arrington, was also the earliest, appearing in *The Utah Alumnus* before the first volume arrived in the bookstores. Although generally satisfied with the work, Arrington complained that Juanita's annotation had unduly emphasized Stout as a man of violence by providing "additional accounts of others engaged in similar activities." He also found Juanita too punctilious in maintaining "fidelity to the written document. The present rendering is a little on the 'fussy' side."[115] Citing the editorial liberties permitted by *The Harvard Guide to American History*, Arrington endorsed a more tolerant adaptation of the conventions of modern English – an alternative which of course Juanita had avoided on principle.

Without exception all reviewers agreed that Stout's diary was a paramount source for the history of the Mormons and the West. According to Dale Morgan, it constituted "one of the most magnificent windows upon Mormon history ever opened, an enduring contribution to American history."[116] The large majority also praised Juanita's performance as an editor. In an essay review of some eleven pages, Harold Shepherd, distinguished professor emeritus from the Stanford school of law, voiced strong satisfaction with her abundant annotation: "For the many important persons who parade in and out of the diary's pages, the editor has provided thumbnail life sketches in footnote form. They constitute a veritable Who's Who of early Mormon history. These notes, together with those explaining matters of Mormon organization and theology and some of Hosea's abbreviated and otherwise enigmatic entries, will be of great assistance to the reader uninitiated in Mormon lore."[117]

The diary is exceptionally important because Stout, an acute observer, was near the center of events throughout much of the formative period of Mormon history. Born in 1810, he joined the Church in 1838. He was expulsed with the Saints from Missouri and became a prominent citizen of Nauvoo. He served as a bodyguard to Joseph Smith, as chief of the Nauvoo police, and as a subordinate officer in the Nauvoo Legion. He married plural wives and fathered numerous children, many of whom died in childhood. He wintered with the Saints on the Iowa plains in 1846 and 1847 and migrated to Salt Lake in 1848. In Utah he practiced law and served as the attorney general of Utah Territory, as U.S. district attorney for Utah, and as a member and president of the House of the Utah territorial legislature.

Stout wrote a vivid, expressive English, his frequent abbreviations, misspellings, and grammatical eccentricities notwithstanding. His diary provides invaluable insight into the activities of the Mormon police in Nauvoo and among the Saints on the plains and into the progress and conflicts of the Utah territorial courts and legislatures—of crucial significance because of the constant efforts by federal appointees to wrest sovereignty from local officials. At $17.50, the volumes were priced beyond the general reader, yet not infrequently their pages contained matter of dramatic as well as historical interest. An excerpt from the diary would in fact be reprinted in an anthology of Mormon literature, *A Believing People*, in 1974. The excerpt recorded the death of Stout's son in a wagon on the Iowa plains, an experience made doubly horrible by Stout's belief that his dying child was possessed of evil spirits:

> At times I felt almost to cowl at his fierce ghastly & horrid look and even felt to withdraw from the painful scene for truly the powers of darkness now prevailed here. We were shut up in the waggon with nothing to behold or contemplate but this devoted child thus writhing under the power of the destroyer. It was now late in the night & he getting worse when we came to the conclusion to lay hands on him again that the powers of darkness might be rebuked if he could not be raised up. Thus alone my wife & me over our only and dearest son struggled in sorrow and affliction with this last determination that we would not yield with the portion of the Priesthood which we had to the evil spirits.[118]

Encouraged by the success of the Stout diary, Everett Cooley and Richard Thurman proposed other cooperative ventures for the Utah Historical Society and the University of Utah Press. Accordingly, they set an eager Juanita to work on the journal of Thomas D. Brown. Juanita had first seen an edited copy of this journal in the Church Historian's Office in 1936, and in 1941 Dale Morgan had given her an improved typescript of it. It was this typescript which during the late summer and fall of 1965 Juanita transcribed and annotated. She also wrote Brown's descendants in an effort to gather materials for a biographical introduction.[119] In mid-October, deeming the editorial labor finished, she submitted her manuscript to Thurman, who assured her of "an early publication." Then came a thunderbolt. Cooley informed her that they could not proceed to publish the journal because, as Juanita wrote, "it is an official Church record and cannot be published without the consent of the Authorities."[120]

In the meantime Juanita traveled by means of her grant from the American Philosophical Society. In October she attended the conference of the Western History Association in Helena, Montana. Taking a bus to Provo, she continued on by automobile with LeRoy and Ann Hafen, who were now associated with BYU. The conference was a heady experience. In the corridors were old friends and deferential strangers wishing to make the acquaintance of the famous historian from St. George. Juanita reported to Alfred Bush: "I came home all stimulated and renewed and eager to get on. I'm still tingling with it."[121]

A week later she flew to New Mexico to orient herself to the geography of John D. Lee's diary detailing his journey to Santa Fe to take possession of the payroll of the Mormon Battalion, this being the only Lee diary which she had permission to publish. Peg Gregory met her with a car, and the two women convivially toured Albuquerque, Santa Fe, and Taos. In Santa Fe Juanita was impressed by the palace of the governors, which "stood much as it was on that same date 112 years ago, when the Mormon Battalion arrived there." She responded intensely to the Catholic churches: "In every one I had a deep sense of reverence—the feeling that these people are as sincere as we, trying to reach the same great SOURCE, but using different methods and symbols."[122] Best of all, Peg had arranged for the publication of the Mormon Battalion mission diary in *The New Mexico Historical Review.*

Saying good-bye to Peg, Juanita dropped in on Willa for a day in Clovis. She found Willa hopeful that by Thanksgiving Thales would return from Viet Nam, where he had flown more than 125 combat missions. Juanita traveled on to Denver to stand by with Ernest and Margie as their son Gerry, who had stayed a winter with Juanita and Will, underwent surgery for the removal of a brain tumor. "The operation was successful," a relieved Juanita wrote, "in that he has come through with all his faculties and with his limbs unimpaired. The worry was that he might be paralyzed on the right side."[123] She then flew to Salt Lake for a meeting of the board of the Utah Historical Society. While in Salt Lake, she made new arrangements for the publication of the biography of George Brooks, having retrieved the manuscript from the procrastinating printer in St. George. Her affairs in Salt Lake settled, Juanita took a night bus and at ten-thirty the next morning taught a Sunday School class in St. George.

In November Juanita flew to Washington, D.C. In the National Archives she searched the correspondence of James K. Polk for letters from leading Mormons, bringing away photocopies of letters as yet untapped by Mormon historians.[124] She also visited Alfred Bush at Princeton University, who showed her a unique draft of Charles Kelly's biography of Porter Rockwell, originally entitled *Sword of the Prophet.* Kelly's collaborator, Hoffman Birney, had, as Juanita later wrote Harold Schindler, "evidently made sweeping changes" as he revised the work which would be published as *Holy Murder.* "I'm not sure whether or not Kelly knows that Bush has it [the draft], and if he does not, I don't want to be the one to enlighten him."[125]

In January 1966, Juanita reported her travels to the American Philosophical Society. She reiterated her intention of editing a volume of Lee's early diaries as a complement to *A Mormon Chronicle,* having received some encouragement in this project by the fact that the Church Historian's Office, in exchange for a verifax copy of Lee's missionary diary of 1841–43, had provided her with a verifax copy of the "full 1846 account from the Mississippi River to establishment at Winter Quarters!"[126] She had expected a verifax copy of merely the Mormon Battalion mission diary. However, still lacking permission to publish the other diaries, she would proceed—not immediately, but by spring—to edit only the Mormon Battalion document.[127]

Shortly before she reported her travels, Juanita had completed a minor article about Mountain Meadows as a pasture where

early travelers to and from California revived their jaded stock. In
November, Russell Mortensen had solicited the article for *The American West*, a recently founded journal of which he was editor. In March
1966, Mortensen forwarded the article to George Pfeiffer III of *Sunset
Magazine*, a major stockholder in *The American West*. Pfeiffer, who
had suggested the article in the first place, rejected it with a scribbled
note: "poorly written, dull as dishwater, adds up to nothing."[128] Embarrassed, Mortensen mailed Juanita a mollifying honorarium. Though
disappointed, she gamely replied, "As I long ago learned, 'There's many
a slip twixt the cup and the lip,' and I must count this as one of
them."[129]

While she worked on this article, it was her pleasure to see
in print *George Brooks: Artist in Stone*. The Salt Lake printer to whom
she had given the manuscript in early November had worked with
dispatch, delivering the finished product by December 21, 1965. Juanita
had ordered a first binding of 500 copies.[130] Within a few months she
would report the sale of 300 copies and would thereafter order the
binding of another 500 copies. She gave numerous copies as gifts at
Christmas and other occasions. The work received a single brief, positive review in the *Utah Historical Quarterly*, which was perhaps one
more than Juanita expected.[131] It is not to be ranked among her best
books, if for no other reason than that in writing it she disposed of
meager sources. Yet it gives substance to an otherwise vanished life.

George Brooks and his siblings, Frank and Mary, were born
at Point of Ayr, Wales, where their father, Samuel, kept a lighthouse.
Having converted to Mormonism, the family immigrated to Utah in
1856. Both of the parents succumbed to the rigors of the pioneer trail,
the mother, Emma Blinston, dying in Florence, Nebraska, and Samuel
dying in Salt Lake shortly after arriving. Separated from his brother
and sister, George moved to St. George in 1862 with the family of his
foster father, Edward L. Parry, a stonemason. Demonstrating a gift for
stone carving, George found steady employment for many years in
the construction of the St. George social hall, tabernacle, and temple.
In 1874 he married Cornelia Branch, the petite daughter of another
Dixie pioneer, and with her raised twelve children. Following the completion of the St. George temple, George earned a living through law
enforcement, serving for many years as sheriff of Washington County.
When after more than fifty years of marriage Cornelia died, George
was inconsolable. He died a year later in 1930.

As a stone carver, he contributed substantially to the solid dignity and simple harmony that qualify the tabernacle and the old college building as Utah classics. Of special note among his carvings are the lintels of the tabernacle windows and the lamp of learning over the entrance of the college. By folk standards, George Brooks merited the tribute offered by early Dixie chronicler Albert E. Miller, which Juanita quoted in the frontispiece of her book: "He was an artist, and whatever he touched was a work of art."

In its later chapters the biography is rich with anecdotes, which Will and his siblings had provided Juanita. They all remembered Uncle Frank, the bachelor brother whom George brought to live with his family not long after he married. A vivid storyteller, Frank delighted in recounting an incident when, as a lone boy on a ranch at night, he had caught a glimpse of a hulking, prowling animal: "At this point he always brought in the sentence: 'I didn't know what in hell to DO!' This would be repeated through the story with the emphasis on a different word each time: 'I didn't know what in hell TO do,' 'I didn't know what in HELL to do,' 'I didn't know WHAT in hell to do,' and so on. But he shot at the object, ran back, and locked himself in the house. The next morning he found the body of a big bear beside the pig pen."[132] Will and his siblings had innumerable tales about one another. There was the occasion when George deputized Dub—John Pace, Josephine's fiancé—to assist him in raiding an illicit chicken roast Will and his teenaged friends were having. "Dad walked in among them, asked what they were doing here, where they got their chickens, and what about the wine? He and Dub sampled each so that they could testify as to just what kind of meat was in the ovens, and something as to the strength of the wine." One of the boys claimed his father had donated the chickens, another that his father had donated wine so weak that "it would take a lot more than a gallon of this kind . . . to make any difference." As soon as George and Dub had departed, these boys raced home to enlist their fathers in their alibi. "Dad didn't make any arrests after that party. The families lied their boys free."[133]

The biography also documents the construction of the rock house on the hill where Juanita and Will made their home. The house was built in 1877: its basement dug, a black rock foundation laid, walls built of rough-hewn stones rejected from the temple construction, joists and rafters fixed, laths nailed, lime slaked, plaster spread,

roof shingled. Much of the material and labor was bartered. For example, George paid the carpenter who did the woodwork with sixteen
loads of manure, several loads of hay, a gravestone, beef, flour, labor
from craftsmen for whom George had worked, and five dollars cash.
In 1879, in honor of the birth of his first son, George, Jr., George
planted two locust saplings, one at the side of the house, the other on
the street. The first tree was removed in 1955 to make way for the
wing which Juanita and Will added; the second is standing today.

CHAPTER TEN

OLD LOVERS GENTLY ROCKED

In January 1966, Juanita committed herself to write a history of the Jews in Utah and Idaho. At a meeting in Salt Lake during the previous October, Louis Zucker, Ben M. Roe, and Sterling McMurrin had proposed the project. Zucker, a prominent Jewish professor of English, would serve as consultant. Roe, a Jewish attorney, would represent Myrtle Friedman of Hailey, Idaho, who would finance the endeavor. McMurrin would ensure that the University of Utah, of which he was provost, would administer the funds as a research grant. Juanita was dubious in the extreme. "In the first place," she explained privately, "I know little of the Jews and care less."[1]

At a meeting on January 4, she agreed to the project.[2] She would be paid $150 a month and expenses for eighteen months; in addition, when the book was completed, she would receive a lump sum of $6,750. Remaining in town for several days to gather sources, she quickly learned that the Jews of Utah had never been numerous nor prone to keep records. On a second trip to Salt Lake in February she encountered other obstacles predictive of future frustrations. She grimly made her way about town by bus and taxi in the midst of a blizzard. At the university Zucker failed to keep an appointment, and the payroll office had no authorization to process her paychecks. She took a night bus home and found waiting a letter from Willa. To her great chagrin, she realized that she had forgotten her daughter's birthday.[3]

In April Juanita prepared to hold an open house in honor of Will's approaching eighty-fifth birthday. With flagging energy she confessed that "all the details of cleaning up and preparing almost get me down."[4] Nonetheless, the event went off grandly. Carla, Ida Jean, and Willa helped enormously. On D Day Juanita did not join in the annual festivities at the block letter on the ridge west of town, speaking instead to fifteen seminary teachers and their spouses from Las Vegas. During the day she "carried a heavy heart," as she reflected upon D Day and "all that it has meant to us all through the years." Subsequently she wondered whether her melancholy might not be an intuition that Tony had once again failed his French language examination at Cornell—the only serious obstacle between him and a completed Ph.D.[5]

One is reminded that Juanita worried constantly about her children and grandchildren. She exhorted Gerry Pulsipher, who moved restlessly between St. George and Grand Junction, to equip himself with proper glasses and either find a job or enter college.[6] She mulled Karl's prospects for a job, since he and Carla did not intend to retain their current teaching positions in California. In May she wrote them that Tony had passed his French examination with a high score. "As for you and your future," she reassured Karl, who had seemed despondent, "DON'T WORRY—Things are going to work out fine. You can't lose. . . . Be of good cheer!"[7] On June 4, 1966, Karl and Carla sealed their marriage for eternity in the Los Angeles temple. Regretfully Juanita and Will did not attend, for they had promised on the same day to be at the wedding of their granddaughter Nellie in the St. George temple and that evening to stand in her reception line.

In May, Juanita and Will received an unusual visit from a dozen junior high school students from the Anaheim school district in California. Their instructor, Todd Berens, had recently opened a correspondence with Juanita on historical matters. Berens and his students were tracing portions of the southern pioneer trail to California as a school project. Juanita and Will treated their guests to root-beer floats, then divided them, Juanita telling pioneer stories to the girls, Will to the boys. Berens was delighted. For some years thereafter he would return with other students recruited from his classes.[8]

Throughout the spring and summer of 1966 Juanita continued to gather materials for the history of the Jews in Utah and Idaho. In May, distressed by interruptions at home, she took a night bus to Salt Lake, locked herself in a room in the Belvedere Hotel, and typed from five a.m. to ten p.m. "with short periods twice a day when I walked a block or two for exercise." Three days later she delivered a thirty-page manuscript to Louis Zucker.[9] For many months Juanita would spend one week out of four in Salt Lake, where her headquarters remained the Belvedere. Ben Roe, with whom she became fast friends, thoughtfully provided a spare key to his office, where after hours and on weekends she worked in air-conditioned comfort. Mid-summer Juanita made a trip to Sun Valley, Idaho, where Jewish residents provided her with valuable materials. At nearby Hailey she visited Miss Myrtle H. Friedman, the wealthy patron of the project.[10]

As if she did not have enough to do, Juanita volunteered during the summer of 1966 to assist in compiling the autobiography of Elise Furer Musser, former altruist, Democratic National Committeewoman, and U.S. delegate to international peace conferences in Buenos Aires and Lima during the 1930s. During her sojourn in Salt Lake, Juanita had become close friends with Elise and her husband, Burton. On her frequent returns to the city, she continued to call on them. While Elise's health deteriorated, Juanita pledged a dozen hours a week to the task of arranging the inchoate autobiographical accounts her remarkable friend had dictated: "Elise has had a fruitful life, and one that has been of significance on more than a local level," Juanita wrote in June; "she deserves to be remembered and her history preserved. She must not feel abandoned and cast-off by her friends."[11]

Juanita intended to prepare four chapters progressing from Elise's birth to her wedding, leaving to others her later life, documented by a diary and numerous newspaper clippings. Using scissors and stapler, Juanita assembled three chapters and had them typed. Her task was not easy. Elise had, for example, dictated five versions of her father's death. During the fall, a relative read the chapters aloud to the bedridden Elise and transcribed her corrections. In December Juanita guiltily informed Elise's nephew in the East that she had not managed to fulfill her commitment: "I have promised Elise that I will get Part Four done before the New Year, but how I am going to do it without literally working around the clock, I don't know."[12]

Although the nephew had promised $1,000 toward publication, no book would ever appear. In 1978, the *Utah Historical Quarterly* would publish an abbreviated redaction of Juanita's chapters and the diary prepared by Janet G. Butler. Even though it is flawed by enervating elisions and abrupt transitions, this account reveals Elise Furer Musser's spunk and energy. Her independence may be seen, for example, in her experiences in Mexico. As an impoverished Mormon immigrant from Switzerland, Elise accompanied the family of George Naegle to Mexico around 1900. Hitherto unaware of the continuing practice of polygamy in the Mormon colonies, she was astonished to discover that those around her expected her to marry Naegle. She took a bookkeeping job with a mining company, which required her to cross a river every day and spend long hours in the company of Mexicans, a dangerous situation according to Anthony W. Ivins, the Mormon leader in Mexico. Elise disagreed. "I never had the slightest fear, and the Mexicans were so lovely to me. . . . I felt strictly on a par with them, for they were working for a living and so was I."[13] Shortly she returned to Salt Lake. Eventually she abandoned Mormonism and allied herself with a Unitarian congregation.

Two deaths touched Juanita in the summer of 1966. In mid-July, Jillyn Woodbury, a young wife and mother, died of a lingering, painful disease. Walking up the hill on a May evening, Juanita had felt impressed to enter the Woodbury home. There she found Jillyn, just returned from treatments in Salt Lake, suffering from an excruciating rash over her entire body. Juanita bathed her in a tepid solution of baking soda and gave her a massage and words of encouragement. Juanita returned daily until the rash had subsided and Jillyn showed other signs of improvement. "Sometimes I wonder if I should do it, because it takes me from what I am supposed to be doing and paid for doing," she wrote to Tony and Janet, referring to her neglect of the Jewish history; "and yet it is a place where Christianity certainly needs to be a matter of action rather than words."[14] When Jillyn died, Juanita was asked to speak at her funeral. "There are no words to express the deepest emotions—no words for love, for grief. The well-springs of these lie too deep," she began. She described the attachment that had formed between her and Jillyn during the preceding weeks: "But I was doing more for myself than I was for her. I was becoming really acquainted with a most precious person, I was seeing into her innermost heart and realizing a wonderful strength of character, an unshaken integrity. I really loved her." Refusing to speculate on the particulars of immortality, Juanita asserted her faith that Jillyn "still remains an entity, and that she still knows."[15] In the entire episode one observes again the indissoluble bond between Juanita and the community called Dixie. The grief of a neighbor was her grief, and her voice was apt at speaking for many.

The other death which touched Juanita closely in the summer of 1966 was that of Wesley Williamson. Some time before, he and Sana had moved from Whittier to St. George. Wesley's health failed rapidly, his habits becoming so erratic that in August 1966 his sons took him and Sana back to California. As he left, he put into Karl's keeping a valuable collection of military guns and a thoroughbred mare, which was in foal. Within a few days of his return to California, he died. Juanita and Karl drove to Whittier, where Juanita spoke at his funeral. Although Wesley's brother reclaimed the guns, his son confirmed the gift of the mare, which Karl corralled with his other horse in his parents' barnyard.[16]

In September, Juanita and Will flew east to visit Tony and Janet in Ithaca and Kay and Ida Jean in Hackensack, New Jersey. Tony, who was completing his dissertation at Cornell, would shortly move to Albuquerque, where he would take a research position with the Atomic Energy Commission. Mid-summer Ernest and Margie had moved to Las Vegas. As summer ended, Karl and Carla moved into the little house at 98 U Street in Salt Lake, and Karl entered a doctoral program at the University of Utah. Soon Juanita reported that Karl's new mare had given birth to "a little buckskin colt, the cutest thing you ever saw, with black mane & tail & feet, black ear points & nose like a maltese kitten. It is so frisky and full of life." Not long afterward the mare injured herself on the end of a pipe, ripping off "a piece of skin as big as a mush bowl—just like it had been taken out of dough with a biscuit cutter."[17] Juanita was heartsick over the injury and couldn't bring herself to phone Karl about it until she saw that the wound had begun to heal.

The deer hunt of 1966 was satisfactory. From out of town came Clair, Karl, Tony, and Ernest with a retinue of wives, children, and friends. Granddaughter Nellie bagged a buck on opening day. Will, who jumped three large bucks and overexerted himself in an unsuccessful pursuit, came home at the end of the first day to recuperate. Throughout the fall, Will attended every high school and college athletic event. He had adopted the habit of sitting in the midst of the high school Pep Club, distributing candy from his bulging coat pockets. On November 4, 1966, the Pep Club declared Uncle Will, as everyone in town now affectionately called him, an honorary member, presenting him "with an official, framed scroll to prove it, a special cushioned seat to put on the bench in the center of the group, a pompom, and a hat."[18]

Despite long interruptions, the Jewish history remained Juanita's major project through the winter and spring of 1967. In December she confided to Dale Morgan that she and Louis Zucker could not agree "even on basics." She wished to place the Jews in a context of general Utah history; Zucker feared that she would thereby neglect them. She believed that "the contribution of Jews in civic and cultural areas, in medicine, education, business, etc. would be important whether or not the persons observed the Holy Days"; he wished to consider "only practicing Jews."[19] She wanted to bring the study up to the latest moment; he desired to close it in 1948. She scored a minor triumph when Zucker, having insisted that he should write an announcement of the project for the Utah Historical Society newsletter, procrastinated so long that the staff instead ran an announcement she had written.

Juanita continued to make frequent public appearances. In March, she joined three other historians for a video taping session at the studios of KUTV in Salt Lake.[20] She also met with the history committee of the Utah Heritage Foundation, whose purpose was to identify historical sites worthy of preservation and to solicit local donations to match federal funds. Although Juanita thought it proper to travel without recompense to attend committee meetings, she resisted making cash contributions to projects outside Dixie. In fact, during 1966 and 1967 she advocated, as a means of concentrating effort, the immediate development of a single historical site in St. George, the old county courthouse. Recently saved from destruction, this structure would be converted into a museum, art gallery, and home for the Chamber of Commerce. In it would be a John D. Lee memorial area.[21]

In the meantime Juanita carried on her private battle to make the site of the Mountain Meadows massacre into a dignified public memorial. In April 1966 the Church had acquired from Ezra Lytle a two-and-a-half-acre plot containing the existing monument. Juanita had first responded with disbelief to rumors that the Church intended to discourage visitors at the site, wryly commenting, "That would be like trying to gather up the scattered feathers of the pillow in the old folk tale."[22] Later events, however, made her suspicious. The sign pointing the way from the nearby highway disappeared in June 1966; the Forest Service, through whose jurisdiction the highway ran, did not replace the sign until Juanita made a second complaint in December. At that time, learning that a summer flash flood had damaged the picnic site attached to the monument, Juanita and Will drove out and were dismayed by what they saw. The access road had not been graded since the storm. Worse, the picnic tables, which the local ranger believed had been washed away by the flood, had stood on high ground and had actually been removed by human beings. "Only ghosts or heavy hoisting equipment could lift them out, but they are gone—stolen and taken no-one-knows-where."[23] In February 1967 Juanita returned to the site with colleagues from Dixie College. Because snow made it impossible to drive down the access road, she and history instructor Melvin Smith elected to hike the steep mile-and-a-half stretch. "It was rather strenuous but interesting," reported the sixty-nine-year-old Juanita.[24]

Although the damaged access road was repaired during the summer of 1967, Juanita remained disgruntled by the fact that the road lacked an all-weather surface and was next to impassable when wet. She had other cause for alarm. The slaughtered women and children had not been buried at the site marked by the monument but in a mound about a half mile distant, readily discernible because "the sage brush grew there so tall and lush—over six feet high amid scrub brush all around."[25] It worried Juanita that Ezra Lytle, who was preparing to farm the surrounding land, could if he wished farm the mound itself. She wrote J. K. Fancher urging that the Fancher family organization petition the United States senators from Arkansas to establish a memorial to the murdered women and children. "After all, the State of Arkansas did give the Mormon Church permission to erect a monument to their Apostle Parley P. Pratt who was killed there. Why should not the State of Arkansas erect one to their slain people in Utah?"[26] Shortly she urged Fancher to enlist his friends and relatives in writing the general authorities of the Church protesting the threatened farming of the mound. "Human decency should demand that these remains be NOT disturbed, but descendants and loved ones should have the privilege of marking the spot and beautifying it. It should be a shrine at which they might gather."[27]

As a part of her campaign in behalf of a dignified memorial Juanita proposed an article to Everett Cooley. The nucleus of the article, the little piece on early pasturage at Mountain Meadows which *The American West* had rejected, already sat in her files. Cooley proving amenable, she expanded the article during the winter of 1967 to include an account of the massacre and the subsequent memorialization of its victims. The article appeared in the spring 1967 issue of the *Utah Historical Quarterly* as "The Mountain Meadows: Historic Stopping Place on the Spanish Trail." A culling of her earlier writings, it was distinguished only by her concluding plea for a reverent treatment of the massacre site.

In January 1967, Will's sister Rozilla died. The funeral was comforting—although Juanita found herself wishing "someone would learn some new funeral songs, or else leave off singing altogether and have instead some lovely string or organ music."[28] During the spring Grant's daughter Susie married, and Juanita and Will hosted a reception in their home. On Memorial Day 1967 the descendants of George Brooks held a reunion in St. George. Ironically, the proverbially bright St. George weather failed as a rainstorm interrupted a dinner in the park "just before we were ready to serve dessert, so everyone came up here [to Juanita's and Will's house] & visited & sang & had the dessert later."[29]

During the summer of 1967 a first installment of John D. Lee's Mormon Battalion mission diary appeared in the *New Mexico Historical Review*, to be followed by a second installment during the fall. From time to time Juanita would reiterate her desire to edit Lee's other unpublished diaries and to combine them with *A Mormon Chronicle* in order to make a comprehensive three-volume collection. However, the Mormon Battalion mission diary would remain the only tangible result of that ambition.

This diary is Lee's daily account of a journey he and two companions made during the late summer and fall of 1846 to overtake the Battalion at Santa Fe and carry back a payroll of $1,200 to Brigham Young in Iowa. Of great interest is Lee's narration of angry conflicts between the men and their tactless non-Mormon officers, altercations to which Lee himself made a substantial contribution. Even its routine entries, recording Lee's progress through uninhabited prairies in a light wagon drawn by mules, reveal much of the hardiness and vigilance by which frontiersmen survived. When his journey began on August 30, 1846, Lee wrote: "Called a halt, discovered that we had forgoten to bring Dr. R [Richards?] little Dog Trip which we purposed taken with us to guard the waggon while we slept in case an attempt should be made to rob and plunder by Indians &c—as our journey was not only arduous but dangerous—Pres Young & Richards returned to camp, brought little Trip in the meanwhile we turned our mules out to feed on the grass & arrainged the loading in our waggon."[30]

On July 1, 1967—the day when her stipulated eighteen months for finishing the Jewish history had elapsed—Juanita arrived in Salt Lake with eight of twelve projected chapters. Louis Zucker was in Logan, so she forwarded the chapters by mail. She went on to Boise, where Alexander Simons, grandson of Idaho governor Moses Alexander, gave her materials relating to the Jews of Idaho and conducted her on a tour of Idaho's capital. "The ride around the city of Boise, to the cemetery, to the hill for a survey of the whole area, but most of all to the Temple, was an experience I shall never forget," she wrote Simons. "I was much impressed with the Temple—its symmetry and beauty and its general air of invitation to worship appealed to me. It should be kept as a holy place for a shrine where people may go singly or in groups to receive spiritual strength."[31]

Between August and November 1967 Juanita kept a sketchy diary in a memo book published by the Anti-Defamation League of the B'nai B'rith. Its entries show that she was busily at work on both the Jewish history and the autobiography of Elise Musser and that she was plying the night buses with the frequency and energy of a much younger person. On Saturday, September 23, she attended the day-long sessions and banquet of the Utah Historical Society in Salt Lake. In the evening she went to a tea at the Kearns Mansion honoring Dale Morgan and Fawn Brodie. On Monday evening, she accompanied Harold Schindler to dinner at an Italian restaurant and to the musical *Oklahoma*. The musical, she recorded, was "*good* but not outstanding."[32] On Friday, October 6, she returned to Salt Lake. She had, she wrote, "a fairly good night," by which one knows she slept better than usual as the bus rumbled on. She arrived in time for breakfast with Karl and Carla before devoting herself to a weekend of work. On Sunday evening she had dinner with Ben Roe, Louis Zucker, their wives, and a visiting Rabbi Rivkin, whose lecture she would attend on Monday evening. Monday, Tuesday, and Wednesday she worked on both the Musser piece and the Jewish history. On Wednesday she delivered the Musser manuscript to Burton Musser. She spent the afternoon with Karl and Carla, made an evening speech before a university class, and took a midnight bus for St. George.

For at least two months Louis Zucker did not respond to the Jewish manuscript Juanita had delivered on July 1. When at last he replied, she could report that he "was not at all pleased with what I had done."[33] In the meantime she had begun revising the manuscript in light of new material that she was steadily accumulating. Modifying her custom of keeping notes on a motley variety of papers and used envelopes, she carefully compiled material on four-by-six note cards. She was inhibited now as later by a paucity of sources. She lamented in an impromptu report which she probably sent to no one: "In all this study, the chief problem has been lack of material."[34] By way of explanation, she pointed out that the *American Jewish Yearbook* for 1966 showed only 1,600 Jews residing in Utah and only 120 in Idaho.

The paucity of materials which she lamented accounts for the nature of a paper she delivered before a session of the Utah Academy on September 8, 1967, a paper entitled "Abraham the Jew and the Mormon War." In 1856, a Jewish convert to Mormonism named Levi Abrams (called Abraham the Jew) maintained a mercantile in Fillmore, the new capital of the territory of Utah. Abrams quarreled with Judge W. W. Drummond while the two played cards. Drummond, a federal appointee unpopular with the Mormons, ordered his servant, a black slave, to give Abrams a caning. The Jew retaliated first by threatening to shoot the judge and finally by filing a complaint against him. Drummond was arrested and arraigned before a Mormon-controlled probate court, an ironic fact because Drummond had bitterly contested the powers granted the probate courts by the territorial legislature. Shortly Drummond fled Utah. His accusations added to the clamor which influenced President Buchanan's decision to send a large military escort with the next group of federal appointees, thus precipitating the Utah War of 1857–58.

This was not Jewish history of which Louis Zucker could approve. In Zucker's eyes, a convert to Mormonism was no longer a Jew. Furthermore, Abrams was overshadowed by the conflict between the Mormons and the federal government. Although Juanita had ferreted out enough detail to establish his identity – for example, he was listed in 1875 as owning a saloon near Temple Square in Salt Lake – he remained an obscure, unimportant figure, as she noted in the eloquent conclusion of her paper: "It was as if he had stepped onto a darkened stage, someone had lighted the tableaux-powder at his feet, and for a minute he stood illumined and in full view of all the people. Then, after the brief sputtering, the stage was dark again, and he was lost in the crowd."[35]

In early November, the Leavitt siblings celebrated the ninetieth birthday of their mother, Mary. Descendants gathered from faraway places: a granddaughter flew from New York City, two others from Portland; a grandson drove from New Jersey. On Friday night Juanita and Will provided beds for thirteen visitors and on Saturday morning served "endless hot cakes."[36] On Saturday there was a family program in a local meetinghouse, and on Sunday, November 5, 1967 – Mary's birthday – there was a public reception in Juanita's and Will's home.[37] As a part of the Saturday program, Juanita presented a first-person narrative of her mother's life, which concluded with a brief summary of Mary's recent activities: "I enjoy working in the temple and go regularly. As a result I have been able to do the work for some 4,050 names. I love to visit my children and grandchildren and am made welcome wherever I go. I am proud to see in almost every home some of my handwork in quilts or baby quilts or netting. I now have living ten children, 51 grandchildren, 115 great-grandchildren, and 2 great-great-grandchildren. I am proud of my descendents, each and all."[38]

In early January 1968, Juanita mailed Louis Zucker a revised manuscript of the Jewish history, complete except for two final chapters which she promised to carry to Salt Lake near February 1. To Zucker, Roe, and McMurrin she wrote: "I am sure that further adjustments will have to be made – deletions and additions – but I hope it comes nearer what is desired." She pointed out that since July 1967 she had worked without pay; being "in a financial bind," she now hoped she could have a portion of the lump sum which had been promised her upon completion of the work.[39]

On January 30, 1968, Will had a heart attack. It seemed so mild that he soon accompanied Juanita on her promised trip to Salt Lake, where he "enjoyed himself thoroughly, and came home in fine shape." Then he began to deteriorate, suffering periods of suffocation – "The Smothers," as he called them. "The doctor gave him pills to use in case of pain, but he has no pain – only these smothering spells," Juanita wrote. "He will not resort to taking a pill if he can help it, which the doctor and everyone else tells him is foolish."[40] In April she recorded: "It's a shocking thing to see a man who has been so active and busy and alert suddenly go down in one instant. He did rally some, and was about a little, but he could only make his way from the bed to the front window for so long. Now, though improved, he still can do nothing except read, visit, and walk a short distance twice a day. He has also been driving the old car to the Post Office, but I get out for the mail."[41]

Understandably, Juanita did little research and writing during the winter and spring of 1968. She herself suffered from an unnamed ailment. In February she wrote a report to Dr. A. W. McGregor, apparently never mailed, about her response to medication he had prescribed. On a Monday afternoon she had received "a massive shot of something (I'd like to know what!)," which had brought immediate relief to her tightened neck muscles and her painful scalp. At intervals that evening and the next day she swallowed a course of "little pink pills," which had an unusual effect upon her. At midnight, she awoke "so wet with sweat that I could almost wring out my pajamas." The next day she became hyperactive, running everywhere: "to get the garbage out; to take down and wash out my bed-room curtains; to manage the lawn watering; often to run up and down to the basement half senselessly." That night she couldn't sleep. Her mind being perfectly clear, she lay in bed reorganizing a chapter of the Jewish history and planning a speech she would make before the Westerners in Salt Lake on March 19. Unfortunately, a little after midnight Will "awakened, went to the bath room, and threshed around up and down and round about for the next hours. Sometime between 2:00 and 3:00 I went to sleep and awakened at five. Separate beds tonight."[42]

As spring advanced, Will seemed at least to be holding his own. Although Juanita gradually turned her attention to writing, she did not resume work on the Jewish history because of a stunning turn of events. Having reviewed the chapters she had delivered in January, Zucker announced that he would undertake to rewrite the entire lot. His particular complaint was that she did not understand the Jewish religion; it is probable that he also objected to the rough and inexpressive style which invariably characterized Juanita's preliminary drafts. Zucker had in effect advanced himself to the status of coauthor.[43] Although Sterling McMurrin and possibly Ben Roe protested this move, for the moment Zucker had his way. Juanita wrote in early April that "Dr. Zucker is 'working over' the first eleven chapters of the Jewish history, and we must combine our notes to make up this last one."[44] Profoundly humiliated, she was only too willing to turn her attention to other matters.

The most substantial writing Juanita did during the summer of 1968 was a paper which she read at a folklore conference in Logan in July. Dale Morgan would inform her months afterward that he had heard good things about her paper, and she would modestly reply: "The time had been pretty well taken when I began, and some who had partaken too liberally of the excellent meal, were ready to doze. I did not stay strictly to the written text, assuming that eventually it would be printed, so much of the last and best part was left out. Perhaps that is why they liked it."[45] In 1969 the paper would see publication in *Forms upon the Frontier*, an anthology edited by Austin and Alta Fife and Henry H. Glassie. Entitled "Mariah Huntsman Leavitt: Midwife of the Desert Frontier," Juanita's article detailed the folklore of pregnancy and childbirth in pioneer Bunkerville and Mesquite. Among many prescriptions were the following:

> Do not tickle a baby or make him laugh too much. This will cause him to stutter.
> Do not cut his fingernails with scissors; bite them off with your teeth when they peel down. Cutting them will make him 'sticky-fingered,' so that he will pick up things which do not belong to him, and who wants a natural thief in the house?
> Do not feed the mother rabbitmeat while she is nursing the child, or he will be prone to run away, and perhaps later to even leave home.[46]

During the summer of 1968 Juanita carried on a polemical correspondence with BYU historian Richard L. Anderson. Anderson was in the process of writing a number of articles demonstrating that Oliver Cowdery, following years in excommunication, had been rebaptized into the Church and had reiterated his testimony as one of the Three Witnesses of the Book of Mormon. At her request, Anderson cordially sent Juanita a copy of a preliminary paper he had read in the spring session of the Utah Academy. Anderson held as spurious the "Confession" of an Oliver Overstreet, who declared in an affidavit that he had impersonated Oliver Cowdery at a church conference at Kanesville, Iowa, on October 21, 1848, delivering, in the guise of the former Mormon leader, a speech of contrition and renewed testimony. For her part, Juanita accepted the Overstreet confession as authentic, as she attempted to explain to Anderson in letters written during July and August 1968.

Anderson remained unimpressed. On the one hand, he argued, many contemporaries wrote of Cowdery's presence at Kanesville; on the other hand, there was no corroborating evidence that a man named Oliver Overstreet had ever existed.[47] In the midst of their exchange Juanita irascibly struck Anderson below the belt. "I realize your dilemma," she wrote; "employed at the BYU and writing for a Church publication, you are forced to look at only what you know will build to the point you set out to prove, and carefully bury or ignore anything that will raise questions in the minds of the readers."[48] Indignantly, Anderson declared his independence of mind and his dedication to objective history. For years, he asserted, he had subjected the claims of the witnesses of the Book of Mormon to "a merciless examination," concluding "that they pass the test. After paying such a price, it seems a little too easy to dismiss my convictions with 'slanted' or 'faith-promoting.' "[49] Shortly he wrote a reconciliatory letter in which he emphasized the values which he assumed that, as Mormons and historians, he and Juanita held in common. Apparently Juanita let the correspondence drop at this juncture, but she went on for months quarreling vicariously with "the BYU Boys"—Anderson and other unspecified historians—in letters to her friends.[50] For almost a decade she would continue to make sporadic—and fruitless—inquiries after evidence substantiating the Overstreet confession.

On July 6 Juanita and Will participated in the annual reunion of the descendants of George Brooks. There was a picnic in the park, and "for the day before and a couple of days after," according to Juanita, "my place was almost like Grand Central Station—a place to gather and visit."[51] Afterward, Karl returned to Salt Lake and wrote an affectionate letter to his parents, thanking them for the support they had given to his pursuit of a doctorate, which he would receive in August. Besides major loans, there had been "the 20's and 30's and 50's that you have advanced . . . , not to mention the two years rent free in the house, the care of the horses and colt for two years."[52] With their year-old daughter, Sharla Sue, Karl, and Carla would move to Monticello in September, where Karl would take the position of principal of the high school.

In early September Juanita decided to disengage herself from the Jewish history. After a particularly frustrating encounter with Zucker, she wrote her colleagues in the project: "I made a mistake when I accepted this assignment. I knew that I was ignorant of the subject; I did not guess how ignorant. But I was flattered that I had been asked, and determined to try. Now I find that I have wasted my time and your money, with little accomplished, and that little not accepted." She proposed two alternatives. One was that she would resign permanently, "hand in my source materials and what I have done and permit Dr. Zucker and others to really do the book." The other – the one which became a fact – was that she would take a leave of absence from the project until the following April, at which time she would "pick it up again and devote FULL TIME – eight hours a day, five days a week until it is done."[53]

She was disencumbering herself for other action. Her foremost ambition was to write a redaction of Will's autobiography. During their residence in Salt Lake, she had encouraged Will to record his memoirs in writing and on tape. Following their return to St. George, he had continued the process in a desultory fashion. Now she proposed that he complete his reminiscences, which she would prepare for publication, organizing them into a coherent narrative and providing punctuation and minor grammatical corrections. She wanted *Uncle Will Tells His Story* published while her husband was alive to enjoy it. His enfeebled condition told her she hadn't much time.

Typically Juanita allowed herself to be diverted by other affairs during the fall of 1968. She served on the local arrangements committee for the meetings of the Utah Academy, held on September 13 at Dixie College. The next day, she spoke to a group of Academy members at Mountain Meadows. It was not an entirely happy experience. For one thing, as she explained later to an appreciative member of the audience, the "wind and sun and dust all combined to fluster me a bit." For another, she had grown weary of recounting the narrative to inexhaustible ranks of curious listeners. "I had long ago said that I would not discuss this subject before an audience again. I would invite people to read the book upon which I spent two years of research. But I find times when I cannot refuse, and this was one of them."[54]

The next Saturday, Juanita and Will traveled to Logan, where Juanita delivered the chief address at the annual meeting of the Utah Historical Society. One of her best autobiographical essays – as readable and absorbing as any work of fiction – the address would be published in the *Utah Historical Quarterly* under the title "Jest a Copyin' – Word f'r Word." It was an account of her love affair with pioneer documents, narrating her adventures in collecting, characterizing the persons who assisted her, and describing the attractive qualities of the diaries themselves. She repeated her conviction "that the person handling an original document is honor- bound to reproduce it accurately, whether he thinks it is true or not."[55] Among the anecdotes with which she illustrated her conviction was that of the Emergency Relief Administration typist who complained of the useless repetitions in the diary of Myron Abbott: " 'I can well believe this whole project is just a waste of government money, if this is the kind of thing we are trying to save. This man does nothing but work on the dam. . . . Ditto, ditto, ditto, for two weeks now.' " Later, however, a government engineer informed Juanita "that this little record was worth its weight in gold as the only real history of the Virgin River anyone had found. Though it covered only a few years, it did give tangible and accurate proof of the floods of that time."[56]

Juanita continued to procrastinate her labors on Will's autobiography. In December she did research on the Mormon Desert Mission of 1858. Sometimes called the White Mountain Mission, this was an expedition undertaken by Mormons in May 1858 to locate a supposed oasis in the Nevada desert where the Church at large could find refuge from the United States army which stood poised at Fort Bridger. The group blazed a trail westward from Cedar City to the site of modern Panaca, Nevada. Here they built ditches and planted crops during the early summer of 1858, which they did not remain to harvest.

Juanita's research would eventually result in an article, "A Place of Refuge," published in the *Nevada Historical Society Quarterly*. Her sources included a daily itinerary prepared by the expedition's historian, James H. Martineau, as a guide for later travelers. Her interest in this itinerary, and indeed in the entire expedition, was whetted by the fact that during the preceding spring Todd Berens and a group of junior high school history students from California had retraced the itinerary by Jeep. As was his custom on his annual field trips, Berens had brought his students to visit Juanita and Will, thereby doubling Juanita's interest in their venture. In December 1968, she corresponded with Berens about a mythical mountain range appearing in Nevada on an early Fremont map which Mormon leaders had studied during their trek westward. That nonexistent mountain range, Berens had suggested to Juanita, might have been the oasis which Brigham Young had sought when he called the expedition into being.

As her article would show, not only did the members of the expedition fail to find an ample haven for great numbers of fleeing Mormons, but they came close to perishing from thirst as they traversed a formidable desert. For Juanita, the episode was one more evidence of Brigham Young's heedless sacrifice of his loyal followers. By her reasoning, Young should have known from the tragic experience of the Donner party, who had crossed Nevada before finding themselves trapped in the snow of the Sierras, that the region held no inviting oasis. Considering the approach of Johnston's army, the expedition was a terrible diversion of manpower. "In all our annals," Juanita wrote Berens, "I know of nothing that was such a total waste."[57]

Juanita was also enticed during the late fall of 1968 to resume editorial work on the journal of Thomas D. Brown, a draft of which she had many months before put into a nearly finished condition. In November, Dale Morgan had challenged Everett Cooley's declaration that William Lund of the Church Historian's Office had forbidden publication of the diary. How could that be, Morgan wrote Cooley, when Lund's superior, Joseph Fielding Smith, had himself given permission in a letter of March 27, 1956?[58] Morgan's challenge seemed to have an immediate effect, for within a month Cooley asked Juanita to assist the staff at the University of Utah Press in final preparations of the manuscript. For her part, Juanita declared herself pleased with the delay, since in the meantime she had "learned a great deal more about the man about whom I knew practically nothing before."[59] However, for reasons which Juanita did not record, the latest initiative would prove as futile as earlier attempts to publish this important account of the Southern Indian Mission of 1854.

On December 15, 1968, Juanita attended a reception at the Utah Historical Society in honor of Cooley, who was resigning as director to accept the position of curator of Western Americana at the University of Utah library. The reception was, Juanita wrote Dale Morgan, "a signal success, with a very large crowd in the line for more than two hours. The Governor was impressed, especially after he learned that all these were members of the Society."[60] Also present was the newly appointed director, Charles S. Peterson, with whom Juanita would evolve a cooperative relationship as she had with Russell Mortensen and Everett Cooley.

In January 1969, Juanita suffered a bout of flu. Furthermore, she felt obliged to fend off recommended surgery for a prolapsed uterus. She assured her Salt Lake physician that the pessary with which he had fitted her was an entirely adequate remedy. "I know one man who has plastic heart valves and another with a plastic larynx, both of which are more complicated than this little deal. So I have assumed that I too have found a permanent solution."[61] Near the same time, she also threatened to prosecute two college students who had illegally entered and held parties in her empty rental house in St. George. Although there were bathrooms, someone had defecated in a closet – "a black, stinking mess," Juanita wrote the young men, whom she preferred to confront by letter. "I spent three hours cleaning the popcorn out of the rug, emptying the ashes, and generally trying to put things in place. But I refused to tackle the pile in the closet. Good Old Uncle Will Brooks put in yesterday forenoon at that, and then didn't get all the stain out of the boards."[62]

During January Juanita received word of the death of Peg Gregory's husband, Reginald, who only recently had retired from the navy and joined his wife in New Mexico. Juanita groped for a concept of immortality that might be acceptable to the mourning Peg: "I do feel that the true identity – the personality, the soul, the knowledge – cannot be entirely dissipated, and that in some mysterious way we are eternal, whether to pass on to another sphere or to return, centuries hence, in a new form to this. Greater minds than mine may resolve this: I cannot."[63] Thoughts of her own husband's demise could not have been absent from Juanita's mind. Will now walked with a cane and had lost the use of his right hand. Though he could feed himself with the left, Juanita buttoned his shirts and assumed the unaccustomed duty of keeping the family accounts. Nonetheless, on the day before her seventy-first birthday she optimistically wrote in a general family letter that Will was "right spry and keen." She was happy to report that Willa and her children had moved to St. George to live while Thales fulfilled a six-month tour of duty in Korea. She also reported that the ancient pink Plymouth had "conked out on us, so we walk the hill – down and try to thumb a way back up. Willa and Walt's folks are all very kind to take us where we need to go, but there are times when we just peg down by ourselves."[64]

In the same letter Juanita declared that she had completed 120 pages of *Uncle Will Tells His Story* – about a third of the narrative she and Will had planned. She had in the meantime allowed another interruption. In early December, the managing editor of *The American West* had solicited an article about John D. Lee's part in the Mountain Meadows massacre. The article was to accompany a reprint of an account of Lee's execution published in a nineteenth-century magazine with illustrations made from woodcuts. Despite her declared weariness of the massacre as a topic, Juanita agreed to write the article because she had acquired documents that cast new light on the bloody event.

In late January 1969, she mailed to *The American West* a rough draft of an article entitled "John D. Lee," requesting that the editor "red-pencil it, cut it, suggest anything that you think might help, and fire it back to me."[65] The article would never be revised. After holding the draft for over a year, *The American West* would decide to abandon the entire project. The modified interpretation of the massacre which Juanita expressed in the article would make its way into a preface to *The Mountain Meadows Massacre* when the University of Oklahoma Press emitted a fourth printing in 1970.[66] In that preface Juanita would emphasize that the Indians had been far more prominent in the massacre than she had hitherto thought. "In line with the early plan, the Indians had been gathered from far and near, so many that the Mormons found 'they had started a fire they couldn't put out,' as one expressed it."[67] She would also emphasize the military nature of the episode: "Military orders brought them to the scene; military orders placed each man where he was to do his duty."[68] Finally, she would lower her estimate of the victims to less than 100.

It is notable that letters and notes which Juanita wrote near the time she composed the rejected article give a color lacking in any published account. In one letter she bluntly declared: "I myself have come to feel that Brigham Young was directly responsible for this tragedy, since the company in question had already passed through Salt Lake City and was on its way south, and since the threat of the Indians on the southern settlements might have been more real than I had previously supposed." In the same letter, she accepted as genuine the message which John M. Higbee had attributed to William H. Dame, ordering that the emigrants be allowed to go free yet containing the corollary order "not to precipitate a war with the Indians while there is an army marching against our people."[69] From this corollary order, Dame's subordinates in the field, fearful of the Indians, took license for proceeding with the massacre. Among Juanita's notes is this hand-scribbled statement: "John D. Lee was a major in charge on the ground, taking orders from Col. Com Wm. H. Dame at Parowan."[70] In no published work did she ever come so close to admitting that Lee was indeed predominant among the subordinates who made the decision that the Mormon militia would assist the Indians in slaughtering the emigrants.

In February 1969 Juanita concentrated on *Uncle Will Tells His Story*. She wrote much of the narrative as Will responded to her questions. Some of the episodes, however, were cast in Will's language, for Juanita transcribed the tape recordings he had made of his favorite stories and positioned them chronologically within the narrative. "I am conscious," she would later explain, "that the style varies somewhat when I tell the story."[71] Working long hours, she completed a book-length manuscript in March and entered it in the annual writing contest of the Utah Arts Council.

She now remembered her promise to proceed with the history of the Jews by April 1. In February she wrote Ben Roe that Louis Zucker had assured her that he was "at work on the book. He said he is doing something with Chapter one, and is adding new material to the chapter on the Jews in Idaho." Although she had become doubtful of Zucker's ability to produce, she agreed that "if he IS seriously working, we should not disturb him or embarrass him."[72] However, Zucker proved to have done little more than write an essay about Jewish immigration into Utah under the impress of German persecution shortly before World War II; this piece, entitled "Recollections and Observations," would become a chapter in the published work. Meeting with Zucker, Roe, and university officials at the end of March, Juanita retrieved her largely untouched chapters and promised to revise them by July 1. During April and May she worked on the manuscript at unseasonable hours. "I'm putting in the heart of every night on this machine," she wrote her colleagues. "It is now 3:30 a.m., and I have put in two hours. After two more, I'll go back to bed. It is the only work pattern by which I can give my undivided attention to what I am trying to do."[73]

When she traveled, Juanita recruited others to keep a close watch over Will. "My good husband is alert and clear in his mind," she wrote, "but tottering on his legs."[74] With assistance, Will continued to visit about town and attend college and high school athletic events. The girls of the high school Pep Club had remembered him at Christmas with a cane having a gold band inscribed with "To Uncle Will Brooks, with love, 1968–69." On spring Honor Day the Pep Club presented him a lap robe for use at football games, which they themselves had quilted. On its blue satin background was a large white D; within the D were white letters "Our Uncle Will." "It is so artistic and beautiful and represents so much in time and skill and work," Will commented in his autobiography, "that I can hardly believe that they would do so much for me. Now I feel that I am truly 'Uncle Will' to all the young people of the town."[75]

During the spring of 1969 Juanita found herself pulled into a conflict at Dixie College between President Ferron C. Losee and the Faculty Association. Long-standing issues concerning Losee's autocratic style of administration and low faculty salaries had been suddenly exacerbated when Losee summarily fired the chairman and vice chairman of the Faculty Association, Melvin Smith and Carl Jensen. Smith successfully invoked an investigation by the Utah Education Association, which censured Losee and called for Smith's and Jensen's reinstatement. Backed by the State Board of Education, an intransigent Losee refused to rehire the instructors.[76] Ultimately, Smith and Jensen went elsewhere, as did an astonishing number of junior instructors who resigned in protest. Smith would enter a suit against Losee and the State Board of Education and in time would win significant damages.

Juanita followed the altercation with extraordinary interest because Melvin Smith and Jay Haymond, another history instructor who resigned in protest, belonged to a monthly discussion group with whom she and Will met. She entered the conflict directly when Willa came home one evening from an MIA road show practice reporting a rumor that Smith was a known "trouble-maker" who had been fired from a prior job. Juanita traced the rumor through a tangle of faculty wives, informing each of a favorable letter of recommendation from Smith's former employer and avowing "that I wish one of my own sons could get so flattering a report."[77] Following a campus hearing in May, Juanita wrote letters to the editors of the *Salt Lake Tribune* and the *Washington County News*. She castigated the State Board of Education and the Dixie College Advisory Board for refusing to allow Smith to speak before them—a fact which "sounded more like Russia than the United States of America, where it is considered a man's inalienable right to face his accusers in his own defense." She recommended that Losee reinstate the fired teachers and that both parties thereafter reconcile and cooperate: "'Agree with thine Adversary QUICKLY.' Otherwise both will be killed professionally and our Dixie College will be irreparably damaged."[78] Her letters had no visible effect. She would, however, remain Melvin Smith's close friend. She furnished information about Losee's administrative practices which she hoped would assist Smith in his court action.[79] Furthermore, her recommendation helped Smith attain positions in the Utah Historical Society—as preservation officer in 1969 and as director in 1971.[80]

During May and June 1969, Juanita engaged in a variety of pleasant ceremonial duties. On May 10, she attended the centennial observance of the completion of the transcontinental railway at Promontory Summit. An estimated crowd of 12,000 persons gathered at the site of a recently created national monument, which featured a visitor's center and two nineteenth-century locomotives. The program included anthems by the Mormon Tabernacle Choir, speeches, and a reenactment of the driving of the Golden Spike. Because it was a hot, dusty day, Juanita made herself a hat from a newspaper. When her tall, conical hat fell off, former University of Utah president Ray Olpin exclaimed: "I didn't expect a woman as smart as you to be hidden under a Dunce Cap!"[81] She wished to depart early to catch a plane for Dixie because the following day would be Mother's Day. Obliging officials drafted a highway patrolman to drive her more than a hundred miles to the Salt Lake airport.

At the end of May Juanita received a second honorary doctor of humanities degree, the College of Southern Utah in Cedar City making the award at its annual commencement.[82] In June Juanita and Will attended the dedication of Lake Powell, an impoundment of the Colorado behind Glen Canyon Dam. They stayed overnight in a motel in Page and with other members of the board of trustees of the Utah Historical Society toured the dam and took an all-day voyage on an excursion boat. The boat paused at Rainbow Natural Bridge and again at Hole-in-the-Rock where Mormon pioneers bound for San Juan County had carved a precarious road into the gorge of the Colorado. Will was excited, but also disappointed, as Juanita explained to a friend, for he "had come here as a young man, riding horseback, and it didn't look the same from the lake. He was troubled that he couldn't adjust."[83] From start to finish they voyaged through stunning beauty: sparkling water, towering cliffs, serpentine inlets, and profusely eroded buttes and pinnacles. As the day wore on, Juanita and Will went to sleep seated side by side on a comfortable bench. Her hand clasped his hand; her head rested on his shoulder. Gently the boat rocked the two old lovers.[84]

Juanita decided during this summer to republish her grandfather's biography, *Dudley Leavitt: Pioneer to Southern Utah*, which

had been out of print for some time. In July she let the job to Ogden
Kraut, who operated a Mormon fundamentalist press in remote
Dugway. For some years Juanita had cordially accepted Kraut's arcane
publications. In March 1969, having received *Jesus Was Married*, she
ruminated in a letter of thanks to Kraut: "During my childhood and
early adolescence this topic was much discussed, some of the men certain that Jesus was not only married, but that he had more than one
wife."[85] Made bold by expressions of family interest, Juanita ordered a
printing of 1,000 copies, of which 500 were to be immediately bound.

Mid-summer Juanita received cheering news: *Uncle Will Tells
His Story* had won first place in the long prose narrative category of
the Utah Arts Council competition. Greatly encouraged, she decided
to try to place the manuscript with a prestigious publisher rather than
to publish it by her own means. Undaunted by rejections, she would
persist for many months, submitting to American West Publishing,
Doubleday, and the University of Oklahoma Press. The politely worded
rejection of Doubleday was typical: "Uncle Will, while he certainly
led a useful and representative life, did not have a terribly adventure-
some or unusual one, nor one that would much transcend purely
regional interest in terms of book-buying."[86]

Juanita applied the $750 awarded by the Utah Arts Coun-
cil toward a handsome used Chrysler that Ernest, who was selling cars
in Las Vegas, had located. Now that Will was too feeble to drive, she
felt obliged to learn. By early July she had completed a driver's training course and received a learner's permit. "I take Daddy to the Post
Office," the seventy-one-year-old Juanita wrote to Bob and Florence,
"and Mother to the temple each morning, and drive around town,
but have only tried the Highway once—to Washington and back. I'm
gaining more confidence all the time, but it has been a real test for me.
I've been too afraid of a car for too many years."[87]

In late July, she experienced a terrible fright. As she cau-
tiously entered the intersection at St. George Boulevard and Main, a
speeding car ran the red light and collided with her car. The offending car spun around and demolished itself on a light pole. Juanita's
Chrysler suffered a crumpled fender and a misaligned front end. "I
had my seat belt securely fastened," she wrote Myrtle Friedman, "so
came out without even a shock, that is, physically. I have been emotionally shaken, it is true, for it is clear that there was only a split
second—one more turn of my front wheels—and it would have been

flowers and slow music for me." She was so shaken, in fact, that she amended her holographic will to specify that, in the event of her death, her research materials and manuscripts related to the Jewish history should become the property of Friedman. "I have taken this seriously as a warning. It would not be a bad time for me to leave now except for the one piece of unfinished business—the book on the Jews. I hope that I may stay to see that done."[88] After her car had been repaired, she pluckily resumed driving.

By September Juanita could cheerfully report that Will "has had quite a remarkable come-back. . . . He walks down town once in a while for exercise; he goes to all the ball games, church meetings, Sons of the Pioneers, and Retired Civil Service groups." She was for the moment agitated over her mother. In the late summer, Mary had departed for a visit with her sons in Idaho. When she became dissatisfied and returned prematurely, Juanita addressed a scolding to all her brothers and sisters. Particularly during the month when the St. George temple was in recess, she hoped her siblings would do their part "to see that she gets from one place to another, not to stay for more than two or three days unless we can provide her with work that is meaningful. She can't simply SIT, and she can't read all the time."[89]

Juanita was also perturbed by Ernest's disaffection from the Church. In a touching letter she reminded Ernest of his dying father's hopes: "He was, as you are, perfectly honest, but he had a deep and lasting testimony of the Gospel, and all his life he was active in the Church. During his last week, when he could see that he was not going to make it, he said, 'Well, I leave a wonderful son to carry on my name and have a family.' " Juanita admitted that she herself had her reservations about doctrine and ritual. "I have gone to Sunday School only a few times this last year; to be honest, I just couldn't stomach the lessons." Still, it was important, she asserted, to discern the valid from the invalid: "The Germans had an old saying, 'Don't throw out the child with the bath.' In other words, seeing the dirty water that does get into the tub, don't forget the living, vital truth that is also there. Save it, cherish it, and drain off all the unclean that you can."[90]

In October, Juanita and Will said good-bye to Willa and her sons. Thales had returned from duty in Korea and would now be stationed in Hawaii. As deer season approached, Will bought a license and asked Juanita to unearth his boots and red hunting gear, but when departure time came, he was too tired to go. In November Juanita and Will made a sudden decision to visit Kay and Ida Jean in Washington and, as they returned, Tony and Janet in Albuquerque. "Daddy is like a kid looking forward to Christmas," Juanita wrote, as she discussed Ernest's plans to convey them to Las Vegas and see them safely on an airplane.[91] The visits were pleasant. Juanita was impressed by the "immaculate, beautiful homes, the lovely children, and the whole general atmosphere"—by which she undoubtedly meant the kindness and affection which their children and grandchildren consistently showed them. In Albuquerque Juanita visited Peg Gregory, accompanying her to a ceremonial Indian dance at a nearby pueblo. Later she wrote Peg: "But I must tell you how happy it made me to see you so well and so busily engaged in doing good."[92] On the return flight from Albuquerque to Las Vegas, "the weather was clear and the plane flew low enough for us to see the Grand Canyon, the Boulder Dam, and the general landscape." Charity and Vernon, who had recently moved to Las Vegas, met Juanita and Will at the airport and provided them with a chicken dinner and a good rest before driving them home to St. George. "It was truly good to be back!" Juanita commented. "Especially for Daddy it was, for he went straight to bed and had a good night."[93]

Shortly before Thanksgiving Will came home from church with a chill. By evening he had again developed swollen ankles and "the smothers," and Juanita took him to the hospital where for several days he rested and took oxygen. On Thanksgiving morning Juanita conveyed him from the hospital to the hall of the Daughters of the Utah Pioneers, which the family had rented to accommodate a multitudinous Thanksgiving dinner. Will "pronounced the blessing on the food and at the end of the little program, spoke briefly to the crowd."[94]

One morning near Christmas, Juanita arose at three-thirty to address a printed holiday letter she had ordered for friends and relatives. At breakfast Will reminded her that it was the last day on which she could qualify for her driver's license before the expiration of her learner's permit. The traffic office was so crowded that she had to return in the afternoon. When at three o'clock it was at last her turn to demonstrate her driving ability, she "had been up for twelve hours and was weary & tense"—the more so because she had failed two earlier driving tests with the same examiner. Once when he had asked her to reverse, she had made a U turn; another time, when he had asked her to make a U turn, she had circled the block. "But I went on and took it, and he DID give me a license, though reluctantly. All in all, I put it down as the worst day I had spent in all my life. I must add, though, that I *do* have more confidence now."[95]

She continued to work sporadically on research and writing projects through the fall of 1969. In early September she was a featured speaker at the annual Writers Roundup of the League of Utah Writers in Salt Lake. The theme of the roundup was "Heights to Climb," in light of which Juanita irreverently entitled her remarks "From the Mole Hill Whereon I Sit." She took along a supply of her biography of George Brooks to sell at the book display. At the same display Sam Weller of Zion Book Store sold other books she had written.[96]

In October she flew to Salt Lake by commuter airline for a board meeting. It was her intention to fly on to Hailey, Idaho, to confer with Myrtle Friedman concerning the history of the Jews. However, a major storm caused her to cancel her plan. Because the storm grounded the airline on which she had arrived, she took a Phoenix-bound flight on another airline which would set her down in Cedar City. "The trip up through [the clouds] in the little plane was one of the most traumatic experiences of my life," she wrote Friedman. "The interesting thing was that the younger woman beside me, in her forties, I'd guess, said to me as we came out into the clear, 'Thank you for being so brave. Just to have you sit there so calm and quiet, not saying a word, gave me strength.' Yet there I was, fighting with all my might for composure and just wet with sweat."[97]

It is evident in the same letter that Juanita considered her revision of the manuscript on the Jews to be nearly finished. She had left it in the hands of her friend Fae Dix, associate director of women's programs in the Division of Continuing Education at the University of Utah. Juanita had recently delivered a series of evening lectures which Dix had arranged. Dix promised to persuade Esther Landa, her supervisor, to critique the manuscript. "This is exactly what I have been hoping for," Juanita wrote Friedman, for Landa was prominent in the Salt Lake Jewish community.

By the fall of 1969, the conflict between Juanita and Louis Zucker had resolved itself in Juanita's favor, chiefly, it appears, because of Zucker's procrastination. During the summer, citing his considerable research for the Jewish history, Zucker had asked Friedman for a compensation of $2,000.[98] Friedman turned the matter over to her Salt Lake banker and reminded Zucker: "As you know—Mrs. Brooks was—and still is commissioned to write the history "that I am sponsoring."[99] The banker offered Zucker $1,000, which after a lapse of six months the professor accepted. In October Fae Dix assured Juanita that Zucker bore her no grudge: "He is a great man under stress and I remain his admirer. He told me all of the story behind this recent action—his version. He hopes you will call him when next you are here and he asked me to extend greetings. . . . He spoke only praise for your 'integrity' and 'ambition' etc."[100]

In late October Juanita took delivery of the reprinted _Dudley Leavitt: Pioneer to Southern Utah._ In private she confessed herself to be bitterly "disappointed"[101] with the product: the paper was of poor quality and the print was small, making it hard to read for aging eyes. Nonetheless, she proceeded to vend the book aggressively for $3 a copy, declaring, "It is very clear and readable, and has a beautiful coat-of-arms in the front."[102] She recruited willing brokers among her relatives, sending, for example, a supply of the book to her aunt Selena Leavitt in Mesquite, offering her "6 or eight as your commission for handling them."[103] The little book did not sell as well as Juanita had hoped, totaling considerably fewer than 250 copies by March of 1970.

In early January 1970 Will felt so much better that he accompanied Juanita to Salt Lake to participate in the celebration of Statehood Day. Will "enjoyed every minute of the whole afternoon," Juanita wrote. "The new _Quarterly,_ featuring my talk at Logan two years ago, 'Jest a Copyin'—Word f'r Word,' has been off the press just long enough for everyone to have read it, and their comments to him were very flattering."[104] At home Will again attended the high school games, where he sat in his favored place among the girls of the Pep Club. His nights, and therefore Juanita's too, were restless. Late one night she wrote: "Daddy filled the bath tub full of hot water sometime after midnight, went back to bed and to sleep, so when I got up a while ago—at 2:30—I jumped into it myself, had a good scrubbing, and decided to stay up for a few hours." One night Will's restlessness proved a godsend. Shortly after midnight he woke Juanita and in confusion asked what day and month it was. He went back to sleep, but she couldn't. As she sat at her typewriter composing a letter, she caught a whiff of smoke. On the previous afternoon she had worked in the backyard with a hired man pruning trees and vines and burning weeds. She dashed out of doors in her stockinged feet and looked about. "Sure enough, there was a little glow over near the shed on a cross pole of the fence; an instant more and a shower of sparks fell out. . . . I found [the hose], got to the tap and turned it on full, and got out [to the shed] in time to catch the first little torches of flame. If I had disregarded this prompting, the whole shed would have gone up."[105]

There were other perturbations during the winter of 1970. On her way to the temple Mary twisted an ankle and fell with such impact that her head snapped "until it threw the hair-net off and every hairpin and comb out."[106] Embarrassed more than injured, the stalwart old woman went on to the temple. Of more lasting concern, Ernest and Margie concluded a divorce. Characteristically, Juanita wrote Ernest letters of solace over what seemed an unfair settlement. "You've been stripped and peeled so far as money is concerned, but you have strengthened your manhood by trying to be fair and decent." She also urged him to pray. "Just because you have not conformed to all the outward signs and duties in our particular Church is no reason why you should not seek and get help. God's blessings are not restricted to tithing-paying or preaching Mormons. They are for the least of all, for any who ask. Try it. You'll find that what I say is true."[107]

In February 1970, Juanita was elated by the promise of an immediate publication of *Uncle Will Tells His Story*. As early as October, Richard Thurman of the University of Utah Press had promised to publish the work after he had cleared away a considerable backlog of other projects. In February, alarmed at how rapidly Will was failing, Juanita phoned Thurman and "told him that if he couldn't take the book on at once, I'd have to send it elsewhere." By coincidence, Thurman declared, he had decided within the past day or so to proceed. Within minutes of hanging up the phone, Juanita received visitors: a friend introducing Charles W. Taggart, who was interested in finding manuscripts to fuel a publishing firm which he intended to found. Taggart, whom Juanita described as a wealthy man "who has lost his right hand and wears a mechanical grasping device," seemed particularly concerned with producing handsome, artistically designed volumes.[108]

Because of Thurman's promise, Juanita did not immediately suggest *Uncle Will Tells His Story* to Taggart. Instead, she mentioned other languishing projects, among them the three-volume edition of the diaries of John D. Lee. Within two days of meeting Juanita, Taggart flew to San Marino and secured a tentative release of the copyright of *A Mormon Chronicle* from the Huntington Library. Ecstatically Juanita wrote Ettie Lee, who was confined to a Los Angeles rest home: "Truly God Moves in a Mysterious Way! We are going to get the full writings of John D. Lee in a new edition of THE MORMON CHRONICLE in three volumes! I can hardly believe it myself."[109]

Quickly this project was shunted aside, for within days of writing Ettie, Juanita agreed with equal eagerness to a proposal that Taggart and Thurman collaborate in producing *Uncle Will Tells His Story*. Soon the University of Utah Press dropped out and left the project entirely to Taggart. While in Salt Lake attending a board meeting, Juanita met a number of times with Russell and Dorothy Mortensen and a designer whom Taggart had hired.[110] There was heady talk of high-quality paper, artistic sketches, and adroitly placed photographs. Dorothy, a former assistant whom Russell had married after the death of his second wife, became the copy editor for the book.

Will seemed so ill upon her return that Juanita decided there could be no more overnight trips. The Mortensens, generously concerned to see the work published with dispatch, drove to St. George in late March to help Juanita put finishing touches to the manuscript. "All day yesterday, Saturday, we worked on it," she wrote, "and got it in shape to be put on the gallies—After I got up this morning at 5 o'clock and put in three more hours on it. They are really pleased with it, and I'm so happy and relieved that it has reached this point." That night, Walt and Irene and their sons Ray and George came in to hold their family home evening with Will and Juanita. "We sang 'We Thank Thee O God for a Prophet'—one verse, Ray offered the opening prayer, and Grandpa and I both told some experiences. We asked a special blessing for Daddy at the end, and I feel sure that he will rest better tonight. He really doesn't look at all well."[111]

On Saturday, March 28, 1970, Juanita felt obliged to leave Will. In November she had promised the students of the LDS Institute of Religion in Ogden that she would speak on the Mountain Meadows massacre. Because it was spring vacation, Clair was in St. George and would stay overnight with Will; Walt also promised to look in on him. The night before she left, Juanita gave Will a hot bath and groomed his toenails. "At breakfast I couldn't get through the prayer, but had to break off in the middle of the sentence, cry a bit, and say 'Amen.' And I ran back for a second good-bye after [going] to the door. I left with a sense that all would be well with him—as it was."[112] Juanita flew to Salt Lake, reserved a room at the Belvedere, rode to Ogden with faculty from the LDS Institute there, and delivered her address.

In the meantime, Susie came in and vacuumed and straightened her grandparents' house for a couple of hours. Clair arrived and took Will out for the mail. Later Walt took Will along while he drove to Hurricane to shop for building materials. Dropping him off at home, Walt promised to return soon and drive him to a funeral. Will put on a white shirt and tie and Sunday suit. For a moment he stood at the living room window and waved at a neighbor. Scarcely three minutes later, Walt found him on the floor "on his side, as if he had been sitting on the edge of his big chair and leaned down to tie his shoes, blacked out, and slipped to the floor."[113] Walt carried his father to a bed and began heart massage. A doctor arrived and advised against further attempts to revive him. Soon a hearse arrived, and Will Brooks left forever the house in which, nearly eighty-nine years before, he had been born.

Juanita received news of Will's death by telephone following her address at the Institute. Those who observed were impressed by the composure she displayed.[114] Returning to the Belvedere in Salt Lake, Juanita found Edith, Will's sister, awaiting her with consoling words. Juanita phoned Russell and Dorothy Mortensen, canceling an appointment to confer with them the next morning about the book. The Mortensens would not hear of her waiting for the midnight bus. They brought her home for a bite of supper, put her into the back seat of their Continental, covering her with a blanket, and set out in the stormy night for St. George. They arrived around three in the morning to find that Karl and Kay and their families had already come. The Mortensens declined an invitation to stay in the obviously crowded house; finding no vacancy in the local motels because of a basketball tournament, they slept briefly in their car on the roadside and returned to Salt Lake.[115]

At the evening viewing, a waiting line extended from the mortuary, around a corner, and down half a block. The next afternoon, Tuesday, March 31, the tabernacle bell tolled solemnly as a great number crowded into the historic building for the funeral. Flowers in unbelievable profusion had come from sympathetic friends. The program featured Will's favorite music: a trumpet solo, "How Gentle God's Commands"; a male quartet, "Oh, My Father"; a vocal solo, "A Poor Wayfaring Man of Grief." A girl from the Pep Club spoke of Will's loyalty to Dixie athletics. Alluding to his habit of distributing candy from his coat pockets, she remembered that he had once shown up at a state tournament in which Dixie played at the University of Utah stadium. "This time he had a whole grocery bag full of candy."[116] Ernest also spoke. Describing Will as good-humored, affectionate, and fair, he remembered that, during the years when he had lived with Henry and Mary in Bunkerville, Will had always enclosed a dollar bill in his letters. An impromptu speaker was Governor Calvin Rampton, who had unexpectedly flown in from Salt Lake. Following the service, Will was buried in the St. George cemetery. Persons by the score approached Juanita: "So many said, 'He was the first man I got acquainted with when I came to St. George,' or 'He always had a special interest in me.' The girls he had taken to the Reform School, the boys he disciplined, even his prisoners came to see him."[117]

By Friday the last of her children had left and Juanita was alone. For a week or two she puttered: there were dozens of letters to write, a hundred things to put away. Sorting through a box of papers, she came upon a little agenda book. On its back page, scrawled in Will's shaky hand and displaying his relaxed spelling, was a poem, which Juanita recognized as a tribute to her:

> *Proude Little Woman:*
>
> Excellent woman
> ever modest.
> Proper in behavior
> dress or speech
> Prudent, Discrete
> A feminane name:
> Careful management,
> economy,
> sound judgement in
> practicle matters
> cautious, discrete in
> conduct, sensible;
> not rash.
> Careful, Wise
> ever modest or proper.

Resourceful—
Skilled in many things.

Juanita sent photocopies of the poem to their children with the following comment: "I had prayed for composure, and I think was able to carry myself without too much demonstration. But this completely bowled me over. I found it in the evening while I was here alone, and really had my cry out. Soaked up my pillow. Even now I cannot read it with a straight face. I feel so totally unworthy of the description, for I do sometimes—too often—speak my mind pretty definitely, as you all know. If he had built this picture of me in his own mind, it perhaps says more of what he wished me to be than what I really am."[118]

As April ended, a rare blizzard struck St. George, killing Juanita's grapes. "What looked to be an exceptionally good crop will now be half a dozen vines, some still with a heavy load, others with a few bunches, 20 vines killed entirely."[119] The storm had forced a neighbor to cancel her plans to fly to Salt Lake for a conference; she dropped by Juanita's house and said that she had been praying that the Lord would open the way for her to get there in time for a banquet the next day. "The way is open, if you can get ready to catch the 11 o'clock bus tonight," said Juanita, who wished to confer with the Mortensens regarding her book. Later she wrote: "I went into SLCity earlier than I had intended, just to help the Dear Lord answer Sister Coxes' prayers."[120] There were other ways in which she eased her loneliness. She often took supper next-door with Mary; Aura and Carl, who had moved to St. George and were remodeling their kitchen, were often there too. From Las Vegas Ernest came from time to time to work in her yard. Once he brought his landlady to stay overnight, a kindly woman of eighty-two for whom Ernest had a great deal of affection. "To me she is just another old lady like me," Juanita dryly commented.[121]

For months, freed from Zucker's supervision, Juanita had declared her intention of getting on with the history of the Jews. Constantly she lamented her procrastination: "Seems that every day is so full of THINGS that I don't get any real work done. I have my Jewish material scattered out all over the bed down here [in the basement where she kept her typewriter] to try to stimulate myself to get at it and stay at it. Never was anything harder for me to do! But I'll do it."[122] Briefly in May she made motions toward resuming work, announcing, "I am now back at it and trying very hard to get into my stride."[123] Unfortunately, she did not find that stride; she failed to work on the project with any consistency until near the end of the year.

She suffered no lack of motivation in preparing *Uncle Will Tells His Story* for publication. She consulted regularly with the Mortensens on the manuscript, read galleys both at home and in Salt Lake, and cooperated with Taggart in finding old photographs and taking new ones for embellishing the layout. In early June she spent a day roaming St. George and its vicinity with Taggart, his photographer, his artist, and the pilot of his chartered plane.[124] Later she gave very decided opinions upon which photographs were to be included and upon their placement within the text. As the layout evolved, she was particularly annoyed by photographs that did not relate directly to their context. "Mr. Taggart told me he had already $5,000 tied up in that manuscript and that changes are very expensive," she wrote peevishly. "I answered that I didn't care if it was $20,000—the book could not appear as it was."[125]

On a Sunday in May, Juanita flew to Salt Lake, beginning ten days of pleasant wandering. Though she would sleep at the Belvedere, LaVon met her at the airport and took her home to supper with Clair and the children. Monday morning she proofread galleys and in the afternoon departed for Monticello with Karl, taking along more galleys. She enjoyed Karl's and Carla's children, and she visited with some of Will's friends from long ago. At the request of Dell Taylor, principal of the LDS seminary, she spoke about the Mountain Meadows massacre to each scheduled seminary class throughout an entire day; later Taylor would describe her as "a great lady" who could quote verbatim long passages from pioneer diaries.[126] On Friday evening she delivered the commencement address at Blanding High School—her chief purpose in coming to San Juan County.

On Saturday Karl and Carla conveyed her to the Rim Rock Motel on the edge of Capitol Reef National Monument for a board meeting of the Utah Historical Society. In the afternoon she joined other board members for a drive and a hike. "I've seen rough country and the sheer walls of Zion's Canyon," she wrote her children, "but nothing has been more overwhelming than this, especially as it got so narrow that the hubs of the wagons scratched the sides. Here at 'Register Rock' were many, many names of early travelers and later visitors."

That evening some of her colleagues became congenially drunk, much to the dismay of director Charles Peterson, who had invited several non-drinking Mormon legislators to the evening session.[127] Juanita responded to the evening program with great emotion. Board member Dean R. Brimhall, a retired naturalist who lived within the boundaries of Capitol Reef, presented slides of Indian petroglyphs found on some of its cliffs. "They were to me most exciting—primitive pictures of men, dogs, goats or sheep, birds big and little, trees like cottonwoods—not pines— Their pictured Deity was always large, sometimes ten feet tall. Often he had wide eyes, a snake by the neck in one hand and a spear in the other. Some tiny birds, no bigger than [Brimhall's] thumb-nail, were perfectly done in fine lines. From their high positions—Dean got iron scaffolding much higher than that we put together to wash our south windows—they must be not thousands but *millions* of years old."[128]

Juanita returned to Salt Lake and continued to proofread galleys. Monday evening she attended *Man of La Mancha*, a musical based on the adventures of Don Quixote. "I wouldn't have missed it!" she wrote. "He was so like Daddy in that he saw the good in everybody and he brought it out." On Tuesday evening she took a bus for St. George; at two on Wednesday morning she walked up the hill to her empty house. Such homecomings were her worst moments. If she were lucky, she might find an encouraging letter as she riffled through her accumulated mail. Hence she wrote to a friend whose letter greeted her on just such an occasion: "Since the passing of my husband some three months ago, I find times when I need a bit of lift. And last night, thanks to you, I got it."[129]

On a Thursday in June, Juanita lectured at a western history workshop at the University of Utah. Thereafter she spent a pleasant weekend at the summer cabin of Ione Bennion, a friend from Logan. Returning to St. George she continued to distract herself with family affairs. In early June Karl's tiny son was in the hospital for tests; he had run a fever and lost weight. "I think we should have a concerted fast for him on Sunday," Juanita wrote her children. "I've put his name into the temple."[130] In early July she attended the reunion of the George Brooks family. The following week she accompanied Janet and her children, who had come to the reunion, to their home in Albuquerque, where she visited for a few days. Tony arrived shortly from Europe where he had traveled briefly following his delivery of a scientific paper at the Fourth International Congress of Radiation Research in France.[131] When she returned to St. George, Juanita hastened to report this proud fact to the *Washington County News*.

Juanita was also distracted during the summer of 1970 by a painful dispute with a neighbor over their common property line. There was a discrepancy of twenty feet between the southern Brooks property line as it had been traditionally defined by a fence erected in pioneer times and as it had been redefined by a recent city survey. One morning in June, Juanita found survey stakes at her south door. "Well, I was just stunned," she wrote. "What could I do? I made myself walk down to the new house to talk to Mrs. Cottam. She informed me that she held the deeds to this property and it belonged to her, but that she would permit me to use it as a driveway, because she herself only wanted it for a roadway."[132]

Juanita's lawyer advised her to pull up the stakes—advice she was quick to follow. For a couple of days she researched county and city records and wrote letters to persons involved in prior transactions concerning the disputed property. One morning she awoke with the idea of putting a carport on the swath of land claimed by Mrs. Cottam. She had discussed that possibility with Will before he died, for her car, parked beneath the giant trees on the street, was constantly soiled by bird droppings. Her lawyer endorsed the plan, and Juanita proceeded quickly. Within a week workmen had placed uprights and prepared forms for pouring the concrete driveway—this after Mrs. Cottam had "ordered them off her land, and I told them to stay put."[133] Mrs. Cottom soon entered a suit against Juanita, claiming the carport. For nearly a year and a half the altercation would cause Juanita, and presumably Mrs. Cottam too, recurring anxiety and irritation.

At the end of July 1970, Juanita made the momentous decision to move to Salt Lake. Such a move, she believed, would greatly facilitate her research and writing. "I have held out stubbornly against it," she wrote her children, "but it seems the only sensible thing to do. I'm wearing myself out and getting nowhere shuttling back & forth. It's too expensive in time and strength and money. Another hunch? Yes. Plain and clear. I hope you will feel that I'm doing the right thing. It's not going to be easy. I can hardly stand to think about it, but I see no other way out."[134]

Near the end of August she rented her St. George home to college boys and moved to her house at 98 U Street in Salt Lake, which renters had freshly vacated. Immediately she had visitors—a niece and her husband and then, as that couple departed, another niece and her husband. There was, she realized, no special room for her research materials in the little house. "Of course, I must expect a lot of company wherever I go—we've had a house by the side of the road in St. George for the last thirty years. But I must have a home with a special room for my books and desk and files, where I can shut myself in."[135] Shortly before moving she had told her children that the recent weeks had been "the darkest hours of my whole life."[136] She continued to be perturbed and depressed as she scanned the classifieds and drove out to inspect one house after another. "They say the darkest hour is just before the dawn," she wrote her children as she recounted the following episode. On a Sunday afternoon, she had spoken in a Sacrament Meeting at the invitation of the man doing the layout work for Will's book. He had conveyed her to the meeting but had mistakenly assumed she had other means for returning to her house. She took a taxi home and brooded over the slight. The next morning, she could muster such little courage that she merely glanced at the classifieds: "I said to myself, 'What the H——l does it matter!' and started to fold the paper up, when just at the very bottom of the last section of houses, I saw this ad."[137]

The instant she saw it, she fell in love with the house at 1731 South 1400 East. She agreed to pay $16,500, as well as an additional $800 for elegant furniture already in the house, and set about raising a large down payment. She was so eager that, when she failed to sell her house at U Street as quickly as she had planned, she wrote a humiliating letter requesting a loan from Myrtle Friedman.[138] Whatever Friedman's response may have been, Juanita soon proceeded without her help. The house at U Street sold, and she rounded out the required amount by borrowing against the equity in her St. George rental and by borrowing from a brother-in-law.

In early October she began loading her Chrysler with books, clothing, and bedding and making cautious drives between U Street and 1400 East. "I reminded myself of an old red ant, carrying a kernel of barley bigger than she was and engineering it along as best she could." Howard Pulsipher and his son hauled her beds and dressers in a truck, and Clair and LaVon helped her transport odds and ends

and arrange the furniture in the new house. She concluded her description of these efforts by alluding to an adage: "As Dad used to say:
'Hard work ain't easy.' How true! How true!" Immediately she experienced an adventure. On a Saturday morning, when she went out for
the paper in her housecoat and woolen socks, the front door locked
behind her. Finding the kitchen door also locked, she tried the bedroom door and found "the screen neatly cut and fitted back into place.
I reached through, unlatched the screen, and, Glory Be! it was not
locked."[139]

As Thanksgiving approached, Juanita's children gave her
an automatic clothes washer. "You can't imagine the difference it has
made," she wrote: "just put 'em in, press a button, and forget 'em."
On Thanksgiving Day, she boldly drove her car to Clair's and LaVon's
house for dinner. "I felt quite heroic, for I think it's my longest trip in
Salt Lake City. Of course, the streets were all practically deserted—
everybody too over-fed to move, I guess. That's the way we were, as
you all can guess who know LaVon's cooking."[140] On the day after
Thanksgiving Howard Pulsipher enlarged the entrance to her garage
to compensate for her uncertain steering. She planned on Saturday
or Sunday to ride with Clair to Provo, where she intended to stay a
few days with LeRoy Hafen, whose wife Ann was near death from
cancer. While still at home on Saturday afternoon, she had a vision of
Will, which comforted her immensely. It seemed so intimate and sacred
that only with reluctance did she describe it for her children:

> I had lain down on the little bed in the back bedroom, just turned
> back the 'Family Tree' quilt which Dawn made for us in 1966, and I am
> using as a show piece because I don't have a spread to fit. I pulled it up
> to partially cover my face and keep the light out of my eyes. I was
> awake, lying flat on my back, eyes closed. There came into my vision a
> street, or a side of a street into which pulled a light-colored van, closed
> like the one Edith's Floral drives. The door opened and Daddy stepped
> out and stood facing me. He saw me and I saw him—there was no
> doubt about that! The word that came into my mind on the instant
> was *radiant.* That describes it better than anything else, radiant with
> vitality, with happiness, with a sense of well-being. I have no memory
> of his clothes, but just of him, and it was only for a flash but long
> enough for us to recognize and greet each other, for he saw me as surely
> as I saw him. Then it was gone. I lay quiet, so full of joy that I could
> scarcely contain myself. Certainly, most certainly, all was well with him;
> he *knew* and was pleased with things here too. So, as I said, I try to

remember and not get too tense about anything. If I do my best, I think he will be pleased with it.[141]

Juanita continued to make frequent speeches and to attend board meetings. In October she attended an address by Fawn Brodie in the ballroom of the Hotel Utah. At her side sat Dale Morgan, for whom, as she later wrote Brodie, she "explained the reactions of the audience by pointing out in his printed copy where you were and what the ad-lib happened to be." After the meeting Morgan let Juanita read a letter from his sweetheart, "a warm, pleasant letter in which she expressed her love for him, but which ended with 'but NO wedding bells, please.' He seemed confident that he could change her mind." The courtship was not news to Juanita. About two years earlier she had spent a day touring historic trails with Morgan and the daughter of his sweetheart, who "was so kind and considerate and pleasant that I almost wondered why he didn't propose to her rather than to her mother."[142] Morgan would not marry his beloved, though he would be near her when, within a half year, he would die of cancer. It was fortunate that on the last day of 1970 Juanita wrote Morgan a final word of respect: "In my mind, you are the only true historian that Utah has yet produced. You stand like a Colossus among all the little people, your achievements like mountains in the midst of mole-hills."[143]

Through the fall of 1970 Juanita's writing gained momentum. She spent long hours in a spacious, unadorned basement room where she had placed her files, desk, and typewriter. By late November she was at last making progress on the Jewish history and hoping that she could "wind it off within a couple of months."[144] She had, she reminded a correspondent, purchased her new house "so that I could be near the sources of material and so that I could work without a lot of interruptions. I have neither dog, nor cat, nor canary. I have neither radio nor television. I have left most of my books and files at home [in St. George]. And I think I have callouses on my be-hind." Yet, haunted by the impossibility of the project, she concluded her letter: " 'The Jews of Utah!' I can hardly learn who they were—and are. Truly, Fools rush in where angels fear to tread."[145]

During the fall she also worked on a contribution to a women's issue of *Dialogue*. Her essay, "I Married a Family," treated the early years of her marriage to Will when they had composed a family from her son, his sons, and their daughter and sons. At first she simply adapted a chapter of her autobiography completed in the 1940s. The essay would be, she wrote Claudia Bushman, editor of the women's issue, a further step toward telling her own often deferred story: "I'll make it a part of my chapter 'I Married a Family' of my projected QUICKSAND AND CACTUS, which may never appear."[146] Bushman later goaded Juanita into a substantial revision. Among Bushman's suggestions was a plea for "a less didactic conclusion, maybe something commenting finally on what I like to think is a major theme here: the synthesis of your family and writing lives."[147]

This synthesis is evident in the essay appearing in a 1971 issue of *Dialogue*. With a mixture of nostalgia and candor, Juanita discussed the perplexities and joys of harmonizing the members of the growing family and of pursuing her research and writing without disturbing the tenor of her household. Often the latter endeavor had involved a frustrating search for a secluded place in which to write— so often, in fact, that she concluded the essay thus: "I think I might, with a little different slant, have called it, 'A Corner of My Own.' " In each of the houses where the family had lived, "I had a small room, if only shoebox size, which all the children knew was not for them. What Mother did there was none of their concern, unless, by chance, she sold an article. Even then she usually forgot to mention it."[148] In this essay, more completely than in any other writing, Juanita touched upon the disparateness that made her unique. It was not simply that she published important scholarly works, nor even that through her innumerable public appearances she became the tragic minstrel of the Mountain Meadows massacre. It was that she wrote, published, and spoke while performing the duties of a mother in such a way as to give her children every advantage of a stable Mormon upbringing; in such a way, indeed, as to shelter them entirely from the perturbations inherent in the difficult subject she had chosen to study.

CHAPTER ELEVEN

PERENNIAL SPUNK

O n December 11, 1970, Charles Taggart put a printed copy of *Uncle Will Tells His Story* into Juanita's hands. On December 22 she autographed copies at Sam Weller's Zion Book Store. Although she conceded that "it *is* a beautiful book, and one we can be proud of,"[1] Juanita had only a month earlier, upon examining the blueline, complained to Taggart: "The art work is a potpourri, a little of everything, photographic, line drawings, impressionistic panels, assorted capital letters. These seem to be an after-thought, starting as they do past the middle of the book and appearing where they are for no apparent reason. Every one is different. They range from a gigantic Y to a dim and dripping F, five or six in all. For me they cheapen the book."[2] She also scolded Taggart—and herself—for failing to copyright the work. "How could we have been so stupid?" she wondered, lamenting that television and movie rights were now compromised.[3]

It is indicative of Juanita's practical personality that she was unimpressed by the artistry Taggart's staff had achieved. The off-white paper was of rich texture. Photographs and sketches of persons and frontier objects varied in size, hue, and finish. Sometimes the photographs carried captions, sometimes not. Sometimes they clearly related to their context; even when they did not, they effectively added to the work's frontier and rural ambiance. The book was in fact a handsome visual object, by far the most esthetically produced of any of Juanita's works and entirely worthy of the man whose life it celebrated.

The book outlined Will's life in a sketchy, anecdotal fashion, without any pretense to a comprehensive summary. Two periods received detailed treatment: his years as an experimenter in dry farming and his years as sheriff. From his early teens Will aspired to be a farmer. When he arrived at BYU in 1906, he was attracted to Professor John A. Widtsoe, who taught the practice and theory of dry farming—the current national rage for getting rich in the unpreempted lands of the West. Under Widtsoe's supervision, Will worked for two summers on an innovative dry farm in Juab County, and in 1907 he followed Widtsoe to Utah Agricultural College at Logan. In 1909, in partnership with two beloved friends, Will undertook the development of a large dry farm in remote San Juan County. The partners purchased 1,000 acres of inexpensive land from the state of Utah and took out homesteads of 360 acres each on adjacent federal land. It was perhaps fortunate that Nellie, whom Will married in 1911, could not tolerate the primitive conditions of Monticello and in 1912 drew him back to St. George. Although he believed that he took a loss when he sold his portion of the enterprise, he left with happy memories, undisillusioned by the reverses that would surely have followed. For the rest of his life San Juan County represented the romance of his youth.

Juanita was as responsible as Will for the abundance of anecdotes from his years as sheriff. Shortly following their marriage, she had written and unsuccessfully submitted them to magazines. Later it was easy to interpolate those tales into the story of Will's life. She devoted a chapter to Lew Fife, sheriff of Iron County, and Jack Weston, a notorious outlaw. Fife apprehended Weston and his mistress Daisy Butler in a remote juniper forest. After wounding Weston, he negligently allowed him to pull a gun, whereupon Butler handcuffed Fife to a juniper sapling and the pair left him to die. Fife saved himself through incredible effort, awkwardly severing an impeding tree limb with a rock held in his manacled hands: "After an hour or so, he could see he was getting a little of the bark off. . . . By this time his hands had lost all feeling, and were perfectly numb. He knew the longer it took him, the weaker he would get, so he kept it up, all afternoon, all evening, all night. After about twenty-two hours of steady work, he pushed at the limb with his shoulder hard enough to break it off!"[4] Fife then climbed the tree, passed his encircling arms over its top, and fell to the ground, free. Later he recruited other officers, including Will, to assist him in capturing Daisy Butler, Weston having in the meantime died of his wounds.

A startling if innocuous anecdote involved a prostitute from Silver Reef who became decrepit with age while Will's father was sheriff. County officials moved her house intact to St. George and placed it on George Brooks' lot. The Brooks family cared for the old woman until she died. It was one of life's minor ironies that following her death, the house became a bedroom for George Brooks' daughters. Other anecdotes reveal a youthful Will who was bellicose to a degree surprising to those who knew only the older Will. While he worked as a freighter in Modena, a much larger man attempted to put him out-of-doors; hours later friends found them still wrestling. "I know I would have stayed the night before I would have let him put me out, as long as I had an ounce of strength left," Will recorded.[5] On another occasion, he punished a brother-in-law for striking his sister: "Instantly I whirled loose and hit him, and really gave him a good beating up before I was through with it."[6] One winter while he ran a trading post in San Juan County, Will forced an Indian youth to give up a credit ticket he had stolen: "I cuffed him on each side of the head with my bare hands. He put his head down and came at me to resist, and I pommeled him good and finally knocked him down."[7] Strength, pugnacity, and a fundamental decency were the traits that made Will Brooks a successful sheriff.

As friends wrote their congratulations for her latest book, Juanita was honored by an Award of Merit from the American Association for State and Local History, given "for an outstanding contribution to local history." Although the award was officially dated September 24, 1970, it was ceremonially delivered January 19, 1971, at a monthly dinner of the Westerners, an association of historical buffs who met in the then exclusively male Alta Club in downtown Salt Lake. Utah Historical Society director Charles Peterson and his wife Betty accompanied Juanita to the gathering.[8] As was expected of parties which included women, Juanita and the Petersons rang to gain admittance through a side door of the venerable building.[9]

Juanita would shortly play a role in selecting a successor to Peterson, who was negotiating a professorship at Utah State University. In February Juanita recorded in her diary: "Charles Peterson tells me of his plans to leave the Historical Society and to put Melvin T. Smith in as top man! I am to spearhead the action!"[10] Ironically, when the board met to consider Smith's appointment, Juanita was not in a condition for lively debate. Several hours before the meeting, she underwent oral surgery for the removal of flesh under her tongue in order to improve the fit of her dentures. She parked her car at the Kearns Mansion and walked a block to a dental clinic. "After I got into the chair and was *all out* under the gas, I thought how utterly crazy I was! Here I hadn't told a living soul about this—not my neighbors or friends or any of the Staff at the society."[11] During the subsequent meeting of the board Juanita sat numbly listening while her colleagues debated and finally gave unanimous approval to Smith's nomination. She performed a more crucial service a few days later by writing a letter to Milton Weilenmann of the state government, assuring him that Smith's altercation with President Losee of Dixie College was not a reason for refusing his appointment, concluding, "I think he should be permitted to hold the position and serve the state well as he has demonstrated that he can."[12]

During the cold, snowy winter of 1971 Juanita's difficulties with her automobile multiplied. After the vehicle had been immobilized for a couple of weeks by a defunct starter, she paid Ernest's air fare from Las Vegas so that he could repair it. She joined Ernest for dinner at the home of a woman with whom he had corresponded. Afterward the three attended a movie; as luck would have it, Juanita found the movie to be unsavory, recording in her diary, "NO GOOD— vulgar & dirty."[13] Following her son's departure, she forced herself to venture abroad in her automobile as a matter of discipline. On February 1, as she backed from her driveway, she became rattled by a car turning a nearby corner and rammed broadside into an old vehicle that had sat parked across the street for many months. "I don't know what a nervous break-down is," she wrote Carla, "but I literally fell apart. I had the man who was coming up take my car into the garage for me and park it. I felt that I could NEVER get into it to drive again. I couldn't stop shaking and chilling for an hour."[14] Although she recovered her spunk and continued to drive occasionally, she sold her handsome Chrysler to Tony in early April. "It almost breaks my heart to see it go," she told her diary, "but I am sure that it is better so."[15]

With or without a car, Juanita was highly mobile. She frequently traveled to St. George, usually by night bus. In March her travels extended to Hawaii. After weeks of vacillation, she suddenly made up her mind to go. Willa, Thales, and their children met her at the airport, "everyone carrying a lai—positively gorgeous. We rode home through a fine rain—waterfalls everywhere."[16] In the days which followed she went on picnics, took in Polynesian entertainments, and even helped with the Derricks' yard work. She toured the Mormon temple grounds and Pearl Harbor and at a beach observed "blow holes where the surf shoots into the air."[17] One evening, she addressed a group of about thirty guests in the Derrick home concerning her historical writings, a presentation which she judged to be very successful.

Immediately upon her return, although she had come down with what would prove a stubborn case of the flu, she attended a memorial service for Dale Morgan. In mid-April she read a tribute to Morgan at the banquet of the Utah Academy in Ogden, where a Distinguished Service Award was posthumously granted the deaf historian. "His brilliant mind," she said, "turned back into itself, cut off from all distractions of sound, became literally an encyclopedia of information which could be brought forth on demand. . . . As Beethoven, stone deaf at the age of thirty-one, continued to compose and did his best works during his last years of silence and sorrow, so Dale Morgan's inner ear developed a sensitivity to sound and rhythm. His writing is not only exact and accurate; it is full of life and color, and most effective when read aloud."[18]

During the afternoon recess of the Academy sessions in Ogden, Juanita went to the home of John A. Shaw, "who insisted that I tell his children some pioneer stories."[19] An Ogden businessman, Shaw desired especially that his children hear the story which would eventually be published in *Frontier Tales* as "The Buckskin Pants." Having heard the story long before, Shaw had stood up in an audience at a cookout in Logan Canyon and requested it; later he had invited Juanita to repeat it before the Kiwanis Club of Ogden. So contagious was his enthusiasm that on the morning following her attendance at the Academy meeting, she awoke "with an idea for Xmas—Booklet of pioneer stories for my grandchildren. Ten or twelve stories at least." The morning after that, a Sunday, she arose from a restless night and "wrote The Buckskin Pants story. Started on Sammy Reber's courtship."[20] During the months which followed she continued to refer to the incipient volume as "the Xmas book."

On a Saturday in April Juanita had a long telephone conversation with Myrtle Friedman about the Jewish history. Juanita had worked on the manuscript in a desultory fashion during the winter. Now she agreed to mail it for Friedman's scrutiny. For several frantic days she enlarged and rearranged; as she mailed the document, she recorded "Happy day!" in her diary.[21] In a cover letter she proposed that her accounts of the Jews in Utah and of the Jews in Idaho be published as different volumes. "If we try to combine them, we'd need to put some of the Idaho story in each of the several chapters, as the dates correspond. This will mean a lot of re-writing, of course." Perhaps to deflect Friedman's interest in an integration of the accounts, she suggested that the project be abandoned entirely. "I think it would be the simplest for all concerned. You would have wasted considerable money, and I a great deal of time, but then WE'D BOTH BE FREE OF IT!"[22] Although Friedman would not abandon it, for the moment Juanita could put the Jewish history from her mind.

In early June she made a pleasant tour of southern Utah with friends from Logan, Ione Bennion and Mary Washington. On their way south by automobile, the trio inspected the territorial statehouse in Fillmore and the old church in Parowan. After pausing in St. George while Juanita watered her trees and vines, the women drove eastward through Short Creek, Bryce Canyon, and Boulder, where Juanita had only to identify herself to secure beds at a motel supposedly having no vacancy. The next day they descended the Waterpocket Fold via the switchbacks of the Burr Trail, which Juanita described as "absolutely the most dangerous & precipitous place I have ever seen."[23] They drove by tedious graveled roads to Hite's Crossing of the Colorado and on to Monticello, where they found hospitable lodging with Karl and Carla. As they traveled, the three conversed incessantly. Among the topics of their conversation was Juanita's manuscript of the Thomas D. Brown diary. Months earlier, Mary Washington had, as director of the new Utah State University Press, expressed an interest in the work. Juanita had been reticent, having hoped to place the manuscript with the University of Utah Press. In the afterglow of the happy outing, she promised the work to Washington. Within a week of their return to their homes, Washington secured the manuscript from Juanita and set in motion the process of publication.[24]

In the meantime the dispute over the boundary of her St. George home continued to agitate Juanita. In June her attorney informed her that the information she had been gathering for the pending trial was worthless: "not notarized," she told her diary. "Now I must begin all over again."[25] She made frequent trips to St. George to ferret out facts that would give credibility to the property line which she claimed. Following one such sortie she wrote Karl, who had recently moved to St. George, asking that he "learn approximately the date of the barbed wire fence which was still there in 1934 when we bought the property." Doubting that he could discover when the fence had been built, she dispiritedly declared herself "sick with the whole mess." Furthermore, the bus on which she had returned to Salt Lake had been freezing—"they *refrigerate* like we were all dead beef that need to be preserved."[26]

In late July she made a miraculous find. She was for the moment in a good mood, having had a heartwarming visit from Tony and Janet and having observed the speedy recovery of Linda Brooks, the young wife of Walt's and Irene's son Paul, who had undergone open heart surgery in a Salt Lake hospital. One morning Juanita awoke and sat on the edge of her bed in her nightgown. Suddenly an inspiration seized her. She went to her writing room in the basement, got into a closet where she kept files, and opened a small metal box containing records which Will's father had kept. Immediately at hand was a record book dated 1878–79. Leafing through it, she came upon entries for the purchase of cedar posts for a fence and gate. Instantly her experienced eye recognized their meaning. "I wanted to shout for joy," she wrote her children, "but I just said a fervent 'THANK YOU: THANK YOU,' without knowing exactly who or what I was thanking. But anyway the date of the fence- building can be definitely set in court, which should close the case."[27]

In August 1971 Juanita participated in a three-day writing workshop at BYU. For an honorarium of $300, she conducted afternoon classes in the writing of biography and delivered an evening address. Upon arriving in Provo, she discovered she had forgotten her clothes bag. She persuaded a young man to drive her to town where she bought "a new dress—Got a blue & white one—too expensive, but pretty."[28] Returning to Salt Lake, she entered upon one of the most diversely productive periods of her life. She submitted to the juvenile *Ranger Rick's Magazine*—futilely, as it turned out—a story demonstrating the mother instinct in birds and animals.[29] She also expanded her projected Christmas book of pioneer stories into two volumes. By late August she had entitled one volume "Wide, Wonderful World" and had put the manuscript into the hands of Sam Weller, proprietor of Zion Book Store. She submitted the other volume, untitled, to Bookcraft of Salt Lake; among these stories was "The Buckskin Pants." She also submitted to Bookcraft several Indian stories written at an earlier date. Acknowledging the Mormon respectability of this firm, she wrote that she had not submitted these stories before "because I was conscious that my name was then in ill-repute among the Brethren. . . . Now the climate has changed a little, so I venture to offer it to you."[30]

During September she continued to improve the stories which she had already submitted and to create others with which to augment the two collections. One of the latter was "Griz," the story of her father's heroic dog, which would appear in *Frontier Tales*. At first she thought of including "Griz" in the collection she had submitted to Bookcraft. For unapparent reasons, she changed her mind and decided to include it in the collection in Weller's possession. Her vacillation was immaterial, for after a time both Bookcraft and Weller rejected her offerings. From the first she had been ill at ease over submitting her stories to Weller; in September she called by his store and failed to carry away her manuscript only because he was not there. "While I know you are an expert copyist and dealer," she candidly wrote him, "I didn't know that you ever really published anything—I mean, I didn't think that publishing is your business."[31] She also despaired of Bookcraft from the beginning, believing, as she wrote in her diary, that her stories were "not *slanted* enough,"[32] by which she meant that they were not sufficiently didactic.

In mid-October Juanita attended the conference of the Western History Association in Santa Fe. She stayed at night with Tony and Janet in Albuquerque and rode to the conference sessions each day with Peg Gregory. While in Santa Fe, Juanita roused the interest of a representative of the University of Oklahoma Press in her Jewish history. In early September, Myrtle Friedman had returned the manuscript and Juanita had settled down to a week of concentrated revision. On September 10 she had delivered the manuscript to Friedman's agent, Frank Diston. Upon her return from Santa Fe in October, she inquired about the manuscript and was dismayed to learn that Diston had placed it with Sam Weller. "Sam is essentially a 'Book Dealer' rather than a publisher," Juanita wrote the University of Oklahoma Press. "But he has it, and I can do nothing about that."[33] Weller, cheerfully projecting a 1972 publication, requested Juanita's assistance, which she promised. It was a measure of his respect that in December 1971 he invited her to address the Exchange Club of Salt Lake.

Juanita's trip to New Mexico also fired her with enthusiasm for getting on with "Quicksand and Cactus." She left a chapter for Peg Gregory's critique and soon afterward wrote a letter discussing the difficulties she faced in continuing her autobiography. She was uncertain as to the order she should impose upon the assorted chapters she had finished long ago. As for picking up the chronicle of her life where those early chapters ended, she had only a timid ambition. She declared herself unable to write about her marriage to the dying Ernest. "I must skip it, either by ending the book entirely, . . . [or by] later picking myself up a widow with a year-old baby boy going back to school."[34] If she went on, she conjectured, she could quickly summarize her years as a self-supporting widow and could perhaps adequately account for her life with Will by interpolating "I Married a Family," the essay soon to appear in *Dialogue*. She made no mention of an account of her career as a writer and researcher.

In November Juanita went on with her multiple projects. She proposed a revision of her biography of John D. Lee as Arthur H. Clark prepared a third printing of that work. Clark proving agreeable, she made slight changes: additional emphasis upon the role of the Indians in the Mountain Meadows massacre and a definitive identification of Nancy Ann Vance as one of Lee's nineteen wives.[35] Juanita also inquired whether Clark would be interested in a short biography of Emma Batchelor Lee, one of John D. Lee's most stalwart and faithful wives. As early as January 1971, she had declared herself at work on Emma's life and had on several occasions throughout the year talked to audiences on the topic. Undeterred by Clark's indifference, Juanita went forward intermittently with this biography.

As the winter of 1971 approached, Juanita allied herself with Cornerstone, a small group of preservation-minded Mormons who wished to forestall the destruction of historic Mormon meetinghouses. The recent decision of Mormon authorities to raze rather than renovate the splendid pioneer tabernacle of Coalville in northeastern Utah had brought the group into being. "After the Coalville incident," Juanita had written in a letter, "my own faith in our present leaders is almost shattered."[36] She attended Cornerstone meetings and wrote letters aimed—vainly, as it turned out—at saving the pioneer meetinghouse in Washington, slated for replacement by a more capacious modern structure. Her ultimate fear was that sooner or later the St. George tabernacle would also go.

In December she expanded her social life by accepting Fae Dix's invitation to join a Great Books group. On a Sunday night she listened to a discussion of Gogol's short story "The Overcoat" and went away instructed to read in Sigmund Freud for the January meeting. The January session would prove, as she wrote in her diary, "a very rewarding evening. I got a new appreciation for this man."[37] Fae, who had become one of Juanita's closest and most loyal friends, considerately called by and drove her to the monthly meetings.

As Christmas approached, Juanita wrote, as a gift for her loved ones, a little story about a mescrew bush which she and Charity had brought from the desert to serve as a Christmas tree in their childhood home. On the morning she finished the story, Kay and Ida Jean brought their three sons to stay with Juanita while they closed their purchase of a new home in nearby Bountiful. Much to Juanita's delight, Kay had been transferred to the FBI office in Salt Lake. While babysitting her grandsons, Juanita made a batch of candy to include in her Christmas packages. That night she slept poorly. She "got up at 2 a.m. & wandered around but did nothing." During the day she made another batch of candy. "It turned out well, but I had to take time out and lie down on the floor—nauseated & weary."[38] The next day she felt better. A few days later she fell on a sidewalk: "Caught my heel on some up-sticking cement and made a 4 point landing, took the knees out of my stockings, but had on heavy gloves which protected my hands."[39]

She spent Christmas Eve in Kay's new home "where we sang carols, Kay read the account from the Bible. Brian & Bradley were shepherds, Julie Mary. Each of the little boys sang. A happy evening."[40] She returned to her own house for the night. She arose early and opened her gifts: a cameo on a gold chain from Ernest, a blue floor-length house coat from Willa and Thales, a set of Corning Ware from Clair and LaVon, and many others. Then began a busy day as relatives drove her about town for visits and the exchange of gifts. In the evening she returned to Kay's house for dinner with a happy crowd composed of both Kay's and Ida Jean's relatives. As 1971 ended, she could not complain that she led a lonely or joyless life.

On January 3, 1972, a bitterly cold day, Juanita took a bus into town and learned from Frank Diston that $700 would be her final portion of the funds with which Myrtle Friedman had endowed the Jewish history project; a considerably larger sum would go to Sam Weller as a publication subsidy. To make his offer seem equable, Diston proposed that they consider her reimbursements for travel and lodging as part of her total payment. Returning home, Juanita wrote a bitter protest to Myrtle Friedman and walked seven blocks in the subzero weather to post it. She particularly resented the subsidy Weller would receive. "After all the time and labor that I have put in on the

project, the night trips up and back on the bus, the digging in libraries and old magazines, the writing and re-writing, I think he is not the
one to make the profit. Not all of it, at least."[41] A couple of days later
she wrote Diston protesting "the attitude that the travel expense should
be counted as advantage to me. Those night bus trips were not pleasure tours; the room and lodging was as reasonable as I could get." In
conclusion she played her only trump: "I will not work with Sam Weller
under this contract. He may take it from here and print it any way he
wishes, but I withdraw. He should NOT print my name as author,
but give credit to Miss Friedman, who is the one to whom all credit is
due."[42]

A few days later Juanita had lunch at the university with
Sterling McMurrin, Jack Adamson, and Ben Roe, who conversed "on
how to get my Jewish book into the hands of the university Press for
publication."[43] The next day McMurrin and Adamson met with Diston
and Weller, and Weller graciously conceded the project to the University of Utah Press. A couple of weeks later, Adamson, professor of
English and chairman of the press advisory committee, made a formal
report to McMurrin, now dean of the graduate school. Juanita's manuscript was basically acceptable, although it stood in need of "a copy
editor who has sufficient authority to make the grammar and punctuation uniform and to make minor stylistic changes here and there for
the sake of clarity and grace." He proposed that, of $7,000 remaining
from Friedman's original sum, $1,000 be paid Juanita as a stipend and
another $500 for expenses, "the amount that she has said would fully
satisfy her."[44] The remainder would accrue to the press as a publication subsidy.

In early February Juanita cheerfully resumed work on the
manuscript. In late February Weller informed her that Myrtle Friedman, refusing to comply with the new arrangement, had instructed
Diston to recover the manuscript from Adamson and return it to
Weller. Friedman's intransigence appears to have derived from her continuing pique with Louis Zucker, whom, although he was retired, she
indelibly associated with the university. "I have resolved to say nothing,"
Juanita wrote in her diary. "Whatever is done or not done, I'm not
going to break a blood-vessel over."[45] In late March she met with Weller
and Diston in the latter's office in Tracy-Collins Bank, recording afterward: "Horrible! Horrible! But I can do nothing."[46] She emerged from
the meeting knowing she would receive $1,000 less than she had recently

expected, a fact which she told Friedman in a letter written months later "cut pretty deep." She went on ironically: "I am always mildly amused by the fact that I had to pay 40c a page to the copyist. Of course, I do get the fun of the writing."[47] Nonetheless, she promised to assist Weller with final preparations of the manuscript.

In the meantime she had other literary irons in the fire. In early January she mailed Gibbs Smith of Peregrine Press a copy of her story about the Christmas tree. Smith liked the story and proposed that he publish it as a small paperback with artwork and photographs, timing it for the Christmas trade.[48] With great energy Juanita set about gathering photographs and physical specimens of small mescrew trees and their peculiarly spiraled seedpods. "I know I am slightly *demented*," she exclaimed as she asked Verl Frehner, a nephew in Las Vegas, to assist her by taking photographs.[49] On February 8 she flew to Las Vegas. Ernest met her at the airport and drove her into the desert where they found branches and seeds but no trunks suitable for photography: "All too old and bush-like," she wrote.[50] Shortly after her return, Verl mailed the desired photographs. These she boxed with her branches and pods and mailed to Gibbs Smith.

She also submitted to Smith the Jacob Hamblin biography she had written in 1952 as the basis for a movie. "The scribbling on this was put there by my sweet husband to indicate parts that he enjoyed," she wrote. "He read and re-read it, and passed it around his little circle."[51] Smith proved uninterested. Juanita pondered submitting to *Dialogue* one of the pioneer stories she had written during the preceding summer and fall but prudently decided to hold it "until I learn whether or not the magazine will fold. They want $100 donations to keep afloat—or better still, $1,000.00 ones."[52] She also scrambled to touch up her brief biography of Emma Lee for the annual writing competition of the Utah Arts Council. "Worked over time & around the clock & mailed it in the morning of March 25. Deadline midnight. . . . Gambled $50 on it."[53]

Juanita also expended considerable effort on final preparations of the Thomas D. Brown journal. In January she stayed several days in Logan working with Mary Washington to perfect the manuscript. Again in April she spent several days in Logan proofreading galleys, a labor which she continued after returning to Salt Lake. Her visits to Logan were pleasant social affairs. Her January visit got under way when Austin and Alta Fife picked her up at home and dined her at the officers' club at nearby Fort Douglas before proceeding to Logan. She lodged with Ione Bennion, with whom she had long and confidential conversations. She and Ione were invited out to dinner one evening, and the next morning Ione put on a breakfast for friends. Juanita also visited briefly with Bob and Frances.[54]

On January 13 Juanita happily traveled from the frigid north into the sunshine of St. George. At an evening banquet, the Soil Conservation Society of America awarded her a plaque in recognition of the contribution her historical writings had made to conservation in Dixie.[55] Throughout the winter and spring, Juanita continued to speak frequently. At a dinner in Richfield on March 10 she addressed some 152 members of the Sevier Valley chapter of the Utah Historical Society. Entitling her remarks "United States Marshals and the Polygamy Raids," she entertained her enthusiastic audience with the maneuverings of the federal marshals and the evasive tactics of the polygamists during the 1880s.[56] The next evening, sponsored by the Sanpete County chapter, she spoke to a large crowd at Snow College in Ephraim. "They had scheduled it for the room in the library, but had to move to the Auditorium because there was not room. They said they had double the number they had expected."[57]

There was an extraordinary intensity about Juanita's relations with her family during the winter and spring of 1972. In January, Karl called to say that Mary had fallen while on her way to the temple and had been taken to the St. George hospital. Juanita immediately alerted a number of relatives, preparing them for the worst. Then she phoned Mary at the hospital, who informed her that she had merely cracked a rib and was about to depart for the temple.[58] Juanita worried about her loved ones who were giving birth—Willa, Ida Jean, Janet, and granddaughter Katie. She rose in the middle of the night and wrote them a letter warning them against allowing strong light to shine into their newborn's eyes. In January she mailed a baby book to Katie. The next Sunday she attended church in Bountiful and witnessed the blessing of Kay's and Ida Jean's infant Benjamin. Two days later Thales called to say that Willa had given birth to a son, Douglas. "They had wanted a girl so bad," Juanita recorded in her diary. "I know just how she felt, for I was the same when Tony was born. Now I wouldn't change him for twin girls."[59]

One evening shortly afterward, Juanita felt lonely. She called Kay's house and found that he was walking his dog. She called Willa's and learned that she was taking a bath. Then, dialing Tony's, she had good luck. Having gathered his family for home evening, Tony put each child on the phone.[60] In February Juanita was plagued by a persistant cold: "Miserable all night," she recorded. "A heavy cold such as I have not had in many years. My nose is a living fountain."[61] Before she had fully recovered, she received a request to speak at the funeral of Will's sister Edith. As the funeral approached, Juanita suffered insomnia and she found herself unable to concentrate. Then from Albuquerque came news of a stillbirth: "Tony calls to say that their baby was born *dead*. I have been troubled with a premonition that it would be subnormal. He is very sad, as are Janet and the children, for it was more than seven pounds."[62]

Other deaths followed. On April 6 Juanita attended the funeral of Willa's father-in-law. On April 20 she flew to Los Angeles to attend the funeral of Will's brother Llewellyn. On the day after her return she reported her trip to Winnie, widow of her brother-in-law Sam. The following day, April 23, was Will's and Kay's birthday. Early that morning, perhaps stirred by the extraordinary coincidence of births and deaths, Juanita had a strange dream reminiscent of the Mountain Meadows massacre: "Another recession into the past this morning. A wide open grassy meadow stretching into every direction. Men (soldiers & priests etc.) in background. Three long bundles or closed sacks carried in and laid on the grass. I saw two opened, the third too far away to recognize—the first a Barton boy & second my son Antone. He opened his eyes, spoke to say 'What an experience' and stepped out stark naked (about 17 years old). The impression was that they were to be sacrificed."[63]

In early May Carla's father died of a heart attack. Before attending the funeral in Kamas, Juanita flew to St. George to help Karl with the children, one of whom was ill with chicken pox.[64] Several days later, she enjoyed a pleasant distraction in the visit of Peg Gregory. She gave Peg a tour of the Kearns Mansion, treated her to lunch at the mountain resort of Brighton, and took her to hear the Tabernacle Choir at Temple Square. Upon Peg's departure, Juanita learned that fellow board member Dean Brimhall had died and that she was requested to speak at his memorial service. This duty came inconveniently, for on the same day Tony would arrive for a brief visit and Juanita was expected to speak at BYU. For several days she worked on her funeral speech. In its polished form, it was eloquent with praise

and high resolve: "Our business is not to grieve his passing, but to live
with added purpose and renewed determination to do as he has done—
to push back, if only for a little way, the bounds of ignorance and
superstition."[65]

Brimhall's body was not present at the service, for it had
been cremated and his ashes released over Mt. Timpanogos near Provo.
The program consisted of five speakers; there were no prayers or music.
When her turn came, Juanita did not rely on the speech she had drafted
but discoursed confusingly upon the diary of Brimhall's grandfather.
During most of the previous night, she had sleeplessly perused that
document, a copy of which she had recently acquired. Some of her
friends thought her performance a disaster. According to Fae Dix: "I
was there [at the service] and she became, well, just not Juanita, not
following her usual classical style, and finally she said that she had
stayed up all night till four o'clock reading someone else's autobiography. . . . There was quite a bit of distress among her friends then
because they recognized it wasn't like Juanita."[66] Afterward the mourn-
ers repaired to the home of Brimhall's widow, Lila, for refreshments.
By evening Juanita was in Provo, where, following a meal in the BYU
cafeteria, she made a speech before a large, friendly crowd. In the
meantime, Kay had picked up Tony at the Salt Lake airport, and
Juanita's homecoming was made pleasant by her waiting sons. She
wrote in her diary that she felt good about her speech at BYU. Of her
remarks at Brimhall's memorial service she wrote: "I was not too pleased
with my performance."[67]

On June 15, Juanita joined Willa, Karl, Kay, and Tony and
their families in an informal reunion in St. George. It was the first
time in many years that the four siblings had been together in their
childhood home. While there Juanita was agitated anew by the pending litigation over her property line. She was particularly incensed
that Mrs. Cottam had planted a garden in the disputed strip below
the Brooks retaining wall. Early one morning, as she explained in a
subsequent letter, Juanita believed herself prompted by her guardian
intuition to strike a protesting blow. "IT said, 'You've been trying to
get Karl to clear that 30 foot strip. Why don't you do it yourself.' I
didn't put on any shoes, I pulled my robe over my nightgown, and
was hardly awake when I had pulled the 4th vine. That seemed enough
to remind her that she is encroaching on my land. And I'm glad that
I did it."[68]

In the same letter Juanita cited other notable moments when her intuition had served her well, among them her decision to get rid of her car. That decision often seemed regrettable, as when she stood forty minutes at a bus stop in freezing weather or got on the wrong bus and had to ride to the end of the line. Yet its soundness was confirmed on the day following her return from St. George. As she laboriously made her way to Bountiful via city buses, she witnessed a terrible auto accident at an intersection. The front door of one of the autos "flew open, and a tall, red-haired- about 18-year-old girl sprang out waving her arms and screaming, 'Help my Mother! SOMEONE! HELP MY MOTHER!' " Unfortunately, her mother was dead. " 'There but for the grace of God, go I,' " Juanita wrote in her diary that evening. "My 30c fare into town, and 45c fare to Bountiful seemed cheap, cheap indeed."[69]

During the early summer of 1972 Juanita decided to donate a carillon to Dixie College. She wished to dignify the college and at the same time to assist Karl, whose duties at Dixie consisted of not only recruiting students but also soliciting contributions. By June 23, when Karl stayed overnight with her while on a recruiting trip, she had determined to make a gift of $8,000. "I shall make a down payment of $1,000.00," she recorded; "borrow $5,000.00 from the bank with payments of $100.00 or more per month. Must mortgage the Provo house to do it. The remaining $2,000 can be paid from rent on the St. George home."[70]

Despite such resolution, financing the gift remained a perplexity through most of the summer. It was, in fact, this necessity that reawakened a vain attempt to rectify her inadequate compensation for writing the Jewish history. In May Ben Roe made Juanita a gift of $500 for her efforts. "You wonderful person!" Juanita wrote in a letter. "To think that you would do this for me! Thank you a thousand times."[71] The unexpected gift did not go far toward the cost of the carillon. In July she wrote a letter to Myrtle Friedman and Frank Diston, ostensibly to complain of Sam Weller's procrastination in publishing the book; more pertinently, she also reminded them that at the meeting in Diston's office in March she had been "refused the $1,000 for the last ten months of my work."[72] Within a few days she phoned Weller and "told him I had $1,000.00 coming from the Jews. He promised to get it, but I doubt that he will."[73]

Juanita also briefly regarded her long deferred plan to produce John D. Lee's diaries in three volumes as a way of increasing her income. In June a lengthy telephone conversation with Raymond Lee elicited his promise to underwrite the project. Quickly Juanita wrote the good news to Peg Gregory, asking her assistance. Peg returned a sobering reminder that Juanita should have a publishing firm prepare a realistic estimate of costs and that she should warn Raymond Lee that it would be years before the project could be finished.[74] In late July Juanita reached an agreement with Lee that for her editorial labors she would be paid $175 a month, "which is my monthly payment to the Bldg & Loan company on the carillon for Dixie College."[75] A few days later she called on Jack Adamson and came away with a premature understanding that the University of Utah Press would publish the work.[76] Nothing further would come of this initiative, possibly because the other parties to the project could detect a lessening of Juanita's competence.

In July Juanita entered upon a comic vendetta against unknown nocturnal assailants—dogs which left large and noisome deposits upon her lawn. Although Juanita often pretended ignorance of protocol and elegance, she in fact took pride in the furnishing of her house and the grooming of her yard. "Juanita had fun in that home," Fae Dix would remember. "She lived mostly downstairs working. . . . She would have fun there saying, 'Look at this bowl,' some association had given her. She would say, 'I know it's something but I just fill it with paper clips and stamps.' I said, 'Juanita, you treasure that.' It was an elegant bowl. Rare in fact."[77] It was therefore no inconsiderable matter when shortly after new neighbors had moved in next door, she returned from a two-night absence to find "10 deposits on just the half of the lawn to the north of the front walk. I spoke to my neighbors, but they were very smart-alecky, 'It wasn't OUR dogs!' " Angrily, Juanita wrote Ernest and Tony asking them to provide her with thorny limbs from desert trees which she could align at the borders of her lawn. "I'm sick to my stomach all day after I clean up; the big piles kill the grass if they are left; the whole place stinks. I'd almost threaten to kill the beasts, but I'm too chicken-hearted for that. I'm really a dog lover until they choose my front lawn for the community out-house."[78]

Juanita brooded about extreme remedies: lassoing the offending animal or giving it a lash with a bullwhip or shooting it. She went so far as to tell a city animal officer that "I had serious intentions of lying in wait for that dog and killing it. My son in the FBI here might not let me use anything of his, but I would buy a small pistol of my own." Once she stayed awake all night watching her front lawn and the street. A man came by with two dogs on a leash; two small dogs trotted by; a neighbor drove away in his car and returned several hours later in an apparent state of inebriation. Unfortunately no offending dog appeared. Finally, following further talks with animal control officers, Juanita shoveled a pile of droppings onto the next door neighbor's porch. Shortly an investigating officer discovered that these neighbors were keeping four or five dogs, a violation of a city law allowing only two. "This morning," Juanita recorded, "the young man next door faced me in a white rage. They must move some of their dogs, and he hopes that I will burn in hell!"[79] Apparently convinced that the young couple were not the owners of the offending animals, Juanita wrote them a contrite letter: "Here I must apologize to you. I was wrong in putting this last mess on your porch. I let myself react too strongly to the frustration of the whole situation—this shadow-boxing with an animal that has a set pattern of returning to the same spot to do his chores. I'm sorry."[80] Whether the neighbors were mollified is not clear. Juanita at least had resigned herself to the continuing nocturnal violations of her lawn.

On July 11 Juanita was delighted to receive copies of the *Journal of the Southern Indian Mission: Diary of Thomas D. Brown*, fresh off the press at Utah State University. The work would be affirmatively reviewed in the *Utah Historical Quarterly*, and loyal friends would write their congratulations. "Thanks for patient, objective scholars who quietly uncover gold nuggets where the general public is often content to enjoy the glitter of fools gold," wrote fellow historian Gustive O. Larson of BYU.[81] It was far shorter than the diaries of John D. Lee and Hosea Stout and much less concerned with the general affairs of pioneer Mormonism; furthermore, Juanita had long before published substantial excerpts from it. Yet the complete journal—138 printed pages—comprised a document of unquestionable worth.

The twenty-one hopeful men who journeyed south in the spring of 1854 were confronted by enormous difficulties. They spent the first summer of their mission at Harmony attempting, with only partial success, to cultivate crops for their own sustenance. Later they split into small groups, each locating near a band of Indians whom they hopefully would teach to farm, thereby civilizing them and making them amenable to conversion. Sometimes they quarreled among themselves, and they often found excuse to travel to other settlements where they could dance, counsel, and worship with the local Saints. Their chief disillusionment was not the lonely, arid country but the tenacity with which even converted Indians clung to what for the missionaries was a filthy, degraded way of life. It is not surprising that only ten of the original group remained in the field of labor after their specified two years had elapsed.

The record of their venture was infused with the vitality of the mission's official historian, Thomas Dunlop Brown. (Besides some eighty-one footnotes and nine appendices, Juanita provided a sketch of Brown's life. An English convert, he was a Salt Lake merchant before and after his mission. In later life he fell away from the Mormon faith.) With poetic flair, Brown described the sleeping accommodations offered the missionaries by Toker, a minor Paiute chief: "Cap. Toker then very courteously led us to our suite or apartments in the great mansion of our common parent, in the sandy bottoms about 30 yards north of their 3 Wickeups—warning us to keep our horses off his grape vines, some 5 or 6 bunches of which intertwined their tendrils with the tall bunch grass."[82] Viewing the magnificent erosions near the boundaries of what would become Zion National Park, Brown broke into rhetorical effusions: "But see over Ash Creek to the east, what table lands are these broken off so abruptly? by some floods of water? what loftly spires! what turrets! what wallls! what bastions! what outworks to some elevated Forts!"[83] He celebrated his forty-seventh birthday, following a day of hard labor, by writing a poem tabulating the overwhelming evils of the world and separating himself from them:

> A Saint I am, or try to be indeed,
> Of heavenly parentage, of noble seed,
> What is my destiny? A martyr's crown?
> If so, oh, God, Amen, says Thomas Brown.[84]

Juanita's literary life took another successful turn when Mary Washington expressed eagerness to publish a collection of Juanita's pioneer stories selected from the submissions she had made to Bookcraft and Sam Weller in 1971. Titled *Frontier Tales*, it would hopefully be ready for the 1972 Christmas market.[85] In early September Gibbs Smith assured her that her little book, *The Christmas Tree*, would appear in time for Christmas. In late September, after Smith had returned the manuscript, she devoted a day to putting a final polish on it. She also cooperated closely with Weller who, undaunted by a fire which had destroyed his bookstore, proceeded with the publication of the Jewish history. In October she proofread galleys of the early chapters until, as she wryly told her diary, "my eyes are ready to fall out of my head."[86] In November, she revised a couple of chapters of the Jewish history and wrote a brief biographical sketch of Ben Roe to be included as an addendum. As had happened so often before while she worked on this manuscript, she seemed to lose all inspiration. As she left her typewriter late one evening, she declared she had had a "ghastly, horrible Day!"[87]

Juanita's effort on the foregoing projects was minor. Always impatient with herself for succumbing to the distractions of family and friends, she was eager to get on with a large, significant new project. In early August she recorded that she had been "looking through the *Dudley Leavitt* book with the idea of putting out a new edition."[88] As a naive, untrained historian when she had written the biography of her grandfather thirty years earlier, she had been ignorant of a multitude of available facts. She now determined to rectify that dearth in a new version entitled *On the Ragged Edge: The Life and Times of Dudley Leavitt*. The appeal of the project was compulsive. Throughout the remainder of 1972 and well into 1973, her diary would reveal her at work with a verve and regularity which she had not shown for some years. She would fret over interruptions as she had long ago and would report herself to have "worked through the wee hours on my D. Leavitt book – To bed at 4 a.m. and not up again until nine."[89] In September she momentarily grew dubious over the project and wondered whether she should instead devote herself to her autobiography. After a frustrating search among the boxes and cabinets that constituted her files – which were, it is to be noted, divided between her Salt Lake and St. George homes – she gratefully surrendered to her grandfather's biography. "I'm angry & upset with myself," she recorded, "because I've put my 'Quicksand and Cactus' away so well that I cannot find it. Will go back to Dudley again with more determination."[90] Day after day, night after night, she pieced together a new manuscript, writing new chapters and sections as necessary and cannibalizing pages torn from Kraut's printing of the original biography when she deemed no rewriting to be mandatory.

In September Juanita attended a meeting of the Utah Historical Society at the University of Utah, where she recognized more completely her status as a venerable senior among Utah historians. There was a session on folk dancing in the Bear Lake region of Utah and Idaho—"so much like ours in the south that it's hard to believe," she commented in her diary. It was withal an absorbing and enheartening day: "I was so warmly received everywhere that I was quite overcome." A day later she wrote: "So worn out after the excitement of yesterday. I can hardly believe the attention I got from everyone."[91] A more formal, though not more valued, honor came in October when Juanita was made a Fellow of the Utah Academy.[92]

In mid-October Karl stayed with Juanita for several nights as he recruited northern Utah students for Dixie College. One evening Kay drove in from Bountiful and joined Karl in an attempt to unclog Juanita's bathtub drain. She noted their success with some ambivalence: "The boys did get the tub so that it drains, only now I use a flat rubber stopper for it. The toilet is not *quite* operating, but I think I'll wait for Ernest."[93] As October ended Juanita traveled to Dixie to celebrate her mother's ninety-fifth birthday and to attend the hearing of the boundary dispute with her neighbor. The birthday observance was held in Mesquite on a Saturday morning in conjunction with Virgin Valley homecoming day. "Such a large crowd as there was!" Juanita wrote. "So many old friends & relatives. They gave Mother a seat on the stand. She had a new dress & an orchid. I spoke briefly; Eva's group sang her original song, composed much ealier. Mom was very pleased."[94]

On Tuesday, October 31, 1972, the hearing on Juanita's property line took place in the county courthouse before a district judge, who tried the case without a jury. The lawyers, presenting documents and calling witnesses, seemed preoccupied with technicalities and precedents. Unable to predict an outcome, Juanita worried greatly. At last, however, the judge rendered a decision distinctly in her favor. The property line, he declared, should be that which the defendant, Juanita Brooks, had claimed; the plaintiff was entitled to no damages; each party to the lawsuit should pay its own costs.[95] Before leaving St. George the next day, Juanita ordered a chain link fence installed along her now legally defined property line, about three feet south of her retaining wall. In Salt Lake, she hosted her attorneys at lunch at the

Lion House and afterward accompanied them to their law firm where she was introduced to their associates.

Juanita was disappointed in November 1972 to learn of the destruction of the Washington church. For over a year she had attended meetings of Cornerstone, the tiny group of Mormons who hoped to effect the preservation of endangered meetinghouses. Early in 1972 she and Maureen Ursenbach, a young Salt Lake historian, toured the antique churches of Spring City, Washington, and Parowan. Soon afterward she consulted with professional house movers regarding the cost of relocating the Washington church: "$10,000 to $15,000 to move just the upper story. More than double the amount for the whole thing."[96] In March she huddled with Ursenbach and a man who was interested in funding the renovation of the threatened building. In August, after she and Ursenbach had inspected the Eighth Ward chapel in Salt Lake, she hopefully recorded: "MAYBE after the Coalville disaster there is a change in attitude among the 'Higher-ups.'"[97] The Washington church was nonetheless razed to make way for a modern building. Following a lengthy conversation with Ursenbach on the matter, she wrote: "We both are grieved at the loss of the beautiful little church in Washington, Utah. Such a gem! And we might have saved it! NO – it was hopeless."[98]

In mid-November she returned to St. George to participate in homecoming at the college. She delivered a brief address at the dedication of the carillon she had donated. Summarizing her career as a student and teacher at Dixie, she recalled that, while taking her sabbatical at Columbia, she had found comfort in the vespers played upon a carillon near her apartment. She hoped her carillon bells would have similar meaning for Dixie students: "They will be valuable only as they are used, and it is my hope that they will be used often and to good purpose, so that the graduates will carry lifelong memories of the Carillon at Dixie."[99]

Juanita celebrated Christmas 1972 at Willa's home in Las Vegas. For Christmas she gave gifts of homemade candy and books. One of the books she gave was *The Christmas Tree*, which Peregrine Press had begun to distribute near the first of December. This thin volume, bound in a white cloth cover, narrated a charming tale. Dismayed that the town of Bunkerville would have no communal Christmas tree, the girls Juanita and Charity scavenged a small mescrew tree from the desert. Illuminated by the flames of the pitchy Yule log, it took on a transcendent glimmer: "I have seen many Christmas Trees since, trees of every shape and kind, but not one so lovely as this. Without electric light bulb or candle, without tinsel or colored balls, it stood a shining, elegant filigree, breath-taking in its symmetry and beauty. Every thorn was a pearl, a shining, precious gem around which all the colors of the rainbow played: coral, pink, flame red, blue, green, yellow, orange—a symphony of color against illuminated white."[100]

The little book sold for $4.50—an exorbitant price, as far as Juanita was concerned. She was surprised that it fared rather well: by December 1973, it would sell 541 copies.[101] She was dismayed by the scenes of village and desert which illustrated its pages. Shortly after seeing the first copies, she wrote the illustrator a letter, lamenting that his rendering of desert plants was inaccurate and that his sketch of the tree showed it as severely asymmetrical and planted in a barrel quite unlike the handsome bucket of varnished slats and brass hoops of her childhood experience: "Here the container looks like a 20 gallon swill barrel or open-headed pickle barrel!" She particularly lamented that during the production of the book she had been unable to reach either the publisher or the illustrator by phone: "Whatever this one little, unimportant publication may mean to anyone else, I hope it will mean to all three of us that people who are sharing the responsibility for bringing out a book should have some communication with each other. A voice over the telephone, if nothing else."[102]

The other book which came off the press in time for Juanita's Christmas giving was *Frontier Tales: True Stories of Real People*. It was produced by Utah State University Press and appeared in both cloth and paperback versions. The eight informal sketches within its fifty-seven pages featured personalities and incidents drawn from the pioneer history of Dixie and from Juanita's childhood. Like many of her other narratives, these were a mingling of fact, folklore, and fiction.

"Sam's Courtship" recounts the adventures of a young Swiss convert who arrived in Santa Clara in 1861, persuaded a girl to marry him, and settled down to a life of hardship and devotion. Simple in the extreme, this biographical narrative lacks the conflict and climax of conventional fiction. In contrast, "The Buckskin Pants" is a well-developed story about a pioneer youth who, deceived into trading new homespun trousers for ragged buckskin pants, made a whip from the buckskin, sold the whip, and bought even better factory-made pants. The longest and best narrative, "The Story of Griz," features the dog from Juanita's childhood whose intelligence, affection, and loyalty had become legendary among the descendants of Henry and Mary Leavitt. Griz made himself the guard of the family's little children, on one occasion preventing the baby from falling into a canal by seizing the seat of its pants in his teeth and on another occasion standing valiantly between the baby and a renegade cow. Collapsing time, Juanita's account has Griz grow old with Henry and shows the elderly Henry telling a town official who wished to dispose of the animal, "I could shoot you a lot easier than I could shoot that dog."[103]

After the holidays, Juanita faced the rigors of a Salt Lake January with the distaste of a native desert dweller. "Snow and more snow! all day yesterday and now this morning. It's impossible to keep any walks open," she recorded.[104] On the evening of January 4, 1973, she set out with friends for a meeting in Ogden; she was "much relieved to be back alive" after icy roads and fog forced the travelers to abort their trip.

Indoors she continued to write. Although a February deadline loomed for a paper on Silver Reef, she found it difficult to tear herself away from the Dudley Leavitt biography. With her perennial eagerness for discovery, she perused her brother Francis's thesis on Bunkerville and studied the federal censuses which enumerated Dudley and his dependents. In early January she had thought to pause, but found she could "hardly stop." Following a restless night in late January, she had a bath and a shampoo while she debated over "what I shall plunge into today." The decision went to the biography.[105] By then she had produced over 100 pages recounting Dudley's life before 1861. In March she would readily secure a contract with the Utah Historical Society for the publication of the revised work.

When at last Juanita paid attention to the Silver Reef project, she found herself equally interested. Traveling to Dixie for a funeral in January, she toured the site of Silver Reef with Eva and Walter—"a very valuable trip for me," she wrote. "Greatly surprised by the number of new homes going up."[106] On a snowy day a week later she went to the Kearns Mansion ostensibly to do her part as a board member in greeting visiting legislators. "I did not even see them," she confessed to her diary, so busy had she become upstairs reading a thesis on Silver Reef.[107]

On the evening of February 21, 1973, she delivered her paper in Provo. "Silver Reef: Fact and Folklore" was one of a series of monthly

lectures sponsored by the Charles Redd Center for Western Studies at
BYU; it would appear in a publication of the series in 1974. In it
Juanita followed the fortunes of the non-Mormon mining town in northeastern Washington County between its founding in 1875 and its
decline in the late 1880s. Predictably, she provided valuable facts in
abundance: bachelor miners often lived in dugouts in the hillsides
near the mills; white women were forbidden to consort with Chinese
laborers; local authorities broke a strike by arresting fractious Irish
miners. However, not even in its published version was the article notable for polish and proportion. Juanita prefaced it with a largely irrelevant chronology of events in early Utah history. In keeping with her
usual practice, she failed to document her sources closely. There were
abrupt transitions and instances of obscure reasoning. "The 1880
census," she declared in a puzzling non sequitur, "is not a true picture
of Silver Reef at its peak, but there were few people there in 1870, and
by 1890 only 177 remained. Nor do I wish to go into detail in the
study of the 1880 records; I need only a man's birthplace, occupation,
and age. The total population numbered 1,112. All are listed as belonging to the white race except thirty-six Chinese, one Indian, and one
Black."[108] At a moment when her mind was beginning to fail and she
stood most in need of constructive criticism, her reputation was such
that editors tended to print her drafts as she submitted them.

In mid-March Juanita flew to Albuquerque and stayed a
weekend with Tony and Janet, who displayed enthusiasm for the hunting, husbandry, and cuisine of gamebirds. As she left Juanita hid cur-
rency in places where Tony and Janet would be sure to find it.
"Antone," she wrote in a subsequent letter, "I'd like it if you would
apply the bill in the bottle towards your new shot gun. . . . And, Janet,
the one in the car was just a contribution to cover extras such as inci-
dentals as prunes and feasts of wonderful game birds." In the same
letter she reported that she had received a letter from her sister Aura,
whose lucidity was an encouraging "sign that she is normal again for a
few weeks. She has these periods of depression that are hard for her to
shake off." Juanita also declared her intention of mailing "a contribution to Aunt Charity & Uncle Vernon,"[109] who were serving as missionaries.

The spring of 1973 brought Juanita an unusual academic
experience. At the urging of Charles Peterson, the Department of History and Geography at Utah State University retained her services

for spring quarter—March 27 to June 9—as a full-time instructor. His purpose in seeing her hired, Peterson wrote, was to expose Utah State students "to your great knowledge and to the special enthusiasm and integrity you bring to the study of history in our locality."[110] She rented an apartment just off campus and on days of instruction climbed the steps onto the campus amid greening lawns and burgeoning trees. On the top floor of Old Main she taught two graduate courses. One was a colloquium in western history with emphasis upon Utah; in this course she discussed books which, by her previous assignment, her students had read. The other was a seminar in which each student pursued a research project, wrote a formal paper, and presented it before the class. In addition, Juanita delivered a number of lectures before Peterson's undergraduate class in Utah history.

It was a strenuous yet gratifying experience. She wrote Willa concerning the stair climbing: "It didn't hurt me any, really, but it made me realize that I am not as young as I used to be."[111] Her remuneration was $5,000—"a real professor's pay. Can't believe it!" she wrote her nephew Carrick and his wife.[112] It is probable that her students and even her fellow instructors accorded her a respect approaching veneration. Her numerous Cache Valley friends crowded close around, inviting her to lunch and dinner and taking her to plays, lectures, and club meetings. She contemplated attending Sunday service in a modernistic Lutheran church which stood near her apartment. Learning of the minister's reputation for militancy against Mormons, she finally decided against that adventure.[113]

As her assignment at Utah State came to a close, Juanita was given formal honors at other institutions. On June 2, 1973, the University of Utah awarded her an honorary doctorate of humane letters. Her photograph appearing in the *University of Utah Review* shows her garbed in a velvet robe and a mortarboard from which dangles a white tassel. Her seamed, bespectacled face wears a grimace in place of a smile. She seems both terrified and profoundly pleased. Four days later, again in academic regalia, she attended the baccalaureate service of Dixie College and received a tribute for her service to that institution.[114]

In the early summer *The History of the Jews in Utah and Idaho* appeared. Juanita's pleasure at seeing the book at long last in print was quickly marred by negative reviews. On July 1 the *Salt Lake Tribune*, which for years had consistently praised her books, asserted that her latest work dealt with its topic "awkwardly, haltingly, tritely—and with a lack of style and a confusion of errors that is at once sad and surprising in a book by Juanita Brooks."[115] Phoning Harold Schindler, an injured and protesting Juanita learned that Jack Goodman, an occasional *Tribune* writer, was the author of the unsigned review.[116] Scholarly reviews appeared more slowly but deprecated the book with equal vehemence. A reviewer for *Western States Jewish Historical Quarterly* was brutal in his belittlement of Juanita's performance. She had ignored a variety of pertinent periodical articles and had failed to use "at first hand the readily available microfilms of English-language Jewish newspapers of nineteenth century America." The acerb critic concluded: "We hope that this inadequate book doesn't close the door on a better one. From our viewpoint, it has left the field wide open."[117]

The History of the Jews in Utah and Idaho was indeed Juanita's worst book. In it she offered a welter of trivial facts, as if evidence had been so difficult to come by that she could not forbear including every morsel. For example, she provided numerous lists of names, noting those in attendance at private gatherings and public meetings and reproducing the mortuary lists of the three Salt Lake congregations over many years. Furthermore, she failed to characterize the Jews methodically. Only incidentally did she allude to the social customs and religious beliefs that distinguished them from other ethnic groups. She also failed to organize her materials with a thoroughgoing logic. She relied excessively upon chronological arrangement, reporting events simply as they happened rather than clustering them according to category, trend, or principle. Often she was careless with transitions, failing to clarify the relationship between some new incident or condition and her ongoing narrative. Finally, her style was pedestrian and repetitious. It did not lack lucidity, yet failed utterly of verve and elegance. The work was not significantly enhanced by the fact that one of its late chapters was written by Louis Zucker, whose name appeared beneath the chapter title. It is ironic that Zucker, a revered writing instructor, responded to Juanita's early drafts with such disapproval that he hindered rather than encouraged improvement.

Its faults notwithstanding, Juanita's book made a contribution to western history. Paying brief attention to the Jews of Idaho and of rural Utah, it emphasized the Jews of Salt Lake, who flourished in sufficient numbers to establish permanent congregations. After B'nai

Israel, the first congregation, was organized in 1884, quarrels over doctrine and ritual quickly arose and the first rabbi departed before completing his contracted year. Although its rabbis came and went with
disturbing regularity for several decades, B'nai Israel eventually emerged
as a Reform congregation. In 1889 Orthodox and Conservative Jews
combined to form the Congregation Montefiore. Around 1918 an
Orthodox-group, splintering from the Congregation Montefiore, created the Sharey Tzedek congregation, which persisted for several
decades before dying out. It was dissension rather than numbers which
led to three congregations and their respective synagogues. "Not only
was there competition between the congregations," Juanita tersely wrote,
"but too often there was a definite bitterness and scorn each for the
other. Nowhere could they come to a meeting of the minds."[118] It was
a hopeful sign, she concluded, that in 1959 Congregation Montefiore
and B'nai Israel at last joined forces in building a Jewish Community
Center.

      The book abounds with interesting particulars. In 1864
Brigham Young donated ground for a Jewish cemetery. In 1877 a rabbi
visiting Salt Lake commented: "All the Jews here are Gentiles."[119] In
the dark days of the federal campaign against polygamy, two prominent Salt Lake Jews, Fred Simon and Isadore Morris, spoke out in
favor of the beleaguered Mormons. The success of Jews as civil leaders
is demonstrated by the fact that both Idaho and Utah elected Jewish
governors, Moses Alexander and Simon Bamberger, respectively. The
chapter devoted to the latter is perhaps the best in the book, giving a
coherent narrative of his remarkable life. As a young man, the German-
born Simon Bamberger maintained a store and banking service at the
construction sites of the advancing transcontinental railroad. Fearing
robbery, he moved to Salt Lake, where he soon made a fortune in
mining investments, thereafter building spur railroads and creating
the Lagoon amusement park. He was elected governor of Utah in 1916
by an impressive majority. Among many useful endeavors, he sponsored legislation establishing a public utilities commission and a
workman's compensation law.

      It is unlikely that Juanita brooded long over the inadequa-
cies of her Jewish history. She had returned from Logan eager to write.
Her first project was an affirmative review of Charles Peterson's recently
published *Take Up Your Mission: Mormon Colonizing Along the Little
Colorado River, 1870–1900*. Her review, which would appear in the

New Mexico Historical Review, expressed her particular interest in Peterson's evidence that scarcely one in ten of the Utah Mormons called into the windswept desolation of northern Arizona remained as a permanent settler. For Juanita, it was a further sign of the callous indifference with which Brigham Young and his successors had condemned their subordinates to poverty and privation. "The human waste, in time, energy, suffering," she wrote, "is beyond measure."[120]

By coincidence, near the time Juanita wrote her review Peterson was writing a critique of her manuscript biography of Emma Lee. Upon her return from Logan, Juanita had forwarded the manuscript to Mary Washington, who in turn passed it on to Peterson for evaluation. Having recommended that Washington publish the work, Peterson wrote Juanita a letter mingling praise and suggestions for improvement. She should, he wrote, divide a certain long chapter and should provide documentation, particularly for the years following the death of John D. Lee.[121] "I am so pleased to have you go over that Emma Lee manuscript," Juanita replied in an acquiescent mood. "I always tell my classes, and remind myself often that: 'There is No such thing as *good* writing; there is only good *re-writing.*' "[122] For the remainder of 1973 this biography was Juanita's chief preoccupation. She researched in archives in Salt Lake and elsewhere, wrote numerous letters, and leafed through her own collection of pioneer accounts. Unfortunately, she would uncover few other sources for Emma Lee's later life than unauthenticated stories told by the modern Lee family.[123]

As the summer progressed, Juanita cooperated with the editorial staff at the Utah Historical Society in rounding out her facts and polishing her style in the revision of the Dudley Leavitt biograpy. In late August, having agreed that a copious offering of family pictures would be appropriate, she gathered photographs from her Leavitt relatives.[124] During August she came to an understanding with the Utah Historical Society that she would edit the diary of pioneer Martha Spence Heywood. This extraordinary diary had first come into Juanita's hands while she collected for the Emergency Relief Administration in 1935. After having copied it, she had returned the original diary to its owner in Panguitch and had thereafter lost sight of it. Since early 1971, staff members at the Kearns Mansion had expressed interest in an edition based upon the typed copy. Now, in 1973, the society's publications director officially promised "to provide the necessary editorial backup including . . . the indexing and proof reading."[125]

Another important project to which Juanita committed herself during the summer of 1973 was "Quicksand and Cactus." For years
she had exhorted herself to resume serious work on the aborted autobiography. In early 1972 she submitted old chapters to the University
of Oklahoma Press, which proved uninterested.[126] In April of 1972
she wrote a brief reminiscence entitled "All on a Summer Day," which
she intended to enter in a short story contest. "Even if it does not get
a prize," she consoled herself, "it will make a short chapter in my
'Quicksand & Cactus,' which, by the way, I should get at."[127] In March
1973 Juanita reported that an unspecified party at the University of
Utah was interested in underwriting the publication of the work.[128]
In July, she delivered "about 150 pages—the opening chapters of 'Quicksand & Cactus,' up to the loss of my pony" to Everett Cooley, Brigham
Madsen, and Lyman Tyler at the university.[129] Cooley soon clarified
that he and his colleagues were serving as intermediaries for Obert C.
Tanner. In his usual discreet manner, this scholarly businessman and
philanthropist had asked the three to persuade Juanita to go forward
with her autobiography on a stipend which he would provide. He had
also agreed to their recommendation that the finished work be published by the University of Utah Press. Accordingly, Cooley gave the
manuscript to Norma Mikkelsen, who had recently replaced Richard
Thurman as director of the press. With this, Juanita was indubitably
engaged, although this project, like the Martha Spence Heywood diary,
would have to wait until she had satisfied other obligations.

During the late summer Juanita joined her Logan friends
at Ione Bennion's cabin in the Uinta Mountains. While the men har-
dily fished in the rain, the women enjoyed the comforts of a blazing
fire and relaxed conversation in the cabin. In October Juanita delivered an address before the Utah Library Association in the Hotel
Utah. A satisfied official warmly complimented her "outstanding"
remarks.[130] During the following week Juanita was awarded an honorary life membership in the Western History Association at its annual
conference in Fort Worth, Texas.[131] Such satisfactions were diminished by the return of fall weather and cold feet. As October ended,
Ernest mailed his mother a heating pad from Las Vegas with solicitous instructions: "I'd turn it to either Med. or Low and put it between
the sheets prior to going to bed, and when my feet got warm enough I
would simply move them away, leaving the pad on till morning. I would
also use it to drape over my feet while I was sitting at the typewriter.

There is no reason to ever have cold feet for more than a few moments any more as long as you are home. You might even take to carrying it with you on trips away from home."[132]

In February 1974 Juanita was honored by a reception at the Kearns Mansion for her latest book, *On the Ragged Edge: The Life and Times of Dudley Leavitt*. Sales were brisk; by April 1,200 copies had sold.[133] Numerous copies moved through Juanita's own network of cousins strategically placed among the multitudinous descendants of Dudley Leavitt. In Juanita's estimation, the book had a single irritating flaw. Amid some eighteen pages of photographs of the extended Leavitt family was a portrait of Janet Smith, Dudley's Indian wife. Juanita was alarmed lest the spots and smears on the old tintype, accentuated by the printing process, be interpreted as a belittlement of her cousins who bore Indian blood. "I was so whopping *MAD* when that ugly thing came out," she wrote to one of Janet's descendants, "that I had enough made up of these others to go in every book that has been printed." She ordered that the tintype be restored and that the improved image of Janet be reproduced in some several thousand copies. She inserted the picture in each of the unsold copies of the book and mailed packets to relatives asking that they distribute the picture "to all of Grandpa Dudley's descendants who do not have them." She was careful to give instructions "to lay them cross-wise on the bottom of the page, so they won't cover the print of Uncle Lister's family picture."[134] In the picture Juanita so widely disseminated, Janet stands in a full skirt, an attractive young woman with a sheen in her long black hair and a slight, bemused smile on her face. Behind this native of the Great Basin desert is an incredible backdrop, the painted shoreline of a lake in the Italian Alps.

In her preface Juanita alluded to the unsatisfactory reprint of the first edition. With an uncharacteristic disregard for truth, she asserted that it had been the unnamed printer (Ogden Kraut), rather than she herself, who had initiated and vended that printing. "I now believe that he had it all done before he approached me on the subject," she fibbed.[135] Her reason for revising the first edition, she went on to explain, was to make available "much new material" regarding Dudley and the extended Leavitt families and to give "a better overall picture of the times and places in which the families lived."[136] Unquestionably, the new edition amplified the fund of published facts about Dudley and his relatives and described in richer detail the activities of frontier

Mormonism in which the youthful Dudley took part. Yet in proportion and effect the second edition was manifestly inferior to the first. Many of the new facts Juanita supplied were trivial. For example, she provided a tedious catalog of each wagon and its occupants among a numerous company of Leavitts and other Mormon converts who migrated from Canada to Illinois in 1837. Sometimes her transitions were abrupt or her arrangement illogical. For instance, she introduced the summary which Dudley's father had made of his ancestry and conversion, not when her own narrative treated these subjects, but at the moment of his death on the Iowa plains. Juanita was too old and ailing to treat new facts and episodes in a graceful, compelling way. This version of the biography of her grandfather would not displace the original version from its rank among her finest works.

During the winter and spring of 1974 Juanita worked many hours on the biography of Emma Lee, which was scheduled for immediate production at Utah State University Press. At the same time she geared up for her autobiography. Norma Mikkelsen of the University of Utah Press had by this time given a tentative arrangement to the disparate chapters which had come into her hands during the preceding summer; these, composed long ago, brought Juanita's life to the threshold of adolescence with the loss of her pony Selah and her entrance into high school. Mikkelsen had assigned Trudy McMurrin, daughter of Sterling McMurrin, to serve as a developmental editor who would advise and encourage Juanita in her task. To celebrate the relationship, Juanita took Mikkelsen and McMurrin to the Lion House for lunch where, in McMurrin's words, "Juanita got the biggest kick out of having a pass because it meant she was a Mormon in good standing. She was just tickled to death; she felt very naughty [although] we were all making this big effort to be professional. . . . "[137] There were other meetings at the press and lengthy telephone conversations in which McMurrin listened to Juanita's ideas and made suggestions about new chapters which would take Juanita's life forward through her education, her marriage to Ernest, and her teaching career as a young widow. Following such discussions, McMurrin sometimes prepared written outlines for Juanita, who seemed notably bereft of direction and procedure. Even in those happier, more vigorous days when Dale Morgan had been her mentor, Juanita had been loath to attribute significance to her own life. Furthermore, she had on many occasions declared that she could never write about her brief, anguished marriage to Ernest. Responding to the gentle prodding of Mikkelsen and McMurrin, who sometimes wept with her, she accepted that painful duty.

As she began to write, Juanita gathered memories from her mother and siblings. In March and April 1974 she exchanged reminiscing letters with Aura, who, despite her frequent bouts of depression, possessed an excellent memory and had as a young woman kept a detailed diary: "You ask about our years in Las Vegas," Aura wrote. "Charity & Velma Waite went down there, to work in Lambert's Cafe. Soon after arriving there, they wrote for me to come—Lambert needed a dish washer. I was young but strong and tickled pink to think my parents gave their consent for me to go. Pa warned me and talked to me about going to that wicked place—for me to hold my head and not get taken up with flattering words of men that was just laying around Las Vegas, to entice young, green girls, to listen to their tales."[138]

In April, Juanita gave an interview which would usefully adumbrate the episodes of "Quicksand and Cactus." Her interviewers were Maureen Ursenbach and Davis Bitton, both employed at the Church Historian's Office, which had recently come into an encouraging liberalization under Church Historian Leonard J. Arrington. From Juanita's rambling dicussion, Ursenbach and Bitton condensed and polished a piece that would appear in *Dialogue* as "Riding Herd: A Conversation with Juanita Brooks." The interviewers returned in June with a photographer, from whose photographs an artist created sketches of Juanita. Reproduced with the interview, the sketches revealed Juanita in transition: elderly and uncertain, yet reflective, resigned, and wise.

Of great interest is the raw typescript of the April interview. One sees that Ursenbach and Bitton performed an enormous reconstruction in the published piece: culling and combining episodes, recomposing sentences, adding transitions. Mercilessly, the chaotic typescript reveals Juanita's mumblings, shifts, and confusions. She was aware, she told her interlocutors, "that I'm aging and I'm afraid I'm not going to last this thing ['Quicksand and Cactus'] out. Where I've been well in my life, but now lately I make a batch of candy that you have to stir all the time and my arm will just ache will ache all night. I'll have to get up and rub the darn thing." She was reluctant to speak of the incredible incident when the eccentric little man, guided by an uncanny force, had found and blessed the suffering Ernest. "But I tremble at this thing I've undertaken," she said. "I don't want it to be ridiculous and I don't want to presume to tell things that are better untold."[139]

In June 1974 Juanita enjoyed an adventure. At the invitation of Claudia Bushman, she flew to Massachusetts where, in suburban Belmont, she addressed a formal gathering sponsored by *The Woman's Exponent 2*. Because the Church had recently abandoned the *Relief Society Magazine*, liberal Mormon women had established this journal, named for a Mormon women's publication of the nineteenth century. Perhaps a month before her departure, Juanita became anxious about the distant journey among strangers and experienced a "terrible night when I struggled with indecision and doubt, such a night as I have never had before."[140] With daylight her equanimity returned. As she traveled, she had two hours to change planes in Chicago: "I almost needed them," she reported, "for the distance seemed like a 10-mile cross-country run."[141] When she had returned, Juanita reported great satisfaction. She had been impressed by Bushman's attainments, which included teaching a university course in the history of American women, and had responded warmly to her children and to her husband, who was a stake president. "Your husband reminds me of my own in his attitude toward you and your work," she wrote Bushman. "That is the highest praise I can give any man." She also admired the determination of the staff of *The Women's Exponent 2*, whom she called "all true Pioneers, bound to arrive!" She predicted success for the journal although certain women in Salt Lake had told her "that not until it is accepted by the [all-male] Priesthood can it ever succeed! We shall see! They MUST accept it, I think."[142] The dissenter had by no means died in the aging Juanita.

Within days of her return, Juanita attended the western writers conference at Utah State University. Following that, she settled in for an extended period of concentrated work on "Quicksand and Cactus"—which, sensing her growing debility, she had come to think of as her final work. Testily she wrote her children: "I feel strongly that if I am ever to get this last book into print, I must stay with it, and not be running hither & yon on some silly errand or another."[143] She continued to consult her relatives about their common past. To her mother she wrote: "Thank you so much for this nice, long letter. It was exactly the kind of thing that I want, because it tells so much of your early life. In school did the teachers require you to memorize very much, or did you mostly just read? Did you have many books, or were you kept close to your Readers? I'm sure you put on last-day-of-school programs, or Christmas Programs. Tell me about some of them."[144] By early August, Juanita had produced a substantial manuscript covering her later teen years, her marriage to Ernest, and the early years of her widowhood. "I must contact Norma at the University Press today, also," she wrote Todd and Betty Berens. "Now that I have myself working in the dining room of the boarding-house at the Gyp Mine and plaster mill I can summarize the season in a few sentences. Writing the account of the winter with one dress will be, I think, fun to do. I'm never sure when to go into detail."[145]

Juanita's disposition for movement soon exerted itself. Her letter to the Berens came on the heels of a pleasant mid-summer visit to their lovely home in Santa Ana, California. The Berens gave Juanita a tour, with knowledgeable commentary, of the historic Catholic missions of southern California. "Pictures, printed words, or talk-talk with slides," she wrote, "can never come as near the reality as actually walking over the ground and seeing the furniture, the precious treasures of gold and jewels, the evidence of the wise guidance of those first Christian missionaries." As she wrote her letter of thanks to the Berens, Juanita was already planning another trip. Despite evident inconveniences, she intended to escort her mother, who had been staying with Juanita's brothers in Idaho, to a family wedding in Dixie. Her brothers, she reported, thought "that it's just silly to spend all that time and money just to get Grandma to a wedding. I admit all of it, but insist that if it is important to her, I'm going to see that she gets there. So I'll fly to Boise—only a 45 minute journey—and one of them can bring her to there in his de lux car, we'll fly back to here [Salt Lake], change planes and go on to Cedar City. For her, it will be quite an adventure. She'll love it!"[146] Juanita did as she had planned, and when the wedding was over, she reversed the complicated itinerary and accompanied Mary to the home of Melvin and Myrtle in Nampa, Idaho. Juanita paused with her brother and sister- in-law long enough to inspect their immaculate, well-tilled farm where the principal crop was hybrid seed corn. As for the ninety-seven-year-old Mary, Juanita could inform a correspondent that she was in good health. "She reads and writes very well, indeed, but her fingers will not play the guitar or net and sew as they did when she was young."[147]

One assumes that Juanita went on through the fall of 1974 in a customary fashion—answering questions posed by the staff at Utah

State University Press about the Emma Lee manuscript; working as her mood allowed on "Quicksand and Cactus"; thinking a good deal about the Martha Spence Heywood project; and permitting herself to be enormously distracted by friends and relatives, by visits, plays, and funerals. What she actually did is not evident. The record becomes sparse because her habit of preserving correspondence had faltered.

If her personal powers declined, her fame did not. When she had received the honorary doctorate from the University of Utah, Wendell J. Ashton, director of public communications for the Church, wrote of his high esteem: "I have long admired your fairness, your thoroughness, your courage, and your skill as a writer in giving to us some of our finest literature in Utah history."[148] It was significant that a high-ranking Mormon official could accord her his sincere congratulations. Of perhaps greater significance was the fact that in November 1974 Juanita autographed 100 copies of *The Mountain Meadows Massacre* at Deseret Book Store in Salt Lake, the central official retail book outlet of the Church.[149] One imagines Juanita at a table in the store, busily scribbling her name. One hopes she was not too old and tired to relish the victory she had won.

CHAPTER • TWELVE

IN THE PERSPECTIVE OF
THE CENTURIES

As 1975 opened, Juanita worried increasingly about her mother, who could no longer live alone. Juanita felt especially guilty over the stress Mary underwent as she rotated among the homes of her offspring. On a February morning Juanita awoke with a firm resolve. Karl should act immediately to raze Mary's little house, which sat next to Juanita's, and on the site construct a new house for his family. Then, when he had vacated Juanita's house, she would return to St. George and take in Mary and live with her "until one or both of us steps out over the edge."[1]

It was not to be hoped, Juanita wrote her children from Salt Lake, that the construction of Karl's new house could advance with the speed of Willa's and Thales'. The Derricks had moved in November 1974 to St. George, where Thales, now retired from the air force, had taken a position in the college administration. Their handsome new house, overlooking the town from the slope of Black Ridge, would be ready in May. Nonetheless, Juanita had been instructed by "the Little Man on My Shoulder"—by an imperative intuition, that is—that Karl should proceed immediately. "This may come as something of a surprise to some of you. It does to me, in fact, for I really love this little house, too. My time here has been happy and rewarding, and things just might work out so that I can come back to it. I'll probably rent or lease it—but then, I'll cross that bridge when I get to it."[2]

In early March Juanita traveled to St. George to help remove Mary's goods so that her little house could be torn down. Thales, who had drawn plans for his new house, drew the plans for Karl's, and by mid-summer construction would be in progress. In the meantime, Juanita vacillated over her promise to return to St. George. "Life presses too close on me—too many pulls in opposite directions—too many decisions," she wrote with a weak, scrawling pen to Todd and Betty Berens in June. She was "trying desperately to finish this 'Quicksand

& Cactus' deal, but find it hard to stay with it—hard to follow my own advice to others 'Glue the seat of your pants to the seat of the chair and *Stay There.'*"³ This narrative, the completion of which seemed her sole reason for remaining in Salt Lake, had come to a standstill at the point of her marriage to Will. She could think of little to add to the account of her later years which had already appeared in the final chapters of *Uncle Will Tells His Story.*

Her inertia also derived from a painful debility. In April she returned to the physician who had fitted her with a pessary some seven years earlier. The doctor removed the pessary and ordered her to go a month without a replacement. "Alone, I'd pray, and cry, and curse, and just almost lose consciousness," she confided to Ione Bennion. Grimly, she tried "to endure to the end of the month to which I was sentenced, to spend periods of suffering which I had not experienced since my last baby was born." She heroically departed with her mother for Albuquerque to pay a visit to Tony and Janet. "Mother is a wonderful traveller," she continued. "I managed, and the trip was a delight—except for the bad times for me. She knew nothing of these." Mercifully refitted with the device before the end of the thirty day period, Juanita declared herself " 'cured' or 'healed' and all normal again. But don't ask me when I'll go back. . . . I've lived almost long enough now, and undisturbed again I think I will last several years."⁴

In June Juanita was awarded an honorary membership in Phi Beta Kappa at the University of Utah. According to the president of the local chapter, this recognition was "reserved for a distinguished individual in the community who, by contributions in the fields of liberal and humanistic studies, has demonstrated allegiance to the ideals of scholarship which Phi Beta Kappa seeks to nurture. The special nominating committee which reviewed candidates for honorary election this year submitted your name with enthusiasm, and it was approved by acclamation of the Chapter membership."⁵On the same day, June 6, 1975, Juanita received in absentia an award cosponsored by Dixie College and Southern Heritage Writers' Guild for, according to her citation, "scholarly documentary writing and ability to epitomize pioneer background."⁶

Another matter for good cheer in the early summer of 1975 was the appearance of *Emma Lee* under the imprint of Utah State University Press. Cast in a lean, prosaic style, this biography sketched a life remarkable for heroic endurance. At twenty-one Emma Batchelor emigrated from England to Utah, unfortunately attaching herself to the ill-fated Martin handcart company, which suffered well over a hundred deaths in early storms on the Wyoming plains. A plucky survivor, Emma shortly became the seventeenth wife of John D. Lee. She proved one of the few of his spouses who remained loyal during the period of his excommunication and exile. It was she whom he established, with her children, in the sterile wastes of Lonely Dell, where, in her husband's frequent absences, she maintained a garden and operated the ferry. Two years after Lee's execution, Emma sold the ferry and migrated to Arizona with the assistance of a kindly prospector, Franklin H. French. Ostracized by the Mormons because of her connection with the disgraced Lee, she soon married French and cast her lot with the gentile population of the railroad town of Winslow. There she maintained a maternity home to which wives from roundabout ranches could come for delivery. Known as Doctor French, she also became a self-taught general practitioner who set bones and sutured wounds.

For the scholarly and the fastidious, this biography left much to be desired. It lacked footnotes and an index. Fictional qualities—intimate descriptions, dialogue, and introspection—alternated with objective narrative. Often the narrative suffered from abrupt transitions, repetition, and incoherence. It suffered, too, from Juanita's reticence to describe rigorously the exceptional privations which Emma experienced. Quickly summarizing the losses of the Martin handcart company in Wyoming, Juanita failed to mention certain grisly facts: a desperate emigrant removed the shawl from a dead baby whose mother had placed it on a pile of corpses; Emma herself salvaged the clothes from a corpse. Juanita alluded to these horrors at a later, less effective point in her narrative. When describing the death of two children in the collapse of a rain-sodden fort, Juanita was again unable to confront the full impact of the tragedy to which Emma was a witness. Of the crushed children she moralized: "The sweet little things went instantly without fear or pain—transported into another life in the twinkling of an eye. They would be happy in their new home."[7]

Yet *Emma Lee* was a useful, even compelling book, a notable addition to Juanita's treatment of the pioneer past. From its pages emerged a woman of exceptional courage and endurance. For example, in October of 1873 Emma gave birth to a daughter at Lonely Dell attended by only her children. She made her preparations, endured the contractions, tied the baby's cord, and had her eldest son bury the placenta. When Jacob Hamblin came by three days later, he found Emma at her regular work. The book also demonstrated the rippling effect of the Mountain Meadows massacre upon those related to John D. Lee. Juanita attributed the suicide of Victoria, Emma's teen-aged daughter, to ostracism resulting from the scapegoating of her father: "To the third and fourth generation, descendants of John D. Lee were rejected: refused admittance to clubs, kept out of offices, never considered on the same social level as others. Children in the lower grades could not join in the games at recess. One does not need to guess the cause of this [Victoria's] desire to escape."[8] To the end of her writing career Juanita remained the minstrel of the Mountain Meadows massacre.

As the fall of 1975 approached, she found herself able to research and write with a renewed concentration. Her work on the life of Martha Spence Heywood, hitherto desultory, now steadied. From a great-granddaughter of Heywood she learned of the whereabouts of the original diary, which she had not seen since 1935. According to this descendant, the present owner, a grandson, was curious as to the provenance of Juanita's copy. "He will appreciate it very much if you will put in writing the details of how you obtained the Martha Spence Heywood Journal and how it was taken from you. He thought the Journal had always been in the family. How it left the family and how it got back to the family intrigues him."[9] In September the great-granddaughter forwarded a photocopy of a small portion of the original. "I'm so grateful that I can't express it for the assurance this bit of a photostat gives me. They had a minor celebration at the Mansion House, I understand," Juanita wrote, alluding to the jubilation among the staff of the Utah Historical Society, who were assisting in editing the diary.[10] Her expression of gratitude aroused a greater generosity. Soon the family sent her the complete diary on temporary loan. By its means she could correct the typescript, whose accuracy she had good reason to doubt.

Although Juanita worked with some of her former eagerness and dedication, she was in fact suffering from a progressive senility. She was, at it were, a wounded warrior, baffled by the swarm of details which her topic presented and susceptible to periods of confusion. In September she agreed to accompany Fae Dix to the funeral of professor Jack Adamson. She arrived at Fae's door at seven-fifteen in the morning, frantic lest she be late. "I brought her in," Fae recorded, "cooked some cereal, and made her rest awhile before driving her back home. She had been up all night writing, and had gotten 'off center' as she calls it. I later dressed and returned her for the service which was at noon. . . . We later came to my house for soup and salad . . . and spoke of the beautiful Mozart work played at the Memorial—and of the poetic tributes."[11] This incident was indicative of Juanita's altered habits. She often worked through the night in her barren basement workroom and slept through the day in another barren basement room—although there were handsomely furnished bedrooms on the ground floor. Her refrigerator was typically unstocked, and to visitors she made a joke of the minuscule meals which she irregularly prepared for herself.

Juanita's impulse to work on the Heywood diary had spent itself by mid-fall. She could not now evade turning her attention to "Quicksand and Cactus." She had no zest for carrying the narrative beyond her wedding to Will, where she had halted months earlier. For one thing, she was at a loss to apportion an equable treatment among the nine children who belonged to the compound-complex family she and Will had created. For another, her own doings seemed now, as they always had, trivial and unworthy of serious consideration. Gently goaded by Trudy McMurrin, she resumed her onerous task. In October she reviewed Will's diaries. "I'm far behind where I should be in this 'Quicksand & Cactus' deal," she wrote Ernest, adding nostalgically: "Uncle Will kept daily diaries of our stay in Salt Lake, our trip to the fair, and our association with your family—such happy days for us all. He certainly is great for detail."[12] Slowly a few sparse episodes emerged from her typewriter. McMurrin constantly urged her to expand, rendering scenes in greater detail, interpolating other incidents, citing further examples. Sometimes, in a mood to talk, Juanita phoned McMurrin in the late afternoon. From her desk at the press, McMurrin waved good-bye to her departing colleagues. Phone at her ear, she patiently jotted notes on Juanita's rambling reminiscences, from which hopefully would emerge suggestions for further revisions.[13]

As usual, Juanita maintained a steady round of visits and outings with friends and relatives. On a June evening she and Fae Dix attended a reception in honor of Ben Roe. "When we came out a flaming sunset enchanted us," Fae recorded, "so we went for a drive in the sweet air. Juanita [was] vivacious and happy."[14] In August Juanita took Todd and Betty Berens, who had traveled from California, to lunch at the Lion House and afterward conducted them to her home and offered them a bed for an afternoon nap. In the evening she introduced the Berens to Clair and LaVon and listened to the shop talk in which the two couples engaged regarding junior high school teaching. In September, Todd Berens mailed Juanita a copy of her biography of John D. Lee and a pre-stamped mailer, requesting that she inscribe and mail it to one of the students who had participated in a trail-finding field trip. "And," he added, "if the spirit should move you, feel free to add any of your comments which will encourage her in her research work."[15]

In October Juanita flew to Cedar City, stayed a night with her brother Dudley, and rode with him to Mesquite to attend the Virgin Valley homecoming. As the sister and brother descended the Virgin Narrows by the recently completed freeway, they conjectured about the route their father might have followed when as a boy he had driven the mail buckboard between St. George and Bunkerville.[16] Near the same moment, Juanita adapted to the fact that Ernest had become seriously attached to a woman who was not a Mormon. A pretty Chicana of Catholic background, Maria worked as a waitress in the casino where Ernest worked as a guard. "All roads may lead to God if the person involved tries to find one," Juanita reassuringly wrote Ernest and Maria, concluding: "Well, let's keep in touch as we can. You're a Great Couple in my Book."[17]

In December Juanita's friend Geneva Larson died in Provo. "She was sitting in her big chair, the shovel on the floor, dead. She had been shoveling the snow from her walks," Juanita wrote to her mother, perhaps mindful that she herself, nearly seventy-eight, often shoveled snow from her walks. Karl, who happened to be in Salt Lake, put Juanita on a bus for Provo, where she attended an evening viewing and, the next morning, the funeral. After the viewing, friends from the BYU faculty took Juanita to a meeting of the local chapter of the Utah Historical Society, where everyone, as Juanita wrote her mother, "made quite a fuss of my being there." As 1975 ended Juanita still planned to move to St. George and take Mary into her home as soon as she had completed "Quicksand and Cactus." Concluding her letter to her mother, she apologized for not having yet lived up to her promise. "Don't get too out of patience with me. I'll try to stay-put and see if I can wind this silly thing off. It is really labor, though. I make so many errors. May hire a typist."[18]

Juanita's remorse was sharply intensified in early 1976 when Mary suffered a stroke. In March Juanita visited Mary in a St. George nursing home. Noting that the unconscious woman had a strong pulse and normal temperature, Juanita concluded that she was being unnecessarily sedated. Traveling on to visit Tony and Janet in Albuquerque, she struggled with herself. At last she sat at Tony's typewriter and addressed a letter to all her children, confessing that she carried "a heavy load of guilt. I should have been [t]here all the time and kept her in my home as I promised to do. Now, after two night's arguing with myself, I'm ready to do that." She was determined, she declared, to dispose of her Salt Lake house, buy a wheelchair for Mary, and settle down to care for her in the house which Karl had now vacated. "The big house on the hill is a good place to be, and once she is there she can at least be moved around from one window to another—maybe even carried out in a chair and taken to some park for an afternoon hour or so. If we manage, we can make these last years good ones."[19]

Mary remained in a partial coma for many weeks. Then miraculously she began to improve. Soon Charity and Vernon took her into their home, where her memory slowly reasserted itself. With time she became as lucid and clear minded as she had ever been—at least she seemed so to Juanita: "She remembers everything clearly: birthdays of the grandchildren, the few married out of the Temple, all of whom are remembered in her prayers."[20] Juanita willingly postponed her promised return to St. George. Near the end of May she wrote Mary a chatty letter describing her gardening activities in her Salt Lake yard. On the previous day she had wrestled with a heavy lawnmower and had set plastic bags full of clippings onto the street. Promising to visit Mary soon, Juanita concluded: "I just wanted to tell you how happy I am that you are so well set up."[21]

Consciously Juanita resisted what subliminally she knew to be a fact: that she herself needed care and attention. She could not readily admit that she no longer had the capacity for concentrated research and writing. Throughout 1976 she maintained a running subterfuge, going through the motions of discussing, planning, and projecting, and assuring those who inquired that she was steadily at work upon one project or another.

She luckily disengaged herself from the Martha Spence Heywood diary without disturbing the illusion that she had satisfactorily completed her part of the task. For some time Miriam Murphy of the Utah Historical Society editorial staff had noted that during their consultations Juanita forgetfully repeated herself.[22] So when, in late 1975 or early 1976, Juanita declared herself satisfied with her manuscript, the staff accepted it as finished and offered her an honorarium for her work. This she declined, stating that she had considered it "a labor of love."[23] Thereafter Murphy went quietly on with the editorial labor.

At the University of Utah Press, Trudy McMurrin employed a different strategy. Gratified by Juanita's trust and confidentiality, McMurrin was reluctant to intervene directly in the writing of the autobiography. Furthermore, she did not view Juanita's tendency to repeat herself as a liability. A retelling of an experience from Juanita's past often provided valuable new details, which McMurrin noted and later urged her to add to her written account. Yet by the summer of 1976 McMurrin could see that, despite Juanita's asseverations of progress, few if any pages were emerging from her typewriter. One morning McMurrin went to Juanita's home equipped with a tape recorder, prepared to stay the entire day. "But we talked about five minutes," McMurrin narrated, "and then she wanted to tell me something real and she asked me to turn it off. . . . " McMurrin subsequently took notes in ink. At noon McMurrin proposed that they go out for lunch. Demurring, Juanita led the editor to her nearly empty refrigerator, extracted carrots and apricots, and blended a puree. It was a concoction in whose salubrity Juanita had for some years believed. Gamely McMurrin partook of the meager lunch: "So we managed to stand at the sink and eat, you know, just eat enough to keep us alive till help came, as my dad would say. . . . "[24]

Typically reinvigorated as the summer of 1976 came on, Juanita indulged herself in fantasies about other projects. When the original diary of John D. Lee's first mission came into her hands, she roused her old ambition to produce a three-volume set of Lee's diaries, going so far as to elicit a cost estimate from the University of New Mexico Press.[25] Soon she turned her enthusiasm to a long delayed article defending the authenticity of the alleged Oliver Overstreet impersonation of Oliver Cowdery.[26] This too quickly passed from her mind.

Juanita continued to be sought after as a public speaker throughout 1976. Vivified by her audiences, she often gave creditable performances. In February she talked to a group of student writers at the LDS Institute attached to the University of Utah. "I like what you exuded about your feeling for the past," wrote the grateful director of the seminar, "your understanding of the struggles and feelings of those tough and courageous pioneer peoples, who—you reminded us—made so many sacrifices to the church."[27] In October she delivered the keynote address at the president's luncheon of the convention of the Daughters of the Utah Pioneers. Some years earlier the officers of the DUP had resented Juanita's criticism of the sanitized rendition of the pioneer past which they had openly advocated. Now a reformed organization demonstrated that it had acceded to the kind of history which Juanita advocated. Officers and members alike applauded her address entitled "Your Pioneer's History—Keep It Authentic."[28]

The senility which advanced upon Juanita did not quickly anesthetize her senses. She could by moments make light of her forgetfulness. On a summer evening, Juanita and Fae were invited to a dinner at which Fae would introduce Juanita and Juanita would talk about her adventures in writing upon forbidden historical topics. Fae arrived at Juanita's home early and found her "standing there in a slip and her bathrobe on a chair. I said, 'Nita, you're not ready.' She said, 'What was I to do?' I said, 'We're to talk at Ernie Poulsen's house.' She said, 'Really? I knew there was some reason I took a bath.' "[29] Despite Juanita's levity, Fae knew it was no laughing matter. On the frequent occasions when Juanita phoned asking what day it was, Fae informed her without making an issue of the matter. She had first been moved to pity by an incident occurring when she accompanied Juanita and other friends to the Lion House for a luncheon honoring a prominent woman suffering from Alzheimer's disease. "I had driven five of them in my car and I could see how uneasy Juanita was. Juanita just couldn't be beside the lady who was ill, just could not. I missed her and found she was out in my car. I said, 'Where did you vanish to?' She was so white and her eyes so wide and frightened. She said, 'Take me away from here.' It just grieved me, it broke my heart to see her so full of fear."[30]

By moments Juanita realized that she must soon renounce an independent life. When Ione Bennion dropped by during the early fall, Juanita gave her a decorative cookie platter, overcoming her friend's protest by saying that shortly she would have to divest herself of most of the beautiful things in her house and return to St. George, as her children were urging her to do.[31] In late August she wrote an anguished letter to Todd and Betty Berens. She lamented that she had had company when the Berens had dropped by on a recent visit to Salt Lake. Thinking they would return, she had supplied herself with the makings of root-beer floats and had prepared a packet of seeds of a curious desert plant which she called a "Dollar Tree." With enormous disappointment she wrote: "I don't know in all my long life a single time that I wanted to find anyone as badly as I wanted to see you for only a few minutes." Briefly she wrote of a project she thought of pursuing. Then, as if her spirits had immediately sagged, she added: "My only worry is that I am more and more aware that OLD AGE has stepped around the corner, grabbed me, and said, 'I Got You!' "[32]

November 1976 found Juanita still in Salt Lake. On a Friday, Fae drove her to ZCMI to buy black shoes to go with a new black velvet skirt which she wished to wear to a banquet celebrating Governor Rampton's birthday. "Then we decided she needed a red velvet vest to go over the white blouse," Fae recorded. "We found that at ZCMI and had a riotous time getting her purse out and money paid."[33] After shopping, they had supper at Fae's apartment and then drove to Juanita's house where they fitted her new outfit. The next evening, the two friends attended the banquet—for which Juanita had purchased tickets at $25 each. Fae was impressed with "how graciously Juanita accepted the accolades of the many people who came to our table to speak to her. She was immensely popular in Salt Lake always."[34] Juanita continued to blame social events for her inability to get on with "Quicksand and Cactus." "I'm discouraged with myself," she wrote Tony and Janet, "for not having this little silly book done long ago, but I'm like the little girl in the play who kept saying, 'I caint say NO,' so I get invited to so many things that there's hardly time to live."[35] Predictably she soon went to Dixie to attend homecoming at the college. She fell ill and remained in St. George till the end of November. "When I came in from church," Fae wrote in her diary, "I called my dear friend, Juanita Brooks in St. George. She has been so very ill, but is improving physically. Her memory is failing far too fast—that very wonderful mind just cannot be damaged. She who has given so much to the world—"[36]

Over the protest of Karl and Willa, Juanita returned to Salt Lake in early December. She found in her mail a critique Fawn Brodie had made for the publisher of a new history of the Mountain Meadows massacre. Brodie denounced the soon-to-appear book as superficial, biased, and ungenerous in its recognition of Juanita's book on the same topic, from which it had drawn heavily. The author, Brodie wrote, "is less effective in stimulating dismay and horror about the Mountain Meadows massacre than Juanita Brooks, who communicates her understanding of the roots of Mormon fanaticism in cooler terms. She is believed because she is in total command of the documents she has seen, and she makes no pretense that she has seen everything."[37]

On December 29, 1976, Juanita wrote her thanks to Brodie. She chatted about the new edition of the Lee diaries she hoped to do and alluded with disparagement to "Quicksand and Cactus," which "was never designed to be anything very exciting or important, but the girls at the Press want me to fill in places before I hand it in. It's just the desert background."[38] This letter was perhaps the last Juanita wrote in her beloved little Salt Lake house. Kay had recently visited there—perhaps to take her to his home for Christmas. On the stove was a pot of sour peas to which Juanita had been periodically adding water. Otherwise there was no evidence of food preparation. Kay phoned Karl and Willa, and on New Year's Day or shortly after, Karl arrived from St. George, insisting that Juanita return with him. She wept, protesting that he was taking her home to die.[39] A few days later her furniture arrived at her St. George home in "a block-long van"— "beautiful, lovely things coming to fill the place," she wrote in a letter to Trudy McMurrin.[40] In March 1977 a savings and loan institution forwarded a check for a little more than $30,000 from the sale of her Salt Lake house.[41] Near the same moment she informed Melvin Smith that she did not wish to be reappointed to the Board of State History. "It will seem strange trying to run State History without you directly involved," Smith wrote as he thanked her for her many years of dedicated service.[42]

Soon after her arrival, Juanita received a letter from McMurrin asking her, as she unpacked, to be alert for stray pieces of "Quicksand and Cactus." McMurrin promised that, as soon she had processed "the huge pile of manuscript" in her possession, she would come to St. George so that she and Juanita could conclude the autobiography.[43] Juanita's reply revealed the desperation of a disoriented mind. "Do you know what it is to be in HELL?" she wrote. "Well, I'll tell you: It's being in a confusion, where nothing seems important, where there are so many THINGS and nothing seems important, but is to somebody else. It's being in the midst of all kinds of unrelated Things."[44]

During the spring of 1977 Juanita suffered a severe blockage of the bowels which required stomach pumping and surgery. For days her survival was doubtful, and it took her many weeks to convalesce.[45] With summer her strength returned, and she settled into a way of life which, continuing without radical change for some five or six years, was not altogether unhappy. She was mistress of her own home, where she slept and, if she wished, prepared her own food. Next door was the new home of Karl and Carla, where she frequently took her meals. She was of course in no condition to care for her mother, as she had once hoped to do. Although Mary had regained her mental alertness, she returned permanently to a nursing home not long after Juanita's return to St. George. Mary would die in July 1980, a few months short of one hundred three years old.

Karl and Carla found it no easy task to respect Juanita's independence yet give her safe, decent care. After Juanita had scolded her several times, Carla became cautious about cleaning her neglected house during her absence. Juanita spent considerable time in her backyard, where there were fruit trees, grapevines, a garden, and an expanse of handsome lawn. It was a domain she shared with Karl, with whom she occasionally came into conflict. In general, her hours in the yard were satisfying. She dragged the hose hither and yon, irrigating her vines and spraying the lawn. She roamed the lawn plucking dandelion blossoms before they matured. She devoted a plot of the garden to alfalfa, which she used for greens. After she had cut her leg with a sickle while harvesting alfalfa, Karl quietly hid the dangerous instrument.[46]

She continued to receive mail from relatives, friends, and admirers. She often replied and probably in lucid moments made some attempt to resume her serious writing. She was ashamed that her control over the keyboard of her typewriter had become uncertain. "I look back over this page and wonder how I could leave such a MESS—Like a First Grader," she wrote to Ernest and Maria. "They tell me that I used to correct Tony's letters with a red pencil and send them back to him to correct and do over. But I knew that if he was to ever make his way into a top place anywhere, he'd have to be able to write a decent page. I know that I should destroy this, and not have my name on it at all. . . . "[47]

Willa dropped in on Juanita almost daily. Numerous other relatives frequently visited her, took her to church meetings and social gatherings, and invited her into their homes for dinners and parties. Maxine, Grant's widow, came by with her new husband, Jesse Phillips. Charmed by the amiable Jesse, Juanita took his face in her two hands and expressed her pleasure that he had become a member of the Brooks family.[48] Characteristically, the family at large welcomed Jesse as warmly as if Maxine had been a Brooks by blood rather than by marriage. Not infrequently Juanita visited her out-of-town relatives. In August 1978 she traveled by air to Idaho, where she spent a week with Laurel and Melva at Homedale. From Idaho she flew to Las Vegas, where she visited Ernest and Maria. She returned to St. George in a small commuter plane which she called "a little 'puddle-jumper', which gave me—if not exactly fear, a great feeling of gratitude for the solid earth under me."[49]

Travelers passing through frequently called at her home: Sterling and Natalie McMurrin, Todd and Betty Berens, Richard and Claudia Sadler, Charles and Betty Peterson, and others. In town for several days, Ione Bennion spent long hours with Juanita. The two friends exchanged confidences, took walks, and went out to dinner.[50] Alison and Wynne Thorne, also from Logan, called by and found Juanita at work among her grapevines. Juanita went on with her labor, conversing more fluently for having something for her hands to do. "We did go right down to the Tabernacle," Alison wrote later, "after you told us about the workmen and their stippling patterns on the stones, and we saw patterns on the stone we hadn't been aware of before."[51] Juanita responded positively to the warm interest of her friends. Though she might vent her nervousness through excessive laughter or move to new topics unexpectedly, she remained basically sensible in her conversations with visitors.

On December 30, 1977, the family held a reception in honor of Juanita's eightieth birthday—a little early on the assumption that her out-of-town friends and relatives could attend more readily during the holiday season. In preparation Juanita sat for a formal portrait photograph, one of the most beautiful of her life. She wears a flowered dress; her short hair is elegantly coifed; her eyes are bemused; a slight,

quizzical smile plays on her face. There are also snapshots of the reception. In one Juanita stands in a long blue dress; in another she sits
next to Ernest, who holds her hand. She looks sober and depressed,
as if she will be relieved to have finished. Undoubtedly the formality
of the occasion has triggered the confusion to which she is susceptible.

The public continued to bestow honors upon the afflicted
historian. In April 1978 the Dixie College library, celebrating National
Library Week, honored her for her contribution to the college and
her region. As the audience gathered in the library, the carillon played.
Karl, by now vice-president for development and college relations,
gave a summary of his mother's life and achievements. "I remember
well taking a class from her, writing a theme that I thought was quite
good," Karl said as he explained his mother's strict standards as an
English teacher. "[I remember] turning it in and having it turned back
with the report that 'Surely you don't want to turn that in in the
present form. I find it unacceptable.' At the end of the course she gave
me a C and I said, 'Why did you give me a C?' 'Because I didn't want
to give you a D.' "[52] Juanita wept a little as she responded in a feeble
yet intelligent voice. Echoing Karl's commentary on good teaching,
she praised her colleagues at Dixie College, perceptively declaring,
"School is not buildings or surroundings but the quality of
teachers."[53]

In November 1978 the Utah Academy of Sciences, Arts
and Letters awarded Juanita its Charles Redd Prize in Humanities and
Social Sciences, which included a cash grant of $1,500. Attending the
luncheon of the academy at Snow College in Ephraim, Juanita listened as the reader of the citation declared that her major historical
works had "required of Mrs. Brooks a rare combination of courage, of
simple but insistent objectivity, of compassionate desire to rectify old
wrongs, and of profound sympathy with those who might wish she
had never stirred these difficult subjects."[54]

In 1981, the BYU Alumni Association honored Juanita with
a University Emeritus Club Award. As long ago as 1975, Juanita had
received the certificate of membership in the Emeritus Club accorded
any living graduate of BYU whose class had passed the fiftieth anniversary of its graduation. At that time, in a letter to the Alumni Association, Juanita recounted the university's humiliating refusal to grant
her a loan with which to buy graduation shoes and a yearbook. "Then

later," she went on, "when I was called an *Apostate* in classes where my son had to stand and defend me in one, and my daughter in another, a niece in a third, I was not happy."[55] The contrite director made an attempt at restitution: "I am interested in knowing if you ever were able to obtain a yearbook for the Class of 1925. If not, I would like to send you one as the Alumni Association has an extra copy."[56] On April 23, 1981, she attended the Emeritus Club luncheon as a recipient of one of the two awards the organization made each year to members who had distinguished themselves. Her citation read: "Her commitment to probe and inquire in order to tell the truth, to narrate and interpret history honestly made it easier for fellow Mormon scholars to pursue church-related history more objectively."[57] On January 4, 1985, Juanita's name was entered into the Beehive Hall of Fame among the names of illustrious politicians, businesspersons, scientists, inventors, and athletes, who were for the most part men. Inscribed on a plaque on display in the foyer of the Marriott Hotel in Salt Lake was a citation calling her "the dean of Utah historians."[58]

Unquestionably Juanita took consolation from these and other honors. Even more she might have found consolation during her declining years in the publication and republication of an impressive number of her writings. Even as her physical person faded, her literary career flourished, having a life and momentum of its own.

In June 1977, Trudy McMurrin paid her a working visit, having first declared in a letter that Juanita's part in "Quicksand and Cactus" was nearly finished. "Do you realize we've got 518 pages on our hands! I think it's time to stop writing and start editing."[59] Of the three sections into which McMurrin had divided the work, the first two, covering Juanita's childhood and her first marriage and widowhood, were virtually complete. McMurrin cheerfully listed some nine completed chapters of the third section, which covered the years of Juanita's marriage to Will. She hoped that Juanita could locate several of these which seemed to be missing and that she could write several new chapters. In her private feelings, however, McMurrin was far from cheeful about the supposedly finished chapters of the third section. She and Juanita had, she would write later, "struggled with approaches (in fact I started doing research on autobiographical methodology), but the manuscript at the time of her removal to St. George was spotty, open-ended, and unreliable chronologically."[60]

McMurrin was accompanied on her visit by Richard Howe, marketing manager for the University of Utah Press. To orient themselves further to Dixie, McMurrin and Howe took Juanita on an excursion to Bunkerville. They also paused at the Jacob Hamblin home in Santa Clara where Juanita took delight in correcting the superficial explanations of an unwitting guide. She was in fine fettle—of a puckish humor and entirely lucid. On another day, McMurrin and Juanita leafed through Juanita's files in search of manuscripts of any nature that might fit into the scheme of "Quicksand and Cactus." Subsequently, McMurrin hoped to assemble the conglomeration of chapters and pieces in her possession into a coherent whole. When that had been accomplished, she intended to send a copy to Fawn Brodie, who had promised to write a foreword.

In the spring of 1978, *Not By Bread Alone: The Journal of Martha Spence Heywood 1850–56* appeared in a modest printing of 1,200 copies. To celebrate its advent, the Utah Historical Society hosted a reception for Juanita in May at its new quarters in the Crane Building in Salt Lake. The experience was probably both fearful and gratifying for Juanita. Greeting old friends with pleasure, conversing guardedly with admiring strangers, she autographed copies with a shaky hand. A woman from Logan asked her to autograph a gift copy for their mutual friend, Alison Thorne. Thorne would later write to Juanita: "She stopped by with your book *Not by Bread Alone*, inscribed to me with love from you, and told how she had stood in line at the reception for you in Salt Lake City, and had asked you to inscribe the book to me, and your face had lit up and you said that Alison Thorne was a child of God."[61]

The book she inscribed predictably revealed a notable personality. According to a daguerreotype, Martha Spence possessed a long face, a prominent mouth, determined eyes, and large, competent hands. An Irish immigrant of a fervent religious nature, she preached Adventism in Canada before converting to Mormonism in 1848. In 1850, penniless and nearing forty, she made her way to Salt Lake in the wagons of Joseph L. Heywood, a merchant. Soon she became Heywood's third wife and persuaded him to establish her in a humble home in Nephi, where she earned her own living by sewing caps and muffs and by teaching school. She was often ill and suffered constant anxiety over the health of her son and daughter. Following the death of her daughter, Martha returned to Salt Lake to live with her sister wives. There she participated in theatrical and literary societies and listened eagerly to the sermons of Brigham Young. In 1861, her husband having been called to the Cotton Mission, she moved to Dixie, establishing a final home in Washington, where she raised her son and made her living as a much respected schoolteacher.

Her diary, dating from 1850 to 1856, is distinguished by her expressive style, her honest introspection, and her vivid delineation of persons and incidents. As the wagon train approached Salt Lake in the fall of 1850, she responded to the landscape with a modern sensitivity: "The scenery has been very grand for the last few days, the rocks are so magnificent looking and the mountains so high and perpendicular that it delights, especially being interspersed with shrubbery and small wood in their coats of rich autumnal grandeur."[62] With a stark eloquence she recorded the irreparable loss of her daughter. "I washed her little body myself on my lap and dressed her in her own clothes and the last sewing I did for her was to make her a pair of shoes of white cloth. Oh, my dear little Sarepta Marie my joy and my comfort by day and by night. Your precious voice that so often cheered my heart to its inmost recesses by its singing and interesting prattle, had gone from my sight."[63]

This informative, fervent diary generated a respectable number of reviews, which without exception praised its author. Most of them praised its editor as well. Harold Schindler paid special tribute to Juanita in the *Salt Lake Tribune*. "As with all writers, some of her published work was extremely good with an occasional piece of mediocrity," Schindler wrote. "But her latest effort, *Not by Bread Alone*, is one of Mrs. Brooks's finer contributions to history." With this achievement as a "fitting capstone" to her literary career, she could, he continued, "relax in her beloved St. George surroundings and be assured that Utah's history has been well served by her."[64] However, a reviewer in *The Colorado Magazine* grumbled about the inadequacies of the editing. The index was "incompletely composed of proper names, thus making it impossible to refer readily to Heywood's detailed comments on particular aspects of Mormon life and practices." Furthermore, the footnotes failed to give the non-Mormon reader a sufficient explanation of Mormon customs, and the work offered no comprehensive sketch of Martha's life.[65]

The most substantive of these complaints was the absence of an overview of Martha's life; her scattered references to her prior experiences did not adequately substitute for a coherent biographical sketch. The index and footnotes, for their part, were detailed and useful. Interestingly, one of the footnotes renewed Juanita's indictment of Brigham Young for callousness. This note, having identified a Dr. Samuel L. Sprague, mentioned by Heywood as attending the dying nephew of her future husband, went on to reveal that when Dr. Sprague had completed a new house for his family, "Brigham Young came and coolly told him that he would like it for his wife Emeline for three or four years until he could build her another. The Spragues could live in the house formerly owned by Jedediah M. Grant which would be repaired and cleaned for their use."[66]

Unknown to most readers, Miriam Murphy of the Utah Historical Society staff shared Juanita's achievement, for she had taken an inadequate manuscript from the ailing historian and had shaped it into a respectable publication. In recognition of what Juanita had been, if not of what she was, Murphy allowed her the undivided attribution of this final work. During the forty-five years since the journal had first come into her hands, Juanita had admired it, cited it, and otherwise promoted it. A large and unstinting part of her historical vocation had been to see into print such splendid original documents. As an editor as well as a historian and biographer, she had been a midwife to the past.

Juanita's connection with the Utah Historical Society expanded in another direction in 1978. For years ambitious librarians and archivists had solicited her private collection of diaries, manuscripts, and letters. As early as 1973, director Melvin Smith had let Juanita know, by means of a delicately worded letter, that the Utah Historical Society "would be very honored to be the repository for your papers and historic memorabilia when their disposition becomes a matter of concern to you."[67] In December 1978, at the invitation of Juanita and her children, Melvin Smith and Jay Haymond, the society's coordinator of collections and research, brought away from St. George a truckload of chests, boxes, and filing cabinets filled with Juanita's papers.[68] Gary Topping, curator of manuscripts, organized the materials. Topping readily imposed a chronological order upon the thousands of letters, original and carbon, which Juanita had saved over a period of nearly fifty years. With greater perplexity, he created a various filing by authors, titles, and topics for the hundreds of manuscripts—typescripts of diaries and other pioneer documents, her own unpublished writings, the unpublished writings of acquaintances—which Juanita had accumulated. Staff members microfilmed the collection during 1980 and early 1981. The collection, neatly foldered in archival boxes, was then returned to the keeping of Kay Brooks in Mapleton, where he had recently moved. Juanita's children soon decided to return the collection to the Utah Historical Society for permanent keeping.[69] Today it occupies more than seventeen linear feet of shelf space in the society's archives in its latest home, the Rio Grande building in Salt Lake.

In March 1979 Juanita was featured in a documentary televised on Salt Lake's KSL-TV. Early that month a television crew descended on Dixie, taking footage of Juanita in her backyard and making excursions to Mountain Meadows and Bunkerville. In one shot Juanita declared in halting language that following the publication of *The Mountain Meadows Massacre* she had been disfellowshipped from the Church.[70] For years a widespread folklore had rumored that Juanita had been either disfellowshipped or excommunicated (disfellowshipment being a formal discipline only a little less severe than excommunication). Actually she had not been. Symbolically, the quiet ostracism she had experienced for many years following the appearance of her history of the massacre had amounted to disfellowshipment. In her old age her tongue spoke what long before her heart had felt.

Juanita's literary career took another fortuitous turn in the fall of 1979 when Richard Howe reached an agreement with Karl to publish the biography of Jacob Hamblin which Juanita had written in 1952 to serve as the basis of an unrealized movie. Resigning from his position at the University of Utah Press, Howe proceeded with crisp efficiency, forwarding galleys to Karl by late November 1979.[71] Except for a few slight changes, the printed text appearing in 1980 followed Juanita's manuscript precisely. Undocumented, partially fictionalized, and slanted toward juvenile readers, the work failed to attract serious scholarly attention. Among general readers it sold well, entering a third printing by 1985, in part because a few loyal reviewers gave it an enthusiastic boost.

Pleased with the Hamblin biography, Karl made arrangements with Howe during the fall of 1980 for the publication of "Quicksand and Cactus," a disappointing but perhaps not unexpected turn of events for the University of Utah Press. By the end of 1978 Trudy

McMurrin had become convinced that the manuscript, composed of numerous pieces as yet not fitted into a single coherent pattern, required—as she would later write—"more substantial work than was really appropriate for the publisher, and an amount that was impossible for anyone on the Press staff at that time." In order to persuade Karl that "further work had to be done by the author or her assistant(s) to produce a publisher-ready manuscript," McMurrin sent the materials south slightly before Christmas 1978.[72] Delayed by an auto accident, they arrived in Karl's hands during the spring of 1979.[73] It is possible that Karl toyed with the idea that he himself would finish the work; if so, he was discouraged by his busy schedule as a vice-president of Dixie College. For a time he placed the materials with a free-lance editor residing in Salt Lake. When that arrangement proved unsatisfactory, he delivered them to an agreeable Richard Howe, placing in his hands a disorganized stack of chapters and fragments some eighteen inches high.

In preparing "Quicksand and Cactus" for publication Howe performed an act of creative editing. For months he left a litter of pages upon the living room floor of his bachelor quarters as he sought to date the incidents narrated within the chapters and to determine a priority of composition for the many incidents existing in several versions. Ingeniously he collated the chapters by the apparent age of the paper, by the distinctive typeface of the various typewriters Juanita had used, and by the frequent appearance of carbon copies on the backs of ruined pages of other manuscripts Juanita was known to have been working on.[74]

For a time Howe naively hoped that he could assemble a coherent narrative of Juanita's entire life. However, he found accounts following her marriage to Will to be so fragmentary that he eventually reached an agreement with Karl that the work would end with her second wedding.[75] By way of partial compensation for the missing chapters, Howe secured an introductory essay by Charles Peterson. Besides outlining her life from 1934 to about 1962, Peterson's introduction placed Juanita among other notable Utah writers and emphasized the cathartic effect of her study of the massacre and the scapegoating of John D. Lee.

There was, Howe sensed, a serious discrepancy between the chapters Juanita had finished in the 1940s and those she had written in the 1970s. With Karl's approval, he made a selection from the former group, which covered her childhood to the loss of her pony Selah and her entrance into high school. Only rarely did he alter the selected chapters by interpolating passages borrowed from alternate versions. In contrast, the chapters composed in the 1970s, which covered from Juanita's high school years until her wedding to Will, were sparse in detail and unpolished in style. "Therefore, I edited this rather heavily," Howe would later write, "inasmuch as I felt we ought to retain a commitment to the style and theme development of the pre-Selah period of the manuscript."[76] Again he drew upon passages from alternate versions. Sometimes he wrote brief passages, amounting according to his later estimate to "no more than a total of maybe a paragraph or two. Any time that I felt a transition was needed, I know I would do this: a couple of times I went to that third person narrative [the version featuring the girl Sal] and picked a transition up from there and stuck that in a place or two and I think I consulted with Karl when I did that."[77] However, the discrepancy of style remained; the second half of "Quicksand and Cactus" amounted, as Howe accurately noted, to "a remembrance, rather than a literary memoir."

The truncation of Juanita's life and the disparity of style were not lost upon the public who greeted *Quicksand and Cactus: A Memoir of the Southern Mormon Frontier* upon its appearance in the fall of 1982. It was, one reviewer declared, "disappointing to expect so much from the 'memoirs' of a writer of the caliber of Juanita Brooks and to be given so much less."[78] Another lamented the formless quality of the work, pointing out that "many chapters consist of two or three stories lacking any apparent unity but that of time."[79] On the whole, however, reviewers and readers were pleased with the autobiography. A first printing quickly sold out, and the Mormon History Association gave the work its Best Book Award of 1982. Despite their disparity, insisted one reviewer, "the book's two halves add up to a satisfactory whole. . . ."[80] "The Brooks work," declared another, "is so honest in the telling, so free of stylistic ornament and narrative complexity that some may wonder if the author did not intend more. It is in fact something of a gentle comedy, a charming parable of life in Dixie. The author does not provide the rolling thunder of great history or a dramatic yardstick for the past. Rather she miniaturizes, domesticates, reduces the grand scheme to the small manageable detail."[81]

The chapters which compose the first half of the published work (discussed in chapter five of this biography) demonstrate traits of the memoir, the folktale, the short story, and the personal essay. Although they are highly episodic, they are fast paced and rich in human interest. They often demonstrate a felicitous style, offering rhythmical sentences and a wry, concrete diction. The sixteen chapters which compose the second half cannot be mistaken for short stories, folktales, or personal essays. Of a lesser literary quality, they are a sparse conventional narrative of Juanita's personal life from her thirteenth to her thirty-fifth year. Too often these chapters are chary of detail and abbreviated in treatment, as if in composing them Juanita had wanted to forget rather than to remember. For example, from other sources one knows of the bizarre and pitiable events surrounding Ernest's funeral. Even as the service was scheduled to begin, Ernest's father and brother had insisted that the bishop attempt to raise the dead Ernest, and Juanita herself had knelt and implored God aloud to bring him back to life. All of that is obliterated in her published account, the funeral having been reduced to "a blur in my memory. Somehow one lives through these crises, walking in a daze through the crowds that come, all eager to be of some assistance, sitting through the meeting with its songs and talk-talk, hearing the sound of earth being shoveled into the open grave."[82]

Nonetheless, even these chapters have some share of kinetic style, fascinating incident, and vivid characterization. By means of select detail, Juanita infused the events preceding Ernest's funeral with a compelling sorrow. Furthermore, she evoked laughter with an encouraging frequency. There was the comic story of Henry Leavitt's first car. On his first drive, Henry attempted to stop the vehicle by pulling back on the steering wheel and shouting, "Whoa!" That good story led Juanita to another about a neighbor who, employing the same method of stopping his car, repeatedly knocked out the rear end of his garage. "It was said," she wrote, "that after replacing that lumber wall a few times, he decided to leave the end open."[83] Juanita continued in this last section of her autobiography, as she had in the first, to depict herself in the ambivalent light of picaresque comedy. When her horse accidentally carried her beneath a projecting pole at her aunt's Pine Valley ranch during the summer following her graduation from high school, she braced herself in the stirrups, grasped the pole, and with incredible luck broke off the firm, new post to which it was attached. " 'I'm sorry. I didn't mean to do it," she said to her dumb-founded male cousins.

"Sorry! Sorry and be damned!" Ral broke in. "You'd better fall on your knees and thank God you're alive to tell it. Where would you have come out if that pole *hadn't* give way? Just turn that over in your mind!"

"Well, if you ask me, either your pituitary gland or your guardian angel, or both, were on the job. There's more here than meets the eye." That was Mart's conclusion.[84]

Thus Juanita expressed both chagrin and pride that, despite her under-nourished stature, her anomalous femininity was not of the kitchen and parlour but of the corral and pasture.

Despite its unfinished nature, *Quicksand and Cactus* is one of the best of Mormon autobiographies. One hopes that when the printed work was placed in her hands during the fall of 1982, Juanita found pleasure in it. One hopes that from time to time she still reflected upon her published works and took consolation from the fact that in them she had built herself an exceptional monument. For truly her literary life continued to flourish. In 1982 the University of Utah Press and the Utah Historical Society collaborated in reprinting *On the Mormon Frontier: The Diary of Hosea Stout – 1844–1861*. In 1983 the University of Utah Press reprinted *A Mormon Chronicle: The Diaries of John D. Lee – 1848–1876*. In 1984 Utah State University Press issued a second edition of *Emma Lee*. Dissatisfied with the quality of the 1975 edition, the new director of that press, Linda Speth, engaged Charles Peterson not only to to write an introductory essay but also to assist her in copyediting the first edition, correcting typos and harmonizing internal inconsistencies.[85] Peterson's introduction declared that Juanita had not followed either the tendency of faith-promoting Mormon historians to cast Mormon history as the workings of God upon the earth or the tendency of nationally prominent historians to romanticize it as a part of the grand sweep of Manifest Destiny. She was, he asserted, an "unadorned realist" who, in place of the foregoing approaches, "substituted the realism of the commonplace and an affinity for the unadorned truth."[86]

In early 1985 Richard Howe emitted his third Brooks title, a paperback reprint of the 1972 edition of *John Doyle Lee: Zealot-Pioneer Builder-Scapegoat*. That Mormon classic, *The Mountain Meadows Mas-*

sacre, continued to be available through the University of Oklahoma Press. Also to be noted was the republication of various chapters from *Quicksand and Cactus* in regional magazines. The perennial favorite, "The Outsider," appeared again in 1984 in *Westward the Women: An Anthology of Western Stories by Women*, augustly positioned among stories by Willa Cather, Mary Austin, Mari Sandoz, and Leslie Silko.

By late 1982 Juanita's moments of lucidity were increasingly rare, and those rare moments were marked by frustration, anger, and despondency. Karl began to dissuade out-of-town friends from visiting her because she wept long after her visitors had departed. She often interrupted a sensible discourse with nonsensical and incoherent statements and frequently confused the past and present. She worried about babies, real or imaginary, whom she conceived to have been abused or abandoned. One night she declared that the ill-fated Donner Party, who had resorted to cannibalism on the snowy slopes of the Sierras, were camped on her front lawn. She had become untrustworthy in turning off the stove or faucet and once or twice had been found wandering the street at night.

One day she slipped on her basement stairs and dragged herself to a bed where she lay for some time before being discovered. Thereupon Karl and Willa agreed to hire a live-in caretaker. The first, Eva's daughter Margaret, proved to be excellent. But after she had gone on to other employment, there were several who were less satisfactory. One of these women irresponsibly took Juanita along in her automobile as she pursued her private purposes. Occasionally she left her elderly charge sitting for hours in her car parked on St. George streets. Once she took her as far away as Las Vegas. Shortly Karl and Willa dismissed her. Finally they succeeded in hiring a kind, efficient woman who lived with Juanita twenty-four hours a day Monday through Friday. On weekends Karl and Carla alternated with Willa and Thales in caring for their mother.[87]

By 1984 Juanita's mobility and speech had worsened drastically. Her balance and coordination had so deteriorated that she spent her out-of-bed hours in a wheelchair. She had also lost her ability to enunciate words. Sometimes, as she tried futilely to enter the conversation of those about her, she wept from sheer frustration. At other times she jabbered, gesticulating and making facial expressions as if carrying on a reasonable discourse, all the while voicing unintelligible sounds. When Charity and Eva visited her, they found that they could cheer her up by reminiscing about events from their girlhood. Juanita responded with a mixture of tears and laughter as her sisters poured out a sunlight from their past.[88]

Increasingly Juanita slipped into a stupor in which she failed to respond to or recognize her loved ones. In November 1984, her children and their families gathered at her home for Thanksgiving dinner. Amidst the excited chatter, Juanita sat in a corner in her wheelchair, disengaged and absent, yet not unhappy. It was a precious final moment, for never again would they all gather with her in this venerable house. On January 3, 1985, Juanita left the house on the hill for the last time and entered a St. George nursing home, a modern facility with semi-private rooms, carpeted floors, and professional personnel dressed in white uniforms.

The move to the nursing home was momentarily traumatic. On one occasion when Maxine and Jesse Phillips visited her as she lay in her bed, she clutched Jesse by his bolo tie, pulled his face close to hers, and with wide frightened eyes made inarticulate sounds of distress.[89] Before a year had elapsed, she had sunk into a semicoma, passing her hours in a condition resembling sleep. At mealtimes, seated in her wheelchair and strapped so that she would not fall out, she received her food and liquid from a spoon. Although her eyes ordinarily remained shut, she obligingly opened her mouth to receive the nourishment, eating heartily and maintaining her weight. Her loved ones continued to visit, although Juanita rarely recognized their presence. At different moments at least once a week Karl and Willa replaced the attendant who normally fed their mother and spooned the food and liquid into her mouth. While he fed her, Karl made it a point to talk with a cheerful volubility in hopes that she comprehended more than she revealed. From time to time she gave slight gestures that fueled his hope. Once he put his cheek against hers and in a facetious voice said: "Don't you remember me, Mom? This is Karl, your son. Don't you remember what a good son I was? Don't you remember what scoundrels your other sons were?" Juanita slapped his hand lightly, a sign of mock maternal reproof of his mock egotism. On another occasion Carla offered Juanita a cup of water, which she angrily knocked to the floor. Taking it as a sign that her mother-in-law was hungry rather than thirsty, Carla promised to bring food, whereupon Juanita, with closed eyes, began to weep.[90]

In March 1987 Willa took a friend into the house on the hill, which for the moment was unrented. She and the friend viewed the old kitchen where sometimes in the winter Juanita had sat on the oven door of the wood-burning range, now long gone. Passing through the old living room, which had been converted to a bedroom, they examined the termite trails in the baseboard—a common phenomenon in Dixie. Standing in the new kitchen, they talked about Juanita. Weeping, Willa called her mother's condition a living death. A little later on the same day this friend accompanied Eva to the nursing home and looked in on the sleeping historian. She lay curled on her side in a semi-fetal position. Her hair was neatly combed and tied; a bare arm lay upon the counterpane; her breathing was deep and regular. Eva hurried the friend away immediately, as if she had suddenly realized that she could not tolerate having him see her sister in this plight.[91]

As this book goes to press, the ninety-year-old Juanita remains in a light coma in the nursing home. One remembers that it was never like her to do an expedient thing. When it would be a mercy to herself and her loved ones to give up the ghost and die, she clings to life with an obverse tenacity. One thinks of her achievement as historian, tragedian, and dissenter. She leaves her books and articles as a monument in which readers will find her forever courageous, intelligent, and kind. She also leaves a monument less tangible than her writings. Because of her, the collective mind of Mormondom is more liberal and more at peace with itself than it might otherwise be. The Mountain Meadows massacre is no longer a repressed, subliminal disturbance in the Mormon psyche. Modern Latter-day Saints accept that those pioneers who committed the massacre were among the best and most representative Mormons. Although modern Mormons thereby take on a sense of communal guilt and contrition, they also understand the exceptional circumstances by which their errant predecessors were tried. They therefore pity and forgive them; they experience catharsis. Equally important, Juanita helped make Mormondom a little less suspicious about nonconformity in general. Voicing her contrary opinions unequivocally, she confronted scolding apostles with a courageous assertion of her faithfulness. The fame of her loyal dissent spread widely, and covert protesters of many varieties took heart.

The human race need not apologize for the life of Juanita Brooks. In the perspective of the centuries, the lingering of her comatose body is of little significance, for within this seemingly ordinary rural house-wife dwelt a spirit remarkable for curiosity, integrity, and tolerance and for the ability to reconcile faith and critical reason.

Juanita Brooks died on August 26, 1989. Her funeral was held in the St. George tabernacle on August 30. The author of this biography counts it one of the great honors of his life to have been invited to speak at her funeral. She lies buried beside Will Brooks in the St. George cemetery.

Juanita, ca. 1975.

Photographs not otherwise attributed are used with permission from
Karl F. Brooks, executor of Juanita Brooks's estate. Many of them
derive from the Juanita Brooks Collection in the Utah State
Historical Society.

Juanita and Charity, 1900.

Left to right: Leah Leavitt, Laman Leavitt, Ann Woodbury Hafen, Norma Hafen, Juanita. Berkeley, California, summer 1917.

Juanita and prize-winning Dixie College debate team, spring 1927.

Leonard Ernest Pulsipher (right) and missionary companion, 1914.
Courtesy of Ernest Pulsipher.

Juanita and her son Ernest, ca. 1926. Courtesy of Ernest Pulsipher.

Juanita, ca. 1927.

Thirza Riding Leavitt and Ernest, Bunkerville, 1927. Courtesy of Ernest Pulsipher.

Henry Leavitt, ca. 1935.

The family of Henry Leavitt, left to right, standing: Francis, Charity, Melvin, Mary, Laurel, Daisy, Dudley; seated: Eva, Aura, Mary Hafen Leavitt, Juanita, ca. 1946.

The compound-complex family of Juanita and Will, left to right, back row: Ernest, Walt, Maxine (Grant's wife), Grant; middle row: Clair, Will, Juanita, Willa, Bob; front row: Tony, Karl, Kay, ca. 1941.

Juanita and Dixie College debate team, ca. 1955.

The house on the hill in St. George as it appeared near the time Juanita and Will moved into it in May 1943.

Will and Juanita, ca. 1945.

Juanita and Dale Morgan, May 1948.

Ettie Lee, 1948.

Juanita at dedication of Lee's Ferry Monument, October 1961.

Juanita signing copies of Uncle Will Tells His Story *at Sam Weller's Zion Book Store, December 1970.*

On Will's eightieth birthday, left to right, back row: Bob and Florence, Ernest and Margie, Walt and Irene, LaVon and Clair; middle row: Thales and Willa, Will and Juanita, Mary Hafen Leavitt; front row: Karl, Tony, Kay, April 1961.

Will and ancient locust tree at the house on the hill, ca. 1969.

NOTES

Abbreviations and Diary Locations

The following abbreviations are consistently used throughout the note sections.

BAN	Bancroft Library, University of California at Berkeley
DMCol	Dale Morgan Collection, Bancroft Library
HL	Huntington Library
JB	Juanita Brooks
JBCol	Juanita Brooks Collection, Utah State Historical Society
JBCol Ad	Materials added to the Juanita Brooks Collection in 1986
LSP	Originals or photocopies in possession of Levi S. Peterson
"Q&C"	Manuscript "Quicksand and Cactus"
Q&C	Published *Quicksand and Cactus*
StanUPress	Stanford University Press
UHS	Utah State Historical Society
UofU	University of Utah Special Collections Library
USU Press	Utah State University PRess
WSC	Weber State College Special Collections Library

The location of approved photocopies of the following diaries is clarified here in order to avoid repetition in the notes. The originals of these diaries reside with the descendants of Juanita Brooks.

Juanita Brooks	Diary 1920–21	JBCol 19:7, UHS
Juanita Brooks	Diary 1933–36	JBCol 7:13, UHS
Juanita Brooks	B'nai B'rith Diary 1967	JBCol 20:9, UHS
Juanita Brooks	Diary A 1971	JBCol Ad, UHS
Juanita Brooks	Diary B 1971–73	JBCol Ad, UHS
Will Brooks	Diary 1961	JBCol Ad, UHS
Will Brooks	Diary 1962	JBCol Ad, UHS
Will Brooks	Diary 1963	JBCol Ad, UHS
Will Brooks	Trans-Atlantic Diary 1963	JBCol 20:16, UHS
Will Brooks	World's Fair Diary 1964	JBCol 20:9, UHS

Chapter One

1. Levi S. Peterson, "Juanita Brooks: The Mormon Historian as Tragedian," *Journal of Mormon History* 3 (1976): 47–54.

2. Levi S. Peterson, "The Civilizing of Mormondom: The Indispensable Role of the Intellectual," *Sunstone* 7 (May-June 1982): 8–15.

3. Obert C. Tanner to JB, 7 October 1968, JBCol, UHS.

4. Sterling McMurrin, interview by Levi Peterson, 4 February 1986, Salt Lake City, UHS Oral History Project.

5. Mary H. Leavitt, account of her life, unpublished, JBCol Ad, UHS.

6. Charity Rowley, account in "Reminiscences of Juanita Brooks," compiled by Eva Miles, unpublished, JBCol Ad, UHS.

7. Henry Leavitt, "A Sketch of the Life of Dudley Henry Leavitt," December 1936, Bunkerville, Nev., unpublished, JBCol Ad, UHS.

8. Mary H. Leavitt, account of her life.

9. Charity Rowley and Eva Miles, interview by Levi Peterson, 20 December 1985, St. George, Utah, UHS Oral History Project.

10. JB to Mary Leavitt, 5 November 1972, JBCol, UHS.

11. Mary Leavitt to Albert Hafen, 7 November 1906, JBCol 34:10, UHS.

12. JB, "The Water's In!" *Harpers* 182 (May 1941): 608.

13. Charity Rowley to Henry Leavitt, n.d.; JBCol 1:3, UHS.

14. JB, "Hen Leavitt's Boy," unpublished chapter, "Quicksand and Cactus" (hereafter "Q&C"), JBCol Ad, UHS.

15. Ibid.

16. JB to Ettie Lee, 28 November 1947, JBCol, UHS.

17. JB, *Quicksand and Cactus: A Memoir of the Southern Mormon Frontier* (Salt Lake City: Howe Brothers, 1982), 92 (hereafter *Q&C*).

18. Juanita L. Pulsipher L.D.S. Family and Individual Record, JBCol 19:7, UHS.

19. See Leonard J. Arrington and Davis Bitton, *The Mormon Experience: A History of the Latter-day Saints* (New York: Alfred A. Knopf, 1979), for a succinct treatment of Mormon history, doctrines, and customs.

20. JB, *Q&C*, 96.

21. JB, "The 'Seeing Eye' in Reading History," unpublished article, JBCol 8:25, UHS.

22. JB to Henry Leavitt, 20 April 1937, JBCol, UHS.

23. JB to Pansy Hardy, 14 August 1963, JBCol, UHS.

24. JB, "Let Us Be United," version #1, "Q&C," JBCol 9:19, UHS.

25. JB, "More Than Meat," "Q&C," JBCol Ad, UHS.

26. Mary H. Leavitt, account of her life.

27. Charity Rowley to Henry Leavitt, n.d., JBCol 1:13, UHS.

28. Pansy L. Hardy, "The Influence of Southern Nevada and Southern Utah Folklore upon the Writings of Dr. Juanita Brooks and Dr. Leroy R. Hafen," M.A. thesis, BYU, 1965, 23. This thesis demonstrates that in her writing JB drew extensively upon the folklore of her native region.

29. JB, "Mariah H. Leavitt: Midwife of the Desert Frontier," in *Forms upon the Frontier*, ed. Austin and Alta Fife and Henry H. Glassie (Logan: Utah State University Press, 1969), 120.

30. Hardy, 24.

31. Charity Rowley, conversation with Levi Peterson, 22 December 1985, St. George, Utah.

32. JB, "Let Us Be United," version #1.

33. Ibid.

34. JB, "Let Us Be United," version #2, "Q&C," JBCol Ad, UHS.

35. JB to Henry Leavitt, 20 April 1937, JBCol, UHS.

36. JB, "Five Grandmas," "Q&C," JBCol Ad, UHS.

37. Mary Ann Hafen, Diary, n.d., JBCol 19:2, UHS.

38. JB, "Riding Herd: A Conversation with Juanita Brooks," *Dialogue* 9 (Spring 1974): 14.

39. JB, "A Close-Up of Polygamy," *Harper's* 168 (February 1934): 303–4.

40. JB, *Q&C*, 152.

41. JB, "Five Grandmas."

42. JB, *Q&C*, 47.

43. JB, "A Close-Up of Polygamy," 302.

44. JB, *Q&C*, 159.

45. JB, "Juanita Brooks Remembers," interview by P. T. and E. R. Reilly, 30 September 1973, Salt Lake City, MS 486, UofU.

46. JB, *Q&C*, 131.

47. Irvine McQuarrie to JB, 22 January 1951, JBCol, UHS.

48. JB, "Please Arise!" "Q&C," JBCol 10:18, UHS.

49. JB to Pansy Hardy, 14 August 1963, JBCol, UHS.

50. JB, "The Look Ahead," unpublished speech, 31 May 1959, JBCol 8:23, UHS.

51. JB, "Mariah H. Leavitt," 121–22.

52. JB, "Let's Preserve Our Records," *Utah Humanities Review* 2 (July 1948): 259.

53. JB, *Q&C*, 173.

54. Ibid., 176.

Chapter Two

1. JB, fragment, "Q&C," JBCol Ad, UHS.

2. Charity Rowley and Eva Miles, interview by Levi Peterson, 20 December 1985, St. George, Utah, UHS Oral History Project.

3. Grant Hardy, "Short History of Bunkerville, Clark County, Nevada, from 1877–1960," mimeographed article, 10 December 1960, Las Vegas, Nev.

4. JB, "Roxie S. Romney," unpublished speech, JBCol 8:13, UHS.

5. JB, "More Than Meat," "Q&C," JBCol Ad, UHS.

6. JB, "Roxie S. Romney."

7. JB, "Let Us Be United," version #1, "Q&C," JBCol 9:19, UHS.

8. *Las Vegas Age,* 26 January 1915.

9. JB, *Q&C*, 169.

10. Ibid., 183–84.

11. JB to Pansy Hardy, 14 August 1963, JBCol, UHS.

12. Mary H. Leavitt, account of her life, unpublished, JBCol Ad, UHS.

13. JB, "More Than Meat."

14. Charity Rowley to Henry Leavitt, n.d., JBCol 1:3, UHS.

15. JB to Henry Leavitt, 20 April 1937, JBCol, UHS.

16. JB, "Archie Gubler," unpublished speech, JBCol 8:6, UHS.

17. JB, *Q&C*, 194.

18. Daisy Reber, "Juanita," in "Reminiscences of Juanita Brooks," compiled by Eva Miles, unpublished, JBCol Ad, UHS.

19. LeRoy R. Hafen and Ann W. Hafen, *The Joyous Journey: An Autobiography* (Glendale, Calif.: The Arthur H. Clark Co., 1973), 132.

20. JB, "The Look Ahead," unpublished speech, 31 May 1959, JBCol 8:23, UHS.

21. JB, outline to chapter 5, "Q&C," JBCol 11:11, UHS.

22. JB, "Add to Untravell'd World," fragment, "Q&C," JBCol Ad, UHS.

23. JB, "Riding Herd (Excerpt from a Letter)," *Dialogue*, 1 (Summer 1966):141.

24. JB, *Q&C*, 198.

25. Ibid., 199–201.

26. Ibid., 207.

27. Trudy McMurrin, interview by Levi Peterson, 14 August 1985, Ogden, Utah, UHS Oral History Project.

28. JB, *Q&C*, 210–12.

29. JB to A. C. Lambert, 29 August 1971, JBCol, UHS.

30. JB to Elmer Leavitt, 4 December 1971, JBCol, UHS.

31. Charity Rowley, conversation with Levi Peterson, 22 December 1985, St. George, Utah.

32. JB, *Q&C*, 198.

33. Ibid., 214–15.

34. Ibid., 217–19.

35. Eva Miles, "My Sister Juanita," in "Reminiscences of Juanita Brooks," compiled by Eva Miles, unpublished, JBCol Ad, UHS.

36. Daisy Reber, "Juanita," in "Reminiscences of Juanita Brooks," compiled by Eva Miles, unpublished, JBCol Ad, UHS.

37. JB, "Riding Herd: A Conversation with Juanita Brooks," *Dialogue*, 9 (Spring 1974): 26.

38. Nephi Johnson, "A Blessing Given by Nephi Johnson, Patriarch, upon the head of Juanita Leone Leavitt," 22 September 1918, JBCol 20:20, UHS.

39. JB, *Q&C*, 219.

40. Ibid., 225.

41. Howard Pulsipher, "Leonard Ernest Pulsipher," unpublished reminiscence, September 1985, JBCol Ad, UHS.

42. JB to Ernest Pulsipher, 29 September 1969, JBCol, UHS.

43. Howard Pulsipher, "Leonard Ernest Pulsipher."

44. Howard Pulsipher to Levi Peterson, 24 March 1986.

45. JB, *Q&C*, 230.

46. JB, "Riding Herd: A Conversation with Juanita Brooks," 26.

47. JB, *Q&C*, 229.

48. JB to Charles Kelly, 23 November 1945, JBCol, UHS.

49. Dudley M. Leavitt, interview by Levi Peterson, 19 December 1985, Cedar City, Utah, UHS Oral History Project.

50. Charity Rowley and Eva Miles, interview by Levi Peterson, 20 December 1985, St. George, Utah, UHS Oral History Project.

51. JB, *Q&C*, 231.

52. JB, "An Incident in the Life of Juanita Leavitt and Leonard Ernest Pulsipher," unpublished account, JBCol 9:7, UHS.

53. Ibid.

54. JB, *Q&C*, 234.

55. JB, outline to chapter 6, "Q&C," JBCol 11:11, UHS.

56. JB to A. C. Lambert, 12 August 1971, JBCol, UHS.

57. JB, *Q&C*, 234.

58. JB to Leland R. Cowan, 3 August 1954, JBCol, UHS.

59. JB to Stewart R. Wyatt, 4 December 1974, JBCol, UHS.

60. JB, Preface to "History of Sarah Studevant Leavitt," mimeographed, Bunkerville, Nev., 1919.

61. Sarah Studevant Leavitt, *History of Sarah Studevant Leavitt* (n.p.: private printing of 1919 edition, [1969]), 23.

62. JB, Diary 1920–21, JBCol 19:7, UHS.

63. Joseph I. Earl, "A Blessing Given by Joseph I. Earl upon the head of Juanita Leon [sic] Leavitt Pulsipher," 14 November 1919, JBCol 20:20, UHS.

64. JB, Diary 1920–21.

65. Ibid.

66. Ibid.

67. JB to Lynn Pulsipher, 6 March 1975, JBCol, UHS.

68. JB, "Riding Herd: A Conversation with Juanita Brooks," 15–16.

69. JB, *Q&C*, 237.

70. JB, Diary 1920–21.

71. Hyrum G. Smith, patriarchal blessing, 2 February 1920, JBCol 20:20, UHS.

72. JB, Diary 1920–21.

73. JB, *Q&C*, 239.

74. Charity Rowley, account in "Reminiscences of Juanita Brooks," compiled by Eva Miles, unpublished, JBCol Ad, UHS.

75. Mary Frehner, "Juanita," in "Reminiscences of Juanita Brooks," compiled by Eva Miles, unpublished, JBCol Ad, UHS.

76. JB, "An Incident in the Life of Juanita Leavitt and Leonard Ernest Pulsipher."

77. JB, *Q&C*, 240–41.

78. JB to Lynn Pulsipher, 12 January 1974, JBCol, UHS.

79. JB, Diary 1920–21.

80. JB, *Q&C*, 242.

81. Ibid., 244–45.

82. Howard Pulsipher, conversation with Levi Peterson, 2 April 1986, Salt Lake City, Utah.

83. JB, Diary 1920–21.

84. Ibid.

85. Howard Pulsipher, conversation with Levi Peterson.

86. William E. Abbott, *The Story of My Life* ([St. George, Utah]: privately published, n.d.), 52–53.

87. Howard Pulsipher, conversation with Levi Peterson.

88. Emily Abbott Hughes, conversation with Levi Peterson, 26 March 1986, St. George, Utah.

Chapter Three

1. JB, Diary 1920–21, 26 November 1921.

2. Ibid., 12 December 1921.

3. JB, outline to chapter 7, "Q&C," JBCol 11:11, UHS.

4. JB to Bruce Furr, 7 August 1967, JBCol, UHS.

5. JB, *Q&C*, 244.

6. JB, Diary 1920–21, 6 November 1921. The autobiography and the

diary give contradictory accounts of Juanita's movements in the spring and summer of 1921. Where it is possible, I have reconciled them. Where it is not, I have relied on the diary.

7. JB to Aura Allen, 26 June 1974, JBCol, UHS.

8. JB, *Q&C*, 255.

9. Ibid., 257

10. Lloyd W. Covin, "The Rise, Progress, and Development of Dixie Junior College," M.S. thesis, UofU, 1962, 34

11. "College Notes," *The Dixie 1922*, n.p.

12. JB to Tony and Janet Brooks, 9 November 1976, JBCol, UHS.

13. JB, *Q&C*, 260.

14. Aura Allen, "Juanita," in "Reminiscences of Juanita Brooks," compiled by Eva Miles, unpublished, JBCol Ad, UHS.

15. JB, *Q&C*, 261.

16. JB, "The Usual Dilemma," *The Dixie – The Girl's Edition 1922*, n.p.

17. JB to Tony and Janet, 9 November 1976, JBCol, UHS.

18. JB, *Q&C*, 264.

19. Ibid., 264

20. JB to Ernest Pulsipher, 29 September 1969, JBCol, UHS.

21. JB, *Q&C*, 267.

22. Ibid., 269.

23. Ibid., 273.

24. JB, "Report to Dr. A. W. McGregor," fragment, JBCol Ad, UHS.

25. JB, *Q&C*, 279.

26. JB, "Home for Christmas – 1924," fragment, "Q&C," JBCol Ad, UHS.

27. JB, *Q&C*, 285.

28. Ibid., 288.

29. Charity Rowley, account in "Reminiscences of Juanita Brooks," compiled by Eva Miles, unpublished, JBCol Ad, UHS.

30. JB, *Q&C*, 288.

31. Aura Allen to JB, 16 March 1973, JBCol, UHS.

32. JB to Parker M. Neilson, 20 May 1966, JBCol, UHS.

33. Augusta Flake, interview by Levi Peterson, 2 September 1985, Snowflake, Ariz., UHS Oral History Project.

34. BYU Records Office to Levi Peterson, 13 February 1986.

35. JB to Ray R. Canning, 9 August 1964, JBCol, UHS. The incident is detailed in *Q&C*, 291–92. That account mistakenly claims that Joseph K. Nicholes offered her a job; he was not then president of Dixie College. It also says his offer came the day after commencement. I rely for my contrary dating on JB's letter to Canning.

36. Ernest Pulsipher, interview by Levi Peterson, 20 December 1985, St. George, Utah, UHS Oral History Project.

37. JB, *Q&C*, 293–94.

38. JB, "But Thinking Makes It So," unpublished story, JBCol 8:40, UHS.

39. JB, *Q&C*, 295.

40. Ernest Pulsipher, "A Few Personal Glimpses of Juanita Brooks," *Utah Historical Quarterly* 55 (Summer 1987): 270.

41. JB, outline to chapter 9, "Q&C," JBCol 11:11, UHS.

42. JB, *Q&C*, 295–96.

43. JB to Joseph and Tina Walker, 31 December 1952, JBCol, UHS.

44. JB to Gladys [Harrison], 9 December 1963, JBCol, UHS.

45. JB, "Jest a Copyin'–Word f'r Word," *Utah Historical Quarterly* 37 (Fall 1969): 378.

46. Ernest Pulsipher, interview.

47. Daisy Reber, "Juanita," in "Reminiscences of Juanita Brooks," compiled by Eva Miles, unpublished, JBCol Ad, UHS.

48. Eva Miles, "My Sister Juanita," in "Reminiscences of Juanita Brooks," compiled by Eva Miles, unpublished, JBCol Ad, UHS.

49. JB, *Q&C*, 296.

50. JB, "Jest a Copyin'–Word f'r Word," 377–78.

51. Francis Leavitt, conversation with Levi Peterson, 3 June 1986, Sacramento, Calif.

52. Daisy Reber, "Juanita."

53. JB, *Q&C*, 297.

54. Pansy L. Hardy, "The Influence of Southern Nevada and Southern Utah Folklore upon the Writings of Dr. Juanita Brooks and Dr. Leroy R. Hafen," M.A. thesis, BYU, 1965, 25.

55. JB, *Q&C*, 299.

56. JB, Roll Book: 1927–28, Dixie Junior College Archives, St. George, Utah.

57. JB, *Q&C*, 301.

58. JB to Henry and Mary Leavitt, 16 September 1928, JBCol, UHS.

59. JB, "The Bells," fragment, "Q&C," JBCol 35:16, UHS.

60. JB to Henry and Mary Leavitt, 16 September 1928, JBCol, UHS.

61. Ibid.

62. JB, *Q&C*, 304.

63. Mary Frehner, "Juanita," in "Reminiscences of Juanita Brooks," compiled by Eva Miles, unpublished, JBCol Ad, UHS.

64. Ernest Pulsipher, "Some Christmases That Stand Out In My Memory," unpublished fragment, JBCol Ad, UHS.

65. JB to Dale Morgan, 13 December 1945, DMCol, BAN.

66. JB, outline to chapter 10, "Q&C," JBCol 11:11, UHS.

67. JB, "The Unmarried Woman and Polygamy," unpublished article, JBCol 11:15, UHS.

68. JB, "Riding Herd: A Conversation with Juanita Brooks," *Dialogue* 9 (Spring 1974): 19.

69. JB, "Founder's Day, Dixie College," unpublished speech, JBCol 8:27, UHS. The version of this incident in *Q&C* differs; unpublished sources support the Founder's Day speech.

70. JB, outline to chapter 10, "Q&C."

71. JB, *Q&C*, 308.

72. JB, outline to chapter 10, "Q&C."

73. Francis Leavitt, "Life with Juanita," in "Reminiscences of Juanita Brooks," compiled by Eva Miles, unpublished, JBCol Ad, UHS.

74. Dudley Leavitt, "Juanita," in "Reminiscences of Juanita Brooks," compiled by Eva Miles, unpublished, JBCol Ad, UHS.

75. JB, *Q&C*, 316–17.

76. Ibid., 311.

77. Eva Miles, "My Sister Juanita."

78. Francis Leavitt, "Life with Juanita."

79. JB, *Q&C*, 318.

80. JB to Brother and Sister Esplin, 11 September 1939, JBCol, UHS.

81. Ibid.

82. JB, *Q&C*, 319–22.

83. Daisy Reber, "Juanita."

84. Francis Leavitt, "Life with Juanita."

85. JB, *Q&C*, 323.

86. Ernest Pulsipher, "A Few Personal Glimpses of Juanita Brooks," 274.

87. JB, "Excerpts of a Tribute to John T. Woodbury, Jr.," unpublished speech, JBCol 8:16, UHS.

88. JB, *Q&C*, 326.

89. Mary Frehner, "Juanita."

90. JB, *Q&C*, 328.

Chapter Four

1. Certificate of Marriage, JBCol 21:20, UHS.

2. JB, "The Adventures of a Sheriff's Wife," outline to chapter 11, "Q&C," JBCol 11:11, UHS.

3. JB, "I Married a Family," version #1, "Q&C," JBCol 9:6, UHS.

4. JB, "I Married a Family," version #2, fragment, "Q&C," JBCol Ad, UHS.

5. JB, "I Married a Family," *Dialogue* 6 (Summer 1971): 15.

6. JB, Diary 1933–36, 27 June 1933.

7. JB, "I Married a Family," version #2, "Q&C."

8. JB, "I Married a Family," *Dialogue*, 16.

9. JB, "I Married a Family," version #1, "Q&C."

10. JB, Diary 1933–36, 5 July 1933.

11. Ibid., 13 July 1933.

12. Ibid., 22 November 1933.

13. Ibid., 19 July 1933.

14. JB, "Jest a Copyin'–Word f'r Word," *Utah Historical Quarterly*, 37 (Fall 1969): 380.

15. JB, Diary 1933–36, 22 November 1933.

16. Francis Leavitt, "Life with Juanita," in "Reminiscences of Juanita Brooks," compiled by Eva Miles, unpublished, JBCol Ad, UHS.

17. JB, Diary 1933–36, 6 December 1933.

18. JB, "I Married a Family," *Dialogue*, 16.

19. Walter Brooks, "Memoir: Juanita and Will Brooks," unpublished reminiscence, August 1985, JBCol Ad, UHS.

20. Ernest Pulsipher, "The Evolution of a Deer Camp," *St. George Magazine* 3 (Fall 1985): 93.

21. JB, Diary 1933–36, 29 June 1933.

22. Mary C. Kimball to JB, 27 November 1933, JBCol, UHS.

23. JB, Diary 1933–36, 27 November 1933.

24. JB, "A Close-up of Polygamy," *Harper's* 168 (February 1934): 306.

25. Harold W. Bentley to JB, 22 January 1934, JBCol, UHS.

26. A. J. Ashman to JB, 7 February 1934, JBCol, UHS.

27. Joseph K. and Olive Nicholes to JB, 31 January 1934, JBCol, UHS.

28. Newell K. Young to JB, 16 February 1934, JBCol, UHS.

29. Ibid., 3 March 1934, JBCol, UHS.

30. Ibid., 10 February 1934, JBCol, UHS.

31. JB, "So You've Married a Family," unpublished article, JBCol 11:3, UHS.

32. JB, Diary 1933–36, 16 August 1934.

33. Ibid., 28 August 1934.

34. Ibid., 5 September 1934.

35. Walter Brooks, "Memoir: Juanita and Will Brooks."

36. Ibid.

37. Nels Anderson to JB, 1 November 1934, JBCol, UHS.

38. JB, Diary, 1933–36, 29 December 1934.

39. JB, "Jest a Copyin'—Word f 'r Word," 381–82.

40. "Report of Project for Collection of Social and Historical Data in Washington County—Juanita Brooks, Supervisor," Utah Emergency Relief Administration, 1935, Man A2356, UHS.

41. Ernest Pulsipher, "Some Cows I Won't Forget," *Nevadan*, 29 December 1985, 11(L).

42. JB, "Power to You!," unpublished article, JBCol 10:20, UHS.

43. Nels Anderson to Darrell J. Greenwell, 18 October 1935, JBCol, UHS.

44. JB to Marian Hibbert, 27 November 1966, JBCol, UHS; see also Grace Winkleman, "Record of Program Operation and Accomplishment: Writers' Program," in Darrell J. Greenwell, "Final Report of the State Administrator, WPA, Utah, 1935–1943," Mic 3, UHS.

45. JB, Diary 1933–36, 19 August 1936.

46. JB, "I Married a Family," *Dialogue*, 20.

47. Ernest Pulsipher, "A Few Personal Glimpses of Juanita Brooks," *Utah Historical Quarterly* 55 (Summer 1987): 274.

48. JB to Nels Anderson, 25 March [1936], JBCol, UHS.

49. Ibid., 14 November 1936, JBCol, UHS.

50. JB to Maurice L. Howe, 19 June 1936, JBCol, UHS.

51. JB to Nels Anderson, 14 November 1936, JBCol, UHS.

52. JB to Preston B. Albright, 26 July 1936, JBCol, UHS.

53. JB to Luther H. Evans, 1 October 1936, JBCol, UHS.

54. Ernest Pulsipher, "A Few Personal Glimpses of Juanita Brooks," 271.

55. Ernest Pulsipher, interview by Levi Peterson, 20 December 1985, St. George, Utah, UHS Oral History Project.

56. Ibid.

57. Walter Brooks, "Memoir: Juanita and Will Brooks."

58. JB, *Uncle Will Tells His Story* (Salt Lake City: Taggart & Co., 1970), 221.

59. JB to Wanda Burnett, 31 July 1936, JBCol, UHS.

60. Luther H. Evans to JB, 2 September 1936, JBCol, UHS.

61. JB to Mary W. Shumway, 22 July 1936, JBCol, UHS.

62. See *Name Index to the Library of Congress Collection of Mormon Diaries*, Western Text Society Series (Logan: Utah State University Press, 1971.)

63. Kate B. Carter, comp., *Heart Throbs of the West*, vol. 1 (Salt Lake City: Daughters of the Utah Pioneers, 1939), 6.

64. For example, there is in JBCol 30:6, UHS, a typed manuscript reading: "Indians of Iron and Washington Counties. Copy made for BYU library, Prof.

M. Wilford Poulson, from Mrs. Wm. Brooks, Sept. 1938."

65. JB, "Jest a Copyin'–Word f 'r Word," 384.

66. JB to Erma ?, 14 November 1936, JBCol, UHS.

67. JB to Mildred Bowler, 2 August 1937, JBCol, UHS.

68. Walter Brooks, "Memoir: Juanita and Will Brooks."

69. JB, "The Arizona Strip," unpublished article, JBCol 8:35, UHS.

70. JB to William R. Palmer, 17 March 1938, JBCol, UHS.

71. JB to Ward Relief Society Presidents, 7 June 1937, JBCol, UHS.

72. JB, "In the Balance–Mormon Social Security," unpublished article, JBCol 10:7, UHS.

73. Zora S. Jarvis and Juanita Brooks, "The L.D.S. Welfare Plan in St. George Stake," unpublished article, JBCol 9:18, UHS.

74. Ernest Pulsipher, "A Few Personal Glimpses of Juanita Brooks," 274.

75. JB, "I Married a Family," version #1, "Q&C."

76. Walter Brooks, "Memoir: Juanita and Will Brooks."

77. D. R. Wheelwright to JB, 10 November 1937, JBCol, UHS.

78. JB, "Backgrounds for Mormon Social Security," unpublished article, WSC.

79. Julian Dana to JB, 20 April 1937, JBCol, UHS.

80. JB, "Whose Business is Recreation?" *The Improvement Era* 41 (October 1938): 597.

81. JB, "Lucy," unpublished story, JBCol 9:22, UHS.

82. M. C. Nelson to JB, 3 June 1939, JBCol, UHS.

83. Mrs. Scott P. Stewart to JB, 16 September 1940, JBCol, UHS.

84. William R. Palmer to Sarah Crosby, 17 March 1930, JBCol, UHS.

85. JB to Emma Seegmiller Higbee, 10 August 1936, JBCol, UHS.

86. "Bull Valley Snort," carbon manuscript, JBCol 26:10, UHS.

87. JB to Emma Seegmiller Higbee, 11 December 1936, JBCol, UHS.

88. JB to Myron F. Higbee, 7 September 1937, JBCol, UHS.

89. Ibid., 28 October 1937, JBCol, UHS.

90. JB, "Sidelight on the Mountain Meadows Massacre," abstract, *Proceedings of the Utah Academy of Sciences, Arts and Letters* 17 (1940): 12. The complete article is not extant.

Chapter Five

1. JB to Dale Morgan, 10 September 1941, DMCol, BAN.

2. Ibid., 25 July 1943, DMCol, BAN.

3. JB, "I Married a Family," *Dialogue* 6 (Summer 1971): 21.

4. JB to Dale Morgan, 9 April 1941, DMCol, BAN.

5. JB, "Power to You!" unpublished article, JBCol 10:20, UHS; also see JB to Gladys [Harrison], 9 December 1963, JBCol, UHS.

6. JB, "The Water's In," *Harper's* 182 (May 1941): 608.

7. Ed. R. Tuttle to JB, 30 June 1941, JBCol, UHS.

8. JB to Dale Morgan, 14 August 1941, DMCol, BAN.

9. Dale Morgan to JB, 12 April 1942, JBCol, UHS.

10. JB to Dale Morgan, 11 August 1941, DMCol, BAN.

11. Ibid., 25 November 1941, DMCol, BAN.

12. JB to Charles Kelly, 7 September 1941, MS 100, UofU.

13. Dale Morgan to JB, 21 May 1942, JBCol, UHS.

14. Ibid., 16 July 1942, JBCol, UHS.
15. JB to Dale Morgan, 28 October 1941, DMCol, BAN.
16. Ibid., 27 December 1941, MS 143, UofU.
17. Ibid., 25 November 1941, DMCol, BAN.
18. Ibid., 6 November 1941, DMCol, BAN.
19. Dale Morgan to JB, 29 December 1941, DMCol, BAN.
20. JB to Dale Morgan, 5 February 1942, DMCol, BAN.
21. Ibid., 20 January 1942, DMCol, BAN.
22. Ibid., 5 February 1942, DMCol, BAN.
23. Ibid., 16 February 1942, DMCol, BAN.
24. Ibid., 7 March [1942], DMCol, BAN.
25. Ibid., 5 April [1942], DMCol, BAN.
26. Dale Morgan to JB, 12 April 1942, JBCol, UHS.
27. JB to Dale Morgan, 5 June 1942, DMCol, BAN.
28. Ibid., 27 May [1942], DMCol, BAN.
29. Ibid., 5 June 1942, DMCol, BAN.
30. Nels Anderson to JB, 29 May 1942, JBCol, UHS.
31. JB to Ettie Lee, 2 May 1949, JBCol, UHS.
32. JB to Dale Morgan, 23 September 1942, DMCol, BAN.
33. Dale Morgan to JB, 27 June 1942, JBCol, UHS.
34. LeRoy R. Hafen to JB, 29 June 1942, JBCol, UHS.
35. JB, *Dudley Leavitt: Pioneer to Southern Utah* (St. George, Utah: By the author, 1942), 105.
36. Laurel and Melva Leavitt, "Tribute of Love and Appreciation to Our Sister Juanita L. Brooks," in "Reminiscences of Juanita Brooks," compiled by Eva Miles, unpublished, JBCol Ad, UHS; also Melva Leavitt to Levi Peterson, 24 August 1986.
37. JB to Dale Morgan, 23 September 1942, DMCol, BAN.
38. Ibid., 11 September [1942], DMCol, BAN.
39. Dale Morgan to JB, 27 September 1942, DMCol, BAN.
40. JB to Dale Morgan, 13 December 1942, DMCol, BAN.
41. Ibid., 25 November 1942, DMCol, BAN.
42. Nels Anderson to JB, 16 May 1943, JBCol, UHS.
43. JB to Dale Morgan, 20 October 1941, DMCol, BAN.
44. Ibid., 23 September 1942, DMCol, BAN.
45. Ibid., 25 November 1942, DMCol, BAN.
46. Dale Morgan to JB, 5 December 1942, MS 486, UofU.
47. JB to Dale Morgan, 13 December 1942, DMCol, BAN.
48. Ibid., 11 January 1943, DMCol, BAN.
49. Ibid., 27 February 1943, DMCol, BAN.
50. Ibid., 20 May 1943, DMCol, BAN.
51. Dale Morgan to JB, 15 January 1943, JBCol, UHS.
52. Ibid.; compare JB, "Indian Relations on the Mormon Frontier," *Utah Historical Quarterly* 12 (January-April 1944): 3.
53. Wallace Stegner to JB, 26 January 1943, JBCol, UHS.
54. JB to Dale Morgan, 11 February 1943, DMCol, BAN.
55. Ibid.
56. Ibid., 21 February 1943, DMCol, BAN.
57. Ibid., 27 February 1943, DMCol, BAN.
58. Ibid., 9 March 1943, DMCol, BAN.

59. Ibid., 21 March 1943, DMCol, BAN.
60. Ibid., 6 April 1943, DMCol, BAN.
61. JB, "Jest a Copyin'–Word f'r Word," *Utah Historical Quarterly* 37 (Fall 1969): 389.
62. JB to Dale Morgan, 21 March 1943, DMCol, BAN.
63. Dale Morgan to JB, 21 April 1943, JBCol, UHS.
64. JB to Dale Morgan, 6 April 1943, DMCol, BAN.
65. JB, "Jacob Hamblin: Apostle to the Indians," *Arizona Highways* 19 (April 1943): 35.
66. JB, "The Mormon Battalion," *Arizona Highways* 19 (May 1943): 39.
67. JB to Dale Morgan, 6 April 1943, DMCol, BAN.
68. Ibid., [? May 1943], DMCol, BAN.
69. Ibid.
70. Ibid., 14 June 1943, MS 143, UofU.
71. Agreement between Wilford W. and Josephine B. Knight and Miss Clara Hamblin, 23 July 1943, JBCol 21:16, UHS.
72. JB, "Ten Days in the County Hospital," unpublished article, JBCol 11:9, UHS.
73. JB to Dale Morgan, 25 July 1943, DMCol, BAN.
74. Ibid., 23 August 1943, DMCol, BAN.
75. Ibid.
76. Dale Morgan to JB, 10 September 1943, JBCol, UHS.
77. JB to Dale Morgan, 14 September 1943, DMCol, BAN.
78. Ibid., 7 October 1943, DMCol, BAN.
79. Marguerite L. Sinclair to JB, 21 July 1943, JBCol, UHS.
80. JB to Dale Morgan, 13 August 1943, DMCol, BAN.
81. JB quotes Alter in JB to Dale Morgan, 14 September 1943, DMCol, BAN.
82. JB to Dale Morgan, 14 September 1943, DMCol, BAN.
83. Ibid., 7 October 1943, DMCol, BAN.
84. Ibid., 8 November 1943, DMCol, BAN.
85. Ibid., 21 February 1944, DMCol, BAN.
86. Ibid., 7 October 1943, DMCol, BAN.
87. Ibid., 7 January 1944, DMCol, BAN.
88. Ibid.
89. Ibid., 2 February 1944, DMCol, BAN.
90. Dale Morgan to Madeline McQuown, 11 February 1944, MS 143, UofU.
91. Dale Morgan to JB, [11 February 1944], JBCol 7:12, UHS.
92. JB to Dale Morgan, 25 February 1944, DMCol, BAN.
93. Dale Morgan to JB, 29 February 1944, JBCol, UHS.
94. JB to Huntington Library, 16 February 1944, Institutional Archives, HL.
95. Leslie E. Bliss to JB, 18 February 1944, Institutional Archives, HL.
96. JB to Dale Morgan, 19 March 1944, DMCol, BAN.
97. Ibid., 21 February 1944, DMCol, BAN.
98. Ibid., 20 March 1944, DMCol, BAN.
99. Ibid., 11 April [1944], DMCol, BAN.
100. Dale Morgan to JB, 12 April 1944, JBCol, UHS.
101. JB to Dale Morgan, 27 March [1944], DMCol, BAN.

102. Dale Morgan to JB, 12 April 1944, JBCol, UHS.

103. JB to Dale Morgan, 8 May 1944, DMCol, BAN.

104. Ibid.

105. Ibid., 16 May [1944], DMCol, BAN.

106. Ibid., 30 May 1944, DMCol, BAN.

107. Ibid., 20 June 1944, DMCol, BAN.

108. Dale Morgan to JB, 20 June 1944, JBCol, UHS.

109. JB to Dale Morgan, 3 July 1944, DMCol, BAN.

110. Louis B. Wright to JB, 7 July 1944, JBCol, UHS.

111. JB to Leslie Bliss, 24 July 44, Institutional Archives, HL.

112. Ibid., 4 August 1944, JBCol, UHS.

113. JB to Dale Morgan, 25 August 1944, DMCol, BAN.

114. Ibid., 1 August 1944, DMCol, BAN.

115. Dale Morgan to Bernard DeVoto, 4 August 1944, Juanita Brooks Miscellaneous File, UofU Press.

116. JB to Dale Morgan, 13 August [1944], DMCol, BAN.

117. Fred T. Marsh to JB, 11 August 1944, DMCol, BAN.

118. JB to Dale Morgan, 19 August [1944], DMCol, BAN.

119. Ibid., 21 September 1944, DMCol, BAN.

120. Ibid., 25 August 1944, DMCol, BAN.

121. JB to Leslie Bliss, 27 August 1944, Institutional Archives, HL.

122. Ann Elizabeth Pulsipher to JB, 5 September 1944, Institutional Archives, HL.

123. JB to Leslie Bliss, 18 September 1944, Institutional Archives, HL.

124. Willa Derrick, interview by Levi Peterson, 20 December 1985, St. George, Utah, UHS Oral History Project.

125. Lynn Pulsipher, conversation with Levi Peterson, 25 May 1986, Ogden, Utah.

126. JB to Leslie Bliss, 18 September 1944, Institutional Archives, HL.

127. JB to Dale Morgan, 21 September 1944, DMCol, BAN.

128. JB to Marba C. Josephson, 20 September 1944, JBCol, UHS.

129. Marguerite Sinclair to JB, 30 September 1944, JBCol, UHS.

130. JB to Dale Morgan, 11 October 1944, DMCol, BAN.

131. Ibid., 30 October 1944, DMCol, BAN.

132. Ibid., 20 November [1944], DMCol, BAN.

133. Ibid., 21 September 1944, DMCol, BAN.

134. Ibid., 11 October 1944, DMCol, BAN.

135. Dale Morgan to JB, 19 October 1944, JBCol, UHS.

136. Ibid., 13 November 1944, JBCol, UHS.

137. JB to Dale Morgan, 20 November [1944], DMCol, BAN.

138. JB to Ivy ?, 1 December 1944, JBCol, UHS.

139. JB to Dale Morgan, 13 December 1944, DMCol, BAN.

140. Mary Leavitt, quoted in "100 Years of Melody: A Brief Biographical Sketch of the Lives of Dudley Henry and Mary Hafen Leavitt," unpublished, compiled by Lana Frehner Larkin, St. George, Utah, 1977, 43.

141. JB to Leslie Bliss, 29 January 1945, Institutional Archives, HL.

142. JB to Dale Morgan, 10 March 1945, DMCol, BAN.

143. Ibid., 10 March 1944, DMCol, BAN.

144. Joseph K. Nicholes to JB, 18 May 1945, JBCol, UHS.

145. Charles S. Peterson, "Juanita Brooks, Unadorned Realist," intro-

duction to JB, *Emma Lee*, 2d ed. (Logan: Utah State University Press, 1984), 8.

146. JB, "Indian Relations on the Mormon Frontier," *Utah Historical Quarterly* 12 (January-April 1944): 47–48.

147. Dale Morgan to JB, 14 April 1945, JBCol, UHS.

148. JB to Dale Morgan, 18 April 1945, DMCol, BAN.

149. Ibid., 21 September 1944, DMCol, BAN.

150. JB to Robert Glass Cleland, 10 April 1945, JBCol, UHS.

151. JB to Dale Morgan, 18 April 1945, DMCol, BAN.

152. JB to Robert Glass Cleland, 22 May 1945, JBCol, UHS.

153. Robert Glass Cleland to JB, 24 May 1945, JBCol, UHS.

154. JB to Robert Glass Cleland, 28 May 1945, JBCol, UHS.

155. Ibid., 5 June 1945, JBCol, UHS.

156. Robert Glass Cleland to JB, 9 June 1945, JBCol, UHS.

157. Robert Glass Cleland to Whom It May Concern, 9 June 1945, JBCol, UHS.

158. JB to Dale Morgan, 4 June 1945, DMCol, BAN.

159. Ibid., 6 July 1945, DMCol, BAN.

160. Ibid., 18 July [1945], DMCol, BAN.

161. Ibid., 9 April 1945, DMCol, BAN.

162. Ibid., 18 July [1945], DMCol, BAN.

163. Ibid., 16 September 1945, DMCol, BAN.

164. Ibid., 18 July [1945], DMCol, BAN.

165. Ibid., 15 August 1945, DMCol, BAN.

166. Dale Morgan to JB, 26 April 1945, JBCol, UHS.

167. Ibid., 5 July 1945, JBCol, UHS.

168. JB to Dale Morgan, 10 August [1945], DMCol, BAN.

169. Ibid., 16 September 1945, DMCol, BAN.

170. Dale Morgan to Fred T. Marsh, 6 December 1945, DMCol, BAN.

171. John Selby to JB, 19 April 1948, JBCol, UHS.

172. JB to D. L. Chambers, 10 February 1949, JBCol, UHS.

173. JB, *Quicksand and Cactus: A Memoir of the Southern Mormon Frontier* (Salt Lake City: Howe Brothers, 1982), 107.

174. Ibid., 108.

175. Ibid., 108–9.

176. Ibid., 87.

177. JB to George Albert Smith, 9 October 1945, JBCol, UHS.

178. George Albert Smith to JB, 16 October 1945, JBCol, UHS.

179. JB to Dale Morgan, 22 October 1945, DMCol, BAN.

180. Ibid.

181. Ibid., 13 December 1945, JBCol, UHS.

182. Ibid., 18 December 1945, DMCol, BAN.

183. Ibid., 26 November [1945], DMCol, BAN.

184. Dale Morgan to JB, 15 December 1945, JBCol, UHS.

185. JB to Dale Morgan, 28 December 1945, DMCol, BAN.

186. Dale Morgan to JB, 11 November 1945, JBCol, UHS.

187. JB to Dale Morgan, 9 December 1945, JBCol, UHS.

188. Dale Morgan to JB, 15 December 1945, JBCol, UHS.

189. Dale Morgan to Fawn Brodie, 22 December 1945, MS 360, UofU.

190. JB to Dale Morgan, 28 December 1945, DMCol, BAN.

Chapter Six

1. JB, "Beauty Beckons in the Parks of Southern Utah," *Utah Magazine* 8 (June 1946): 33.

2. JB to Dale Morgan, 22 January 1946, DMCol, BAN.

3. W. L. Cook to JB, 9 February 1946, Institutional Archives, HL.

4. JB to Dale Morgan, 1 March 1946, DMCol, BAN.

5. JB to Leslie Bliss, 5 June 1946, Institutional Archives, HL.

6. JB to Dale Morgan, 1 March 1946, DMCol, BAN.

7. Ibid., 19 May 1946, JBCol, UHS.

8. JB to Leslie Bliss, 29 April 1946, JBCol, UHS.

9. JB to Dale Morgan, 4 April 1946, JBCol, UHS.

10. Ibid., 31 May 1946, JBCol, UHS.

11. Ibid., 25 June 1946, DMCol, BAN.

12. Ibid., 18 July 1946, DMCol, BAN.

13. Kay Brooks to Levi Peterson, 10 September 1985.

14. JB to Leslie Bliss, 2 August 1946, Institutional Archives, HL.

15. JB to Dale Morgan, 20 August 1946, DMCol, BAN.

16. Ibid., 29 October 1946, JBCol, UHS.

17. JB to Hugh Nibley, 7 November 1946, JBCol, UHS.

18. JB to Dale Morgan, 30 November 1946, JBCol, UHS.

19. Ettie Lee to JB, 25 November 1946, JBCol, UHS.

20. JB to Ettie Lee, 28 November 1946, JBCol, UHS.

21. Ettie Lee to JB, 2 December 1946, JBCol, UHS.

22. Dale Morgan to JB, 15 January 1947, JBCol, UHS.

23. JB to Dale Morgan, [? January 1947], JBCol 2:1, UHS.

24. JB, "To the Glory of God," *Arizona Highways* 23 (April 1947): 32.

25. JB to Dale Morgan, 6 March 1947, JBCol, UHS.

26. Ibid., 29 March 1947, DMCol, BAN.

27. Austin E. Fife to Dale Morgan, 14 May 1947, JBCol 38:36, UHS. The article was eventually published in *Journal of American Folklore* (January-March 1948): 19–30.

28. JB to Dale Morgan, 4 June 1947, JBCol, UHS.

29. Ibid., 25 April [1947], JBCol, UHS.

30. JB to ? Mitchell, 11 February 1947, JBCol, UHS.

31. JB to Dale Morgan, 6 March 1947, JBCol, UHS.

32. Ibid.

33. JB to Leslie Bliss, 24 March 1947, JBCol, UHS.

34. JB to Dale Morgan, 25 April [1947], JBCol, UHS.

35. Ibid.

36. JB, "The First One Hundred Years of Southern Utah History," *Proceedings of the Utah Academy of Sciences, Arts and Letters* 24 (1946–47):71.

37. Ibid., 77.

38. Ibid., 79.

39. JB to [Manetta] Henrie, 2 July 1947, JBCol, UHS.

40. Will Brooks to Robert Brooks, 15 August 1947, JBCol, UHS.

41. JB to Leslie Bliss, 20 October [1947], JBCol, UHS.

42. Ibid., 10 November 1947, JBCol, UHS.

43. Ettie Lee to JB, 11 November 1947, JBCol, UHS.

44. JB to Robert Glass Cleland, 16 December 1947, JBCol, UHS.

45. JB to Dale Morgan, 6 January 1948, JBCol, UHS.
46. Robert Glass Cleland to JB, 9 February 1948, JBCol, UHS.
47. Edith R. Mirrielees to JB, 4 November 1947, JBCol, UHS.
48. JB, "Jacob Hamblin: Apostle to the Lamanites," *The Pacific Spectator* 2 (1948): 320.
49. Ibid., 321.
50. Ibid., 329.
51. JB to Dale Morgan, 20 May 1948, JBCol, UHS.
52. Dale Morgan to Fawn Brodie, 22 May 1948, MS 360, UofU.
53. JB to Leslie Bliss, 20 May 1948, JBCol, UHS.
54. JB to Kate B. Carter, 20 May 1948, JBCol, UHS.
55. Mary H. Leavitt, Application for Membership, The Society of Daughters of the Utah Pioneers, JBCol Ad, UHS.
56. JB, "Let's Preserve Our Records," *Utah Humanities Review* 2 (July 1948): 263.
57. JB, "Ye Who Are Called to Labor," *The Improvement Era* 51 (September 1948): 594, 596.
58. JB, "Trippingly Off the Tongue," *Deseret News*, 12 September 1948, 6(F).
59. JB to Ettie Lee, 23 July 1948, JBCol, UHS.
60. Dale Morgan to JB, 2 September 1948, MS 486, UofU.
61. Wallace Stegner to JB, 16 September 1948, JBCol, UHS.
62. JB to Wallace Stegner, 24 September 1948, JBCol, UHS.
63. JB to Leslie Bliss, 16 October 1948, JBCol, UHS.
64. Will Brooks to Robert Brooks, 25 October [1948], JBCol 20:22, UHS.
65. JB to Leslie Bliss, 16 October 1948, JBCol, UHS.
66. Ibid., 27 October 1948, JBCol, UHS.
67. JB to Ettie Lee, 12 November 1948, JBCol, UHS.
68. Ibid., 21 January 1949, JBCol, UHS.
69. JB to Stanton Schmutz, 18 January 1949, JBCol, UHS.
70. JB to Harold B. Lee, 18 January 1949, JBCol, UHS.
71. Harold B. Lee to JB, 24 January 1949, MS 486, UofU.
72. Mary Frehner to Levi Peterson, 22 September 1986.
73. JB to Joseph and Tina Walker, 16 March 1949, JBCol, UHS.
74. Dale Morgan to JB, 23 March 1949, MS 486, UofU.
75. Donald Bean to JB, 10 March 1949, JBCol, UHS.
76. JB to Donald Bean, 14 March 1949, JBCol, UHS.
77. Ibid., 13 April 1949, JBCol, UHS.
78. Donald Bean to JB, 20 April 1949, JBCol, UHS.
79. Ettie Lee to JB, 29 April 1949, JBCol, UHS.
80. JB to Ettie Lee, 2 May 1949, JBCol, UHS.
81. JB to Edith R. Mirrielees, 26 May 1949, JBCol, UHS.
82. JB, "The Arizona Strip," *The Pacific Spectator* 3 (Summer 1949): 301.
83. JB to Leslie Bliss, 9 June 1949, Institutional Archives, HL.
84. JB to Ettie Lee, 19 June 1949, JBCol, UHS.
85. Ibid., 3 June 1949, JBCol, UHS.
86. Dale Morgan to JB, 3 July 1949, MS 486, UofU.
87. Donald Bean to JB, 8 July 1949, JBCol, UHS.
88. JB to Donald Bean, 11 July 1949, Operational Files, StanUPress.
89. JB to Ettie Lee, 12 July 1949, JBCol, UHS.

90. JB to Donald Bean, 15 July 1949, JBCol, UHS.

91. Ibid., 16 July 1949, JBCol, UHS.

92. Donald Bean to JB, 18 July 1949, JBCol, UHS.

93. JB Folder, Operational Files, StanUPress.

94. JB to Dale Morgan, 28 July [1949], DMCol, BAN.

95. JB to Ettie Lee, 13 September 1949, JBCol, UHS.

96. Ibid., 20 September 1949, JBCol, UHS.

97. Pamela Faust to JB, 2 November 1949, JBCol, UHS.

98. ? to Donald Bean, 19 January 1949, Operational Files, StanUPress.

99. Donald Bean to Charles Allen, 24 October 1949, Operational Files, StanUPress.

100. Pamela Faust to Donald Bean, 31 October 1949, Operational Files, StanUPress.

101. JB to Pamela Faust, 11 November 1949, JBCol, UHS.

102. Pamela Faust to JB, 23 November 1949, JBCol, UHS.

103. JB to Pamela Faust, 1 December 1949, JBCol, UHS.

104. Dale Morgan to JB, 15 November 1949, MS 486, UofU.

105. JB to Donald F. Whistler, 25 February 1950, JBCol, UHS.

106. JB to Pamela Faust, 4 October 1950, JBCol, UHS.

107. "Minutes, Convention Utah Chapter National Association of Postmasters," 23 to 25 May 1950, St. George, Utah, JBCol 20:17, UHS.

108. Robert J. Twiggs to Will and Juanita Brooks, 3 June 1950, JBCol, UHS.

109. Leslie Bliss to JB, 1 August 1950, JBCol, UHS.

110. JB to Leslie Bliss, 8 June 1950, Institutional Archives, HL.

111. A. Russell and Dorothy Mortensen, interview by Levi Peterson, 9 September 1985, Escondido, Calif., UHS Oral History Project.

112. JB to LeRoy and Ann Hafen, 11 February 1951, JBCol, UHS.

113. JB, Roll Book: 1950–51, Dixie Junior College Archives, St. George, Utah.

114. Joseph Walker to JB, 22 November 1950, JBCol, UHS.

115. JB, *The Mountain Meadows Massacre* (Stanford, Calif.: Stanford University Press, 1950), vi.

116. Ibid., 67.

117. Ibid., 146.

118. Ibid., 160.

119. "Historical Volume Tells Story of Pioneer Massacre in Utah," *San Francisco Examiner*, 2nd News Sec., 10 December 1950, 10.

120. "Case Book of a Tragedy," *The Oregonian*, 15 December 1950.

121. Henry Nash Smith, "A Scholarly, Dramatic Narrative of the Tragedy at Mountain Meadows," *New York Herald Tribune Book Review*, 11 March 1951, 5.

122. JB to Robert Glass Cleland, 29 April 1951, JBCol, UHS.

123. Ettie Lee to JB, 1 December 1950, JBCol, UHS.

124. Fawn Brodie to JB, 9 December 1950, JBCol, UHS.

125. Dale Morgan to JB, 20 December 1950, JBCol, UHS.

126. Charles Kelly to JB, 5 January [1951], JBCol, UHS.

127. J. Golden Taylor to JB, 24 January 1951, JBCol, UHS.

128. Milton R. Hunter to Frank H. Jonas, 2 February 1951, MS 508, UofU.

129. JB to Frank H. Jonas, 9 February 1951, MS 508, UofU.
130. Albert R. Lyman to Whom It May Concern, 17 January 1951, JBCol, UHS.
131. Charity Rowley to Albert R. Lyman, 3 February 1951, JBCol, UHS.
132. Charity Rowley to JB, 10 [February] 1951, JBCol, UHS.
133. JB to Albert R. Lyman, 12 February 1951, JBCol, UHS.
134. JB to Charity Rowley, 12 February 1951, JBCol, UHS.

Chapter Seven

1. Charity Rowley, "Juanita," in "Reminiscences of Juanita Brooks," compiled by Eva Miles, unpublished, JBCol Ad, UHS.
2. JB to Dale Morgan, 2 June [1951], JBCol, UHS.
3. Ibid., 10 June 1951, JBCol, UHS.
4. Ibid., 20 June 1951, JBCol, UHS.
5. Dale Morgan to JB, 26 July 1951, MS 486, UofU.
6. JB to William R. Palmer, 14 August 1952, LSP.
7. Sterling McMurrin, interview by Levi Peterson, 4 February 1986, Salt Lake City, UHS Oral History Project.
8. William Mulder to JB, 3 October 1951, JBCol, UHS.
9. Thomas A. Blakely, "The Swearing Elders: The First Generation of Modern Mormon Intellectuals," *Sunstone* 10 (1985): 11.
10. Richard D. Poll, "The Swearing Elders: Some Reflections," *Sunstone* 10 (1985): 16.
11. JB to Dale Morgan, 9 September [1951], JBCol, UHS.
12. JB to Donald P. Bean, 11 September 1951, JBCol, UHS.
13. JB to Brian Foy, 10 September 1951, JBCol, UHS.
14. Finlay McDermid to JB, 2 October 1951, MS 486, UofU.
15. JB to Finlay McDermid, 15 October 1951, MS 486, UofU.
16. Finlay McDermid to JB, 19 October 1951, MS 486, UofU.
17. Donald P. Bean to JB, 24 October 1951, JBCol, UHS.
18. JB to Finlay McDermind, 22 October 1951, MS 486, UofU.
19. Dale Morgan to JB, 12 September 1951, MS 486, UofU.
20. JB to Gladys Harrison and Elise Musser, 11 February 1965, JBCol, UHS.
21. D. Michael Quinn, *J. Reuben Clark: The Church Years* (Provo: Brigham Young University Press, 1983), 170.
22. Donald Bean to JB, 20 November 1951, JBCol, UHS.
23. JB to Leslie Bliss, 1 November 1951, JBCol, UHS.
24. JB to Richard A. Nelson, 9 March 1973, JBCol, UHS.
25. Donald P. Bean to JB, 5 March 1952, JBCol, UHS.
26. Louis C. Zucker to JB, 17 December 1951, JBCol, UHS.
27. JB to Charles Kelly, 5 January 1952, JBCol, UHS.
28. Stephen L. Richards to JB, 7 January 1952, LSP.
29. JB to Stephen L. Richards, 15 January 1952, LSP.
30. Ettie Lee to JB, 10 March 1952, JBCol, UHS.
31. Dale Morgan to JB, 23 February 1952, MS 486, UofU.
32. Grant D. Hanson to JB, 16 September 1952, JBCol, UHS.
33. JB to Leslie Bliss, 1 August 1952, JBCol, UHS.
34. JB to Morton Grant, 23 November 1952, JBCol, UHS.

35. JB, review of *Jacob Hamblin, Buckskin Apostle,* by Paul Bailey, in *Utah Humanities Review* 2 (July 1948): 287.

36. Dale Morgan to JB, 29 November 1952, MS 486, UofU.

37. JB, review of *Jacob Hamblin, the Peacemaker,* by Pearson H. Corbett, in *Pacific Historical Review* 22 (1953): 181.

38. JB to Leslie Bliss, 2 September 1952, Institutional Archives, HL.

39. JB to L. L. Merrill and G. H. Tolman, 9 September 1952, JBCol, UHS.

40. Will Brooks to Robert Brooks, 5 September 1952, JBCol, UHS.

41. JB, "A Community Portrait," in "Symposium on Mormon Culture," Utah Academy of Sciences, Arts and Letters, 14 November 1952, Logan, Utah, 4.

42. Robert Glass Cleland to JB, 15 January 1953, JBCol, UHS.

43. Dale Morgan to JB, 15 March 1953, MS 486, UofU.

44. JB to Robert Glass Cleland, 8 February 1953, JBCol, UHS.

45. Pauline Syler to JB, 4 September 1953, JBCol, UHS.

46. Will Brooks to Ettie Lee, 28 July 1953, JBCol, UHS.

47. Dorothea Lange and Ansel Adams, "Three Mormon Towns," *Life,* 6 September 1954, 91-100.

48. JB to Claudia Bushman, 21 December 1971, JBCol, UHS.

49. "Arizona Raids Polygamist Colony," *Salt Lake Tribune,* 27 July 1953, 17, 20.

50. Joseph Walker to JB, 15 August 1953, JB Col, UHS.

51. JB, "Short Creek: Arizona's Grand Pre," unpublished essay, JBCol 10:31, UHS.

52. "UEA Votes 2 to 1 to Open School," *Salt Lake Tribune,* 29 August 1953, 1.

53. JB, "Governor Lee and the Schools of Utah," unpublished fragment, JBCol 33:22, UHS.

54. Charity Rowley, conversation with Levi Peterson, 22 December 1985, St. George, Utah.

55. JB, *Uncle Will Tells His Story* (Salt Lake City: Taggart & Co., 1970), 233.

56. JB to Arthur H. Clark, 27 October 1963, JBCol, UHS.

57. Caroline Keturah Parry to JB, 18 July 1956, JBCol, UHS.

58. Glenn S. Dumke to JB, 22 October 1953, JBCol, UHS.

59. JB to Glenn S. Dumke, 27 October 1953, JBCol, UHS.

60. Russell Mortensen to JB, 15 December 1953, JBCol, UHS.

61. JB to Russell Mortensen, 14 December 1953, JBCol, UHS.

62. JB to Dale Morgan, 15 January [1954], DMCol, BAN.

63. JB to Leland R. Cowan, 28 August 1954, JBCol, UHS.

64. Ibid., 3 August 1954, JBCol, UHS.

65. Leland R. Cowan to JB, 1 September 1954, JBCol, UHS.

66. Jospeh Walker to JB, 3 February 1954, JBCol, UHS.

67. Two Lee diaries had been previously published: Charles Kelly, ed., *Journals of John D. Lee 1846-47 and 1859,* Salt Lake City: Western Printing Co., 1938; and Gustive O. Larson, ed., "The Journal of the Iron County Mission [1850-51], John D. Lee, Clerk," *Utah Historical Quarterly* 20 (1952): 109-134, 253-82, 353-83. Kelly's edition, long out of print, was reissued by the University of Utah Press in 1984 with an introduction by Charles S. Peterson.

68. Robert Glass Cleland to JB, 26 February 1954, JBCol, UHS.

69. JB to Robert Glass Cleland, 22 March 1954, JBCol, UHS.
70. Ibid., 5 May 1954, JBCol, UHS.
71. Robert Glass Cleland to JB, 17 May 1954, JBCol, UHS.
72. JB to Hamilton Gardner, 15 September 1954, JBCol, UHS.
73. JB, "Everyman and the Humanities: Unsatisfied," unpublished report, JBCol 11:17, UHS.
74. JB, review of *Orderville, Utah: A Pioneer Mormon Experiment in Economic Organization*, by Leonard J. Arrington, in *The Western Humanities Review* 8 (1954): 169.
75. JB to Robert Glass Cleland, 12 June 1954, JBCol, UHS.
76. JB to Dale Morgan, 11 August 1954, JBCol, UHS.
77. JB to Virginia Sorensen, 15 October 1954, JBCol, UHS.
78. Dale Morgan to JB, 16 November 1954, JBCol, UHS.
79. JB, *Uncle Will Tells His Story* (Salt Lake City: Taggart & Co., 1970), 234.
80. Ibid., 235.
81. Glenn A. Duncan to JB, 10 November 1954, JBCol, UHS.
82. JB, *Uncle Will Tells His Story* (Salt Lake City: Taggart & Co., 1970), 233.
83. Ibid., 234.
84. JB to L. Robert Gardner, 9 March 1956, JBCol, UHS.
85. "Dedication Program," *Harrison Daily Times*, 2 September 1955, 1.
86. J. K. Fancher to JB, 10 May 1965, JBCol, UHS.
87. JB, "Dedicatory Speech," *Utah Historical Quarterly* 24 (Winter 1956):76.
88. J. K. Fancher to JB, 10 September 1955, JBCol, UHS.
89. Sugar House Press to JB, 6 September 1955, JBCol, UHS.
90. JB to Joseph C. Columbus, 26 June 1956, JBCol, UHS.
91. Karl Brooks to Levi Peterson, 4 December 1985.
92. Robert Glass Cleland and Juanita Brooks, eds., *A Mormon Chronicle: The Diaries of John D. Lee – 1848–1876* (San Marino, Calif.: Huntington Library, 1955), 2:103.
93. Ibid., 2:91–92.
94. Ibid., 2:92–93.
95. Ibid., 1:7.
96. "A Splendid Saga," review of *A Mormon Chronicle*, in *Time*, 19 December 1955, 101.
97. Carl Carmer, "A Pioneer In Utah," review of *A Mormon Chronicle*, in *New York Times Book Review*, 25 December 1955, 1 (sec. 7).
98. Russell Mortensen, review of *A Mormon Chronicle*, in *Utah Historical Quarterly* 24 (Winter 1956): 89.
99. Russell Mortensen to Ettie Lee, 13 January 1956, JBCol, UHS.
100. Russell Mortensen to JB, 11 January 1956, JBCol, UHS.
101. Virginia Sorensen to JB, 6 January 1956, JBCol, UHS.
102. Leonard Arrington to JB, 13 December 1955, JBCol, UHS.
103. JB to Leonard Arrington, 28 December 1955, JBCol, UHS.
104. Martha Padve to JB, 29 December 1955, JBCol, UHS.

Chapter Eight

1. JB to LeGrand Richards, 29 November 1955, LSP.

2. LeGrand Richards to JB, 30 November 1955, LSP.

3. JB to LeGrand Richards, 5 December 1955, LSP.

4. LeGrand Richards to JB, 7 December 1955, LSP.

5. Ibid., 13 January 1956, LSP.

6. Marjorie Walker to Levi Peterson, 26 August 1985.

7. JB to Virginia Sorensen, 15 October 1954, JBCol, UHS.

8. JB to Elsa Harris, 17 January 1956, in *Truth* 21 (March 1956): 313.

9. JB to Editors, *Deseret News*, 1 February 1956, in *Truth* 21 (March 1956):310.

10. Samuel W. Taylor to JB, 6 March 1956, JBCol, UHS.

11. JB, review of *I Have Six Wives*, by Samuel W. Taylor, in *Utah Historical Quarterly* 24 (1956): 367.

12. "State to Return Children of Cult Member Mother," *Salt Lake Tribune*, 12 June 1956, 17-18.

13. JB to Anthony I. Bentley, 2 February 1956, JBCol, UHS.

14. JB to Ettie Lee, 14 February 1956, JBCol, UHS.

15. Ibid., 28 February 1956, JBCol, UHS.

16. Turnley Walker to JB, 21 February 1956, JBCol, UHS.

17. JB to Dale Morgan, 5 March 1956, JBCol, UHS.

18. Dorothy O. Riedel to JB, 21 May 1956, JBCol, UHS.

19. Turnley Walker to JB, 22 May 1956, JBCol, UHS.

20. Joseph Walker to JB, 1 June 1956, JBCol, UHS.

21. Ettie Lee to JB, 2 June 1956, JBCol, UHS.

22. Ibid., 13 May 1956, JBCol, UHS.

23. JB to Russell Mortensen, 18 July 1956, JBCol, UHS.

24. Gweneth Mulder to JB, 16 August 1956, JBCol, UHS.

25. JB, "Reading Around the West: English 270," unpublished report, JBCol 11:21, UHS.

26. Ibid.

27. JB to Ettie Lee, 24 October 1956, JBCol, UHS.

28. William Mulder to JB, 24 October 1956, JBCol, UHS.

29. JB, "Report on *The Log of a Cowboy*," unpublished report, JBCol 11:21, UHS.

30. JB to Henry J. Webb, 26 December 1956, JBCol, UHS.

31. Ibid., 20 January 1957, JBCol, UHS.

32. Ibid., 7 March 1957, JBCol, UHS.

33. Ibid., 7 May 1957, JBCol, UHS.

34. "A Tentative Examination of Some Basic Mormon Concepts," unpublished report, JBCol 11:21, UHS.

35. Henry J. Webb to JB, 24 June 1957, JBCol, UHS.

36. JB to J. K. Fancher, 20 July 1957, JBCol, UHS.

37. Ibid., 1 August 1957, JBCol, UHS.

38. "Missionary Testimonial," 15 December 1957, printed brochure, JBCol 35:19, UHS.

39. JB to Family, 17 January 1958, JBCol, UHS.

40. Leonard J. Arrington to JB, 5 May 1958, JBCol, UHS.

41. JB to Dale Morgan, 2 November 1958, JBCol, UHS.

42. JB to Mary Leavitt, 12 August 1971, JBCol, UHS.

43. JB to Virginia Christensen, 10 January 1973, JBCol, UHS.

44. JB to Dale Morgan, 2 November 1958, JBCol, UHS.

45. JB, "The Land That God Forgot," *Utah Historical Quarterly* 26 (July 1958): 215.

46. "Vandals Cut Down Historic S.L. Tree," *Deseret News*, 22 September 1958, 1.

47. "Desecration of a Landmark," *Deseret News*, 25 September 1958, 14(A).

48. "Youth, Note, Key, Sack, Ash, Probe," *Salt Lake Tribune*, 4 October 1958, 17.

49. "Leaders Rap Vandals for Felling Tree," *Salt Lake Tribune*, 28 September 1958, 4(B).

50. "Minutes, Board of Trustees," 4 October 1958, UHS.

51. Russell Mortensen, interview by Levi Peterson, 9 September 1985, Escondido, Calif., UHS Oral History Project.

52. JB to Stanley Ivins, 18 October 1958, JBCol, UHS.

53. Winifred Gregory to JB, 1 June 1960, JBCol, UHS.

54. JB to Carmen ?, 25 October 1958, JBCol, UHS.

55. Wayne Hinton, interview with Levi Peterson, 22 December 1985, Cedar City, Utah, UHS Oral History Project.

56. JB to O. Boyd Mathias, 27 May 1957, JBCol, UHS.

57. Ibid., 8 February 1959, JBCol, UHS.

58. JB to Dale Morgan, 22 January 1959, JBCol, UHS.

59. JB, "The Look Ahead," 31 May 1959, unpublished speech, JBCol 8:23, UHS.

60. Ira N. Hayward to JB, 1 July 1959, JBCol, UHS.

61. "Juanita Brooks Will Talk in Provo Wednesday," *Daily Herald*, 23 August 1959, 5.

62. JB to Dixie Lee Powell, 16 August 1959, JBCol, UHS.

63. Kay Brooks to Juanita and Will Brooks, 27 July 1959, JBCol, UHS.

64. JB to Marion Hughes, 7 September 1959, JBCol, UHS.

65. JB to J. Lewis Pulsipher, 7 September 1959, JBCol, UHS.

66. JB to Alfred A. Knopf, 1 November 1959, JBCol, UHS.

67. Alan C. Collins to JB, 10 December 1959, JBCol, UHS.

68. Winifred Gregory to JB, 1 June 1960, JBCol, UHS.

69. Ibid., 7 July 1960, JBCol, UHS.

70. Will Brooks, Diary 1961, irregular initial entry, 16 June 1960, JBCol Ad, UHS.

71. Statement of Appointment as Research Associate, JBCol 20: 19, UHS.

72. Will Brooks, Diary 1961, irregular initial entry, no date.

73. Winifred Gregory to JB, 7 July 1960, JBCol, UHS.

74. JB to A. C. Lambert, 11 December 1961, JBCol, UHS.

75. Will Brooks, Diary, 28 June 1961.

76. Marjorie Walker to Levi Peterson, 26 August 1985.

77. Ibid., 6 January 1986.

78. Marjorie Walker, conversation with Levi Peterson, 6 December 1986, Salt Lake City.

79. A. C. Lambert, "Professional Information Sheet: A. C. Lambert," unpublished vita, JBCol 12:22, UHS.

80. A. C. Lambert, "A Bibliography of Some of the Productive Work of A. C. Lambert," unpublished bibliography, JBCol 12:22, UHS.

81. Ibid.

82. JB to A. C. Lambert, 13 January 1961, JBCol, UHS.
83. Ibid.
84. Will Brooks, Diary, 12 January 1961.
85. Ibid., 13 January 1961.
86. Ibid., 14 January 1961.
87. Marjorie Walker to Levi Peterson, 6 January 1986.
88. Ray R. Canning, conversation with Levi Peterson, 9 December 1986, Salt Lake City.
89. Will Brooks, Diary, 25 March 1961.
90. Ibid., 23 March 1961.
91. Ibid., 5 April 1961.
92. Ernest Linford to JB, [24 April 1961], JBCol, UHS.
93. Will Brooks, Diary, 23 April 1961.
94. Ibid., 1 April 1961.
95. Russell and Dorothy Mortensen, interview by Levi Peterson, 9 September 1985, Escondido, Calif., UHS Oral History Project.
96. Will Brooks, Diary, 28 July 1961.
97. Joseph Walker, "Portrait of a Country Doctor," *Utah Historical Quarterly* 29 (July 1961): 293–94.
98. Will Brooks, Diary, 2 June 1961.
99. "Merit and Respect," unpublished citations from Dixie College, JBCol Ad, UHS.
100. Ettie Lee to JB, 12 May 1961, JBCol, UHS.
101. JB to Arthur H. Clark, 15 May 1961, JBCol, UHS.
102. JB to Merrit L. Norton, [? May 1961], JBCol 4:10, UHS.
103. Jesse A. Udall to Ettie Lee, 8 June 1961, JBCol, UHS.
104. JB to Everett Cooley, 31 January 1969, JBCol, UHS.
105. JB to Ida Hamblin, 7 August 1961, JBCol, UHS.
106. JB to A. C. Lambert, 11 December 1961, JBCol, UHS.
107. Ettie Lee to JB, 15 June 1961, JBCol, UHS.
108. Jesse A. Udall to JB, 20 June 1961, JBCol, UHS.
109. JB to Jesse A. Udall, 23 June 1961, JBCol, UHS.
110. Will Brooks, Diary, 27 June 1961.
111. Ibid., 7 July 1961.
112. JB, 1 February 1969, unpublished fragment, JBCol 7:12, UHS.
113. JB to Ida Hamblin, 7 August 1961, JBCol, UHS.
114. Will Brooks, Diary, 9 July 1961.
115. JB to Arthur H. Clark, 17 July 1961, JBCol, UHS.
116. Ray R. Canning, conversation with Levi Peterson, 9 December 1986, Salt Lake City.
117. Will Brooks, Diary, 22 August 1961.
118. Ibid., 30 August 1961.
119. JB to Ettie Lee, 3 September 1961, JBCol, UHS.
120. JB, "Indian Sketches from the Journals of T. D. Brown and Jacob Hamblin," *Utah Historical Quarterly* 29 (October 1961): 349–50.
121. JB to Richard C. Angell, 16 October 1961, JBCol, UHS.
122. JB to Wallace Stegner, 26 October 1961, JBCol, UHS.
123. Wallace Stegner to JB, 1 November 1961, JBCol, UHS.
124. JB to Wallace Stegner, 4 November 1961, JBCol, UHS.
125. JB, "The Diaries of Hosea Stout," unpublished abstract, attached

to Everett L. Cooley to JB, 8 November 1961, JBCol, UHS.

126. JB to Reed A. Stout, 30 July 1961, JBCol, UHS.

127. Will Brooks, Diary, 10 September 1961.

128. Ibid., 9 October 1961.

129. JB to Winifred Gregory, 16 October [1961], JBCol, UHS.

130. JB to Ettie Lee, 15 October 1968, JBCol, UHS.

131. JB to Arthur H. Clark, 5 December 1961, JBCol, UHS.

132. Paul Hubbard, review of *John Doyle Lee*, in *Arizona and the West* 4 (Autumn 1962): 281.

133. Norman F. Furniss, review of *John Doyle Lee*, in *The Mississippi Valley Historical Review* 49 (June 1962): 142.

134. Review of *John Doyle Lee*, in *San Francisco Chronicle*, 7 December 1961; quoted in John Wesley Williamson, Sr., "Review of Book Reviews," mimeographed pamphlet, JBCol 13:25, UHS.

135. Robert R. Kirsch, review of *John Doyle Lee*, in *Los Angeles Times*, 21 January 1962; quoted in John Wesley Williamson, Sr., "Review of Book Reviews," mimeographed pamphlet, JBCol 13:25, UHS.

136. Dale L. Morgan, review of *John Doyle Lee*, in *Southern California Quarterly* 45 (December 1963): 365.

137. Leonard J. Arrington, review of *John Doyle Lee*, in *Montana, the Magazine of Western History* 14 (April 1964): 114.

138. Paul Bailey, review of *John Doyle Lee*, in *Journal of the West* 2 (January 1963): 104.

139. JB, *John Doyle Lee: Zealot–Pioneer Builder–Scapegoat*, 2d ed. (Glendale, Calif.: Arthur H. Clark Co., 1962), 347.

140. Ibid., 364.

141. Axel J. Andresen to Paul W. Galleher, 27 December 1961, JBCol, UHS.

142. Paul A. Foulger to JB, 5 December 1961, JBCol, UHS.

Chapter Nine

1. Will Brooks, Diary, 29 November 1961.

2. Ibid., 1 January 1962.

3. Ibid., 15 January 1962.

4. JB to Arthur H. Clark, 29 December 1961, JBCol, UHS.

5. JB to Dale Morgan, 15 January 1962, JBCol, UHS.

6. Dale Morgan to JB, 16 January 1962, JBCol, UHS.

7. JB, ed., *On the Mormon Frontier: The Diary of Hosea Stout 1844–1861* (Salt Lake City: University of Utah Press and the Utah State Historical Society, 1964), 2:368.

8. JB to Klaus Hansen, 12 March 1962, JBCol, UHS.

9. Wallace Stegner to JB, 9 March 1962, JBCol, UHS.

10. JB to William Carlson, 5 May 1962, JBCol, UHS.

11. JB to John W. Fitzgerald, 16 January 1962, JBCol, UHS.

12. Will Brooks, Diary, 6 May 1962.

13. Ibid., 3 June 1962.

14. JB to Winifred Gregory, 30 June 1962, JBCol, UHS.

15. Will Brooks, Diary, 29 June 1962.

16. Ibid., 3 July 1962.

17. Wilson C. Wood to JB, 30 July 1962, JBCol, UHS.

18. Aldin O. Hayward to JB, 11 July 1963, JBCol, UHS.

19. JB to Evan Woodbury, 24 January 1963, JBCol, UHS.

20. Will Brooks, Diary, 6 September 1962.

21. Ibid., 8 September 1962.

22. Ibid., 6 October 1962.

23. Parker M. Nielson to JB, "Memorandum of Agreement," 8 October 1962, JBCol, UHS.

24. JB to Dale Morgan, 24 October 1962, JBCol, UHS.

25. Will Brooks, Diary, 18 October 1962.

26. JB to O. Boyd Mathias, 19 October 1962, JBCol, UHS.

27. Ibid., 8 November 1962, JBCol, UHS.

28. JB to Dale Morgan, 4 October 1962, JBCol, UHS.

29. JB to George T. Boyd, 13 November 1962, JBCol, UHS.

30. Ibid., 11 December 1962, JBCol, UHS.

31. JB to Aura and Carl Allen, 5 December 1962, JBCol, UHS.

32. JB to Alfred L. Bush, 17 January 1963, JBCol, UHS.

33. Will Brooks, Diary, 19 January 1963.

34. Ibid., 2 February 1963.

35. JB to Alfred L. Bush, 17 January 1963, JBCol, UHS.

36. JB to Mary Isabel Fry, 10 January 1963, JBCol, UHS; JB to Wayne C. Grover, 22 January 1963, JBCol, UHS.

37. JB to A. C. Lambert, 9 January 1963, JBCol, UHS.

38. JB to Savoie Lottinville, 10 January 1963, JBCol, UHS.

39. Robert R. Kirsch, "One of the West's Most Tragic Events Lives Anew," review of The Mountain Meadows Massacre, 2d ed., in Los Angeles Times, 23 January 1963, 2(IV).

40. T. A. Larson, review of The Mountain Meadows Massacre, 2d ed., in New Mexico Historical Review 39 (January 1964): 83.

41. Merlin Stonehouse, review of The Mountain Meadows Massacre, 2d ed., in Southern California Quarterly 45 (September 1963): 281.

42. Savoie Lottinville to JB, 11 March 1963, JBCol, UHS.

43. George W. Bauer to Levi Peterson, 2 January 1986.

44. Will Brooks, Diary, 20 February 1963.

45. Ibid., 19 February 1963.

46. Ibid., 23 February 1963.

47. JB, "A Report on the History and uses of the Green River from the Point Where It Enters the State of Utah to Its Confluence with the San Rafael," unpublished report, JBCol 10:23, UHS, 143.

48. JB to Parker M. Nielson, 6 October 1963, JBCol, UHS.

49. United States v. State of Utah, Judgment, Salt Lake City, C 201-62, 8 January 1965.

50. JB to Parker M. Nielson, 20 May 1966, JBCol, UHS.

51. Will Brooks, Diary, 9 April 1963.

52. Ibid., 5 May 1963.

53. JB to Washington County News, 7 May 1963, JBCol, UHS.

54. Austin E. Fife to JB, 2 May 1963, JBCol, UHS.

55. JB to John and LaVora Tucker, 4 March 1963, JBCol, UHS.

56. JB to Alfred L. Bush, 1 May 1963, JBCol, UHS.

57. JB to Wallace Stegner, 13 June 1963, JBCol, UHS.

58. Wallace Stegner to JB, 20 June 1963, JBCol, UHS.
59. JB to Winifred Gregory, 1 July 1963, JBCol, UHS.
60. JB to Laura and Glen Snow, 1 July 1963, JBCol, UHS.
61. Publisher's Contract, University of Utah Press, July 1963, Hosea Stout Publication Section, Box 2, UHS.
62. Everett L. Cooley to Savoie Lottinville, 16 August 1963, Hosea Stout Publication Section, Box 2, UHS.
63. Will Brooks, Trans-Atlantic Diary, 28 July 1963.
64. JB to Ann Smith, 16 September 1963, JBCol, UHS.
65. Will Brooks, Trans-Atlantic Diary, 5 August 1963.
66. Ibid., 9 August 1963.
67. JB to Family, 19 August 1963, JBCol, UHS.
68. Will Brooks, Trans-Atlantic Diary, 13 August 1963.
69. JB to Winifred Gregory, 1 November 1963, JBCol, UHS.
70. Will Brooks, Diary, 9 September 1963.
71. Ibid., 21 September 1963.
72. Ibid., 28 September 1963.
73. JB to Winifred Gregory, 1 November 1963, JBCol, UHS.
74. JB to Grace Woodbury, 22 October 1963, JBCol, UHS.
75. JB to Burton and Elise Musser, 9 December 1963, JBCol, UHS.
76. JB, "Roxie S. Romney," unpublished speech, JBCol 8:13, UHS.
77. JB to Wesley and Sana Williamson, 30 January 1964, JBCol, UHS.
78. J. Golden Taylor to JB, 4 December 1963, JBCol, UHS.
79. John Greenway to JB, 15 December 1963, JBCol, UHS.
80. J. Golden Taylor to JB, 7 January 1964, JBCol, UHS.
81. JB to John Greenway, 21 March 1964, JBCol 10:29, UHS.
82. John Greenway, Editor's Note, in JB, "Memories of a Mormon Girlhood," *Journal of American Folklore* 77 (July-September 1964): 195.
83. Inez S. Cooper to JB, 11 March 1964, JBCol, UHS.
84. JB, "Women in the Arts," unpublished speech, JBCol 8:29, UHS.
85. JB to Winifred Gregory, 5 May 1964, JBCol, UHS.
86. JB to Russell R. Elliott, 11 May 1964, JBCol, UHS.
87. JB to Winifred Gregory, 5 April 1964, JBCol, UHS.
88. JB to Wesley and Sana Williamson, 2 July 1964, JBCol, UHS.
89. "Citation, Juanita Leavitt Brooks," 6 June 1964, Logan, Utah, unpublished, JBCol Ad, UHS.
90. JB to Ellvert H. Himes, 27 June 1964, JBCol, UHS.
91. Ettie Lee to JB, 30 June 1964, JBCol, UHS.
92. Will Brooks, World's Fair Diary, 23 July 1964.
93. JB to Gordon and Alta Howard, 8 August 1964, JBCol, UHS.
94. JB, Program, Twelfth Annual Meeting, Utah Historical Society, unpublished marginalia, JBCol 39:6, UHS.
95. JB to Dale Morgan, 10 January 1965, JBCol, UHS.
96. Ibid.
97. JB to Thomas E. Cheney, 27 August 1964, JBCol, UHS.
98. Thomas E. Cheney to JB, 28 November 1964, JBCol, UHS.
99. JB, "Pranks and Pranksters," in *Lore of Faith and Folly*, ed. Thomas E. Cheney (Salt Lake City: University of Utah Press, 1971), 59.
100. JB, "The Role of Woman in a Changing World," unpublished speech, JBCol 8:24, UHS.

101. JB to Willa and Thales Derrick, 7 February 1965, JBCol, UHS.

102. JB to Kay and Ida Jean, Tony and Janet Brooks, 8 February 1965, JBCol, UHS.

103. JB to Gladys Harrison, 11 February 1965, JBCol, UHS.

104. JB to Dale Morgan, 10 January 1965, JBCol, UHS.

105. Leonard J. Arrington to JB, 18 March 1965, JBCol, UHS.

106. George W. Corner to JB, 9 June 1965, JBCol, UHS.

107. JB to Winifred Gregory, 16 June 1965, JBCol, UHS.

108. JB to Robert and Florence Brooks, 31 March [1965], JBCol, UHS.

109. JB to Melvin and Laurel Leavitt, 10 May 1965, JBCol, UHS.

110. JB to Willa Derrick, 10 March 1965, JBCol, UHS.

111. Milan B. Robbins to JB, 28 June 1965, JBCol 21:23, UHS.

112. Board of Trustees to Alvin Gittins, 27 January 1965, Hosea Stout Publication Section, Box 2, UHS.

113. Everett L. Cooley, conversation with Levi Peterson, 30 January 1987, Salt Lake City.

114. Richard Y. Thurman to S. J. Quinney, 23 June 1965, Hosea Stout Publication Section, Box 2, UHS.

115. Leonard J. Arrington, "The Penetrating Eye," review of *On the Mormon Frontier*, in *The Utah Alumnus* 41 (April 1965): 13–14.

116. Dale Morgan, "A Western Diary," review of *On the Mormon Frontier*, in *The American West* 2 (Spring 1965): 46.

117. Harold Shepherd, review of *On the Mormon Frontier*, in *Utah Law Review* 9 (Summer 1965): 816.

118. JB, ed., *On the Mormon Frontier: The Diary of Hosea Stout – 1844–1861* (Salt Lake City: University of Utah Press and Utah State Historical Society, 1964), 1:171.

119. JB to George A. Brown, 18 September 1965, JBCol, UHS.

120. JB to Burton and Elise Musser, 4 November 1965, JBCol, UHS.

121. JB to Alfred L. Bush, 18 October 1965, JBCol, UHS.

122. JB to Family, 3 November 1965, JBCol, UHS.

123. JB to Winnie Brooks, 6 November 1965, JBCol, UHS.

124. JB to George W. Corner, 17 January 1966, JBCol, UHS.

125. JB to Harold Schindler, 11 December 1965, JBCol, UHS.

126. JB to Alfred L. Bush, 18 October 1965, JBCol, UHS.

127. JB to George W. Corner, 17 January 1966, JBCol, UHS.

128. Russell Mortensen to George Pfeiffer III, 9 March 1966, MS 201, UofU.

129. JB to Russell Mortensen, 18 June 1966, JBCol, UHS.

130. JB to Burton and Elise Musser, 4 November 1965, JBCol, UHS.

131. S. Lyman Tyler, review of *George Brooks: Artist in Stone*, in *Utah Historical Quarterly* 34 (Fall 1966): 345.

132. JB, *George Brooks: Artist in Stone* (St. George, Utah: By the author, 1965), 94.

133. Ibid., 133–34.

Chapter Ten

1. JB to Alfred L. Bush, 18 October 1965, JBCol, UHS.

2. JB to Robert W. Olsen, Jr., 26 December 1965, JBCol, UHS.

3. JB to Willa Derrick, 17 February [1966], JBCol, UHS.

4. JB to Tony and Janet Brooks, 3 April [1966], JBCol, UHS.

5. JB to Janet Brooks, 18 April 1966, JBCol, UHS.

6. JB to Gerry Pulsipher, 25 February 1966, JBCol, UHS.

7. JB to Karl and Carla Brooks, 20 May 1966, JBCol, UHS.

8. Todd I. Berens, interview by Levi Peterson, 7 September 1985, Santa Ana, Calif., UHS Oral History Project.

9. JB to Gertrude Richards, 3 June 1966, JBCol, UHS.

10. JB to Burton and Elise Musser, 18 July 1966, JBCol, UHS.

11. JB to Gertrude [Richards], 3 June 1966, JBCol, UHS.

12. JB to Louis Roberts, 16 December 1966, JBCol, UHS.

13. JB and Janet G. Butler, eds., "Utah's Peace Advocate, the 'Mormona': Elise Furer Musser," *Utah Historical Quarterly* 2 (Spring 1978): 155.

14. JB to Tony and Janet Brooks 23 May [1966], JBCol, UHS.

15. JB, "For Jillyn Woodbury," unpublished speech, JBCol 8:15, UHS.

16. JB to Willa and Thales Derrick, Kay and Ida Jean Brooks, 1 October 1966, JBCol, UHS.

17. Ibid.

18. JB, *Uncle Will Tells His Story* (Salt Lake City: Taggart & Co., 1970), 247.

19. JB to Dale Morgan, 15 December 1966, JBCol, UHS.

20. LaMar Smith to JB, 27 February 1967, JBCol, UHS.

21. JB to Gustive O. Larson, 6 February 1967, JBCol, UHS.

22. JB to Dale Morgan, 1 December 1966, JBCol, UHS.

23. JB to Winifred Gregory, 18 March 1967, JBCol, UHS.

24. JB to R. J. and Marilyn Snow, 5 February 1967, JBCol, UHS.

25. JB to Everett L. Cooley, 28 March 1967, JBCol, UHS.

26. JB to J. K. Fancher, 5 September 1967, JBCol, UHS.

27. Ibid., 16 September 1967, Russell Fancher, Green Forest, Ark.

28. JB to Howard Cottam, 21 January 1967, JBCol, UHS.

29. JB to Gerry Lynn Pulsipher, 1 June 1967, JBCol, UHS.

30. John D. Lee, "Diary of the Mormon Battalion Mission," ed. JB, *New Mexico Historical Review* 42 (1967): 176.

31. JB to Alexander Simons, 10 July 1967, JBCol, UHS.

32. JB, B'nai B'rith Diary, 25 September 1967.

33. JB to Ben Roe, Louis Zucker, and Sterling McMurrin, 20 January 1968, MS 139, UofU.

34. JB, "Lack of Material," unpublished fragment, JBCol 29:17, UHS.

35. JB, "Abraham the Jew and the Mormon War," unpublished article, JBCol Ad, UHS.

36. JB, B'nai B'rith Diary, 4 November 1968.

37. JB to J. K. Fancher, 5 September 1967, LSP.

38. JB, "This Is Your Life – Mary Hafen Leavitt," unpublished narrative, JBCol 11:12, UHS.

39. JB to Ben Roe, Louis Zucker, and Sterling McMurrin, 20 January 1968, MS 139, UofU.

40. JB to Winifred Gregory, 17 March 1968, JBCol, UHS.

41. JB to LaVell ?, 2 April 1968, JBCol, UHS.

42. JB, "Report to Dr. A. W. McGregor," unpublished fragment, JBCol Ad, UHS.

43. Sterling McMurrin, interview by Levi Peterson, 4 February 1986, Salt Lake City, UHS Oral History Project.

44. JB to Lavell ?, 2 April 1968, JBCol, UHS.

45. JB to Dale Morgan, 11 December 1968, JBCol, UHS.

46. JB, "Mariah Huntsman Leavitt: Midwife of the Desert Frontier," in *Forms upon the Frontier*, ed. Austin and Alta Fife and Henry H. Glassie, Monograph Series (Logan: Utah State University Press, 1969), 120.

47. Richard L. Anderson to JB, 18 July 1968, JBCol, UHS.

48. JB to Richard L. Anderson 12 August 1968, JBCol, UHS.

49. Richard L. Anderson to JB, 14 August 1968, JBCol, UHS.

50. JB to Miss Noya, 2 February 1969, JBCol, UHS.

51. JB to Gertrude Richards, 12 July 1968, JBCol, UHS.

52. Karl Brooks to Will and Juanita Brooks, [8 July 1968], JBCol, UHS.

53. JB to Richard Thurman, Ben Roe, and Louis Zucker, 5 September 1968, MS 139, UofU.

54. JB to Lavor K. Chaffin, 5 October 1969, JBCol, UHS.

55. JB, "Jest a Copyin'–Word f'r Word," *Utah Historical Quarterly* 37 (Fall 1969): 392.

56. Ibid., 391–92.

57. JB to Todd Berens, 12 December 1968, Todd I. Berens, Santa Ana, Calif.

58. Dale Morgan to Everett L. Cooley, 11 November 1968, JBCol, UHS.

59. JB to Dale Morgan, 11 December 1968, JBCol, UHS.

60. Ibid., 16 December 1968, JBCol, UHS.

61. JB to J.C. Warenski, 14 January 1969, JBCol, UHS.

62. JB to Joe Terry and Rick Wright, 10 January 1969, JBCol, UHS.

63. JB to Winifred Gregory, 14 January 1969, JBCol, UHS.

64. JB to Family, 14 January 1969, JBCol, UHS.

65. JB to T. H. Watkins, 27 January 1969, JBCol, UHS.

66. Edward A. Shaw to JB, 3 October 1969, JBCol, UHS.

67. JB, *The Mountain Meadows Massacre*, 3d ed. (Norman: University of Oklahoma Press, 1970), x.

68. Ibid., xii.

69. JB to Robert B. Mathison, 21 November 1968, MS 486, UofU.

70. JB, handwritten note, JBCol 9:16, UHS.

71. JB to T. H. Watkins, 11 July 1969, JBCol, UHS.

72. JB to Ben Roe, 5 February 1969, JBCol, UHS.

73. JB to Richard Thurman, Ben Roe, and Louis Zucker, 4 May 1969, MS 139, UofU.

74. JB to Myrtle Friedman, 28 March 1969, JBCol, UHS.

75. JB, *Uncle Will Tells His Story*, 248.

76. "Dixie College President Flays UEA Campus Probe," *Salt Lake Tribune*, 15 May 1969, 29(A).

77. JB to Milton L. Weilenmann, 35 [sic] March 1971, JBCol, UHS.

78. JB, Letter to the Editor, *Washington County News*, 15 May 1969.

79. JB to Melvin Smith, undated, JBCol Ad, UHS.

80. JB to Charles S. Peterson, 10 June 1969, JBCol, UHS.

81. JB to Theron Luke, 22 May 1969, JBCol, UHS.

82. "CSU to Award Honor Degrees to Dr. Daryl Chase, Juanita Brooks," *Iron County Record*, 22 May 1969, 1.

83. JB to Hardy Redd, 23 July 1969, JBCol, UHS.

84. Charles S. Peterson, conversation with Levi Peterson, 9 September 1985, Logan, Utah.

85. JB to Ogden Kraut, 5 March 1969, JBCol, UHS.

86. Luther Nichols to JB, 16 August 1969, JBCol, UHS.

87. JB to Robert and Florence Brooks, 11 July 1969, JBCol, UHS.

88. JB to Myrtle Friedman, 28 July 1969, JBCol, UHS.

89. JB to Family, 14 September 1969, JBCol, UHS.

90. JB to Ernest Pulsipher, 29 September 1969, JBCol, UHS.

91. JB to Kay and Ida Jean Brooks, 30 October 1969, JBCol, UHS.

92. JB to Winifred Gregory, 2 December 1969, JBCol, UHS.

93. JB to Kay, Ida Jean, Tony, and Janet Brooks, 14 November 1969, JBCol, UHS.

94. JB to Winifred Gregory, 2 December 1969, JBCol, UHS.

95. JB to Ernest and Margie Pulsipher, 23 December 1969, JBCol, UHS.

96. Bonnie Emmertson to JB, 1 August 1969, JBCol, UHS.

97. JB to Myrtle Friedman, 5 October 1969, JBCol, UHS.

98. Louis C. Zucker to Myrtle H. Friedman, 30 July 1969, MS 139, UofU.

99. Myrtle H. Friedman to Louis C. Zucker, 1 August 1969, MS 139, UofU.

100. Fae D. Dix to JB, [24 October 1969], JBCol, UHS.

101. JB to Willa and Thales Derrick, [20] October 1969, JBCol, UHS.

102. JB to Mildred L. Last, 20 October 1969, JBCol, UHS.

103. JB to Selena Leavitt, 10 February 1970, JBCol, UHS.

104. JB to Willa and Thales Derrick, 8 January 1970, JBCol, UHS.

105. Ibid., 13 February 1970, JBCol, UHS.

106. JB to Family, 30 January 1970, JBCol, UHS.

107. JB to Ernest Pulsipher, 19 March 1970, JBCol, UHS.

108. JB to Willa and Thales Derrick, 13 February 1970, JBCol, UHS.

109. JB to Ettie Lee, 18 February 1970, JBCol, UHS.

110. JB to Family, 2 March 1970, JBCol, UHS.

111. Ibid., 21 March 1970, JBCol, UHS.

112. JB to Russell and Dorothy Mortensen, 3 April 1970, JBCol, UHS.

113. JB to Ettie Lee, 14 April 1970, JBCol, UHS.

114. Richard W. Sadler, conversation with Levi Peterson, 20 March 1986, Ogden, Utah.

115. Russell and Dorothy Mortensen, interview by Levi Peterson, 9 September 1985, Escandido, Calif., UHS Oral History Project.

116. Mary Jo Shurtliff, "Will Brooks 1881-1970," unpublished speech, JBCol 20:18, UHS.

117. JB to Calvin L. Rampton, 6 April 1970, JBCol, UHS.

118. JB to Family, 19 April 1970, JBCol 20:18, UHS.

119. Ibid., 3 May 1970, JBCol, UHS.

120. JB to Ernest Pulsipher, 5 May 1970, JBCol, UHS.

121. JB to Family, 15 May 1970, JBCol, UHS.

122. JB to Tony and Janet Brooks, 20 January 1970, JBCol, UHS.

123. JB to Jessie M. Perry, 13 May 1970, JBCol, UHS.

124. JB to Family, 12 June 1970, JBCol, UHS.

125. Ibid., 17 August 1970, JBCol, UHS.

126. Dell Taylor, conversation with Levi Peterson, 25 March 1986, St.

George, Utah.
   127. Charles S. Peterson, conversation with Levi Peterson, 26 June 1985,
Logan, Utah.
   128. JB to Family, 28 May 1970, JBCol, UHS.
   129. JB to Hortense Y. Hammond, 11 July 1970, JBCol, UHS.
   130. JB to Family, 12 June 1970, JBCol, UHS.
   131. JB to Karl and Carla Brooks, 8 July 1970, JBCol, UHS.
   132. JB to Family, 12 June 1970, JBCol, UHS.
   133. Ibid.
   134. Ibid., 3 August 1970, JBCol, UHS.
   135. JB to Gary Knudsen, 29 August 1970, JBCol, UHS.
   136. JB to Family, 17 August 1970, JBCol, UHS.
   137. Ibid., 10 September 1970, JBCol, UHS.
   138. JB to Myrtle Friedman, 10 October 1970, JBCol, UHS.
   139. JB to Family, 4 October 1970, JBCol, UHS.
   140. Ibid., 27 November 1970, JBCol, UHS.
   141. JB to Willa and Thales Derrick, 18 December 1970, JBCol, UHS.
   142. JB to Fawn Brodie, 4 May 1971, MS 360, UofU.
   143. JB to Dale Morgan, 31 December 1970, JBCol, UHS.
   144. JB to Family, 27 November 1970, JBCol, UHS.
   145. JB to Leonard Rice, 9 December 1970, JBCol, UHS.
   146. JB to Claudia Bushman, 25 August 1970, JBCol, UHS.
   147. Claudia Bushman to JB, 3 February 1971, JBCol, UHS.
   148. JB, "I Married a Family," *Dialogue* 6 (Summer 1971): 21.

Chapter Eleven

   1. JB to Willa and Thales Derrick, 18 December 1970, JBCol, UHS.
   2. JB to Charles W. Taggart, 10 November 1970, JBCol, UHS.
   3. Ibid., 28 December 1970, JBCol, UHS.
   4. JB, *Uncle Will Tells His Story* (Salt Lake City: Taggart & Co., 1970),
207.
   5. Ibid., 81.
   6. Ibid., 85.
   7. Ibid., 134.
   8. JB, Diary A, 19 January 1971.
   9. Charles S. Peterson, conversation with Levi Peterson, 28 March 1987,
Logan, Utah.
   10. JB, Diary A, 22 February 1971.
   11. JB to Family, 19 March 1971, JBCol, UHS.
   12. JB to Milton L. Weilenmann, 35[sic] March 1971, JBCol, UHS.
   13. JB, Diary A, 23 January 1971.
   14. JB to Carla Brooks, 2 February 1971, JBCol, UHS.
   15. JB, Diary A, 9 April 1971.
   16. Ibid., 25 March 1971.
   17. Ibid., 26 March 1971.
   18. JB, Citation: Distinguished Service Award to Dale L. Morgan, *Proceedings of the Utah Academy of Sciences, Arts and Letters* 48, pt. 1 (1971): 8.
   19. JB, Diary A, 16 April 1971.
   20. Ibid., 18 April 1971.

21. Ibid., 14 April 1971.
22. JB to Myrtle Friedman, 13 April 1971, JBCol, UHS.
23. JB, Diary A, 17 June 1971.
24. Ibid., 23 June 1971.
25. Ibid., 21 June 1971.
26. JB to Karl and Carla Brooks and Willa and Thales Derrick, 22 July 1971, JBCol, UHS.
27. JB to Willa and Thales Derrick and Kay and Ida Jean Brooks, 6 August 1971, JBCol, UHS.
28. JB, Diary A, 9 August 1971.
29. JB to *Ranger Rick's Magazine*, 22 September 1971, JBCol, UHS.
30. JB to Marvin Wallin, 25 August 1971, JBCol, UHS.
31. JB to Sam Weller, 10 September 1971, JBCol, UHS.
32. JB, Diary A, 26 August 1971.
33. JB to Mary E. Stuth, 10 November 1971, JBCol, UHS.
34. JB to Winifred Gregory, [17] October [1971], JBCol, UHS.
35. JB to Arthur H. Clark, 14 November 1971, JBCol, UHS.
36. JB to Austin and Alta Fife, 6 March 1971, JBCol, UHS.
37. JB, Diary B, 9 January 1972.
38. Ibid., 14 December 1971.
39. Ibid., 22 December 1971.
40. Ibid., 24 December 1971.
41. JB to Myrtle H. Friedman, 3 January 1972, JBCol, UHS.
42. JB to Frank E. Diston, 6 January 1972, MS 139, UofU.
43. JB, Diary B, 10 January 1972.
44. Jack H. Adamson to Sterling M. McMurrin, 24 January 1972, MS 139, UofU.
45. JB, Diary B, 19 February 1972.
46. Ibid., 27 March 1972.
47. JB to Myrtle H. Friedman, 5 July 1972, JBCol, UHS.
48. JB to Gibbs M. Smith, 18 January 1972, JBCol, UHS.
49. JB to Verl Frehner, 3 February 1972, JBCol, UHS.
50. JB, Diary B, 8 February 1972.
51. JB to Gibbs M. Smith, 18 January 1972, JBCol, UHS.
52. JB, Diary B, 5 February 1972.
53. Ibid., 22 March 1972.
54. Ibid., 23 January 1972.
55. "Tribute to Juanita Brooks," Soil Conservation Society of America, 13 January 1972, unpublished, JBCol Ad, UHS.
56. Program, Sevier Valley Chapter of the Utah State Historical Society, 10 March 1972, unpublished, JBCol Ad, UHS.
57. JB to Mary Leavitt and Charity Rowley, 15 March 1972, JBCol, UHS.
58. JB, Diary B, 21 January 1972.
59. Ibid., 2 February 1972.
60. Ibid., 7 February 1972.
61. Ibid., 13 February 1972.
62. Ibid., 24 February 1972.
63. Ibid., 23 April 1972.
64. Ibid., 6 May 1972.

65. JB, Untitled remarks in "Memorial Service Dean R. Brimhall," unpublished, MAN A1605, UHS.

66. Fae Dix, conversation with Levi Peterson, 4 March 1986, Salt Lake City.

67. JB, Diary B, 18 May 1972.

68. JB to Family, 21 June 1972, JBCol, UHS.

69. JB, Diary B, 20 June 1972.

70. Ibid., 23 June 1972.

71. JB to Ben Roe, 20 May 1972, MS 139, UofU.

72. JB to Myrtle H. Friedman and Frank Diston, 5 July 1972, JBCol, UHS.

73. JB, Diary B, 11 July 1972.

74. Winifred Gregory to JB, 28 June 1972, JBCol, UHS.

75. JB, Diary B, 21 July 1972.

76. Ibid., 23 July 1972.

77. Fae Dix, interview by Levi Peterson, 4 February 1986, Salt Lake City, UHS Oral History Project.

78. JB to Ernest Pulsipher and Tony Brooks, 28 July [1972], JBCol, UHS.

79. JB, Diary B, 9 August 1972.

80. JB to My neighbors next door, [10 August 1972], JBCol, UHS.

81. Gustive O. Larson to JB, 20 November 1972, JBCol, UHS.

82. JB, ed., *Journal of the Southern Indian Mission: Diary of Thomas D. Brown*, Western Text Society No. 4 (Logan: Utah State University Press, 1972), 44.

83. Ibid., 46.

84. Ibid., 102.

85. JB, Diary B, 11 July 1972.

86. Ibid., 6 October 1972.

87. Ibid., 13 November 1972.

88. Ibid., 6 August 1972.

89. Ibid., 3 December 1972.

90. Ibid., 23 September 1972.

91. Ibid., 17 September 1972.

92. Ibid., 13 October 1972.

93. Ibid., 17 October 1972.

94. Ibid., 28 October 1972.

95. Helen S. Cottam v. Juanita Brooks, 5th District Court, 3 November 1972, JBCol Ad, UHS.

96. JB, Diary B, 28 February 1972.

97. Ibid., 6 August 1972.

98. Ibid., 28 November 1972.

99. JB, "The Carillon Bells," lithographed pamphlet, Dixie College Press, n.d., JBCol Ad, UHS.

100. JB, *The Christmas Tree* (Salt Lake City: Peregrine Smith, 1972), n.p.

101. Gibbs M. Smith to JB, 30 November 1973, JBCol, UHS.

102. JB to David Crockett, 7 December 1972, JBCol, UHS.

103. JB, "The Story of Griz," in *Frontier Tales: True Stories of Real People*, Western Text Society Special Publication (Logan: Utah State University Press, 1972), 57.

104. JB, Diary B, 3 January 1973.

105. Ibid., 30 January 1973.

106. Ibid., 13 January 1973.

107. Ibid., 19 January 1973.

108. JB, "Silver Reef: Fact and Folklore," in *Essays on the American West, 1972–73: Charles Redd Monographs in Western History No. 3,* ed. Thomas G. Alexander (Provo: Brigham Young University Press, 1974), 95.

109. JB to Tony and Janet Brooks, 19 March 1973, JBCol, UHS.

110. Charles S. Peterson to JB, 14 November 1972, JBCol, UHS.

111. JB to Willa Derrick, 15 July 1973, JBCol, UHS.

112. JB to Martha and Carrick Leavitt, 12 March [1973], JBCol, UHS.

113. Mary Washington, conversation with Levi Peterson, 24 April 1987, Logan, Utah.

114. Ferron C. Losee to JB, 4 May 1973, JBCol, UHS.

115. "Jewish Book Falls Short of Promise," review of *The History of the Jews in Utah and Idaho,* in *Salt Lake Tribune,* 1 July 1973, 2(E).

116. Harold Schindler, conversation with Levi Peterson, 1 May 1987, Salt Lake City.

117. William M. Kramer, review of *The History of the Jews in Utah and Idaho,* in *Western States Jewish Historical Quarterly* 6 (January 1974): 155.

118. JB, *The History of the Jews in Utah and Idaho* (Salt Lake City: Western Epics, 1973), 183.

119. Ibid., 77.

120. JB, review of *Take Up Your Mission: Mormon Colonizing Along the Little Colorado River, 1870–1900,* by Charles S. Peterson, in *New Mexico Historical Review* 49 (April 1974), 180.

121. Charles S. Peterson to JB, 2 July 1973, JBCol, UHS.

122. JB to Charles S. Peterson, 5 July 1973, JBCol, UHS.

123. JB to P. T. Reilly, 24 July 1973, JBCol, UHS.

124. JB to Sue ?, 28 August 1973, JBCol, UHS.

125. Glen M. Leonard to JB, 9 August 1973, JBCol, UHS.

126. Mary E. Stith to JB, 20 January 1972, JBCol, UHS.

127. JB, Diary B, 27 April 1972.

128. JB to Carrick and Martha Leavitt, 12 March [1973], JBCol, UHS.

129. JB to Willa Derrick, 15 July 1973, JBCol, UHS.

130. Gerald A. Buttars to JB, 19 October 1973, JBCol, UHS.

131. "Western Writers Honor Noted Utah Historian," *Salt Lake Tribune,* 21 October 1973, 2(E).

132. Ernest Pulsipher to JB, 30 October 1973, JBCol, UHS.

133. JB to Lovina ?, 3 April 1974, JBCol, UHS.

134. JB to Zuna Barnum, 18 May 1974, JBCol, UHS.

135. JB, *On the Ragged Edge: The Life and Times of Dudley Leavitt* (Salt Lake City: Utah State Historical Society, 1973), ix.

136. Ibid., x.

137. Trudy McMurrin, interview by Levi Peterson, 14 August 1985, Ogden, Utah, UHS Oral History Project.

138. Aura Allen to JB, 12 April 1974, JBCol, UHS.

139. JB, interview by Maureen Ursenbach and Davis Bitton, 3 April 1974, Salt Lake City, unpublished typescript, Maureen Ursenbach Beecher, Salt Lake City, Utah.

140. JB to Claudia Bushman, 15 May 1974, JBCol, UHS.

141. JB to Family, 15 June 1974, JBCol, UHS.

142. JB to Claudia Bushman, 14 June 1974, JBCol, UHS.

143. JB to Family, 15 June 1974, JBCol, UHS.

144. JB to Mary Leavitt, 28 August 1974, JBCol, UHS.

145. JB to Todd and Betty Berens, 4 August, 1974, Todd I. Berens, Santa Ana, Calif.

146. Ibid.

147. JB to Sheriff Armin Brandt, 16 August 1974, JBCol, UHS.

148. Wendell J. Ashton to JB, 5 June 1973, JBCol, UHS.

149. JB to David S. Grow, 16 December 1974, JBCol, UHS.

Chapter Twelve

1. JB to Ernest Pulsipher, 13 February 1975, JBCol, UHS.

2. JB to Family, 11 February 1975, JBCol, UHS.

3. JB to Todd and Betty Berens, 21 June 1975, Todd I. Berens, Santa Ana, Calif.

4. JB to Ione Bennion, 2 June 1975, JBCol, UHS.

5. Arvo Van Alstyne to JB, 22 May 1975, JBCol, UHS.

6. Recognition of JB, Dixie College and Southern Heritage Writers' Guild, 6 June 1975, Karl Brooks, St. George, Utah.

7. JB, *Emma Lee*, Western Text Society Series (Logan: Utah State University Press, 1975), 20–21.

8. Ibid., 99.

9. Mary H. Lewis to JB, 18 August 1975, Operational Files, UHS.

10. JB to Mary H. Lewis, 9 September 1975, JBCol, UHS.

11. Fae Dix, Diary, 12 September 1975, Fae D. Dix, Salt Lake City.

12. JB to Ernest and Maria Pulsipher, 22 October 1975, JBCol, UHS.

13. Trudy McMurrin, interview by Levi Peterson, 14 August 1985, Ogden, Utah, UHS Oral History Project.

14. Fae Dix, Diary, 13 June 1975, Fae D. Dix, Salt Lake City.

15. Todd and Betty Berens to JB, 22 September 1975, JBCol, UHS.

16. JB to Mary Leavitt, 3 December 1975, JBCol, UHS.

17. JB to Ernest and Maria Pulsipher, 22 October 1975, JBCol, UHS.

18. JB to Mary Leavitt, 3 December 1975, JBCol, UHS.

19. JB to Family, 19 March 1976, JBCol, UHS.

20. JB to Trudy McMurrin, undated, JBCol, UHS.

21. JB to Mary Leavitt, 24 May 1976, JBCol, UHS.

22. Miriam B. Murphy, conversation with Levi Peterson, 4 May 1987, Salt Lake City.

23. Stanford J. Layton to JB, 19 March 1976, Operational Files, UHS.

24. Trudy McMurrin, interview by Levi Peterson, 14 August 1985, Ogden, Utah, UHS Oral History Project.

25. JB to Elaine McPhie, 21 June 1976, JBCol, UHS.

26. JB to Todd and Betty Berens, 30 August 1976, Todd I. Berens, Santa Ana, Calif.

27. Dale C. LeCheminant to JB, 27 February 1976, JBCol, UHS.

28. Emma R. Olsen to JB, 4 October 1976, JBCol, UHS.

29. Fae Dix, interview by Levi Peterson, 4 February 1986, Salt Lake City, UHS Oral History Project.

30. Ibid.

31. Ione Bennion, conversation with Levi Peterson, 28 April 1987, Logan, Utah.

32. JB to Todd and Betty Berens, 30 August 1976, Todd I. Berens, Santa Ana, Calif.

33. Fae Dix, Diary, 5 November 1976, Fae D. Dix, Salt Lake City.

34. Fae Dix to Levi Peterson, 21 April 1987.

35. JB to Tony and Janet Brooks, 9 November 1976, JBCol, UHS.

36. Fae Dix, Diary, 27 November 1976, Fae D. Dix, Salt Lake City.

37. Fawn M. Brodie to Cynthia Vartan, 18 November 1976, JBCol, UHS.

38. JB to Fawn Brodie, 29 December 1976, JBCol, UHS.

39. Karl and Carla Brooks, conversation with Levi Peterson, 23 March 1987, St. George, Utah.

40. JB to Trudy McMurrin, undated, JBCol, UHS.

41. Ardith Johnson to JB, 7 March 1977, JBCol, UHS.

42. Melvin T. Smith to JB, 3 March 1977, JBCol, UHS.

43. Trudy McMurrin to JB, 24 January 1977, JBCol, UHS.

44. JB to Trudy McMurrin, undated, JBCol, UHS.

45. Willa Derrick, conversation with Levi Peterson, 15 May 1987, St. George, Utah.

46. Ibid., 23 March 1987, St. George, Utah.

47. JB to Ernest and Maria Pulsipher, 3 January ?, JBCol 7:10, UHS.

48. Maxine and Jesse Phillips, conversation with Levi Peterson, 22 March 1987, St. George, Utah.

49. JB to Guy and Pamela Walker, 1 September 1978, JBCol, UHS.

50. Ione Bennion, conversation with Levi Peterson, 28 April 1987, Logan, Utah.

51. Alison Thorne to JB, 20 June 1979, JBCol, UHS.

52. Karl Brooks, Speech at Dixie College, 4 April 1978, tape transcription, UHS Oral History Project.

53. "Juanita Brooks Honored at Dixie College," *Washington County News*, 13 April 1978.

54. Levi Peterson, Citation for the Charles Redd Award, *Encyclia* 55 (1978): 108.

55. JB to Ronald G. Hyde, 23 May 1975, Alumni Association Files, BYU.

56. Ronald G. Hyde to JB, 1 March 1976, JBCol, UHS.

57. Emeritus Club Luncheon Program, 23 April 1981, Alumni Association Files, BYU.

58. "Beehive Hall of Famer," *St. George Magazine* 3 (Spring 1985): 58.

59. Trudy McMurrin to JB, 2 June 1977, Operational Files, UofUPress.

60. Trudy McMurrin to Norma Mikkelsen, 12 August 1981, Operational Files, UofUPress.

61. Alison Thorne to JB, 20 June 1979, JBCol, UHS.

62. JB, ed., *Not by Bread Alone: The Journal of Martha Spence Heywood 1850-56* (Salt Lake City: Utah State Historical Society, 1978), 31.

63. Ibid., 117-18.

64. Harold Schindler, "Juanita Brooks: 'Not by Bread Alone,' " review of *Not by Bread Alone*, in *Salt Lake Tribune*, 8 April 1979, 2(E).

65. Judith Austin, review of *Not By Bread Alone*, in *The Colorado Magazine* 56 (Winter and Spring 1979): 95.

66. JB, ed., *Not by Bread Alone*, 36.

67. Melvin T. Smith to JB, 6 March 1973, JBCol, UHS.

68. Jay M. Haymond to JB, 3 January 1979, JBCol, UHS.

69. Gary Topping, conversation with Levi Peterson, 14 March 1986, Salt Lake City.

70. *Juanita Brooks: Utah Historian*, videocasette, 15 min., produced and directed by Louise Degn, KSL-TV, 1979, Salt Lake City.

71. Richard Howe to Karl Brooks, 23 November 1979, Operational Files, Howe Brothers.

72. Trudy McMurrin to Norma Mikkelsen, 12 August 1981, Operational Files, UofUPress.

73. Trudy McMurrin to JB, 2 February 1979, Operational Files, UofU Press.

74. Richard Howe, interview by Levi Peterson, 20 August 1985, Salt Lake City, UHS Oral History Project.

75. Richard Howe to Karl Brooks, 17 November 1981, Operational Files, Howe Brothers.

76. Richard Howe to Charles Peterson, 14 January 1982, Operational Files, Howe Brothers.

77. Richard Howe, interview by Levi Peterson, 20 August 1985, Salt Lake City, UHS Oral History Project.

78. Loretta L. Hefner, "February Book Review," review of *Quicksand and Cactus*, in *Utah Endowment for the Humanities Newsletter*, February 1983, n.p.

79. Richard W. Etulain, "Going Out to Meet Life," review of *Quicksand and Cactus*, in *Sunstone Review* (March 1983): 19.

80. Ronald W. Walker, review of *Quicksand and Cactus*, in *Arizona and the West* 26 (Spring 1984): 74.

81. Wilbur S. Shepperson, review of *Quicksand and Cactus*, in *The Pacific Historian* 27 (Spring 1983): 88.

82. JB, *Quicksand and Cactus: A Memoir of the Southern Mormon Frontier* (Salt Lake City: Howe Brothers, 1982), 243.

83. Ibid., 283.

84. Ibid., 192–93.

85. Linda E. Speth to Charles S. Peterson, 1 August 1983, Operational Files, USUPress.

86. Charles S. Peterson, introduction to *Emma Lee*, by JB, 2d ed. (Logan: Utah State University Press, 1984), 6.

87. Willa Derrick, conversation with Levi Peterson, 23 March 1987, St. George, Utah.

88. Eva Miles, conversation with Levi Peterson, 23 March 1987, St. George, Utah.

89. Maxine and Jesse Phillips, conversation with Levi Peterson, 22 March 1987, St. George, Utah.

90. Karl and Carla Brooks, conversation with Levi Peterson, 23 March 1987, St. George, Utah.

91. Levi Peterson, personal notes, 23 March 1987, Ogden, Utah.

JUANITA BROOKS:
A BIBLIOGRAPHY

I. Works by Juanita Brooks*

Books

Dudley Leavitt: Pioneer to Southern Utah. St. George, Utah: By the author, 1942. Reprint 1955, 1969.

The Mountain Meadows Massacre. 1st ed. Stanford: Stanford University Press, 1950. 2d ed., Norman: University of Oklahoma Press, 1962. New preface 2d ed., 1970.

John Doyle Lee: Zealot—Pioneer Builder—Scapegoat. 1st ed. Western Frontiersman Series. Glendale, Calif.: Arthur H. Clark Co., 1961; reinstatement version, 1962. 2d ed., 1972. Reprint 2d ed., Salt Lake City, Utah: Howe Brothers, 1985.

George Brooks: Artist in Stone. St. George, Utah: By the author, 1965.

Uncle Will Tells His Story. Salt Lake City: Taggart & Co., 1970.

Frontier Tales: True Stories of Real People. Western Text Society Special Publication. Logan: Utah State University Press, 1972.

The Christmas Tree. Salt Lake City: Peregrine Smith Inc., 1972.

History of the Jews in Utah and Idaho. Salt Lake City: Western Epics, 1973.

On the Ragged Edge: The Life and Times of Dudley Leavitt. Salt Lake City: Utah State Historical Society, 1973. (Redaction of *Dudley Leavitt: Pioneer to Southern Utah.*)

Emma Lee. Western Text Society Series. 1st ed. Logan: Utah State University Press, 1975. 2d ed., with an Introduction by Charles S. Peterson, 1984.

Jacob Hamblin: Mormon Apostle to the Indians. Salt Lake City: Westwater Press (later Howe Brothers), 1980.

Quicksand and Cactus: A Memoir of the Southern Mormon Frontier. With an Introduction by Charles S. Peterson. Salt Lake City: Howe Brothers, 1982.

Edited Books and Articles

"History of Sarah Studevant Leavitt."* Bunkerville, Nev.: By the editor, 1919. (Mimeographed.) *History of Sarah Studevant Leavitt,* n.p., private printing of 1919 edition, [1969].

"Journal of Thales H. Haskell." *Utah Historical Quarterly* 12 (January-April 1944): 69–98.

"Journal of John Pulsipher." *Utah Humanities Review* 2 (October 1948): 351–79; *Western Humanities Review* 3 (January 1949): 38–55.

*Asterisked works were published under the name of Juanita Pulsipher.

A Mormon Chronicle: The Diaries of John D. Lee—1848–1876. Coedited by Robert Glass Cleland. 2 vols. San Marino: Huntington Library, 1955. Reprint with a Preface by Everett L. Cooley, Salt Lake City: University of Utah Press, 1983.

"Biographies: Federal Heights Ward." Salt Lake City: Federal Heights Ward Genealogical Committee, 1963. (Multilithed.)

On the Mormon Frontier: The Diary of Hosea Stout—1844–1861. 2 vols. Salt Lake City: University of Utah Press and Utah State Historical Society, 1964. Reprint with a Preface by Everett L. Cooley, 1982.

"John D. Lee: Diary of the Mormon Battalion Mission." *New Mexico Historical Review* 42 (1967): 165–209, 281–332.

Journal of the Southern Indian Mission: Diary of Thomas D. Brown. Western Text Society No. 4. Logan: Utah State University Press, 1972.

"Utah's Peace Advocate, the 'Mormona': Elise Furer Musser." Coedited by Janet G. Butler. *Utah Historical Quarterly* 46 (Spring 1978), 151–66.

Not By Bread Alone: The Journal of Martha Spence Heywood—1850–1856. Salt Lake City: Utah State Historical Society, 1978.

Articles, Essays, Sketches, and Stories

"The Usual Dilemma."* *The Dixie—The Girl's Edition*, St. George, Utah: Dixie Normal College, 1922: n.p. (Story.)

"A Close-up of Polygamy." *Harper's* 168 (February 1934): 299–307.

"Back to the Scriptures Project: The Old Testament." *Relief Society Magazine* 21 (December 1934): 760–62.

"With New Vision." *Relief Society Magazine* 22 (1935): 403–5.

"Romance of Highway 91." *The Utah* 2 (May 1936): 12, 38–39; (July 1936): 10–11, 52.

"St. George: The City with a Heritage." *The Utah* 2 (August 1936): 13, 28, 38.

"Whose Business Is Recreation?" *Improvement Era* 41 (October 1938): 596–97.

"Recreation of the Pioneers." *Relief Society Magazine* 26 (July 1939): 439–42.

"The St. George Temple Renewed." *Improvement Era* 42 (July 1939): 414, 435.

"Sidelights on the Mountain Meadows Massacre." *Proceedings of the Utah Academy of Sciences, Arts and Letters* 17 (1940): 12. (Abstract.) Reprint in *Encyclia: Journal of the Utah Academy of Sciences, Arts and Letters* 75th Anniversary Retrospective Issue (1983): 81–82.

"Washington County, Utah." *Democratic Digest*, Democratic National Committee (March 1941): 21.

"A Bonanza for Writers." *Writer's Year Book*. Cincinnati: Writer's Digest, 1941.

"The Water's In!" *Harper's* 182 (May 1941): 608–13. Condensed in *Reader's Digest* 38 (June 1941): 101–3.

"Jacob Hamblin: Apostle to the Indians." *Arizona Highways* 19 (April 1943): 31–35. Reprint in *Improvement Era* 47 (April 1944): 210–11, 249, 251–55.

"The Mormon Battalion." *Arizona Highways* 19 (May 1943): 38–40, 42.

"Indian Relations on the Mormon Frontier." *Utah Historical Quarterly* 12 (January-April 1944): 1–48.

"The Southern Indian Mission." *Improvement Era* 48 (April, May, June 1945): 188, 212–15; 262–63; 342, 368–69.

"Old Toab." *Utah Magazine* 8 (April 1946): 20–21, 46–47.

"Beauty Beckons in the Parks of Southern Utah." *Utah Magazine* 8 (June 1946): 10–13, 33, 35.

"The St. George Temple." *Improvement Era* 49 (June 1946): 370–71, 410–13.

"Symbol of a People's Faith." *Utah Magazine* 9 (July 1947): 20–21, 40–42.

"To the Glory of God: The Story of the St. George Temple." *Arizona Highways* 23 (April 1947): 1, 32.

"The First One Hundred Years of Southern Utah History." *Proceedings of the Utah Academy of Sciences, Arts and Letters* 24 (1946–1947): 71–79. Reprint in *Encyclia: Journal of the Utah Academy of Sciences, Arts and Letters* 75th Anniversary Retrospective Issue (1983): 89–98.

"Jacob Hamblin: Apostle to the Lamanites." *Pacific Spectator* 2 (1948): 315–30.

"Ye Who Are Called to Labor." *Improvement Era* 51 (August, September 1948): 498–99, 532–33; 564–65, 593–94, 596–97.

"Trippingly Off the Tongue." *Deseret News* 12 September 1948, 6(F).

"Let's Preserve Our Records." *Utah Humanities Review* 2 (July 1948): 259–63.

"The Arizona Strip." *Pacific Spectator* 3 (Summer 1949): 290–301.

"The Southern Indian Mission [Alternate Version]"; "Regarding the 'RETURN' of New Harmony to Iron County." In *Under Dixie Sun: A History of Washington County*, ed. Hazel Bradshaw. St. George, Utah: Washington Co. Daughters of Utah Pioneers, 1950. Reprint, 1978, 23–33; 140–41.

"St. George, Utah: A Community Portrait." In "Symposium on Mormon Culture." Logan: Utah Academy of Sciences, Arts and Letters, 1952, 1–8. (Mimeographed.)

"Way Out West in Dixie." *Ford Times*, May 1953, 53.

"Fort Pierce." *Sons of Utah Pioneers News* 2 (October 1955): 16.

"Speech Given at the Dedication of a Monument Honoring the Victims of the Massacre at the Mountain Meadows." *Utah Historical Quarterly* 24 (January 1956): 72–77. Reprint in *Among the Mormons: Historic Accounts by Contemporary Observers*, ed. William Mulder and A. Russell Mortensen. New York: Alfred A. Knopf, 1958; paperback reprint Lincoln: University of Nebraska Press, 1973, 315–20.

"Unpublished Letters [regarding Vera Black]." *Truth* 21 (March 1956): 310–13.

"Lee's Ferry at Lonely Dell." *Utah Historical Quarterly* 25 (1957): 283–95.

"There's a Dixieland in Utah." *Westways* 50 (December 1958): 12–13.

"The Land That God Forgot." *Utah Historical Quarterly* 26 (July 1958): 207–19. Excerpted as " 'Dixie'–Land of Enchantment" in *Deseret News*, 1 August 1959, 10(A).

"The Face of the Land"; "The Cotton Mission"; "Early Buildings"; "Silver Reef"; "Vignettes." *Utah Historical Quarterly* 29 (July 1961): 193–97; 201–21; 241–53; 281–87; 289–302. Reprint in special St. George centennial pamphlet, *Utah's Dixie: The Cotton Mission*, Salt Lake City: Utah State Historical Society, 1961.

"Indian Sketches from the Journals of T. D. Brown and Jacob Hamblin." *Utah Historical Quarterly* 29 (October 1961), 346–60.

"Memories of a Mormon Girlhood." *Journal of American Folklore* 77 (July-September 1964): 195–219. Reprint in *Folklore of the Great West*, ed. John Greenway, 17–46. Palo Alto, Calif.: American West Publishing, 1969.

"The Mormons in Carson County, Utah Territory." *Nevada Historical Society Quarterly* 8 (Spring 1965): 3–23.

"Riding Herd (Excerpt from a Letter)." *Dialogue* 1 (Summer 1966): 141.

"The Mountain Meadows: Historic Stopping Place on the Spanish Trail." *Utah Historical Quarterly* 35 (Spring 1967): 137–43.

"The Outsider." In *Great Western Short Stories*, ed. J. Golden Taylor, 393–404. Palo Alto, Calif.: American West Publishing, 1967.

"Jest a Copyin'–Word f'r Word. *Utah Historical Quarterly* 37 (Fall 1969): 375–95.

"Mariah Huntsman Leavitt: Midwife of the Desert Frontier." In *Forms upon the Frontier: Folklife and Folk Arts in the United States*. Monograph Series, ed. Austin and Alta Fife and Henry H. Glassie, 119–31. Logan: Utah State University Press, 1969.

"Frontier Birth Beliefs." *Western Folklore* 29 (January 1970): 53–55.

"A Place of Refuge." *Nevada Historical Society Quarterly* 14 (Spring 1971): 13–24.

"I Married a Family." *Dialogue* 6 (Summer 1971): 15–21.

"Our Annual Visitors"; "Pranks and Pranksters." In *Lore of Faith and Folly*, ed. Thomas E. Cheney, assisted by Austin E. Fife and Juanita Brooks, 5–13; 57–60. Salt Lake City: University of Utah Press, 1971.

"Citation: Distinguished Service Award to Dale L. Morgan." *Proceedings of the Utah Academy of Sciences, Arts and Letters* 48, pt. 1 (1971): 7–8.

"The Carillon Bells." St. George, Utah: Dixie College Press, [1972]. (Pamphlet.)

"Riding Herd: A Conversation with Juanita Brooks." Interview by Davis Bitton and Maureen Ursenbach. *Dialogue* 9 (Spring 1974): 11–33.

"Silver Reef: Fact and Folklore." In *Essays on the American West, 1972–1973*. Charles Redd Monographs in Western History, no. 3, ed. Thomas G. Alexander, 87–104. Provo, Utah: Brigham Young University Press, 1974.

"The Outside Comes In." *Beehive History* 7, Utah State Historical Society (1981): 2–5. (Reprint from *Q&C*.)

"Quicksand and Cactus." *Utah Holiday* 11 (August 1982): 34–37, 54. (Reprint from *Q&C*.)

"The Outsider: A Stranger Comes to Bunkerville." *Nevada* 44 (July-August 1984): 44–46. (Reprint from *Q&C*.)

"The Outsider." In *Westward the Women: An Anthology of Western Stories by Women*, ed. Vicki Pierkarski, 158–167. Garden City, N.Y.: Doubleday & Co., 1984. (Reprint from *Q&C*.)

"To Columbia." *St. George Magazine* 3 (Spring 1985): 55–58, 81, 89, 96. (Reprint from *Q&C*.)

Poems

"Your Cover Is Faded and Torn, Old Book."* In Juanita Pulsipher, ed., "History of Sarah Studevant Leavitt." Bunkerville, Nev.: By the editor, 1919. (Mimeographed.)

"Sunrise from the Top of Mount Timp."* *Improvement Era* 29 (September 1926): 1124. Reprint in *Under Dixie Sun: A History of Washington County*, ed. Hazel Bradshaw. St. George, Utah: Washington Co. Daughters of Utah Pioneers, 1950. Reprint, 1978, 360.

"Resignation."* *Improvement Era* 36 (April 1933): 363.

"Awakening."* *Improvement Era* 36 (April 1933): 370.

Book Reviews

Review of *Nikoline's Choice*, by Margaret Maw. In *Utah Humanities Review* 1 (October 1947): 410.

Review of *Jacob Hamblin, Buckskin Apostle*, by Paul Bailey. In *Utah Humanities Review* 2 (July 1948): 287–89.

Review of *Jacob Hamblin, the Peacemaker*, by Pearson H. Corbett. In *Pacific Historical Review* 22 (1953): 180–82.

Review of *Orderville, Utah: A Pioneer Mormon Experiment in Economic Organization*, by Leonard J. Arrington. In *Western Humanities Review* 8 (1954): 168–69.

Review of *I Have Six Wives*, by Samuel W. Taylor. In *Utah Historical Quarterly* 24 (1956): 366–67.

Review of *The Mormon Conflict, 1850–1859*, by Norman F. Furniss. In *Utah Historical Quarterly* 29 (1961): 77–80.

Review of *The Mormon Conflict, 1850–1859*, by Norman F. Furniss. In *New Mexico Quarterly* 31 (Autumn 1961): 258–60.

Review of *The Life and Times of Joseph Fish, Mormon Pioneer*, ed. by John H. Krenkel. In *Colorado Magazine* 48 (1971): 167–68.

Review of *Take Up Your Mission: Mormon Colonizing Along the Little Colorado River, 1870–1900*, by Charles S. Peterson. In *New Mexico Historical Review* 49 (April 1974): 179–80.

II. Writings about Juanita Brooks

Articles, Introductions, and Theses

Hardy, Pansy L. "The Influence of the Southern Nevada and Southern Utah Folklore upon the Writings of Dr. Juanita Brooks and Dr. LeRoy R. Hafen." Master's thesis, Brigham Young University, 1965.

Jarvik, Elaine. "Utah Historian Now Writing Her Own Story." *Deseret News*, 30 June 1976, 3(A).

Lowe, Ellen M. "Juanita Brooks: Utah Historian." Bound research paper, Utah State Historical Society MAN A 1166.

Morgan, Dale L. "Juanita Brooks." *Utah Historical Quarterly* 25 (1957): 193–95.

Peterson, Charles S. Introduction to *Quicksand and Cactus*, by Juanita Brooks. Salt Lake City: Howe Brothers, 1982.

————. Introduction to *Emma Lee*, by Juanita Brooks. 2d ed. Logan: Utah State University Press, 1984.

Peterson, Levi S. "Juanita Brooks: The Mormon Historian as Tragedian." *Journal of Mormon History* 3 (1976): 47–54.

————. "Juanita Brooks's *Quicksand and Cactus*: The Evolution of a Literary Memoir." *Dialogue* 20 (Spring 1987): 145–55.

Pulsipher, Ernest. "A Few Personal Glimpses of Juanita Brooks." *Utah Historical Quarterly* 44 (Summer 1987): 268–77.

Winkler, Lorna M. "Censorship and the Freedom of Information in Mormon Society: The Research of Juanita Brooks." Bound research paper, Brigham Young University, 1981.

Reviews of *The Mountain Meadows Massacre*

Bailey, Paul. *The Branding Iron* 64 (March 1963): 11–12.

Edwards, Paul M. *Courage* 5 (Winter-Spring 1973): 156–57.

Frazier, Charles E., Jr. *Journal of the West* 2 (1963): 482–83.

Geiser, S. W. *Southwest Review* (Spring 1952): 169–71.

Hafen, LeRoy R., Robert G. Athearn, Myrl V. Walker, and L. H. Kirkpatrick. *Western Humanities Review* 5 (Spring 1951): 209–15.

Handy, R. T. *Journal of Religion* 31 (October 1951): 285.

Hutcheson, Austin E. *Pacific Northwest Quarterly* 42 (July 1951): 248–49.

Johnson, Barry C. *English Westerners' Tally Sheet* 9 (September-October 1965): 6–8.

Larson, T. A. *New Mexico Historical Review* 39 (January 1964): 81–83.

Mortensen, A. R. *Pacific Historical Review* 20 (May 1951): 180–81.

Mortensen, A. R. *Utah Historical Quarterly* 31 (Spring 1963): 164.

Reeder, Armand W. *Denver Westerners' Roundup* 19 (April 1963): 14, 21.
Robertson, Frank C. *Utah Historical Quarterly* 20 (January 1952): 96–97.
Smith, Henry Nash. *New York Herald Tribune Book Review*, 11 March 1951, 5.
Stonehouse, Merlin. *Southern California Quarterly* 45 (September 1963): 280–81.
Wallace, William S. *Library Journal*, 15 January 1963, 219.
San Francisco Chronicle, 4 December 1950.
San Francisco Examiner, 10 December 1950.
San Francisco Argonaut, 15 December 1950.
Portland Oregonian, 15 December 1950.
Newsweek Magazine, 18 December 1950.
Iron County [Utah] Record, 21 December 1950.
San Jose Mercury News, 7 January 1951.
Denver Post, 21 January 1951.
Provo [Utah] Daily Herald, 28 January 1951.
Long Beach Press-Telegram, 25 February 1951.
Saints' Herald, 2 April 1951.
Dallas Morning News, 2 July 1952.
Los Angeles Times, 23 January 1963.
Riverside [Calif.] Enterprise, 3 February 1963.
Arizona Republic, 10 February 1963.
Grand Junction [Colo.] Sentinel, 17 February 1963.
Dallas Times-Herald, 3 March 1963.
Bridgeport [Conn.] Post, 3 March 1963.
Salt Lake Tribune, 10 March 1963.
Tulsa World, 10 March 1963.
El Paso Times, 17 March 1963.
Oklahoma City Oklahoman, 31 March 1963.
San Francisco Chronicle, 14 April 1963.
Wichita Falls [Texas] Times, 12 May 1963.
Washington Post and Times Herald, 11 August 1963.
Sacramento Bee, 22 September 1963.

Reviews of *A Mormon Chronicle: The Diaries of John D. Lee – 1848–1876*

Banfield, Edward C. *Mississippi Valley Historical Review* 43 (June 1956): 122–24.
Blankenship, Russell. *Pacific Northwest Quarterly* 47 (July 1956): 93.
Carmer, Carl. *New York Times Book Review*, 25 December 1955, 1(Sec. 7).
McNiff, W. J. *American Historical Review* 61 (April 1956): 751–52.
Mortensen, A. R. *Utah Historical Quarterly* 24 (1956): 88–90.
Smith, Melvin T. *Utah Historical Quarterly* 52 (Fall 1984): 401–2.
Deseret News, 24 November 1955.
Washington County [Utah] News, 24 November 1955.
Salt Lake Tribune, 25 November 1955.
Time Magazine, 19 December 1955.
Salt Lake Tribune, 8 January 1956.
Pasadena Star-News, 26 February 1956.

Reviews of *John Doyle Lee: Zealot – Pioneer Builder – Scapegoat*

American Book Collector 12 (March 1962): 29.
Arrington, Leonard J. *Montana, the Magazine of Western History* 14 (April 1964): 114.
Atkinson, J. H. *Arkansas Historical Quarterly* 21 (Spring 1962): 85–86.

Bailey, Paul. *The Branding Iron* 58 (September-October 1961): 6.
Bailey, Paul. *Journal of the West* 2 (January 1963): 103-4.
Edwards, Paul M. *Courage* 3 (Winter-Spring 1973): 156-57.
Furniss, Norman F. *Mississippi Valley Historical Review* 49 (June 1962): 141-42.
Gregory, Winifred W. *New Mexico Quarterly* 32 (Summer 1963): 230-32.
Hager, Everett G. *California Historical Society Quarterly* 41 (December 1962): 348-49.
Hubbard, Paul. *Arizona and the West* 4 (Autumn 1962): 280-81.
Kirkpatrick, L. H. *Utah Libraries* 5 (Spring 1962): 9-10.
Larson, Gustive O. *Utah Historical Quarterly* 30 (Spring 1962): 175-77.
Madsen, Brigham D. *Western Humanities Review* 17 (Winter 1963): 97-98.
Missouri Historical Review 56 (October 1961-July 1962): 308.
Morgan, Dale L. *Southern California Quarterly* 45 (December 1963): 364-66.
Paul, Rodman Wilson. *Pacific Historical Review* 31 (November 1962): 417-18.
Stewart, Omer C. *Colorado Magazine* 39 (July 1962): 224-27.
Wells, Merle W. *American Association for State and Local History News* 19 (December 1963): 32-33.
Wright, Muriel H. *Chronicles of Oklahoma* 41 (Summer 1963): 226-27.
San Francisco Chronicle, 7 December 1961.
Salt Lake Tribune, 10 December 1961.
Decatur [Illinois] Review, 19 December 1961.
Los Angeles Examiner, 24 December 1961.
Arizona Republic, 24 December 1961.
Provo [Utah] Daily Herald, 28 December 1961.
Glendale [Calif.] News-Press, 12 January 1962.
Los Angeles Times, 21 January 1962.
San Bernardino Sun-Telegram, 21 January 1962.
Omaha World Herald, 25 February 1962.
Washington County [Utah] News, 5 April 1962.
Salt Lake Tribune, 3 March 1985.
Utah Endowment for the Humanities News, May 1986.
Murray [Utah] Green Sheet, 24 July 1985.

Review of *George Brooks: Artist in Stone*

Tyler, Lyman S. *Utah Historical Quarterly* 34 (Fall 1966): 345.

Reviews of *On the Mormon Frontier: The Diary of Hosea Stout – 1844-1861*

Allen, James B. *California Historical Society Quarterly* 46 (1967): 257-59.
Andrews, Thomas F. *Journal of the West* 5 (January 1966): 130.
Arrington, Leonard J. *Utah Alumnus* 41 (April 1965): 12-14.
DePillis, Mario S. *Southern California Quarterly* 48 (June 1966): 195-201.
Ellsworth, S. George. *Utah Historical Quarterly* 33 (Summer 1965): 272-73.
Fife, Austin E. *Journal of the Illinois State Historical Society* 59 (Summer 1966): 190-92.
Hansen, Klaus J. *Journal of American History* 52 (March 1966): 833-34.
Hubbard, Paul. *Arizona and the West* 8 (Autumn 1966): 280-82.
Jennings, Warren A. *Missouri Historical Review* 60 (1965-1966): 254-56.
Miller, David E. *Nebraska History* 47 (1966): 221-22.
Morgan, Dale L. *American West* 2 (Spring 1965): 46-47, 93.
Paul, Rodman Wilson. *American Historical Review* 71 (July 1966): 1442-43.
Shepherd, Harold. *Utah Law Review* 9 (Summer 1965): 816-27.

Shipps, Jan. *Pacific Historical Review* 35 (May 1966): 229–30.
Salt Lake Tribune, 29 August 1965.
San Francisco Chronicle, 5 December 1965.
Ogden [Utah] Standard-Examiner, 3 April 1983.
Deseret News, 17 April 1983.

Reviews of *Uncle Will Tells His Story*

Batman, Richard. *Journal of the West* 10 (April 1971): 382.
Cheney, Thomas E. *Dialogue* 7 (Summer 1972): 67–69.
Weller, Sam. *Utah Historical Quarterly* 39 (Fall 1971): 379–80.
Salt Lake Tribune, 24 January 1971.

Review of *Frontier Tales: True Stories of Real People*

Lambert, Neal E. *Utah Historical Quarterly* 42 (Spring 1974): 202–03.

Review of *Journal of the Southern Indian Mission: Diary of Thomas D. Brown*

Roske, Ralph J. *Utah Historical Quarterly* 41 (Spring 1973): 202–3.

Reviews of *History of the Jews in Utah and Idaho*

Crowder, David L. *Pacific Northwest Quarterly* 67 (January 1976): 40.
Kramer, William M. *Western States Jewish Historical Quarterly* 6 (January 1974): 155.
Levinson, Robert E. *American Jewish Historical Quarterly* 65 (December 1975): 183–85.
Taylor, Samuel W. *Dialogue* 9 (Spring 1974): 94–95.
Salt Lake Tribune, 1 July 1973.

Reviews of *Emma Lee*

Ahrens, Ronald. *St. George Magazine* (Fall 1985): 102.
Anderson, Thayle. *American West* 13 (September-October 1976): 55.
Roske, Ralph J. *Utah Historical Quarterly* 44 (Spring 1976): 185–86.
Smiley, Winn Whiting. *The Journal of Arizona History* 16 (Winter 1975): 432–33.

Reviews of *Not By Bread Alone: The Journal of Martha Spence Heywood*

Austin, Judith. *Colorado Magazine* 56 (Winter-Spring 1979): 94–96.
Campbell, Eugene E. *Western Historical Quarterly* 10 (April 1979): 239–40.
Herndon, Jerry A. *American West* 16 (March-April 1979): 52–53.
Hinckley, Ted C. *Montana* 27 (Autumn 1978): 60–61.
May, Cheryll Lynn. *Dialogue* 12 (Spring 1979): 113–15.
Pacific Historian 22 (Fall 1978): 319.
Salvato, Jeanne. *Utah Holiday* 8 (October 1978): 102–4.
Stark, Helen Candland. *Exponent II* 5 (Winter 1979): 13.
Zieglowsky, Debby. *Annals of Iowa* 47, no. 5: 479–81.
Deseret News, 19 May 1978.
Salt Lake Tribune, 8 April 1979.

Reviews of *Jacob Hamblin: Mormon Apostle to the Indians*

Agnew, T. L. *Journal of the West* 20 (January 1981): 90.
Cooper, Inez S. *Utah Historical Quarterly* 48 (Fall 1980): 409–10.
Peterson, Charles S. *Western American Literature* 16 (Spring 1981): 59–61.

Smith, Melvin T. *Annals of Iowa* 3d series, 46 (Summer 1981): 75–76.
El Paso Times, 15 June 1980.
Deseret News, 28 June 1980.
Salt Lake Tribune, 13 July 1980.

Reviews of *On the Ragged Edge: The Life and Times of Dudley Leavitt*

Jenson, Harold H. *The Pioneer* 22 (January-February 1975): 19.
Trafzer, Clifford. *Journal of the West* 13 (October 1974): 146–47.

Reviews of *Quicksand and Cactus: A Memoir of the Southern Mormon Frontier*

Choice 21 (October 1983): 342.
Etulain, Richard W. *Sunstone Review* (March 1983): 18–19.
Gibson, Arrell M. *Chronicles of Oklahoma* 61 (Winter 1983–84): 430–31.
Greever, William S. *Western Historical Quarterly* 14 (October 1983): 476.
Hefner, Loretta L. *Utah Endowment for the Humanities News*, February 1983, n.p.
Johnston, David. *Los Angeles Times Book Review*, 22 May 1983, 8.
Lythgoe, Dennis L. *Journal of the West* 23 (April 1984): 105–6.
Mulder, William. *Western American Literature* 19 (Summer 1984): 167–68.
Sadler, Richard W. *Dialogue* 16 (Summer 1983): 133–35.
Shepperson, Wilbur S. *Pacific Historian* 27 (Spring 1983): 87–88.
Smith, Melvin T. *Utah Historical Quarterly* 51 (Winter 1983): 93–94.
Walker, Ronald W. *Arizona and the West* 26 (Spring 1984): 73–74.
Deseret News, 9 October 1982.
Salt Lake Tribune, 19 December 1982.

INDEX